Communications in Computer and Information Science 2027

Rationale
The CCIS series is devoted to the publication of proceedings of computer science conferences. Its aim is to efficiently disseminate original research results in informatics in printed and electronic form. While the focus is on publication of peer-reviewed full papers presenting mature work, inclusion of reviewed short papers reporting on work in progress is welcome, too. Besides globally relevant meetings with internationally representative program committees guaranteeing a strict peer-reviewing and paper selection process, conferences run by societies or of high regional or national relevance are also considered for publication.

Topics
The topical scope of CCIS spans the entire spectrum of informatics ranging from foundational topics in the theory of computing to information and communications science and technology and a broad variety of interdisciplinary application fields.

Information for Volume Editors and Authors
Publication in CCIS is free of charge. No royalties are paid, however, we offer registered conference participants temporary free access to the online version of the conference proceedings on SpringerLink (http://link.springer.com) by means of an http referrer from the conference website and/or a number of complimentary printed copies, as specified in the official acceptance email of the event.

CCIS proceedings can be published in time for distribution at conferences or as post-proceedings, and delivered in the form of printed books and/or electronically as USBs and/or e-content licenses for accessing proceedings at SpringerLink. Furthermore, CCIS proceedings are included in the CCIS electronic book series hosted in the SpringerLink digital library at http://link.springer.com/bookseries/7899. Conferences publishing in CCIS are allowed to use Online Conference Service (OCS) for managing the whole proceedings lifecycle (from submission and reviewing to preparing for publication) free of charge.

Publication process
The language of publication is exclusively English. Authors publishing in CCIS have to sign the Springer CCIS copyright transfer form, however, they are free to use their material published in CCIS for substantially changed, more elaborate subsequent publications elsewhere. For the preparation of the camera-ready papers/files, authors have to strictly adhere to the Springer CCIS Authors' Instructions and are strongly encouraged to use the CCIS LaTeX style files or templates.

Abstracting/Indexing
CCIS is abstracted/indexed in DBLP, Google Scholar, EI-Compendex, Mathematical Reviews, SCImago, Scopus. CCIS volumes are also submitted for the inclusion in ISI Proceedings.

How to start
To start the evaluation of your proposal for inclusion in the CCIS series, please send an e-mail to ccis@springer.com.

KC Santosh · Aaisha Makkar · Myra Conway ·
Ashutosh K. Singh · Antoine Vacavant ·
Anas Abou el Kalam ·
Mohamed-Rafik Bouguelia · Ravindra Hegadi
Editors

Recent Trends in Image Processing and Pattern Recognition

6th International Conference, RTIP2R 2023
Derby, UK, December 7–8, 2023
Revised Selected Papers, Part II

Springer

Editors
KC Santosh
University of South Dakota
Vermillion, SD, USA

Aaisha Makkar
University of Derby
Derby, UK

Myra Conway
University of Derby
Derby, UK

Ashutosh K. Singh
Indian Institute of Information Technology
Bhopal, India

Antoine Vacavant
University of Clermont Auvergne
Aubière, France

Anas Abou el Kalam
ENSA - Cadi Ayyad University
Marrakesh, Morocco

Mohamed-Rafik Bouguelia
Halmstad University
Halmstad, Sweden

Ravindra Hegadi
Central University of Karnataka
Kalaburagi, India

ISSN 1865-0929 ISSN 1865-0937 (electronic)
Communications in Computer and Information Science
ISBN 978-3-031-53084-5 ISBN 978-3-031-53085-2 (eBook)
https://doi.org/10.1007/978-3-031-53085-2

This Springer imprint is published by the registered company Springer Nature Switzerland AG
The registered company address is: Gewerbestrasse 11, 6330 Cham, Switzerland

Preface

We are delighted to present this compilation of research papers in Springer's Communication in Computer and Information Science (CCIS) series from the 6th International Conference on Recent Trends in Image Processing and Pattern Recognition (RTIP2R 2023). RTIP2R 2023 was hosted in-person at the University of Derby, UK, from December 07–08, 2023, in collaboration with the Applied AI Research Lab at the University of South Dakota, USA (URL: https://rtip2r-conference.org/).

As highlighted in the call for papers, RTIP2R 2023 attracted a wealth of current and recent research in image processing, pattern recognition, and computer vision across diverse applications, including document understanding, IoT, biometrics, healthcare informatics, and security. With a total of 216 submissions, we carefully selected 62 papers for presentation during the conference. Unlike the last event, we diligently reviewed revised submissions to arrive at final decisions, resulting in an acceptance rate of 28.70%. Each selected/accepted paper underwent a rigorous evaluation process with an average of three single-blind reviews per selection.

In essence, the conference provided a valuable platform that brought together research scientists, academics, and industry practitioners. We firmly believe that the event encapsulated a wealth of innovative ideas. We extend our gratitude to Girijesh Prasad from the School of Computing, Engineering, and Intelligent Systems at Ulster University, UK for delivering an insightful keynote address. During the conference, KC Santosh spearheaded a workshop titled "AI for Good - How about the Carbon Footprint?," featuring speakers including Vinaytosh Mishra (Gulf Medical University, UAE), Wajahat Ali Khan (University of Derby, UK), and Mabrouka Abuhmida (University of South Wales, UK).

Our heartfelt thanks go out to all contributors who made RTIP2R 2023 a success.

November 2023

KC Santosh
Aaisha Makkar
Myra Conway
Ashutosh K. Singh
Antoine Vacavant
Anas Abou el Kalam
Mohamed-Rafik Bouguelia
Ravindra Hegadi

Organization

Patrons

Warren Manning	University of Derby, UK
Louise Richards	University of Derby, UK
Stephan Reiff-Marganiec	University of Derby, UK

Honorary Chairs

Farid Meziane	University of Derby, UK
Alistair McEwan	University of Derby, UK
Xi-zhao Wang	Shenzhen University, China
Laurent Wendling	Université Paris Cité, France
KC Santosh	University of South Dakota, USA

General Chairs

Aaisha Makkar	University of Derby, UK
Myra Conway	University of Derby, UK
Ashutosh Kumar Singh	IIIT Bhopal, India

Program Chairs

Antoine Vacavant	University of Clermont Auvergne, France
Anas Abou el Kalam	Cadi Ayyad University, Morocco
M.-R. Bouguelia	Halmstad University, Sweden
Ravindra Hegadi	Central University of Karnataka, India

Special Track Chairs

Mickael Coustaty	Université de La Rochelle, France
Yassine Sadqi	University Sultan Moulay Slimane, Morocco
Abdul Wahid	University of Galway, Ireland
Aditya Nigam	IIT Mandi, India

Deepika Saxena	University of Aizu, Japan
Jitendra Kumar	NIT Tiruchirappalli, India
Longwei Wang	University of South Dakota, USA
Abdelkrim Haqiq	Hassan 1st University, Morocco

Workshop Chairs

Hubert Cecotti	California State University, Fresno, USA
Rodrigue Rizk	University of South Dakota, USA
Alice Othmani	Université Paris-Est Créteil, France
Nibaran Das	Jadavpur University, India
Manju Khari	JNU, India
Gaurav Jaswal	IIT Mandi, India
Satish K. Singh	IIIT Allahabad, India
Sushma Venkatesh	AiBA AS, Norway

Local Workshop Chairs

Alaa AlZoubi	University of Derby, UK
Maqbool Hussain	University of Derby, UK
Wajahat Ali Khan	University of Derby, UK
Asad Abdi	University of Derby, UK

Core Technical Program Committee (TPC)

Abdul Wahid	University of Galway, Ireland
Abdullah Kaleem	MPGI SOE, Nanded, India
Abhilasha Jain	MIET, India
Abhinav Muley	SVPCET, India
Abhishek Verma	PDPM IIITDM, Jabalpur, India
Abhishek Hazra	IIIT Sri City, India
Agha Husian	ITS Engineering College, India
Ajay Kumar	MIET, India
Akhilesh Pandey	MIET, India
Ali Nazarizadeh	Islamic Azad University Central Tehran Branch, Iran
Alok Aggarwal	UPES, India
Amarpreet Singh	Chandigarh University, India
Amit Saini	MIET, India

Amol Vibhute	SICSR, Symbiosis International (Deemed University), India
Anas Abou El Kalam	Cadi Ayyad University, Morocco
Aniket Muley	Swami Ramanad Teerth Marathwada University, India
Ankur Nagori	CIAE Bhopal, India
Antoine Vacavant	Université Clermont Auvergne, France
Anurag Malik	Uttaranchal University, India
Arkajyoti Mitra	University of Texas at Arlington, USA
Ashutosh Dhar Dwivedi	Aalborg University, Denmark
Badr Hssina	Hassan II University of Casablanca, Morocco
Bhanu Chander	IIIT Kottayam, India
Bimal Mandal	IIT Jodhpur, India
Bouchaib Cherradi	CRMEF Casablanca-Settat (S. P. d'El Jadida), Morocco
Brian Keith Norambuena	Universidad Católica del Norte, Chile
Chetan Pattebahadur	Dr. B.A.M. University, India
Chitra Gaikwad	Government College of Engineering Aurangabad, India
Dattatray Sawat	HCLTech, India
Deepak Sharma	University of Petroleum and Energy Studies, India
Deepak Gupta	GIIT, India
Deepak Rakesh	University of Economics and Human Sciences in Warsaw, Poland
Deepika Saxena	University of Aizu, Japan
Digvijay Singh	Uttaranchal University, India
Dipak Sah	IITISM Dhanbad, India
Gaurav Yadav	IAMR Group, India
Ghanshyam Bopche	NIT Tiruchirappalli, India
Gurjot Gaba	Linköping University, Sweden
Harsimran Kaur	Chitkara University, India
Himadri Mukherjee	West Bengal State University, India
Jatinder Kumar	National Institute of Technology Kurukshetra, India
Joana Sousa	NOS Inovação, Portugal
João Baptista Cardia Neto	UNESP, Brazil
Kalman Palagyi	University of Szeged, Hungary
Kamaljeet Kaur	Star Academy, India
Kaushik Roy	WBSU, India
Kavita Chaudhary	ABESEC, India
Kishu Gupta	National Institute of Technology Kurukshetra, India
Lorenzo Putzu	University of Cagliari, Italy

Madhu Arora	Sri Balaji University, India
Mahadev Patil	Bharati Vidyapeeth's Abhijit Kadam Institute of Management and Social Sciences, Solapur, India
Maheswaran S.	Kongu Engineering College, India
Mallikarjunaswamy M. S.	JSSSTU, India
Mansi Poonia	IAMR Group, India
Manwinder Singh	Lovely Professional University, India
Midhula Vijayan	National Institute of Technology, Tiruchirappalli, India
Mohamed-Rafik Bouguelia	Halmstad University, Sweden
Mohammod Naimul Islam Suvon	University of Sheffield, UK
Mohan Rawat	Chameli Devi Group of Institutions, India
Mohd. Saifuzzaman	Daffodil International University, Bangladesh
Muhammad Adeel Hafeez	University of Galway, Ireland
Mukesh Khandelwal	Govt. Women Mahila Engineering College Ajmer, India
Muntazir Mehdi	University of Derby, UK
Nahid Sami	University of Derby, UK
Narottam Patel	VIT Bhopal, India
Navjot Rathour	Chandigarh University, India
Navneet Kaur	Guru Nanak Dev Engineering College, India
Neeraj Joshi	MIET, India
Neeraj Kumar	GNIOT, India
Niharika Singh	University of Helsinki, Finland
Onel López	University of Oulu, Finland
Pankaj Dhiman	JUIT, India
Parbhat Gupta	SRM Institute of Science and Technology Modinagar, India
Parminder Kaur	Guru Nanak Dev University, India
Peter Dolan	University of Minnesota, Morris, USA
Pooja Janse	Dr. B.A.M. University, India
Pooja Rani	National Institute of Technology, Kurukshetra, India
Pooja S.	Galgotias University, India
Prabhakar S.	ITSEC, India
Prabhakar C. J.	Kuvempu University, India
Prakash Hiremath	KLE Technological University, India
Pranav Kumar Singh	Central Institute of Technology Kokrajhar, India
Prashant Kumar	National Institute of Technology Durgapur, India
Prasun Tripathi	University of Sheffield, UK
Rahul Kumar	BIT Meerut, India

Rajat Singh	Uttaranchal University, India
Rajat Balyan	Uttaranchal University, India
Ranit Kishore	Tula's Institute, India
Ravi M.	GFGC, Raichur, India
Ravinder Kumar	Guru Nanak Dev University, India
Ravindra Hegadi	Central University of Karnataka, India
Ravindra Sharma	Swami Rama Himalayan University, India
Rimjhim Rimjhim	Jain University, India
Rodrigo Nava	AstraZeneca, UK
Rodrigue Rizk	University of South Dakota, USA
S. S. Patil	University of Agricultural Sciences, Bangalore, India
Sachin Kumar	Vidya College, India
Samson Anosh Babu Parisapogu	Chaitanya Bharathi Institute of Technology, India
Sandeep Arora	Lovely Professional University, India
Sandhya Pundhir	DSEU, India
Sanjay Jain	ITM University Gwalior, India
Sara Arezki	University Hassan First, Morocco
Satender Kumar	National Institute of Technology Kurukshetra, India
Saurabh Singhal	Chandigarh University, India
Shaik Vaseem Akram	SRU, India
Shalini Aggarwal	Graphic Era Hill University, India
Sharad Saxena	Thapar Institute of Engineering and Technology, India
Shashank Agnihotri	MIET, India
Shilpa Sharma	JIMSEMTC, India
Shivam Chaudhary	MIET, India
Shubham Mahajan	Ajeenkya DY Patil University, India
Shweta Pandey	Uttaranchal University, India
Siddharth Dabhade	National Forensic Sciences University, India
Smruti Swain	National Institute of Technology, Kurukshetra, India
Sumanth Sharma	Government College for Women, Kolar, India
Sumit Sharma	National Institute of Technology Kurukshetra, India
Sunil Nimbhore	Dr. Babasaheb Ambedkar Marathwada University, India
Swarnika Swarnika	NGI, India
Thomas Monoth	Mary Matha Arts & Science College, Kannur University, India
Uruj Jaleel	Alliance University, India

V. Malemath	KLE Dr. M. S. Sheshgiri College of Engg. and Technology, Belagavi, India
Vikas Humbe	SRTM University, India
Vinay Singh	UPES, India
Vinay T. R.	Nitte Meenakshi Institute of Technology, India
Vinaytosh Mishra	Gulf Medical University, UAE
Vineet Vishnoi	Shobhit University Meerut, India
Vivek Singh	Sharda University, India
Yusera Khan	Shri Mata Vaishno Devi University, India
Zakaria Rguibi	FST Settat, Morocco

Conference Secretaries

Jose David Cortes	Applied AI Research Lab, USA
Siddhi K. Bajracharya	Applied AI Research Lab, USA

Webmaster

KC Santosh	Applied AI Research Lab, USA

Contents – Part II

Healthcare Informatics

Contents – Part I

Healthcare Informatics

Leveraging Handwriting Impairment as a Biomarker for Early Parkinson's Disease Diagnosis

Anish Mathew Chacko, Rodrigue Rizk(✉), and KC Santosh(✉)

Applied AI Research Lab, Department of Computer Science,
University of South Dakota, Vermillion, SD 57069, USA
anishmathew.chacko@coyotes.usd.edu, {rodrigue.rizk,santosh.kc}@usd.edu

Abstract. Parkinson's Disease (PD) is a progressive neurodegenerative condition that significantly impacts motor function, leading to symptoms such as tremors, bradykinesia, and rigidity. However, diagnosing PD in its early stages remains challenging due to the absence of specific biomarkers, often resulting in delayed treatment and symptom management. Handwriting changes serve as a dependable marker of disease severity in PD patients, who exhibit significantly slower and lighter writing or drawing. In this paper, we aim to develop a cost-effective, non-invasive diagnostic tool utilizing handwriting samples, specifically spiral and wave drawings. We introduce a classification model incorporating a convolutional neural network (CNN) to extract relevant features from these drawings and distinguish individuals with Parkinson's disease from healthy ones. Our study holds promising results, with the VGG-19 model achieving an accuracy of 91.33%, specificity of 90.45%, and sensitivity of 92.6%. These outcomes underscore the potential of our approach to facilitate early PD diagnosis and treatment, ultimately enhancing the quality of life for affected individuals. The use of handwriting as a unique biomarker underlines the importance of leveraging advanced AI techniques for accurate and accessible PD diagnosis.

Keywords: Parkinson's Disease Diagnosis · CNN · Handwriting Impairment

1 Introduction

Parkinson's Disease (PD) is a well-recognized neurological disorder characterized by the degeneration of dopamine-producing neurons, leading to movement impairments [1]. This condition results from the disruption of dopamine's communication between the substantia nigra and the corpus striatum, causing asymmetrical neural functioning and motor control disturbances. PD, primarily affecting individuals over 60 years of age, presents symptoms such as tremors, gait difficulties, and behavioral changes [1]. Recent research suggests a complex interplay of genetic predisposition and environmental toxins influencing PD, emphasizing

KC Santosh et al. (Eds.): RTIP2R 2023, CCIS 2027, pp. 3–11, 2024.
https://doi.org/10.1007/978-3-031-53085-2_1

the need for a comprehensive understanding of its etiology [2]. PD advances through distinct stages of severity, progressively impeding an individual's ability to function independently [3]. In recent years, research efforts have explored the application of machine learning techniques in PD detection, including image-based tremor measurement and cascaded learning frameworks [6,7]. Among the observable alterations in PD, handwriting impairment stands out as a potential biomarker, characterized by slower drawing speeds and diminished pen pressure [8]. The tremors and muscular rigidity characteristic of PD disrupt smooth drawing, resulting in distinct patterns in patient sketches. Handwriting is a complex motor task that relies on the coordination of multiple neural circuits, including those affected by PD. Studies have shown that individuals with PD exhibit distinctive handwriting changes, including slower and lighter writing or drawing, even in the early stages of the disease. This alteration in handwriting is believed to be linked to the underlying motor control deficits in PD, providing a unique opportunity for early disease detection [8]. While the clinical manifestations of PD are well-documented, diagnosing the disease in its early stages remains a challenging task. Early diagnosis is crucial for timely intervention and improved patient outcomes. The current lack of specific and easily accessible biomarkers often leads to delayed diagnosis and treatment. This paper explores the potential of handwriting impairment as a viable non-invasive biomarker for early PD diagnosis, potentially streamlining diagnostic procedures and reducing the need for supplementary hardware. Figure 1 illustrates handwriting samples highlighting the key differences between individuals with PD and healthy controls in two common handwriting tasks. Figure 1a) showcases a representative spiral drawing by an individual with PD, clearly displaying the characteristic handwriting impairment associated with PD, such as slower and lighter strokes. In contrast, Fig. 1b) presents a spiral drawing from a healthy control subject, showing smoother and more regular handwriting patterns compared to the PD sample. Figure 1c) depicts a wave drawing completed by an individual with PD, emphasizing distinctive handwriting characteristics related to the disease. Lastly, Fig. 1d) features a wave drawing by a healthy individual, serving as a reference for the typical handwriting style of individuals without PD. These handwriting samples visually represent the differences in handwriting impairment between PD patients and healthy individuals, forming the foundation for our diagnostic approach. In this context, our research employs preprocessing, data augmentation, and the utilization of the Spiral and Wave models in conjunction with pre-trained convolutional neural networks (CNNs) such as VGG-19, ResNet-50, and DenseNet-121 to classify between PD patients and normal individuals [8]. This combination of techniques enhances diagnostic accuracy for early PD detection. Through this interdisciplinary approach, our study aims to advance non-invasive tools for early PD detection, aligning with the objective of improving diagnostic accuracy and patient care. The findings underscore the potential of handwriting as a biomarker and emphasize the importance of sophisticated neural network architectures in achieving precise classification.

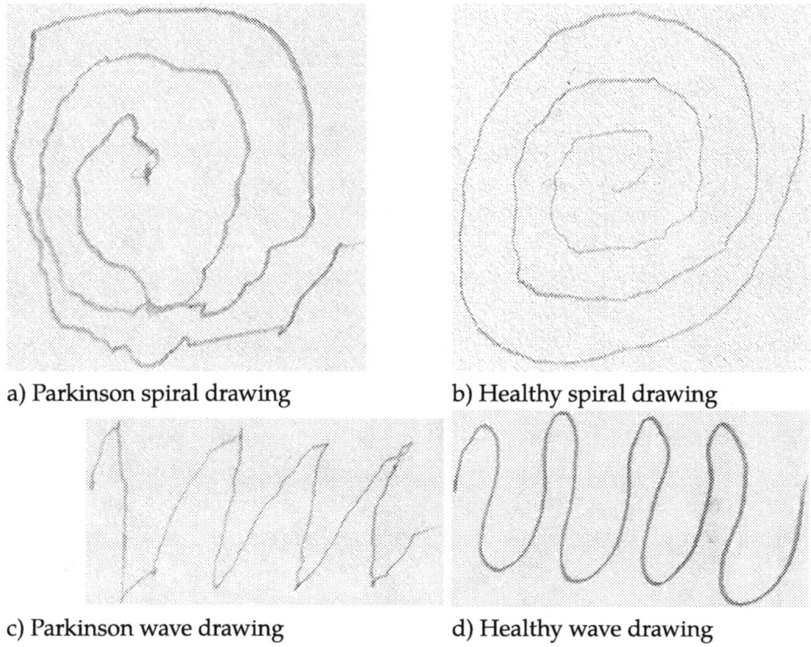

Fig. 1. Handwriting samples illustrating the key differences between individuals with PD and healthy controls in two common handwriting tasks.

2 Related Works

Free-hand sketches are known for their exceptional illustrative qualities and have been extensively employed in human behavior analysis [10–16]. They serve as a valuable tool for understanding human actions and interactions in a variety of application, and PD is no exception.

The detection of PD has been the subject of significant research efforts, with a variety of approaches and markers employed for diagnostic purposes. This section provides an overview of relevant studies in the literature that address the challenge of PD detection.

Zham et al. [2] conducted a study that utilized speed and pen-pressure criteria during sketching to differentiate individuals with PD at various disease stages. They extracted features from the drawings and established a technique to correlate these features with the severity of PD. The Mann-Whitney test was employed to validate their findings, demonstrating that these methods can effectively distinguish between different stages of PD. Notably, substantial changes in the correlation factor were observed at different PD stages, underscoring the diagnostic potential of handwriting characteristics. Pereira et al. [4] introduced their "HandPD" handwriting dataset and leveraged computer vision algorithms for PD recognition. They evaluated the dataset using supervised techniques, including OPF, SVM, and Naive Bayes (NB) classifiers, with the NB classifier achieving the highest accuracy of 78.9%. Kotsavasiloglou et al. [8] conducted an investigation based on the trajectory of the pen tip on a drawing pad when healthy subjects and PD patients drew simple horizontal lines. Features were extracted from these drawings and used to train machine learning algorithms for the identification of PD participants among healthy subjects. Various classifiers, including Naive Bayes, AdaBoost, Logistic Regression, J48, Support Vector Machine (SVM), and Random Forest, were employed to build an automated system. The model's performance was evaluated using metrics such as the Area under the Curve (AUC), True Positive (TP), True Negative (TN), and accuracy. The system achieved an accuracy of 91%, TP of 0.88, and TN of 0.95. Memedi et al. [3] proposed an automatic spiral analysis for the objective assessment of motor symptoms in PD. This study used machine learning techniques to differentiate between "off" episodes and peak dosage dyskinesia based on spiral data obtained from telemetry touch screen devices. Features were extracted from the data and used to train machine learning classifiers, including Support Vector Machine, Logistic Regression, Random Forest, and Multi-Layer Perceptron (MLP). The MLP classifier outperformed others, achieving an accuracy of 84%. Hatamino et al. [5] introduced a deep learning-CNN-based system for medical diagnosis, focusing on PD. They implemented the AlexNet architecture of a convolutional neural network (CNN) while simplifying the network due to a relatively small dataset. The model achieved an accuracy of 72.5%.

Our work extends these existing efforts by introducing a non-invasive method for early PD detection based on handwriting impairment. By concentrating on this distinct marker, we contribute to the evolving body of research aimed at enhancing the accuracy and accessibility of PD diagnosis, ultimately benefiting patient care and overall quality of life.

3 Methodology

In this study, we introduce a deep learning model aimed at harnessing handwriting impairment as a biomarker for early PD diagnosis, with a particular focus on two common handwriting tasks: spiral and wave drawings. Figure 2 presents an overview of the methodology employed for classifying individuals as either PD patients or healthy controls. This proposed deep learning model integrates multiple layers and four distinct pre-trained deep learning models, namely VGG-19, InceptionV-3, DenseNet121, and ResNet50, to perform the classification task. The proposed model's collective capacity to leverage a rich set of features extracted from the augmented and preprocessed data aids in more accurate early diagnosis and intervention, potentially improving the lives of individuals with PD.

3.1 Data Acquisition and Pre-processing

Our dataset was sourced from RMIT University in Melbourne [9], serving as the cornerstone of our research. Initially comprising 102 images (51 spiral and 51

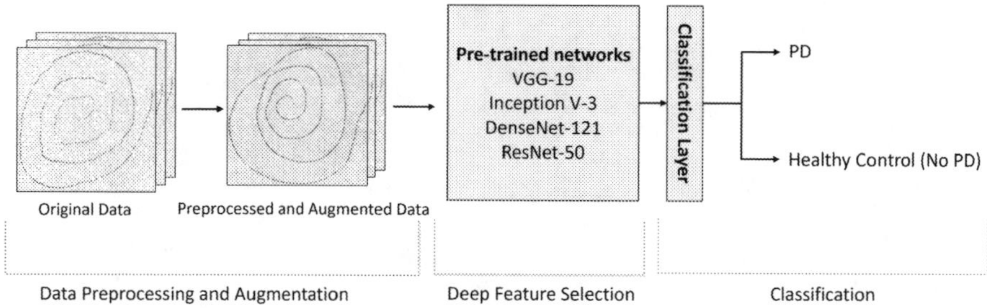

Fig. 2. Proposed Deep Learning Model for PD Classification

wave drawings), we significantly expanded and diversified the dataset using data augmentation techniques. This resulted in a total of 5112 images for both spiral and wave categories. The dataset was gathered from 55 individuals, divided into two groups: the Control Group (28 participants without PD) and the Parkinson Group (27 individuals diagnosed with PD). Both groups underwent the Spiral and Wave drawing tests, providing an extensive pool of handwriting samples for thorough analysis and comparison.

To ensure data uniformity and quality, a series of pre-processing steps were applied. The process begins with the preprocessing of original image data, comprising samples from both healthy controls and PD patients. These data are subjected to various preprocessing techniques to enhance image quality, remove noise, and standardize features, ensuring that they are suitable for deep learning analysis. The images were resized to a standardized format of (229, 229) pixels to provide consistent inputs. Additionally, the images were transformed into grayscale, reducing color details while preserving essential features. Techniques such as histogram equalization and Contrast Limited Adaptive Histogram Equalization (CLAHE) were employed to enhance image contrast and brightness [7]. These pre-processing steps collectively aimed to prepare the data for subsequent analysis.

3.2 Data Augmentation

Data augmentation was a crucial strategy for enhancing dataset diversity and improving model performance. By applying transformations such as rotation, horizontal flipping, and vertical flipping using the Keras ImageDataGenerator, multiple versions of each image were created with different orientations and perspectives. These augmented samples were appropriately labeled and integrated into the dataset for both model training and comprehensive evaluation.

Through data pre-processing and augmentation, the dataset was refined and readied for training the classification models. These steps played a pivotal role in ensuring that the models could effectively capture subtle handwriting patterns associated with PD. Figure 3 illustrates sample images after applying

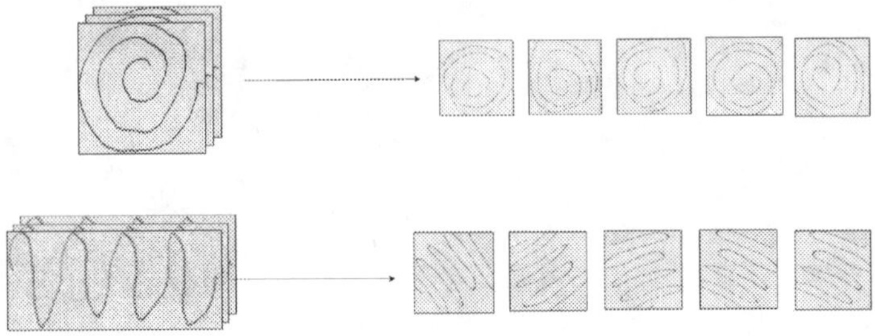

Fig. 3. Sample images after applying pre-processing and data augmentation techniques to handwriting data from individuals with PD and healthy controls.

pre-processing and data augmentation techniques to handwriting data from individuals with PD and healthy controls.

3.3 Model Definition and Training

In this phase of the study, we defined and trained a robust deep learning model with the objective of accurately classifying PD based on handwriting impairment. The model architecture leveraged a pre-trained VGG19 convolutional neural network (CNN) as the foundation for feature extraction from the augmented and preprocessed handwriting images. Supplementary layers, including Global Average Pooling and fully connected layers, were incorporated to facilitate binary classification. The model was compiled using the Adam optimizer and binary cross-entropy loss. To prevent overfitting on the limited dataset, the model's layers were initially frozen, enabling transfer learning.

To further enhance the model's generalization and performance, data augmentation was incorporated during training. Augmentation helps diversify the dataset by introducing variations in handwriting samples. These variations include changes in stroke patterns, writing speed, and pen pressure. Data augmentation aims to improve the model's ability to handle diverse handwriting styles and enhance its generalization. An image data generator was utilized to produce augmented images with rotations, shifts, and flips. The augmented dataset was then used for model training, allowing it to learn from a broader range of handwriting patterns and improving its ability to differentiate between healthy and Parkinson's-afflicted handwriting.

Throughout the training process, the model iteratively processed the augmented training dataset over a predetermined number of epochs. Progress was continuously monitored, and the model's performance was evaluated on the augmented testing dataset to assess its accuracy in disease classification. Upon completing training, the model weights were saved for future use.

This phase of model definition and training played a pivotal role in creating a robust and effective classification tool for early PD diagnosis using handwriting impairment as a biomarker. The utilization of transfer learning, data

Table 1. Model Performance

Model	Accuracy	Specificity	Sensitivity
VGG-19	91.33%	90.45%	92.6%
Inception V-3	85.64%	84.2%	83.2%
DenseNet-121	81.22%	82.15%	80.2%
ResNet-50	83.37%	84.25%	81.54%

augmentation, and comprehensive training strategies collectively contributed to the model's enhanced accuracy and potential for practical application.

4 Results and Discussion

In this section, we present the outcomes of the study, which involved the utilization of four different pre-trained deep learning models for the classification task, namely VGG-19, InceptionV-3, DenseNet121, and ResNet50. The training process was conducted on a single node HPC[1]. The evaluation of the model's performance included standard metrics such as accuracy, specificity, and sensitivity. These metrics provide a comprehensive assessment of the model's proficiency in distinguishing between individuals with PD and healthy controls. A summary of the results is presented in Table 1.

Among the employed models, VGG-19 exhibited the highest accuracy, achieving an impressive accuracy of 91.33%. It also demonstrated a well-balanced performance in terms of specificity (90.45%) and sensitivity (92.6%), highlighting its effectiveness in correctly classifying both healthy and Parkinson's-afflicted individuals based on their handwriting impairment.

In comparison, the InceptionV-3 model achieved an accuracy of 85.64%, with a specificity of 84.2% and sensitivity of 83.2%. The DenseNet121 model followed with an accuracy of 81.22%, a specificity of 82.15%, and a sensitivity of 80.2%. Lastly, the ResNet50 model attained an accuracy of 83.37%, accompanied by a specificity of 84.25% and sensitivity of 81.54%.

The results emphasize the potential of utilizing deep learning techniques for the early diagnosis of PD through the analysis of handwriting impairment. The remarkable performance of the VGG-19 model suggests its suitability as an effective tool for identifying individuals at risk of PD at an early stage. The comparative performance of the other models provides valuable insights into their applicability in this context.

These findings underscore the significance of leveraging deep learning and handwriting analysis as a non-invasive and accessible approach for the timely identification of PD. The development of accurate classification models offers the potential to revolutionize the landscape of PD diagnosis and significantly

[1] Computation was performed on Lawrence Supercomputer at University of South Dakota awarded by NSF.1626516.

enhance patient care, ultimately leading to improved outcomes and quality of life. The source code for our implementation is available on GitHub for reproducibility[2].

5 Conclusion

Parkinson's Disease is a complex neurodegenerative condition that poses significant challenges in early diagnosis. The absence of specific and easily accessible biomarkers often results in delayed treatment and symptom management, impacting the quality of life for affected individuals. In response to this critical need, our study explored the potential of leveraging handwriting impairment as a non-invasive and accessible biomarker for early PD diagnosis.

Through an interdisciplinary approach, we developed a robust methodology that harnessed deep learning techniques and four pre-trained models, including VGG-19, InceptionV-3, DenseNet121, and ResNet50, to analyze handwriting samples from individuals with PD and healthy control subjects. The results of our investigation demonstrated the feasibility of using handwriting as a diagnostic tool for PD.

The VGG-19 model emerged as the top-performer, achieving an accuracy of 91.33%, with balanced specificity (90.45%) and sensitivity (92.6%). This remarkable performance underscores the potential of utilizing handwriting impairment analysis as an early diagnostic tool for PD. While the other models exhibited slightly lower accuracy rates, they still provided valuable insights into the applicability of various deep learning models in this context.

The study's findings highlight the promise of machine learning and handwriting analysis as a non-invasive approach for the timely identification of PD. By successfully distinguishing individuals with PD from healthy controls based on their handwriting impairment, our research represents a significant step forward in improving the accuracy and accessibility of PD diagnosis.

Ultimately, our work contributes to the broader landscape of PD research, offering a cost-effective and non-invasive method that could revolutionize the diagnostic process. By enabling early diagnosis and intervention, we can significantly enhance patient care and ultimately improve the quality of life for those affected by PD. This study not only demonstrates the potential of handwriting as a valuable biomarker but also paves the way for future advancements in the field of PD diagnosis and management.

[2] https://github.com/2ai-lab/PD.

References

1. Bosch, J., Barsainya, R., Ridder, A., Santosh, K.C., Singh, A.: Interval timing and midfrontal delta oscillations are impaired in Parkinson's disease patients with freezing of gait. J. Neurol. **269**(5), 2599–2609 (2022). PMID: https://doi.org/10.1007/s00415-021-10843-9. Epub 21 Oct 2021
2. Zham, P., Arjunan, S.P., Raghav, S., Kumar, D.K.: Efficacy of guided spiral drawing in the classification of Parkinson's disease. IEEE J. Biomed. Health Inform. **22**(5), 1648–1652 (2017)
3. Memedi, M., et al.: Automatic spiral analysis for objective assessment of motor symptoms in Parkinson's disease. Sensors **15**(9), 23727–23744 (2015)
4. Pereira, C.R., et al.: A step towards the automated diagnosis of Parkinson's disease: analyzing handwriting movements. In: 2015 IEEE 28th International Symposium on Computer-Based Medical Systems, Sao Carlos, pp. 171–176 (2015)
5. Hatamino et al.: Introduced a Deep Learning-CNN system for diagnosing Parkinson's disease through handwriting. "Parkinson's Disease", National Institute on Aging (2020). Accessed 01 Oct 2020
6. Thomas, M., Lenka, A., Kumar Pal, P.: Handwriting analysis in Parkinson's disease: current status and future directions. Mov. Disord. Clin. Pract. **4**, 806–818 (2017)
7. Deuschl, G., Fietzek, U., Klebe, S., Volkmann, J.: Chapter 24 clinical neurophysiology and pathophysiology of Parkinsonian tremor. In: Hallett, M. (ed.) Handbook of Clinical Neurophysiology, vol. 1, pp. 377–396. Elsevier, Amsterdam (2003)
8. Kotsavasiloglou, C., Kostikis, N., Hristu-Varsakelis, D., Arnaoutoglou, M.: Machine learning-based classification of simple drawing movements in Parkinson's disease. Biomed. Signal Process. Control **31**, 174–180 (2017)
9. Zham, P., et al.: Distinguishing different stages of Parkinson's disease using composite index of speed and pen-pressure of sketching a spiral. Front. Neurol. **8**, 435 (2017)
10. Santosh, K.C., Nattee, C., Lamiroy, B.: Relative positioning of stroke-based clustering: a new approach to online handwritten Devanagari character recognition. Int. J. Image Graph. **12**(2), 1250016 (2012)
11. Xu, P., Hospedales, T.M., Yin, Q., Song, Y.Z., Xiang, T., Wang, L.: Deep learning for free-hand sketch: a survey. IEEE Trans. Pattern Anal. Mach. Intell. **45**, 285–312 (2022)
12. Li, Y., Hospedales, T.M., Song, Y.-Z., Gong, S.: Free-hand sketch recognition by multi-kernel feature learning. Comput. Vis. Image Underst. **137**, 1–11 (2015)
13. Zhang, X., Li, X., Liu, Y., Feng, F.: A survey on freehand sketch recognition and retrieval. Image Vis. Comput. **89**, 67–87 (2019)
14. Santosh, K.C., Lamiroy, B., Wendling, L.: DTW-Radon-based shape descriptor for pattern recognition. Int. J. Pattern Recognit Artif Intell. **27**(3), 1350008 (2013)
15. Guha, R., Das, N., Kundu, M., Nasipuri, M., Santosh, K.C.: DevNet: an efficient CNN architecture for handwritten Devanagari character recognition. Int. J. Pattern Recognit. Artif. Intell. **34**(12), 2052009:1–2052009:20 (2020)
16. Ghosh, T., Sen, S., Md Obaidullah, S.K., Santosh, K.C., Roy, K., Pal, U.: Advances in online handwritten recognition in the last decades. Comput. Sci. Rev. **46**, 100515 (2022)

Enhancing CT Image Visualization and Analysis Through Rescaling Raw Pixel Values to Hounsfield Units

Rohini A. Bhusnurmath and Shivaleela Betageri(✉)

Department of Computer Science, Karnataka State Akkamahadevi Women University, Vijayapura 586108, Karnataka, India
shivaleela.betageri@gmail.com

Abstract. Medical images are useful in the study and diagnosis of a wide range of medical problems. The human body can be imaged using several different imaging techniques, such as X-ray, CT, MRI, and ultrasound. The significant challenge in the process of successful disease identification and diagnosis is separating the required part of the person from the background of medical images and it is achieved by the Hounsfield unit. The Hounsfield unit (HU) is a measurement of relative radio density. DICOM (Digital Imaging and Communications in Medicine) is a standard for the storage and transmission of medical images. The pixel data read from the DICOM file is the raw attenuation coefficient present in the file which is usually used for the visualization purpose. This study aims to rescale raw pixel values to the Hounsfield unit. To achieve this, the abdominal CT scan image of the CHOAS dataset is used. Each raw pixel of the DICOM image is rescaled to the Hounsfield unit using rescale intercept and rescale slope values. The obtained results are analyzed for the same Hounsfield unit range before and after Hounsfield scaling. By converting the raw pixel values into Hounsfield units, CT images can be displayed and analyzed with greater clinical significance.

Keywords: Medical imaging · Hounsfield unit · Hounsfield unit scaling · DICOM

1 Introduction

Medical imaging [1] is a technique for photographing the human body to diagnose, monitor, and treat health issues. Medical imaging developed rapidly to play an important role in medicine today, assisting in illness diagnosis and therapy. Medical imaging plays an important role in a variety of medical situations and at all levels of health care. Diagnostic imaging services are crucial in confirming, analyzing, and documenting the course of a variety of disorders and their response to therapy [2]. Although a substantial portion of medical imaging technology is employed in the healthcare business, it also has applications in areas such as spot diagnosis, illness monitoring, treatment planning, assessing treatment efficacy, and age-related calculations, among others. Medical imaging is a noninvasive or invasive procedure that uses physical phenomena such as light,

KC Santosh et al. (Eds.): RTIP2R 2023, CCIS 2027, pp. 12–20, 2024.
https://doi.org/10.1007/978-3-031-53085-2_2

electromagnetic radiation, radioactivity, nuclear magnetic resonance (MR), and sound to create visual representations or images of the exterior or interior tissues of the human body or a portion of the individual's body [3]. X-ray radiography, computed tomography (CT), magnetic resonance imaging (MRI), ultrasound, and digital pathology are the most often used imaging modalities in clinical practice [4].

Computed tomography (CT) [5] is one of the most used diagnostic imaging methods [5]. Using X-rays to measure an object's projection from all angles, it then reconstructs the linear attenuation coefficient throughout the whole object. Even though the images are frequently compiled as a sequence of parallel axial slices, the CT image's result is a three-dimensional representation of the anatomy [6]. The basis for CT imaging is the attenuation of X-rays as they travel through various tissues in the body. X-rays are a form of electromagnetic radiation. The attenuation is determined by the density and atomic composition of the tissues encountered [7]. CT scan data is typically stored in a digital format using a specific file format known as DICOM (Digital Imaging and Communications in Medicine) [8].

The DICOM format organizes CT scan data into a structured set of information that includes both the image data and associated metadata. A DICOM file is primarily made up of a 'header' and 'image pixel intensity' data that is compressed into a single file. The data in the header is organized using a standardized set of tags. Data extracted from these tags can provide crucial information on the patient, study parameters, image data, and metadata [9, 10]. The pixel data read from the DICOM file is the raw bytes present in the file which is usually used for the visualization purpose [11]. Analysis of body parts based on these values is very difficult. Therefore, this problem needs to be addressed.

In this research work, the aim is to address the problem of DICOM image analysis. Firstly, the importance of Hounsfield units in CT images is discussed. Secondly, the impact of Hounsfield scaling on the analysis of different body parts using Hounsfield unit values is explored. Lastly, the results before and after Hounsfield scaling are compared to conclude.

2 Hounsfield Unit

Radiologists evaluate computed tomography (CT) images using the Hounsfield unit (HU) [12], a relative quantitative measurement of radio density. A grayscale picture is created during CT reconstruction using the radiation absorption/attenuation coefficient within a tissue. The amount of the X-ray beam that is absorbed or attenuated depends on the physical density of the tissue [13]. HU is a dimensionless value that is calculated based on the attenuation coefficient of a particular tissue or substance compared to that of water. Water is assigned a HU value of zero, and the HU scale extends from −1000 HU (air) to 1000 HU (dense bone). The following standard equation is used to convert each material's linear attenuation coefficient at the chosen effective energy to CT numbers Hounsfield units. Here μ stands for CT linear attenuation coefficient.

$$\mathrm{HU} = \left(\frac{\mu_{\mathrm{material}} - \mu_{\mathrm{water}}}{\mu_{\mathrm{water}}}\right) \times 1000 \tag{1}$$

HU values are used to differentiate between various types of tissues and help in the diagnosis of diseases and conditions. For example, air-filled structures such as the lungs will have a low HU value, while dense bone will have a high HU value. Soft tissues such as muscles and organs will fall in between these values. Overall, Hounsfield units are a key measurement used in CT imaging to quantify the radio density of tissues and structures within the body [14–16]. Table 1 illustrates the range of HU values for different tissues/organs.

Table 1. Maximum and minimum HU for various tissues/organs of the human body

Tissue/Organs	Minimum HU	Maximum HU
Bone	226	3071
Compact Bone(Adult)	662	1988
Compact Bone(Child)	586	2198
Soft tissue	−700	225
Liver	40	60
White matter	−37	−45
Water	0	
Fat	−50	−100
Air	−1000	
Muscle tissue (Adult)	−5	135
Muscle tissue (Child)	−25	139
Fat tissue (Adult)	−205	−51
Fat tissue (Child)	−212	−72

HU values in computed tomography (CT) imaging can be influenced by various factors, including the characteristics of the X-ray beam used. The non-monochromatic nature of X-ray beams in CT imaging can introduce several effects that impact HU values [17].

3 Hounsfield Unit Scaling

Hounsfield scaling, also known as HU scaling or CT number scaling, is a technique used in computed tomography (CT) imaging to convert the raw attenuation values obtained from CT scans into Hounsfield units [18]. This scaling allows for the visualization and interpretation of the different tissues and structures in the scanned area. The Hounsfield unit scale was developed by Sir Godfrey Hounsfield [19], who invented the CT scanner. It is a quantitative scale that assigns numerical values to the radio density of various tissues and substances within the human body. The scale is based on the linear attenuation coefficients of X-rays passing through different materials compared to water and air [20].

The pixel data read from the DICOM file is the raw bytes present in the file which is usually used for the visualization purpose [11]. Hence, segmenting the body parts based on these values is very difficult. So, these are converted to a linear scale (Hounsfield unit scale) by using Eq. (2)

$$Rescaled\ pixel = Pixel \times Rescale\_Slope + Rescale\_Intercept \tag{2}$$

where rescale slope and rescale intercept values are provided in the DICOM image header and can be used to rescale raw attenuation coefficients of the DICOM image. By applying the rescaling formula to each pixel of the CT image, the raw pixel values are multiplied by the scaling factor (Rescale_Slope) and then adjusted by the intercept value (Rescale_Intercept). This process maps the raw pixel values to the desired scale, such as Hounsfield units, allowing for accurate interpretation and analysis of the CT image.

4 Results and Discussion

The purpose of this experiment is to understand how the Hounsfield unit scaling affects its impact on analyzing medical images. The experiment aimed to determine how the Hounsfield unit rescaling plays a role in medical image processing.

To carry out this experiment, the CHAOS dataset [20], consisting of 20 CT images of different patients is used. The CT images are in the DICOM format. The study involved using these images, which are experimented with at different Hounsfield units ranges as in the Table 1, before and after scaling. The results were analyzed and validated based on the standard Hounsfield units mentioned in the Table 1 and also with the medical practitioners. Further, for the better understanding and representation purpose one sample image is shown in the Fig. 1. A detailed analysis of the image revealed various insights such as the minimum pixel value in the image was found to be 0, and the maximum pixel value was 2291. Furthermore, the image had a rescale intercept of –1200 and a rescale slope of 1. In addition to these parameters, Fig. 2 provided extensive information about several other parameters associated with this image. As mentioned above, the pixels in the current image range from 0 to 2291, which can be observed from the histogram plot shown in Fig. 3.

Upon a thorough examination of Fig. 3, the major observation is that the majority of the pixel values are spread between 100 and 200, as well as between 1100 and 1400. Based on this information, an attempt is made to extract specific parts of the human body, such as bones, liver, fat, muscles, etc. Standard Hounsfield unit values are used to identify the range of 300 to 1000 for bone markings, the range of 100 to 200 for fat and muscle presence, and subsequently, the range of 200 to 300 for liver presence. The findings obtained through this study are depicted in Figs. 5, 7, and 9.

Upon analyzing the obtained results, we have discovered that it is not possible to extract various body parts from Fig. 1, based on the HU. Therefore, when examining the cause of this issue, we found that DICOM, a medical imaging format, provides a medium to display medical images along with additional information generated by the scanner. Additionally, the pixels in the DICOM image are stored as raw pixels and are primarily intended for visualizing medical images. Due to these reasons, even though the Standard HU range is used, accurate results could not be achieved.

Therefore, to address this issue, a Hounsfield scaling method has been proposed to convert the raw pixels in the DICOM image to Hounsfield units. In this Hounsfield scaling

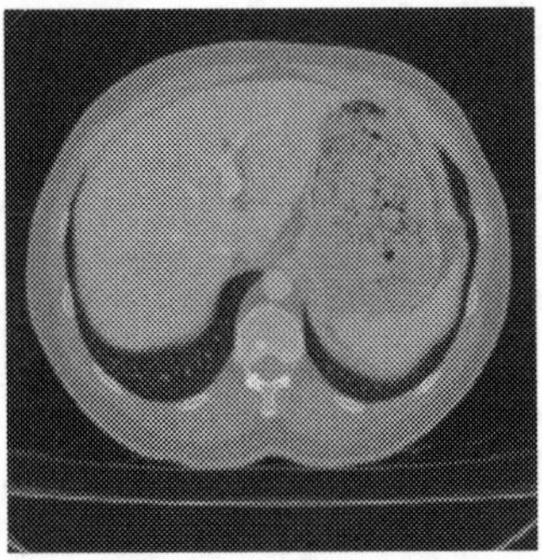

Fig. 1. Sample Abdominal CT scan image of CHAOS dataset [20]

```
(0028, 0103) Pixel Representation                    US: 0
(0028, 0106) Smallest Image Pixel Value              US: 0
(0028, 0107) Largest Image Pixel Value               US: 2291
(0028, 1050) Window Center                           DS: [45, 100]
(0028, 1051) Window Width                            DS: [350, 200]
(0028, 1052) Rescale Intercept                       DS: '-1200.0'
(0028, 1053) Rescale Slope                           DS: '1.0'
```

Fig. 2. Information present in the 'header' file of Fig. 1.

method, rescaling slope and rescaling intercept parameters are required to convert raw pixels to Hounsfield units. These two parameters are part of the DICOM image metadata and are found in the header section of the DICOM image. This information has already been provided in Fig. 2. To rescale raw pixels into the Hounsfield unit using rescale intercept and rescale slope following algorithm is employed.

Algorithm for rescaling Hounsfield unit:

Step 1: Read the DICOM Image.
Step 2: Convert the DICOM image into pixel array.
Step 3: Read the rescale slope and rescale intercept values from the DICOM image header.
Step 4: Convert raw pixel values to Hounsfield units using the formula mentioned in Eq. (2).

When the raw pixels are converted to Hounsfield units, we discovered some information. In the rescaled image, pixel values ranged from -1200 to 1091. This means that the minimum pixel value is -1200 and the maximum pixel value is 1091. This distribution of pixel values is shown in Fig. 4. Further, we analyzed various parts of the body using the standard Hounsfield ranges. We began the process of extracting different regions of the body by utilizing the pixel values we had initially established. The resulting interpretations are shown in Figs. 6, 8, and 10.

Results before HU scaling

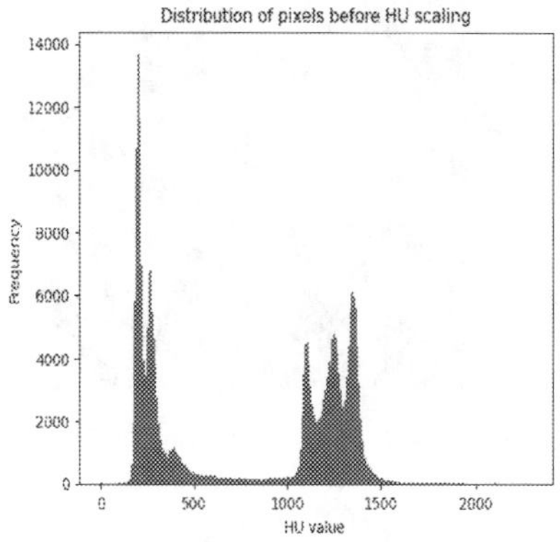

Fig. 3. Histogram representation of distribution of pixels before HU scaling

Results after HU scaling

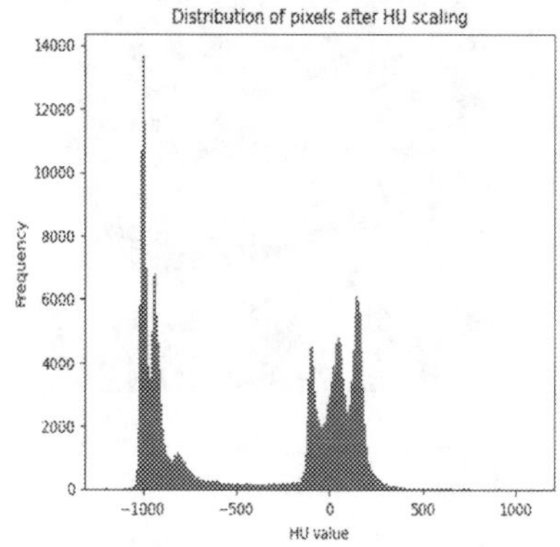

Fig. 4. Histogram representation of distribution of pixels after HU scaling

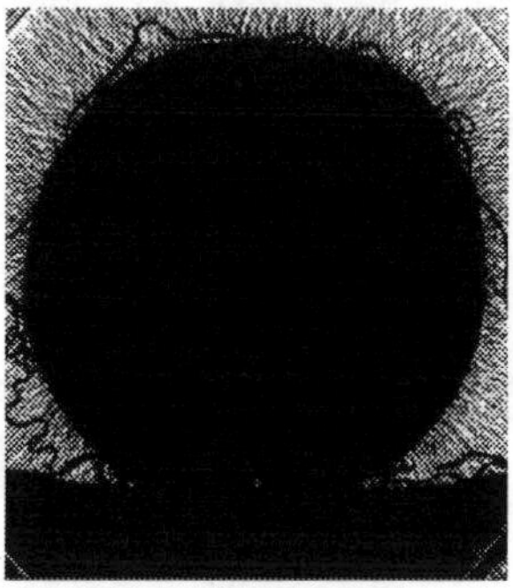

Fig. 5. View between 300 and 1000 before HU scaling

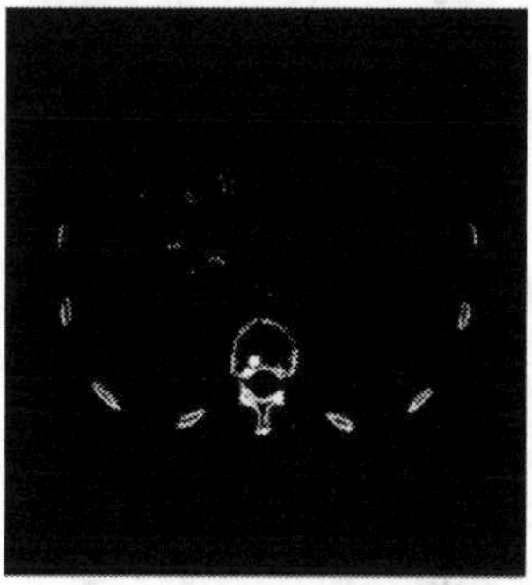

Fig. 6. View between 300 and 1000 after HU scaling

Fig. 7. View between −800 and −200 before HU scaling

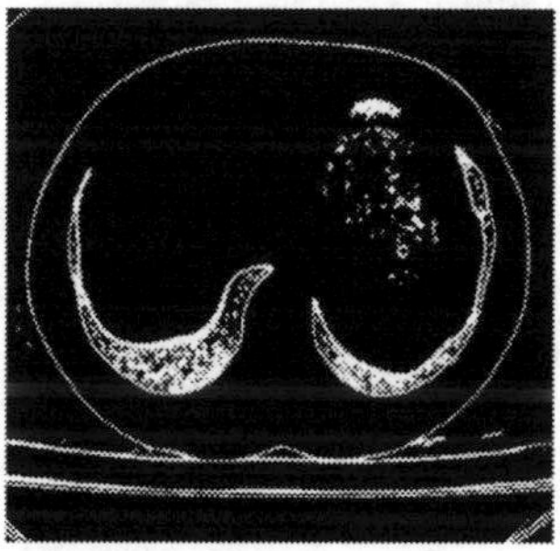

Fig. 8. View between −800 and −200 after HU scaling

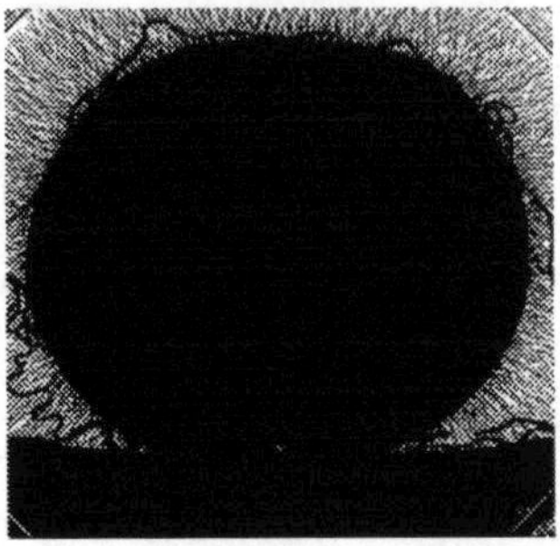

Fig. 9. View between 100 and 200 before HU scaling

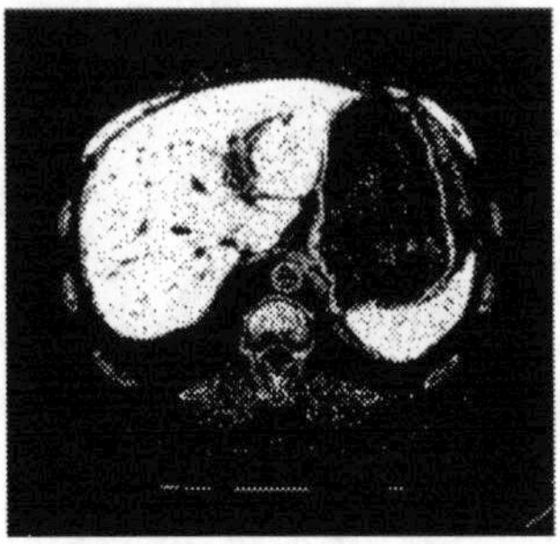

Fig. 10. View between 100 and 200 after HU scaling

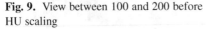

When observing the results mentioned above, it is noticeable that different results are obtained for the same Hounsfield unit range before and after Hounsfield scaling. It is observed that Fig. 5 of the before HU scaling, curves of the scanner are observed. Whereas in Fig. 6 of the after scaling, structures of the bones are obtained for the same range. Similarly, in the range of −800 to −200 where more pixels are saturated, we cannot see any parts of the body in Fig. 7, which is the before scaling. However, after scaling, as shown in Fig. 8, outlines are visible. Furthermore, in the range of 100 and 200, in the before Hounsfield scaling, counters of the scanners and in the after HU scaling liver, fat, and muscles can be seen. It can be observed in Fig. 9 and Fig. 10 respectively. From these observations, it is noted that it is difficult to extract different parts of the body using raw pixels of the DICOM image. Hence, rescaling the raw pixels of the DICOM image to Hounsfield units (HU scaling) may help identify parts of the body based on the Hounsfield unit range.

5 Conclusion

In conclusion, this study aimed to enhance CT image visualization and analysis by rescaling raw pixel values to HU, a relative quantitative measurement of radio density used in CT imaging for differentiating tissues and aiding disease diagnosis. The study utilized the DICOM format and employed a rescaling method using rescale intercept and rescale slope values from the DICOM image header. The results revealed limitations in analyzing CT images based on raw pixel values, making it challenging to accurately extract specific body parts due to the DICOM format's nature and the visualization purpose of raw pixels. To address this, a Hounsfield scaling method was proposed, converting raw pixels to Hounsfield units using rescale intercept and rescale slope. The application of the Hounsfield scaling method demonstrated significant improvements in image analysis and visualization. The rescaled images facilitated the identification of body parts based on the Hounsfield unit range, such as bones, liver, fat, and muscles. Comparing results before and after Hounsfield scaling showed enhanced visibility and accuracy of extracted body parts. These findings emphasize the importance of rescaling raw pixel values to Hounsfield units for CT image analysis, enabling clinicians and researchers to interpret images with greater clinical significance. Utilizing the Hounsfield unit scale can provide valuable insights for disease identification and diagnosis. Advancements in

Hounsfield scaling techniques may further improve CT imaging and its application in medical diagnostics.

Acknowledgements. Authors are thankful to reviewers valuable comments and suggestions which improved the quality of the manuscript. The authors are grateful to Dr. Siddaroodha Sajjan, Associate Professor, Department of Radiology, BLDE(DU) Shri B M Patil Medical college, Vijayapura for his valuable suggestions and support in validating the experimental results.

References

1. van Veelen, A., van der Sangen, N.M.R., Delewi, R., Beijk, M.A.M., Henriques, J.P.S., Claessen, B.E.P.M.: Detection of vulnerable coronary plaques using invasive and non-invasive imaging modalities. J. Clin. Med. **11**(5), 1361 (2022)
2. Liu, X., et al.: A comparison of deep learning performance against health-care professionals in detecting diseases from medical imaging: a systematic review and meta-analysis. Lancet Digit. Health **1**(6), e271–e297 (2019)
3. Smith, N.B., Webb, A.: Introduction to Medical Imaging: Physics, Engineering and Clinical Applications. Cambridge University Press, Cambridge (2010)
4. Elangovan, A., Jeyaseelan, T.: Medical imaging modalities: a survey. In: 2016 International Conference on Emerging Trends in Engineering, Technology and Science (ICETETS), pp. 1–4. IEEE (2016)
5. Basu, S., Kwee, T.C., Surti, S., Akin, E.A., Yoo, D., Alavi, A.: Fundamentals of PET and PET/CT imaging. Ann. N. Y. Acad. Sci. **1228**(1), 1–18 (2011)
6. Pelc, N.J.: Recent and future directions in CT imaging. Ann. Biomed. Eng. **42**, 260–268 (2014)
7. Moses, D.A.: Deep learning applied to automatic disease detection using chest x-rays. J. Med. Imaging Radiat. Oncol. **65**(5), 498–517 (2021)
8. Fajar, A., Sarno, R., Fatichah, C., Fahmi, A.: Reconstructing and resizing 3D images from DICOM files. J. King Saud Univ.-Comput. Inf. Sci. **34**(6), 3517–3526 (2022)
9. Rakocz, N., et al.: Automated identification of clinical features from sparsely annotated 3-dimensional medical imaging. NPJ Digit. Med. **4**(1), 44.Q (2021)
10. Manjunath, K.N.: Re: How can I convert pixel intensity values to housefield (CT number)? (2015). https://www.researchgate.net/post/How_can_I_convert_pixel_intensity_values_to_housefield_CT_number/5577b8735cd9e3a94e8b4591/citation/download
11. Vija, A.H., Desh, V.: Method for converting CT data to linear attenuation coefficient map data. U.S. Patent 6,950,494. Issued 27 September 2005
12. Phan, A.-C., Cao, H.-P., Trieu, T.-N., Phan, T.-C.: Detection and classification of brain hemorrhage using Hounsfield unit and deep learning techniques. In: Dang, T.K., Küng, J., Takizawa, M., Chung, T.M. (eds.) FDSE 2020. CCIS, vol. 1306, pp. 281–293. Springer, Singapore (2020). https://doi.org/10.1007/978-981-33-4370-2_20
13. DenOtter, T.D., Schubert, J.: Hounsfield unit (2019)
14. Eguren, M., et al.: Can gray values be converted to Hounsfield units? A systematic review. Dentomaxillofac. Radiol. **51**(1), 20210140 (2022)
15. Razi, T., Niknami, M., Ghazani, F.A.: Relationship between Hounsfield unit in CT scan and gray scale in CBCT. J. Dental Res. Dental Clin. Dental Prospects **8**(2), 107 (2014)
16. Shah, J.P., Mann, S.D., McKinley, R.L., Tornai, M.P.: Characterization of CT Hounsfield units for 3D acquisition trajectories on a dedicated breast CT system. J. Xray Sci. Technol. **26**(4), 535–551 (2018)

17. Hounsfield, G.N.: Computed medical imaging. Science **210**(4465), 22–28 (1980)
18. Huda, W., Slone, R.M.: Review of Radiologic Physics. Lippincott Williams & Wilkins, Philadelphia (2003)
19. Bushberg, J.T., Boone, J.M.: The Essential Physics of Medical Imaging. Lippincott Williams & Wilkins, Philadelphia (2011)
20. Kavur, A.E., Selver, M.A., Dicle, O., Barış, M., Gezer, N.S.: CHAOS - Combined (CT-MR) Healthy Abdominal Organ Segmentation Challenge Data (Version v1.03), April 2019. Zenodo. https://doi.org/10.5281/zenodo.3362844

Diabetic Retinopathy Blood Vessel Detection Using Deep-CNN-Based Feature Extraction and Classification

Anita Murmu(✉) and Piyush Kumar

Department of Computer Science and Engineering, National Institute of Technology Patna, Patna 800005, Bihar, India
{anitam.phd20.cs,piyush.cs}@nitp.ac.in

Abstract. Diabetic Retinopathy (DR) is the main cause of blindness and harms the retina due to the accumulation of glucose in the blood. Therefore, early DR detection, diagnosis, segmentation, and classification prevent patients with diabetes from losing their vision. However, the main challenge is the test takes time, lots of procedure, and money for proliferative stage of DR and identifying the proper glucose level that is present in the blood vessel. To address this problem, a unique and hybrid method, namely Deep Convolutional Neural Network (CNN) with EFficientNetB0 (Deep-CNNEF-Net), is used for earlier detection and classification of DR. Furthermore, the proposed scheme follows the pre-processing, input feature extraction, and classification phases. The pre-processing stage improves the presence of abnormalities and segmentation of DR by using the CNN with mean orientation technique. Moreover, the input feature extraction step uses CNN to obtain features that are important for training purposes. Furthermore, a novel modification to the VGG16 pooling layer uses the Global Average Pooling Layer (GAP) without a fattening layer for the boundary box of infected retinal blood vessels. The experimental results are obtained using two databases, namely the Digital Retinal Images for Vessel Extraction (DRIVE) and the STructured Analysis of the Retina (STARE) datasets, for the classification and detection of DR. The simulation results have been examined by evaluation metrics, such as accuracy, precision, recall, F1-score, specificity, and Mean Process Time per Frame (MPTF) for proper validation. The evaluation analysis outperforms the existing State-Of-The-Art (SOTA) models on the same eye retinal DR datasets.

Keywords: Retinal blood vessel · vessel classification · deep learning · retinopathy image · diabetic

1 Introduction

The DR is one of the leading causes of eye blindness due to the dilation and scarring of retinal blood vessels [1]. Therefore, loss of vision in the initial phases of diabetes is often prevented by early detection and treatment of DR biomarkers [2]. Ophthalmologists use a traditional fundus imaging technique to identify microaneurysms (MAs) in

KC Santosh et al. (Eds.): RTIP2R 2023, CCIS 2027, pp. 21–33, 2024.
https://doi.org/10.1007/978-3-031-53085-2_3

order to diagnose DR [3]. MAs are the main indicator of DR. However, contains significant drawbacks such as a conventional screening procedure. For instance, it is time-consuming, highly error-prone (since it is manual screening), and not a cost-effective option. Additionally, misclassifications may happen when some fundus image elements are identified as MAs, and additional errors happen when MAs are grouped together with other elements. Computer-aided automated diagnostic (CAD) techniques have a high rate of precision and can quickly determine DR. Therefore, convolutional techniques can be simply replaced when manual visual examination and observation become required [4]. Proliferative diabetic retinopathy (PDR) and Nonproliferative diabetic retinopathy (NPDR) are the two DR types. The PDR level shows a clear optic disk and normal blood vessel function [5]. The little veins in the retina (blood vessels) begin to leak fluid (substances) or blood, causing the retina to retain the exudates. This type of NPDR is thought to be a fundamental DR stage, and its abnormalities are classified depending on severity (moderate, mild, and severe). This condition should collapse under the influence of vision, resulting in swelling or thickening of the retina. Also clearly perceive minor components because of a tiny region in the retina's focus point [6]. However, several types of Deeo Learning (DL) [7] and Machine learning (ML) with Transfer Learning (TL) [8] approaches have been given and developed for classifying the severity of DR (mild, moderate, or severe) and early recognition.

Usman et al. [9] have proposed a Principal Component Analysis (PCA) to accomplish feature extraction. A pre-trained CNN-based Deep Learning MultiLabel Feature Extraction and Classification (ML-FEC) technique. Then, using three novel CNN architectures with transfer learning - ResNet50, SqueezeNet1, and ResNet152 with parameters used to train a subset of images to identify and categorize the lesions. Kumar et al. [10] have proposed an efficient hybrid DL technique for RBV segmentation and vessel classification. Saranya et al. [11] have proposed the proliferative phases of diabetic retinopathy, which are also distinguished by their distinctive characteristic known as neovascularization to be detected and recognized. This model uses color retinal images to accurately detect the existence of neovascularization. The detailed literature survey with a limitation table is shown in Table 1.

The novel Deep-CNNEF-Net is a combination of Deep-CNN with EfficientNetB0 approach for retinal blood vessel classification and detection from DR. In this work, to enhance image quality by applying a median filter. Additionally, to classify DR using the proposed Deep-CNNEF-Net system. Moreover, to detect the boundaries of DR using the deep learning-based VGG16-GAP approach. Therefore, by modifying the normalization steps within the Deep CNN framework. The Deep-CNN enhances the inherent functionality of Deep CNNs by modifying the normalization stages of the ReLU activation function within the deep framework. This approach enhances the intrinsic self capabilities of Deep CNNs without introducing extra learning layers. This enhancement emphasizes meaningful image features, leading to improved classification accuracy. Moreover, this enables Deep-CNN to operate efficiently without requiring an additional layer, which is critical for computing efficiency and classification accuracy. In this proposed approach, EfficientnetB0 improves performance while improving efficiency of computation by decreasing the number of parameters and Floating point Operations Per Second (FLOPs). The CNN layers have been utilized to extract features from the DR input images by using the EfficientNetB0 approach to train it faster and mitigate overfitting. Additionally, including the VGG16-GAP used for DR boundary boxes vessels. Specifically, the following contributions are included:

- The lack of samples to identifying the proper glucose level that is present in the blood vessel and test takes time, lots of procedure, and money for proliferative stage of DR. A novel method is proposed to overcome these issues.
- In the proposed system, design a novel Deep-CNNEF-Net model for classifying DR vessels. Furthermore, CNN with mean orientation segmentation techniques is used during training and improves feature maps in an upsampling layer.
- Additionally, the VGG16-GAP approach is used to vessel boundary boxes of DR.
- The experimental evaluation shows the proposed model outperforms SOTA for retinal blood vessel.

The rest sections of the paper are organized as follows: in Sect. 2 outlines the proposed approach. The description of the results of the experiment and discussion are in Sect. 3. Finally, the conclusion and future work of the paper are in Sect. 4.

Table 1. Literature survey

Ref.	Objective	Datasets	Techniques	Advantage	Limitations
[9]	Detection of diabetic retinopathy	DR and CSME	ML-FEC	Performance better	A single network cannot evaluate properly
[10]	Classification of retinal blood vessel image	DRIVE and STARE	EFCM	Increase performance	The preprocessing was not done
[11]	Segmentation of blood vessel image	DRIVE and STARE	CNN-VGG16	Performance increase	More time required
[15]	Retina vessels segmentation	DRIVE, STARE, IOSTAR, RC-SLO	VA-UFL	Easily integrated	Not able to detect tiny blood vessel
[16]	Blood vessel fundus segmentation	DRIVE, CHASEDB1, HRE, STARE	FC-CRF	Potential to connect with server	Not able to run in unlabeled image
[17]	Segmentation of retinal vessels	DRIVE, CHASE, STARE	MSIF	Improve performance	Not obtained the deeper features
[18]	Segmentation of retainal blood image	DRIVE, CHASE, STARE	Line dector	Performance increases	Missing of small vessel

2 Methodology

The proposed hybrid method, namely Deep Convolutional Neural Network (CNN) with EFficientNetB0 (Deep-CNNEF-Net), is shown in Fig. 1. The framework of the proposed scheme contains convolutional nodes, max-pooling, batch normalization, EfficientnetB0 as a backbone, and an activation function in downsampling. The details should be described in depth in this section, starting with the network architecture and essential network components. Furthermore, an overview of the proposed boundary box of the infected region of the retinal blood vessel image.

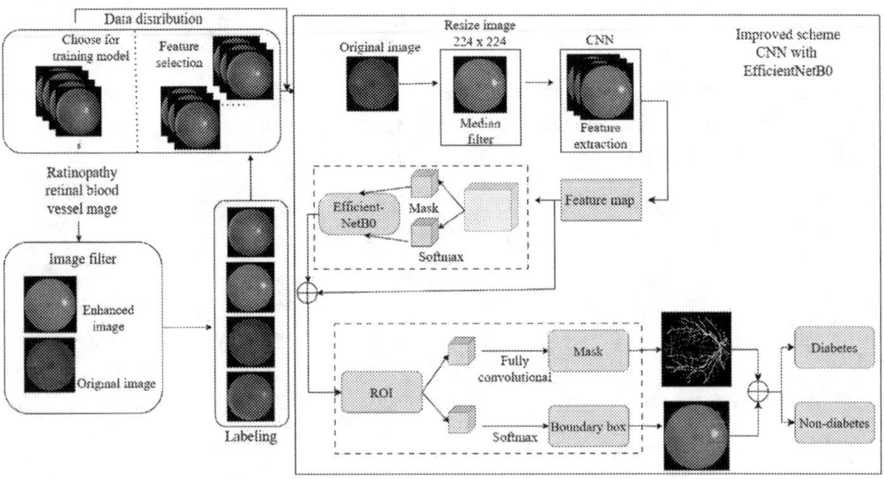

Fig. 1. The proposed methodology.

2.1 Dataset Details

We estimate the proposed scheme for DR blood vessel classification and detection tasks by using two datasets: STARE [12] and DRIVE [13], sample images of datasets are shown in Fig. 2.

- **STARE:** The STARE collection consists of 20 retinal images with a resolution of 700 × 605 pixels, 10 of which are pathologically affected. The STARE dataset received leave-one-out cross-validation.
- **DRIVE:** The DRIVE datasets contain a total of 40 color retinal images at resolutions of 565 × 584 pixels. The dataset is split into test and train sets, each containing 20 images.

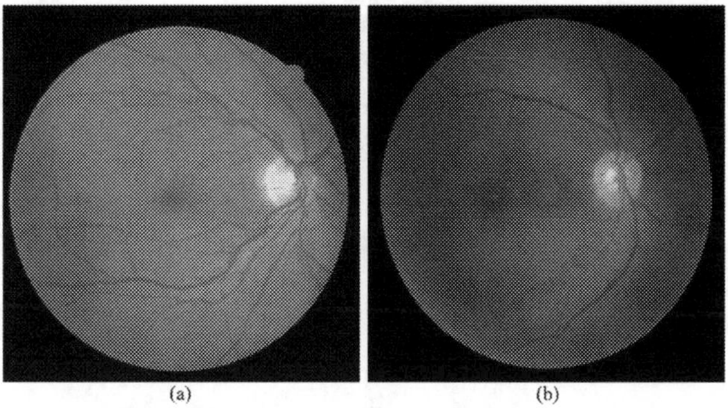

Fig. 2. Sample image of (a) DRIVE, and (b) STARE datasets.

2.2 Pre-processing

The vessel edge-preserving smooth filter classes include non-linear filters like the median filter. The fundus of images is quickly smoothed using the median filter, and the normalized image retains its crisp features. The median represents the average of all neighborhood pixel values. A stronger "central value" exists for the median value than for the average value. The middle-value calculation mathematical equation is shown in Eq. (1).

$$medianfilter[P(z) + R(z)] \neq median[P(z)] + median[Q(z)] \tag{1}$$

where the two different P(z) and R(z) retinal images.

Particularly, a median estimate is highly good in removing many noises between the neighborhood pixels that have low numerical variances. A median filter takes along every vessel pixel in the visual retinal image, regardless of the degree to which it accurately represents its surroundings. The median filter modifies the value of pixels with mid-way values rather than modifying the neighborhood mean pixel values. By dividing adjacent pixel values in the numerical sequence, the median is calculated. Then, substitute the center pixel value for the original value. If the neighborhood pixel has an even number of pixels, the average of the two middle pixels is used. Furthermore, apply the augmentation technique to increase the size and diversity of a training dataset.

2.3 Classification

CNN with Mean Orientation Based Segmentation and Boundary Box: The mean orientation approach is used in CNN for segmenting the exacted area from the DR retinal cells image using the mean orientation approach. The mean shift gives accurate information about the objects, combines regions, and frequently leads to extensive segmentation. The means shift represents a clustering approach that also does a non-parametric density gradient evaluation using a thorough kernel process. The mean shift determines the range of values for each data point before calculating its mean. Moreover, move the pixels to mean and keep using the same strategy until convergence. Mean shift is used for a variety of tasks including visual tracking, image segmentation, clustering, mode searching, and space analysis. The most common way for estimating density is by using kernel density. Given k points of data i = 1, 2, 3, … , k in d-dimensional region Q^b, the multiple-variate density estimates with the kernel are denoted as Q(z), and symmetric positively with the M matrix bandwidth. The point z, which is provided in Eq. (2), is calculated

$$f(z) = \frac{1}{k}\sum\nolimits_{i=1}^{k} K_M(z - z_i) \tag{2}$$

where

$$Q_M(z) = |M|^{\frac{-1}{2}} Q(M^{\frac{-1}{2}} z) \tag{3}$$

A multiple-variate kernel is produced from a symmetrical univariate kernel Q1(x) in two alternative methods, as shown mathematically in Eq. (4).

$$Q^s(z) = \prod\nolimits_{i=1}^{b} Q_1(z_i) Q^s(z) = a_{q,b} Q^1(z) \tag{4}$$

where $Q^p(z)$ is obtained from the multivariate kernel product and $Q^s(z)$ is radially symmetric since it is formed by rotating $Q_1(z)$ *in* $Q^b.a_{q,b}^{-1} = \int_{Q^b} Q_1(z)dz$ a constant implies that $Q^s(x)$ combines into one. The radially symmetrical kernels are more appropriate in this scenario. By using Eq. (5), a certain class of radially symmetrical kernels is achieved.

$$Q(z) = c_{q,b} q\left(z^2\right) \tag{5}$$

where Q(z) is a kernel shape, however only if X is greater than 0. Q(z) integrated a single influence of the normalization factor cq, b, which is taken to be positive. However, it has been shown in Eq. (3), it is important to first check the feature space's Euclidean metric validity. One bandwidth factor is used, the Eq. (2) becomes as follows:

$$f(\hat{z}) = \frac{1}{km^b}\sum_{i=1}^{k} Q(\frac{z - z_i}{m}) \tag{6}$$

The mean square error (MSE) is used as a proxy for a kernel density estimator's performance. The density estimation in Eq. (6) has been rewritten using the curve notation, and it is shown in Eq. (7).

$$f_{m,q}(\hat{z}) = \frac{c_{q,b}}{km^b}\sum_{i=1}^{k} Q(\frac{z - z_i^2}{m}) \tag{7}$$

The segmentation of DR retinal blood vessels provided by Eq. (7) is shown in Fig. 3 and Fig. 4, respectively.

Deep-CNN with EfficientNet: The proposed hybrid version of Deep-CNN with an EFficientNetB0 Network architecture (Deep-CNNEF-Net) is used to enhance the vessels classification and detection while maintaining the model's portability (shown in Fig. 1 and Algorithm 1 with time complexity $O(n^2)$). EfficientNetB0 provides a novel

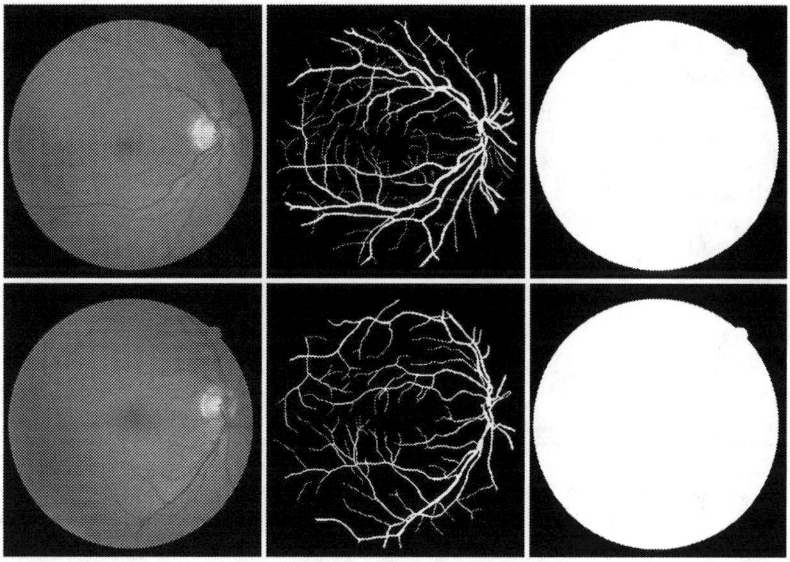

(a) (b) (c)

Fig. 3. Performance results (a) original image, (b) masked image, and (c) segmented image

approach to expanding a CNN convolutional layer structure without having the issue of gradients vanishing by using the concept of shortcut connections. Moreover, EfficientnetB0 improves performance while improving the efficiency of computation by decreasing the number of parameters and FLOPs. The CNN layers have been utilized to the extract features from the input colonoscopy images and choose the ROI using the EfficientNetB0 approach to train it faster. In order to recover spatial information and enhance the boundary classification of vessels, the CNN with EfficientNetB0 network incorporates an encoder-and-decoder structure. The decoder layers are used to extract specifics, while the encoder layers are designed to minimize feature loss and collect higher-level semantic data.

The depth, breadth, and cardinality of the frameworks affect the performance of CNN architecture. In addition to these components, network architecture design also has to be taken into consideration in order to improve the expressiveness of a model. A low-level feature map focusing on relevant traits and suppressing unneeded ones boosts expressiveness. To choose the parameters and emphasize significant features in the spatial and medium components of the retinal blood vessels image, we employ channel and low-level feature maps modules. Moreover, the dice loss and sigmoid function are used for improving the performance, Eq. (8) shows the dice loss:

$$LSdice = 1 - DSC(true\_y, pred\_y) \tag{8}$$

Algorithm 1: Training process of vessel classification

Input : Retinal blood vessels extracted features
Output: Classification of diabetic vessels from retinopathy image
Initialize the number of features $F_1, F_2, F_3, ..., F_n$ and number of layers LN
for *every feature* **do**
  Calculate CNN function using $(CNNL_a)_i^m = CNNL_a(q_i^m)$
  for *all features* **do**
    Calculate pooling function using $Py_i^m = PL_0(CNN_a)_i^m$
  end
end
for *every features* **do**
  Calculate the output of the Deep-CNNEF-Net using $\emptyset(F) = \sum_{i=1}^{m} dip(\,||F - f_i||\,)$
end
return classified diabetic retinal blood vessel i.e $\emptyset(F)$

Infected Region Boundary Box: The experiment demonstrates that the DeepCNNEF-Net model is significantly more effective at classifying blood vessels than other classification methods. For evaluating the quality of the qualitative evaluation of the retinopathy imagine visualization using VGG16-GAP. The VGG16GAP gets applied to calculate the importance of the spatial position in the convolution layers using the gradient. The Deep-CNN technology allows us to concentrate more on an images key components. VGG16 improves the capacity of the network for learning and discriminative representations. The final convolutional outputs are computed using the VGG16-GAP visualization of the infected blood vessels boundary box. The VGG16 of the model has variable locations and concentrations, as seen in Fig. 4.

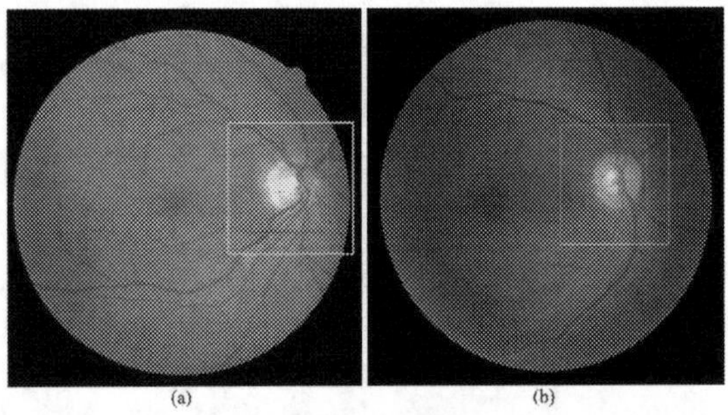

Fig. 4. The performance boundary box results (a) DRIVE and (b) STARE

3 Results and Discussion

The proposed system evaluates results by using STARE dataset and DRIVE dataset. The proposed model is tested and trained on an Intel Core i5 processor running at 2.8 GHz, 8 GB of RAM, and the graphics processor Unit (GPU) [14]. In addition to TensorFlow and Python 3.8.1, used Keras library to implement the proposed approach. The publically available dataset has been resized to 224 × 224 pixels. All the collected samples are used in training, and only 30% of the data is used in the testing process. The proposed system is trained by using the Adam optimizer with a 0.0001 learning rate, a 0.1 dropout, and a 16 mini-batch size. Figure 6 shows the proposed model loss and accuracy graph.

3.1 Experimental Results

Quantitative Analysis by Using DRIVE Dataset: The DRIVE dataset is used in this subsection to compare the performance evaluation of the proposed system to various SOTA classification approaches. The F1-score and accuracy of the proposed methodology performance evaluation are used in Table 2 to validate it.

Table 2. The performance results of proposed scheme

Datasets	Deep-CNN backbone	Accuracy	Recall	Precision	F1-score	Specificity	MPTF (ms)
DRIVE	EfficientNetB0	97.23	96.77	95.05	97.55	93.10	430
	Mean	0.972	0.967	0.950	0.975	0.931	0.430
	± SD	0.072	0.064	0.098	0.049	0.021	0.008
STARE	EfficientnetB0	98.89	95.91	95.23	97.95	93.83	390
	Mean	0.988	0.959	0.952	0.979	0.938	0.0390
	± SD	0.098	0.084	0.097	0.062	0.048	0.009

Here, the performance analysis has been verified using 30% training images and 70% testing images using retinal images from a random sample. According to the validation results, the proposed approach performed better VAUFL [15], conditional random field [16], DNet [17], LDVS-MWDS [18], GVF [19], and CNNVGG16-Net [11] than alternative classification approaches. However, though the comparable classification techniques give 95.89%, 97.09%, 95%, 97%, and 96% of accuracy, respectively, the proposed approach (CNN-EfficientNetB0) has a accuracy of 97.23%. However, the ELEMENT [20] is better in terms of proposed model accuracy. The proposed methodology F1-score is 97.55%, compared to F1-score of 76.07%, 78.57%, 82.46%, 75%, 83%, 85.79%, and 97% for the comparative classification approaches. Figure 5 shows a visual depiction of proposed scheme.

Quantitative Analysis by Using the STARE Dataset: The STARE dataset is used to compare the proposed technique's performance evaluation with the results of existing classification approaches. The validation result in Table 2 demonstrated that the proposed approach performed better than previous classification techniques. The proposed technique has a accuracy 98.89%, whereas other SOTA approaches give a accuracy of 95.02%, 97.81%, 95%, 96%, 98.27%, and 95%, respectively. Similar in that the proposed technique achieves a F1score is 97.95%, the comparative classification approaches obtain F1-score of 76.90%, 76.40%, 84.82%, 76%, 82%, 89.10%, and 95%, respectively. Figure 5 show a graphical depiction of the STARE dataset's recall, precision, F-score, specificity, accuracy, and Mean Process Time per Frame (MPTF).

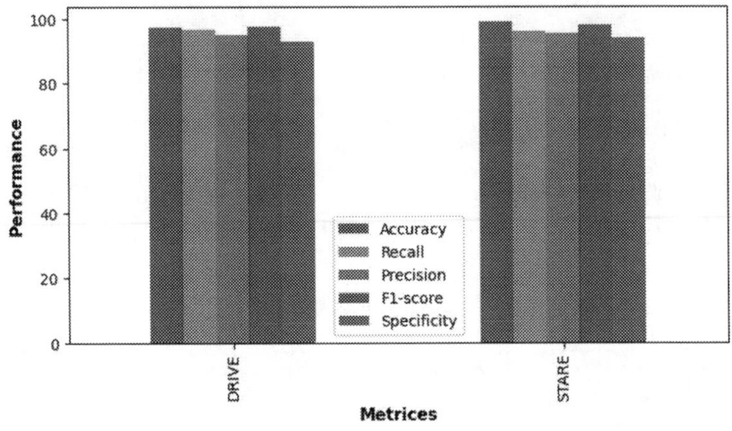

Fig. 5. The performance graph of proposed Deep-CNNEF-Net model

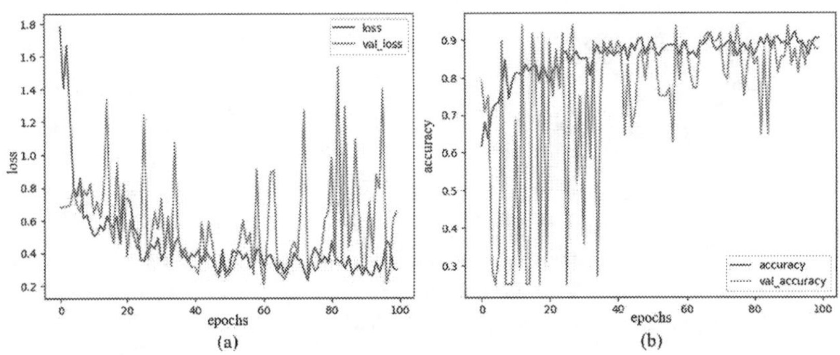

Fig. 6. Performance (a) loss and (b) accuracy verse epoch graph

3.2 Results Comparison

This demonstrates that the proposed technique has a lot of possibilities for helping diabetics classify and identify retinal blood vessels during retinopathy. The proposed Deep-CNNEF-Net performance has improved the accuracy in comparison to the other existing models. The result comparison of blood vessel classification accuracy, recall, precision, F1-score, specificity, and MPTF with the proposed models with existing SOTA approaches. As demonstrated in Table 3 and Fig. 2(a)-(b) accuracy of STARE and DRIVE, and Fig. 2(c)-(d) F1-score of STARE and DRIVE, the proposed Deep-CNNEF-Net outperforms present models. Moreover, Fig. 7 shows the proposed model comparison with existing SOTA model (a)-(b) accuracy of STARE and DRIVE, and (c)-(d) F1-score of STARE and DRIVE. Additionally, Deep-CNNEF-Net increases dataset accuracy by 6.29% and 4.75% overall due to EfficientNetB0 and mean orientation in an upsampling layer. Moreover, the proposed scheme outperforms better in comparison to VAUFL [15], conditional random field [16], DNet [17], LDVS-MWDS [18], GVF [19], ELEMENT [20], and CNNVGG16-Net [11] in terms of F1-score and accuracy due to the EfficientNetB0 in upsampling layer and dropout being added in the channels. However, in terms of accuracy ELEMENT DRIVE dataset is better than the proposed model. Moreover, the biomedical imaging technique has used many modalities namely, X-ray, Computer Tomography (CT), and ultrasound, and so on [21].

Table 3. The performance comparison with other existing state-of-the-arts models for vessel classification

S. No	Models	STARE dataset		DRIVE dataset	
		Accuracy	F1-score	Accuracy	F1-score
1	VAUFL [15]	95.02	76.90	95.89	76.07
2	Conditional random field [16]	–	76.40	–	78.57
3	DNet [17]	97.81	84.82	97.09	82.46
4	LDVS-MWDS [18]	95	76	95	75
5	GVF [19]	96	82	97	83
6	ELEMENT [20]	98.27	89.10	**97.40**	85.79
7	CNNVGG16-Net [11]	95	95	96	97
8	**Deep-CNNEF-Net (Proposed)**	**98.89**	**97.95**	97.23	**97.55**

4 Conclusion and Future Work

The proposed Deep-CNNEF-Net scheme provided for classifying and detecting retinal blood vessels from DR images. The proposed CNN feature extraction is extracted from DR images. Furthermore, an CNN with mean orientation is used to handle scale variation during training and improve feature selection of vessel segmentation. Moreover, the VGG16-GAP approach is used to vessels boundary boxes of the retina. As a result, the Deep-CNNEF-Net learns additional specifics about the target area of DR vessels. In the future, Deep-CNNEF-Net will be tested on other medical modality-related tasks including secured feature detection in order to increase the effectiveness of medical image security.

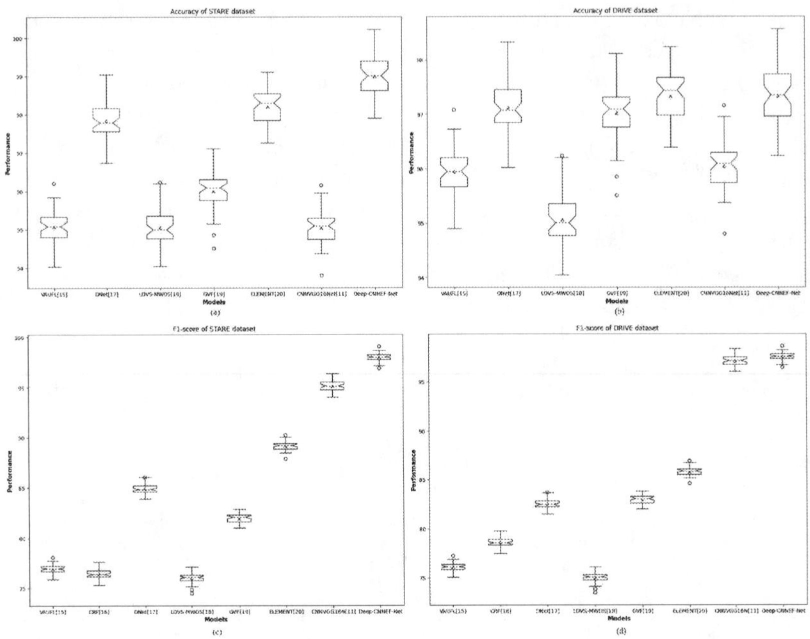

Fig. 7. The performance model comparison with existing SOTA model (a)-(b) accuracy of STARE and DRIVE, and (c)-(d) F1-score of STARE and DRIVE

References

1. Diabetic Retinopathy. https://www.nei.nih.gov/learnabout-eye-health/eye-conditions-and-diseases/diabetic-retinopathy. Accessed 9 July 2023
2. Ahsan, H.: Diabetic retinopathy–biomolecules and multiple pathophysiology. Diabetes Metab. Syndr. **9**(1), 51–54 (2015)
3. He, A., Li, T., Li, N., Wang, K., Fu, H.: CABNet: category attention block for imbalanced diabetic retinopathy grading. IEEE Trans. Med. Imaging **40**(1), 143–153 (2020)
4. Dai, L., et al.: Clinical report guided retinal microaneurysm detection with multi-sieving deep learning. IEEE Trans. Med. Imaging **37**(5), 1149–1161 (2018)
5. Zang, P., et al.: DcardNet: diabetic retinopathy classification at multiple levels based on structural and angiographic optical coherence tomography. IEEE Trans. Biomed. Eng. **68**(6), 1859–1870 (2020)
6. Math, L., Fatima, R.: Adaptive machine learning classification for diabetic retinopathy. Multimed. Tools Appl. **80**(4), 5173–5186 (2021)
7. Murmu, A., Kumar, P.: Deep learning model-based segmentation of medical diseases from MRI and CT images. In: TENCON 2021 IEEE Region 10 Conference (TENCON), pp. 608–613 (2021)
8. Murmu, A., Kumar, P.: A novel Gateaux derivatives with efficient DCNN-Resunet method for segmenting multi-class brain tumor. Med. Biol. Eng. Comput., 1–24 (2023)
9. Usman, T.M., Saheed, Y.K., Ignace, D., Nsang, A.: Diabetic retinopathy detection using principal component analysis multi-label feature extraction and classification. Int. J. Cogn. Comput. Eng. **4**, 78–88 (2023)
10. Kumar, Y., Gupta, B.: Retinal image blood vessel classification using hybrid deep learning in cataract diseased fundus images. Biomed. Signal Process. Control **84**, 104776 (2023)

11. Saranya, P., Prabakaran, S., Kumar, R., Das, E.: Blood vessel segmentation in retinal fundus images for proliferative diabetic retinopathy screening using deep learning. Vis. Comput., 1–16 (2022)
12. STARE Dataset. https://www.kaggle.com/datasets/vidheeshnacode/stare-dataset. Accessed 9 July 2023
13. DRIVE Digital Retinal Images for Vessel Extraction. https://www.kaggle.com/datasets/andrewmvd/drive-digital-retinal-images-forvessel-extraction. Accessed 9 July 2023
14. Kumar, P., Agrawal, A.: GPU-based focus-driven multi-coordinates viewing system for large volume data visualisation. Int. J. Comput. Syst. Eng. **4**(2–3), 86–95 (2018)
15. Srinidhi, C.L., Aparna, P., Rajan, J.: A visual attention guided unsupervised feature learning for robust vessel delineation in retinal images. Biomed. Signal Process. Control **44**, 110–126 (2018)
16. Orlando, J.I., Prokofyeva, E., Blaschko, M.B.: A discriminatively trained fully connected conditional random field model for blood vessel segmentation in fundus images. IEEE Trans. Biomed. Eng. **64**(1), 16–27 (2016)
17. Jiang, Y., Tan, N., Peng, T., Zhang, H.: Retinal vessels segmentation based on dilated multi-scale convolutional neural network. IEEE Access **7**, 76342–76352 (2019)
18. Biswal, B., Pooja, T., Bala, S.N.: Robust retinal blood vessel segmentation using line detectors with multiple masks. IET Image Proc. **12**(3), 389–399 (2018)
19. Karn, P.K., Biswal, B., Samantaray, S.R.: Robust retinal blood vessel segmentation using hybrid active contour model. IET Image Proc. **13**(3), 440–450 (2019)
20. Rodrigues, E.O., Conci, A., Liatsis, P.: Element: multi-modal retinal vessel segmentation based on a coupled region growing and machine learning approach. IEEE J. Biomed. Health Inform. **24**(12), 3507–3519 (2020)
21. Murmu, A., Kumar, P.: A novel GAN with DNA sequences and hash-based approach for improving Medical Image Security. Int. J. Image Graph. Signal Process. (IJIGSP) (2023, in press)

Detection of COVID-19 Disease Using Federated Learning

Saurabh Dixit(✉) and C. L. P. Gupta

Bansal Institute of Engineering and Technology, Lucknow, India
saurabh.dixit.21@gmail.com

Abstract. The study investigates the use of Federated Learning (FL) in combination with the AlexNet architecture for the early confirmation of COVID-19 from chest radiography data. A thorough literature review highlights the potential of FL in healthcare and its application in COVID-19 detection, emphasizing privacy preservation and data security. The methodology involves collecting and 80% preprocessing a diverse dataset, partitioning the data among multiple clients, and iteratively training a global model. Experimental results demonstrate the effectiveness of the FL-based AlexNet model, achieving a high accuracy of 92% on a test dataset. Future research should focus on expanding datasets, exploring advanced privacy techniques, optimizing and scaling FL models, developing real-time applications, and integrating FL models with other modalities for improved COVID-19 detection. These advancements can contribute to early detection and diagnosis, supporting healthcare professionals in combating the pandemic.

Keywords: Deep learning · CNN · AlexNet · Federated learning

1 Introduction

Since its emergence in late 2019, the global landscape has been profoundly impacted by the outbreak of COVID-19. This unprecedented pandemic has brought about significant changes to various aspects of society, including public health, economies, and daily life. It has rapidly spread across continents, leading to millions of infections and fatalities globally [16]. The disease exhibits a many symptoms like cold and cough, chest congestion etc. with some cases resulting in organ failure and death. Efforts to control the spread of the virus have included widespread testing, contact tracing, lockdowns, and the development of vaccines. The long-term effect of this on public health, economies, and society as a whole continues to be a subject of ongoing research and analysis [2]. ML and DL have played pivotal roles in various aspects of COVID-19 detection, diagnosis, risk assessment, contact tracing, treatment development, and vaccine optimization. These technologies continue to contribute to our understanding of the virus and support efforts to combat the pandemic [15]. The conflict between machine learning and privacy, particularly in the health sector where data is

KC Santosh et al. (Eds.): RTIP2R 2023, CCIS 2027, pp. 34–43, 2024.
https://doi.org/10.1007/978-3-031-53085-2_4

often stored in multiple organizations due to regulations like HIPAA and GDPR redefine the data management policy. Machine learning, especially deep learning models, require access to large datasets to performed well. However, privacy concerns and liability risks make it difficult to obtain such data [4]. Internet of Medical Things (IoMT) is used to improve the healthcare operations during Covid-19 pandemic [1]. The Internet of Medical Things (IoMT) has revolutionized healthcare by utilizing wearable sensors and devices to collect medical data for intelligent data analytics. These devices enable real-time monitoring and analysis of patient health parameters, leading to more personalized and timely healthcare interventions. Unlike traditional smart healthcare systems that rely on centralized AI functions located in the cloud or data centers, IoMT leverages edge computing to process data locally, reducing communication latency and improving response times [11]. The author leveraging the Internet of Medical Things (IoMT) and applying ML and DL techniques face challenges related to communication latency, network scalability, data privacy, and the unavailability of appropriate datasets. To address these issues, we propose a novel model that combines the base model of AlexNet with Federated Learning. This approach aims to overcome the limitations posed by communication latency and network scalability in IoMT, while also addressing data privacy concerns and the scarcity of suitable datasets in ML and DL traditionally [10]. Due to communication latency and network scalability issues while using IoMT and data privacy and proper dataset unavailability issues while using machine learning and deep learning, we proposed a model to overcome these issues with the base model of AlexNet using Federated Learning.

Further article are organized in following way. In Sect. 2, a comprehensive review of the existing work is presented. The research methodology, including the base model of AlexNet using Federated Learning and its evaluation is described Sect. 3. The experiment results, describing the accuracy comparison of base model and with FL, ROC-AUC comparison for all the models and the comparison between epoch and loss, accuracy is shown in Sect. 4, Finally, we conclude this with future scope Sect. 5.

2 Literature Review

In [13] The author discusses Federated Learning (FL) as a decentralized approach to address privacy concerns in healthcare. It highlights real-world cases in COVID-19 scenarios and examines the limitations of FL. The paper emphasizes the potential of FL in fighting the COVID-19 pandemic and advancing data-driven precision medicine. In [7] FedFocus is a federated learning framework for COVID-19 detection on CXR images. It improves training efficiency and accuracy by using the training loss for parameter aggregation weights. The framework includes a dynamic factor to stabilize the aggregation process as the training deepens. Real-world CXR images are divided based on population and infection data from three cities, resulting in a dataset that closely represents reality. Extensive experiments demonstrate that FedFocus outperforms baselines in terms of training efficiency, accuracy, and stability. In [9] author reviews recent advances in deep learning and federated learning for COVID-19 detection, focusing on the latter. It presents a simple FL implementation for COVID-19 detection using CXR image datasets. The paper explores the potential of FL in medical research and addresses implementation challenges. It concludes with suggestions for future work in this area. In [18] the paper highlights the criticality of privacy in healthcare and proposes a privacy-preserving federated learning algorithm that utilizes homomorphic encryption. The evaluation of the algorithm demonstrates its effectiveness in maintaining data security while achieving satisfactory performance. This work contributes to the advancement of privacy-preserving techniques in healthcare applications and underscores the need for robust privacy measures in the domain. In [5] presents Genetic Clustered Federated Learning (Genetic CFL), an algorithm for privacy-preserving early detection of COVID-19. It optimizes parameters using genetic algorithms and outperforms conventional AI approaches. The study discusses limitations, deployment conditions, and suggests future research areas such as scalability and real-time datasets in various applications. In [19] Yang et al. introduces FLOP, a new algorithm for privacy-preserving FL on used datasets. A partial model shared by FLOP, mitigating privacy and security risks. It achieves comparable or superior performance in benchmark and real-world healthcare tasks, including COVID-19 detection. The paper addresses privacy attacks in federated learning and highlights FLOP's ability to address vulnerabilities. In summary, FLOP provides a solution for privacy protection in federated learning with medical datasets. In [3] Durga and Poovammal presents FLED-Block, a novel framework for privacy-preserving COVID-19 prediction using lung CT images. It combines blockchain and federated learning, achieving accurate predictions while maintaining data privacy. Comparative analysis shows superior performance compared to existing models. FLED-Block offers a concise and unique solution for privacy-preserving COVID-19 prediction. In [8] Lu et al. introduces a weakly-supervised framework that enables federated learning without direct data sharing which is attention based. The approach achieves accurate classification and survival prediction across multiple institutions while preserving differential privacy. Results demonstrate the effectiveness of the method in developing accurate models without data sharing, and an easy-to-use software package for computational pathology is made available. In [11] the author initiate a FL approach for detection using GANs. It enables collaboration among institutions without sharing data by employing model averaging and a reputation-based incentive mechanism. The approach surpasses standalone GANs in terms of accuracy and convergence speed. In [17] Ved et al. evaluates FL for predicting mortality of this disease using EHR data from 5 hospitals. The study demonstrates that federated models outperform local models in most hospitals.

From the above literature review we found that their are various approaches and algorithms in the context of COVID-19 detection using federated learning and related techniques. The studies explore the potential of federated earning in addressing privacy concerns, improving training efficiency and accuracy, and maintaining data security. Different algorithms such as FedFocus, Genetic CFL, FLOP, FLED-Block, and GAN-based approaches are proposed to enhance COVID-19 detection while preserving privacy. The studies demonstrate superior performance compared to convolutional AI methods and highlight the importance of privacy preservation in healthcare. Overall, the literature review showcase the advancements and potential of federated learning in the fight against COVID-19.

In the following section, we will discuss the methodology used in a study focused on developing a AlexNet model to detect COVID-19 from chest radiography images using federated learning. Specifically, we will cover the data collection and preprocessing process, which involved gathering images from various publicly accessible datasets and some of the dataset is created by our own. We will also discuss how the collected data was split into training and test sets, and the AlexNet model that was developed using full architecture having 7 layers. Additionally, we will dive into the model's high accuracy achieved on both training and test sets. Lastly, we will explore how AlexNet architecture was used to reduce the loss without compromising its accuracy, and provide an overview of the steps followed in the model.

3 Methodology

3.1 Data Collection and Preprocessing

The data is collected from various publicly accessible datasets, online sources, and published papers. Specifically, 2437 Chest images were collected from the Padchest, 179 from a medical school in Germany, 558 from SIRM, Github, Kaggle, and Twitter, and 400 CXR images from another Github source. In addition, 10192 non-COVID-19 CXR images were collected from three different datasets, including 8851 from RSNA and 1341 from Kaggle. From these images 1811 images are covid-19 affected images, 1029 images are affected with viral pneumonia, 10781 images are healthy and 1624 images are affected with Bacterial Pneumonia. After the collection of dataset these images are split in test, train and validate for model processing. Details of the split dataset are given in Table 1.

Table 1. Number of images in each class

Class	Train	Test	Val
Covid-19	1500	206	105
Viral Pneumonia	412	412	205
Healthy	901	880	450
Bacterial Pneumonia	650	650	324

The AlexNet architecture lies in its ability to demonstrate the effectiveness of deep learning for large-scale image classification tasks, its pioneering use of deep networks [14] and the introduction of novel techniques that improved model performance. It set the stage for the development of deeper and more powerful CNN architectures, leading to significant advancements in computer vision and deep learning research [6]. Overall, integrating the AlexNet architecture with federated learning offers the potential to leverage the power of deep learning for image classification tasks while preserving data privacy and facilitating collaborative knowledge transfer among multiple institutions. It combines the strengths of both approaches to achieve improved accuracy, scalability, and privacy in large-scale image classification scenarios [20].

The steps in implementing the AlexNet architecture using Federated Learning are as follows [4]:

- Data Partitioning: Divide the dataset into multiple non-overlapping partitions, where each partition is distributed among different clients (e.g., hospitals or institutions) in a federated learning setting. Ensure that the data is appropriately split while maintaining privacy and data security.
- Model Initialization: Initialize the AlexNet model on each client with the same architecture and parameters. This serves as the starting point for training.
- Local Model Training: Perform model training on clients using their local data partition. Clients independently do model training on its data using the backpropagation algorithm.
- Aggregation: when model training is done, it will aggregate the model parameters from each client to create a global model. This aggregation step can be performed using various methods, such as model averaging or weighted averaging, to combine the knowledge from different clients while preserving privacy.
- Model Update and Iteration: Distribute the updated global model back to the clients. Each client uses the global model as a starting point for the next round of local training. Repeat steps 3–5 for multiple iterations by which model's performance will be improved.
- Evaluation and Testing: Assess the performance of the federated AlexNet model on a separate test dataset. Measure metrics such as accuracy, precision, recall, or F1 score to evaluate the model's effectiveness in detecting the target task (e.g., COVID-19 detection).
- Privacy and Security Measures: Implement techniques for ensuring the confidentiality and integrity of the data during federated learning.
- Fine-tuning and Optimization: Explore techniques to optimize the federated learning process, such as gradient compression, adaptive learning rates, or client selection strategies, to enhance training efficiency and convergence.

– Iterative Refinement: Iterate and fine-tune the federated learning process based on the performance and feedback obtained from evaluation steps. This may involve adjusting hyperparameters, modifying the data partitioning scheme, or incorporating additional privacy or security measures.

As per above given steps, we have utilized AlexNet architecture with FL framework for COVID-19 detection, enabling model training across many clients while maintaining data privacy. We have evaluated the model performance on a test dataset with 2148 pictures. The model has given an accuracy of 92%, which indicates the effectiveness in predicting disease using chest images [12]. The experimental results given by the model for COVID-19 given below.

4 Experimental Results

The model is run on the powerful NVIDIA DGX v100 computer to train our model. In this article, federated learning (FL) is used with Alexnet as base model and also it is run for several clients. A list of hyper parameter is listed in Table 2. In this article it is also compared with AlexNet base model which is run for 500 epochs. During the training of Alexnet model, epoch vs loss and accuracy changes is plotted. It is shown in the Fig. 1 and it is also shown a comparison with Alexnet Base model.

Accuracy is one of the important matrix to measure the model performance. In the Fig. 2, it is shown a comparison of accuracy with federated learning method with AlexNet Base model. In this figure, it is clearly shown that FL with 15 client with AlexNet as base model provide 5.89% higher accuracy than AlexNet base model. Increasing accuracy is very less than expected because lack of availability of dataset but it is clearly seen a increment of result.

AUC-ROC is one of the important matrices that validate the performance of deep learning model. The high area under the curve denotes better performance where lower indicates the less reliable model. ROC plot include true positive rate (TPR) and false positive rate (FPR). In the Eq. 1 and Eq. 2 shows the mathematical representation of FPR, TPR respectively.

$$FPR = FP/(FP + TN) where FP = False positive and TN = True Negative. \tag{1}$$

$$TPR = TP/(TP + FN) where TP = True positive and FN = False Negative. \tag{2}$$

In the Fig. 3, it is showing the ROC curve with area under curve and it is also shown a comparison with AlexNet base model.

Table 2. Parameter used in federated learning model (FL)

Parameters	Range or Value
Client	5,10,15,20
Communication Round	500
Epochs per communication round	100
Learning Rate	0.001
Optimizer	Adam
Batch Size	32

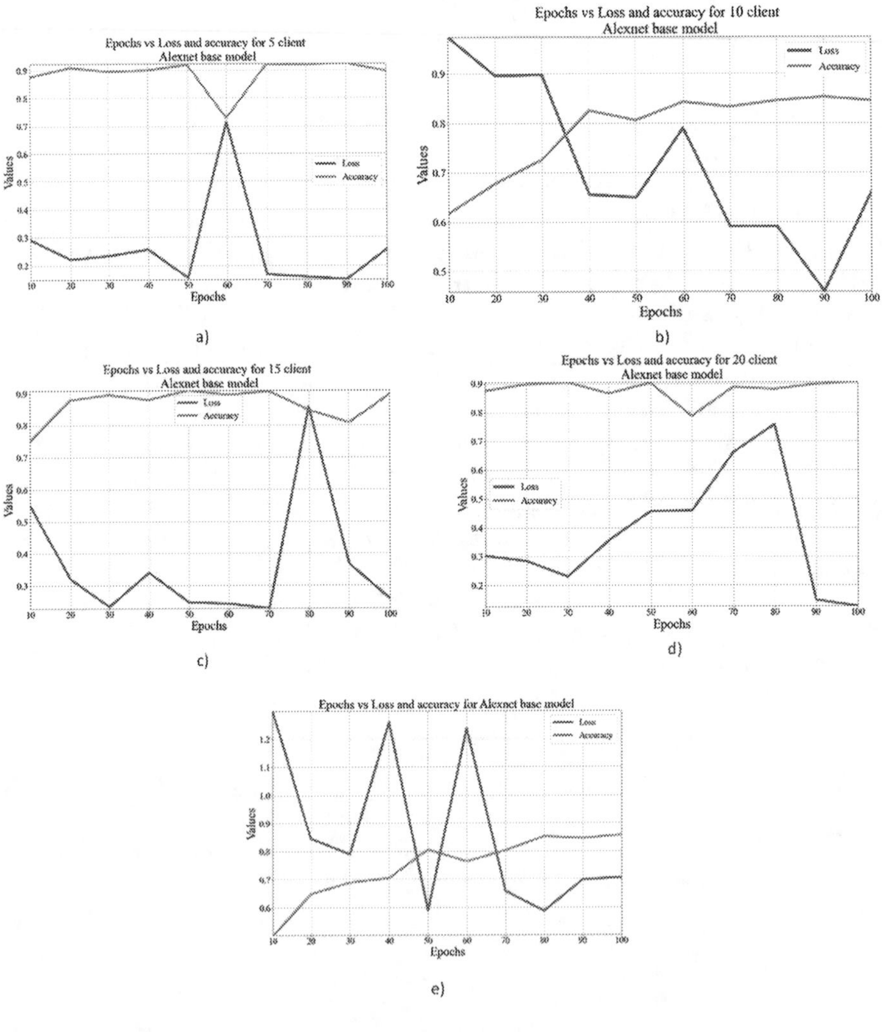

Fig. 1. Epoch vs loss and accuracy

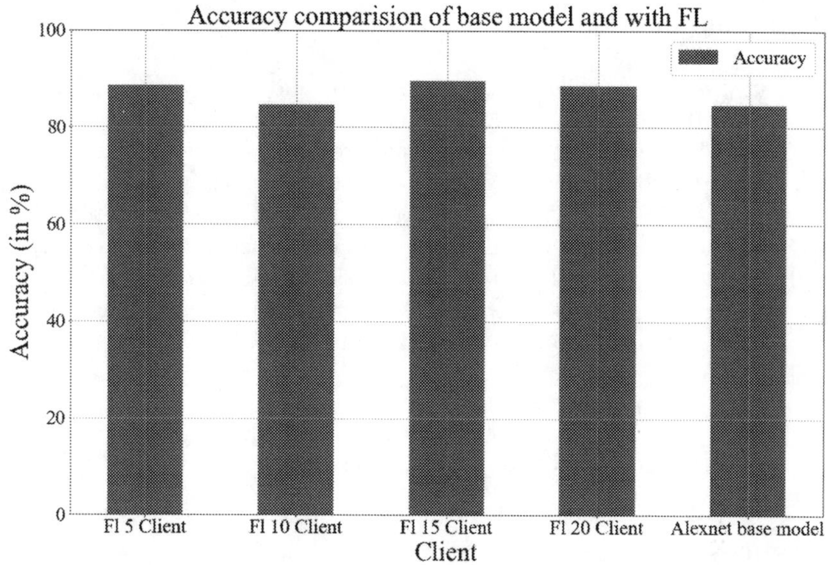

Fig. 2. Comparison of Accuracy for all model.

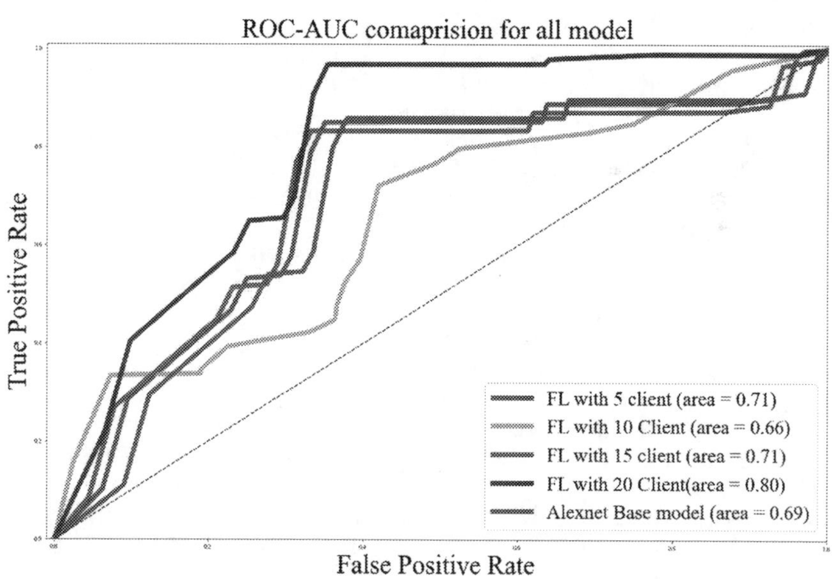

Fig. 3. ROC Curve for all models

5 Conclusion

In this study, we used Federated Learning (FL) and the AlexNet architecture to detect COVID-19 from chest X-ray images. The FL approach allowed us to train the model using distributed data while preserving privacy. We achieved an accuracy of 92% in detecting COVID-19, demonstrating the effectiveness of the FL-based AlexNet model. This has the potential to aid healthcare professionals in early detection and diagnosis. The model showed promising results in predicting COVID-19, indicating its potential in assisting healthcare professionals in early detection and diagnosis. FL with 20 clients showing a good accuracy with high AUC score (.80) which implies that alexnet base model with 20 clients is the best model to classify the covid19 in early stage from radiography Future work includes expanding datasets, exploring advanced privacy techniques, optimizing and scaling FL models, developing real-time applications, and integrating FL models with other modalities for improved COVID-19 detection.

References

1. Chowdhury, D., et al.: Federated learning based Covid-19 detection. Expert Syst. **40**(5), e13173 (2023). https://doi.org/10.1111/exsy.13173. https://onlinelibrary.wiley.com/doi/10.1111/exsy.13173
2. Darzidehkalani, E., Sijtsema, N.M., van Ooijen, P.M.A.: A comparative study of federated learning models for COVID-19 detection, March 2023. http://arxiv.org/abs/2303.16141, arXiv:2303.16141 [cs, eess]
3. Durga, R., Poovammal, E.: FLED-block: federated learning ensembled deep learning blockchain model for COVID-19 prediction. Front. Public Health **10**, 892499 (2022). https://doi.org/10.3389/fpubh.2022.892499. https://www.frontiersin.org/articles/10.3389/fpubh.2022.892499/full
4. Feki, I., Ammar, S., Kessentini, Y., Muhammad, K.: Federated learning for COVID-19 screening from Chest X-ray images. Appl. Soft Comput. **106**, 107330 (2021). https://doi.org/10.1016/j.asoc.2021.107330. https://linkinghub.elsevier.com/retrieve/pii/S1568494621002532
5. Kandati, D.R., Gadekallu, T.R.: Genetic clustered federated learning for COVID-19 detection. Electronics **11**(17), 2714 (2022). https://doi.org/10.3390/electronics11172714. https://www.mdpi.com/2079-9292/11/17/2714
6. Li, S., Wang, L., Li, J., Yao, Y.: Image classification algorithm based on improved AlexNet. J. Phys. Conf. Ser. **1813**, 012051 (2021)
7. Li, Z., et al.: Integrated CNN and federated learning for COVID-19 detection on chest X-ray images. IEEE/ACM Trans. Comput. Biol. Bioinf., 1–11 (2022). https://doi.org/10.1109/TCBB.2022.3184319. https://ieeexplore.ieee.org/document/9800698/
8. Lu, M.Y., et al.: Federated learning for computational pathology on gigapixel whole slide images. Med. Image Anal. **76**, 102298 (2022). https://doi.org/10.1016/j.media.2021.102298. https://linkinghub.elsevier.com/retrieve/pii/S1361841521003431
9. Naz, S., Phan, K.T., Chen, Y.P.: A comprehensive review of federated learning for COVID-19 detection. Int. J. Intell. Syst. **37**(3), 2371–2392 (2022). https://doi.org/10.1002/int.22777. https://onlinelibrary.wiley.com/doi/10.1002/int.22777

10. Nguyen, D.C., Ding, M., Pathirana, P.N., Seneviratne, A., Zomaya, A.Y.: Federated learning for COVID-19 detection with generative adversarial networks in edge cloud computing. IEEE Internet Things J. **9**(12), 10257–10271 (2022). https://doi.org/10.1109/JIOT.2021.3120998. https://ieeexplore.ieee.org/document/9580478/
11. Nguyen, D.C., et al.: Federated learning for smart healthcare: a survey. ACM Comput. Surv. **55**(3), 1–37 (2023). https://doi.org/10.1145/3501296. https://dl.acm.org/doi/10.1145/3501296
12. Nilsson, A., Smith, S., Ulm, G., Gustavsson, E., Jirstrand, M.: A performance evaluation of federated learning algorithms. In: Proceedings of the Second Workshop on Distributed Infrastructures for Deep Learning, pp. 1–8 (2018)
13. Qian, F., Zhang, A.: The value of federated learning during and post-COVID-19. Int. J. Qual. Health Care **33**(1), mzab010 (2021). https://doi.org/10.1093/intqhc/mzab010. https://academic.oup.com/intqhc/article/doi/10.1093/intqhc/mzab010/6128587
14. Sharma, N., Jain, V., Mishra, A.: An analysis of convolutional neural networks for image classification. Procedia Comput. Sci. **132**, 377–384 (2018)
15. Suri, J.S., et al.: Systematic review of artificial intelligence in acute respiratory distress syndrome for Covid-19 lung patients: a biomedical imaging perspective. IEEE J. Biomed. Health Inform. **25**(11), 4128–4139 (2021)
16. Ulhaq, A., Burmeister, O.: COVID-19 imaging data privacy by federated learning design: a theoretical framework, October 2020. http://arxiv.org/abs/2010.06177, arXiv:2010.06177 [cs]
17. Vaid, A., et al.: Federated learning of electronic health records to improve mortality prediction in hospitalized patients with COVID-19: machine learning approach. JMIR Med. Inform. **9**(1), e24207 (2021). https://doi.org/10.2196/24207. http://medinform.jmir.org/2021/1/e24207/
18. Wibawa, F., Catak, F.O., Kuzlu, M., Sarp, S., Cali, U.: Homomorphic encryption and federated learning based privacy-preserving CNN training: COVID-19 detection use-case. In: EICC 2022: Proceedings of the European Interdisciplinary Cybersecurity Conference, pp. 85–90. ACM, Barcelona, June 2022. https://doi.org/10.1145/3528580.3532845. https://dl.acm.org/doi/10.1145/3528580.3532845
19. Yang, Q., Zhang, J., Hao, W., Spell, G.P., Carin, L.: FLOP: federated learning on medical datasets using partial networks. In: Proceedings of the 27th ACM SIGKDD Conference on Knowledge Discovery & Data Mining, pp. 3845–3853. ACM, Virtual Event Singapore, August 2021. https://doi.org/10.1145/3447548.3467185. https://dl.acm.org/doi/10.1145/3447548.3467185
20. Yuan, Z.W., Zhang, J.: Feature extraction and image retrieval based on AlexNet. In: Eighth International Conference on Digital Image Processing (ICDIP 2016), vol. 10033, pp. 65–69. SPIE (2016)

Breast Cancer Detection Using Optimal Machine Learning Techniques: Uncovering the Most Effective Approach

Tanmay Joshi[1](✉) and Ravindra Hegadi[2]

[1] MGM's Jawaharlal Nehru Engineering College, Aurangabad, India
ytanmayjoshi1234@gmail.com
[2] Central University of Karnataka, Kalaburagi, India

Abstract. This research paper aimed to identify the most effective machine-learning approach for breast cancer detection. The study utilized the Breast Cancer Wisconsin (Diagnostic) Data Set and evaluated five different algorithms: Logistic Regression, Support Vector Machine (SVM), Decision Tree, Random Forest, and K-Nearest Neighbours (KNN). After thorough analysis, all five algorithms demonstrated high accuracy rates, ranging from 93% to 97.37%. The SVM and Random Forest models achieved the highest accuracy, F1-score, recall, and precision values, making them the most effective approaches for breast cancer detection. These models successfully classified benign and malignant tumours, reducing unnecessary treatments and improving patient safety. Additionally, the research reviewed other studies in the field of breast cancer detection using machine learning. These studies highlighted the potential of uncertain expert systems, deep learning models, microarray analysis, and multi-classifier approaches to enhance breast cancer diagnosis and prognosis prediction. The findings of this research have significant implications for healthcare. SVM and Random Forest, as machine learning techniques, can be leveraged to develop accurate and efficient breast cancer detection systems. Implementing these models in clinical practice can improve early detection rates, minimize unnecessary surgeries, and enhance patient outcomes. This research contributes to the existing knowledge on breast cancer detection using machine learning techniques and offers valuable insights into the most effective approach for improving early diagnosis and treatment outcomes for breast cancer patients.

Keywords: Breast Cancer Prediction · Machine Learning · Data Analysis · Correlation Analysis

1 Introduction

Breast cancer remains a significant public health concern worldwide, affecting a considerable population of women on a global level. Detecting breast cancer at

KC Santosh et al. (Eds.): RTIP2R 2023, CCIS 2027, pp. 44–53, 2024.
https://doi.org/10.1007/978-3-031-53085-2_5

an early stage is crucial for successful treatment and improved patient outcomes. In recent years, there has been a growing interest in utilizing machine learning techniques to enhance breast cancer detection and diagnosis. This research paper aims to uncover the most effective approach for breast cancer detection using optimal machine learning techniques. The timely identification of breast cancer plays a crucial role in lowering mortality rates and enhancing the prospects of successful treatment. The development of sophisticated machine learning algorithms has provided new avenues for improving breast cancer detection accuracy and efficiency.

With the exponential growth of healthcare information, including medical records and clinical data, large databases have been established to store and manage these valuable resources. Governments and public organizations have taken significant steps toward making this data more accessible and actionable, allowing researchers to utilize it for various studies [1]. For this research, the publicly available Breast Cancer Wisconsin (Diagnostic) Data Set, also known as the Wisconsin Diagnostic Breast Cancer (WDBC) dataset from Kaggle, has been employed to investigate the effectiveness of different machine-learning techniques [2]. Various techniques have been employed by medical practitioners to detect breast cancer at an early stage, with surgical biopsy being one of the most accurate methods, exhibiting approximately 100% correctness [3]. Nonetheless, surgical biopsies can be an invasive process, potentially causing discomfort for patients and, in certain instances, resulting in unnecessary surgical interventions. Therefore, the exploration of non-invasive methods, such as machine learning, holds great promise in improving the accuracy and efficiency of breast cancer detection. The objective of this research work is to identify the best machine learning technique for breast cancer detection, utilizing a comprehensive evaluation based on various metrics such as F1 score, accuracy, precision, and recall.

In total, five different machine learning techniques will be employed to compare their performance and determine the most accurate method. The machine learning process will follow three main strategies: pre-processing, feature selection or extraction, and classification [4]. By accurately classifying benign tumours, patients can avoid undergoing unnecessary treatments, reducing potential risks and medical costs. The utilization of data mining techniques in the medical field holds immense potential for predicting diverse outcomes, minimizing expenses, and enhancing healthcare value, ultimately saving lives.

2 Literature Survey

Breast cancer detection is an area of research that has gained considerable attention in the healthcare field, particularly in terms of prediction. With machine-learning techniques emerging as powerful tools for analysing complex data patterns and providing accurate predictions. Over the past few years, numerous research studies have introduced diverse methods to improve breast cancer detection through the utilization of machine learning algorithms. These methodologies have displayed encouraging outcomes and hold the promise of advancing the field.

D. Selvathi et al. [5], focuses on an automated system that achieves accurate breast cancer detection using a Sparse Autoencoder (SAE). The SAE learns features from mammograms, and a classifier, combined with the SAE, performs classification based on these learned features. This approach demonstrates the potential of deep learning techniques in achieving precise breast cancer detection. By leveraging the power of deep learning and feature learning, this method shows promise in improving the accuracy of breast cancer detection systems.

M. J. Van De Vijver et al. [6] propose the use of microarray analysis to evaluate a well-established 70-gene prognosis profile for breast cancer. This analysis categorizes a series of 295 consecutive patients with primary breast carcinomas into groups based on gene-expression signatures associated with either a poor prognosis or a good prognosis. By examining the molecular characteristics and prognosis prediction for breast cancer patients, this approach contributes to a deeper understanding of the disease and aids in more personalized treatment strategies. Microarray analysis allows for comprehensive gene expression profiling, enabling researchers to identify potential biomarkers and predict patient outcomes accurately.

Salama et al. [7] conducted a study on titled breast cancer diagnosis on three different datasets using multi-classifiers using the WEKA data mining tool. In their research, they employed five machine learning classifiers, including NB, MLP, J48, SMO, and IBK, for binary classification tasks on multiple breast cancer datasets. The SMO classifier achieved the highest accuracy of 96.9957%. Furthermore, by combining J48 and MLP with Principal Component Analysis (PCA), the researchers were able to further improve the accuracy to 97.568%. This study showcases the effectiveness of using multiple classifiers and data mining techniques for accurate breast cancer diagnosis. By leveraging the strengths of different classifiers and utilizing dimensionality reduction techniques, the researchers achieved significant improvements in classification accuracy.

In the field of breast cancer detection, Bhavya et al. [8] research has explored innovative wearable devices designed to enhance early diagnosis. These devices, including iTBra, EVA, iSonoHealth, and Celesstia Health, have emerged as promising contenders. iTBra, developed by Cyrcadia Health, uses thermistor sensors to monitor breast temperature variations and detect circadian patterns, achieving an accuracy rate of 87%. In contrast, EVA, envisioned by Julian Rios Cantu, offers a user-friendly approach with thermal and tactile sensors, yielding an impressive 89% sensitivity. iSonoHealth integrates ultrasound scans with artificial intelligence, achieving an 80% sensitivity and specificity. Celesstia Health's multi-sensor chip-based wearable scrutinizes biometric patterns tied to temperature and moisture. These cutting-edge wearables hold substantial promise for advancing early breast cancer detection, providing convenience and the potential for heightened accuracy. Ongoing research efforts aim to further optimize their performance.

In addition to the studies mentioned above, numerous researchers have explored different machine-learning techniques to enhance the accuracy of breast cancer detection. Deep learning models such as Convolutional Neural Networks

(CNNs) have shown promise in effectively analyzing mammographic images and extracting relevant features for accurate classification. Ensemble methods, which combine multiple models, have also been utilized to improve the robustness and generalization of breast cancer detection systems.

3 Materials and Methodology

3.1 Data Preparation

In the data preparation phase, several essential libraries such as numpy, pandas, os, matplotlib, seaborn, and sci-kit-learn are imported to facilitate various tasks related to data manipulation, visualization, and machine learning. These libraries offer a broad range of functionalities that greatly assist in data analysis. To begin, the 'os. walk' function is employed to navigate through the dataset directory and retrieve the file paths. This enables efficient access to the relevant data files. Once the desired file, "data.csv," is located, it is loaded into a pandas Data Frame called 'data' using the 'read-csv' function. This allows for convenient manipulation and analysis of the dataset. Next, to eliminate an unnamed column that might have been present in the data, the 'drop' function is utilized with the 'axis=1' parameter. This ensures that the unnecessary column is removed from the Data Frame. In order to gain insights into the structure and contents of the dataset, the 'display' function is employed. By applying this function, the initial rows of the Data Frame can be displayed, providing a quick overview of the dataset's characteristics. The described process involves importing the necessary libraries, locating the dataset file, loading it into a Data Frame, removing any extraneous columns, and examining the dataset's initial rows. These steps are essential in preparing the data for subsequent analysis and modeling tasks.

3.2 About Dataset

The dataset used in this research is the Breast Cancer Wisconsin (Diagnostic) dataset, which is publicly accessible through the UCI Machine Learning Repository and the University of Wisconsin's FTP server. It comprises features extracted from digitized fine needle aspirate (FNA) images of breast masses, characterizing cell nucleus properties. These features include measures like radius, texture, and symmetry, with computed means, standard errors, and "worst" values, resulting in 30 features per image. The dataset is vital for our study as it allows us to discriminate between benign and malignant diagnoses based on these cell nucleus characteristics. It consists of 357 benign and 212 malignant cases, making it a valuable resource for our exploratory data analysis (EDA) and subsequent research, aiding in the understanding of breast cancer diagnosis.

3.3 Exploratory Data Analysis (EDA)

During the exploratory data analysis (EDA) phase, various tasks were undertaken to gain insights and visualize essential information about the dataset. The seaborn library's 'counterplot' function was initially utilized to create Fig. 1, which displayed the counts of diagnoses for both the Malignant and Benign categories. This plot effectively showcased the distribution of the target variable, providing a clear understanding of the proportions of malignant and benign diagnoses within the dataset. To further explore the dataset, subplots, and Seaborn's 'distplot' function were employed to visualize the distributions of each feature. These plots offered valuable insights into the range and spread of values present in each feature. Additionally, certain machine learning algorithms require data to have a normal distribution, so a log transformation was applied to specific features in order to address skewed distributions. This transformation aimed to normalize the distributions and make the data more suitable for the chosen algorithms. To compare the effects of the log transformation, another set of subplots was created to display the transformed distributions alongside the original distributions. This allowed for a deeper understanding of how the log transformation influenced the shape and spread of the feature distributions.

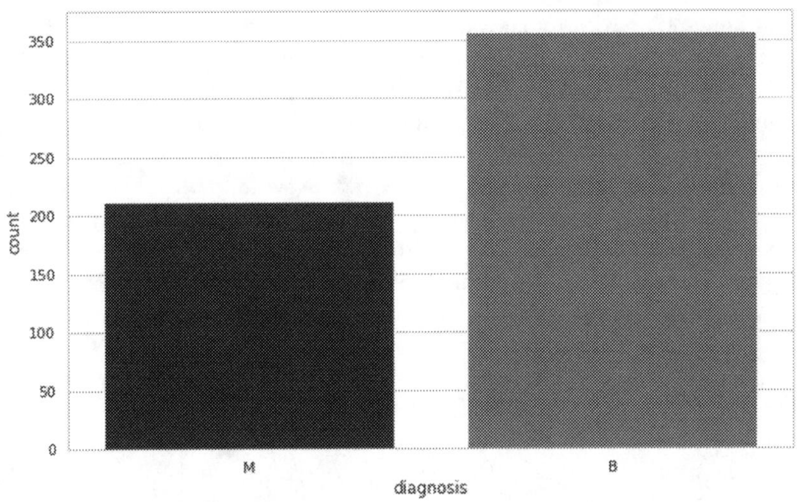

Fig. 1. Number of malignant and benign

3.4 Feature Selection

In the process of selecting the most relevant features for predicting the diagnosis, a series of steps were undertaken. Initially, the code calculated the correlation between the features and the diagnosis by using the 'corr' function on the 'data' Data frame. This computation produced correlation values for each feature-target pair, indicating the strength of their relationship. The correlation values were then sorted in descending order using the 'sort-values' function, enabling the identification of the top 20 features with the highest correlation

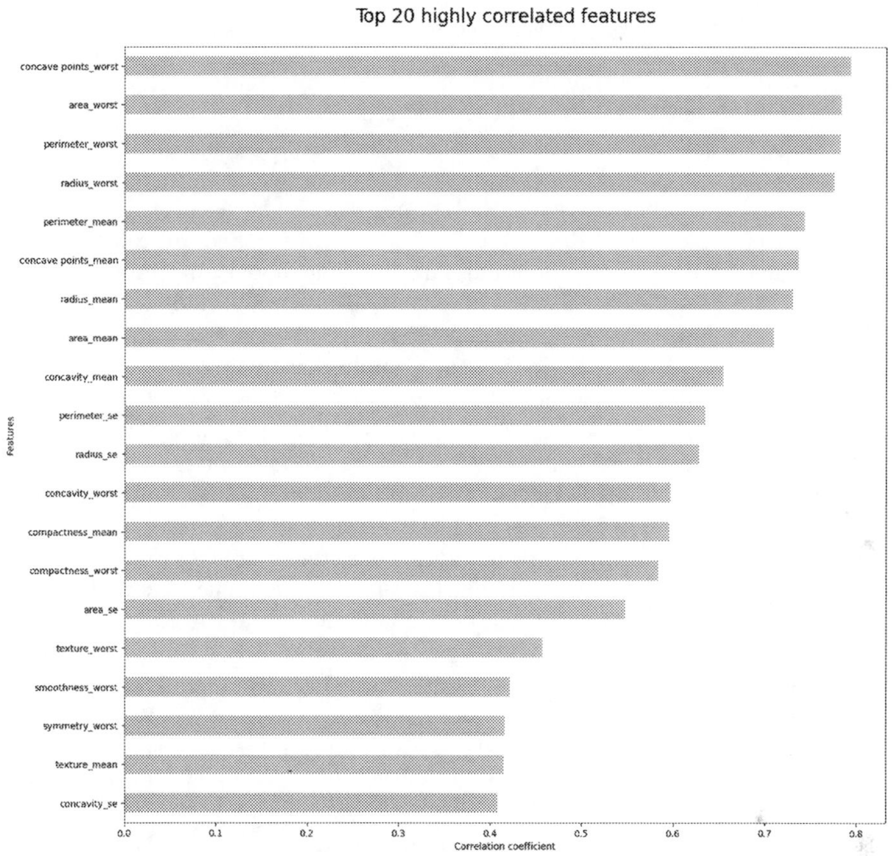

Fig. 2. Highly Correlated Features

coefficients. To visually represent the association between these selected features and the target variable, a bar chart as shown in Fig. 2 was generated. This chart displayed the correlation coefficients of the 20 features derived from the Wisconsin Breast Cancer Dataset. By examining the chart, it became easier to discern which features had the most significant positive or negative correlations with the diagnosis. A high correlation coefficient signified a stronger relationship with the diagnosis, while a lower coefficient indicated a weaker association. Through these steps, the feature selection process aimed to identify the most meaningful features for predicting the diagnosis in the given dataset. By considering the correlation coefficients and their visual representation in the bar chart, it became possible to gain insights into the features that exhibited the strongest relationships with the diagnosis.

3.5 Model Training and Evaluation

During the model training and evaluation phase, the code proceeds to train and evaluate multiple classification models using scikit-learn. The dataset is divided into training and testing sets using the 'train-test-split' function from scikit-learn, following a 75% to 25% split ratio for training and testing, respectively. This allows for a reliable assessment of the models. To ensure consistent scaling, the features undergo standardization using scikit-learn's 'StandardScaler', resulting in features with zero mean and unit variance. The models, including Logistic Regression, Support Vector Machine (SVM), Decision Tree, Random Forest, and K-Nearest Neighbors (KNN), are instantiated using their corresponding scikit-learn classifier classes and trained on the training data using the 'fit' method. Logistic Regression is a linear classification algorithm that models the relationship between the input features and the probability of a binary outcome. It uses the logistic function to map the linear regression output to a probability score. 'random-state': This parameter sets the random seed for reproducibility. It ensures that the results can be reproduced when the algorithm is run multiple times with the same data. It helps maintain consistency in the results. Support Vector Machine is a powerful algorithm used for both classification and regression tasks. It aims to find an optimal hyperplane that separates the data points of different classes with the largest margin. 'kernel': The kernel function specifies the type of decision boundary to be created by SVM. 'Random-state': Similar to logistic regression, this parameter sets the random seed for reproducibility. It ensures that the same random operations, such as shuffling the data or initializing weights, will yield the same results when the code is run multiple times. Decision Tree is a non-parametric supervised learning algorithm that creates a flowchart-like model of decisions based on the features of the data. It splits the data based on different features to create nodes and branches, leading to a final decision at the leaf nodes. 'random-state': This parameter sets the random seed for reproducibility. By setting a specific random seed, the same sequence of random numbers will be generated during the tree-building process, ensuring that the results can be reproduced. Random Forest is an ensemble learning method that combines multiple decision trees to make predictions. It creates an ensemble of decision trees and aggregates their predictions to obtain a final prediction. Hyperparameter 'n-estimators' is used for the number of decision trees to be included in the random forest. Increasing the number of trees generally improves the performance of the model, but it also increases the computational time. It is important to find an optimal value that balances accuracy and efficiency. 'random-state' Similar to the previous algorithms, this parameter sets the random seed for reproducibility. K-Nearest Neighbors is a simple and intuitive classification algorithm. It assigns a new data point to the majority class among its K nearest neighbors, based on a distance metric such as Euclidean distance. 'n-neighbors' is the number of nearest neighbors to consider when making predictions. It determines the sensitivity of the model to the data. A smaller value makes the model more sensitive to local variations, while a larger value makes it more robust but potentially less accurate. The hyperparameters associated with each algorithm allow for fine-tuning the models to achieve the best performance on the dataset. Predictions are made on the testing data using the 'predict' method for each model. Evaluation metrics such as accuracy, precision, recall, and F1-score are calculated using the appropriate functions from sci-kit-learn. The performance of these models can be observed in Table 1, which presents a table showcasing the accuracy, F1-score, recall, and precision values for each algorithm.

$$\text{Accuracy} = \frac{(\text{Number of correctly classified instances})}{(\text{Total number of instances})}$$

Accuracy measures the proportion of correctly classified instances to the total number of instances

$$\text{F1} - \text{Score} = \frac{2 \times (\text{Precision} \times \text{Recall})}{(\text{Precision} + \text{Recall})}$$

The F1-Score is a measure of a model's accuracy that considers both precision and recall. It provides a balance between precision and recall

$$\text{Recall} = \frac{(\text{TruePositive})}{(\text{TruePositive} + \text{FalseNegatives})}$$

Recall measures the proportion of actual positive instances that are correctly identified by the model.

$$\text{Precision} = \frac{(\text{TruePositive})}{(\text{TruePositive} + \text{FalseNegatives})}$$

Precision evaluates the ratio of accurately identified positive instances to the total instances predicted as positive. True Positives (TP) represent instances correctly classified as positive, while False Positives (FP) correspond to instances incorrectly classified as positive. Additionally, False Negatives (FN) pertain to instances incorrectly classified as negative.

Table 1. Performance of Algorithms

Algorithm	Accuracy	F1-Score	Recall	Precision
Logistic Regression	93%	0.93	0.92	0.88
Support Vector Machine (SVM)	97.37%	0.968	0.957	0.978
Decision Tree	94.71%	0.935	0.915	0.956
Random Forest	97.37%	0.968	0.957	0.978
K-Nearest Neighbours (KNN)	96.49%	0.957	0.936	0.978

3.6 Model Comparison

During the phase of model comparison, a crucial step involves visually assessing the accuracies of the SVM, KNN, and Decision Tree models. This is achieved through the creation of a bar chart that serves as a graphical representation of the performance of these models. The accuracies of each model are stored in a dictionary called 'accuracies', where the model names act as keys and the corresponding accuracies serve as their respective values. The bar chart, referred to as Fig. 3, plays a pivotal role in presenting a comprehensive and concise summary of the model performances. The x-axis of the chart displays the names of the models, while the y-axis represents the accuracies achieved by each model. By visually comparing the heights of the bars, one can quickly evaluate and distinguish the accuracies of the different models. The significance of this visual representation lies in its ability to provide decision-makers with a clear and intuitive understanding of the relative performances of the models under consideration. By observing the bar chart, one can easily identify which model exhibits the highest accuracy, thus facilitating informed decision-making during the model selection process. Moreover, the bar chart offers a succinct summary of the comparative accuracies of the models, enabling a quick assessment of their relative strengths and weaknesses. This aids in streamlining the decision-making process, as decision-makers can readily identify the most accurate model without delving into complex numerical analyses.

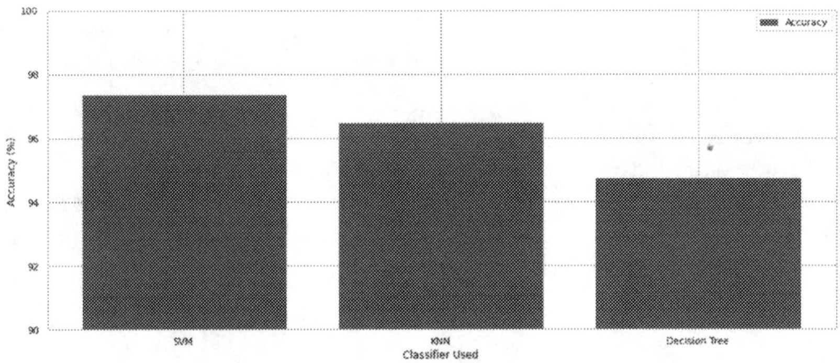

Fig. 3. Comparison of Ml Algorithm's

4 Results, Conclusion, and Future Scope

Based on the research findings, it can be concluded that Support Vector machines (SVM) and Random forest are highly effective machine-learning methods for detecting breast cancer. These models demonstrated impressive accuracy and robust performance in correctly classifying breast tumors, with SVM achieving an exceptional accuracy rate of 97.37%. The results highlight the significant potential of SVM as a powerful tool in breast cancer detection. These research findings provide valuable insights into the application of machine-learning techniques in breast cancer detection. The results suggest that SVM and Random Forest can be valuable tools for healthcare professionals, improving the accuracy and efficiency of breast cancer diagnosis. However, further research and validation on larger and more diverse datasets are necessary to ensure the reliability and generalizability of these findings. In conclusion, this study emphasizes the promising prospects of machine learning techniques, particularly SVM with an accuracy rate of approximately 98%, in the field of breast cancer detection. By utilizing SVM and Random Forest models, accurate diagnosis can be achieved, leading to early detection, improved treatment outcomes, and ultimately saving lives. It is important to continue advancing research in machine learning algorithms to further enhance the capabilities of breast cancer detection systems, benefiting both patients and healthcare providers.

References

1. Kayyali, B., Knott, D., Van Kuiken, S.: The 'big data' revolution in healthcare. Center for US Health System Reform Business Technology Office (2013)
2. Breast Cancer Wisconsin (Diagnostic) Data Set, UCI Machine Learning Repository. https://www.kaggle.com/uciml/breast-cancer-wisconsin-data
3. Abdulkareem, S.A., Abdulkareem, Z.O.: An evaluation of the Wisconsin breast cancer dataset using ensemble classifiers and RFE feature selection technique. IJSBAR **55**(2), 67–80 (2021)
4. Eltalhi, S., Kutrani, H.: Breast cancer diagnosis and prediction using machine learning and data mining techniques: a review. IOSR J. Dental Med. Sci. **18**(4), 85–94 (2019)
5. Selvathi, D., Aarthypoornila, A.: Performance analysis of various classifiers on deep learning network for breast cancer detection. In: International Conference on Signal Processing and Communication (ICSPC)
6. Van De Vijver, M.J., et al.: A gene-expression signature as a predictor of survival in breast cancer. New Engl. J. Med. **347**, 19992009 (2002)
7. Salama, G.I., Abdelhalim, M., Zeid, M.A.-E.: Breast cancer diagnosis on three different datasets using multi-classifiers. Breast Cancer (WDBC) **32**(569), 2 (2012)
8. Bhavya, G., Manjunath, T.N., Hegadi, R.S., Pushpa, S.K.: A study on personalized early detection of breast cancer using modern technology. In: Sridhar, V., Padma, M., Rao, K. (eds.) Emerging Research in Electronics, Computer Science and Technology. Lecture Notes in Electrical Engineering, vol. 545. Springer, Singapore (2019). https://doi.org/10.1007/978-981-13-5802-9-33

Compressed Deep Learning Models with XAI for COVID-19 Detection Using CXR Images

Deepanshi[1], Namo Jain[1], Prakhar Consul[1(✉)], Ishan Budhiraja[1], and Deepak Garg[2]

[1] School of Computer Science Engineering and Technology, Bennett University, Noida, Uttar Pradesh, India
{e20soe819,e21soep0004,ishan.budhiraja}@bennett.edu.in

[2] SR University, Ananthasagar, Hasanparthy Hanumakonda, Siddipet, Telangana, India
deepak.garg@sru.edu.in

Abstract. Significant global disruptions brought on by the COVID-19 pandemic call for fast and accurate detection techniques to stem the disease's spread. Due to its non-invasiveness and reasonable cost, chest X-ray (CXR) imaging has become a useful technique for diagnosing COVID-19. The analysis of CXR images using compressed deep learning models combined with explainable artificial intelligence (XAI) is a novel method for COVID-19 identification presented in this paper. To lower the computational complexity and memory needs of the deep learning models without compromising performance, our suggested approach uses model compression techniques including pruning and quantization. The incorporation of XAI increases transparency and makes it easier to identify key features for COVID-19 detection in CXR pictures by giving insights into the models' decision-making process. On a sizable dataset of CXR images, we test our method, and we show that it is effective in obtaining high detection accuracy while keeping a small model size and low computing cost. Our study contribute the creation of effective, open, and trustworthy COVID-19 detection tools, which can be particularly helpful in resource-constrained environments and for enhancing confidence in AI-driven diagnostics.

Keywords: Deep learning(DL) · Compression · XAI · COVID-19

1 Introduction

The current global health crisis caused by the COVID-19 pandemic has exerted significant strain on healthcare systems across the globe, underscoring the significance of fast and accurate diagnostic techniques. The utilization of Chest X-ray (CXR) imaging has become increasingly significant as a diagnostic modality for COVID-19, owing to its non-invasive nature, extensive accessibility, and comparatively lower expenses. The analysis of CXR images demands specialized knowledge and can require a significant amount of time, potentially constraining its effectiveness in widespread screening and timely identification of medical

KC Santosh et al. (Eds.): RTIP2R 2023, CCIS 2027, pp. 54–66, 2024.
https://doi.org/10.1007/978-3-031-53085-2_6

conditions. The application of deep learning models has demonstrated notable achievements in the automation of medical image analysis, specifically in the context of COVID-19 detection through CXR images. The lack of transparency of deep learning models, commonly referred to as "black-box" models, can hinder their extensive execution by healthcare practitioners owing to a lack of transparency and interpret-ability [1].

Compressed deep learning models for COVID-19 detection through CXR images presents various benefits in comparison to conventional deep learning models. The model architecture is simplified through the utilization of techniques such as pruning and quantization. The act of diminishing the dimensions of deep learning models, resulting in a reduction of memory demands. The simplification of the models leads to expedited processing duration and enhances their compatibility with devices that possess restricted computational capabilities, such as edge devices or mobile phones. Compressed models exhibit reduced computational and memory requirements, thereby leading to decreased energy consumption. It provide faster inference times owing to their reduced complexity. The rapidity of diagnosis is crucial for efficient patient management and virus containment, especially in time-sensitive scenarios like COVID-19 detection. They possess the advantage of reduced computational and memory demands, rendering them easier to adapt to scaling for larger datasets or distribution across multiple devices. As such, they represent a promising solution for the implementation of extensive COVID-19 screening initiatives [2].

XAI in conjunction with deep learning models for COVID-19 detection presents numerous benefits, providing it a valuable strategy in the area of medical diagnostics. Artificial intelligence techniques aid in enhancing the transparency and interpretability of deep learning models by offering valuable insights into their decision-making mechanisms. Comprehending the reasoning behind a diagnosis is of utmost significance in medical contexts, as it is imperative for both healthcare practitioners and patients. XAI has the potential to assist healthcare practitioners in their decision-making process by offering supplementary information and visual representations that clarify the model's reasoning. The utilization of this approach can assist healthcare professionals in making well-informed decisions regarding patient care and treatment strategies, which can ultimately result in improved patient outcomes.

The present study introduces a novel strategy to tackle the aforementioned obstacles by creating compact deep learning architectures that incorporate the Grad-CAM++ XAI technique for detecting COVID-19 through CXR images. The methodology utilized model compression methodologies such as pruning and quantization, to decrease the computational complexity and memory demands while maintaining the models' efficacy. The utilization of Grad-CAM++ as an XAI methodology provides evident explanations for the model's reasoning process, thereby enhancing clarity and comprehensibility [3] (Fig. 1).

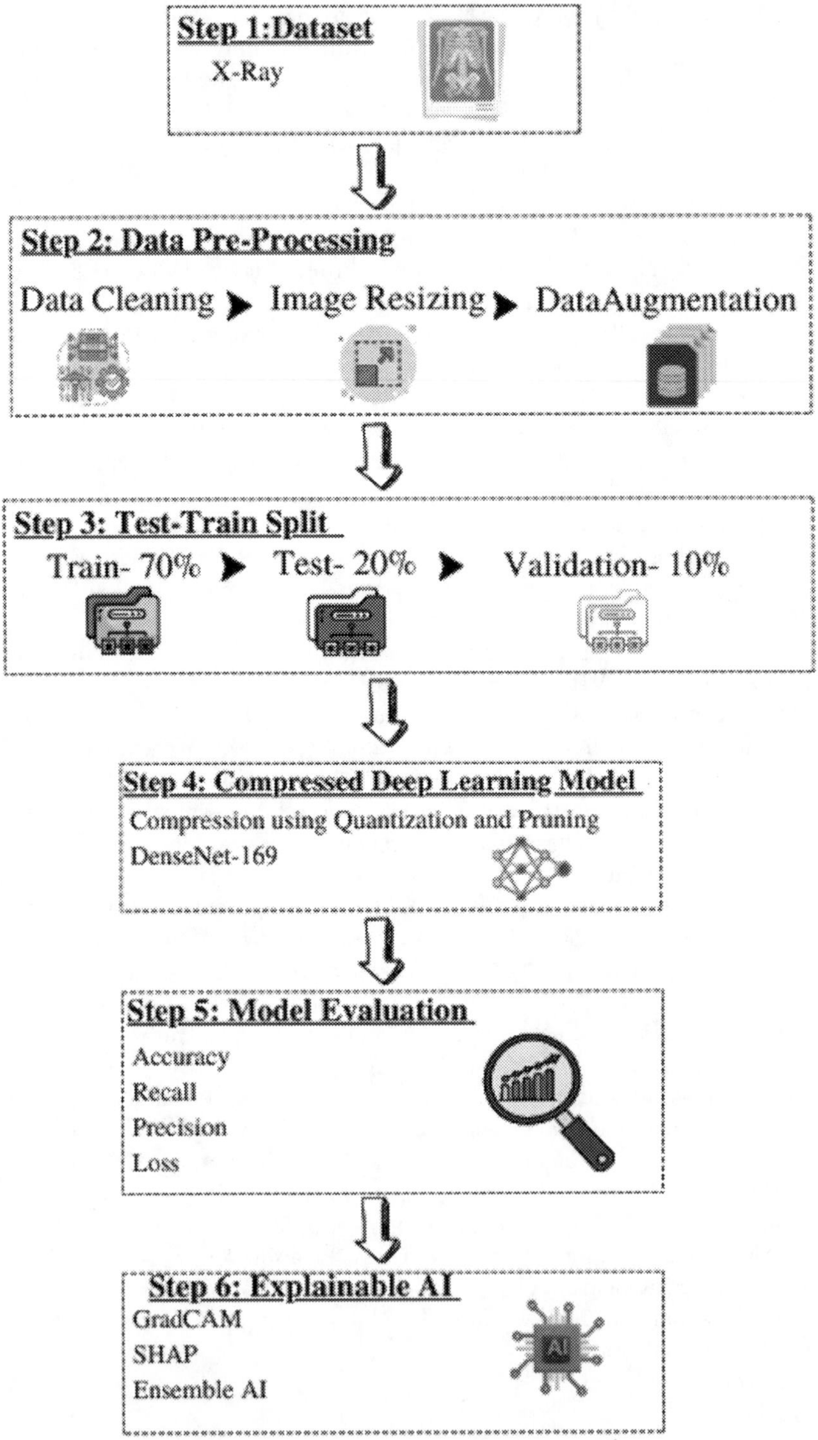

Fig. 1. Methodology

1.1 Motivation and Contribution

Our objective is to create deep learning models that are effective in diagnosing COVID-19, while minimizing computational complexity. We will also integrate XAI techniques to improve the transparency and interpretability of the models. This will aid in the practical implementation and acceptance of the models by medical practitioners. The main contributions of the proposed work are summarized in what follows:

- Compressing deep learning models to reduce computational complexity and memory needs while maintaining high detection accuracy makes them ideal for deployment in resource-constrained environments and on devices with restricted computational capabilities.
- Integrating XAI tools like Grad-CAM++ to visualize the deep learning models' decision-making process for healthcare practitioners.
- Evaluating the suggested approach on a large dataset of CXR images shows that compressed models can achieve excellent detection accuracy while reducing model size and computational complexity.

2 Related Work

Several investigations have utilized deep learning architectures, including convolutional neural networks (CNNs), to identify COVID-19 through the analysis of CXR and CT images. These models have exhibited favorable outcomes with regards to their ability to accurately detect and display sensitivity. An example of this can be seen in the research conducted by Wang et al. (2020), where they proposed the COVID-Net framework, which was tailored to identify COVID-19 in chest X-ray images [4]. The authors Han et al. (2015) introduced a technique that employs pruning, trained quantization, and Huffman coding to achieve notable reductions in both model size and computational complexity through deep compression [5]. In their 2017 publication, Liu et al. introduced the concept of network slimming, which involves the pruning and scaling of a deep neural network to achieve notable reductions in both model size and computational complexity, while simultaneously preserving high levels of accuracy [6]. The study conducted by Cheng et al. (2018) presents an all-encompassing overview of various methods for compressing and accelerating deep neural networks. These techniques include pruning, quantization, knowledge distillation, and model architecture design [7]. Several XAI techniques have been devised, including LIME, SHAP, and Grad-CAM. Selvaraju et al. (2017) proposed the Grad-CAM technique as a means of visualizing regions in deep learning models that are discriminative of specific classes [8,9]. Chattopadhay et al. (2018) subsequently expanded upon this method with Grad-CAM++, which provides enhanced visual interpretations of model decisions [10]. The authors Li et al. (2020) introduced a compressed deep learning model that incorporates explainable artificial intelligence (XAI) for the purpose of detecting pneumonia in chest X-ray (CXR) images [11]. Their findings suggest that the integration of model compression and XAI can lead to efficient and interpretable analysis of medical images. The scope of the research includes the domains of deep learning models for detecting COVID-19, techniques for compressing models, and methods for explainable artificial intelligence. The objective of this study is to devise a proficient, lucid, and comprehensible methodology for identifying COVID-19 through the utilization of CXR images, by incorporating and enhancing these domains.

3 Methodology

The present section defines the methodology employed for the creation of compressed deep learning models integrated with XAI for the purpose of COVID-19 detection through the analysis of CXR images. The procedure involves a series of sequential stages: Data collection and pre-processing of data, development of a model, compression of the model, and integration of explainable AI (Fig. 2).

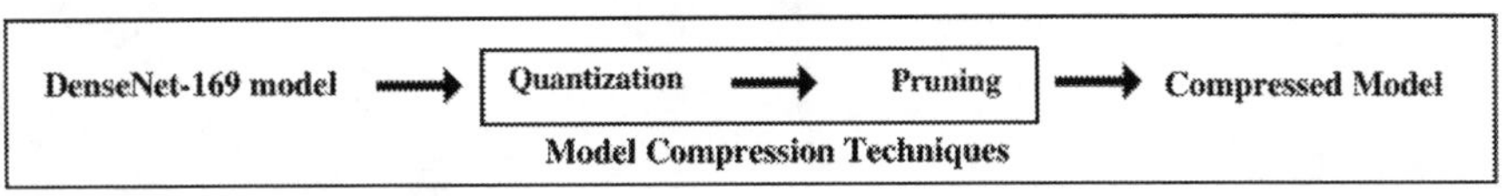

Fig. 2. Compression Flow Diagram

3.1 Preprocessing

The preprocessing stage is a vital component in the development of deep learning models, as it facilitates the preparation of raw data for model input through the implementation of transformations and standardization techniques. Typically, the procedure comprises multiple phases. Initially, the act of resizing images to a standardized size guarantees that the model is provided with uniform input dimensions, irrespective of the initial sizes of the images.

Table 1. Comparative analysis of Results on Dense-Net-201 with and without model and image compression.

S. No.		Original Dataset	Dataset Compression	Original Ensembled Model	Compressed Ensembled Model	Accuracy
DenseNet-201	X-Ray	Yes	No	Yes	No	96.72%
		Yes	No	Yes	Yes	97.07%
		Yes	Yes	Yes	No	96.11%
		Yes	Yes	Yes	Yes	96.72%

Normalization is a process that rescales the pixel values to a predetermined range, such as 0 to 1 or -1 to 1. This technique is employed to enhance the learning process of the model by mitigating the impact of inconsistent brightness and contrast levels. The utilization of data augmentation techniques, such as rotation, flipping, and zooming, serves to artificially increase the size of the dataset, thereby enhancing its variability and facilitating the acquisition of more resilient features by the model.

3.2 Compression of Model

In order to create compressed deep learning models using XAI for COVID-19 identification using CXR pictures, model compression via quantization and pruning is required. These methods minimize the complexity and size of models while maintaining high performance. Quantization reduces the accuracy of weights and activations to lower numerical representations, while pruning gets rid of unnecessary neurons or connections in the model. When these methods are combined, a compact and efficient model is produced that can be used in real-time or low-resource settings. Iterative experimentation and fine-tuning are required to find the optimal combination of size reduction, computational efficiency, and maintained performance when implementing both pruning and quantization, but the resulting deep learning model for COVID-19 detection in CXR images is more accessible and deployable as a result [12].

Densenet169. Based on the work of Gao Huang et al. in 2016, DenseNet-169 is an extension of the DenseNet architecture. CNNs like DenseNet have been developed to facilitate the training of deeper networks by enhancing information flow and gradient propagation. The "169" in DenseNet-169 indicates the network's total number of layers. DenseNet is able to accomplish its dense connection by feeding information from the previous layer into the current layer in a feed-forward method within the dense block. The several benefits of such extensive connection include The vanishing gradient problem is mitigated and deeper networks can be trained more quickly thanks to the improved gradient flow made possible by the dense connections used in backpropagation. Promotes the reuse of features: The network can learn and utilise its parameters more effectively since it can recycle features thanks to the concatenation of feature maps from earlier layers. Fewer network parameters:-DenseNet promotes feature reuse, cutting down on the need for many network parameters. This reduces the need for memory and processing, and helps prevent overfitting [13]. Multiple dense blocks are interconnected by transition layers in the DenseNet-169 design. There are multiple convolutional layers in each dense block, and their growth rate is fixed, such that the total number of feature mappings grows at a constant rate. Both the spatial dimensions and the number of feature maps can be reduced with the aid of the transition layers, which typically comprise of a convolutional layer followed by an average pooling layer. DenseNet-169 has been shown to be effective in a number of image recognition tasks, and it is a good option for tasks like COVID-19 identification utilizing CXR pictures due to its efficient use of parameters and improved gradient flow [14,15].

Performance Evaluation. In order to determine how efficient and trustworthy deep learning models are, performance evaluation is essential. Depending on the work at hand and the desired outcomes, a variety of assessment methods and indicators can be used to assess the effectiveness of a model [16]. Some common methods for evaluating a deep learning model's efficacy are listed below.

- Confusion Matrix:- The amount of right and incorrect predictions made by the model, broken down by class, is displayed in a table called a confusion matrix. It is useful for determining the percentages of correct classifications in binary or multi-class jobs.
- Accuracy:- The accuracy of a model is measured by how many of its predictions were accurate out of a total of predictions. It's a popular metric, but it could not be accurate for datasets with bias because it doesn't account for how the model does with underrepresented groups.
- Precision:- It is the rate at which a model makes correct positive predictions relative to the total number of positive predictions it makes. When the number of false positives is important, this metric can be used to evaluate the model's efficacy.
- Recall:- It is the fraction of cases correctly predicted as positive compared to the total number of positive instances in the dataset. When the number of false negatives is a major concern, this metric can be used to evaluate the model's efficacy.
- F1-Score:- It is the optimal metric because it strikes a middle ground between precision and recall. This method's ability to account for both false positives and false negatives makes it particularly effective in situations when classes are distributed unevenly.

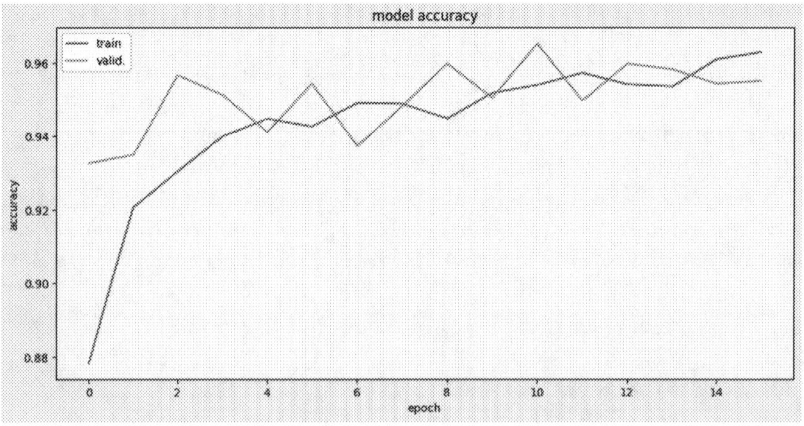

Fig. 3. Compressed Dense-Net Accuracy Graph

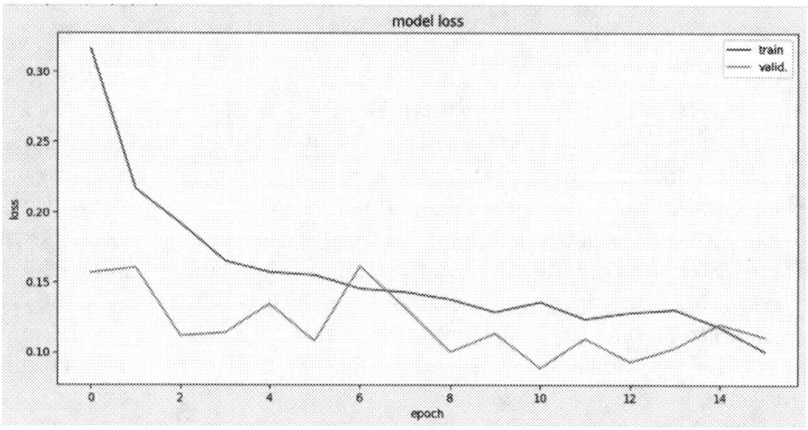

Fig. 4. Compressed Dense-Net Loss Graph

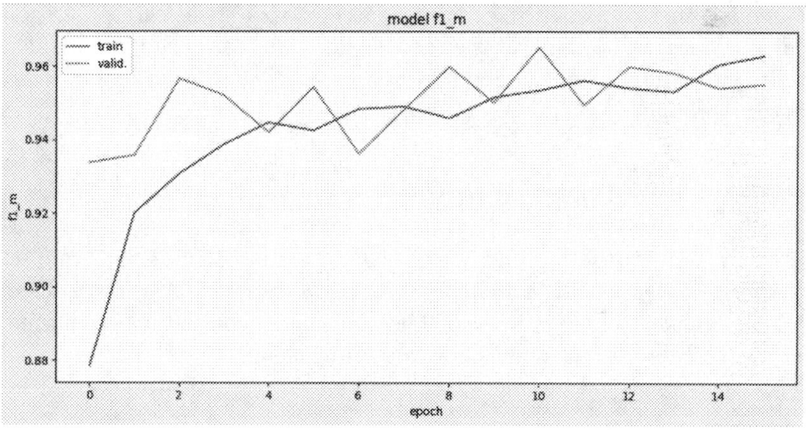

Fig. 5. Compressed Dense-Net F1-Score Graph

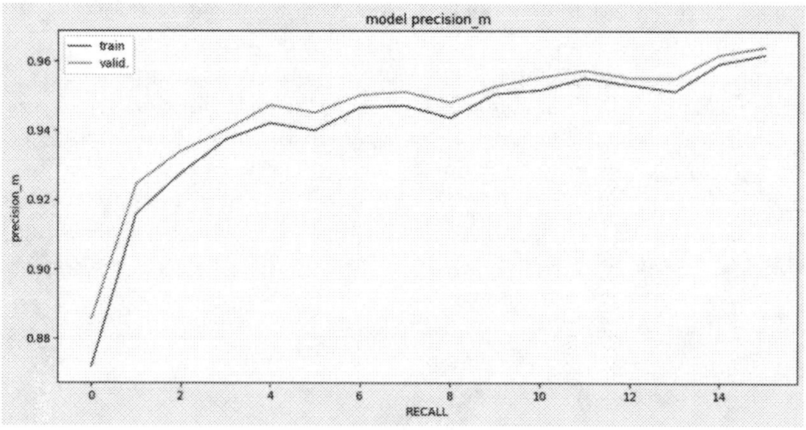

Fig. 6. Compressed Dense-Net Precision Graph

3.3 XAI

Grad-CAM++ is an enhanced iteration of the Gradient-weighted Class Activation Mapping (Grad-CAM) [17] methodology, which offers visual justifications for the determinations provided by deep learning models. Utilize the Grad-CAM++ methodology on the calculated gradients, encompassing: The determination of significance weights for individual feature maps is achieved through the consideration of higher-order derivatives. The generation of a coarse heatmap (class activation map) involves the computation of importance weights, which are then used to take a weighted combination of the feature maps. Rescale the primitive heatmap to match the dimensions of the input CXR image and superimpose it onto the unaltered image. The visualization obtained from the analysis emphasizes the areas within the image that have the greatest impact on the model's forecast, thereby offering valuable understanding into the model's cognitive process. The integration of Grad-CAM++ into the compressed deep learning model outlined in the paper can provide enhanced insight into the predictions generated by the model, thereby benefiting both researchers and healthcare practitioners. The enhanced interpretability of the model's decisions can foster confidence and credibility, potentially resulting in broader acceptance of the model for detecting COVID-19 through CXR images.

4 Results and Discussion

This section outlines the findings of our experimentation involving compressed deep learning models and XAI techniques for the purpose of COVID-19 detection through the analysis of CXR images. The study was centered on evaluating the efficacy of the compressed models and the XAI visualizations.

4.1 Dataset

This section outlines the dataset employed in the development and assessment of compressed deep learning models with XAI for the purpose of COVID-19 detection through the analysis of CXR images. The dataset comprises of CXR images that have been gathered from various publicly accessible sources. The dataset comprises of CXR images that have tested positive for COVID-19, images that exhibit pneumonia, which can serve as a substitute for COVID-19 negative images, and normal images. The final dataset comprises a total of 1300 images, comprising 400 cases of COVID-19 positive cases, 480 cases of COVID-19 negative cases, and 420 cases of pneumonia. The dataset is curated from a publicly available kaggle dataset.

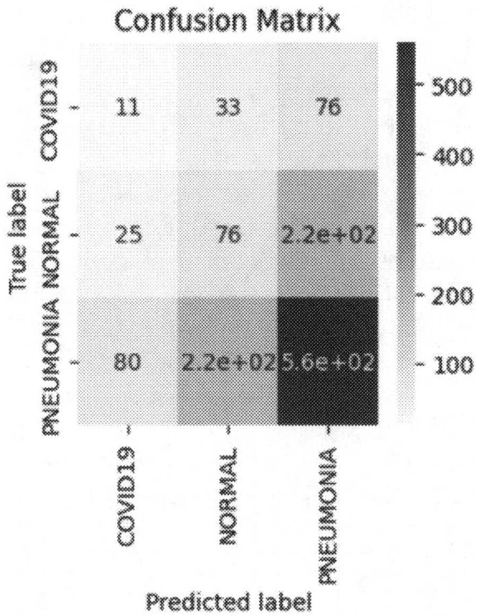

Fig. 7. Compressed Dense-Net Confusion metrics Graph

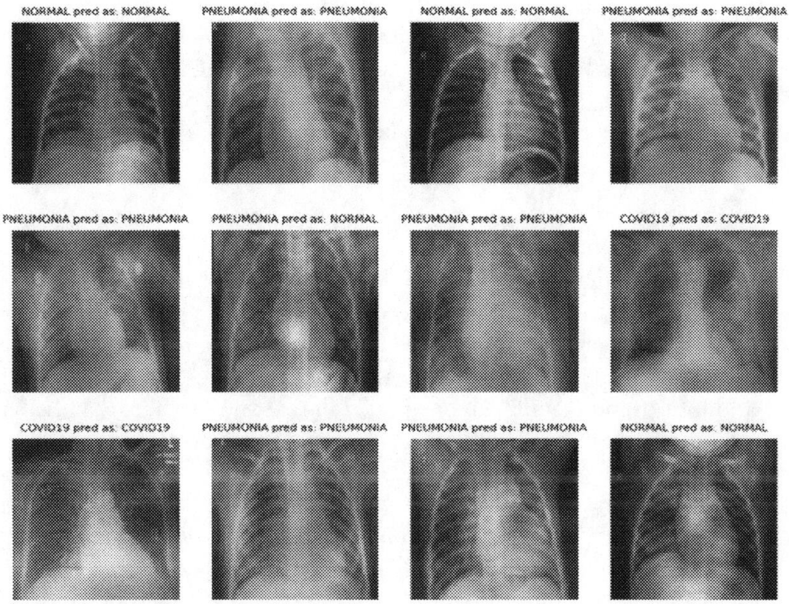

Fig. 8. Comparative Analysis of XAI model COVID-19, pneumonia and normal X-ray images corresponding XAI explanation

4.2 Experimental Results

The DenseNet-169 model went through compression through the utilization of pruning and quantization techniques. Various levels of pruning and quantization were tested to determine the most effective trade-off between reducing model size, improving computational efficiency, and preserving performance. The findings of our study suggest that a compressed model that reduces the number of parameters by 40% can attain a level of performance that is comparable to that of the original DenseNet-169 model. The compressed model's performance was assessed through the utilization of various metrics, including but not limited to accuracy, precision, recall, F1-score, and AUC-ROC. The training of the model was conducted on a dataset comprising of CXR images, encompassing instances of COVID-19 positive, COVID-19 negative, and other respiratory ailments. The compressed model's performance metrics were obtained through our experimental procedures and are as follows in 1 The findings indicate that the compressed model is effective in identifying COVID-19 cases through the utilization of CXR images, with performance levels comparable to those of the uncompressed model. Figs. 3 and 4 Shows the accuracy and loss graph of the compressed Denesnet-169 model respectively. Figs. 5 and 6 shows the F1 Score and precision graph of the model. Fig. 7 shows the confusion metrics of the model. In order to improve the comprehensibility of the compressed model, we utilized the Grad-CAM++ methodology to produce visual justifications for the model's prediction. The heatmaps generated were effective in identifying the areas within the CXR images that had the greatest impact on the model's determinations, thereby offering significant revelations into the model's decision-making mechanism. The utilization of visual representations facilitated the comprehension and acceptance of the model's prediction by healthcare professionals, thereby enhancing the likelihood of the model's implementation for the identification of COVID-19 through CXR images (Fig. 8).

5 Conclusion

Our study outlines a methodology for constructing compressed deep learning models augmented with XAI to facilitate COVID-19 detection through the analysis of CXR images. The main objective was to develop a model that is both efficient and interpretable, and can be applied in real-time scenarios and environments with limited resources, while also ensuring optimal performance. Model compression techniques, such as pruning and quantization, were utilized in order to decrease the computational demands and model size. Our model utilized the DenseNet-169 architecture as its backbone, exhibiting exceptional efficacy in identifying COVID-19 cases from CXR images. In order to improve the interpretability of the model, we integrated the Grad-CAM++ methodology, which produced visual justifications for the model's prediction. The utilization of visualizations enabled healthcare professionals to enhance their comprehension of the decision-making mechanism of the model, thereby augmenting their confidence in the model's prognostications and optimizing the possibility of incorporating it for COVID-19 detection via CXR images.

The findings of our experiments indicate that the compressed model exhibited a level of performance that was comparable to that of the original, uncompressed DenseNet-169 model. However, the compressed model achieved this while significantly reducing the model size and computational requirements. In summary, our study showcases the viability of employing compressed deep learning models in conjunction with XAI methodologies for the purpose of detecting COVID-19 in CXR images. This methodology achieves an optimal balance between the efficacy of the model, its computational efficiency, and its interpretive capacity, providing it a beneficial instrument for healthcare professionals in their endeavors to combat the persistent COVID-19 outbreak. Potential future research activities may involve investigating alternative model compression and XAI methods, in addition to incorporating supplementary data sources and techniques to enhance the model's effectiveness and functionality.

References

1. Hryniewska, W., Bombiński, P., Szatkowski, P., Tomaszewska, P., Przelaskowski, A., Biecek, P.: Checklist for responsible deep learning modeling of medical images based on covid-19 detection studies. Pattern Recogn. **118**, 108035 (2021)
2. Hu, Q., Gois, F.N.B., Costa, R., Zhang, L., Yin, L., Magaia, N., de Albuquerque, V.H.C.: Explainable artificial intelligence-based edge fuzzy images for covid-19 detection and identification. Appl. Soft Comput. **123**, 108966 (2022)
3. Consul, P., Budhiraja, I., Garg, D., Bindle, A.: Power allocation scheme based on DRL for CF massive MIMO network with UAV. In: Garg, D., Kumar, N., Iqbal, R., Gupta, S. (eds.) Innovations in Information and Communication Technologies. Algorithms for Intelligent Systems, Springer, Singapore, pp. 33–43 (2023). https://doi.org/10.1007/978-981-19-3796-5_4
4. Budhiraja, I., Garg, D., Kumar, N., Sharma, R., et al.: A comprehensive review on variants of SARS-COVS-2: challenges, solutions and open issues. Comput. Commun. **197**, 34–51 (2022)
5. Chattopadhay, A., Sarkar, A., Howlader, P., Balasubramanian, V.N.: Grad-cam++: generalized gradient-based visual explanations for deep convolutional networks. In: IEEE Winter Conference on Applications of Computer Vision (WACV), vol. 2018, pp. 839–847. IEEE (2018)
6. Sundararajan, M., Taly, A., Yan, Q.: Axiomatic attribution for deep networks. In: International Conference on Machine Learning, PMLR, pp. 3319–3328 (2017)
7. Gupta, P.K., Mittal, S., Consul, P., Jindal, J.K.: A review of different vulnerabilities of security in a layered network. In: Advances and Applications in Mathematical Sciences, pp. 227–236, December 2020
8. Jacobi, A., Chung, M., Bernheim, A., Eber, C.: Portable chest x-ray in coronavirus disease-19 (covid-19): a pictorial review. Clin. Imaging **64**, 35–42 (2020)
9. Consul, P., Budhiraja, I., Chaudhary, R., Garg, D.: FLBCPS: federated learning based secured computation offloading in blockchain-assisted cyber-physical systems. In: 2022 IEEE/ACM 15th International Conference on Utility and Cloud Computing (UCC), pp. 412–417, December 2022

10. Ozturk, T., Talo, M., Yildirim, E.A., Baloglu, U.B., Yildirim, O., Acharya, U.R.: Automated detection of covid-19 cases using deep neural networks with x-ray images. Comput. Biol. Med. **121**, 103792 (2020)
11. Ucar, F., Korkmaz, D.: Covidiagnosis-net: Deep bayes-squeezenet based diagnosis of the coronavirus disease 2019 (covid-19) from x-ray images. Med. Hypotheses **140**, 109761 (2020)
12. Li, L., et al.: Artificial intelligence distinguishes covid-19 from community acquired pneumonia on chest CT, Radiology (2020)
13. Ramanjaneyulu, K., Kumar, K.H., Snehith, K., Jyothirmai, G., Krishna, K.V.: Detection and classification of lung cancer using VGG-16. In: 2022 International Conference on Electronic Systems and Intelligent Computing (ICESIC), pp. 69–72. IEEE (2022)
14. Wang, S., et al.: A fully automatic deep learning system for covid-19 diagnostic and prognostic analysis. Eur. Respiratory J. **56**(2), 76–79 (2020)
15. Nehra, A., Consul, P., Budhiraja, I., Kaur, G., Nasser, N., Imran, M.: Federated learning based trajectory optimization for UAV enabled MEC. In: ICC 2023 - IEEE International Conference on Communications, pp. 1640–1645, October 2023
16. Quan, T.M., et al.: Xpgan: x-ray projected generative adversarial network for improving covid-19 image classification. In: IEEE 18th International Symposium on Biomedical Imaging (ISBI), vol. 2021, pp. 1509–1513. IEEE (2021)
17. Tahir, H., Iftikhar, A., Mumraiz, M.: Forecasting covid-19 via registration slips of patients using ResNet-101 and performance analysis and comparison of prediction for covid-19 using faster R-CNN, mask R-CNN, and ResNet-50. In: 2021 International Conference on Advances in Electrical, Computing, Communication and Sustainable Technologies (ICAECT), pp. 1–6. IEEE (2021)

HLB Disease Detection in Omani Lime Trees Using Hyperspectral Imaging Based Techniques

Jacintha Menezes[1(✉)], Ramalingam Dharmalingam[1], and Palaiahnakote Shivakumara[2]

[1] Majan University College, Muscat 112, Sultanate of Oman
{jacintha.menezes,ramalingam.d}@majancollege.edu.om
[2] University of Malaya, 50603 Kuala Lumpur, Malaysia
shiva@um.edu.my

Abstract. In the recent years omani acid lime cultivation and production has been affected by Citrus greening or Huanglongbing (HLB) disease. HLB disease is one of the most destructive diseases for citrus with no remedies or countermeasures to stop the disease. Currently used Polymerase chain reaction (PCR) and Enzyme-linked immunosorbent assay (ELISA) HLB detection tests require lengthy and labor-intensive laboratory procedures. Furthermore, the equipment and staff needed to carry out the laboratory procedures are specialized hence making them a less optimal solution for the detection of the disease. The current research uses hyperspectral imaging technology for automatic detection of citrus trees with HLB disease. Omani citrus tree leaf images were captured through portable Specim IQ hyperspectral camera. The research considered healthy, nutrition deficient and HLB infected leaf samples based on the Polymerase chain reaction (PCR) test. The high-resolution image samples were sliced to into sub cubes. The sub cubes were further processed to obtain RGB images with spatial features. Similarly, RGB spectral slices were obtained through a moving window on the wavelength. The resized spectral-spatial RGB images were given to Convolution Neural Network for deep feature extraction. The current research was able to classify a given sample to the appropriate class with 92.86% accuracy indicating the effectiveness of the proposed techniques. The significant bands with a difference in three types of leaves are found to be 560 nm, 678 nm, 726 nm and 750 nm. This research offers a promising and effective approach utilizing cutting-edge technology to address the critical challenge of HLB disease in Omani citrus trees, providing a potential pathway for more efficient disease identification and management in the citrus industry.

Keywords: Huanglongbing (HLB) · Hyperspectral Imaging (HSI) · Omani Citrus · Deep Learning · CNN

Supported by The Research Council (TRC), Sultanate of Oman.

KC Santosh et al. (Eds.): RTIP2R 2023, CCIS 2027, pp. 67–81, 2024.
https://doi.org/10.1007/978-3-031-53085-2_7

1 Introduction

Citrus greening disease, often known as huanglongbing (HLB), is a serious hazard to citrus farming all over the world. The bacteria Candidatus Liberibacter spp., which are spread by the Asian citrus psyllid (Diaphorina citri), are responsible for this terrible disease. Citrus trees infected with HLB experience a loss in tree health, a reduction in fruit production, and eventually mortality (Singerman and Useche, 2017; Gottwald, 2010; Bassanezi et al., 2020; Wangithi, 2019). In order to prevent disease spread and reduce financial losses in citrus-producing regions, rapid and accurate diagnosis of HLB is essential. At present, the Polymerase chain reaction (PCR) and enzyme-linked immunosorbent assay (ELISA) are the two common methods used for detecting HLB. Both these methods however, require lengthy and labor-intensive laboratory procedures. Furthermore, the equipment and staff needed for these procedures are specialized making them unfeasible for widespread surveillance and early detection of the disease. Hyperspectral imaging has emerged as a viable method for the quick and non-destructive identification of numerous plant diseases to overcome such constraints (Wan et al., 2022; Bock et al., 2010).

The diagnosis and control of HLB are of the utmost importance in the context of Omani lime trees, which constitute an essential part of Oman's citrus economy. Given that Omani lime trees are particularly vulnerable to HLB infection, the disease has a potentially serious impact on the nation's economy. Lime exports and imports, specifically items coming under commodity group 805, are the second largest in Oman's citrus fruit industry, as per Trade Economy's Annual International Trade Statistics by Country. In general, only 9% of limes are exported, with the remaining 91% coming from foreign sources (UN Comtrade, 2022). A recent article with the headline "New Disease Threatens Citrus Trees in Oman" reports the emergence of a disease that puts citrus trees in the Sultanate of Oman at risk. The importance of citrus trees, especially Omani limes, in terms of productivity and cultivated land in the nation is emphasized in the text. The northern part of Oman has the highest concentration of acid lime cultivation, a particular variety of citrus that is widely grown throughout the country (Observer, 2019).

On October 2, 2018, the United Nations Food and Agriculture Organization (FAO) and the Sultanate of Oman's government launched a programme to develop the citrus industry sector. The main goal of this project, titled "Development, Production, Multiplication and Dissemination of Certified Citrus Propagating Materials" is to increase the production and multiplication of certified citrus plant propagative materials by producing pathogen-free citrus plants (FAO, 2018). This is an initiative to create disease-free citrus plants has been put into place by the Omani Ministry of Agriculture, Fisheries Wealth, and Water Resources, notably the Directorate-General of Agricultural and Animal Research. The goal of this project, which was supported by the Agriculture and Fisheries Fund, is to grow mother trees free of disease. The goal of this initiative is to protect various citrus varieties, particularly those that are economically viable and grown all over the Sultanate of Oman (Observer, 2017). Therefore, the development of effective and precise methods for HLB detection is essential for prompt intervention and halting of the disease's spread to healthy citrus groves.

Hyperspectral imaging enables early diagnosis and monitoring of HLB-infected trees, even before obvious symptoms appear by leveraging the distinctive spectral signatures of healthy and diseased plants (Mahlein et al., 2018). The purpose of this study is to examine the possibility of hyperspectral imaging as a method for detecting HLB disease in Omani lime trees. The spectral properties of healthy and HLB-infected lime plants will be examined with an emphasis on the major spectral bands that show notable changes between the two groups. This will enable the creation of a reliable and automated HLB detection system. The research will also examine how well different predictive algorithms perform in identifying healthy and diseased lime trees based on hyperspectral data.

The results of this study will advance the field of precision agriculture and offer citrus farmers, agronomists, and plant pathologists' insightful information about the efficient management and control of HLB. It can improve disease surveillance capabilities, enable early intervention, and lessen the effect of HLB on the productivity of Omani lime trees by utilizing hyperspectral imaging technology. Ultimately, this research aims to safeguard the citrus sector, save agricultural livelihoods, and guarantee HLB-affected citrus agriculture is sustainable.

2 Literature Review

Lan et al., (2020) conducted a comparative study for citrus greening detection on acquired UAV multispectral images using machine learning methods. The research used calculated vegetation indices (VIs) followed by PCA (principal components analysis) for correlation analysis and dimensionality reduction. Further potential features were discovered using AutoEncoder. The results showed that the highest accuracy could be achieved by combining the features obtained through PCA and the VIs with the original DN (digital numbers) values. The machine learning methods Random Forest and K-Nearest Neighbors (KNN) were applied by (Chavarro-Mesa et al., 2020) for disease monitoring and HLB incidence prediction in the Columbian context. The performance of Random Forest model was effective compared to KNN. Soini, Fellah and Abid, (2019) extracted sub-images of fruit from a tree image to detect HLB infection using computer vision and deep leaning techniques' inception model. Further signs of a citrus greening infection were determined using trained machine learning functions. The research found that the worst (around 80%) accuracy was obtained by using computer vision fruit sub-image extraction. Therefore, tree images were manually calibrated to detect a specific range of orange color values. However, deep learning model was able to provide 93.3% in identifying whether HLB disease exists or not. A Genetic Algorithm (GA) based Feature Optimization method was used by (Kaur et al., 2020) to distinguish between healthy and unhealthy citrus fruit images. Among the different machine learning approaches GA-SVM using color, shape and texture features was able to achieve accuracy of 90.4%. Hyperspectral remote sensing data was used by (Deng et al., 2020) to extract canopy spectral samples based on single pixels. The genetic algorithm extracted feature bands at 468 nm, 504 nm, 512 nm, 516 nm, 528 nm, 536 nm, 632 nm, 680 nm, 688 nm, and 852 nm for the HLB detection. The research used canopy spectral feature parameters obtained through a stacked autoencoder (SAE) neural network and multi-feature fusion of vegetation index for HLB detection. The approach was able to identify diseased and healthy citrus canopies. A hyperspectral imaging software (ENVI, ITT VIS) was used for the analysis in (Lee, 2012). The research used an image-derived spectral library for HLB infected areas for spectrum identification and used mixture tuned matched filtering (MTMF), spectral angle mapping (SAM), and linear spectral unmixing for classification. MTMF was able to achieve accuracy of 80%. Deng et al., (2019) used HSI based band selection approach to extract characteristic features for the classification of healthy and symptomatic HLB leaves. The research obtained 13 bands after eliminating redundancy and provided 90.8% of classification accuracy for three group classification using SVM. Yang et al., (2022) predicted the carbohydrate concentration using the combination of micro-FTIR spectroscopy and machine learning algorithm in two citrus varieties. They found that intensity peaks were higher in HLB infected navel orange and Ponkan leaf midribs as compared to healthy and nutrition deficient samples. The spectrum of citrus plants gets affected by the morphological effects of the disease. The increased magnitude is evident in the diseased leaves (Hariharan et al., 2023).

2.1 Summary

It can derived from the literature review is that, most of the published research has focused on classification of citrus leaves into only two classes namely HLB infected or not. In the current research three different classes namely HLB infected, healthy and nutrition deficient are considered. Moreover, the current research focuses on making use of spectral and spatial features of healthy, nutrition deficient and HLB infected leaves classification through a deep learning approach in the Omani lime context. To the best of our knowledge, this is the first research that focuses on HLB detection in Omani lime trees using hyperspectral imaging. The following sections provide details on materials and methods used for sample collection, methodology adopted, results obtained, discussions, conclusion, and future directions.

3 Materials and Methods

3.1 Study Site

The samples for the current research were obtained from Oman's Ministry of Agriculture, Fisheries Wealth, and Water Resources, Liwa Sohar, Oman and Barka, Oman. The ministry has maintained lime tree orchards and identified trees as healthy or infected. Figure 1 shows the HLB infected trees and fruit.

Fig. 1. HLB infected tree leaves and fruit.

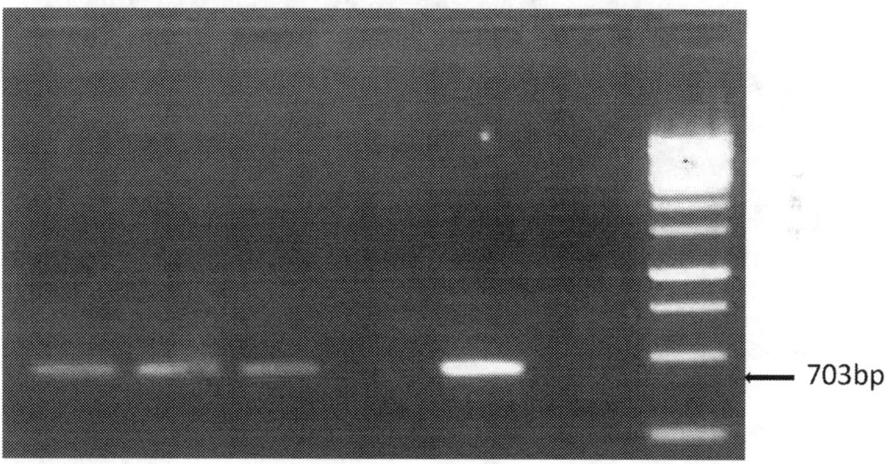

Fig. 2. Polymerase chain reaction (PCR) test for the HLB infected leaf

Initially, the samples were taken from both HLB infected and healthy orchards and polymerase chain reaction (PCR) test was used to detect the presence of HLB bacterium in each leaf. The PCR test result of the HLB infected leaf is provided in Fig. 2.

Referring to Fig. 2 the gel under UV light shows the success of rplKAJL-rpoBC operon (β-operon) region amplification using A2/J5 primer pairs producing bands of 703 bp. Lanes 1,2 and 3 samples infected with HLB. Lane 4 negative sample, Lane 5 positive control and Lane 6 negative control, M:1 kb Ladder.

According to the PCR test, all the tree leaves from the healthy orchard were negative however the leaves from some of the infected trees orchard were found to be positive. The three sample classes namely healthy, nutrition deficient and HLB infected were created based on the PCR test. Further, the samples were captured in a controlled room with halogen lights using Specim IQ hyperspectral cameras manufactured by Spectral Imaging Ltd, Finland. Specim IQ cameras are equipped with a high-resolution hyperspectral sensor that captures images at many different wavelengths typically between 400 and 1000 nm. The Spatial resolution is typically between 1 and 3 megapixels. Spectral resolution is typically between 10 and 20 nm. Calibration was done prior to the sample capture using the calibration tile provided. Moreover, a white reflectance panel was used during the image capture of the samples. Fig. 3 provides gray scale image of the 50 spectral band samples. The typical spectra of citrus leaf pixels of different classes are provided in Fig. 4. The typical spectra for each class was obtained by averaging a group of 15 spectra of a given class.

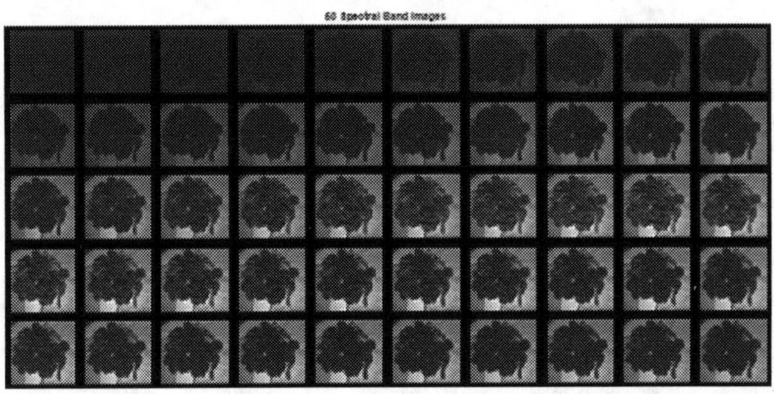

Fig. 3. Gray scale of the image 50 band samples

The captured images were read into the MATLAB environment as hyperspectral image cubes and the following methodology (Fig. 5) was used to process the image samples for three different classes.

4 Proposed Methodology

In the proposed methodology, the hyperspectral image samples were read into the MATLAB 21a version software environment and stored as hypercubes. As part of preprocessing the region of interest (ROI) was chosen by eliminating non-essential background. The ROI was segmented into eight sub slices with

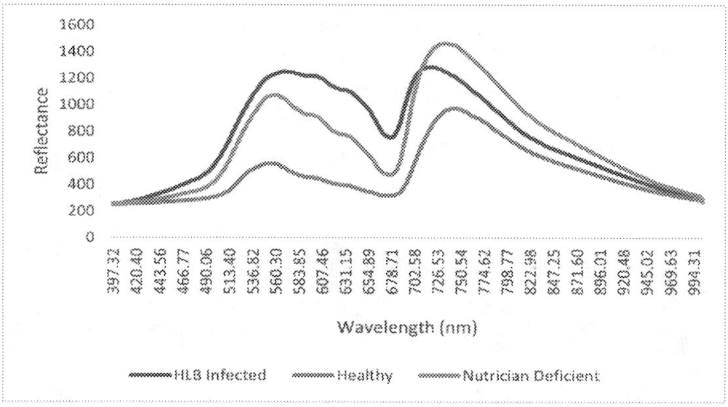

Fig. 4. Typical spectra of citrus leaf pixels of different classes

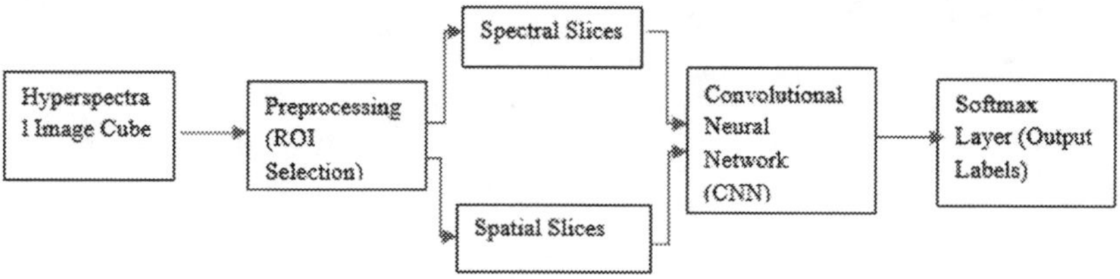

Fig. 5. Proposed methodology

spatial features. Figures 6, 7 and 8 show the segmented images of the samples. Similarly, the ROI was segmented into sub slices of ten bands each to capture spectral features. Figures 9, 10 and 11 show the segmented spectral slices of the image samples. Further, the combined images samples were given as input to Convolutional Neural Network (see the description of CNN below and Table 1 for CNN parameters) for deep learning and classification. The details of the procedure followed are given in the following sections.

4.1 Algorithm

1. **Read and Store Hyperspectral Image Samples**
   - Read hyperspectral image samples into the MATLAB Environment.
   - Store the samples as hypercubes in the software environment.
2. **Preprocessing: Region of Interest Selection**
   - Choose the region of interest (ROI) to exclude non-essential background.
   - Segment the ROI into eight sub-slices based on spatial features.
   - Segment the ROI into sub-slices, each containing ten bands to capture spectral features using a moving window.
3. **Input Preparation for Convolutional Neural Network (CNN)**
   - Combine the segmented image samples obtained from the previous steps.

   - Use the combined sliced image samples as input data for CNN.
4. **CNN Processing (Deep Learning and Classification)**
   - Apply Convolutional Neural Network (CNN) for deep learning and classification.

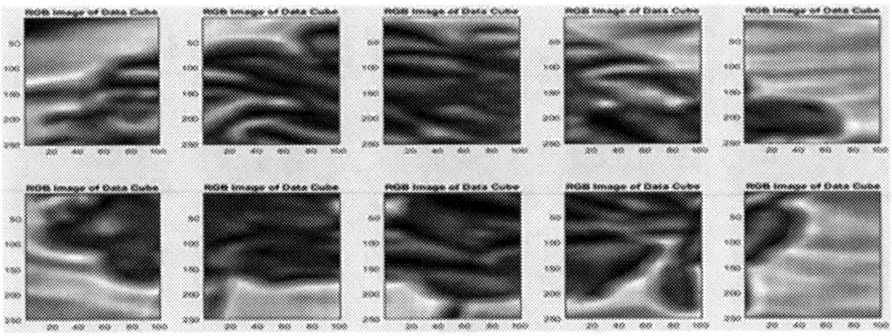

Fig. 6. Segmented healthy leaf images

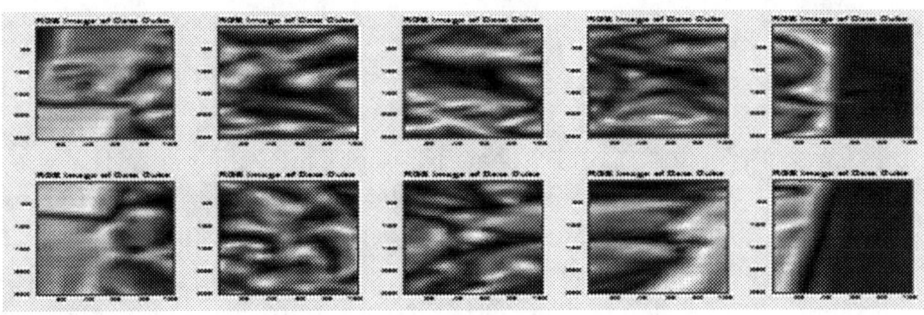

Fig. 7. Segmented nutrition deficient leaf images

4.2 Convolutional Neural Network (CNN)

CNN network is created using image input layer, convolution layer, batch normalization layer, ReLu layer and softmax layer. Softmax assigns an input datum to the appropriate class label. The convolution layer applies a 2D filter on the inputs in each image region. The train network function calculates a dot product for the input and weights and further the bias term is added. Here the weights are called the filter. The moving filters with the same set of weights and bias will create a feature map. The batch normalization layer is used to speed up the training of the CNN and reduce the sensitivity to network initialization. The batch normalization layer is used between the convolutional layers and nonlinear

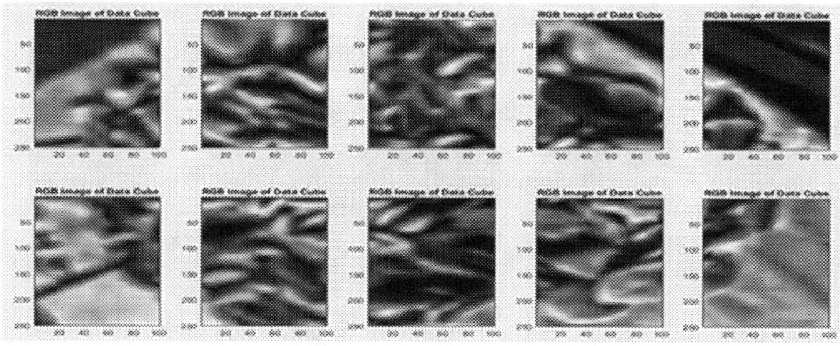

Fig. 8. Segmented HLB infected leaf images

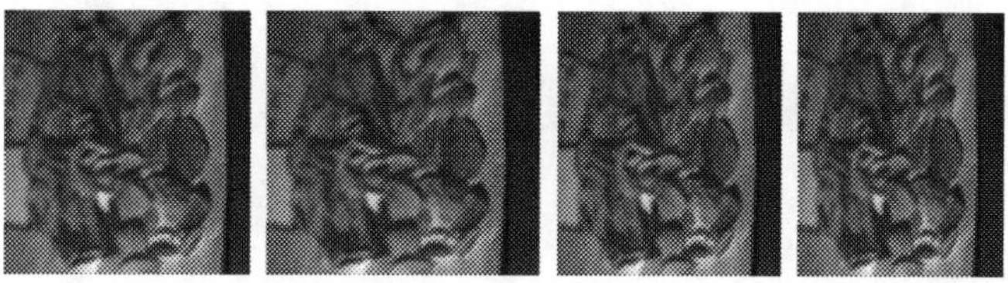

Fig. 9. Spectral Slices of HLB infected leaf images

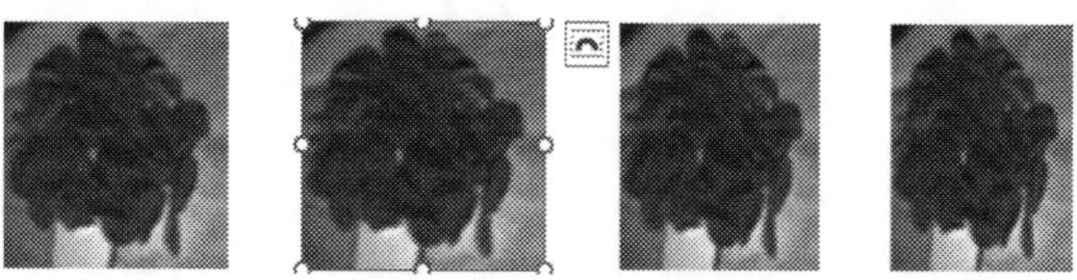

Fig. 10. Spectral Slices of healthy leaf images

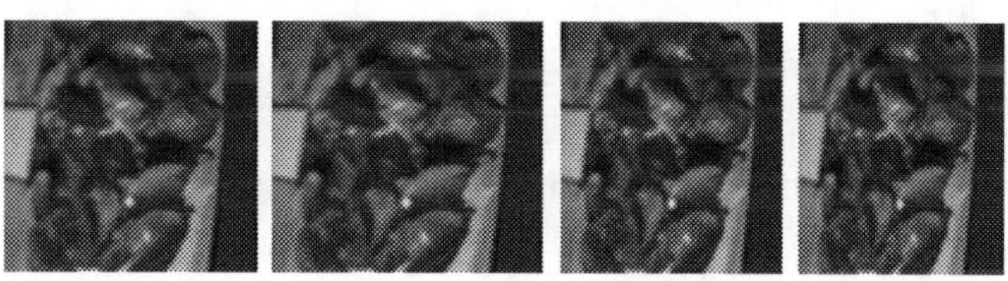

Fig. 11. Spectral Slices of nutrition deficient leaf images

layers like ReLu layer. Normalization can be done by subtracting the *mini_batch* mean and dividing by the *mini_batch* standard deviation. The ReLu layer performs a threshold operation based on the following condition.

$$f(x) = \begin{cases} \text{x}, & \text{if } x \geq 0 \\ 0, & \text{otherwise} \end{cases}$$

Relu layer does not change the size of the input. The fully connected layer multiplies the input by a weight matrix (W) and then adds a bias vector (b) as shown in Eq. 1.

$$f(x) = WX_t + b \tag{1}$$

where t is time step of X. The softmax layer and classification layer are the output layers. The Softmax layer applies the softmax function. The classification layer calculates the cross-entropy loss for classification and weighted classification with mutually exclusive classes.

The softmax function y_r is given as

$$y_(r) = \frac{exp(a_(r)(x)}{\Sigma_{j=1}^{k} exp(a_(j)(x)} \tag{2}$$

where $0 \leq y_r \leq 1$ and $\Sigma_{j=1}^{k} y_j = 1$ The softmax function is the output unit activation function after the fully connected layer. The conditional probability of a sample for a given class r is given by Eq. 3.

$$p(c_r \mid\} x, \theta) = \frac{p(x, \theta \mid\} c_r) p(c_(r)}{\Sigma_{j=1}^{k} \{p(x, \theta \mid\} c_j) p(c_(j)} \tag{3}$$

where c_r is called the class prior probability.

$$p(c_r \mid\} x, \theta) = \frac{exp(a_r(x, \theta))}{\Sigma_{j=1}^{k} \{exp(a_j(x, \theta))} \tag{4}$$

Here $0 \leq p(c_r|x, \theta) \leq 1$ and $\Sigma_{(j=1)}^{k} p(c_j|x, \theta) = 1$ hence $a_r = \ln(p(x, \theta c_r) p(c_r))$ The softmax function which is also called the normalized exponential can be treated as the multi class generalization of the logistic sigmoid function.

$$loss = -\frac{1}{N} \Sigma_{m=1}^{N} \sigma_{i=1}^{K} W_i t_m i \ln(y_m i) \tag{5}$$

where N is the number of samples, K is the number of classes, W_i is the weight for class i and $t_m i$ is the indication that the $m^t h$ sample belongs to the $i^t h$class. $y_m i$ is the output for sample m for $i^t h$ class which means to say that $y_m i$ is the probability that the network associates the $m^t h$ input with $i^t h$ class. For a single observation the mean squared error (MSE) is given by Eq. 6.

$$MSE = \Sigma_{i=1}^{R} \frac{(t_i - y_i)^2}{R} \tag{6}$$

where R is the number of responses, t_i is the target output and y_i is the network prediction for response i.

5 Experimental Results and Analysis

The experiments were conducted on a laptop with specifications 15.6" FHD 300 Hz, Core i7-10750H, 16 GB RAM, 1 TB SSD, 8 GB Nvidia GeForce RTX 2070. The sample images were read as hypercubes and sub cubes were created with a dimension of 250X100X204. The obtained sub cubes were subjected to automatic color contrast enhancement. One image sample contained around 50 leaves. Each image sample provided 8 sub cubes. Further, spectral indices of the sub cubes were obtained. In the present work Enhanced vegetation index (EVI) was used. The selected sub cubes were saved as RGB images retaining only the spatial features. In order to obtain the spectral features of the same image sample, only the spectral dimension was considered with a moving window size of 10. A minimum wavelength of 400 nm and maximum wavelength of 1000 nm were considered. As per the literature, neighboring bands of a hyperspectral image have high correlation which increases computational complexity hence in the current research neighboring spectral values were eliminated using a step size of 3. The obtained spectral slices were stored as RGB colored images.

Each of the three classes (HLB infected, nutrition deficient and healthy) had samples of 5 images and each image had around 50 leaves totaling 250 leaf image samples for each class. The obtained spectral and spatial RGB images for the three classes were resampled and given as input to the CNN network. The parameters shown in the following Table 1) were used for the experiments. Among the total samples 70% were used for training and for 30% for validation.

Table 1. CNN parameters.

S.No	Parameter	Value
1	**Network Type**	CNN
2	**Epoch**	10
3	**Input layer neuron**	250X100X3
4	**Total Number of Layers**	7
5	**Activation Function** Text follows	ReLU

Figure 12 provides an overview of the CNN network training and validation results. The overall validation accuracy of 92.86% was obtained for the proposed approach. The classification accuracy reached above 90% by epoch 4. Similarly, the loss became zero by 4th epoch. The training smoothness is also obtained by epoch 4.

In the current experiments, it is observed that feeding images to the CNN network with only spatial details was able to provide a classification accuracy of 77.78% which implies the importance of spectral features which have the capability to differentiate materials even with minute difference. Referring to Fig. 4 the spectral signature of the three classes of leaves, it can be observed that

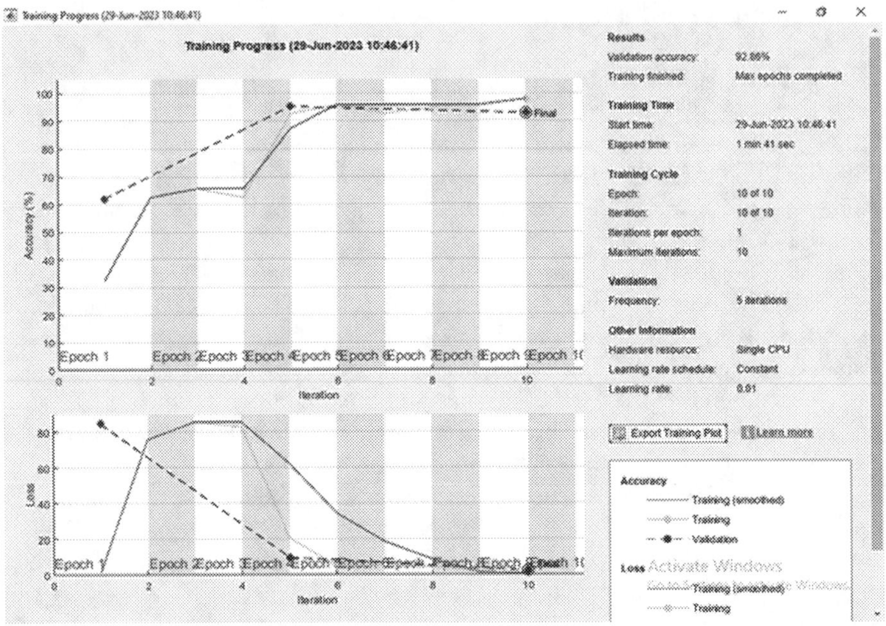

Fig. 12. CNN Training & Validation Results

the difference is obvious starting from the green band as there is less chlorophyll absorption in infected and nutrition deficient leaves. The significant bands with a difference in the three types of leaves are 560 nm, 678 nm, 726 nm and 750 nm. The stress level nutrition deficient leaves are higher which is evident in bands 700 nm to 720 nm. Although there is a very slight difference between HLB infected and nutrition deficient leaves, the current research was able classify the images with a high validation accuracy rate.

5.1 Contributions

The following are the contributions of the proposed research. Introduction of Innovative Detection Method: This research pioneers the application of hyperspectral imaging technology for the automatic identification of Citrus greening or Huanglongbing (HLB) disease in Omani acid lime trees. It marks a significant shift from manual identification methods by leveraging high-resolution leaf images captured through a portable Specim IQ hyperspectral camera.

Classifying Citrus Leaves with High Accuracy: The study categorizes Omani citrus tree leaves into three distinct classes: healthy, nutrition deficient, and HLB infected, determined through Polymerase chain reaction (PCR) tests. Employing Convolution Neural Networks and deep features extraction techniques, the research achieves an impressive classification accuracy of 92.86%. This high accuracy showcases the effectiveness and reliability of the proposed approach in distinguishing between the different leaf types.

Identification of Discriminatory Spectral Bands: The research identifies specific spectral bands at 560 nm, 678 nm, 726 nm, and 750 nm that demonstrate discernible differences among the three leaf categories. These findings signify the potential use of these spectral bands as distinguishing markers for classifying healthy, nutrition-deficient, and HLB-infected citrus leaves.

Advancing Disease Detection in Citrus Cultivation: By introducing a novel methodology that surpasses manual tree inspection, this research represents a significant leap in disease detection in Omani acid lime cultivation. It offers a more efficient, automated, and precise means to identify and quarantine infected trees, ultimately aiding in the prevention of HLB disease transmission to healthy trees.

5.2 Delimitations

The present study concentrated solely on a single type of HLB-infected leaves without distinguishing between symptomatic or asymptomatic ones. It primarily focused on the detection of HLB presence without delving into the specific percentage of the disease occurrence. The leaves classified within the third category were denoted as nutritionally deficient without specifying the exact type of deficiency.

6 Conclusion

In the current research, Citrus greening or Huanglongbing (HLB) disease infected Omani lime trees were studied for the automatic identification of the disease through hyperspectral imaging technology. Images captured through a Specim IQ HSI camera were preprocessed and fed into a CNN network for deep feature extraction and classification. The research considered three classes namely HLB infected, nutrition deficient and healthy. The current research used both spectral and spatial features of the said image samples and through deep feature extraction the classification accuracy was able to reach above 90% just in 4 epochs. Future research could study the life cycle of HLB infected trees to determine the stage at which a healthy leaf gets infected. This will help the concerned authorities to take preventive measures at an early stage and stop the spread of the disease. Moreover, comparative study of spectral signatures could be carried out for the citrus leaves with HLB disease and other types of diseases.

Acknowledgements. The research leading to these results has received funding from the Research Council (TRC) of the Sultanate of Oman under the Block Funding Program. TRC Block Funding Agreement No BFP/RGP/EBR/21/332. The authors would like to thank Mr. Mohammed, Lab technician, Ministry of Agriculture, Fisheries Wealth, and Water Resources, Liwa, Sohar in conducting the Polymerase chain reaction (PCR) test.

References

Bassanezi, R.B., et al.: Overview of citrus huanglongbing spread and management strategies in Brazil. Trop. Plant Pathol. **45**(3), 251–264 (2020). https://doi.org/10.1007/s40858-020-00343-y

Bock, C.H., et al.: Plant disease severity estimated visually, by digital photography and image analysis, and by hyperspectral imaging. Crit. Rev. Plant Sci. **29**(2), 59–107 (2010). https://doi.org/10.1080/07352681003617285

Chavarro-Mesa, E., et al.: Preliminary machine learning model for citrus greening disease (Huanglongbing-HLB) prediction in Colombia. In: 2020 IEEE Colombian Conference on Applications of Computational Intelligence, ColCACI 2020 - Proceedings, Colombia. IEEE (2020). https://doi.org/10.1109/ColCACI50549.2020.9247900

Deng, X., et al.: Field detection and classification of citrus huanglongbing based on hyperspectral reflectance. Comput. Electron. Agric. **167**(9), 105006 (2019). https://doi.org/10.1016/j.compag.2019.105006

Deng, X., et al.: Detection of citrus huanglongbing based on multi-input neural network model of UAV hyperspectral remote sensing. Remote Sens. **12**(17), 2678 (2020). https://doi.org/10.3390/RS12172678

FAO and Oman work to develop the national citrus industry. https://www.fao.org/neareast/news/view/en/c/1155823/. Accessed 4 May 2023

Hariharan, J., et al.: An AI-based spectral data analysis process for recognizing unique plant biomarkers and disease features. Comput. Electron. Agric. **204**(12), 107574 (2023). https://doi.org/10.1016/j.compag.2022.107574

Gottwald, T.R.: Current epidemiological understanding of citrus Huanglongbing. Annu. Rev. Phytopathol. **48**, 119–39 (2010). PMID: 20415578, https://doi.org/10.1146/annurev-phyto-073009-114418

Kaur, B., et al.: A genetic algorithm based feature optimization method for citrus HLB disease detection using machine learning. In: Proceedings of the 3rd International Conference on Smart Systems and Inventive Technology, ICSSIT 2020, India. IEEE (2020). https://doi.org/10.1109/ICSSIT48917.2020.9214107

Lan, Y., et al.: Comparison of machine learning methods for citrus greening detection on UAV multispectral images. Comput. Electron. Agric. **171**, 105234 (2020). https://doi.org/10.1016/j.compag.2020.105234

Lee, W.S.: Citrus greening disease detection using aerial hyperspectral and multispectral imaging techniques. J. Appl. Remote Sens. **6**(1), 063542–063542 (2012). https://doi.org/10.1117/1.jrs.6.063542

Mahlein, A.K., et al.: Hyperspectral sensors and imaging technologies in phytopathology: state of the art. Annu. Rev. Phytopathol. **56**, 535–558 (2018). https://doi.org/10.1146/ANNUREV-PHYTO-080417-050100

Project aims at citrus plants free of diseases - Oman Observer. https://www.omanobserver.om/article/80944/Local/project-aims-at-citrus-plants-free-of-diseases. Accessed 14 May 2023

New disease threatens citrus trees in Oman - Oman Observer. https://www.omanobserver.om/article/35039/Business/new-disease-threatens-citrus-trees-in-oman. Accessed 14 May 2023

Singerman, A., Useche, P.: Florida citrus growers' first impressions on genetically modified trees. AgBioforum **20**(1), 67–83 (2017)

Soini, C.T., Fellah, S., Abid, M.R.: Citrus greening infection detection (CIGID) by computer vision and deep learning. In: ACM International Conference Proceeding Series, pp. 21–26. ACM, USA (2019). https://doi.org/10.1145/3325917.3325936

Annual International Trade Statistics by Country (HS02). https://trendeconomy.com/data/h2/Oman/0805. Accessed 22 Apr 2023

Wan, L., et al.: Hyperspectral sensing of plant diseases: principle and methods. Agronomy **12**(6), 1–19 (2022). https://doi.org/10.3390/agronomy12061451

Wangithi, C.M.: Evaluation of the magnitude of Citus yield losses due to African Citrus Triozid, False Codling Moth, the Greening Disease and other pests of economic importance in Kenya. J. Econ. Sustain. Dev. **10**(20), 87–97 (2019). https://doi.org/10.7176/jesd/10-20-11

Yang, B., et al.: Citrus Huanglongbing detection and semi-quantification of the carbohydrate concentration based on micro-FTIR spectroscopy. Anal. Bioanal. Chem. **414**(23), 6881–68897 (2022). https://doi.org/10.1007/s00216-022-04254-6

A Stack Ensemble Approach for Early Alzheimer Classification Using Machine Learning Algorithms

Amit Kumar[1], Neha Sharma[1](✉), Rahul Chauhan[2], Akhilendra Khare[3], Abhineet Anand[4], and Manish Sharma[5]

[1] Chitkara University Institute of Engineering and Technology, Chitkara University, Rajpura, Punjab, India
nehasharma0110@gmail.com
[2] Department of CSE, Graphic Era Hill University, Dehradun, India
[3] School of Computing Science and Engineering, Galgotias University, Noida, India
[4] Chandigarh University, Mohali, India
abhineet.e13847@cumail.in
[5] Computer Science and Engineering, Graphic Era Deemed to Be University, Dehradun, Uttarakhand, India
manishsharma.cse@geu.ac.in

Abstract. The incorporation of machine learning techniques in medical research has facilitated the exploration of novel avenues for the timely identification of diseases. The continuous progress in medical technology has facilitated the acquisition of complex and complete datasets, which in turn enhances the ability to identify medical diseases in their early stages. Alzheimer's disease, a significant and hard problem, is characterised by the slow degeneration of brain cells and has a profound impact on cognitive functions, namely memory. It occupies a prominent position within this domain. In the middle of these exciting promises, there remains a significant research gap that pertains to the absence of thorough empirical evidence about the effectiveness of machine learning algorithms in the early identification of Alzheimer's disease. The primary objective of this study is to address the existing research gap by conducting a comprehensive and meticulous series of experiments. A comprehensive examination of data obtained from sophisticated neuroimaging technologies is performed by utilising a wide range of machine learning models, such as Logistic Regression, Naive Bayes, Neural Networks, Random Forest, and the Stack ensemble. The primary objective is to facilitate the prompt detection of Alzheimer's disease, hence enabling expedited interventions and therapeutic approaches. As one embarks on the journey of research, the unfolding narrative is shaped by the use of empirical evidence, establishing a strong foundation in the convergence of state-of-the-art technology and the urgent healthcare need to detect early stages of Alzheimer's disease. Furthermore, this research not only addresses existing gaps in the literature but also ends in the identification of the most effective machine learning model, specifically the Neural Network, which has an accuracy rate of 87%. This significant advancement represents a critical juncture in the diagnosis of Alzheimer's disease and sets a hopeful trajectory for its treatment and control.

KC Santosh et al. (Eds.): RTIP2R 2023, CCIS 2027, pp. 82–96, 2024.
https://doi.org/10.1007/978-3-031-53085-2_8

Keywords: Machine learning · Alzheimer's disease · cognitive impairments · neuroimaging · CT · MRI · PET · EEG · Logistic Regression · Naive Bayes · Neural Networks · Random Forest · early detection · intervention · treatment

1 Introduction

Alzheimer's disease (AD), a widely widespread form of dementia, is a significant and intricate health burden. The condition under consideration is a progressive syndrome that is distinguished by the steady decline of cognitive capacities, ultimately impacting an individual's memory and ability to carry out everyday activities [1]. This incapacitating condition not only presents a considerable hardship to people and their families but also carries enormous consequences for public health. Alzheimer's disease (AD) is widely recognised as a prominent contributor to the development of dementia on a global scale. It instigates the degeneration of brain cells, leading to the deterioration of memory, cognitive abilities, and the manifestation of behavioral alterations. It is noteworthy to mention that the likelihood of having Alzheimer's disease escalates with advancing age. Regrettably, although diligent study endeavors, a conclusive remedy or preventative approach for this ailment remains elusive. However, there exist potential therapeutic interventions that demonstrate efficacy in mitigating the advancement of the ailment and enhancing the overall well-being of persons afflicted by it. Dementia, a condition frequently associated with Alzheimer's disease, is a growing global health issue. It is concerning to see that around 70% of persons diagnosed with Alzheimer's disease also exhibit symptoms of dementia. Significantly, despite the higher prevalence of dementia compared to some types of cancer, it has not garnered an equivalent degree of attention, research funding, or public health measures. The aforementioned disparity highlights the pressing want for comprehensive study aimed at enhancing comprehension and mitigation of this escalating health concern. In the endeavor to discover more efficacious interventions for Alzheimer's disease, researchers are increasingly using the potential of machine learning, a state-of-the-art approach to data analysis. Machine learning algorithms facilitate the construction of prediction models that possess the ability to identify patterns and connections across extensive and intricate datasets, often with little human interaction. The use of this technology exhibits substantial potential in augmenting our capacity to properly detect and forecast Alzheimer's disease with more precision and at earlier developmental phases. The primary objective of our study is to develop and refine machine learning models, such as logistic regression [5], Naive Bayes [6], Neural Networks [7], and Random Forest [8], with the purpose of accurately predicting the occurrence of Alzheimer's disease. In brief, our research aims to leverage the capabilities of machine learning and comprehensive datasets in order to enhance our comprehension of Alzheimer's disease and dementia. Through the utilization of these sophisticated technologies, our aim is to augment the precision and promptness of Alzheimer's disease diagnosis, thus providing optimism for enhanced patient care and maybe establishing a foundation for more efficacious therapies in subsequent periods.

2 Methodology

In recent years, there has been a significant increase in research efforts dedicated to understanding the intricacies of Alzheimer's disease. This spike can be attributed to a shared determination among researchers to unravel the complexity associated with this debilitating disorder. One significant advancement in this endeavor has been the creation and implementation of a sophisticated algorithm specifically designed to forecast the beginning of Alzheimer's disease. The method utilized in this study incorporates a wide variety of data sources, including crucial variables such as total brain volume, obtained through thorough analysis of MRI images [12], in addition to a comprehensive set of other cognitive and biological characteristics. In conjunction with this anticipatory methodology, scholars have embarked on exploring the domain of clustering algorithms, utilizing their capacity to identify complex patterns within the extensive and intricate datasets linked to Alzheimer's study. In addition, the incorporation of a Fuzzy inference system [11] inside the algorithmic framework has enhanced its predictive capacities [2]. The multidisciplinary character of Alzheimer's research is shown by this complex approach, which integrates the fields of computer science, neurology, and data science in an effort to get a more comprehensive comprehension. The current research environment encompasses a variety of machine learning techniques, each offering unique perspectives on the task of forecasting Alzheimer's disease. The techniques employed in this endeavor include Logistic Regression, Naive Bayes, Neural Networks, and the formidable Random Forest model. The diverse range of computational methods used in this study highlights the need of taking a comprehensive approach to predicting and understanding Alzheimer's disease. This approach recognises the complex and multiple character of the illness. In the wider framework of scientific investigation, the notion of degradation assumes a prominent position. The phenomenon under scrutiny encompasses the complex conundrum of cognitive energy dissipation, which is clearly characterized by a pervasive decrease in cognitive performance. The decrease in performance is not exclusively ascribed to changes in focus, but rather incorporates a wide range of cognitive modifications [3]. The careful examination of the intricate distinctions highlights the thorough methodology employed by researchers in analyzing the significant cognitive changes brought about by Alzheimer's disease [4]. The domain of Alzheimer's research [9] is a dynamic sphere in which novel techniques intersect. Researchers continue to demonstrate their commitment to gaining a deeper understanding of this complex disorder, employing algorithmic prediction frameworks that integrate brain imaging and cognitive data, as well as conducting detailed investigations of cognitive impairment. This multidisciplinary framework has the potential for breakthroughs in the diagnosis, intervention, and overall comprehension of Alzheimer's disease [10].

3 Materials and Methods

Particularly in the context of dementia like Alzheimer's or others that are connected to it, the categories shown in Fig. 1 described seem to relate to various phases of cognitive impairment. Let's sum up these categories in a few words:

Non-Demented: This classification applies to people who do not show a severe cognitive impairment. They are cognitively healthy and do not exhibit the typical signs of dementia, such as forgetfulness, confusion, or difficulty doing everyday tasks [11].

Mild Demented: Individuals who display minor cognitive impairment often fall under the heading of mildly demented. Although they could go through tiny changes in memory, thinking, or behavior that are perceptible to themselves and sometimes others, these changes don't severely affect their capacity to carry out everyday tasks on their own [12].

Very Mild Demented: This is frequently an early stage of dementia in which people have only very slight cognitive impairment. They may occasionally experience mild disorientation, memory lapses, or word finding issues, but they can often handle their everyday tasks without much help.

Moderate Demented: People in this group have more severe cognitive impairment. They could have trouble remembering things, speaking, and making decisions. Individuals frequently need substantial help and supervision as daily tasks grow more difficult.

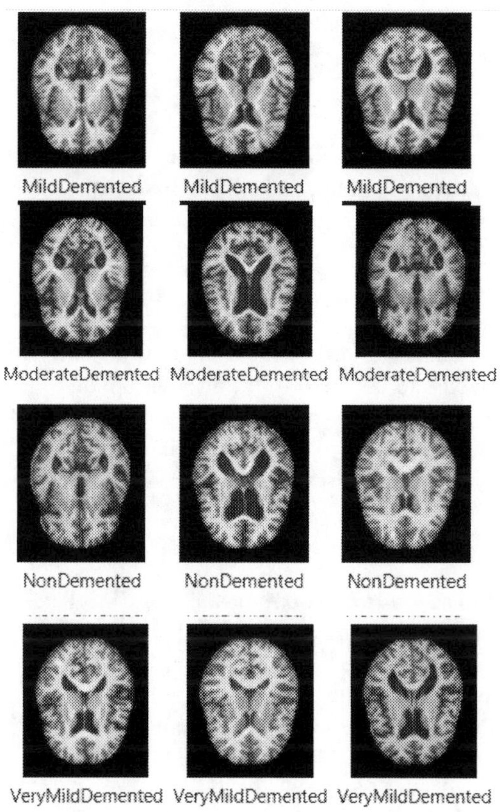

Fig. 1. Categories/Stages of Alzheimer

These classifications are often used in clinical evaluations and scientific studies to categorize the degree of cognitive impairment in people with Alzheimer's disease or other types of dementia [13, 14]. It's crucial to remember that dementia is a degenerative disorder, and over time, people may move from one group to another. The right classification enables medical personnel to specifically target therapies and assistance to the requirements of people experiencing various stages of cognitive decline.

3.1 Logistic Regression

It analyzes the chance of a specific event happening, with the common emphasis being placed on binary or categorical results. Its primary application is in classification processes, such as deciding whether or not an email should be labeled as spam or whether or not it can be trusted as an authentic message. Logical regression analyzes the link between a set of independent factors and a binary dependent variable to calculate the likelihood that a binary dependent variable will take on a particular value. This is done by looking at the correlation between the two sets of variables. The truth value of the dependent variable could either be true or false. The sigmoid function, more often known as the logistic function, is utilized in the execution of this modeling technique. This function converts real-valued inputs to a range between 0 and 1, where 1 represents the expected probability of a binary result. The inputs are converted to a range between 0 & 1 and is mathematically represented as [15]:

$$\mathrm{p} = 1/\left(1 + e\hat{}(-\mathrm{z})\right) \tag{1}$$

p is the likelihood that the result variable will fall into a specific category, z is the linear combination of the predictor variables, and e is the base of the natural logarithm.

The following equation represents the linear combination of the predictor variables (z):

$$\mathrm{z} = \mathrm{b}_0 + \mathrm{b}_1\mathrm{x}_1 + \mathrm{b}_2\mathrm{x}_2 + \ldots + \mathrm{b}_\mathrm{p}\mathrm{x}_\mathrm{p} \tag{2}$$

The linear combination is denoted by z, the coefficients (weights) that are allocated to each predictor variable are denoted by b0 through bp, and the predictor variables themselves are denoted by x1 through xp. During the training phase of logistic regression, the coefficients (b0, b1, b2,..., bp) are determined using maximum likelihood estimation or other optimization procedures. This takes place before the analysis of the data.

3.2 Random Forest

Constructing a set of decision trees is one of the steps involved in a Random Forest model. Each tree is built by applying a randomized portion of the training data as well as a randomized percentage of the features. This ensures that each tree has a unique structure. During the process of training, each tree will make its own individual forecast of the outcome, and the final prediction will be obtained by adding together the results of each of the trees' predictions. While carrying out classification tasks, the class that is predicted by the trees the most number of times is selected; on the other hand, while carrying out regression activities, the average or median of the tree's predictions is utilized. The algorithm works as follows [16]:

Data Preparation: Random Forest requires a labeled dataset in which the input features (predictor variables) are represented as numerical or categorical values, and the target variable is the outcome that is to be predicted in order for the algorithm to work properly.

Building the Forest: The Random Forest technique results in the production of several different decision trees. The number of trees that comprise the forest is a hyperparameter that can be adjusted in accordance with the activity that is currently being performed and the level of performance that is required. Each tree is constructed using a different, random subset of the data used for training. The term "bootstrapping" refers to this method of random sampling with replacement. By providing variance into the training data, it assists in the creation of more diversified trees. A random subset of the predictor variables is examined and taken into consideration for splitting at each node of the decision tree. This randomization helps trees become more independent of one another by lowering the correlation that exists between them.

Growing Decision Trees: A recursive partitioning of the data into subsets depending on the selected predictor variables is used to create each individual decision tree. The objective is to generate splits that either reduce the amount of impurity or increase the amount of information gained. Gini impurity and entropy are two examples of popular impurity measurements that are utilized in Random Forest. These measurements help to quantify the level of variability that exists inside each split, which in turn guides the process of tree construction.

Making Predictions: When performing classification tasks, the results of majority voting are used to integrate the predictions from each tree. The final prediction is going to be based on the class that received the most votes across all of the trees. In order to obtain the final prediction for regression tasks, the predictions obtained from each tree are first averaged.

Evaluating Performance: The performance can be assessed and analyzed in a number of different ways using a range of assessment metrics. These metrics can be used in a number of different combinations to evaluate and study the performance of the Random Forest model. These evaluative criteria can be applied in a variety of different ways, depending on the context.

3.3 Naïve Bayes

In the field of machine learning, Naive Bayes refers to a classification algorithm that makes use of Bayes' theorem. Because of how easy and effective it is to operate, it has a wide range of applications. The assumption that each feature contributes independently to the classification decision is made by the Naive Bayes algorithm. This means that the algorithm operates on the presumption that each feature is independent. The likelihood of each class is computed by the algorithm based on the characteristics that have been seen, and the algorithm chooses the class that has the highest probability as the target for its prediction. It is mathematically represented as [17]:

$$P(C|X) = \left(P(C)*P(X_1|C)*P(X_2|C) * \ldots *P\left(X_p|C\right)\right)/P(X) \tag{3}$$

The posterior probability of class C is denoted by the symbol P(C|X), which is calculated based on the predictor variables X. The value displayed here is the likelihood that an observation with predictor variables X belongs to class C. The prior probability of class C, denoted by the symbol P(C), is the likelihood of class C happening in the absence of any information regarding the variables that predict it. The conditional probabilities of observing the values of the predictor variables X1, X2,..., and Xp given class C are represented by the probabilities P(X1|C), P(X2|C),..., and P(Xp|C), respectively. The evidence, also known as the marginal likelihood, is denoted by the symbol P(X) and is defined as the probability of witnessing the predictor variables in question.

3.4 Neural Network

When information is passed through a neural network, it does so in a direction that is forward through the network. Every neuron takes in information, performs some kind of mathematical operation on it, and then sends the result on to the neuron below it in the hierarchy. While the output layer is responsible for producing the final prediction or outcome, the input layer is responsible for receiving the initial data. The computations that are carried out by the intermediate layers, sometimes referred to as the hidden layers, extract and transform features from the input data. Every neuron in the network executes a computation determined by the weights of its inputs, then applies an activation function to the result and sends it on to the next layer. It is mathematically represented as follows [18]:

$$z = w_1x_1 + w_2x_2 + \ldots + w_px_p + b \tag{4}$$

$$a = f(z) \tag{5}$$

z represents the weighted sum of the inputs. $w_1w_2 \ldots w_p$ are the weights associated with the inputs $x_1x_2 \ldots x_p$, respectively. b is the bias term, which allows shifting the activation function. a is the output of the neuron after applying the activation function f(z).

3.5 Stack Ensemble

A stack ensemble is a machine learning technique that combines the predictions of multiple diverse base models using a meta-model. In this approach, a set of base models, such as decision trees, support vector machines, or neural networks, are trained independently on the same dataset. The predictions generated by these base models serve as input features for a meta-model, which learns how to effectively combine these predictions to produce the final output. Stack ensembles are renowned for their ability to improve predictive accuracy by leveraging the strengths of different models and are frequently employed in tasks where maximizing performance is crucial, such as machine learning competitions and complex real-world applications.

4 Performance Metrics

4.1 AUC

The performance of binary classification models is assessed using the AUC (Area Under the Curve), an important statistic in machine learning (ML). Its goal is to evaluate a model's ability to discriminate between positive and negative classes at various levels of classification. The Receiver Operating Characteristic (ROC) plot, which depicts the connection between the true positive rate (sensitivity) and the false positive rate (1 - specificity) for various threshold values, is the basis for the calculation of AUC.

4.2 CA-Classification Accuracy

It determines the percentage of instances or samples in a dataset that were properly classified out of all the occurrences in the dataset. To achieve this, divide the percentage by the overall dataset's occurrence count. This may be seen as a ratio or percentage. The calculations that must be performed to determine whether or not the categorization is accurate are as follows: Examining the ratio of the number of accurate predictions to all of the predictions made by the classification is one way to gauge the degree of accuracy associated with a given classification. An evaluation of a classification model's utility may be completed quickly and easily in a number of scenarios by using the classification accuracy technique. This holds especially true in circumstances in which the classes in the dataset are dispersed in a manner that is fair to all of the classes. However, if the classes are not balanced—that is, if one class has a disproportionately high number of instances in comparison to the other(s)—then this statistic might not be the most accurate one to use. It is mathematically calculated as [19]:

$$Accuracy = \frac{(TP + TN)}{(TP + TN + FP + FN)} \tag{6}$$

4.3 F1-Score

It offers a more accurate evaluation of a model's overall performance by merging accuracy and recall into a single statistic. It can be thought of as a single number that measures a model's efficacy in a rounded way. The F1 score takes into account both the model's accuracy in identifying positive examples and its completeness in recording positive events. Both precision and recall measure how well a model can recognize good examples and how well it can record all positive events, respectively. It's calculated as the average of two other metrics—accuracy and recall—to account for the compromise between them. The term "precision recall harmonic mean" describes this endpoint. One way to think about this number is as a precision indicator. The F1 score is quite useful when working with skewed datasets or when weighting precision and recall equally. It is mathematically calculated as:

$$F - score = 2 \times \frac{(Precision \times Recall)}{(Precision + Recall)} \tag{7}$$

4.4 Precision

Each base learner is taught using a subset of the training data when using AdaBoost, and weights are applied to each data point as the training proceeds. A binary classification statistic called Precision is used to evaluate various models since it assesses how well a model predicts the future. This is done by calculating the percentage of positive cases that were correctly predicted out of all the positive instances that were anticipated. Precision is an assessment metric in binary classification. A low number of false positives is a sign that the model has a good capacity to avoid wrongly recognizing negative cases as positive. This may be shown by comparing the model's true positive rate to the percentage of false positives.

$$Precision = \frac{TP}{(TP + FP)} \tag{8}$$

4.5 Recall

Recall is an evaluation metric used in binary classification problems that examines the model's ability to catch all actual positive cases. Recall measures how well the model predicts actual positive cases, to put it another way. It is often referred to as the sensitivity or the true positive rate. It also goes by the name "sensitivity." The recall measure is helpful for acquiring an insight of how well the model recognizes positive cases because it does not take into consideration the total number of false positives. It is of utmost significance in circumstances when the occurrence of false negatives (missing positive instances) might have major repercussions. For instance, in medical diagnostics, a high recall means that a larger proportion of real cases are correctly recognized, even if it results in some erroneous positive forecasts. This is true even if it causes some false negative predictions.

$$Sensitivity = \frac{TP}{(TP + FN)} \tag{9}$$

5 Results

The machine learning algorithms are implemented in python and the dataset has been taken from Kaggle.

Table 1 compares the results of various machine learning models using the different performance metrics. The findings show that, in terms of numerous assessment measures, the Neural Network algorithm outperforms all other models. With scores of 0.965, 0.870, 0.869, 0.870,0.870 and 0.785, respectively, it earned exceptional values for AUC, classification accuracy, F1-score, precision, recall and MCC. After the Neural Network model, the next machine learning model is Stack. Then comes logistic regression, random forest and Naïve Bayes algorithm. This analysis will be used in the future work to propose a hybrid model for classification purposes (Fig. 2).

Table 1. Comparative Analysis of existing ML models

Model	AUC	CA	F1	Precision	Recall	MCC
Logistic Regression	0.903	0.766	0.766	0.766	0.766	0.612
Naïve Bayes	0.671	0.430	0.454	0.544	0.430	0.202
Neural Network	0.965	0.870	0.869	0.870	0.870	0.785
Random Forest	0.734	0.589	0.568	0.568	0.589	0.288
Stack Ensemble	0.957	0.868	0.867	0.868	0.868	0.781

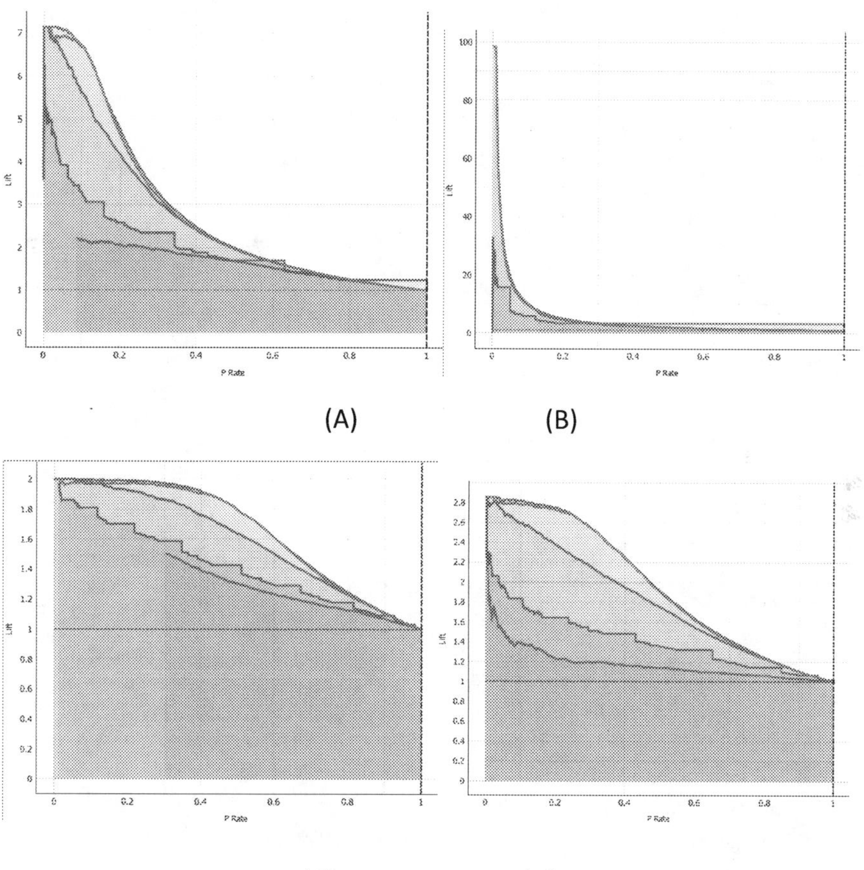

Fig. 2. Performance curve – Lift Curve (A) Mild, (B) Moderate, (C)Very Mild (D)Non-Demented

5.1 Performance Curve – Lift Curve

Figure 3 gives us a visual representation of the cumulative benefits made by the various ML models that were examined. The outcomes show how each model performed when assessed in terms of cumulative gains, a crucial parameter in evaluating ranking or recommendation algorithms. Gains over time measure how well these algorithms prioritize and suggest products to consumers based on their preferences or relevance. These numbers offer important information on how successfully each model delivered cumulative benefits and, as a result, made precise and pertinent recommendations to users (Fig. 4).

5.2 Performance Curve – Cumulative Gains

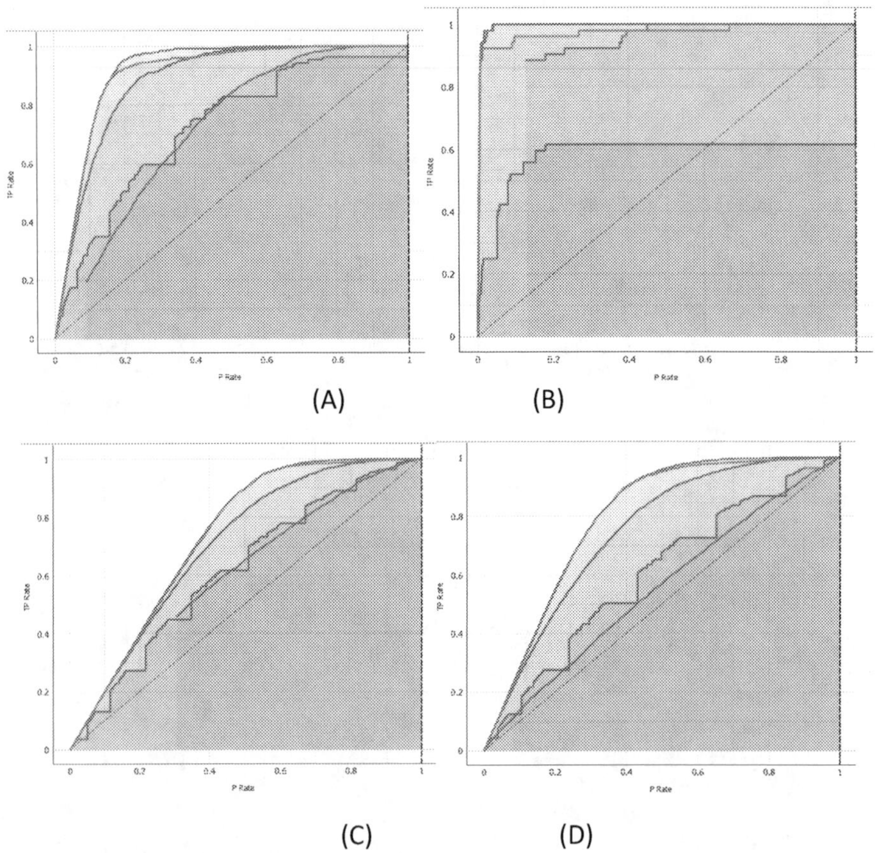

Fig. 3. Performance curve – Cumulative Gains (A) Mild, (B) Moderate, (C)Very Mild (D)Non-Demented

5.3 Performance Curve – Precision-Recall

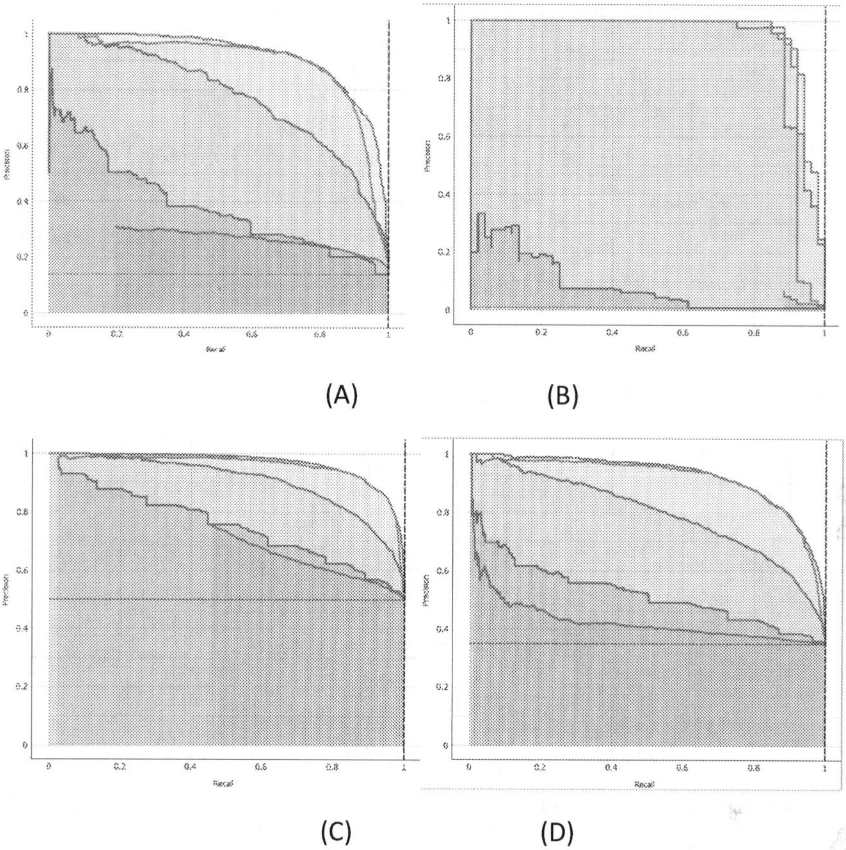

Fig. 4. Performance curve – Precision-Recall (A) Mild, (B) Moderate, (C)Very Mild (D)Non-Demented

5.4 Confusion Matrix Interpretation

A useful tool called a "confusion matrix" is used in the fields of statistics and machine learning to evaluate the effectiveness of a classification model.It does a comparison between the class labels that were predicted and the class labels that were actually assigned to a set of data points.The matrix comprises the following four important values: True Negatives (occurrences that were accurately predicted to be negative), True Positives (occurrences that were properly predicted to be positive), and False Positives (occurrences that were incorrectly predicted to be positive). The model's accuracy and its ability to distinguish between various groups are some of the insights provided by these numbers. In every confusion matrix that was described, the value 1 indicated a prediction of Alzheimer, whereas the value 0 indicated a lack of Alzheimer.

The confusion matrices for the ML modes considered—Logistic Regression, Naive Bayes, Random Forest, and Neural Networks—are shown in Figs. 5, 6, 7, 8 and 9, respectively.

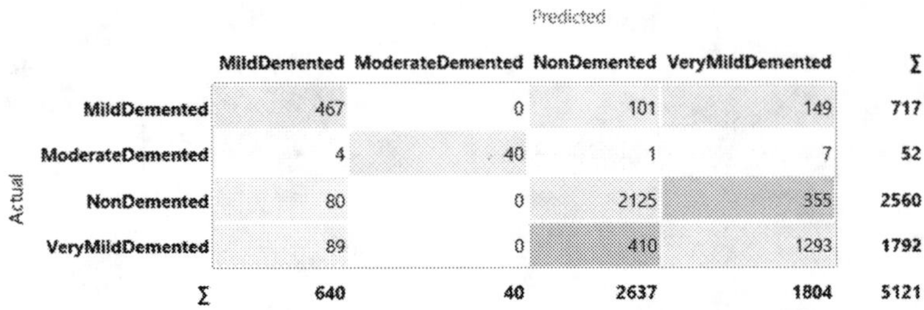

Actual \ Predicted	MildDemented	ModerateDemented	NonDemented	VeryMildDemented	Σ
MildDemented	467	0	101	149	717
ModerateDemented	4	40	1	7	52
NonDemented	80	0	2125	355	2560
VeryMildDemented	89	0	410	1293	1792
Σ	640	40	2637	1804	5121

Fig. 5. Confusion matrix: Logistic regression

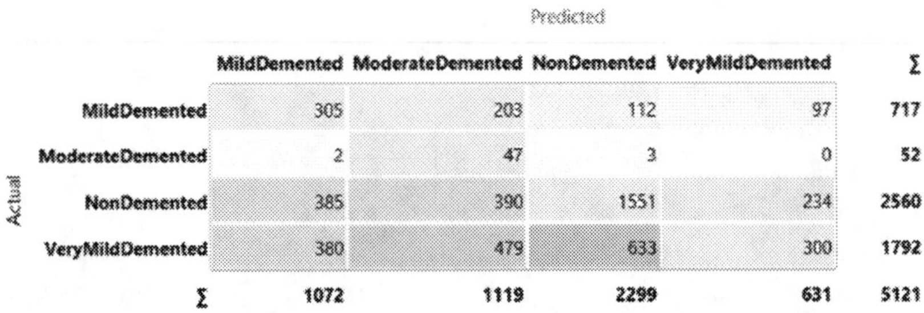

Actual \ Predicted	MildDemented	ModerateDemented	NonDemented	VeryMildDemented	Σ
MildDemented	305	203	112	97	717
ModerateDemented	2	47	3	0	52
NonDemented	385	390	1551	234	2560
VeryMildDemented	380	479	633	300	1792
Σ	1072	1119	2299	631	5121

Fig. 6. Confusion matrix: Naïve Bayes

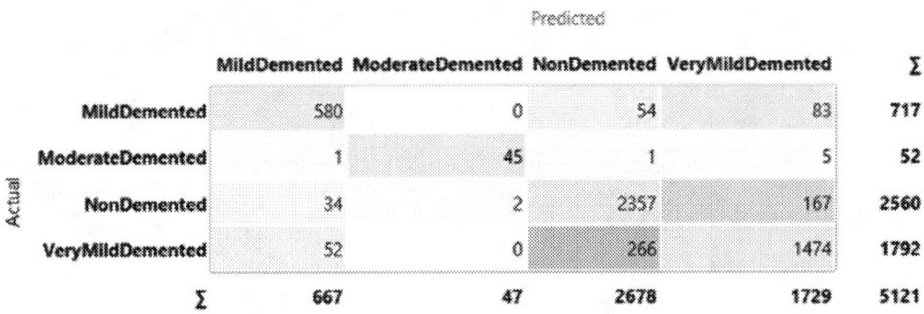

Actual \ Predicted	MildDemented	ModerateDemented	NonDemented	VeryMildDemented	Σ
MildDemented	580	0	54	83	717
ModerateDemented	1	45	1	5	52
NonDemented	34	2	2357	167	2560
VeryMildDemented	52	0	266	1474	1792
Σ	667	47	2678	1729	5121

Fig. 7. Confusion matrix: Neural Networks

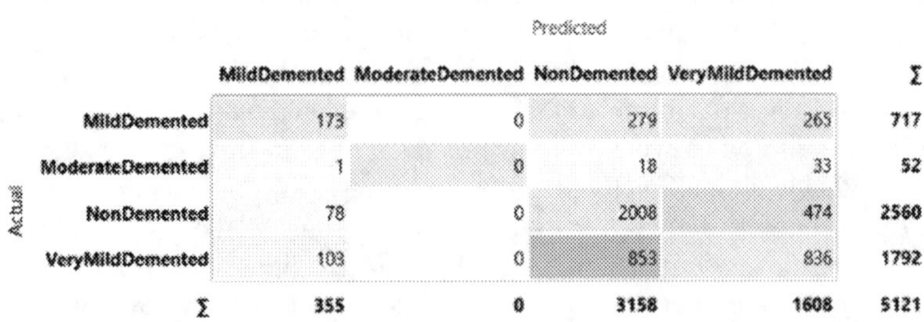

Actual \ Predicted	MildDemented	ModerateDemented	NonDemented	VeryMildDemented	Σ
MildDemented	173	0	279	265	717
ModerateDemented	1	0	18	33	52
NonDemented	78	0	2008	474	2560
VeryMildDemented	103	0	853	836	1792
Σ	355	0	3158	1608	5121

Fig. 8. Confusion matrix: Random Forest

Actual \ Predicted	MildDemented	ModerateDemented	NonDemented	VeryMildDemented	Σ
MildDemented	575	0	59	83	717
ModerateDemented	1	44	1	6	52
NonDemented	34	0	2356	170	2560
VeryMildDemented	52	0	269	1471	1792
Σ	662	44	2685	1730	5121

Fig. 9. Confusion matrix: Stack Ensemble

6 Conclusion

In conclusion, successful care and intervention of Alzheimer's disease depend greatly on its early identification. In order to diagnose Alzheimer's disease using neuroimaging data, this study thoroughly investigated the applicability of four machine learning models: Logistic Regression, Naive Bayes, Neural Networks, and Random Forest. The results of this study shed light on how machine learning algorithms may be used to precisely forecast Alzheimer's disease, particularly in its early stages. Early detection is essential for starting prompt medical treatments and individualised care plans, which ultimately improve patient outcomes and quality of life. This study makes an important contribution to the continuing work to improve Alzheimer's disease diagnosis. It offers a key building piece for enhancing our ability to address this prevalent health concern by leveraging the capabilities of machine learning and neuroimaging data. In conclusion, this study highlights the potential of interdisciplinary research by supporting the fusion of healthcare and technology to further the study of early Alzheimer's disease detection. The combination of machine learning and medical research offers a promising route towards more accurate diagnosis and enhanced patient care as we continue to look for novel solutions.

References

1. Chakraborty, A., de Wit, N.M., van der Flier, W.M., de Vries, H.E.: The blood brain barrier in Alzheimer's disease. Vasc. Pharmacol. **89**, 12–18 (2016)
2. Breitner, J.C.: Dementia—epidemiological considerations, nomenclature, and a tacit consensus definition. J. Geriatr. Psychiatry Neurol. **19**(3), 129–136 (2006)
3. Kiraly, A., Szabo, N., Toth, E., et al.: Male brain ages faster: the age and gender dependence of subcortical volumes. Brain Imaging Behav. **10**, 901–910 (2016)
4. Mesrob, L., Magnin, B., Colliot, O., et al.: Identification of atrophy patterns in alzheimer's disease based on SVM feature selection and anatomical parcellation. Med. Imaging Augmented Reality **5128**, 124–132 (2008)
5. Nusinovici, S., et al.: Logistic regression was as good as machine learning for predicting major chronic diseases. J. Clin. Epidemiol. **122**, 56–69 (2020)
6. Maliha, S.K., Ema, R.R., Ghosh, S.K., Ahmed, H., Mollick, M.R.J., Islam, T.: Cancer disease prediction using naive bayes, K-nearest neighbor and J48 algorithm. In 2019 10th International Conference on Computing, Communication and Networking Technologies (ICCCNT), pp. 1–7. IEEE, July 2019

7. Desai, M., Shah, M.: An anatomization on breast cancer detection and diagnosis employing multi-layer perceptron neural network (MLP) and convolutional neural network (CNN). Clin. eHealth **4**, 1–11 (2021)
8. Murugan, A., Nair, S.A.H., Kumar, K.S.: Detection of skin cancer using SVM, random forest and kNN classifiers. J. Med. Syst. **43**, 1–9 (2019)
9. Biju, K.S., Alfa, S.S., Lal, K., Antony, A., Akhil, M.K.: Alzheimer's detection based on segmentation of MRI image. Procedia Comput. Sci. **115**, 474–481 (2017)
10. Teipel, S., et al.: Multimodal imaging in Alzheimer's disease: validity and usefulness for early detection. Lancet Neurol. **14**(10), 1037–1053 (2015)
11. Jouffe, L.: Fuzzy inference system learning by reinforcement methods. IEEE Trans. Syst. Man Cybern. Part C (Appl. Rev.) **28**(3), 338–355 (1998)
12. Katti, G., Ara, S.A., Shireen, A.: Magnetic resonance imaging (MRI)–a review. Int. J. Dent. Clin. **3**(1), 65–70 (2011)
13. Kukreja, V., Dhiman, P.: A Deep Neural Network based disease detection scheme for citrus fruits. In: 2020 International Conference on Smart Electronics and Communication (ICOSEC), pp. 97–101. IEEE, September 2020
14. Dhiman, P., et al.: A novel deep learning model for detection of severity level of the disease in citrus fruits. Electronics **11**(3), 495 (2022)
15. Panwar, A., Yadav, R., Mishra, K., Gupta, S.: Deep learning techniques for the real time detection of Covid19 and pneumonia using chest radiographs. In: Proceedings of 19th IEEE International Conference on Smart Technologies, EUROCON 2021, pp. 250–253 (2021). https://doi.org/10.1109/EUROCON52738.2021.9535604
16. Bhatt, C., Kumar, I., Vijayakumar, V., Singh, K.U., Kumar, A.: The state of the art of deep learning models in medical science and their challenges. Multimed. Syst. **27**(4), 599–613 (2021). https://doi.org/10.1007/s00530-020-00694-1
17. Sharma, N., Chakraborty, C., Kumar, R.: Optimized multimedia data through computationally intelligent algorithms. Multimedia Syst. 1–17 (2022)

Analyzing Pulmonary Abnormality with Superpixel Based Graph Neural Network in Chest X-Ray

Ronaj Pradhan and KC Santosh(✉)

Applied Artificial Intelligence Research Lab, Department of Computer Science, University of South Dakota, Vermillion, SD 57069, USA
ronaj.pradhan@coyotes.usd.edu, santosh.kc@usd.edu
https://github.com/2ai-lab/Superpixels-in-graph-neural-network

Abstract. In recent years, the utilization of graph-based deep learning has gained prominence, yet its potential in the realm of medical diagnosis remains relatively unexplored. The challenge arises from the inherent irregular and unordered nature of physiological data, making it challenging to depict intricate patterns using conventional methods. Our research focuses on abnormality screening: classification of Chest X-Ray (CXR) as Tuberculosis positive or negative, using Graph Neural Networks (GNN) that uses Region Adjacency Graphs (RAGs) and each superpixel serves as a dedicated graph node. By integrating residual and concatenation structures, our approach effectively captures crucial features and relationships among superpixels, facilitating advancements in tuberculosis identification. Through the amalgamation of state-of-the-art neural network architectures and innovative graph-based representations, our work introduces a new perspective to medical image analysis.

Keywords: Chest X-ray · Region Adjacency Graph · Graph Neural Network · Graph Attention Network · Graph Convolutional Network · Superpixel

1 Introduction

Lung abnormality screening through CXR is a vital diagnostic tool, enabling early detection and intervention for various pulmonary conditions. They exhibit unique visual attributes, including sharp boundaries, specific colors, shapes, and angles when contrasted with natural pictures [1]. Tuberculosis (TB) appears on CXR with various radiological signs such as cavities, consolidations, infiltrations, opacity, and thickening, among other observable manifestations [2,3]. A non-invasive imaging technique such as CXR is essential in improving healthcare outcomes by identifying clinical manifestations in the lungs. Of all, the diseases TB is no exception. TB, an ancient and enduring human affliction, has been intertwined with our species for millennia, potentially spanning several million years [4]. Despite advancements in diagnostic and therapeutic approaches, the

KC Santosh et al. (Eds.): RTIP2R 2023, CCIS 2027, pp. 97–110, 2024.
https://doi.org/10.1007/978-3-031-53085-2_9

global burden of TB remains distressingly high, TB infected 10 million individuals and killed 1.4 million people in 2019 [5]. With approximately one-third of the world's population harboring Mycobacterium Tuberculosis (MTB) infection, the annual tally of new TB cases exceeds 9 million [6]. Encouragingly, this bacterial disease can be effectively treated as consequent administration of proper medication can cure this deadly disease [7]. Automated radiological screening is a progressing area of interest, wherein algorithms and predictive models are employed to identify anomalies in CXR [8]. Radiological methods like CXR have demonstrated their reliability and cost-effectiveness as a means of understanding clinical presentations in medical imaging [9].

CXR, with or without contrast enhancement, may be helpful for better characterization of radiographic findings by helping to distinguish between previous inactive and active disease [10]. The integration of Deep Learning (DL) algorithms has simplified the process of clinical evaluation and the interpretation provided by experts [11]. This has rendered Computer-Aided Diagnosis (CADx) as a potent strategy for mass screening of pulmonary TB via the analysis of CXR images, particularly in regions with few radiologists, in recommending high-risk patients for appropriate treatment [12]. Machine Learning (ML) and DL are the predominant Artificial Intelligence (AI) techniques employed to develop CAD systems for analyzing CXR images. Both techniques have had a significant impact, but the DL approach, such as Convolutional Neural Networks (CNN) has gained increasing attention in the medical field, particularly in the diagnosis of various pulmonary abnormalities, with a notable focus on tuberculosis detection [13].

Even though we have rich state-of-the-art literature for pulmonary abnormality screening using CXR, none of the techniques studied GNN. The GNN has the potential to capture substantial interest from the academic and industrial spheres, sparking swift advancements across a spectrum of disciplines [14]. Emerging as a formidable category of deep learning frameworks, GNNs excel in dissecting datasets characterized by intricate information interconnections manifesting as heterogeneous graphs. This proficiency is particularly evident in domains as diverse as drug development, social networks, traffic flow analysis, and notably, medical diagnostics. Experimental evidence underscores the remarkable potential of GNN architectures to effect transformational changes in these domains [15,16]. Our current endeavor is centered around the segmentation of CXR images into groupings of pixels with shared color and other fundamental attributes, giving rise to what are commonly referred to as 'superpixels.' Subsequently, these superpixels are preprocessed into a graph structure, which serves as input for the GNN. The goal of this approach is to facilitate image classification. By harnessing the potential of GNNs, we aim to yield insights and outcomes that hold promise for enhancing the interpretation of medical images in a novel and impactful manner.

2 Related Work - Graph Neural Networks

The initial endeavors to extend neural networks to graph structures can be attributed to the work of *Scarselli et al.* [17]. The interest in non-Euclidean deep learning has recently surged in computer vision after the seminal work of *Bruna et al.* [18] in which the authors formulated CNN like deep neural architectures on graphs in the spectral domain. Another notable advancement came from Kipf and Welling [19], who introduced simple filters operating on 1-hop neighborhoods of a graph. These filters employed a message-passing mechanism to construct node representations by aggregating local information from neighboring nodes. In the context of image segmentation, paper by Shi and Malik [20] applied graph-based techniques directly to images. Each pixel was treated as a graph node, aiming to achieve image segmentation. However, while this approach had potential, generating accurate segmentation results remained a challenge. An intermediate solution emerged through the concept of superpixels [21]. Superpixels groups pixels similar in color and other low-level properties, like location, into perceptually meaningful representaion [22]. These oversegmented and simplified images can be applied to many common task in computer vision, which includes image classification [14].

Monti et al. [23] introduced the application of GNN to image classification. They proposed the MoNET framework for handling geometric data, incorporating a scale factor for geometric distance in neighborhood aggregation. Their initially experiments employed GNN to the MNIST [24] dataset, which was segmented into superpixels for the image classification task. *Avelar et al.* [21] presented RAG-GAT, that segmented an input image into superpixels and generated RAG by connecting each region to the neighbors and supplying it to the GAT. The RAG-GAT performed better than other GNN models on grayscale images but had very low accuracy on three-channel RGB images because unnecessary information was aggregated due to the forced connection between adjacent areas.

Subsequently, *Matthias et al.* [25] proposed SplineCNN, a graph convolution operator based on the B-spline kernel. This operator served as a means to extract graph features, enabling the construction of an end-to-end deep GNN. Ushasi et al. [26] employed multi-scale superpixels as preprocessing steps for images, coupled with GCN [19] algorithm to develop a siamese graph convolutional network for image retrieval.

Boris et al. introduced a graph attention pooling technique, [27] which they compared with Graph Isomorphism Network (GIN) [28] and GCN on Mnist-75 dataset, This study explored the anti-noise capabilities and robustness of various pooling methods by introducing random Gaussian noise to the Mnist-75 dataset. After that, *Boris et al.* [29] constructed a Hierarchical Multigraph Network (HMN), which takes superpixels with different scale as input and combines different granularities information to complete image classification.

In summary, the evolution of applying graph structures to neural networks in computer vision has been marked by several key advancements, from the early attempts by Scarselli et al. to the introduction of graph-based CNN-like architectures and the incorporation of superpixels, culminating in the development of more sophisticated techniques such as GNNs, attention pooling, and hierarchical multigraph networks.

3 Methodology

3.1 Dataset

CXR scans play a pivotal role in the investigation and exploration of diseases linked to the respiratory system. Our research is centered on the classification of TB, a critical medical challenge. To address this TB classification problem, we curated our dataset from two publicly available and accessible databases. These databases were chosen as reliable sources of medical imaging data that could facilitate our study's objectives. By leveraging these databases, we aimed to ensure the robustness and credibility of our research outcomes in the realm of TB detection and diagnosis.

1. NLM dataset: We opted to utilize the reputable National Library of Medicine (NLM) Tuberculosis Digital Image Database for our dataset selection. This database was established through a collaborative effort between the NLM and Shenzhen No.3 People's Hospital, comprising two distinct sets of CXR images: the NLM-MontgomeryCXRSet and the NLM-ChinaCXRSet.
   The NLM-MontgomeryCXRSet encompasses a collection of 138 CXRs obtained from Montgomery County's TB screening initiative. On the other hand, the NLM-ChinaCXRSet encompasses a larger dataset of 662 CXRs. Each of the X-ray datasets represents patients exhibiting either one of two medical conditions: (a) a normal state, or (b) manifestations indicative of TB. The dataset is further enriched with meticulously crafted gold standard segmentations of the CXRs. These segmentations were meticulously generated under the guidance of a radiologist, ensuring a high degree of accuracy and reliability. For the purpose of our case study, we categorized the cases into a binary classification problem, specifically for two classes: (0) normal cases and (1) cases exhibiting pulmonary TB manifestations. This approach effectively simplifies the problem into a clear-cut non-TB vs. TB classification, allowing for focused analysis and interpretation.
2. Belarus dataset: The Belarus dataset was compiled as part of a pivotal drug resistance investigation, by the collaborative efforts of the National Institute of Allergy and Infectious Diseases and the Ministry of Health in the Republic of Belarus. Every image within this distinctive database was meticulously selected due to its affiliation with TB infection [30]. The dataset encompasses a total of 306 CXR images, derived from a cohort of 169 patients. It is important to highlight that, despite the initial pool of images, a subset of 107 CXR images from the original pool was ultimately incorporated into the study. This careful selection process was guided by the availability of the dataset at that specific juncture.

3.2 Data Preparation

We have gathered a collection of 811 grayscale CXR images, each of varying dimensions. Specifically, the images come from three distinct datasets:

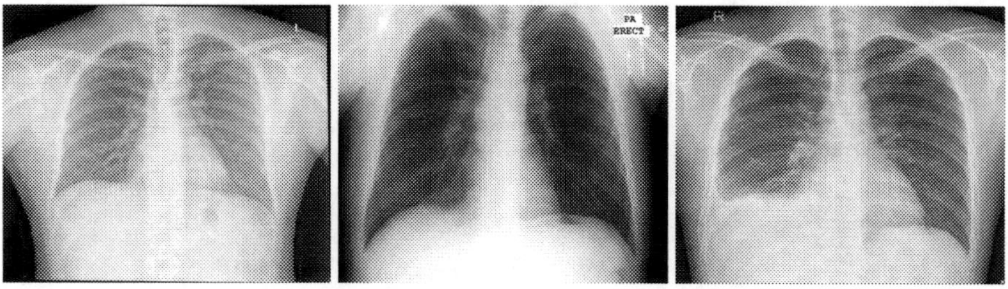

Fig. 1. Chest x-ray from samples, one per dataset (left to right): Montgomery County (USA), Shenzhen (China), and Belarus.

the Shenzen dataset with dimensions of 3000×3000, the Montgomery dataset with dimensions of 4020×4892, and the Belarus dataset with dimensions of 2248×2248. These images have been annotated to indicate the presence or absence of TB, with binary labels of 0 for absence and 1 for presence of TB. We preprocessed the CXR and the masked lung boundaries by overlaying the mask of lung boundaries on the CXR to obtain the region of interest (i.e., only the lungs region in the CXR). Additionally, we uniformly resized all CXR images to a resolution of 512×512 pixels and applied a superpixel algorithm. The process groups pixels into coherent regions, thus replacing the rigid pixel grid structure. This approach allows us to capture more meaningful image features and enhance the overall analysis of the images. The SLIC (Simple Linear Iterative Clustering) algorithm [31] was employed to generate superpixels for each image. These superpixels were then organized into four distinct sets, each with a different number of superpixels. The sets included superpixel images with counts of 75, 200, 300, and 400, providing a range of options for subsequent analysis. While (512×512) pixels can be represented as a node, we follow [32,33] and experiment with the number of superpixels, this is used to represent the nodes and edges between the superpixels (Fig. 1).

3.3 Superpixel Graph

In alignment with prior research in this field, we employed the SLIC algorithm since it was readily available and is recommended among other state of the art over segmentation algorithms [31]. After completing the superpixel segmentation, we created a RAG. In this graph each superpixel was treated as a node representing segmented regions, and we established edge relationship of nodes by considering their K-nearest neighbours which span more than one neighbour level. Every node within the graph can possess associated features, which serve to aggregate information derived from the inherent characteristics of the corresponding superpixel.

Various methods can be employed to generate node features, including utilizing information like coordinate data (the position of superpixels) and statistical attributes like the mean and variance of each superpixel's grey scale channels:

$$X = (x_1, x_2, ..., x_n)^T \text{ and } x_i = [\frac{1}{N_i} \sum_{j=1}^{N_i} (I_j, a_j, b_j)^T], \tag{1}$$

where x_i is the node feature with superpixel label i, N_i is the number of pixels which label is i, I_j is the mean pixel intensity of superpixel, a_j and b_j is pixel's position in the image.

The computation of edge features between nodes relies on calculating the Euclidean distance between their center of masses, employing a fixed-width Gaussian function σ:

$$G_{ij}^K = \exp(-\frac{|x_i - x_j|^2}{\sigma_x^2}), \tag{2}$$

where x_i, x_j are the 2-D coordinates of superpixels i,j and σ_x is the scale parameter defined as the averaged distance x_k of the k nearest neighbours for each node and build adjacency matrix for each sample.

We make an initial assumption that each pair of nodes in the graph can have at most one edge connecting them. However, real-world data can be intricate, with nodes often having diverse relationships that encompass various semantic, physical, or abstract aspects. We propose that there may be additional relationships within the data that are not explicitly represented and could be captured by relaxing the restriction on the number of edges between nodes, allowing for the inclusion of multiple types of edges, beyond those predefined in the dataset. As depicted in Fig. 2, once the original image undergoes SLIC segmentation, we initially extract the relevant features from the resulting superpixel image. Given that the features are not distinct when nodes rely solely on coordinate information for connectivity, we employ a combination of both coordinates and pixel intensity for establishing connections.

This fusion of coordinate and pixel intensity serves as an effective initialization strategy, providing a clearer representation of the target structure within the graph. Since, we connect nodes through a K-nearest neighbour procedure, our dataset has a higher-connectivity graph that could generalize better on the information flow and improve classification problem. For this, we computed a heirarchy of 75, 200, 300 and 400 SLIC superpixels and used mean superpixel intensity and coordinates as node features. The resultant graphs are of size 58–75 nodes for N $\leq$ 75, 168–200 nodes for N $\leq$ 200, 261–300 nodes for N $\leq$ 300 and 354–400 nodes for N $\leq$ 400 (Fig. 3).

3.4 Network Models

The GNN model relies on a propagation module to facilitate information exchange among nodes. This propagation module employs convolution operators to gather information from neighboring nodes, thereby generalizing the concept of convolutions to the realm of graphs. These message passing-based graph convolutional networks, update node representation from one layer to the other as it permits the gradual aggregation of information from neighbouring nodes.

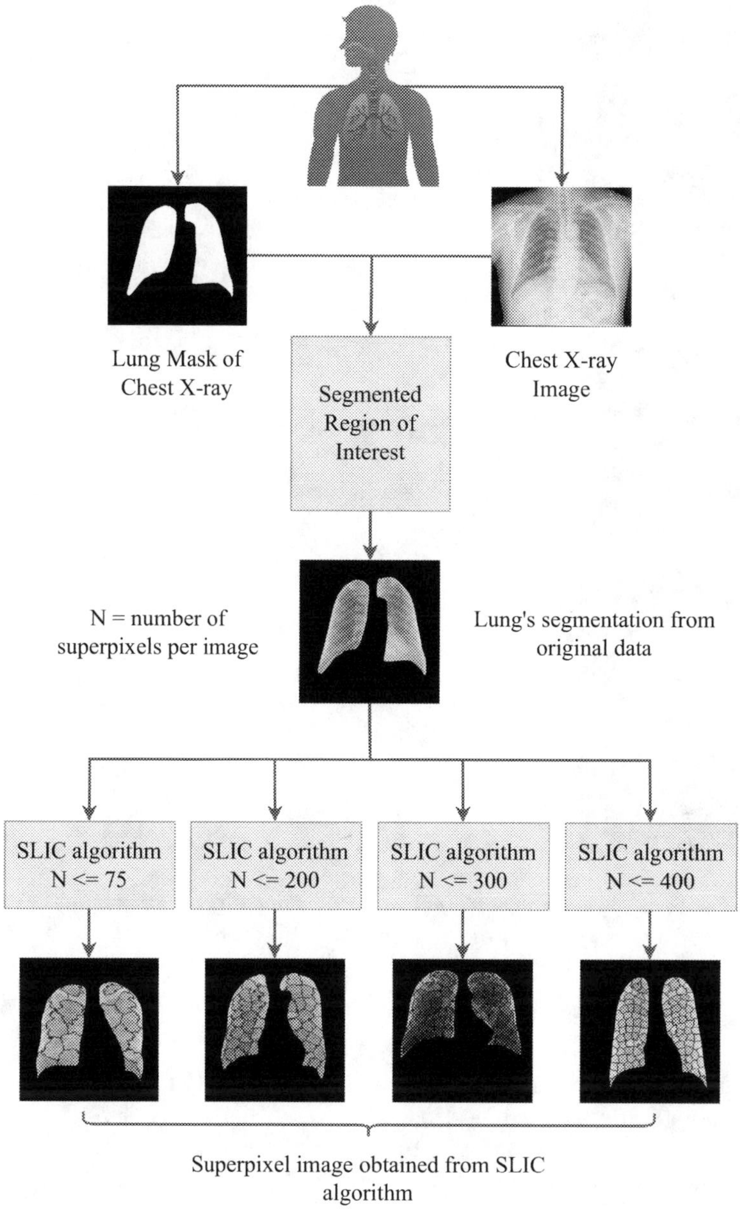

Fig. 2. Chest X-ray images and corresponding masks to delineate the region-of-interest (ROI). Additionally, as part of our data preparation process, we employed the SLIC algorithm to generate four distinct sets of images, each with a different level of superpixel segmentation.

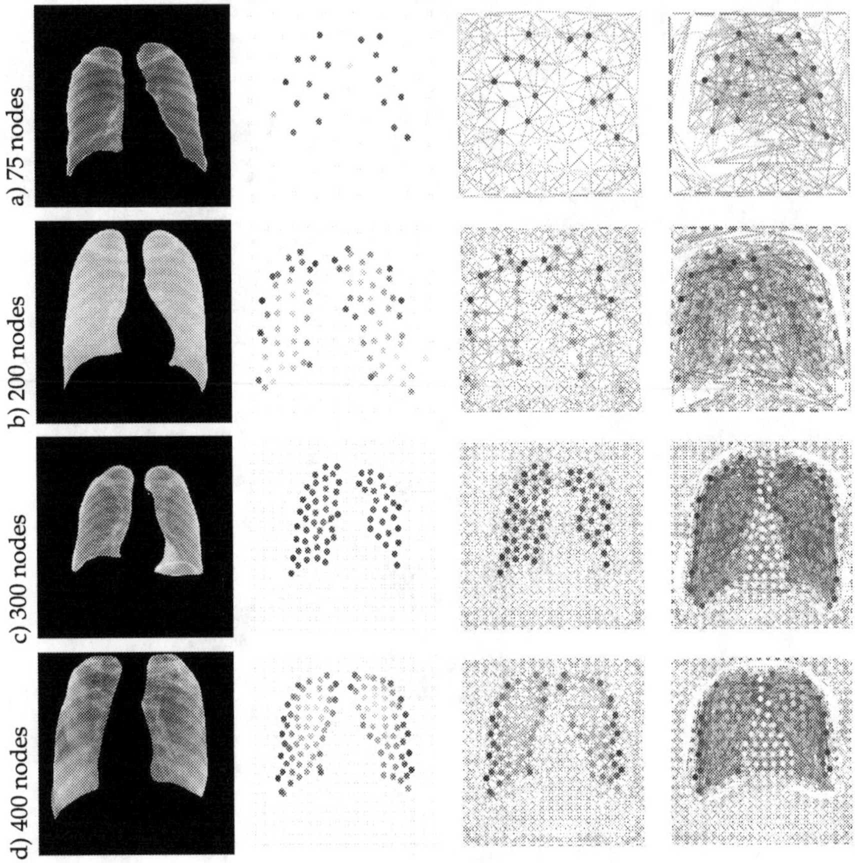

Fig. 3. Visualizing data conversion (left to right): lung segmentation, superpixel nodes (centroids) with SLIC, connectivity (only coordinate) of the graph representation with 75 nodes, and connectivity (feature and coordinate) of the graph representation with 75/200/300/400 nodes.

Input Layer: The information inside a node specifically the pixel intensity, coordinate points and edge connections are passed between neighbouring nodes. This is known as message passing. In the case of message passing-based graph convolutional networks the node gets updated from one layer to the other, and can be expressed as:

$$s_i^{l+1} = f[s_i^l, (s_j^l)_{j \epsilon N_i}]. \quad (3)$$

In a graph, each node is associated with node features represented as $\alpha_i \in R^{aX1}$, where a is the dimensionality of the node features. Additionally, there may be edges connecting nodes, and each of these edges can have edge features $\beta_{ij} \in R^{bX1}$, where b is the dimensionality of the edge features. Before feeding these node and edge features into a GNN, they are projected into d-dimensional

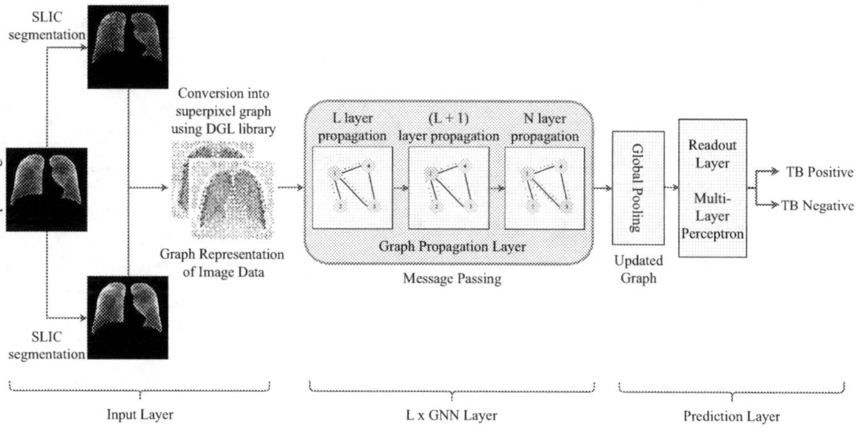

Fig. 4. Workflow of graph neural network layer in classification of TB positive and TB negative.

hidden features, denoted as s_i, and e_{ij}, respectively, through a simple linear transformation:

$$s_i^0 = U^0 a_i + u^0 \quad ; \quad e_{ij}^0 = V^0 \beta_{ij} + v^0, \tag{4}$$

where $U^0 \in R^{dXa}$, $V^0 \in R^{dXb}$ and $u^0, v^0 \in R^d$.

GNN Layers: In each GNN layer, we calculate d-dimensional representations for the nodes and edges within the graph. This is achieved through an iterative process known as neighborhood diffusion or message passing. During this process, each node in the graph collects information from its neighboring nodes, which helps it capture and represent the local structure of the graph. By stacking multiple GNN layers, denoted as L, the network progressively constructs node representations that encompass information from nodes within neighbours of L hops away. In other words, it allows the network to capture and integrate information from nodes that are further and further away from each target node, thereby building richer and more informative node representations. This hierarchical approach is useful for capturing both local and global graph structures in a systematic manner.

As shown in Fig. 4, let s_i^l denote the feature vector at layer l associated with node 1. The updated features s_i^{l+1} at the next layer L+1 are obtained by applying non-linear transformations to the central feature vector s_i^l and all the neighbouring connected nodes j of node 1. We can take Eq. 3 as the generic version of feature vector s_i^{l+1} at vertex i, where $j \in N_i$ denotes the set of neighbouring node and f maps the input vector s_i^l, as well as an unordered set of vectors s_j^l. The choice of the mapping f defines the class of GNNs in the network.

Graph Convolutional Network (GCN): In the simplest form of GNNs, referred to as Graph Convolutional Networks (Graph ConvNets), the node features are updated iteratively. This update involves an isotropic averaging operation over the features of neighboring nodes:

$$s_i^{l+1} = \text{ReLU}(U^l \text{Mean}_{j\epsilon N_i} s_j^l), \tag{5}$$

where $U^l \in R^{dXd}$ is a matrix that updates node features through linear transform, $\text{Mean}_{j\epsilon N_i} s_j^l$ reflects the number of incoming edges to that node. Equation 5 in the context of GNNs is commonly referred to as a convolution. This is because it serves as a linear approximation of a localized spectral convolution, a technique used to aggregate information from neighboring nodes in the graph.

Graph Attention Network (GAT): In GAT, an attention mechanism is utilized to introduce directional emphasis during neighborhood aggregation. GAT also adopts a multi-headed architecture, akin to the transformer model, which enhances its learning capacity, and here is how node update happens:

$$s_i^{l+1} = \text{Concat}_{k=1}^{K}(\text{ELU}(\sum_{j\epsilon N_i} e_{ij}^{k,l} U^{k,l}, s_j^l)), \tag{6}$$

where $U^{k,l} \in R^{\frac{d}{kXd}}$ are the K linear projection heads, and $e_{ij}^{k,l}$ are the attention coefficients for each head defined as:

$$e_{i,j}^{k,l} = \frac{\exp(\hat{e}_{i,j}^{k,l})}{\sum_{j'\epsilon N_i} \exp(\hat{e}_{i,j'}^{k,l})}, \tag{7}$$

$$\hat{e}_{i,j}^{k,l} = \text{LeakyReLU}(V^{k,l}\text{Concat}(U^{k,l} s_i^l, U^{k,l} s_j^l)), \tag{8}$$

where $V^{k,l} \in R^{\frac{2d}{K}}$, learns a mean over each node's neighborhood features sparsely weighted by the importance of each neighbor.

Prediction Layer: It is responsible for generating task-specific outputs. These outputs are then fed into a loss function to train the network parameters in an end-to-end fashion. The input to the prediction layer consists of the outputs from the final message-passing GCN layer for each node in the graph. To conduct graph classification, we begin by creating a d-dimensional graph-level vector representation, denoted as yG. This representation is generated by computing the average of all node features found in the last GCN layer:

$$yG = \frac{1}{\text{V}} \sum_{i=0}^{V} s_i^L, \tag{9}$$

The graph features are then passed to a MLP, which outputs un-normalized logits/scores $y_{\text{pred}} \in R^C$ for each class:

$$y_{\text{pred}} = P\text{ReLU}(QyG), \tag{10}$$

where $P \in R^{dXC}$, $Q \in R^{dXd}$, C is the number of classes. Finally, we minimize the cross-entropy loss between the logits and groundtruth labels.

Table 1. Test Accuracy, sensitivity, specificity, and AUC result of the four datasets N-75, N-200, N-300, and N-400 with the respective models of GCN and GAT.

Dataset	Model	Accuracy	Sensitivity	Specificity	AUC
N-75	GCN	0.69	0.87	0.51	0.70
	GAT	0.68	0.84	0.63	0.74
N-200	GCN	0.70	0.67	0.79	0.75
	GAT	0.77	0.76	0.71	0.73
N-300	GCN	0.78	0.88	0.61	0.76
	GAT	0.77	0.82	0.64	0.72
N-400	GCN	0.76	0.75	0.77	0.75
	GAT	0.74	0.74	0.74	0.76

GCN: Graph Convolutional Network, GAT: Graph Attention Network

4 Results and Discussions

We conducted experiments using two distinct models, GCN and GAT, on four different datasets: N-75, N-200, N-300, and N-400. These datasets were created by segmenting images into varying numbers of super-pixels, resulting in graphs with different sizes in terms of nodes and edges. Our primary objective was to classify the data into two categories: 0 (normal) and 1 (Tuberculosis).

Out of the two GNN models used, the GCN architecture comprised an initial embedding layer with two node features, pixel intensity and coordinates along with edge connections between the nodes. Four layers of GCN layers were stacked, each with 146 input and output channels. As we are dealing with a graph classification problem and aiming to obtain a single label by aggregating transformed node representations (node embeddings), we introduced a readout layer. This readout layer updates node representations using a Multi-Layer Perceptron (MLP) and computes graph representations from node embeddings using a mean operation. In our case, we employ a mean readout layer consisting of three linear layers, ultimately classifying into two categories. Similarly, the GAT architecture also starts with an embedding layer and is followed by four GAT layers, each with 152 input and output channels. Each GAT layer is accompanied by a leakyReLU activation function, batch normalization, and a mean readout layer.

To evaluate the performance of our models, we split the data into three subsets: 598 graphs for training, 163 for testing, and 50 for validation. Initially, we hypothesized that increasing the number of super-pixels in the dataset would lead to improved model performance on the testing dataset. However, our findings deviated from this expectation. As shown in Table 1, we discovered that the N-300 dataset exhibited better performance with an AUC score of 0.76 when using the GCN model. However, the N-400 dataset demonstrated superior results when employing the GAT model with AUC score of 0.76. These results slightly outperformed the other datasets in terms of performance on both GNN models.

Despite the variations in superpixel number in the dataset and GNN models there was no notable improvement seen in the AUC score. One major contributor to lower results could be the lack of dataset with the masked lung boundaries. DL requires a large amount of data to be trained and collecting large amount of data is not trivial [34]. Furthermore, increasing the dataset size alone does not guarantee to make the system robust. Therefore, we require an intelligent tool that can learn with human experts without having to wait for a complete and/or labeled dataset [35]. We could use the concept of Active Learning in GNN to overcome these shortcomings [36].

5 Conclusion and Future Work

We have focused our research on abnormality classification of CXR as TB positive or negative, using graph neural network. The aim was to assess the suitability of GNN for classifying TB positive and negative cases. We have employed two GNN models on four datasets (N-75, N-200, N-300, and N-400) generating super-pixel segmentation, and have achieved the highest AUC of 0.76 and 0.75 on GAT and GCN, respectively. Despite implementing four-layer structures for both GCN and GAT models and experimenting with four datasets that have different superpixel configurations for feature extraction, we have observed that our classification metrics, particularly AUC scores, did not exhibit any noteworthy enhancements compared to the results reported in the state-of-the-art literature. The main reason for this is that in medical imaging, each pixel holds significant clinical pathology-related information, and superpixels are not effectively harnessing this valuable data. Therefore, this gives us an immediate plan to work on.

References

1. Santosh, K.C., Allu, S., Rajaraman, S., Antani, S.: Advances in deep learning for tuberculosis screening using chest X-rays: the last 5 years review. J. Med. Syst. **46**(11), 82 (2022)
2. Vajda, S., Karargyris, A., Jaeger, S., Santosh, K.C., Candemir, S., Xue, Z., Thoma, G.: Feature selection for automatic tuberculosis screening in frontal chest radiographs. J. Med. Syst. **42**, 1–11 (2018)
3. Santosh, K.C., Antani, S.: Automated chest X-ray screening: can lung region symmetry help detect pulmonary abnormalities? IEEE Trans. Med. Imaging **37**(5), 1168–1177 (2017)
4. Hirsh, A.E., Tsolaki, A.G., DeRiemer, K., Feldman, M.W., Small, P.M.: Stable association between strains of mycobacterium tuberculosis and their human host populations. Proc. Natl. Acad. Sci. **101**(14), 4871–4876 (2004)
5. Mahbub, M.K., Biswas, M., Gaur, L., Alenezi, F., Santosh, K.C.: Deep features to detect pulmonary abnormalities in chest X-rays due to infectious diseaseX: Covid-19, pneumonia, and tuberculosis. Inf. Sci. **592**, 389–401 (2022)
6. Ravimohan, S., Kornfeld, H., Weissman, D., Bisson, G.P.: Tuberculosis and lung damage: from epidemiology to pathophysiology. Eur. Respiratory Rev. **27**(147) (2018)

7. Sharma, S.K., Mohan, A.: Tuberculosis: from an incurable scourge to a curable disease-journey over a millennium. Indian J. Med. Res. **137**(3), 455 (2013)
8. Das, D., Santosh, K.C., Pal, U.: Cross-population train/test deep learning model: abnormality screening in chest x-rays. In: 2020 IEEE 33rd International Symposium on Computer-Based Medical Systems (CBMS), IEEE (2020)
9. Makkar, A., Santosh, K.C.: SecureFed: federated learning empowered medical imaging technique to analyze lung abnormalities in chest X-rays. Int. J. Mach. Learn. Cybern. **14**, 1–12 (2023)
10. Rea, G., Sperandeo, M., Lieto, R., Bocchino, M., Quarato, C.M.I., Feragalli, B., Lacedonia, D.: Chest imaging in the diagnosis and management of pulmonary tuberculosis: the complementary role of thoraci ultrasound. Front. Med. **8**, 753821 (2021)
11. Santosh, K.C., GhoshRoy, D., Nakarmi, S.: A systematic review on deep structured learning for covid-19 screening using chest CT from 2020 to 2022. In: Healthcare, vol. 11. no. 17, MDPI (2023)
12. Santosh, K.C., Vajda, S., Antani, S., Thoma, G.R.: Edge map analysis in chest X-rays for automatic pulmonary abnormality screening. Int. J. Comput. Assist. Radiol. Surg. **11**, 1637–1646 (2016)
13. Oloko-Oba, M., Viriri, S.: A systematic review of deep learning techniques for tuberculosis detection from chest radiograph. Front. Med. **9**, 830515 (2022)
14. Long, Jianwu. "A graph neural network for superpixel image classification. In: Journal of Physics: Conference Series, vol. 1871. no. 1. IOP Publishing (2021)
15. Bae, J., Yu, G., Lee, J., Vu, D., Anh, L., Kim, H., Kim, J.: Superpixel image classification with graph convolutional neural networks based on learnable positional embedding. Appl. Sci. **12**(18), 9176 (2022)
16. Dwivedi, V.P., Luu, A.T., Laurent, T., Bengio, Y., Bresson, X.: Graph neural networks with learnable structural and positional representations. arXiv preprint arXiv:2110.07875 (2021)
17. Gori, M., Monfardini, G., Scarselli, F.: A new model for learning in graph domains. In: Proceedings, 2005 IEEE International Joint Conference on Neural Networks, vol. 2, IEEE (2005)
18. Bruna, J., Zaremba, W., Szlam, A., LeCun, Y.: Spectral networks and locally connected networks on graphs. arXiv preprint arXiv:1312.6203 (2013)
19. Kipf, T.N., Welling, M.: Semi-supervised classification with graph convolutional networks. arXiv preprint arXiv:1609.02907 (2016)
20. Shi, J., Malik, J.: Normalized cuts and image segmentation. IEEE Trans. Pattern Anal. Mach. Intell. **22**(8), 888–905 (2000)
21. Avelar, P.H.C., Tavares, A.R., Da Silveira, T.L.T., Jung, C.R., Lamb, L.C.: Superpixel image classification with graph attention networks. In: 2020 33rd SIBGRAPI Conference on Graphics, Patterns and Images (SIBGRAPI), IEEE (2020)
22. Stutz, D., Hermans, A., Leibe, B.: Superpixels: an evaluation of the state-of-the-art. Comput. Vis. Image Underst. **166**, 1–27 (2018)
23. Monti, F., Boscaini, D., Masci, J., Rodolà, E., Svoboda, J., Bronstein, M. M.: Geometric deep learning on graphs and manifolds using mixture model CNNs. In: Proceedings of the IEEE Conference on Computer Vision and Pattern Recognition (2017)
24. LeCun, Y.: The MNIST database of handwritten digits. https://yann.lecun.com/exdb/mnist/ (1998)
25. Fey, M., Lenssen, J. E., Weichert, F., Muller, H.: Splinecnn: fast geometric deep learning with continuous b-spline kernels. In: Proceedings of the IEEE Conference on Computer Vision and Pattern Recognition (20180

26. Chaudhuri, U., Banerjee, B., Bhattacharya, A.: Siamese graph convolutional network for content based remote sensing image retrieval. Comput. Vis. Image Underst. **184**, 22–30 (2019)
27. Knyazev, B., Taylor, G.W., Amer, M.: Understanding attention and generalization in graph neural networks. In: Advances in Neural Information Processing Systems, vol. 32 (2019)
28. Keyulu, X., Weihua, H., Jure, L., Stefanie, J.: How powerful are graph neural networks? In: International Conference on Learning Representations (ICLR) (2019)
29. Knyazev, B., Lin, X., Amer, M.R., Taylor, G.W.: Image classification with hierarchical multigraph networks. arXiv preprint arXiv:1907.09000 (2019)
30. B. P. Health. Belarus Tuberculosis Portal (2020). Accessed 9 Jun 2020. https://tuberculosis.by/
31. Achanta, R., Shaji, A., Smith, K., Lucchi, A., Fua, P., Süsstrunk, S.: SLIC superpixels compared to state-of-the-art superpixel methods. IEEE Trans. Pattern Anal. Mach. Intell. **34**(11), 2274–2282 (2012)
32. Defferrard, M., Bresson, X., Vandergheynst, P.: Convolutional neural networks on graphs with fast localized spectral filtering. In: Advances in Neural Information Processing Systems, vol. 29 (2016)
33. Veličković, P., Cucurull, G., Casanova, A., Romero, A., Liò, P., Bengio, Y.: Graph attention networks. arXiv preprint arXiv:1710.10903 (2017)
34. Santosh, K.C.: AI-driven tools for coronavirus outbreak: need of active learning and cross-population train/test models on multitudinal/multimodal data. J. Med. Syst. **44**(5), 1–5 (2020). https://doi.org/10.1007/s10916-020-01562-1
35. Nakarmi, S. and Santosh, K.C.: Active learning to minimize the risk from future epidemics. In: 2023 IEEE Conference on Artificial Intelligence (CAI), IEEE (2023)
36. Zhang, W., et al.:. Information gain propagation: a new way to graph active learning with soft labels. arXiv preprint arXiv:2203.01093 (2022)

Silicosis Detection Using Extended Transfer Learning Model

Gulshan Kumar Sharma[1], Priyanka Harjule[1(✉)], Basant Agarwal[2], and Rajesh Kumar[1]

[1] Malaviya National Institute of Technology Jaipur, Jaipur, India
priyanka.maths@mnit.ac.in
[2] Central University of Rajasthan Kishangarh, Ajmer, India
basant@curaj.ac.in

Abstract. Silicosis is a prevalent and damaging occupational disease in India. The detection of silicosis on X-ray images heavily relies on the expertise of radiologists, resulting in delayed detection and diagnosis. To overcome this challenge, machine learning-based computer-aided detection methods are being explored. However, due to the lack of publicly available large databases of silicosis images, highly accurate deep-learning models for silicosis detection through X-rays are difficult to obtain. In this study, we propose a method for silicosis detection using transfer learning techniques on X-ray radiographs. We trained and tested well-known deep transfer learning models, including Vgg16, Vgg19, ResNet50, ResNet101, Densenet121, Densenet169, Densenet201, Xception, Mobilnet, InceptionV3, and Efficient B7 models. Our proposed model is based on ResNet50 in which we add additional layers, which achieved an F1 score of 0.8166. Additionally, we applied the Grad-CAM technique to produce heatmap images that highlight the important features extracted from the X-ray images This approach could serve as a feasible alternative in countries with limited access to specialized radiological equipment and trained radiologists for detecting silicosis on X-ray images.

Keywords: Silicosis Detection · Convolutional Neural Networks · X-rays · Transfer Learning · GradCam · ResNet

1 Introduction

Silicosis is a serious lung disease caused by inhaling silica particles in mining environments. The disease results in fibrosis and pleural fluid build-up, leading to reduced surface area for air diffusion in the lungs and serious respiratory problems [1]. Chest X-ray scans are commonly used for the diagnosis of silicosis due to their low cost and non-invasiveness. However, the complexity and non-uniformity of silicosis features in chest X-ray images require highly qualified radiologists to diagnose the disease [2]. Early diagnosis of silicosis is critical for early treatment, but detecting silicosis can be challenging due to its resemblance with other common chest diseases on radiographs.

KC Santosh et al. (Eds.): RTIP2R 2023, CCIS 2027, pp. 111–126, 2024.
https://doi.org/10.1007/978-3-031-53085-2_10

Automation and machine learning have been developed to address the discrepancy between the available experts and the need for human expertise. In recent years, scientists and researchers have partnered to develop intelligent devices that can separate silicosis patients from other similar-seeming cases [3]. Deep learning models, especially convolutional neural networks (CNNs), have shown promising results in detecting silicosis features with high sensitivity and specificity compared to human experts [4].

In this study, we aim to investigate the effectiveness of advanced deep learning techniques and compare their performance using identical parameters and datasets. We propose the use of transfer learning methods in CNNs to leverage pre-trained models on large image datasets and develop an early screening model for distinguishing cases of silicosis from healthy individuals using chest X-ray images. We also utilize the GradCam technique to visualize the regions of the X-ray image contributing most to the model's diagnosis, aiding in the interpretation and explanation of the model's predictions.

Objectives:

1. To leverage transfer learning methods in CNNs for developing an early screening model.
2. To visualize the regions within chest X-ray images that contribute most to the model's diagnostic decisions using GradCam.
3. To compare the performance of the proposed model with a previously developed model for silicosis.

Hypotheses:

1. We hypothesize that transfer learning techniques will enhance the performance of the model in early silicosis detection.
2. We hypothesize that the application of GradCam will provide valuable insights into the model's diagnostic decisions.
3. We hypothesize that the proposed model will yield comparable or superior results to the previously developed model for silicosis

2 Literature Review

Silicosis is a disease of the lungs that develops over time as a result of prolonged inhalation of substantial quantities of dust containing crystalline silica. Diagnosis of silicosis is challenging due to its insidious onset and long progression, but advances in technology, such as deep learning classifiers and medical imaging, are proving more promising than traditional methods for detecting lung diseases.

Recent advances in data-driven deep learning [5–7] have shown promising results in various fields, including medical image analysis. Using texture analysis, Cai et al. were able to accurately diagnose 29 pictures of pneumonia [8] with an accuracy of 0.793. In order to diagnose pneumonia, Kermany [9] developed a deep-learning approach and used it on X-ray and CT datasets. They proved that deep learning diagnosis is just as accurate as human specialists. According to research conducted by Singh et al. [10] in 2018, AI has demonstrated its effectiveness in aiding the diagnosis of various lung abnormalities, including lung nodules, pulmonary TB, cystic fibrosis, and pneumoconiosis. Additionally, Rajpurkar et al. [11] discovered in 2018 that AI systems perform at levels comparable to radiology specialists when it comes to reading radiographs. Wang XH et al. conducted a study to explore the potential of deep learning in the diagnosis of silicosis. They compared Inception-V3 results with that of two registered radiologists and found that the former outperformed the radiologists [12]. Over the years, several methods have been developed to enhance diagnostic efficiency and accuracy in chest radiograph analysis. Hall et al. utilized spatial moments and pattern recognition techniques to analyze radiology images [13]. Texture analysis for chest radiograph classification was developed by Ledley et al. [14], while Savol et al. explored an adaptive object-growing algorithm that relied on image intensity to detect small, rounded opacities [15].

While these methods have shown promise in reducing the workload of radiologists or enhancing their performance in different tasks, they rely on "hand-crafted" feature definition, which can be time-consuming and technically challenging, particularly for complex tasks such as pneumoconiosis diagnosis and staging [16]. To improve the transparency of silicosis detection, By utilizing Grad-CAM, the model's attention during classification is highlighted by emphasizing the regions of the input image it focuses on. This technique relies on spatial information contained in the final convolution layer's feature maps, which are essential for identifying distinct visual patterns that differentiate between different classes. The Grad-CAM technique utilizes the trained model's layers and extracted features [17].

3 Materials and Methods

3.1 Dataset

We have utilized the publicly available dataset [18]. The table shows the description and distribution of the silicosis dataset that was used for training and testing state-of-the-art models. A total of 706 chest X-ray images in PNG format were included in the dataset. The dataset was split into a train and test set, with 114 Silicosis and 452 Normal images in the train set and 112 Silicosis and 28 Normal

Table 1. Pre-trained model configurations used in the study

Silicosis Dataset	Image Count	
	Label	Count
Train	Silicosis	114
	Normal	452
Test	Normal	112
	Silicosis	28
Total		706

images in the test set. The label column shows the two classes of images in the dataset - silicosis and normal. Table 1 depicts the distribution of the dataset utilized for models. Samples of this dataset are given in Fig. 1.

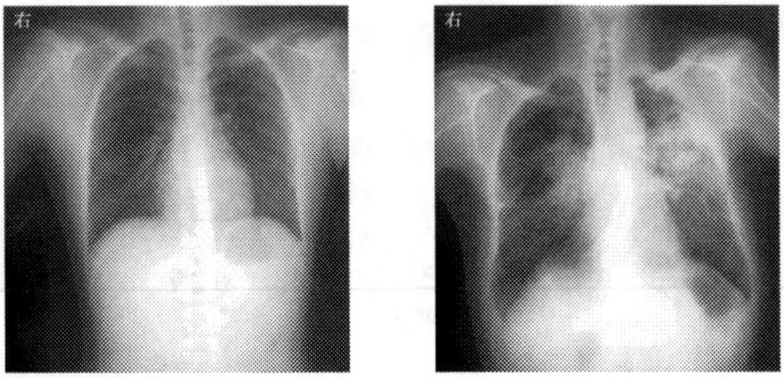

(a) Normal (b) Abnormal

Fig. 1. Sample of chest X-ray images of Normal and Abnormal

3.2 Methodology

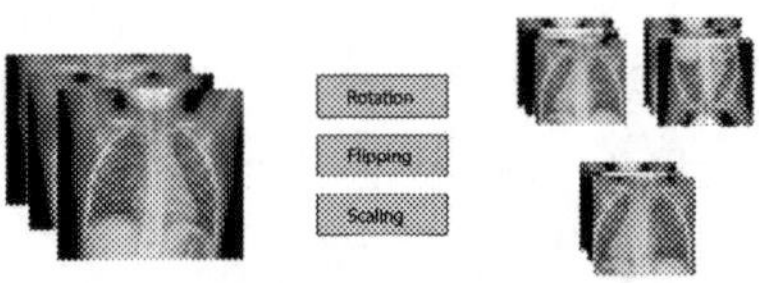

Fig. 2. In this study, various augmentation techniques were utilized to enhance the quality

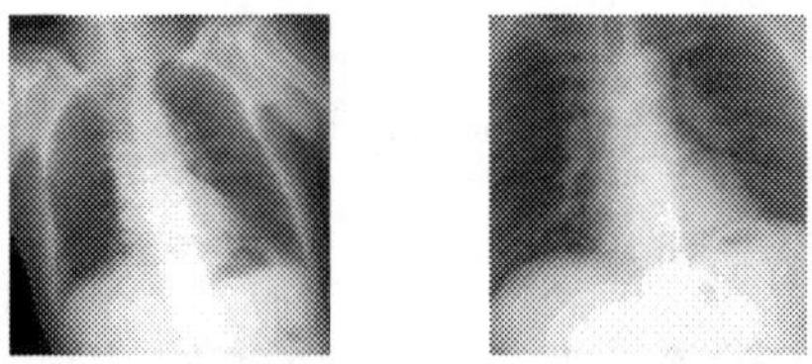

(a) Rotation (b) Zoom

Fig. 3. Post dataset data augmentation

Image Pre-processing and Data Augmentation. In the present study, we have resized all images to a consistent dimension of $224 \times 224 \times 3$, and each pixel was rescaled by a factor of $\frac{1}{255}$ to maintain consistency across all models. To enhance the performance of the image classification model, several data augmentation techniques were employed. These included rotation up to 40°, scaling of height, width, vertical and horizontal flipping, and zoom range. The augmented images were normalized to improve the efficiency of the model's learning process. A validation split of 0.2 was used, with 20% of the images reserved for validation. Moreover, a height shift range of 0.05 was used to enhance the generalization ability of the model. Figure 3 illustrates an example of the data augmentation applied to the training images. Figure 3 displays a sample of the outcomes achieved post-data augmentation (Fig. 2).

Transfer Learning Approach. Transfer learning, a technique of adapting pre-trained neural network parameters to new tasks and datasets, was utilized in this study to overcome data limitations and time constraints [19]. Pre-trained models from the ImageNet dataset were used, and Table 2 provides details of the transfer learning criteria and classification function for each employed CNN. Fine-tuning parameters were determined through experimentation, with frozen layers indicating the number of untrainable layers. The transfer learning mechanism, illustrated in Fig. 4, facilitated the identification and classification of Silicosis.

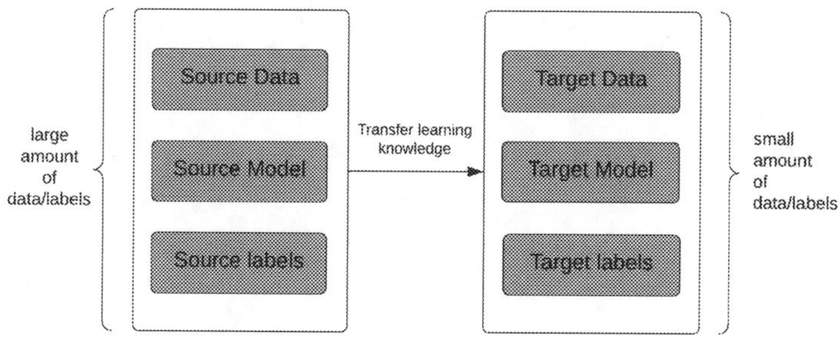

Fig. 4. An overview of the transfer learning approach used in this study for the diagnosis of silicosis

In the case of deep neural networks trained on natural photos, it's worth noting that the earliest layers tend to learn generic characteristics that aren't exclusive to any given dataset or task but can be applied to a wide variety of datasets and tasks. As the neural network goes deeper into the layers, it starts to capture more specific features that are relevant to the current dataset and its intended purpose. Transfer learning can be a beneficial strategy for training a large target network without overfitting while dealing with a substantially smaller target dataset. In this study, ResNet-50, ResNet-101 [20], VGG16 [21], MobileNet [22], DenseNet-121, DenseNet-169, DenseNet-201 [23], VGG19 [24], Xception [25], InceptionV3 [26], and EfficientNetB7 [27] were used as base models. The objective of this study was to achieve high accuracy in the classification of X-ray images using 11 distinct CNN models. Transfer learning was used to improve the models' performance by extracting features from X-ray pictures using pre-trained classifiers. The models include ResNet50, VGG19, MobileNet, DenseNet169, ResNet101, VGG16, DenseNet201, DenseNet121, Xception, InceptionV3, and EfficientNetB7. Each of the models has different numbers of layers and varying numbers of parameters. ResNet-50 has 50 layers and a total of 39 million parameters. VGG16 has 16 layers and a total of 122 million parameters.

MobileNet has 27 layers and a total of 213 million parameters. DenseNet-121 has 121 layers and a total of 217 million parameters. ResNet-101 has 101 layers and a total of 44 million parameters. VGG19 has 19 layers and a total of 143 million parameters. DenseNet-201 has 201 layers and a total of 19 million parameters. DenseNet-169 has 169 layers and a total of 14 million parameters. Xception has 126 layers and a total of 23 million parameters. InceptionV3 has 159 layers and a total of 24 million parameters. Finally, EfficientNetB7 has 800 layers and a total of 66 million parameters. Table 2 shows the parameter of pre-trained models used in this study.

The architecture of the pre-trained models was kept unchanged, and the pre-existing weights from the ImageNet dataset were utilized. To reduce the dimensionality of the data, global average pooling was applied, which was followed by a dense layer with softmax activation for classification. This process ensures that the network learns effectively during training. After conducting experiments and empirical evaluations, we chose a learning rate of 0.001 and a batch size of 4, which resulted in the best performance for our dataset.

Table 2. Pre-trained model configurations used in the study

Model	Total Parameters	Non-Trainable Parameters
ResNet-101	58,366,786	42,760,576
ResNet-50	39,102,818	23,587,712
VGG16	138,357,544	14,714,688
VGG19	143,667,240	20,024,384
Mobiledet	4,253,864	3,228,864
DenseNet-121	8,062,504	209,921,170
DenseNet-169	14,307,880	12,711,176
DenseNet-201	20,242,984	18,646,280
Xception	22,910,480	22,793,176
Inceptionv3	23,851,784	23,695,208
EfficientNetB7	66,658,687	54,125,408

Custom Sequential Model Approach

- **Undersampling:** In the context of the Silicosis dataset, undersampling was used to balance the class distribution between the normal and silicosis classes. This approach was preferred over oversampling because the normal class was significantly larger than the silicosis class in the training set. Randomly removing normal class samples through undersampling helped to address the issue of class imbalance and allowed for more effective training of the classification models. Specifically, the normal class samples were randomly removed,

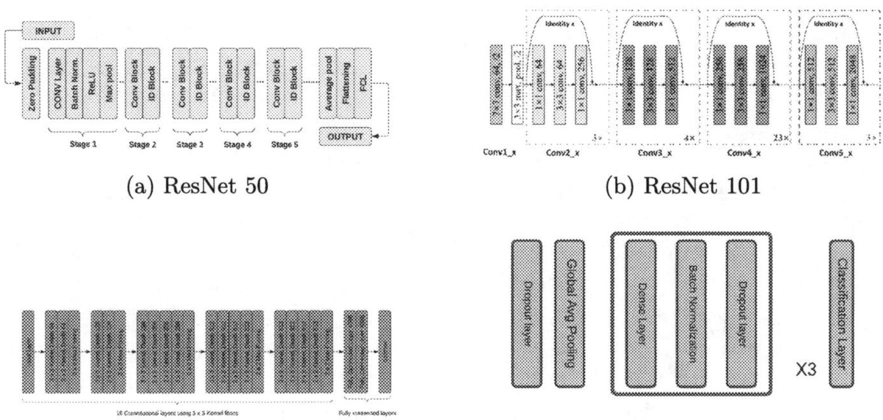

(a) ResNet 50 (b) ResNet 101

(c) VGG19 (d) Proposed Model

Fig. 5. (a) ReseNet 50 (b) ResNet 101 (c) VGG19 (d) Proposed Model

resulting in a training set with 114 silicosis images and 100 normal images. This approach helped to address the issue of class imbalance and allowed for more effective training of the classification models. The test set remained unchanged, with 112 silicosis images and 28 normal images.

- **Proposed approach:** After evaluating the performance of several pre-trained models based on the ROC (receiver operating characteristic) curve, we selected ResNet50, ResNet101, and VGG19 as the top performers. We then applied an additional layer approach to each model to improve their performance. To improve the performance of the model, several additional layers were added. These include a dropout layer, which randomly drops out some of the nodes during training to reduce overfitting; a global average pooling layer, which averages the output of the previous convolutional layer across all spatial locations to obtain a fixed-length feature vector; and batch normalization, which normalizes the activations of each layer to reduce the effects of internal covariate shift and speed up training. The model also includes three blocks, each containing batch normalization, a dropout layer, an activation function (such as ReLU), a dense layer (which computes a linear transformation of the input followed by the activation function), and another dropout layer. The final dense layer uses the softmax activation function, which outputs a probability distribution over the possible classes, to predict the label of the input. For VGG19, we included an L1L2 regularizer at one of the dense layers to prevent further overfitting. Overall, The additional layers were added to the pre-trained models to enhance their ability to extract more discriminative features from the X-ray images, which can improve the overall performance of the model. These modifications aim to improve the generalization performance of the model by reducing overfitting, speeding up training, and normalizing the activations of each layer. The models were trained using an Adam optimizer, with a batch size of 4 and a learning rate of 0.001. These hyperparameters were chosen based on previous research and experimentation to achieve the best possible performance of the model. Figure 5 (a, b, c) displays the ResNet 50, ResNet 101, VGG19 Architecture. Figure 5 (d) shows the proposed model architecture.

- **The Grad-CAM Technique:** The Grad-CAM technique is utilized in this study to generate class-specific heatmaps that highlight the significant features in X-ray images [18]. By employing the ResNet50 model, Grad-CAM is used to visualize the important regions for classification. This technique computes gradients of feature maps and generates a heatmap, which is then normalized and processed to obtain the final discriminative saliency map. This approach enables the interpretation of the CNN model's decision-making process and identification of informative regions for silicosis diagnosis. Figure 6 Shows the mechanism of Grad-CAM technique.

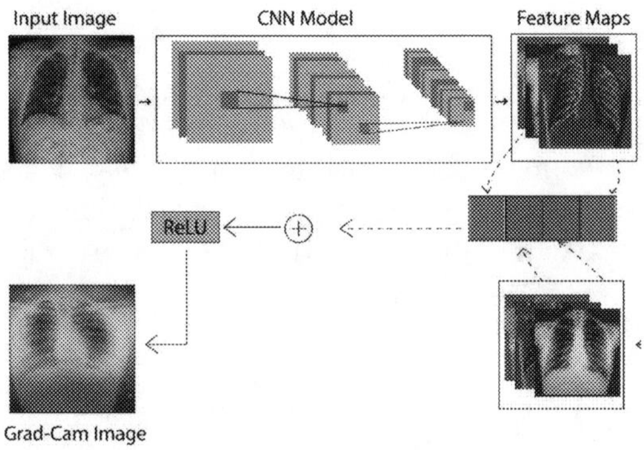

Fig. 6. Architecture to describe the Grad-CAM technique

4 Results

4.1 Transfer Learning Approach

The performance of different classifiers was evaluated based on various metrics such as accuracy, specificity, precision, sensitivity and F1-score, and their corresponding scores are presented in Table 3 Densenet121, EfficienNettB7, and InceptionV3 were the top three classifiers in terms of accuracy, with scores of 0.542857, 0.528571, and 0.535714, respectively. While Densenet169, ResNet101, ResNet50, Vgg16, Vgg19, and Xception achieved perfect sensitivity scores of 1.0, Densenet121, EfficienNettB7, and Mobilenet had sensitivity scores of 0.5, 1.0, and 0.857143, respectively. Densenet121 had the highest specificity score of 0.553571, followed by InceptionV3 with 0.473214 and Xception with 0.401786.

Densenet169 achieved the highest precision score of 0.849558, followed by EfficienNettB7 with 0.859574, and ResNet101, ResNet50, Vgg16, and Vgg19 all achieving a precision score of 0.854902. InceptionV3 had the highest F1-score of 0.57664, followed by Vgg16 with 0.516947 and Xception with 0.516931. The Densenet models (121, 169, and 201) performed relatively poorly compared to other models on most criteria, while EfficienNettB7, InceptionV3, and Vgg16 were the best performing.

Table 3. Showing the performance scores for different image classifiers

Classifiers	Accuracy	Sensitivity	Specificity	Precision	F1-score
Densenet121	0.542857	0.5	0.553571	0.696382	0.588529
Densenet169	0.392857	1	0.241071	0.849558	0.390224
Densenet201	0.471429	0.928571	0.357143	0.814966	0.498124
EfficienNettB7	0.528571	1	0.410714	0.859574	0.557626
InceptionV3	0.535714	0.785714	0.473214	0.772965	0.57664
Mobilenet	0.478571	0.857143	0.383929	0.783528	0.512043
ResNet101	0.471429	1	0.339286	0.854902	0.491487
ResNet50	0.471429	1	0.339286	0.854902	0.491487
Vgg16	0.492857	1	0.366071	0.856566	0.516947
Vgg19	0.478571	1	0.348214	0.855446	0.500067
Xception	0.478571	0.785714	0.401786	0.755321	0.516931

Table 4. Performance of ResNet50, VGG19, and ResNet101 on the test set

Classifiers	Accuracy	Sensitivity	Specificity	Precision	F1-score
ResNet50	0.814286	0.571429	0.875	0.819394	0.816651
vgg19	0.678571	0.714286	0.669643	0.793067	0.709502
ResNet101	0.792857	0.357143	0.901786	0.77423	0.7812

To compare their performance, We evaluated the performance of various models by generating their ROC curves, Fig. 7 shows the ROC analysis, and uses metrics such as Area Under the Curve (AUC) to compare their performance. A higher AUC indicates better performance across all possible thresholds. Among the models tested, ResNet-101 achieved the highest AUC score of 0.848, indicating the best overall performance. Other models had AUC scores ranging from 0.584 (DenseNet121) to 0.791 (EfficientNetB7).

4.2 Results of Proposed Approach

Table 4 shows the performance metrics of three classifiers: ResNet50, vgg19, and ResNet101. ResNet50 has the highest accuracy of 0.814286, followed by

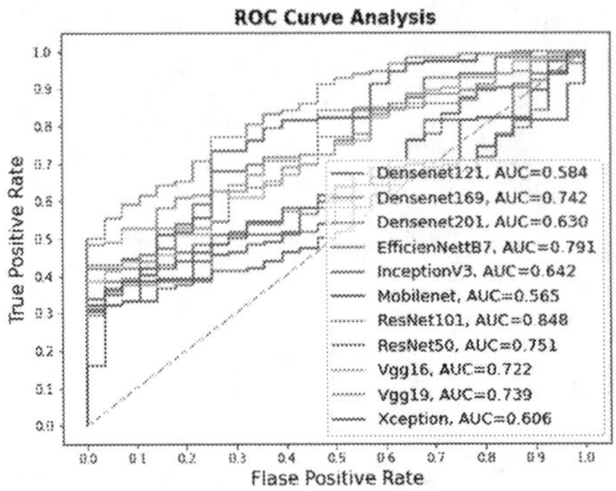

Fig. 7. Roc Curve for Transfer Learning Approach

ResNet101 with 0.792857 and vgg19 with 0.678571. ResNet50 has a sensitivity of 0.571429, which means it correctly identified 57% of the positive cases, followed by vgg19 with a sensitivity of 0.714286 and ResNet101 with 0.357143. ResNet50 has the highest specificity of 0.875, which means it correctly identified 87.5% of the negative cases, followed by ResNet101 with 0.901786 and vgg19 with 0.669643. ResNet50 has the highest precision of 0.819394, followed by vgg19 with 0.793067 and ResNet101 with 0.77423. ResNet50 has the highest F1 score of 0.816651, followed by ResNet101 with 0.7812 and vgg19 with 0.709502. Overall, ResNet50 performs the best in terms of accuracy, specificity, precision, and F1 score, while vgg19 has the highest sensitivity among the three classifiers. However, after careful consideration, we selected ResNet50 as the most promising classifier for further experimentation (Fig. 8).

Plot	Description
0	ResNet 50
1	Vgg19
2	ResNet 101

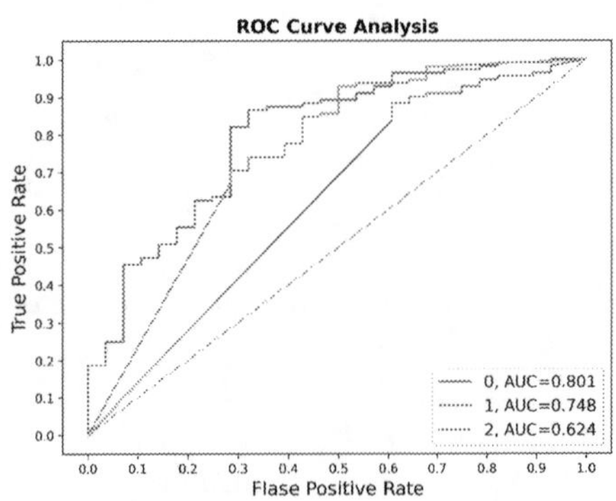

Fig. 8. Roc Curve for Proposed Approach

4.3 Disease Localization Using Grad-CAM Technique

Figure 9 demonstrates the effectiveness of GradCAM visualization in highlighting significant image regions used by the CNN for classification. These highlighted regions provide insights into the important features and patterns used by the model, aiding clinicians in identifying affected areas and understanding the disease pathology. Comparing GradCAM visualizations across images helps identify common patterns and gain insights into the underlying disease mechanisms.

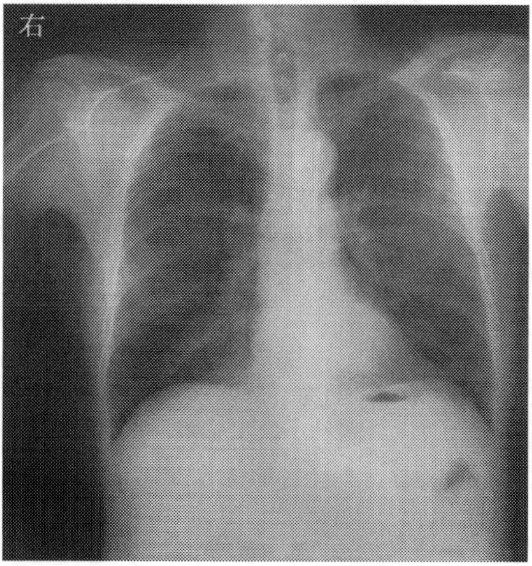

Fig. 9. ResNet 50 Grad-CAM activation map on the silicosis X-ray image

4.4 Discussion

Silicosis is a common occupational disease in India that results in high treatment costs and economic losses for healthcare systems and families. Current diagnosis relies on radiologists, which can delay early detection. Researchers are exploring computer-aided 'diagnosis using deep learning techniques such as convolutional neural networks (CNNs), which have shown promise in accurately predicting and diagnosing diseases and outperforming radiologists [28].

A transfer learning technique was used in this study for the classification of silicosis utilizing chest X-ray images from a frontal perspective. The study involved data preprocessing, which included dataset augmentation and addressing class imbalance issues, followed by training, validation, and testing of the models using pre-trained networks. The performance of each model was evaluated by comparing their ROC curves. Grad-CAM was also utilized to visualize the classification decisions. In this study, several state-of-the-art pretrained neural networks were experimented with using transfer learning technique, including ResNet50, VGG16, MobileNet, DenseNet121, ResNet101, VGG19, DenseNet201, DenseNet169, Xception, InceptionV3, and EfficientNetB7. In summary, the study shows that CNN-based detection models utilizing transfer learning are effective in binary classification tasks for silicosis images. Although transfer learning with fine-tuning has its benefits, it shares some common challenges with the traditional approach of training CNNs. Among these challenges is the selection of hyper-parameters, which are key training parameters such as learning rate, batch size, optimization function, and others. Choosing the appropriate values for these hyper-parameters directly affects the model's ability to train and, as a result, influences its classification performance [29].

The image datasets for silicosis are not sufficient for training a neural network due to their small size. As a result, transfer learning has been employed, Ravishankar et al. used transfer learning to detect ultrasound kidney images [30]. Transfer learning's benefits in medicine were explored using a deep convolutional neural network (DCNN) in [31]. To improve accuracy with small datasets, subspace-based techniques like those in [32] can be used in conjunction with transfer learning. The present study utilized transfer learning technique, employing 11 pre-trained deep neural network models, including ResNet50, VGG19, MobileNet, DenseNet169, ResNet101, VGG16, DenseNet201, DenseNet121, Xception, InceptionV3, and EfficientNetB7. These models were originally pre-trained on the ImageNet dataset, and were subsequently fine-tuned for the task of classifying chest X-rays in this study. This study aimed to enhance the diagnostic accuracy of ResNet 101, ResNet 50, and VGG19 models by refining their structure from different perspectives.

To compare their performance, we have trained the models, generated their ROC curves and compared their performance using metrics such as the Area Under the Curve (AUC), which measures the overall performance of the classifier across all possible thresholds. A higher AUC indicates better performance. AUC for ResNet-101, ResNet-50, VGG19 was reported to be higher 0.848, 0.751, 0.739, respectively in comparison to other models. Subsequently, the three models underwent further enhancement, standardization, and evaluation, with accuracy and receiver operating characteristic (ROC) curves used as the evaluation metrics. The ROC curve was utilized to generate a stable evaluation curve and determine the optimal threshold value, as classifiers with curves closer to the upper-left corner are deemed to perform better. To measure and compare the performance of our models, we employed evaluation metrics, including the F1 score, which is widely used in machine learning. The F1 score assesses the trade-off between precision and recall of a model, making it a valuable evaluation metric, especially for imbalanced datasets. Accuracy may not be suitable for evaluating model performance when the number of positive and negative instances is not equal.

In this study, we have compared different models and found that our proposed method performed better than the method by Hao et al. [18], which was evaluated on the same dataset. In their study the ResNet34 model's performance on the test set was evaluated with scale factors of 1 and 5, resulting in reported F1 scores of 0.681 and 0.667, respectively. The performance of three different DenseNet models, namely DenseNet40, DenseNet53, and DenseNet64, was estimated on the test set. The reported F1 scores for these models were 0.476, 0.652, and 0.625, respectively. Additionally, dropout operations were performed on DenseNet53 with drop rates of 0 and 0.25, resulting in F1 values of 0.652 and 0.476, respectively. Furthermore, the impact of reduction operations was evaluated on DenseNet53 with reduction values of 0.25, 0.5, and 1. The reported F1 scores for these reductions were 0.652, 0.667, and 0.489, respectively. By analyzing the impact of bottleneck blocks with bottleneck values of false and true of DenseNet53. The F1 scores obtained for these configurations were 0.566 and 0.652, respectively. In our study after fine tuning and refinement, we have recorded F1 scores of 0.816, 0.709, and 0.781 for ResNet50, Vgg19, and ResNet 101, respectively. The model with the highest performance achieved an average F1 score of 0.816. The enhanced performance can be attributed to architectural modifications, including the addition of extra layers. These changes increased the model's capacity to capture complex features in chest X-ray images, which are crucial for distinguishing between different chest diseases, including silicosis. Furthermore, our targeted fine-tuning process allowed the model to adapt to the unique characteristics of silicosis, which contributed to the improved accuracy and sensitivity observed in our results.

This shows that our model is performing better than other models on the same dataset in terms of overall accuracy and precision-recall balance. This is a positive indication that our model is able to correctly classify the data points with a higher degree of accuracy.

Utilizing the Grad-CAM technique, class-specific heatmap images were generated, highlighting the key features extracted from X-ray images to aid interpretation. In the context of convolutional neural networks (CNNs), Grad-CAM technique [17], can generate class-specific heatmap. This heatmap visualization can reveal the regions of the input image that the model focuses on during classification.

While these results are promising, it's essential to delve into the model's specific misclassifications to gain insights into its limitations and areas for potential improvement. Our analysis of misclassifications highlights specific challenges, such as distinguishing subtle patterns within the dataset. These findings suggest possible enhancements, including additional feature engineering or fine-tuning of specific model components. By understanding these limitations, we can refine our approach for even better performance in future studies.

5 Conclusion

The study employed transfer learning and pre-trained neural networks to classify chest X-ray images using deep learning, and also utilized Grad-CAM visualization to highlight the regions of the input image where the model focused its attention during classification. The performance of 11 pre-trained convolutional neural networks (CNNs) was compared, and the best-performing models were further fine tune. Evaluation metrics such as F1 Score and ROC curves were used to assess the models. The findings revealed that the ResNet 50 network had superior generalization ability on the testing datasets. Additionally, the Grad-CAM technique was utilized to generate class-specific heatmap images, highlighting the areas where the model focused on during feature extraction.

Early detection of silicosis through automated and accurate methods can lead to timely medical intervention, reducing the severity of the disease and improving the quality of life for affected individuals. Additionally, by automating the detection process, this research can help bridge the gap between the limited availability of specialised radiologists and the growing need for efficient diagnosis. This has significant implications for public health, workplace safety, and healthcare resource utilisation.

Funding. The present study received funding from the Government of Rajasthan under research project number 1000113614, entitled "Artificial intelligence (AI)-based model to assist radiologists in silicosis screening using chest X-rays."

References

1. Thomas, C.R., Kelley, T.R.: A brief review of silicosis in the United States, Environmental Health Insights, vol. 4 (2010)
2. Austin, E.K., James, C., Tessier, J.: Early detection methods for silicosis in Australia and internationally: a review of the literature. Int. J. Environ. Res. Public Health **18**(15), 8123 (2021)
3. Zhu, L., Zheng, R., Jin, H., Zhang, Q., Zhang, W.: Automatic detection and recognition of silicosis in chest radiograph. Biomed. Mater. Eng. **24**(6), 3389–3395 (2014)
4. Wang, X., et al.: Potential of deep learning in assessing pneumoconiosis depicted on digital chest radiography. Occup. Environ. Med. **77**, 597–602 (2020)
5. Kashika, P.H., Venkatapur, R.B.: Deep learning technique for object detection from panoramic video frames. Int. J. Comput. Theory Eng. **14**(1), 20–26 (2022)
6. Chris, L.A., Mulyawan, B., Dharmawan, A.B.: A Leukocyte Detection System using scale invariant feature transform method. Int. J. Comput. Theory Eng. **8**(1), 69–73 (2016)
7. Jawaid, M.M., Narejo, S., Qureshi, I.A., Pirzada, N.: A review of the state-of-the-art methods for non-calcified plaque detection in cardiac CT angiography. Int. J. Comput. Theory Eng. **10**(3), 84–92 (2018)
8. Cai, C.X., Zhu, B.Y., Chen, H.: Computer-aided diagnosis for pneumoconiosis based on texture analysis on digital chest radiographs. Appl. Mech. Mater. **241–244**, 244–247 (2012)
9. Kermany, D.: Labeled optical coherence tomography (OCT) and chest X-ray images for classification, Mendeley Data. https://data.mendeley.com/datasets/rscbjbr9sj/2
10. Singh, R., et al.: Deep learning in chest radiography: detection of findings and presence of change. PLOS ONE **13**(10), e0204155 (2018)

11. Rajpurkar, P., et al.: Deep learning for chest radiograph diagnosis: a retrospective comparison of the CheXNeXt algorithm to practising radiologists. PLOS Med. **15**(11), e1002686 (2018)
12. Wang, X., et al.: Potential of deep learning in assessing pneumoconiosis depicted on digital chest radiography. Occup. Environ. Med. **77**(9), 597–602 (2020)
13. Hall, E.L., Crawford, W.O., Roberts, F.E.: Computer classification of pneumoconiosis from radiographs of coal workers. IEEE Trans. Biomed. Eng. **BME-22**(6), 518–527 (1975)
14. Ledley, R.S., Huang, H.K., Rotolo, L.S.: A texture analysis method in classification of Coal Workers' pneumoconiosis. Comput. Biol. Med. **5**(1–2), 53–67 (1975)
15. Savol, A.M., Li, C.C., Hoy, R.J.: Computer-aided recognition of small rounded pneumoconiosis opacities in chest X-rays. IEEE Trans. Pattern Anal. Mach. Intell. **PAMI-2**(5), 479–482 (1980)
16. Okumura, E., Kawashita, I., Ishida, T.: Computerized analysis of pneumoconiosis in digital chest radiography: effect of artificial neural network trained with Power Spectra. J. Digit. Imaging **24**(6), 1126–1132 (2010)
17. Selvaraju, R.R., Cogswell, M., Das, A., Vedantam, R., Parikh, D., Batra, D.: Grad-CAM: visual explanations from deep networks via gradient-based localization. Int. J. Comput. Vision **128**(2), 336–359 (2020)
18. Hao, C., et al.: Balanced convolutional neural networks for pneumoconiosis detection. Int. J. Environ. Res. Public Health **18**(17), 9091 (2021)
19. Yosinski, J., et al.: How transferable are featured in deep neural networks? In: Advances in Neural Information Processing Systems, pp. 3320–3328 (2014)
20. Wu, Z., Shen, C., van den Hengel, A.: Wider or deeper: revisiting the ResNet model for visual recognition. Pattern Recogn. **90**, 119–133 (2019)
21. Simonyan, K., Zisserman, A.: Very deep convolutional networks for large-scale image recognition. arXiv.org, April 2015. http://arxiv.org/abs/1409.1556
22. Howard, A.G., et al.: MobileNets: efficient convolutional neural networks for Mobile Vision Applications. arXiv.org, April 2017. https://arxiv.org/abs/1704.04861
23. Huang, G., Liu, Z., Van Der Maaten, L., Weinberger, K.Q.: Densely connected convolutional networks. In: IEEE Conference on Computer Vision and Pattern Recognition (CVPR) (2017)
24. Bansal, M., Kumar, M., Sachdeva, M., Mittal, A.: Transfer learning for image classification using VGG19: Caltech-101 Image Data Set. J. Ambient Intell. Humanized Comput. **14**, 3609–3620 (2021)
25. Jinsakul, N., Tsai, C.-F., Tsai, C.-E., Wu, P.: Enhancement of deep learning in image classification performance using exception with the Swish activation function for colorectal polyp preliminary screening. Mathematics **7**(12), 1170 (2019)
26. Szegedy, C., Vanhoucke, V., Ioffe, S., Shlens, J., Wojna, Z.: Rethinking the inception architecture for computer vision. In: 2016 IEEE Conference on Computer Vision and Pattern Recognition (CVPR) (2016)
27. Tan, M., Le, Q.V.: EfficientNet: rethinking model scaling for convolutional neural networks. arXiv.org, September 2020. https://arxiv.org/abs/1905.11946v5
28. Bhandary, A., et al.: Deep-learning framework to detect lung abnormality-a study with chest X-Ray and lung CT scan images. Pattern Recogn. Lett. **129**, 271–278 (2020)
29. Vrbančič, G., Pecnik, S., Podgorelec, V.: Hyper-parameter optimization of convolutional neural networks for classifying COVID-19 X-ray images. J. Comput. Sci. Inf. Syst. **19**(00), 56–56 (2021)

30. Ravishankar, H., et al.: Understanding the mechanisms of deep transfer learning for medical images. In: Proceedings of the International Conference on Medical Imaging with Deep Learning, pp. 188–196 (2016)
31. Alzubaidi, L., et al.: Towards a better understanding of transfer learning for medical imaging: a case study. Appl. Sci. **10**(13), 4523 (2020)
32. Ahmed, S.E., Amiri, S., Doksum, K.: Ensemble linear subspace analysis of high-dimensional data. Entropy **23**(3), 324 (2021)

Automated Make and Model Identification of Reverse Shoulder Implants Using Deep Learning Methodology

Ved Prakash Dubey[1], A. Ramanathan[1], Senthilvelan Rajagopalan[2], C. Malathy[1], M. Gayathri[1], Vineet Batta[3](✉), and Srinath Kamineni[4]

[1] School of Computing, SRM Institute of Science and Technology, Chennai, India
[2] Department of Orthopaedics, MIOT International Hospital, Chennai, India
[3] Department of Orthopaedics and Trauma, Luton and Dunstable University Hospital NHS Trust, Luton, UK
battavineet@doctors.org.uk
[4] Department of Orthopaedic Surgery and Sports Medicine, Elbow Shoulder Research Center, University of Kentucky, UK HealthCare, Lexington, KY, USA

Abstract. Identification of an Orthopaedic Implant before a revision surgery is very important. Failure to identify an implant causes surgical planning delays, inability to plan for the correct equipment requirements, and can result in poorer patient outcomes. This paper proposes a framework to identify, make and model of two different reverse shoulder implants from X-ray images using Deep Learning Techniques. Both Anterior Posterior and Lateral views of X-rays were used in the study and a comparison was made to identify which view enables better results in identification. Various pre-trained deep learning models such as VGG16, VGG19 and InceptionV3 were used for classification of implants. The proposed methodology identifies both the make and model of the implant with an accuracy of 95% using both Anterior Posterior and Lateral Views and an accuracy of 86.67% using only the Anterior view.

Keywords: Reverse Shoulder Implant · Orthopedics · Biomedical · Deep Learning · Medical Images

1 Introduction

Total Shoulder Arthroplasty (TSA) is a surgical operation to treat an irreparable shoulder, either in an anatomic or a reverse configuration. Frequently encountered reasons for TSA are arthritis and shoulder injuries. In this procedure, the shoulder joint is replaced by a prosthesis or an Implant [1]. The procedure is usually recommended when non-surgical treatments do not provide the necessary pain relief and functional outcomes [2]. A common surgical procedure, when the rotator cuff musculature is dysfunctional, is a Reverse Shoulder Arthroplasty (RTSA). The components of RTSA are different from that of an anatomic TSA and include a convex glenosphere and humeral stem with concave liners [3]. From 2004 to 2015, Finland saw a 500% increase in TSA and a

KC Santosh et al. (Eds.): RTIP2R 2023, CCIS 2027, pp. 127–138, 2024.
https://doi.org/10.1007/978-3-031-53085-2_11

4500% increase in RTSA respectively [4]. The number of Reverse Shoulder Arthroplasty procedures performed in the USA during the year 2017 was 62,705 [3]. It is estimated through various mathematical models that shoulder arthroplasty will continue to increase and by 2025 will surpass hip and knee joint replacements with RSA likely to increase by around 349% in over 8 years [5].

Klug et al. projected a continued likely increase in shoulder arthroplasty by 2040, with each year requiring at least 37,000 procedures with an expected increase in revision surgery [6]. Projections by Villatte et al. show progression of shoulder replacements from 18% to 161% by 2050 [7]. It is estimated that by 2030, the necessity for shoulder arthroplasty in people less than the age of 55 years will increase by 333% and for people older than 55 years, the rate of increase is projected to be 755% [8].

The prosthetic implant that replaces the human joint, which is made of metal and plastic components, inevitably wears out and may have to be revised [1]. Glenoid and humeral component loosening, fracture, rotator cuff tear, instability, infection etc. are some of the common reasons for implant revision [9].

Identification of an implant before a revision surgery is important, for reasons of ordering the correct implants/instruments for revision surgery, especially when only one of the components is loose while the others are intact, thereby avoiding full replacement. This is currently accomplished with the help of surgical records and x-ray images of implants. The inability to access medical records, for various reasons such as change of hospitals and doctors, can preclude the attempt to identify the implant [10]. It is often difficult to identify implants solely from plain radiographs as there are numerous makes and models available, and the identification process can be difficult and time-consuming [2].

Failure to identify the implants at the right time yields more pain and trauma to patients due to increased waiting time and enhanced hospital cost and allied charges. This makes surgeons at times postpone the surgery thereby increasing the complexity of the surgery and increase in waiting time of other patients.

To address this clinical problem, we propose a novel framework that uses Deep learning techniques to identify the make and model of 2 different reverse shoulder arthroplasty implants from plain radiographs.

This work is the first of its kind to focus and identify only reverse shoulder implants in a single study. The proposed work also compares the influence of different views-Anterior Posterior (AP) and Lateral (LAT) in implant identification making it the first benchmark performed in a Shoulder implant Identification study.

2 Literature Review

Deep Learning and Image Processing methods were applied to various subfields in medicine, especially in the analysis of radiographic images in orthopedics [11], particularly hip arthroplasty [12], and identification of dental implants [13]. Deep learning based artificial intelligence methods were also used to diagnose knee osteoarthritis from plain knee radiographs [14].

Alireza et al. proposed an accurate pre-trained neural network that is successful in identifying up to 9 different hip implants with a generalized accuracy. This neural network was also tested against actual orthopedic surgeons and yielded desirable results thus proving a practical application of using deep learning methods in implant identification and classification [12].

Urban et al. classified total shoulder implants consisting of 16 models from 4 different manufacturers using 597 X-ray images. Classification was performed using deep learning methods, with NasNet performing the best out of 7 surveyed deep neural networks, obtaining an accuracy of 80.4%. Pre-trained models appear to work well with fine tuning of convolutional neural networks (CNN) [1].

Paul et al. used a custom Deep convolutional neural network (DCNN) based Resnet to obtain an accuracy of 97% in classification of 5 different total shoulder implants to detect the presence of shoulder implants and to differentiate between TSA and RTSA. Grad CAM was applied to highlight the important features in a shoulder implant radiographic image. DCNN detected the presence of a shoulder implant with an AUC (Area under Curve) of 1.0 and differentiated TSA and RTSA, with an AUC of 0.97 respectively [15].

Minh et al. proposed a new model, "X-net", to achieve desirable results in total shoulder implant classification. The model utilized the Squeeze and Excitation (SE) block integrated into the Residual Network (ResNet). The model was tested with a dataset that consisted of 597 radiographic images of implants from 4 manufacturers. The model ResNet 50 achieved an accuracy of 82% in classification of implants [16].

3 Dataset Description

The dataset consisted of the make and model of 2 different reverse shoulder arthroplasty implants. The images were obtained anonymously from individual surgeons. The X-ray images were labeled for make and model only, without any patient specific details or identifiers. The images were obtained for both AP and LAT views respectively. Table 1 describes the implants used in this study.

Table 1. Dataset of Two Different Make And Models.

Make	Model	Images in AP	Images in LAT
Depuy	Delta Xtend	20	10
Evolutis	Unic	30	6

Figure 1 and Fig. 2 displays Depuy Delta and Evolutis Unic implants in both AP and LAT view respectively.

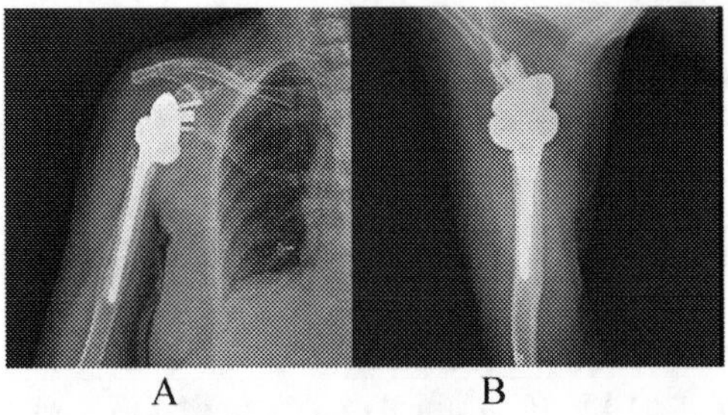

Fig. 1. A–B shows Depuy Delta Implant in AP and LAT view.

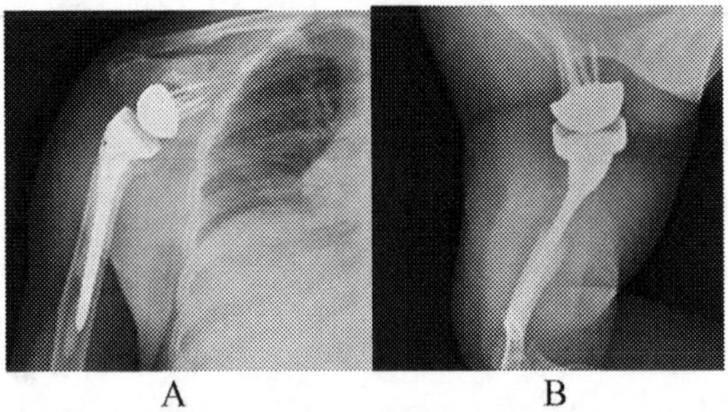

Fig. 2. A–B shows Evolutis Unic Implant in AP and LAT view.

4 Methods and Methodology

4.1 Proposed Approach

The approach attempted to identify the make and model of two implant classes as well as differentiate whether an AP view was only sufficient for classification or whether the use of both AP and LAT views improved results. Hence the databases were separated into (a) AP view and (b) AP and LAT views. The images were resized into 224 × 224 × 3 before the train and test split.

4.2 Training Set

For both the approaches discussed above, from the total set of images, 70% of the images were used for training the deep learning model. Images were taken at random for this process. To increase the number of images before training, augmentation techniques were applied to the raw images.

4.3 Testing Set

The testing set encompassed 30% of the original images (which were different from that of the training images) and did not undergo any augmentation. These images were used for checking the quality of training and to indicate how well the model performs in the classification of the implants.

4.4 Data Augmentation

The data augmentation technique addresses the lack of huge training data. The model becomes more robust when the databases of images are increased by augmentation [17]. Augmentation techniques of Zoom and Rotation [18] were used to increase the count of the initial training images.

To ensure standardization in the methodology, the same augmentation techniques were used for both AP and LAT images-based classification and only AP-images based classification. Data augmentation was applied only on the training images and the testing images were left untouched without any augmentation being performed on it.

Zoom augmentation with various random values after trial and error that resembles real-world patient- based X-ray data was applied to increase the number of images.

Rotations of the images were performed for 4 different angles. The angles used are $+3$, -3, $+5$ and -5 respectively. These angles were chosen on a trial and error basis to ensure images were rotated on the both left and right sides.

4.5 Deep Learning Methods

Deep Learning uses automated feature extraction for classification. Deep learning is highly beneficial when using large amounts of data. To obtain a large amount of data various augmentation techniques discussed above are used. The work used deep learning based convolutional neural networks which learned from the input data without manual feature extraction [19].

The proposed work compares various deep learning models such as VGG16 [20], VGG19 [21] and InceptionV3 [22] for both AP and LAT images and only with AP images alone across the 2 implant classes. The models were selected as they were the most common models that had performed well in various medical image classification problems [23].

4.6 Proposed Approach

The proposed model (Fig. 3) uses VGG16 Architecture pre-trained on ImageNet dataset. Image size of (224 224) was used to train the model. The model was tuned and verified for various optimizers and epochs. The model consisted of 2 convolutional layers of 3×3 kernel size and 64 followed by 1 pooling layer to perform pooling with pool size.

The above pattern of the cycle was repeated one more time. Output of the polling layer was given as input into 3 convolution layers followed by 1 pooling layer. The loop was repeated again for 2 more times. The output was flattened before it reaches the fully connected layers which use 'Softmax Function'.

4.7 Performance Metrics

The final obtained results are evaluated using Accuracy, F1 Score, Confusion Matrix, Precision and Recall [24]. These were obtained from samples of images after classifications that have been categorized as True Negative (TN) and True Positive (TP) and also as False Negative (FN) and False Positive (FP) respectively [25].

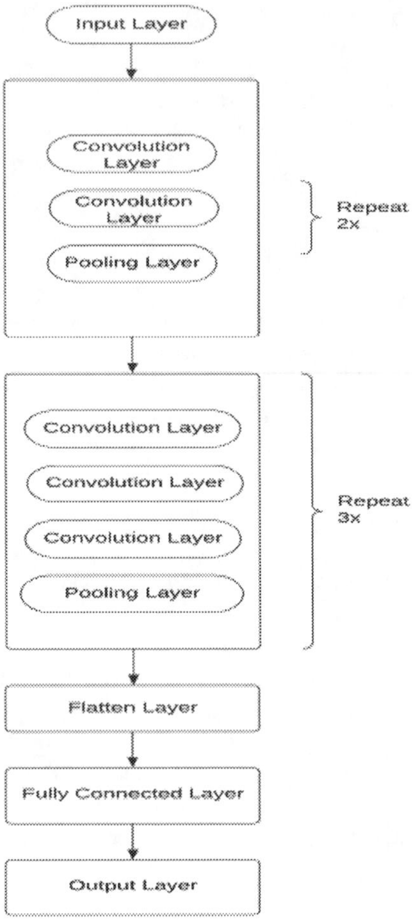

Fig. 3. Block Diagram of the proposed VGG16 Model.

5 Results and Discussion

5.1 Data Augmentation

Data Augmentation has increased the number of training images. Figure 4 shows a batch of images passed to model after augmentation for training.

5.2 Deep Learning Results

Results obtained for different deep learning models are explained below.

Table 2 shows the comparative results for various deep learning models when both AP and LAT view images were used for training and testing.

Table 3 shows the best obtained performance metrics for various deep learning models when both the images are used for training and testing.

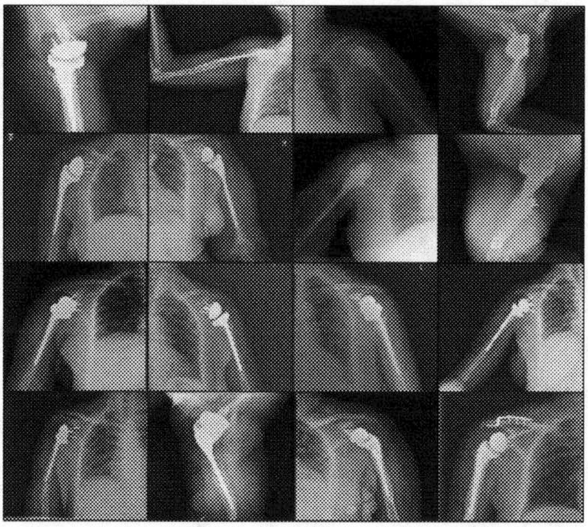

Fig. 4. A batch of augmented AP and LAT images used to train the deep learning algorithm

Table 2. Results for each deep learning model after tuning for both AP and LAT Images

Model	Epochs	Training Loss	Training Accuracy (%)	Testing Loss	Testing Accuracy (%)
VGG 16	25	0.1296	99.56	0.2601	95.00
VGG19	25	0.1653	98.90	0.3106	90.00
InceptionV3	25	0.0157	99.78	0.2744	90.00

Table 3. Performance metrics for each deep learning model for both AP and LAT Images

Model	Epochs	Precision	Recall	F1 Score
VGG 16	25	0.9541	0.9500	0.9498
VGG19	25	0.9000	0.9000	0.9000
InceptionV3	25	0.9241	0.9200	0.9396

From Table 2 and Table 3 it's clearly indicated that VGG16 performs well with an accuracy of 95% and a F1 score of 0.9498 in classification of implants using both AP and LAT images.

Table 4 shows the comparative results for various deep learning models when only AP images were used for training and testing.

Table 5 shows the best obtained performance metrics for various deep learning models when only AP images were used for training and testing.

From Table 4 and Table 5 it is observed that the use of view images produces an accuracy of 86.67% and a F1 Score of 0.9496 using the VGG16 model in classification

Table 4. Results for each deep learning model after tuning for only AP images

Model	Epochs	Training Loss	Training Accuracy (%)	Testing Loss	Testing Accuracy (%)
VGG 16	25	0.2410	98.15	0.3961	86.67
VGG19	25	0.2694	96.49	0.4125	86.67
InceptionV3	25	0.0138	99.98	0.6775	80.00

Table 5. Performance metrics for each deep learning model for only AP Images

Model	Epochs	Precision	Recall	F1 Score
VGG 16	25	0.9541	0.9500	0.9496
VGG19	25	0.8666	0.8666	0.8666
InceptionV3	25	0.8107	0.8000	0.8018

of implants and has better performance metrics compared to VGG19 which provides similar accuracy.

Figure 3 shows the loss graphs of the best obtained VGG16 model for both AP and LAT images.

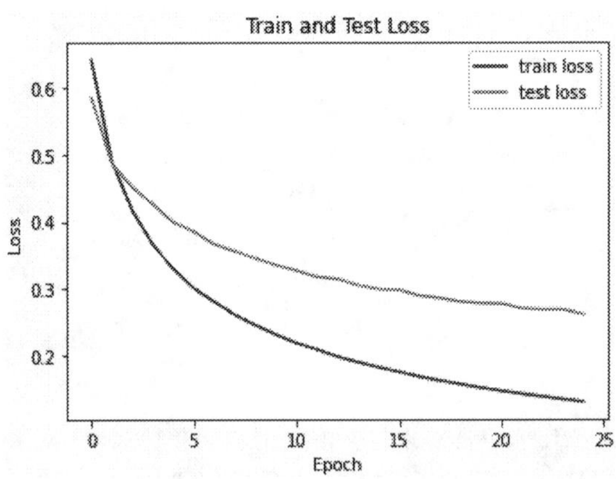

Fig. 5. Loss curve for VGG 16 for both AP and LAT images

As we can see in Fig. 5, both training and testing loss comes down as we tune the model thereby indicating the model performs well.

Figure 6 displays the confusion matrix of VGG16 for both AP and LAT Images. It is indicated from the matrix that there was one misclassification of the Depuy Delta Xtend implant model.

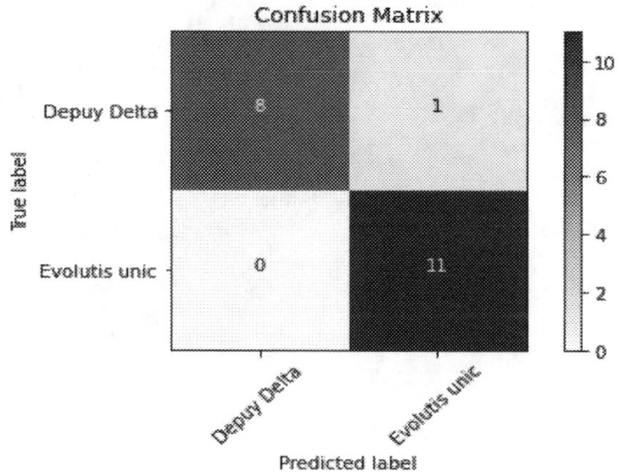

Fig. 6. Confusion Matrix of VGG 16 for both AP and LAT Images

In Fig. 7, plot of loss of VGG16 for only AP view images. The loss comes down there by indicating the model learns well.

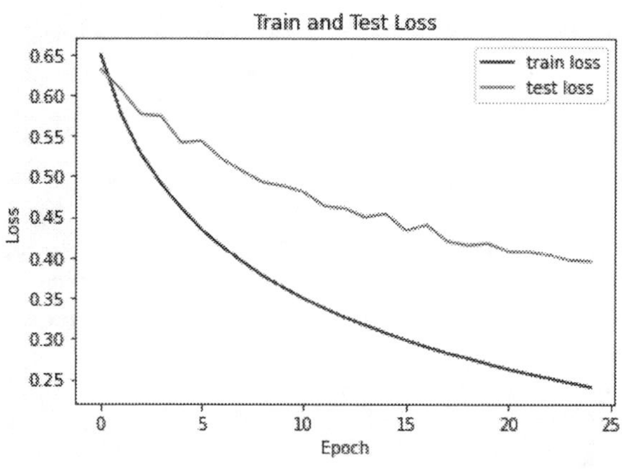

Fig. 7. Loss curve for VGG 16 for only AP Images

In Fig. 8, the confusion matrix of VGG 16 for only AP images indicates misclassification in both Depuy and Evolutis models thereby reducing the accuracy.

All the proposed best results were obtained after tuning each deep learning model intensively with different hyperparameters such as learning rates and optimizers. This study leverages the optimizers such as Adagrad [26], Adam [27] and SGD [28]. Each optimizer was combined with different learning rates such as 0.01, 0.001and 0.0001 for various epochs. Adam optimizer was overfitting increased test loss and gave 100% of training accuracy in many scenarios. SGD reduced the test loss, however failed to generate an enhanced accuracy.

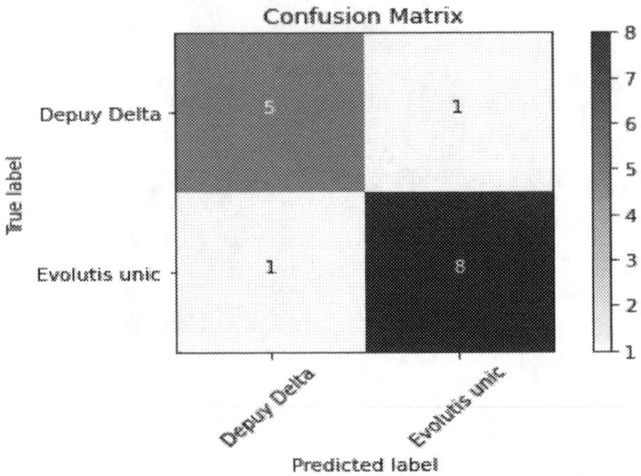

Fig. 8. Confusion Matrix of VGG 16 for only AP Images

Adagrad optimizer performed better with higher accuracy and reduced test loss thereby indicating that the model has learned well and performs better in the testing set. Thus Adagrad optimizer performs better in reverse shoulder implant identification when compared to Adam and SGD optimizers in our experimental studies.

The best results with AP and LAT images were obtained with the Adagrad optimizer with a learning rate of 0.001 for 25 epochs. The use of both AP and LAT view X-ray images of implants gives better results than depending only on AP view for the classification of implants. The potential of LAT images alone in the classification of implants was not considered due to its low initial number of images.

The proposed study is the first of its kind to identify reverse implants with both make and model while the existing studies [1, 15, 16, 29] identify total shoulder implant which is a completely different category/type of implant and also identifies their make/manufacturer only.

Though the study by Geng et al. [30] identifies a few reverse implants including Depuy Delta Extend along with total shoulder implants, the proposed work shows dominance with an accuracy of 95.00% and an F1 Score of 0.9498 which is comparatively better in identifying the reverse shoulder implants. The source of the database and approach of the study incorporated in [30] was also different from that of the proposed one.

The proposed work remains the first study to leverage upon the potential of different views of X-ray images (AP and LAT) together and individually (Only AP) in the classification of shoulder implants which are not present in other exisitng studies [1, 15, 16, 29, 30] in shoulder implant identification.

Since there are numerous models under a single make or company, our study makes the identification clinically significant and impactful before performing a revision surgery by identifying both the make and model of a reverse shoulder implant.

Accurate identification of reverse shoulder implants makes the surgery much more impactful and cost effective without any time delay and helps surgeons for better planning and management for patients by providing enhanced treatment.

6 Conclusion

The proposed novel framework identifies the make and model of the two reverse shoulder implants. The work which is first of the kind in identifying only reverse shoulder arthroplasty also compares the results with both AP and LAT view images of implants where both views together achieves an accuracy of 95% using VGG16 and only the AP view provides an accuracy of 86.67% in classification of implants after rigorous fine-tuning.

This paves way for accurate preoperative planning and helps the surgeon to focus on the operative procedure as implant identification usually takes more time for the doctors. This also subsequently reduces pre hospitalization time for the patients and reduces trauma and pain encountered during the waiting time before accurate implant identification.

Expanding the approach to multiple classes of implants and applying various higher deep learning and machine learning techniques can be performed as future work.

References

1. Urban, G., Porhemmat, S., Stark, M., Feeley, B., Okada, K., Baldi, P.: Classifying shoulder implants in X-ray images using deep learning. Comput. Struct. Biotechnol. J. **18**, 967–972 (2020). https://doi.org/10.1016/j.csbj.2020.04.005
2. Sultan, H., Owais, M., Park, C., Mahmood, T., Haider, A., Park, K.R.: Artificial intelligence-based recognition of different types of shoulder implants in X-ray scans based on dense residual ensemble-network for personalized medicine. J. Personalized Med. **11**(6), 482 (2021)
3. Hermena, S., Rednam, M.: Reverse shoulder arthroplasty, 1 October 2022. In: StatPearls [Internet]. Treasure Island (FL): StatPearls Publishing; PMID: 34662059, January 2023
4. Harrison, A.K., Knudsen, M.L., Braman, J.P.: Hemiarthroplasty and total shoulder arthroplasty conversion to reverse total shoulder arthroplasty. Curr. Rev. Musculoskelet. Med. **13**, 501–508 (2020)
5. Farley, K.X., Wilson, J.M., Daly, C.A., Gottschalk, M.B., Wagner, E.R.: The incidence of shoulder arthroplasty: rise and future projections compared to hip and knee arthroplasty. JSES Open Access **3**(4), 244 (2019)
6. Klug, A., Herrmann, E., Fischer, S., Hoffmann, R., Gramlich, Y.: Projections of primary and revision shoulder arthroplasty until 2040: facing a massive rise in fracture-related procedures. J. Clin. Med. **10**(21), 5123 (2021)
7. Villatte, G., Erivan, R., Barth, J., Bonnevialle, N., Descamps, S., Boisgard, S.: Progression and projection for shoulder surgery in France, 2012–2070: epidemiologic study with trend and projection analysis. Orthop. Traumatol. Surg. Res. **106**(6), 1067–1077 (2020)
8. Padegimas, E.M., Maltenfort, M., Lazarus, M.D., Ramsey, M.L., Williams, G.R., Namdari, S.: Future patient demand for shoulder arthroplasty by younger patients: national projections. Clin. Orthopaedics Relat. Res. **473**, 1860–1867 (2015)
9. Fossati, C., Vitale, M., Forin Valvecchi, T., Gualtierotti, R., Randelli, P.S.: Management of painful shoulder arthroplasty: a narrative review. Pain Ther. **9**, 427–439 (2020)
10. Borjali, A., Chen, A.F., Muratoglu, O.K., Morid, M.A., Varadarajan, K.M.: Detecting total hip replacement prosthesis design on plain radiographs using deep convolutional neural network. J. Orthopaedic Res. **38**(7), 1465–1471 (2020)
11. Olczak, J., et al.: Artificial intelligence for analyzing orthopedic trauma radiographs: deep learning algorithms—are they on par with humans for diagnosing fractures? Acta Orthop. **88**(6), 581–586 (2017)

12. Borjali, A., et al.: Comparing the performance of a deep convolutional neural network with orthopedic surgeons on the identification of total hip prosthesis design from plain radiographs. Med. Phys. **48**(5), 2327–2336 (2021)
13. Takahashi, T., Nozaki, K., Gonda, T., Mameno, T., Wada, M., Ikebe, K.: Identification of dental implants using deep learning—pilot study. Int. J. Implant Dent. **6**, 1–6 (2020)
14. Tiulpin, A., Thevenot, J., Rahtu, E., Lehenkari, P., Saarakkala, S.: Automatic knee osteoarthritis diagnosis from plain radiographs: a deep learning-based approach. Sci. Rep. **8**(1), 1–10 (2018)
15. Yi, P.H., et al.: Automated detection and classification of shoulder arthroplasty models using deep learning. Skeletal Radiol. **49**, 1623–1632 (2020)
16. Vo, M.T., Vo, A.H., Le, T.: A robust framework for shoulder implant X-ray image classification. Data Technol. Appl. **56**(3), 447–460 (2022)
17. Mikołajczyk, A., Grochowski, M.: Data augmentation for improving deep learning in image classification problem. In: 2018 International Interdisciplinary PhD Workshop (IIPhDW), pp. 117–122. IEEE (2018)
18. Khalifa, N.E., Loey, M., Mirjalili, S.: A comprehensive survey of recent trends in deep learning for digital images augmentation. Artif. Intell. Rev. **55**, pp. 1–27 (2022)
19. Sarker, I.H.: Deep learning: a comprehensive overview on techniques, taxonomy, applications and research directions. SN Comput. Sci. **2**(6), 420 (2021)
20. Simonyan, K., Zisserman, A.: Very deep convolutional networks for large-scale image recognition. arXiv preprint arXiv:1409.1556 (2014)
21. Bansal, M., Kumar, M., Sachdeva, M., Mittal, A.: Transfer learning for image classification using VGG19: Caltech-101 image data set. J. Ambient Intell. Human. Comput. **14**, 1–12 (2021)
22. Wang, C., et al.: Pulmonary image classification based on inception-v3 transfer learning model (2019)
23. Sistaninejhad, B., Rasi, H., Nayeri, P.: A review paper about deep learning for medical image analysis. Comput. Math. Methods Med. **2023**, 1 (2023)
24. Vakili, M., Ghamsari, M., Rezaei, M.: Performance analysis and comparison of machine and deep learning algorithms for IoT data classification. arXiv preprint arXiv:2001.09636 (2020)
25. Ramanathan, A., Christy Bobby, T.: Classification of corpus callosum layer in mid-saggital MRI images using machine learning techniques for autism disorder. In: Modeling, Machine Learning and Astronomy: First International Conference, MMLA 2019, Bangalore, India, 22–23 November 2019, Revised Selected Papers, vol. 1, pp. 78–91. Springer Singapore (2020). https://doi.org/10.1007/978-981-33-6463-9_7
26. Lydia, A., Francis, S.: AdaGrad—an optimizer for stochastic gradient descent. Int. J. Inf. Comput. Sci. **6**(5), 566–568 (2019)
27. Kingma, D.P., Ba, J.: Adam: a method for stochastic optimization. arXiv preprint arXiv:1412.6980 (2014)
28. Ruder, S.: An overview of gradient descent optimization algorithms. arXiv preprint arXiv:1609.04747 (2016)
29. Yılmaz, A.: Shoulder implant manufacturer detection by using deep learning: proposed channel selection layer. Coatings **11**(3), 346 (2021)
30. Geng, E.A., et al.: Development of a machine learning algorithm to identify total and reverse shoulder arthroplasty implants from X-ray images. J. Orthop. **35**, 74–78 (2023)

COVID-19 Disease Prediction Using Generative Adversarial Networks with Convolutional Neural Network (GANs-CNN) Model

Kakelli Anil Kumar(✉), Binamra Neupane, Saugat Malla, and Durga Prasad Pandey

Vellore Institute of Technology, Vellore, Tamil Nadu, India
anilsekumar@gmail.com,
{binamra.neupane2018,saugat.malla2018,durgaprasad.pandey2018}@vitalum.ac.in

Abstract. This study primarily focuses on a novel approach to Covid-19 prediction utilizing X-ray images. The images are used for the initial stage of training of the CNN Convolution neural network model. For improved classification and prediction accuracy, images are trained and tested using a hybrid GANs (Generative Adversarial Networks based Convolution neural network) - CNN (Convulational Neural Network) model. The noise cancellation technique of image processing has been used to minimize the noise in images and used for the GANs-CNN hybrid model. Each method of the proposed model has resulted in better accuracy, in which the validation accuracy on every 15 epochs is 79.2%, 85.8%, and 87.1% respectively.

Keywords: Image Processing · Neural Networks · Data Visualization · Generative Adversarial Network (GAN)

1 Introduction

COVID-19 infection was discovered in the year 2019 and it has spread over the world since its inception. Consequently, all nations throughout the world have been struggling and fighting against the COVID-19 outbreak. Limiting the spread of COVID-19 requires the timely diagnosis of affected people. The worldwide impact of the Coronavirus (COVID-19) epidemic has intensified the strain on healthcare and medical systems. Fever, dry cough, weariness, headache, vomiting, sore throat, sneezing, dyspnea, and myalgia are some of the important symptoms that can be seen in the COVID-19 patient. The majority of patients infected with the disease have respiratory conditions. According to the data from Johns Hopkins University, the global death to case ratio was 1.21%

COVID-19 Disease Prediction using GANs-CNN Model.

KC Santosh et al. (Eds.): RTIP2R 2023, CCIS 2027, pp. 139–149, 2024.
https://doi.org/10.1007/978-3-031-53085-2_12

on May 5, 2022 (6,245,354/515,641,293). Early disease detection, patient care, and community programs all benefit from reliable medical database research. Various machine learning algorithms have already been implemented in various medical fields. Machine learning methods have been successfully used in a variety of applications, including disease prediction. In this research work, a hybrid CNN and GANS model is being implemented. Furthermore, the image smoothing technique i.e., Gaussian filter has been used which has improved the model accuracy. The model is trained using X-ray image datasets obtained from the Kaggle repository [1]. Researchers from Qatar University and the University of Dhaka have created a database of chest X-ray pictures in partnership with medical practitioners from Pakistan and Malaysia [1]. These images depict COVID-19 cases as well as Normal and Viral Pneumonia [1]. There has been an exponential advancement in the medical sector which has helped an average citizen and improved the health care system of various countries all across the globe. But there is still a need for an automated system that an average person and the medical worker can use for preliminary purposes.

There are four sections to this study. An introduction is provided in the Sect. 1. Moving forward, the Sect. 2 delves into a comprehensive literature review, a critical component of the research process. This section offers an insightful overview of the various methods and techniques that have been employed in the past to predict COVID-19. The Sect. 3 of the paper constitutes the experimental component, which serves as the heart of the research endeavor. Here, the paper delves into the specifics of the suggested system, offering a detailed exposition of the methodology, data sources, and experimental setup. The results of the study are in-depth reviewed in Sect. 4 discussion of the findings and conclusions.

2 Literature Review

The influence of a modern patient's lungs and the harm to the lung is well explained by many researchers [2]. One of the research's key problems is identifying and selecting appropriate data sets and techniques for analyzing lung illnesses [2]. VDSNet is a new hybrid deep learning framework for detecting lung illnesses from X-ray pictures [3]. The new model is tested using a dataset of NIH chest X-ray images from the Kaggle repository [3]. VDSNet obtained the best validation accuracy of 73% for the complete dataset [3]. Other numerous models, vanilla gray, vanilla RGB, hybrid CNN-VGG basic CapsNet, and modified CapsNet were implemented; however, their accuracy was not promising as the VDSNet model [3].

Based on lung CT scans, a unique coronavirus detection principle has been developed using CNN and AdaBoost classifier logic [4]. The nature of the processing in this presented methodology enables images to be filtered in two ways: edge-based filtering and surface-based filtering [4]. And using this proposed approach known as HDDP gives an accuracy level of 97% [4]. The chest X-ray pictures are segmented using the Un-net model and as a result, slices are created [5]. For prediction, these slices are further processed through several convolution layers and capsule layers [5]. This model is known as the XRCAP model, and it is an ensemble deep learning model. The accuracy, sensitivity, and specificity metrics were used to evaluate the models. For the prediction of COVID-19 using X-ray images, the model had a 93.2% accuracy [5]. Five deep learning models, ResNet, FitNet, IRCNN, EffectiveNet, and Fit-net have been used to create a novel framework [6]. Individually, they are pre-trained utilizing a recurrent CXR-specific technique [6]. The models are fine-tuned with the initialization parameters and are combined using a variety of ensemble procedures, including majority voting, simple averaging, and weighted averaging [6]. With a 64% reduction in clock cycles, the weighted averaging ensemble achieves maximum accuracy, precision, recall, and F1-score of 0.99, 0.98, 0.98, and 0.98 respectively [6].

COVID-CheXNet system for the COVID-19 virus in X-ray images utilizes efficient image processing and deep learning technologies to produce an accurate and real-time diagnostic system [7]. Using this method, poor-quality images were improved and the noise level was lowered using the CLAHE method and Butterworth bandpass filter respectively [7]. With a DAR of 98%, sensitivity of 96%, specificity, accuracy of both 100%, and an F1 score of 98%, the pre-trained ResNet50 model produced the best results [7]. In comparison with the COVID-CheXNet system, the ResNet50 model had the same specificity and precision, but it performed poorly on other quantitative criteria [7]. A system was developed that accurately detected COVID-19-affected persons [8]. Furthermore, it can be integrated into any Internet-connected gadget that has a monitoring feature to connect with medical professionals [8]. To forecast COVID-19 infected patients, a Deep Ensemble Learning Framework is presented that uses the prediction accuracies of individual transfer learning models such as I ResNet50, (ii) DenseNet201, (iii) InceptionV3, (iv) VGG-16, (v) VGG-19, (vi) Exception, and (vii) MobineNetV2 [8]. The accuracy score was 99.87%, and the sensitivity (recall) value was 99.58% [8].

To evaluate the efficacy, the COVID-19 certified data from the United States, India, and Russia are combined [9]. In the case of the United States, the average MAPE, RMSE, and MAE of the hybrid model are lowered by 47.27%, 44.50%, and 55.34%, respectively, when compared to the average MAPE, RMSE, and MAE of the single model [9]. GVMD-ELM-ARIMA reduces the MAPE by 60%, the RMSE by 56.85%, and the MAE by 61.61% to GVMD-ELM-ELM [9]. The experimental results demonstrate that GVMD-ELM-ARIMA has the best prediction accuracy and offers a new strategy for forecasting cumulative COVID-19 confirmed data [9]. 30 research, involving 34 models, met all of the requirements for inclusion [10]. The sum of the sensitivity, specificity, and area under the receiver operating characteristic curves was 0.86, 0.86, and 0.91, respectively [10]. In terms of both sensitivity and specificity, the objective of machine learning models, class imbalance, and feature selection are significant factors relevant to explaining the between-study heterogeneity [10].

3 Experimental Setup

3.1 CNN Model

Based on x-ray scans, a dataset of lung images categorized as "COVID-19" is utilized to predict if a patient has Covid-19 or not. It comprises two main convolutional layer, followed by fully connected layers. The first layer includes a 2D convolutional layer that transforms input grayscale images into 16 feature maps, followed by batch normalization to stabilize training, ReLU activation for introducing non-linearity, and max-pooling to down sample the spatial dimensions. The second layer further refines the features by convolving the 16 feature maps into 32 new feature maps, again followed by batch normalization, ReLU activation, and max-pooling. These layer enable the network to learn hierarchical and abstract features from the input data. The flattened output is then passed through a fully connected layer to create a bottleneck for feature representation, which is followed by dropout regularization to prevent overfitting. The final fully connected layer produces a single output node, indicating the network's prediction, which is transformed through a sigmoid activation function to yield a probability-like output. This CNN architecture is designed to capture intricate patterns within the input images and make informed binary classification decisions based on the learned features (Fig. 1).

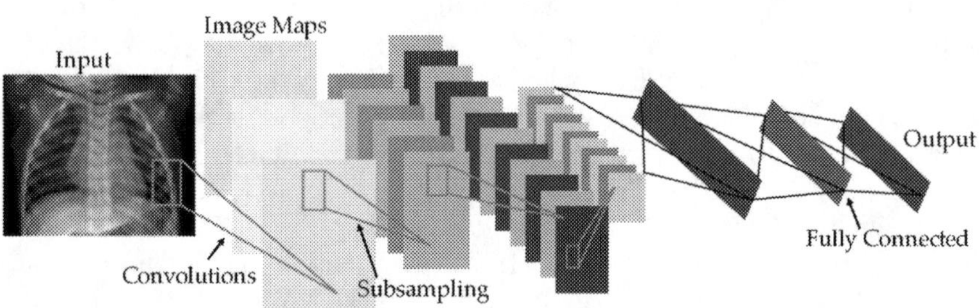

Fig. 1. CNN architecture typically consisting of convolutional, pooling, and fully connected layers for feature extraction and image classification

3.2 GANs Model

The generator functions as a convolutional neural network within the framework of generative adversarial networks (GANs), dedicated to crafting synthetic data. Its primary purpose is to convert a latent noise vector into data that appears remarkably authentic.

The initial layer is a transposed convolutional layer that takes the latent noise vector and expands it into a 4×4 grid featuring 512 channels. Batch normalization is applied to stabilize the training dynamics, and a Rectified Linear

Unit (ReLU) activation function introduces non-linearity while preserving positive values. The subsequent transposed convolutional layers continue the process of enhancing spatial dimensions. This progression occurs sequentially: from 4×4 to 8×8, 16×16, and ultimately culminating in a 32×32 grid (Fig. 2).

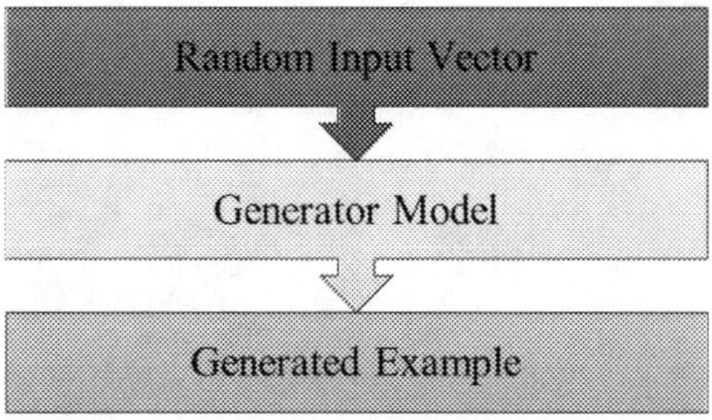

Fig. 2. Generator Model takes random noise as input and transforms it into synthetic data

The terminal transposed convolutional layer is responsible for upscaling the output to a 64×64 grid with 3 channels, representing an RGB image. This layer employs the nn.Tanh() activation function to ensure that pixel values are confined to the range of $[-1, 1]$, aligning with the suitable range for image data. By navigating through these layers, the generator acquires the capacity to translate a latent noise vector into a meticulously constructed synthetic image that bears resemblance to the target data distribution (Fig. 3).

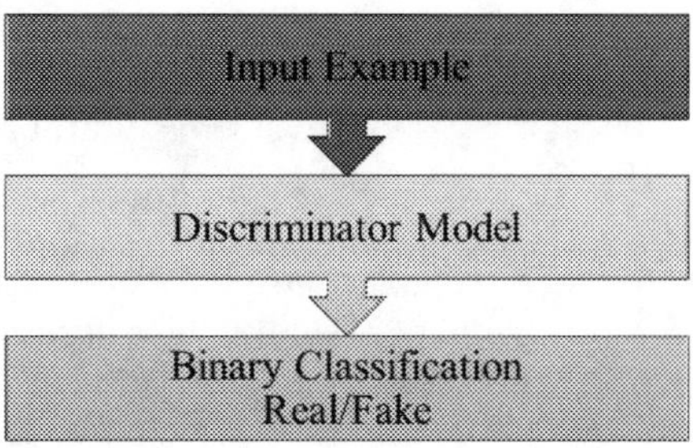

Fig. 3. Discriminator Model for adversarial learning to distinguish between real and generated data in a Generative Adversarial Network (GAN)

The discriminator is a convolutional neural network crucial for distinguishing between real and generated data in generative adversarial networks (GANs). It starts with a convolution layer processing 3-channel 64×64 images, followed by batch normalization and LeakyReLU activation, resulting in 64 feature maps at 32×32 resolution. Subsequent layers expand complexity, generating 128,

256, and 512 feature maps with progressively smaller spatial dimensions. The final layer produces a 1×1 output, which after flattening and sigmoid activation, yields a probability score. This architecture empowers the discriminator to assess input authenticity, contributing significantly to GANs' adversarial training dynamic.

3.3 Image Smoothing Technique

The processing of the images involves a series of steps. To facilitate systematic image manipulation, a loop iterates through the images using the glob.glob function. Within the loop, each image is loaded. To enhance the image quality, a Gaussian blur operation with a kernel size of (5,5) is applied. Subsequently, the processed image is converted into a PIL (Pillow) Image object, and a set of transformations are applied through the transform function to ensure consistent preprocessing. The transformed images are then sequentially saved in the designated directory with distinct filenames generated using a specific formatting pattern. Throughout this process, an incremental counter is employed to manage the naming and tracking of processed images. Ultimately, this approach contributes to the creation of a repository of processed lung images that have undergone Gaussian blurring and other transformations, primed for further investigation or utilization in various computational tasks.

3.4 Proposed System Model

A comprehensive comparison of three distinct approaches for predicting images using Convolutional Neural Networks (CNNs) is undertaken.

1. **Dataset**
   A large dataset of medical images for diverse respiratory conditions has been compiled. For COVID-19, a total of 2473 chest X-ray images have been obtained. In addition, 400 more CXR images have been collected. 10,192 photos have been curated for regular cases. A total of 6012 photos of lung opacity instances have been sourced. Finally, the collection has 1345 photos of Viral Pneumonia cases. This collection is an invaluable resource for scholars and professionals interested in respiratory health.
2. **CNN based approach**
   The first approach involves the implementation of a straightforward CNN model, trained and evaluated on a dataset comprising 500 sample images. The process entails passing the collected images through the CNN architecture, leveraging the model's trained parameters to generate predictions that discern between Covid-19 and normal images.
3. **GAN + CNN based approach**
   In the second approach, the focus shifts to the utilization of Generative Adversarial Networks (GANs) to augment the available dataset. Here, the collected images are subjected to the GANs model, generating additional images that

contribute diversity and richness to the dataset. This expanded dataset, inclusive of GANs-generated images, is subsequently integrated with the existing collection. The composite dataset is then subjected to the CNN model, enabling it to predict the classification of Covid-19 or normal images based on the learned model parameters.

4. **GAN + Image noise filtering + CNN based approach**
The final approach focuses on improving image quality by employing image noise filtering, which successfully eliminates residual noise. The noise-filtered images are fed into the GANs model, which has the ability to understand and work with intricate visual data. By utilizing the improved images, the GANs system generates a fresh collection of images. The CNN model receives this expanded dataset as input. The CNN model produces predictions that successfully distinguish between Covid-19 and normal images. In essence, this paper encompasses a comprehensive evaluation of these three methods, each contributing a unique facet to the predictive capacity of CNNs in the realm of image classification. Through these distinct strategies, the study delves into enhancing dataset diversity, image quality refinement, and ultimately advancing the accuracy of image predictions in the context of Covid-19 diagnosis.

3.5 Evaluation

Binary cross entropy, also known as logarithmic loss, is used to calculate the loss function which is utilized for binary classification jobs. It operates by evaluating the logarithmic difference between the predicted probability of the positive class and the actual label. When a model forecast differs from the true label, Binary Cross Entropy provides a larger loss; when they coincide, it assigns a lesser loss. During the training process, it is the goal to reduce this loss value as much as possible. The model effectively learns to align its predictions with the ground truth labels by reducing the Binary Cross Entropy loss, improving its accuracy in binary classification tasks (Figs. 4 and 5).

Yi represents the actual class and log(p(yi)) is the probability of that class. p(yi) is the probability of one 1-p(yi) is the probability of zero.

For accuracy, binary classification has been implemented. Binary classification is the process of categorizing data items into one of two mutually exclusive groups, sometimes known as positive and negative classes or class 1 and class 0, respectively. The major objective is to evaluate the model's ability to distinguish between these two classes using the traits or attributes associated with each data point.

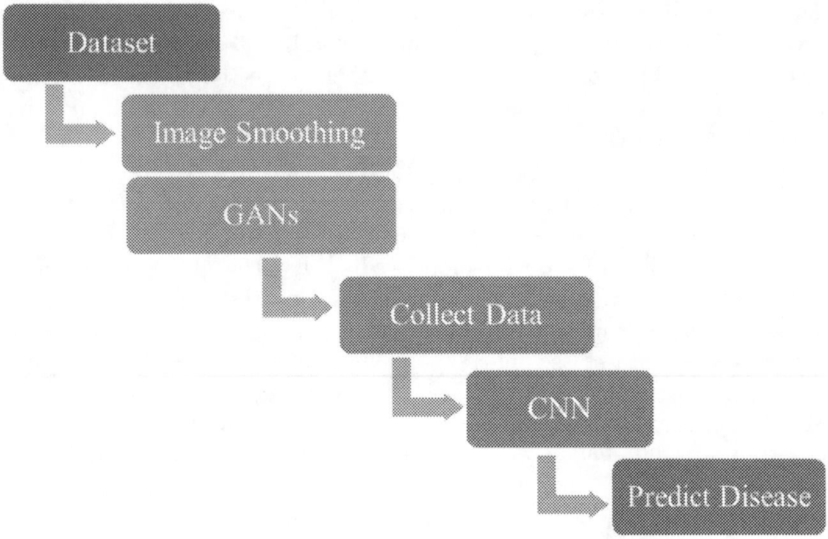

Fig. 4. NN Flow Chart. Prior to collecting the data and passing it to the CNN model to forecast the Covid-19 disease, the dataset is first processed through a GANs model. Second, the Image Smoothing Technique is used, and the results are then passed on to the GANs and CNN model.

$$-\frac{1}{N}\sum_{i=1}^{N} y_i \cdot log(p(y_i)) + (1 - y_i) \cdot log(1 - p(y_i))$$

Fig. 5. Formulae for Binary Cross Entropy

Mathematically, accuracy = (Number of Correct Predictions)/(Total Number of Predictions)

In order to convert this value to a percentage, multiply it by 100. As a result, a greater accuracy rate shows that the model is actually producing more accurate predictions, whereas a lower accuracy rate indicates a need for improvement. In terms of positives and negatives, accuracy can be represented as:

$$Accuracy = (TP + TN)/(TP + TN + FP + FN),$$

where TP = True Positives, TN = True Negatives, FP = False Positives, and FN = False Negatives.

4 Results and Discussion

This study focuses on the comprehensive comparison of three distinct methodologies aimed at predicting instances of Covid-19 disease. The accuracy of these methodologies is meticulously evaluated and tracked across multiple epochs, providing valuable insights into their performance dynamics. The accuracy measurements are documented at regular intervals, as illustrated in Tables 1, 2, and 3, which offer a quantitative representation of the methodologies' predictive capabilities.

Upon examining the results, a notable trend emerges: accuracy tends to improve progressively as the number of epochs increases. The first approach involves the deployment of a straightforward CNN model. This initial model achieves a training accuracy of 90.4% and a validation accuracy of 79.2%, as indicated in Table 1. However, it is observed that the model's validation accuracy remains comparatively lower, suggesting potential challenges in its generalization to new and unseen images. This shortcoming may lead to the exclusion of new images from the dataset.

The second methodology builds upon the preceding one by incorporating images generated using Generative Adversarial Networks (GANs). By integrating these GANs-generated images into the CNN model, significant improvements are observed. Specifically, on the 15th epoch, the model achieves a training accuracy of 91.8% and a validation accuracy of 85.8%, as outlined in Table 2. This demonstrates the value of enhancing the dataset through GANs-generated images in bolstering the model's predictive capacity.

The final approach introduces a pivotal preprocessing step before GANs-generated images are incorporated. Here, an image processing technique-the Gaussian filter-is employed. Applying the Gaussian filter contributes to the enhancement of image quality by mitigating noise. This refined dataset leads to a remarkable advancement in accuracy. On the 15th epoch, the training accuracy elevates to 97.4%, while the validation accuracy reaches 87.1%, as showcased in Table 3.

In summation, this work systematically unveils a comprehensive comparative analysis of three methodologies for Covid-19 prediction. The research underscores the potential of GANs-generated images in augmenting the dataset and highlights the efficacy of image preprocessing techniques like the Gaussian filter. The incremental improvement in accuracy across these methodologies reflects their collective contribution towards enhancing the reliability and precision of Covid-19 prediction, thus facilitating informed medical decision-making.

Table 1. CNN without filter and addition of GANs

EPOCH	Training loss	Validation loss	Training accuracy	Validation accuracy
1	0.698	0.6107	68.533	68.0
5	0.3812	0.9257	82.933	64.8
10	0.262	1.1168	88.2667	68.8
15	0.231	0.6781	90.4	79.2

Table 2. CNN with addition of GANs

EPOCH	Training loss	Validation loss	Training accuracy	Validation accuracy
1	0.3994	0.7355	82.133	73.55
5	0.298	0.4259	87.033	82.5
10	0.2401	0.3519	90.733	85.5
15	0.198	0.3714	91.8667	85.8

Table 3. CNN with Noise filter and addition of GANs

EPOCH	Training loss	Validation loss	Training accuracy	Validation accuracy
1	0.122	0.4342	74.4333	79.8
5	0.1047	0.772	91.8667	83.2
10	0.0907	0.6915	96.2333	86.3
15	0.082	0.7659	97.4	87.1

5 Conclusion

A Hybrid Neural Network Model based on GANs and CNN is utilized in this study to predict whether or not a patient has Covid-19 based on x-ray images. This project is divided into three sections, each of which has a different methodology for classifying x-ray images as Covid-19 or normal. It also examines the precision of three different approaches for predicting Covid-19 disease.

References

1. D. Qatar University, Qatar, and the University of Dhaka, Bangladesh, "COVID-19 Radiography Dataset, 29 May 2021. https://www.kaggle.com/datasets/preetviradiya/covid19-radiography-dataset
2. Gunasinghe, A.D., Aponso, A.C., Thirimanna, H.: Early prediction of lung diseases. In: 2019 IEEE 5th International Conference for Convergence in Technology (I2CT), pp. 1–4, March 2019
3. Bharati, S., Podder, P., Mondal, M.R.H.: Hybrid deep learning for detecting lung diseases from X-ray images. Inform. Med. Unlocked **20**, 100391 (2020)

4. Prabha, B., Kaur, S., Singh, J., Nandankar, P., Jain, S.K., Pallathadka, H.: Intelligent predictions of Covid disease based on Lung CT images using machine learning strategy. Mater. Today Proc. **63** (2021)
5. Darji, P.A., Nayak, N.R., Ganavdiya, S., Batra, N., Guhathakurta, R.: Feature extraction with capsule network for the COVID-19 disease prediction through X-ray images. Mater. Today Proc. **56**, 3556–3560 (2022)
6. Sakthivel, R., et al.: An efficient hardware architecture based on an ensemble of deep learning models for COVID-19 prediction. Sustain. Urban Areas **80**, 103713 (2022)
7. Al-Waisy, A.S., et al.: COVID-CheXNet: hybrid deep learning framework for identifying COVID-19 virus in chest X-rays images. Soft Comput. **27**(5), 2657–2672 (2020)
8. Roy, P.K., Kumar, A.: Early prediction of COVID-19 using an ensemble of transfer learning. Comput. Electr. Eng. **101**, 108018 (2022)
9. Li, G., Chen, K., Yang, H.: A new hybrid prediction model of cumulative COVID-19 confirmed data. Process Saf. Environ. Prot. **157**, 1–19 (2022)
10. Kuo, K.-M., Talley, P.C., Chang, C.-S.: The accuracy of machine learning approaches using non-image data for the prediction of COVID-19: a meta-analysis. Int. J. Med. Informatics **164**, 104791 (2022)

Modified Snapshot Ensemble Algorithm for Skin Lesion Classification

Samson Anosh Babu Parisapogu[1(✉)], Mastan Mohammed Meera Durga[2], Vallela Kaushik Shashank Reddy[3], Boyapati Kalyan Chakravarthi[4], and P. Vasanth Sena[1]

[1] Department of AI and DS, Chaitanya Bharathi Institute of Technology, Hyderabad 500075, Telangana, India
{samsonanoshbabu_aids,vasanthasena_aids}@cbit.ac.in
[2] Department of Computer Science and Engineering, Bapatla Engineering College, Bapatla 522102, Andhra Pradesh, India
[3] Arista Networks, Bellandur, Bengaluru 560103, Karnataka, India
[4] Microsoft, Nalagandla 500019, Telangana, India
https://www.cbit.ac.in/wp-content/uploads/2023/03/Dr_samsonanoshbabu_P_-AI_DS.pdf,
https://www.cbit.ac.in/wp-content/uploads/2023/03/ITD_P-Vasanth-Sena_March-2023.pdf

Abstract. Skin cancer prediction has become an essential task in dermoscopic image analysis. For automatic diagnosis of the skin lesions, the Scientific community. The most crucial part in the cure of skin cancer is the exact identification and classification of the skin lesion types. This paper proposes a modified snapshot ensemble algorithm for skin lesion classification. This method utilizes the advantages of transfer learning approach with ResNet50. The method is shown efficient results for the popular metrics, such as accuracy, F1-score, recall and precision.

Keywords: Skin classification · Snapshot ensemble · Deep learning · Transfer learning

1 Introduction

Skin cancer is a widely recognized disease among most of the human diseases. The malignant growth happens when healthy cells experience a change and develop without typical controls. Basal and squamous cell carcinomas are widely recognized skin cancer types, and Melanoma is the third most regular type of malignant skin growth. The initial two diseases of skin are known as non-melanoma skin cancers. Other uncommon skin cancer types include Merkel cell tumors and Dermatofibrosarcoma protuberans (DFSP) [2]. From 2011 to 2022, various studies conducted by the researchers on Skin Lesion Analysis (SLA) especially lesion segmentation and classification applied different techniques including computer vision algorithms, manual feature engineering, and automated Artificial

KC Santosh et al. (Eds.): RTIP2R 2023, CCIS 2027, pp. 150–159, 2024.
https://doi.org/10.1007/978-3-031-53085-2_13

Intelligence (AI), Machine Learning (ML) and Deep Learning (DL) [1]. According to the Average Annual Number and Rate of Invasive Melanoma incidence Rates by Sex and Race/Ethnicity, the United States, 2012–2016, the highest are non-Hispanic white males (34.9 per 100,000) and the lowest are black (1.0 per 100,000) and Asian/Pacific Islander individuals (1.3 per 100,000). Moreover, non-Hispanic white males also have the highest death rates (4.7 per 100,000). Also, more than 100,000 people in the U.S. expect to diagnose with some skin disease in the year 2020. Also, approximately 7,000 are expected to die [3].

Computer-aided diagnosis (CAD) frameworks have recently developed to classify skin lesions in support of the scientific community [4]. As per the review, the CAD frameworks broadly concentrated yet recognized just particular sorts of pigmented skin lesions [5]. For the most part, in view of the extraction of color and texture features, these frameworks developed and then defined these characteristics through machine learning approaches [6]. A computer-based classification between malignant and benign will be an option for decreasing inter and intraobserver changeability. Recognizing and classifying a skin lesion using dermoscopic images is one of the most critical biomedical engineering problems [7].

Despite these technical advances, however, the absence of a substantial clinical dataset has restricted machine learning or deep learning research in medicine [1,8,19]. Therefore, developing a powerful strategy that could segregate skin cancer from noncancer and classify skin disease types would be beneficial as an underlying screening instrument. This paper proposed a deep learning model using Microsoft ResNet50 as a transfer learning approach and improved the Snapshot ensemble technique. This model builds up a classification framework by utilizing the publicly available HAM10000 dataset [9], containing clinical pictures of 7 skin cancers- Melanocytic-nevi, Melanoma, Basal cell carcinoma, Actinic keratoses, Vascular lesions, Benign-keratosis-like-lesions and Dermatofibroma.

1.1 Contributions

The following elements describes a list of contributions carried by the proposed work:

1. Proposed an modified snapshot ensemble algorithm to enhance model training efficiency.
2. Implementation of popular CNN architecture (ResNet50) as a transfer learning approach, a pre-trained network.
3. Implementation of data augmentation to deal with the small sample-sized datasets and providing efficient performance.

Moreover, the methodology is explained in Sect. 2. Further, Sect. 3 provides the proposed approach details. Section 4 and Sect. 5 details the experimental results and conclusion, respectively.

2 Methodology

The section provides various methods used for the skin lesion classification using modified snapshot ensemble technique.

2.1 Preprocessing

In the preprocessing stage we remove the unwanted observations from the dataset. This step is useful in deleting duplicate, irrelevant and redundant values from the dataset. Duplicate data arise mostly during data collection. Irrelevant observations are those observations that do not fit the certain problem that we are trying to solve. the following equation is applied on all the images for normalization

$$I = \frac{(N - \mu)}{\sigma} \tag{1}$$

where, N represents a pixel value of the image, μ denotes the average of all related pixels and σ denotes the standard deviation of all related pixels. Further, the dataset used in the proposed method does not contain any unwanted or duplicate, so this step can be ignored. Further, the data augmentation techniques [18] and transfer learning using ResNet50 CNN are applied. Because, the transfer learning via fine-tuning obtained exceptional results in Skin lesion classification [10]. Therefore, for better classification of the skin lesions, the proposed approach uses the deep learning-based CNN architecture ResNet50 in the transfer-learning approach.

2.2 Snapshot Ensemble Technique

In general, neural network ensemble models are significantly robust and accurate compared to individual networks. The 'Snapshot Ensembling' provides ensembling number of neural networks with consistent low error rates with no training cost. By using cyclic LR scheduling, the snapshot ensemble technique has proved its adaptability with different network models [11]. Figure 1, illustrates the Stochastic Gradient Descent (SGD) optimization with conventional learning rate schedule and snapshot ensemble technique.

3 Proposed Algorithm

The proposed modified snapshot ensemble technique relies on the working principle of the combination of deep learning-based CNN architecture ResNet50, using the transfer-learning approach and Snapshot ensemble technique. Figure 2 shows the graphical representation of the proposed approach. The proposed approach uses the data, which is collected from the HAM10000 dataset. Further, the data preprocessing techniques are applied to remove the 'unwanted observations'.

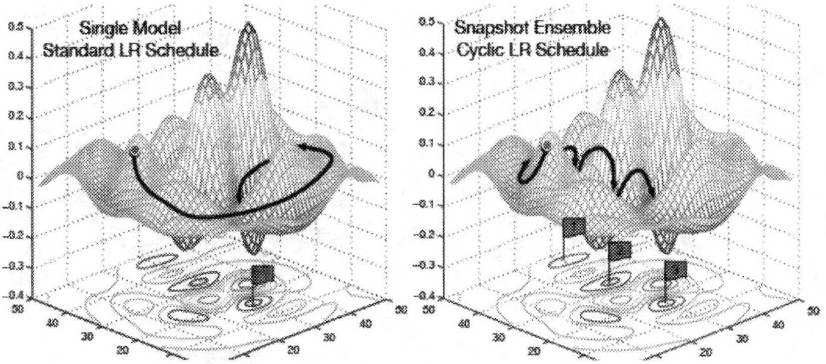

Fig. 1. Visualization of SGD optimization with conventional LR schedule (left), and visualization of Snapshot Ensemble Cyclic LR Schedule (right) [11].

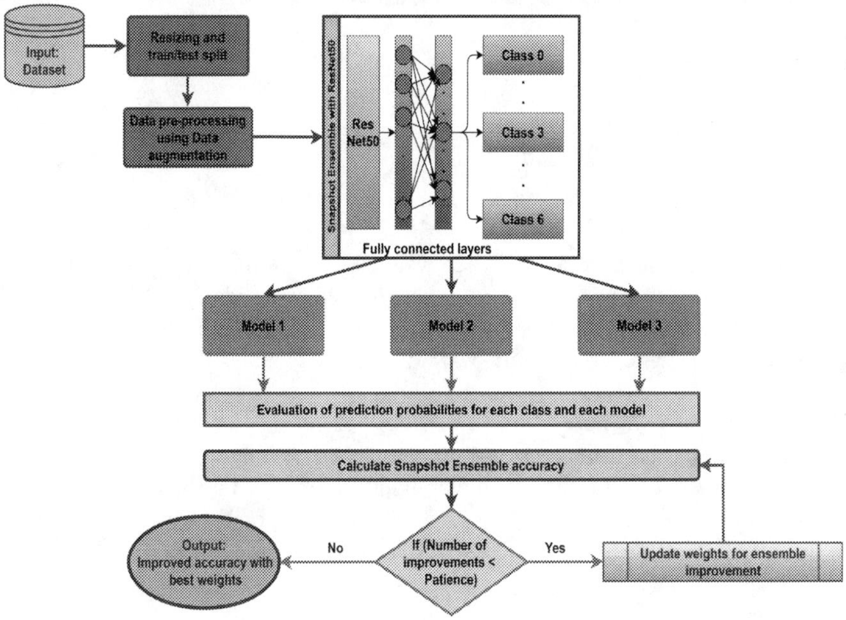

Fig. 2. Graphical representation of the modified snapshot ensemble approach

3.1 Model Creation

Initially, the model uses ResNet50 architecture using the transfer learning technique. The utilized pre-trained model was already trained on the ImageNet data [12]. The proposed approach has chosen ResNet50 [13] pre-trained architecture as a transfer learning approach. Figure 3 displays the proposed model summary.

```
Layer (type)                 Output Shape              Param #
================================================================
resnet50 (Model)             (None, 2048)              23587712
----------------------------------------------------------------
dropout_1 (Dropout)          (None, 2048)              0
----------------------------------------------------------------
dense_1 (Dense)              (None, 128)               262272
----------------------------------------------------------------
dropout_2 (Dropout)          (None, 128)               0
----------------------------------------------------------------
dense_2 (Dense)              (None, 7)                 903
================================================================
Total params: 23,850,887
Trainable params: 9,194,503
Non-trainable params: 14,656,384
```

Fig. 3. Proposed model summary

3.2 Modified Snapshot Ensemble

The existing Snapshot ensemble considers the typical probabilities average of all the models to calculate the accuracy. The accuracy is determined using the recommended approach employing the weighted mean of all the model's probabilities. Furthermore, the random weights initialization was explored to fix the weights for distinct models. After assessing the changes, weights are updated to the best weights. If no betterment was identified, the no. of improvements was increased.

The algorithm continues the process until it reaches the maximum number of improvements. The final accuracy, and updated weights are calculated. Algorithm 1 represents the modified Snapshot ensemble model. Moreover, the performance of the approach is observed by utilizing the popular evaluation metrics including Specificity, Precision, Recall, Accuracy, F1-score, and Jaccard index.

4 Experimental Results

This section provides details of experimental analysis of the proposed approach.

4.1 Dataset Details

The metadata and images used in the proposed work are collected from Harvard Dataverse- HAM10000 dataset, a large collection of multi-source dermatoscopic images of common skin lesions[1]. The data contains 10015 images of seven skin lesion types diagnosed using medical methods, including Melanocytic-nevi,

[1] https://www.kaggle.com/kmader/skin-cancer-mnist-ham10000.

Algorithm 1: Modified Snapshot Ensemble algorithm

```
Input: P= Predict, N= New_weights and E= Ensemble_score
Output: S= Best_score and W= Best_weights
Initialization
Set S = E;
Set W = None;
Set Number_Of_Improvements I = 0;
Set Patience= 5000;
while (I < Patience) do
    Select N randomly;
    Normalize N;
    Evaluate New_score using N and P ;
    if (New_score > S) then
        I = 0;
        S = New_score;
        W = N;
        Print S;
    end
    else
        I= I+1;
    end
end
Print W;
```

Melanoma, Basal cell carcinoma, Actinic keratoses, Vascular lesions, Dermatofibroma, Benign-keratosis-like-lesions. Table 1 provides the details of the utilized dataset.

The obtained data is divided into train set and test set with 80:20 ratio. The training set was further divided into train set and validation set with an 80:20 ratio. Moreover, to avoid data imbalance problem, the proposed approach used the data augmentation technique. Table 2 displays the balanced dataset details.

4.2 Model Training and Testing

The proposed model's training phase contains the combinations of different models. Further, total number of epochs are fixed to 30. Additionally, total $models = 3, epochs\ per\ model = 10$, Maximum learning rate $= 0.001$ and $batch\ size = 10$.

After applying the data augmentation and ResNet50 on the HAM10000 dataset we obtained an overall micro average accuracy of 88% and the micro averages of precision, recall, F1-score, specificity, and Jaccard similarity are found as 88%, 88%, 88%, 98%, and 78%, respectively. In Table 3 the results are visualized.

Table 1. Original dataset

Skin lesion name	Number of samples
Melanocytic-nevi	6705
Melanoma	1113
Benign-keratosis-like-lesions	1099
Basal cell carcinoma	514
Actinic keratoses	327
Vascular lesions	142
Dermatofibroma	115
Total	10015

Table 2. Balanced dataset

Skin lesion name	Number of samples
Melanocytic-nevi	6705
Melanoma	5565
Benign-keratosis-like-lesions	5495
Basal cell carcinoma	5140
Actinic keratoses	4905
Vascular lesions	5680
Dermatofibroma	5750
Total	39240

4.3 Snapshot Ensemble Calculation

An existing snapshot ensemble approach's probability is evaluated by considering the 'average' of all the obtained three probabilities. The ensemble model and ensemble accuracy were then produced by combining the derived class with the highest probability with the projected data. Table 4 visualizes the ensemble accuracy along with three models accuracy. Upon observation, it can find that the ensemble accuracy is less than that of one of the models. It is because of taking an average of all three probabilities. The proposed approach improves the Snapshot ensemble accuracy by taking the 'weighted average' for calculating the best weights.

For selecting the best weights for different models, the weights are initially assigned randomly and checked for improvement; and updated for betterment. The process continues til the no. of improvements reaches its maximum limit. The detailed steps are provided in the Algorithm 1. The improvements to the accuracy after applying the modified snapshot ensemble algorithm are displayed in Table 5.

Table 3. Test accuracy of the existing approach

Skin lesion name	Support	Accuracy	Jaccard Index	Precision	Recall	F1-score	Specificity
Benign-keratosis-like-lesions	199	0.92	0.59	0.62	0.92	0.74	0.94
Melanocytic-nevi	1349	0.88	0.85	0.96	0.88	0.92	0.93
Dermatofibroma	22	0.91	0.67	0.71	0.91	0.80	1
Melanoma	228	0.73	0.63	0.82	0.72	0.77	0.98
Vascular-lesions	33	0.97	0.52	0.53	0.97	0.69	0.99
Basal cell carcinoma	106	0.99	0.89	0.90	0.99	0.94	0.99
Actinic keratoses	66	1	0.94	0.94	1	0.97	1
Average (Micro)/Overall	2003	0.88	0.78	0.88	0.88	0.88	0.98

Table 4. Model wise test accuracy along with Snapshot ensemble accuracy

Model name	Accuracy
Model-1	0.8882
Model-2	0.9051
Model-3	0.9271
Snapshot Ensemble	0.9186

4.4 Comparison and Discussion

Table 6 compares the proposed method with the other approaches using HAM10000 datasets for skin classification. The comparison shown that the proposed method efficiently classified the skin lesion images. The error rate of the model is 0.12. Using the modified snapshot ensemble techniques, the error rate is reduced to 0.0598. The proposed approach uses weighted average of the predicted classes. Using this approach, the error rate can overcome by the model. In the image classification procedure, most of the results depend on the dataset.

Table 5. Modified snapshot ensemble accuracy with final best weights

Improvement/weights	Accuracy/weights
Improvement-1	0.9216
Improvement-2	0.9226
Improvement-3	0.9236
Improvement-4	0.9261
Improvement-5	0.9266
Improvement-6	0.9286
Improvement-7	0.9301
Improvement-8	0.9326
Improvement-9	**0.9402**
Obtained best weights	**0.0480, 0.1456, 0.8064**

In the proposed work, the HAM10000 dataset contains 10,015 images, but most of those images belong to only one single (i.e., Melanocytic Nevi). The dataset has only seven different lesion types, whereas there are many more different types of skin cancer in practice. However, the proposed model shown efficient performance compared to other methods.

Table 6. Comparison of the proposed approach with literature that uses the HAM10000 dataset

Method	Accuracy	Precision	Recall	Specificity	F1-score
Method-1 [14]	91%	92%	87%	92%	89%
Method-2 [15]	83%	81%	81%	84%	81%
Method-3 [4]	84%	84%	79%	84%	81%
Method-4 [8]	86%	85%	84%	86%	85%
Method-5 [16]	83%	80%	78%	86%	79%
Method-6 [17]	87%	86%	85%	86%	86%
Proposed method	**94%**	**95%**	**95%**	**99%**	**87%**

5 Conclusion

The occurrence of skin cancer has increased in recent decades; the need of the hour is to transition to an effective and strong automated skin cancer categorization system capable of providing reliable and timely predictions. The approach demonstrates the effectiveness of deep learning in automated dermoscopic multi-class skin cancer classification by involving the ResNet50 CNN model as a transfer learning approach and modified snapshot ensemble technique. It used the HAM10000 dataset consists of 10,015 dermoscopy images and achieved an overall accuracy of 94% for seven classes in the HAM10000 dataset.

References

1. Hasan, M.K., et al.: A survey, review, and future trends of skin lesion segmentation and classification. Comput. Biol. Med. 106624 (2023)
2. World Health Organization: Who report on cancer: setting priorities, investing wisely and providing care for all (2020)
3. Centers for Disease Control and Prevention: Skin cancer prevention progress report (2019)
4. Bakkouri, I., Afdel, K.: Computer-aided diagnosis (CAD) system based on multilayer feature fusion network for skin lesion recognition in dermoscopy images. Multimedia Tools Appl. 1–36 (2019)
5. Ferris, L.K., et al.: Computer-aided classification of melanocytic lesions using dermoscopic images. J. Am. Acad. Dermatol. **73**(5), 769–776 (2015)

6. Stoecker, W.V., et al.: Detection of granularity in dermoscopy images of malignant melanoma using color and texture features. Comput. Med. Imaging Graph. **35**(2), 144–147 (2011)
7. Abbas, Q., Celebi, M.E.: Dermodeep-a classification of melanoma-nevus skin lesions using multi-feature fusion of visual features and deep neural network. Multimedia Tools Appl. **78**(16), 23559–23580 (2019)
8. Han, S.S., Kim, M.S., Lim, W., Park, G.H., Park, I., Chang, S.E.: Classification of the clinical images for benign and malignant cutaneous tumors using a deep learning algorithm. J. Investig. Dermatol. **138**(7), 1529–1538 (2018)
9. Tschandl, P.: The HAM10000 dataset, a large collection of multi source dermatoscopic images of common pigmented skin lesions (2018). https://doi.org/10.7910/DVN/DBW86T
10. Hosny, K.M., Kassem, M.A., Fouad, M.M.: Classification of skin lesions into seven classes using transfer learning with alexnet. J. Digit. Imaging 1–10 (2020)
11. Huang, G., Li, Y., Pleiss, G., Liu, Z., Hopcroft, J.E., Weinberger, K.Q.: Snapshot ensembles: train 1, get m for free. arXiv preprint arXiv:1704.00109 (2017)
12. Russakovsky, O., et al.: Imagenet large scale visual recognition challenge. Int. J. Comput. Vision **115**(3), 211–252 (2015)
13. He, K., Zhang, X., Ren, S., Sun, J.: Deep residual learning for image recognition. In: Proceedings of the IEEE Conference on Computer Vision and Pattern Recognition, pp. 770–778 (2016)
14. Esteva, A., et al.: Dermatologist-level classification of skin cancer with deep neural networks. Nature **542**(7639), 115–118 (2017)
15. Dorj, U.O., Lee, K.K., Choi, J.Y., Lee, M.: The skin cancer classification using deep convolutional neural network. Multimedia Tools Appl. **77**(8), 9909–9924 (2018)
16. Li, Y., Shen, L.: Skin lesion analysis towards melanoma detection using deep learning network. Sensors **18**(2), 556 (2018)
17. Yu, C., et al.: Acral melanoma detection using a convolutional neural network for dermoscopy images. PLoS ONE **13**(3), e0193321 (2018)
18. Shorten, C., Khoshgoftaar, T.M.: A survey on image data augmentation for deep learning. J. Big Data **6**(1), 1–48 (2019)
19. Alenezi, F., Armghan, A., Polat, K.: Wavelet transform based deep residual neural network and ReLU based extreme learning machine for skin lesion classification. Expert Syst. Appl. **213**, 119064 (2023)

A Residual Learning Approach Towards the Diagnosis of Colorectal Disease Effectively

T. P. Raseena(✉), Jitendra Kumar, and S. R. Balasundaram

Department of Computer Applications, National Institute of Technology, Tiruchirappalli, India
rasi.tp@gmail.com, {jitendra,blsundar}@nitt.edu

Abstract. Colorectal cancer (CRC) is a significant global health concern with substantial morbidity and mortality rates. Early identification and proper diagnosis significantly impact the prognosis of patients with CRC. This study presents an efficient residual learning model using ResNet50 as the underlying architecture with a comprehensive analysis focused on developing a robust computer-aided diagnostic (CAD) system for CRC detection and classification using colonoscopy images. This approach involves extensive preprocessing, data augmentation and hyperparameters tuning techniques to enhance the model's ability to detect subtle abnormalities and overcome potential data deficiency. Furthermore, dropout layers and regularization techniques are introduced to address overfitting issues, improving the model's generalization performance. The study uses four different benchmark datasets: PolypsSet, CP-CHILD-A, CP-CHILD-B, and Kvasir v2. These datasets contain diverse colonoscopy images, including polyps, non-polyps, adenomas, and hyperplastic lesions. The model exhibits remarkable Accuracy, Precision, Recall, and F1-score, effectively on all four datasets. The Recall of the proposed model across all datasets surpassed 87%, which outperformed three benchmark results out of four, validating its ability to effectively classify colorectal polyps. Consequently, this study advances the field of medical image analysis and opens the door to early detection and individualised treatment plans for patients with CRC.

Keywords: Colorectal cancer · Medical images · Residual learning · ResNet50 · Computer aided diagnosis system

1 Introduction

CRC is a prevalent and deadly form of cancer and one of the leading causes of cancer-related deaths worldwide. CRC is a malignant tumour that affects the colon or rectum; both are vital components of the digestive system. The disease typically originates from the development of abnormal growths called polyps, which can gradually become cancerous if left untreated [19]. According

KC Santosh et al. (Eds.): RTIP2R 2023, CCIS 2027, pp. 160–172, 2024.
https://doi.org/10.1007/978-3-031-53085-2_14

to the World Health Organization (WHO), CRC is the third most common cancer worldwide, accounting for a significant number of cancer-related deaths. It affects men and women and occurs in all racial and ethnic groups [1]. The risk of developing colorectal cancer increases with age, with the majority of cases occurring in individuals over 50 years old [17]. However, there has been a concerning rise in cases among younger adults in recent years. Detecting colorectal cancer at an early stage and accurately classifying it is vital for effective treatment and improved patient outcomes. Screening plays a crucial role in detecting colorectal cancer at an early stage when it is more treatable [11]. Common screening methods include colonoscopy, faecal occult blood test (FOBT), and sigmoidoscopy. The primary screening test is colonoscopy, a medical procedure used to examine the inner lining of the large intestine or colon and rectum [2]. It is considered the gold standard for diagnosing and screening for colorectal conditions, including colorectal cancer. During a colonoscopy, the colonoscope, which has a light and a small camera at the end, is gently inserted into the rectum and guided through the colon. The camera transmits real-time images to a monitor, allowing the doctor to visualize the colon's lining and identify any abnormalities, such as polyps or lesions. These polyps can be removed using specialized instruments. This minimizes the risk of these polyps developing into cancer over time. If any suspicious areas are found, the doctor may perform a biopsy, where a small tissue sample is collected for further analysis [22,24]. Traditional methods for diagnosing colorectal cancer are time-consuming, subjective and dependent on the expertise of the physician. This subjectivity can introduce inter-observer variability and lead to a false negative diagnosis [25]. False negatives can result in missed or delayed diagnoses. Early detection significantly increases the chances of successful treatment and improved survival rates.

CRC is a significant global health concern, necessitating effective and efficient diagnostic tools. To address these limitations, there has been a growing interest in utilizing advanced technologies in machine learning and image analysis techniques, particularly deep learning, to classify and detect CRC. Deep learning models have emerged as promising alternatives, leveraging the power of artificial intelligence to automate the diagnosis process and improve diagnostic accuracy [23]. ResNet has become one of the most prominent Convolutional Neural Network (CNN) architectures in recent years, especially for image recognition tasks. Due to its distinctive residual connections and skip connections, the vanishing gradient problem is mitigated during the training of very deep neural networks. ResNet is capable of intricate and informative features from complex medical images by effectively handling hundreds of layers [4].

This study aims to harness the power of ResNet to classify colorectal images efficiently. ResNet's ability to handle the intricacies present in colorectal images renders it a valuable choice. The objective is to develop a robust and accurate detection and classification system that can efficiently differentiate between different classes of colorectal lesions, including polyps, non-polyps, adenomas, and hyperplastic lesions, from colonoscopy images.

2 Related Work

Deep learning, a branch of artificial intelligence, has shown promising results in medical imaging, particularly in classifying medical images. This section presents a comprehensive review of the recent advancements in the classification of colorectal cancer using deep learning models. We discuss the methodologies, datasets, and performance metrics utilized in these studies, highlighting the advancements in this domain.

Recently, Feng et al. [3] developed an accurate system of a modified U-shaped CNN model with a Visual Geometry Group (VGG) to segment and classify various pathological regions within colonoscopy images. There are two main parts to the suggested methodology: segmentation and classification. The classification component employs a deep learning model using a public dataset to classify the segmented regions into specific pathology categories, such as adenomas, hyperplastic polyps, or malignancies. Xinyu Liu et al. [9] introduced a source-free domain adaptation approach with the pre-trained ResNet101 and CNN model to diagnose the polyps, which does not rely on any labelled data from the target domain during the training process. Instead, it leverages unlabeled data from the target domain and labelled data from multiple source domains to learn a domain-invariant representation. This representation captures the common features of polyps across different domains while suppressing domain-specific variations. Shaban et al. [16] presented a context-aware approach within a two-stacked CNN architecture for effectively grading CRC histology images to diagnose colorectal diseases. Jiang et al. [6] introduced a method using ResNet basic architecture to showcase the effectiveness of the proposed approach in accurately identifying tissue types and predicting gene mutations from histopathology images using TCGA-COAD, a public database of CRC. Zhanh et al. [25] conducted a study to classify colorectal polyps into adenoma and hyperplastic using the transfer learning ability of deep CNN by transferring the features learned from a non-medical to a medical domain, which is evaluated on two public datasets. A novel approach for real-time polyp diagnosis in endoscopic videos using EMSEN using deep learning with CSPNet as the main component is proposed by wang et al. [20].

Ren et al. [15] put forward a model CAD-CTC that integrates shape index analysis, multiscale enhancement filters, and radiomic features with a random forest classifier. CAD-CTC is a computer-aided detection scheme using computed tomographic colonography that aims to improve the performance of colorectal polyp detection. Recently, Islam et al. [5] suggested an approach utilising ResNeXt architecture to build a Siamese classification model to analyze pre-treatment and mid-treatment computed tomography (CT) images of colorectal cancer liver metastases. The classifier is trained to extract relevant features from the images and classify them into different response categories, such as complete response, partial response, stable disease, or progressive disease.

In a study by Talukder et al. [18], a hybrid approach consisting of two stages of deep feature extraction and ensemble learning is suggested. In the first stage, a few transfer learning models, such as VGG, MobileNet and DenseNet, are employed to extract high-level features from colon images to indicate the presence of cancer. In the second stage, ensemble learning techniques, such as random forests or gradient boosting, are applied to combine the predictions from multiple individual models and improve the overall classification performance. Yang et al. [23] suggested a predictive deep learning model incorporating fuzzy logic, RNNs, and CoxPH techniques for accurately predicting the mortality risk in patients with rectal cancer using a public dataset. Paing et al. [12] proposed a method previously that FFC-ResNet utilizes a combination of fast Fourier transform (FFT) and ResNet-50 to extract informative features from the polyp images and perform dysplasia grading. The fast Fourier transform is applied to the polyp images to convert them into the frequency domain, capturing spatial and frequency information. FFC-ResNet is evaluated on the benchmark dataset UniToPatho.

This comprehensive review provides an in-depth analysis of the current research landscape in classifying colorectal cancer using deep learning models. The studies discussed in this review explain the potential of deep learning in achieving accurate and automated classification of colorectal cancer. However, challenges such as interpretability, generalizability, and dataset problems need to be addressed to facilitate the clinical translation of these models. Further research is warranted to refine and validate these models in large-scale clinical settings to improve the diagnosis of colorectal cancer.

3 Methods

3.1 Overview

Deep CNN has made so many breakthroughs in computer vision tasks, mainly for image classification. Deep networks have the ability to integrate inner-level features of the data by processing it through multiple layers [10]. However, the approach of stacking more layers will be impeded by the vanishing gradients during training, making it difficult for networks with many layers to converge from the beginning of training; hence, the performance degrades. ResNet has emerged as a breakthrough solution for training deep neural networks by addressing the vanishing gradient problem associated with very deep architectures [4]. In colorectal image classification, augmentation techniques are particularly valuable due to the limited availability of annotated data and the need to account for different imaging conditions, variations in polyp appearance, and diverse patient cases. By applying augmentation techniques, it is possible to artificially expand the dataset and introduce variations that mimic real-world scenarios, making the model more adaptable to different conditions it may encounter during inference. An efficient model is presented in this study utilizing ResNet50 as the underlying architecture and dropout layers and regularization techniques to overcome overfitting problems. The schematic workflow of the study is visually depicted in Fig. 1.

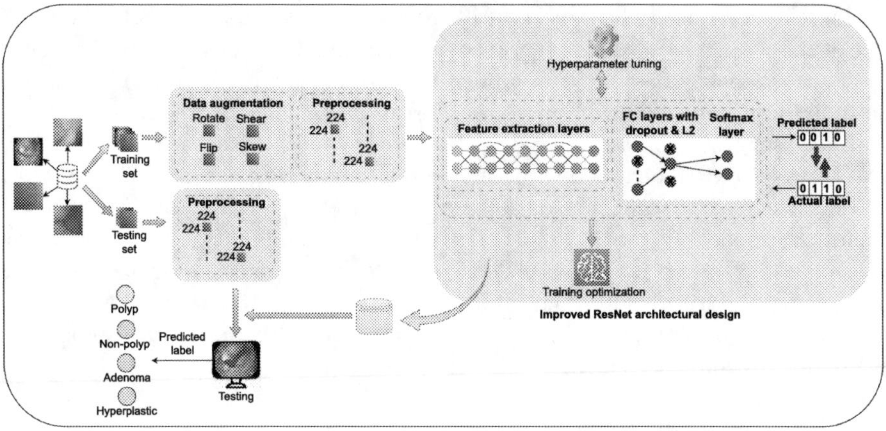

Fig. 1. Workflow of the proposed method

3.2 Preprocessing

Image preprocessing is paramount in achieving accurate and efficient polyp classification in medical images. The quality and size of the training data heavily influence the performance of a deep learning model. Yet, a common challenge in deep learning is needing more data. Optimal model performance is often achieved with a large and diverse dataset. Data augmentation addresses this problem by generating new data samples by applying various mathematical operations to existing ones. This approach effectively expands the dataset and enhances the model's generalisation ability and performance. Generating augmented images involves a combination of rotation, random flipping, shearing, and skew operations, which is defined in Eq. (1),

$$F = T \rightarrow A \tag{1}$$

Let F be the transformation function responsible for performing data augmentation. T represents the training set of the original dataset, and A denotes the augmented set obtained by applying the transformation function F to the samples in T. The augmented training set is given in Eq. (2),

$$T' = T \cup A \tag{2}$$

Here, T' represents the complete training set, encompassing the original and augmented samples. These transformations collectively create diverse variations of the original images, enriching the dataset for improved model training and generalization. The CP-CHILD-B and Kvasir V2 datasets are subjected to data augmentation.

Before feeding the images into deep learning models, it is vital to undergo preprocessing to improve their quality, standardize their format, and optimize model performance. The datasets comprise images of diverse sizes, necessitating preprocessing to standardize them into the appropriate input format for the ResNet model to achieve optimal results. Each image in the dataset is resized to 224×224 pixels before being fed into the proposed model during training. Following the image resizing, the next step involves normalization, which scales the pixel values to a consistent range between 0 and 1. This rescaling guarantees that the images possess comparable intensity distributions, facilitating faster model convergence during training and mitigating numerical instability concerns. Finally, the four datasets are divided into an 80:20 ratio for the training and testing sets.

3.3 Proposed Methodology

Resnet is a deep residual learning framework which alleviates the vanishing gradient problem of training very deep neural networks more effectively by introducing residual connections between layers with increased depth.

Residual Learning. Residual learning is a technique used in deep neural networks to improve accuracy by allowing layers to learn residual functions instead of trying to directly approximate the underlying mapping. Instead of learning the underlying mapping of the input data $H(x)$ directly by the stacked layers, ResNet allows these layers to learn a residual mapping by a different mapping $F(X) = H(x) - x$. the initial mapping $H(x)$ is then reformulated to $F(x) + x$. It is assumed that optimising the residual mapping $F(x)$ is easier than directly optimising the initial mapping $H(x)$. Instead of training the network to learn identity mapping through a stack of nonlinear layers, it is easier to make the residual mapping close to zero if identity mapping is the optimum solution. To implement the formulation of $F(x)+x$, ResNet introduces using feedforward neural networks with shortcut connections. Shortcut connections are connections that skip intermediate layers in the network. Here, the shortcut connections perform an identity mapping, i.e., they pass the input directly to their output. The output of the shortcut connections is added to the output of the stacked layers. Significantly, the identity shortcut connections do not add any extra number of parameters or the network's complexity to the network.

Identity Mapping. The ResNet architecture incorporates residual learning in each couple of stacked layers of the network, which is defined in Eq. (3),

$$y = F(x, W_i) + x \tag{3}$$

where x is the input to the residual block, $F(x, W_i)$ is the residual mapping that needs to be learned, and y is the output. The function F is defined as in Eq. (4),

$$F = W_2 \sigma(W_1 x) \tag{4}$$

where W_1 and W_2 are weight matrices, σ denotes the ReLU activation function, and biases are ignored for the transparency. The operation of residual mapping

$F(x) + x$ is performed as mentioned in Eq. (1) using a shortcut connection, and the output of this connection is added element-wise to the output of the stacked layers. Adding the output of the residual mapping F with the input x, using a shortcut connection and element-wise addition, followed by a nonlinearity. The output of the residual mapping F must have the same dimensions as the input vector x. If not, a linear projection will be performed using the matrix W_s, which helps to match the dimensions of x and F, and the modified equation is given in Eq. (5),

$$y = F(x, W_i) + W_s x \tag{5}$$

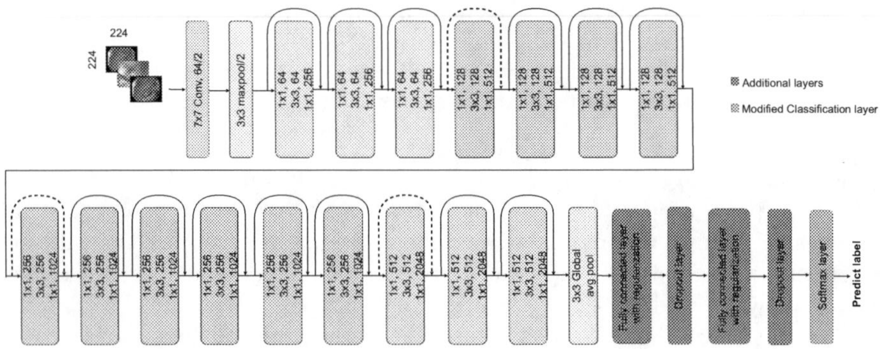

Fig. 2. Architecture of the proposed model.

3.4 Proposed Method Architecture

The architecture proposed in this study comprises a collection of stacked residual blocks. Each block comprises several convolutional layers, followed by batch normalization and ReLU activation. Also, dropout layers are included within the hidden layers at the end, leading to the classification layer (See Fig. 2). The inclusion of skip connections in the proposed method enables the direct flow of gradients by adding the original input to the output of each residual block. This allows the network to learn residual mappings, capturing the difference between the Predicted label and the original label of the colonoscopy image, making it easier to optimize the underlying mapping. The core building blocks of the proposed model are identity blocks, convolutional blocks, and dropout blocks, which make the model capture intricate features, down-sampling the data, and solving overfitting problems. The incorporation of residual connections facilitates the flow of gradients and enables the network to learn residual mappings effectively.

Identity blocks are employed when the spatial dimensions of the feature maps remain unchanged within a block. They consist of three convolutional layers with the same input and output dimensions. Convolutional blocks, on the other hand, are utilized when downsampling is required to reduce the spatial dimensions. They include convolutional layers with a stride of 2, resulting in decreased spatial dimensions and increased channel depth. Transition layers, which involve a 1×1 convolution followed by downsampling operations, are used to match the dimensions between different blocks. These transitions facilitate a smooth transition of information flow between the different block types. The standard ResNet50 model exhibited overfitting issues when applied to the four distinct benchmark datasets. To address this problem, two additional hidden layers were introduced, along with dropout layers with a rate of 0.5. Furthermore, Regularization techniques were incorporated into the hidden layers, utilizing an $l2$ value of 0.001 after the global average pooling layer. This combination of layers and hyperparameter tuning effectively mitigated the overfitting problem, yielding notable improvements.

The proposed architecture concludes with a modified classification layer, which aggregates the spatial information of the feature maps into a fixed-length feature vector after flattening. A softmax activation function is applied to this vector by the classification layer for classification tasks. The proposed architecture utilizes the bottleneck structures of the ResNet50 to reduce computational complexity while maintaining model capacity.

4 Experimental Results and Analysis

4.1 Dataset

Four benchmark datasets consisting of colonoscopy images were employed. These datasets include PolypsSet, CP-CHILD-A, CP-CHILD-B, and Kvasir. Sample images from these datasets are illustrated in Fig. 3.

PolypsSet. The PolypsSet dataset used in this study comprises 16741 hyperplastic and 19240 adenomatous images sourced from multiple datasets, including the KUMC dataset, the CVC-colon DB dataset, the GLRC dataset, and the MICCAI 2017 dataset. All images within this dataset are extracted from diverse frames of colonoscopy videos [7].

CP-CHILD-A and CP-CHILD-B. These datasets consist of images obtained from 1600 colonoscopies conducted on children aged between 0 and 18 years [21]. The CP-CHILD-A dataset comprises 8000 colonoscopy images, including 7000 non-polyp images and 1000 polyp images. On the other hand, the CP-CHILD-B dataset consists of 1500 colonoscopy images, with 1100 non-polyp images and 400 polyp images.

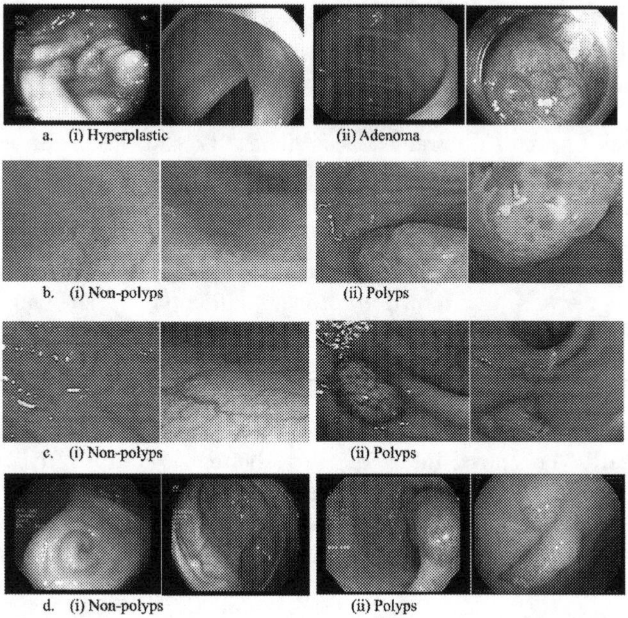

Fig. 3. Different examples of the images in the datasets. (a) is the example of hyperplastic and adenoma from PolypsSet, (b) is the example of non-polyps and polyps from CP-CHILD-A, (c) is the example of non-polyps and polyps from CP-CHILD-B, and (d) is the example of non-polyps and polyps from Kvasir V2.

Kvasir V2. The Kvasir V2 dataset is derived from the Kvasir dataset version 2. Originally, the Kvasir dataset comprises eight classes of endoscopically acquired colour images of the gastrointestinal (GI) tract, meticulously annotated and confirmed by medical professionals [14]. However, for the purpose of this study, only two classes are relevant, namely, polyps and non-polyps (normal cecum), specifically associated with colorectal disease. The other classes within the dataset are unrelated to the objectives of this study. The dataset contains 2000 images of polyps and non-polyps, with an equal distribution of 1000 images in each class.

4.2 Comparison with the Benchmark Results

This section reports the experimental results obtained from evaluating the proposed model on the benchmark datasets. The proposed model's performance evaluation involved assessing the model using key metric Recall, along with additional metrics such as Accuracy, Precision and F1 score. In this study, recall is regarded as the most valuable parameter. This metric is critical because it accounts for false negative classifications, ensuring that individuals with suspected CRC are not misclassified as non-polyp or hyperplastic instances, which indicate regular colon conditions, since lowering the false negative rate is critical. The experiments were conducted on a high-performance computing platform with a specified hardware configuration. Through a series of experiments conducted using four different benchmark datasets, PolypsSet, CP-CHILD-A, CP-CHILD-B and Kvasir V2, the proposed model demonstrated its capability to accurately classify colorectal polyps into different categories, including polyp versus non-polyp and adenoma versus hyperplastic. Table 1 provides a comprehensive summary of the performance metrics achieved by the proposed model on the benchmark datasets. The proposed model achieved Accuracy, Recall, Precision, and F1-score values on the PolypsSet, 79.80%, 73.78%, 87.78% and 80.18%, on the CP-CHILD-A, 97.20%, 91.34%, 95.00% and 93.13%, on the CP-CHILD-B, 98.75%, 96.11%, 99.00% and 97.53% and the Kvasir V2, 95.00%, 92.45%, 98.00% and 95.14% respectively. These results indicate the model's high accuracy and reliability across different datasets. Additionally, this study compared the residual model's performance with existing state-of-the-art approaches on the same benchmark datasets showcased in Table 2. Patel et al. [13] used a basic VGG19 model to train the PolypsSet dataset to classify images into hyperplastic and adenoma classifications. The Accuracy of their study reached 79.78%, the Recall rate reached 78.64%, the Precision reached 78.71%, and the F1-score reached 78.67%. Considering the authors only reported individual Recall, Precision, and F1-score values for each class in their research, these Recall, Precision, and F1-score metrics were manually computed based on the provided true positive, true negative, false positive, and false negative values. Another study by Wei Wang et al. [21] presented a ResNet152-GAP model based on the ResNet architecture, including Global Average Pooling (GAP). This model was tested on two separate datasets, CP-CHILD-A and CP-CHILD-B. ResNet152-GAP exhibited an accuracy of 99.29% and a Recall of 97.55% on CP-CHILD-A, and an Accuracy of 99.35% and a Recall of 97.70% on CP-CHILD-B. However, the authors did not include metrics for ResNet152-GAP, such as Precision and F1-score. Liew et al. [8] proposed a modified ResNet50 model combined with PCA, AdaBoost, and various preprocessing techniques. They evaluated the model on the Kvasir V2 dataset, achieving an Accuracy of 97.91%, Recall of 96.45%, and Precision of 99.35%. Although the authors did not provide the F1-score explicitly, it was estimated as the mean Precision and Recall value, yielding an F1-score of 97.90%. The proposed model's Recall across all datasets exceeded 87%, outperforming all benchmark results except CP-CHILD-A, demonstrating its potency in accurately classifying colorectal polyps. The results clearly indicate that the proposed model outperforms Recall of these existing methods, achieving higher accuracy and superior classification performance.

Table 1. Classification report of the proposed Residual model on four different datasets.

Dataset	Accuracy (%)	Precision (%)	Recall (%)	F1-score (%)
PolypsSet	79.80	73.78	87.78	80.18
CP-CHILD-A	97.20	91.34	95.00	93.13
CP-CHILD-B	98.75	96.11	99.00	97.53
Kvasir V2	95.00	92.45	98.00	95.14

Table 2. Comparison of the proposed Residual model with the existing state-of-the-art methods on four different datasets.

Dataset	Method	Underlying architecture	Accuracy (%)	Precision (%)	Recall (%)	F1-score (%)
PolypsSet	Residual model	ResNet50	**79.80**	73.78	**87.78**	80.18
	Patel et al. [13]	VGG-19	79.78	83.35	83.70	83.52
CP-CHILD-A	Residual model	ResNet50	97.20	**91.34**	95.00	**93.13**
	Wei Wang et al. [21]	ResNet152-GAP	99.29	-	**97.55**	-
CP-CHILD-B	Residual model	ResNet50	98.75	**96.11**	**99.00**	**97.53**
	Wei Wang et al. [21]	ResNet152-GAP	99.35	-	97.70	-
Kvasir V2	Residual model	ResNet50	95.00	92.45	**98.00**	95.14
	Liew et al. [8]	Modified ResNet-50 with AdaBoost	97.91	99.35	96.45	97.87

5 Conclusion

This study introduced an enhanced residual model based on ResNet50, incorporating dropout and regularization techniques to mitigate overfitting. Furthermore, extensive experimental analyses and ablation studies are conducted to investigate the impact of various parameters and techniques on the model's performance. The proposed method has achieved remarkable results across various datasets in high-performance computing. The experimental findings validate the model's efficacy in accurately classifying colorectal polyp images across various classes, including polyp versus non-polyp and adenoma versus hyperplastic, using benchmark datasets such as PolypsSet, CP-CHILDA, CP-CHILDB, and Kvasir V2. The proposed residual model demonstrates outstanding performance in CRC detection and classification, achieving high Accuracy of 79.80%, 97.20%, 98.75% and 95.00%, the Precision of 73.78%, 91.34%, 96.11%, 92.45%, the Recall of 87.78%, 95.00%, 99.00%, 98.00%, and the F1-score of 80.18%, 93.13%, 97.53%, 95.14% on PolypsSet, C-CHILD-A, CP-CHILD-B and Kvasir V2 respectively. The promising outcomes of this study showcase the robustness and reliability of the proposed deep learning framework for CRC detection, and further advancements and investigations in the proposed model will contribute to the accurate real-time diagnosis of colorectal polyps by endoscopists.

Acknowledgment. This study was funded by the University Grants Commission (UGC) of India under UGC-JRF grant 3640/(NET-JULY2018), and C-DAC and the National Institute of Technology (NIT) Tiruchirapalli, India provided the computing resources.

References

1. The International Agency for Research on Cancer: Cancer today. https://gco.iarc.fr/. Accessed 15 Nov 2022
2. Fang, Y., Zhu, D., Yao, J., Yuan, Y., Tong, K.Y.: ABC-Net: area-boundary constraint network with dynamical feature selection for colorectal polyp segmentation. IEEE Sens. J. **21**(10), 11799–11809 (2020)
3. Feng, R., Liu, X., Chen, J., Chen, D.Z., Gao, H., Wu, J.: A deep learning approach for colonoscopy pathology WSI analysis: accurate segmentation and classification. IEEE J. Biomed. Health Inform. **25**(10), 3700–3708 (2020)
4. He, K., Zhang, X., Ren, S., Sun, J.: Deep residual learning for image recognition. In: Proceedings of the IEEE Conference on Computer Vision and Pattern Recognition, pp. 770–778 (2016)
5. Islam, M.M., et al.: Deep treatment response assessment and prediction of colorectal cancer liver metastases. In: Wang, L., Dou, Q., Fletcher, P.T., Speidel, S., Li, S. (eds.) MICCAI 2022. LNCS, vol. 13433, pp. 482–491. Springer, Cham (2022). https://doi.org/10.1007/978-3-031-16437-8_46
6. Jiang, Y., et al.: Identification of tissue types and gene mutations from histopathology images for advancing colorectal cancer biology. IEEE Open J. Eng. Med. Biol. **3**, 115–123 (2022)
7. Li, K., et al.: Colonoscopy polyp detection and classification: dataset creation and comparative evaluations. PLoS ONE **16**(8), e0255809 (2021)
8. Liew, W.S., Tang, T.B., Lin, C.H., Lu, C.K.: Automatic colonic polyp detection using integration of modified deep residual convolutional neural network and ensemble learning approaches. Comput. Methods Programs Biomed. **206**, 106114 (2021)
9. Liu, X., Yuan, Y.: A source-free domain adaptive polyp detection framework with style diversification flow. IEEE Trans. Med. Imaging **41**(7), 1897–1908 (2022)
10. Matthew Zeiler, D., Rob, F.: Visualizing and understanding convolutional neural networks. In: ECCV (2014)
11. Pacal, I., Karaboga, D., Basturk, A., Akay, B., Nalbantoglu, U.: A comprehensive review of deep learning in colon cancer. Comput. Biol. Med. **126**, 104003 (2020)
12. Paing, M.P., Pintavirooj, C.: Adenoma dysplasia grading of colorectal polyps using fast fourier convolutional ResNet (FFC-ResNet). IEEE Access **11**, 16644–16656 (2023)
13. Patel, K., et al.: A comparative study on polyp classification using convolutional neural networks. PLoS ONE **15**(7), e0236452 (2020)
14. Pogorelov, K., et al.: KVASIR: a multi-class image dataset for computer aided gastrointestinal disease detection. In: Proceedings of the 8th ACM on Multimedia Systems Conference, pp. 164–169 (2017)
15. Ren, Y., Ma, J., Xiong, J., Lu, L., Zhao, J.: High-performance CAD-CTC scheme using shape index, multiscale enhancement filters, and radiomic features. IEEE Trans. Biomed. Eng. **64**(8), 1924–1934 (2016)
16. Shaban, M., et al.: Context-aware convolutional neural network for grading of colorectal cancer histology images. IEEE Trans. Med. Imaging **39**(7), 2395–2405 (2020)
17. American Cancer Society: American cancer society guideline for colorectal cancer screening. https://www.cancer.org/cancer/colon-rectal-cancer/detection-diagnosis-staging/acs-recommendations.html. Accessed 15 Nov 2022

18. Talukder, M.A., Islam, M.M., Uddin, M.A., Akhter, A., Hasan, K.F., Moni, M.A.: Machine learning-based lung and colon cancer detection using deep feature extraction and ensemble learning. Expert Syst. Appl. **205**, 117695 (2022)
19. Tan, J., et al.: 3D-GLCM CNN: a 3-dimensional gray-level co-occurrence matrix-based CNN model for polyp classification via CT colonography. IEEE Trans. Med. Imaging **39**(6), 2013–2024 (2019)
20. Wang, D., Wang, X., Wang, S., Yin, Y.: Explainable multitask shapley explanation networks for real-time polyp diagnosis in videos. IEEE Trans. Industr. Inform. (2022)
21. Wang, W., Tian, J., Zhang, C., Luo, Y., Wang, X., Li, J.: An improved deep learning approach and its applications on colonic polyp images detection. BMC Med. Imaging **20**, 1–14 (2020)
22. Xie, X., Xing, J., Kong, N., Li, C., Li, J., Zhang, S.: Improving colorectal polyp classification based on physical examination data-an ensemble learning approach. IEEE Robot. Autom. Lett. **3**(1), 434–441 (2017)
23. Yang, C.H., Chen, W.C., Chen, J.B., Huang, H.C., Chuang, L.Y.: Overall mortality risk analysis for rectal cancer using deep learning-based fuzzy systems. Comput. Biol. Med. **157**, 106706 (2023)
24. Younas, F., Usman, M., Yan, W.Q.: A deep ensemble learning method for colorectal polyp classification with optimized network parameters. Appl. Intell. 1–24 (2022)
25. Zhang, R., et al.: Automatic detection and classification of colorectal polyps by transferring low-level CNN features from nonmedical domain. IEEE J. Biomed. Health Inform. **21**(1), 41–47 (2016)

Realistic Skin Image Data Generation Leveraging Conditional GAN and Classification Using Deep CNN

Jinaga Tulasiram, Balaji Banothu(✉), and S. Nickolas

Department of Computer Applications, NIT Trichy, Tiruchirappalli, Tamilnadu, India
{405120007,balaji,nickolas}@nitt.edu

Abstract. The recent surge in monkeypox (mpox) cases across various nations has escalated into a significant public health challenge, underscoring the imperative for timely detection and diagnosis. In light of this, our research focused on identifying the most efficient deep learning model tailored for mpox detection. Clinically, the progression of monkeypox is characterized by four distinct stages: macular, papular, vesicular, and pustular. In this study, we explore the viability of leveraging a Deep Convolutional Generative Adversarial Network (DCGAN) in conjunction with a conditional vector to strengthen the diagnostic precision of monkeypox. By utilising the remarkable capabilities of GANs, we generate synthetic images mirroring monkeypox skin lesions, thereby amplifying our limited dataset. This approach of utilizing a conditional DCGAN, when paired with stage-specific conditions, results in a significant boost in classification accuracy, elevating it from 0.7532 to 0.8734, complemented by precision 0.91, recall 0.878 F1-score 0.8936. These promising results underscore the advantages of deploying GANs for data augmentation in biomedical image classification tasks, when compared with well known classification models. These models assures the potential of deep learning-assisted diagnostics in dermatology. Especially in therapeutic contexts, where real data may be sparse, the addition of synthetic images can act as a valuable resource, paving the way for enhanced diagnostic instruments.

Keywords: DCGAN · Monkeypox Virus · Deep CNN

1 Introduction

The monkeypox virus (MPXV), a member of the genus orthopoxvirus, is responsible for this contagious disease. The virus was first detected in monkeys in 1959 at a Danish research institute, earning the name Monkeypox virus. A toddler in the Republic of the Congo in 1970 became the first proven human case after displaying smallpox-like symptoms. Close contact with infected people or

Supported by NIT Trichy.

KC Santosh et al. (Eds.): RTIP2R 2023, CCIS 2027, pp. 173–185, 2024.
https://doi.org/10.1007/978-3-031-53085-2_15

infected materials is how the virus is transmitted to humans. Originally confined to Africa, it has now spread to over 50 other nations, where it has caused 3,413 confirmed cases and one fatality.

Both a Central African clade and a West African clade of monkeypox virus have been identified so far. However, monkeypox has no specific cure, thus the creation of a vaccine is still the best option. Both the polymerase chain reaction (PCR) and an electron microscopy skin lesion test are commonly used to identify Monkeypox. The polymerase chain reaction (PCR) is a trusted approach for confirming COVID-19 infections.

In recent years, AI-based approaches have demonstrated promise in viral identification through analysis of medical images. Using deep learning techniques, AI models have been developed for detecting diseases caused by viruses like COVID-19. To improve the accuracy of disease diagnosis from medical pictures, transfer learning has been widely used with pre-trained models such as ResNet-50 and VGG-19. In this work, the paper is organized as follows: Sect. 2 provides a comprehensive literature survey; Sect. 3 introduces our proposed methodology; Sect. 4 discusses the results derived from our experiments; and Sect. 5 concludes the paper, highlighting the implications and suggesting potential future directions for our study.

2 Literature Survey

Although there has been work on virus detection using deep learning, there has been relatively little investigation into the identification of the monkeypox virus. Previous work by Ahsan et al. [17] employing a transfer learning strategy and the VGG-16 model for monkeypox detection showed promising results. However, their method could only be used for binary classification and not very efficient or easy to understand.

The progression of monkeypox is complex and can be broken down into distinct phases [10]. Following an incubation period of 3–17 days during which the patient shows no symptoms, the prodromal stage of the disease begins. Fever, chills, lymphadenopathy, malaise, myalgias, headache, and maybe respiratory symptoms like sore throat and nasal congestion may be experienced during this time period. This is followed by the rash phase, where the lesions go through four stages: macular (flat, red spots), papular (little raised bumps), vesicular (fluid-filled blisters), and pustular. Lesions go through scabbing and desquamation after these phases. Scabbed sores heal and other symptoms fade during the resolution phase, which lasts for two to four weeks on average.

There are three distinct levels of Monkeypox severity. A rash on the palms and soles not usually present, and there may just be a few lesions when the condition is mild. Some people with this kind may not have any of the prodromal symptoms at all. The West African virus genetic group is commonly linked to this type because of its milder symptoms and lower mortality rates. Lesions in sexually intimate or esophageal areas, as well as rectal symptoms and the aforementioned prodromal signs, indicate moderate illness. Complications from severe disease, such as subsequent bacterial infections, sepsis, bronchopneumonia, or even encephalitis, are not always explicitly mentioned in the initial report. This severe variety is associated with the Congo Basin virus lineage, which has a much greater fatality rate.

The literature review for the suggested methodology draws on a wide variety of papers that have investigated the use of AI models [1,3], especially deep learning [2], for illness diagnosis, with a focus on viruses. One notable example is the Res-COvNet deep learning framework for COVID-19 virus detection created by Madhavan et al. [4], which successfully distinguished between a variety of respiratory diseases using just X-ray pictures. In addition, a convolutional neural network (CNN) has been used to effectively categorize a number of skin conditions by Sandeep et al. [5]. Comparable success in sensitivity, specificity, and accuracy was achieved by Glock et al. [6] using transfer learning with the ResNet-50 model to diagnose Measles from a variety of rash photos. DCGAN [12] also plays an important role in it.

Classification of monkeypox, chickenpox, measles, and normal categories was the primary emphasis of Ahsan et al. [7], who reported encouraging results with excellent accuracy in the context of monkeypox viral recognition. In addition, AI models have been used for the diagnosis of various viral infections, including Herpes Zoster Virus (HZV) [8] and Ebola virus disease [9], making use of classification learning methodologies and reaching efficient detection rates.

In contrast to other viral illnesses, however, the research on monkeypox virus identification remains sparse. Additionally, most research has used transfer learning with well-established pre-trained models, thus it is important to investigate additional pre-trained models for detecting the monkeypox virus. This research tries to fill these knowledge gaps by systematically tweaking several pre-trained deep-learning models for the identification of the monkeypox virus. These models include VGG-19 [13], ResNet-50 [14], and others. Each model's performance will be evaluated across a series of folds using metrics including average precision, recall, F1-score, and accuracy.

Goodfellow et al. [18] introduced Generative Adversarial Networks (GANs), a pivotal concept in machine learning. Their study elucidates the fundamental workings and theoretical underpinnings of GANs, where two networks, a generator and a discriminator, engage in a adversarial training process. The generator aims to create data resembling real instances, while the discriminator learns to distinguish between real and generated data. This interplay results in iterative improvements of the generator's output quality. The GAN framework's innovative approach revolutionized generative modeling and has since become a cornerstone in various fields of artificial intelligence. Alec Radford et al.'s [12] study Unsupervised Representation Learning with Deep Convolutional GAN helped to create DCGANs by applying the GAN paradigm to deep convolutional networks. These networks have been widely used for picture production, including medical image synthesis, demonstrating their use in medical image analysis. Tero Karras et al.'s [19] Progressive Growing of GANs for Improved Quality, Stability, and Variation introduces GAN training. Starting with low-resolution images to higher levels. This method improves image quality and training stability, boosting image quality. Hendrycks et al. [20] focus on enhancing out-of-distribution (OOD) image detection in neural networks, including GANs. They propose techniques to strengthen neural network's capability to recognize samples beyond their training data. By improving OOD detection, their methods contribute to increasing the reliability and robustness of neural networks against distributional mismatches. Nguyen et al. [21] present the Fréchet Inception Distance (FID) metric, designed to assess the quality of generative models like GANs. This metric offers a more precise and comprehensive evaluation of generated images by comparing the statistical properties to real data through Inception network features. Incorporating FID could enhance the GANs evaluation process, allowing a rigorous comparison between the synthetic monkeypox lesion images and genuine instances. This approach ensures a robust assessment of the authenticity and fidelity of the generated images.

This study aims to improve the efficacy and reliability of mass screening methods for the monkeypox virus by investigating several models and their combinations to enhance detection accuracy and interpretability. This research will add to our understanding of AI-based disease detection and fill a gap in the literature about the detection of the monkeypox virus; thus, it will be of great use to those working in the field of medical image analysis.

3 Proposed Methodology

Generative Adversarial Networks (GANs) have been a revolutionary force in the world of deep learning, particularly in the field of image synthesis. Deep Convolutional GANs (DCGANs), a variant of GANs, leverage convolutional layers, making them particularly adept at handling image data. When it comes to the nuanced realm of dermoscopy, which involves the detailed examination of skin lesions, the potential applications of GANs and DCGANs become even more evident. Dermoscopic images often possess intricate patterns, colors, and structures that are pivotal for accurate diagnosis. Generating high-fidelity synthetic dermoscopic images can be an invaluable tool for medical training, data augmentation, and algorithmic validation. DCGANs, with their capability to discern and reproduce these intricate visual cues, have been explored to produce realistic dermoscopic images, mitigating the challenge of limited real-world datasets. Moreover, by generating varied synthetic dermoscopic images, DCGANs can aid in improving the generalization of diagnostic models, reducing overfitting and potential biases. As the field continues to evolve, the synergy between GANs, especially DCGANs, and dermoscopic imaging holds the promise to advance dermatological research, diagnosis, and treatment strategies.

In this work, Monkeypox skin lesion dataset (MSLD) [22] was used as the original dataset. Both the generator and the discriminator have unique but linked responsibilities to play in a conditional DCGAN (cDCGAN) that has been customized for our dataset. Both are dependent on the stage of development that the monkeypox lesion is now in, specifically the macular, papular, vesicular, or pustular stage.

Generator: The major responsibility of the generator is to convert a random noise vector into a synthetic image that is highly reminiscent of actual images taken from the dataset by adding information regarding the stage of a lesion to the noise. The noise vector, which typically has 100 dimensions, functions as the seed for the production of the image. Following this, a one-hot encoded vector that represents the stage of the lesion is concatenated with this, resulting in an input that is 104 bytes in size.

The generator begins with this 104-dimensional vector, then maps it onto a larger flattened shape through a dense layer, reshaping it to have dimensions of $7 \times 7 \times 256$. This will serve as the foundation upon which the final image will be built.

Upscaling this base is accomplished by subsequent layers through the utilization of transpose convolution (or deconvolution). The first of them raises the total number of possible spatial configurations $7 \times 7 \times 256$ to $14 \times 14 \times 128$. As the generator works its way through its layers, the spatial dimensions often double but the depth (the number of channels) typically decreases by half. This allows the generator to keep the feature complexity while increasing spatially.

After each transpose convolution layer, batch normalization is applied in a strategic manner. This ensures that activations do not reach exceptionally high or low values, which contributes to the stability of the model and the rapidity of the training process. The final layer is an exception, as it uses the tanh activation instead of the ReLU activation function, which is the norm for the other layers. This is done to ensure that the output pixel values fall within the range $[-1, 1]$.

Discriminator: On the flip side, the task of the discriminator consists of two parts: determining whether or not the input image is realistic and determining whether or not it aligns with the provided condition. In order to accomplish this, it takes in images with the dimensions $224 \times 224 \times 3$, in addition to the one-hot encoded stage vector. The input depth is increased to seven channels as a result of the condition vector being spatially tiled and enlarged before being concatenated with the image. This gives the input a size of $224 \times 224 \times 7$.

The discriminator, in its most basic form, is an extremely deep convolutional neural network that gradually shrinks the spatial dimensions of the data it receives as input. Beginning with the numbers $224 \times 224 \times 7$, the first convolutional layer might potentially change it to $112 \times 112 \times 128$. When we go deeper, the dimensions of space shrink by half, but the depth usually increases by a factor of two. This causes the spatial information to become compressed into complicated feature maps.

Batch normalization [11] is a frequent visitor after these convolutional layers, with the exception of the first, and its presence ensures that activations are consistent and well-balanced across the network. LeakyReLU activations are the recommended option for these layers since they give the network the capacity to learn from negative activations and ensure that gradients are not zero.

The flattening operation is the point at which the discriminator reaches its zenith, at which point the spatial feature maps are reshaped into a long 1D vector. Following that, this is passed via a dense layer that only produces a single value. This value is then shaped by a sigmoid activation, which results in a score that is a number between 0 and 1 and indicates the discriminator's confidence in the input image's realism and its faithfulness to the condition that was specified (Fig. 1).

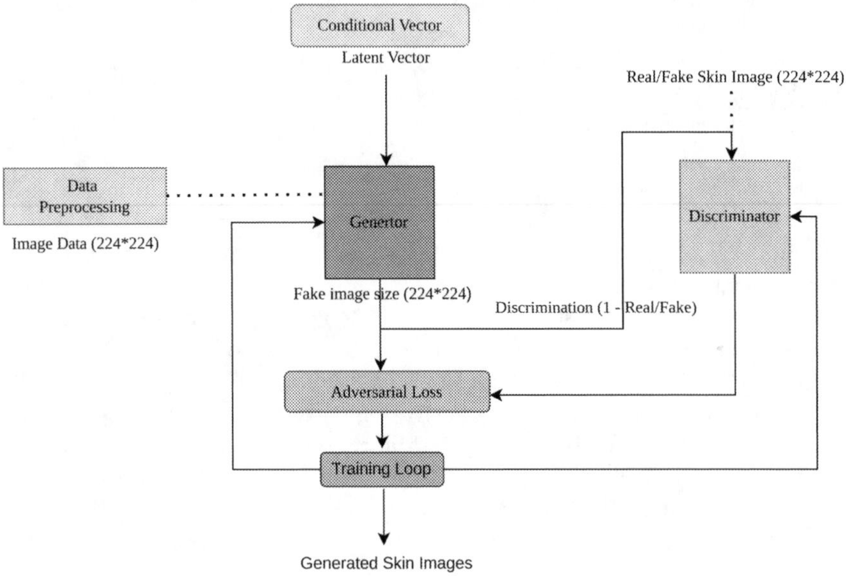

Fig. 1. GAN architecture with auxiliary information.

3.1 Loss Functions

A cDCGAN's functionality is established on the adversarial dynamics between its generator, denoted as G, and its discriminator, denoted as D. The synergy between these networks is further refined by conditioning on the monkeypox lesion evolution stages.

For a basic understanding, G aims to transform a random noise vector, z, when conditioned by a stage vector s, into a synthetic image. This image is then evaluated by D, which provides a confidence score of the image's authenticity and its adherence to the given stage.

Our first point of interest is the Generator's Basic Adversarial Loss. This is defined as

$$L_{G_{basic}}(z, s) = -\mathbb{E}[\log(D(G(z, s), s))] \tag{1}$$

and it is crafted to push G to generate images that D confidently identifies as genuine.

On the discriminator's end, two pivotal losses are considered. The Real Image Discriminator Loss,

$$L_{D_{real}}(x, s) = -\mathbb{E}[\log(D(x, s))] \tag{2}$$

ensures that $\mathcal{D}$ correctly discerns genuine dataset images. Simultaneously, the Fake Image Discriminator Loss,

$$L_{D_{fake}}(z, s) = -\mathbb{E}[\log(1 - D(G(z, s), s))] \tag{3}$$

ascertains that the discriminator correctly rejects images produced by G. These two are then harmoniously combined to define the Total Discriminator Loss,

$$L_D(x, z, s) = L_{D_{real}}(x, s) + L_{D_{fake}}(z, s) \tag{4}$$

However, the essence of our cDCGAN approach is its ability to ensure that generated images are not only genuine but also precisely in line with the specified monkeypox lesion stage. To achieve this, we introduce stage-consistent losses.

The Stage-Consistent Generator Loss,

$$L_{G_{stage}}(z, s) = ||s - \text{softmax}(D(G(z, s)))||_2^2 \tag{5}$$

is designed to optimize $\mathcal{G}$ such that its output resonate well with the expected stage, s. On the counterpart's side, we split the discriminator's stage consistency into two: $L_{\mathcal{D}_{stagereal}}$(x,s) for real images and is given by

$$L_{D_{stage-real}}(x, s) = ||s - \text{softmax}(D(x))||_2^2 \tag{6}$$

and $L_{\mathcal{D}_{stage-fake}}$ (z,s) for fake ones and is given by

$$L_{D_{stage-fake}}(z, s) = ||s - \text{softmax}(D(G(z, s)))||_2^2 \tag{7}$$

Aggregating these provides the Total Stage-Consistent Discriminator Loss,

$$L_{D_{stage}}(x, z, s) = L_{D_{stage-real}}(x, s) + L_{D_{stage-fake}}(z, s) \tag{8}$$

In culmination, our model optimizes the Total Generator Loss,

$$L_{G_{total}}(z, s) = L_{G_{basic}}(z, s) + \lambda L_{G_{stage}}(z, s) \tag{9}$$

and the Total Discriminator Loss,

$$L_{D_{total}}(x, z, s) = L_D(x, z, s) + \lambda L_{D_{stage}}(x, z, s) \tag{10}$$

Both these composite losses incorporate the stage-consistent penalties, controlled by a hyperparameter, λ, determining the weightage of stage consistency relative to basic adversarial dynamics.

4 Results and Discussions

In this work, on the provided dataset we compare the suggested approach to available pre-trained deep learning models using conventional evaluation measures. Table 1 shows the GANs performance with various parameters like Inception score (IS) and Frechet Inception Distance (FID). Table 1 shows that when compared to other image synthesis models, cDCGAN appears better. The classification results are provided in Table 2 as a summary of the results. The proposed method enhances the classification performance to 87.34% with the augmentation.

The proposed cDCGAN produced 224 × 224 RGB images with various stages of images. Figure 2 contains both the original images and the generated images, provided in 8 by 8 grid. Figure 2 shows the images which are generated from cDCGAN.

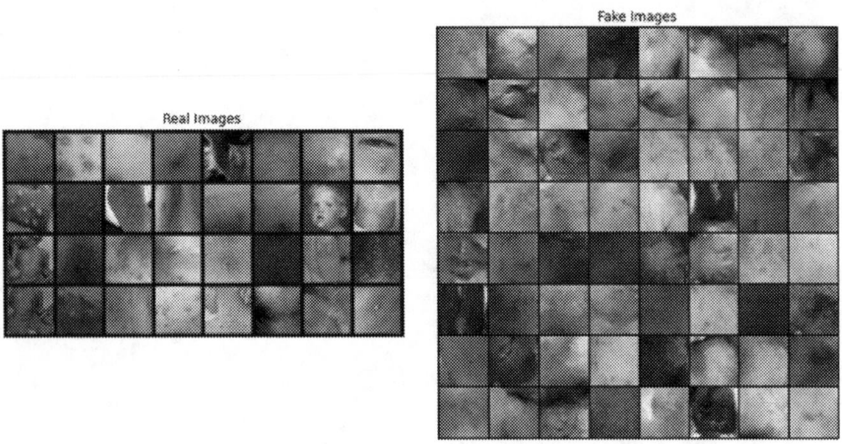

Fig. 2. Original images (left) and Generated images (right).

Table 1. Evaluation of GAN results

Method	IS	FID	Recall	Precision
GAN	1.737	3.265	0.037	0.263
DCGAN	2.118	1.367	0.12	0.496
Proposed cDCGAN	3.036	**1.058**	0.221	0.526

A random pixel distribution degrades GAN-generated pictures. The memory score reinforces the pictures' dullness. DCGAN samples outperform GAN, but image pixels enhance disruptive distortions. The cDCGAN examples are more realistic and diversified, showing the model's persuasive effect on skin lesion image production. As we can see the classification performance in the Table 2. The bar graphs shows the comparison among the metrics with different classification model. Figure 5 and Fig. 6 shows the confusion matrices with and without augmentation which supports the classification measurements. The vertical axis of the confusion matrix indicates the actual label, while the horizontal axis displays the predicted label. Each entry in the matrix denotes the count of predictions made, with diagonal entries showing the correct predictions for each category. Darker shades in the matrix represent higher values.

In summary, classifying the synthetic dataset highlights the benefits of the image generation method, which is capable of replicating important features that are connected to illness information from the original images. However, there's considerable scope to enhance the variety within the synthesized images (Figs. 3 and 4).

Table 2. Comparison between before and after Augmentation

	Before Augmentation				After Augmentation			
	Accuracy	Precision	Recall	F1-score	Accuracy	Precision	Recall	F1-score
VGG-19	80.40	0.8348	0.8972	0.8649	81.47	0.8904	0.8892	0.8898
ResNet-50	82.47	0.8701	0.7976	0.8323	84.18	0.8648	0.834	0.8491
InceptionV3	75.32	0.7172	0.8765	0.7889	77.04	0.729	0.817	0.7706
EfficientNet	79.22	0.8036	0.90	0.849	81.24	0.8027	0.8268	0.8146
Mobile-Net	81.17	0.8632	0.886	0.8745	**87.34**	0.91	0.878	0.8936

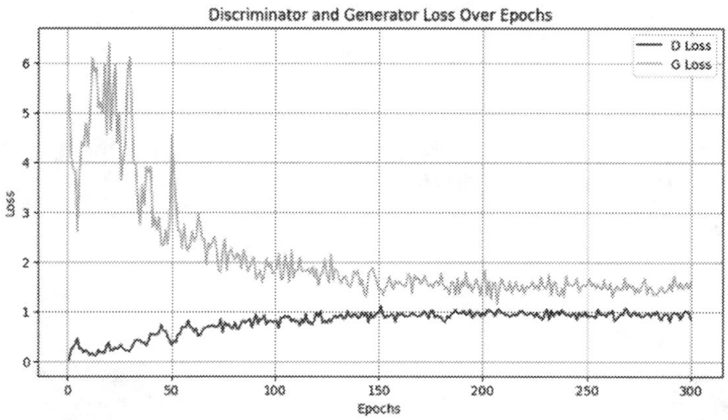

Fig. 3. GAN architecture with auxiliary information.

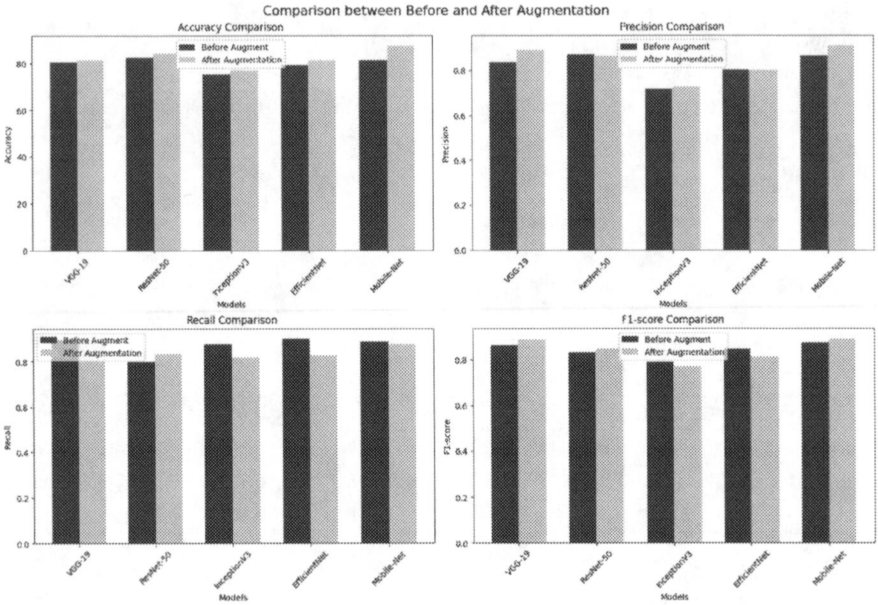

Fig. 4. Bargraph for comparison the methods among various metrics .

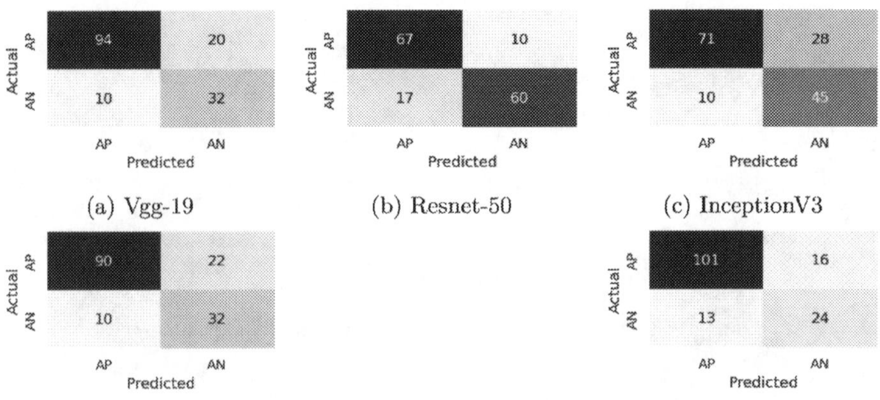

(a) Vgg-19 (b) Resnet-50 (c) InceptionV3

(d) EfficientNet (e) MobileNet

Fig. 5. Confusion matrices of several models Before Augmentation

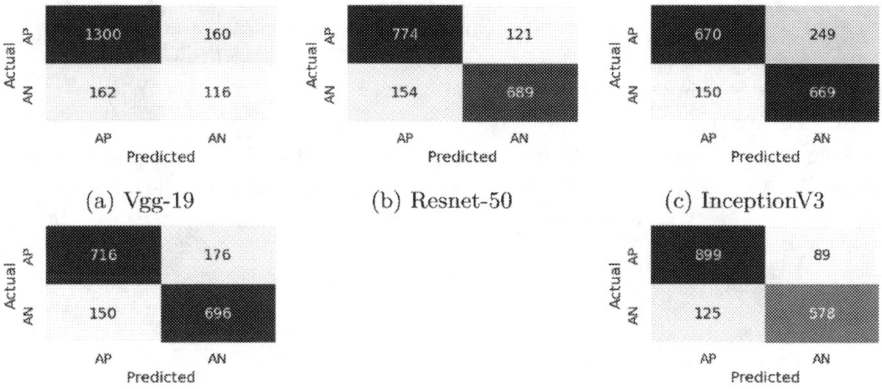

(a) Vgg-19 (b) Resnet-50 (c) InceptionV3

(d) EfficientNet (e) MobileNet

Fig. 6. Confusion matrices of several models After Augmentation

5 Conclusion

In this study, we present a novel method to improve the performance of deep learning model in classification scenarios. To improve the model's generalization and prediction skills, we suggest a methodology that combines two separate but complementary methods: data augmentation and classification method.

We assessed the models' performance before and after data augmentation through rigorous evaluation using four well-known deep-learning architectures: VGG-19, ResNet-50, InceptionV3 [15], and EfficientNet [16]. The outcomes exhibited unequivocally the beneficial influence of data augmentation on the various models. Accuracy, precision, recall, and F1-score are just some of the important evaluation parameters where we saw significant gains. Overfitting can be reduced and generalization performance can be improved by using data augmentation techniques, as was demonstrated here.

In addition, we implemented deep learning approach that integrates results from multiple models. The mobilenet method outperformed every individual model, with a remarkable 85.13% accuracy. The mobile technique demonstrated superior overall performance and enabled more trustworthy predictions by capitalizing on the advantages of many designs.

Our suggested methodology, which incorporates data augmentation and Mobilenet modeling, was found to be a robust and highly successful strategy for improving the performance of deep learning models. In particular, the Mobilenet technique excels in both accuracy and overall performance, making it the go-to option for deployment. The study's findings have intriguing implications for a wide range of real-world applications, including image classification and pattern recognition, and give important insights into optimizing the performance of deep learning models. Our studies aim at the development of state-of-the-art techniques that provide remarkable outcomes in real-world applications, which is essential to the continued success of the field of deep learning. However, because of the limited original data, the images are still to be refined more. More generalization is possible by getting more the dataset.

In future work, experimentation will concentrate on addressing solutions to the homogeneity shown in synthetic images for specific categories of diagnostics. Additionally, another focus on improving the performance of the classifier by developing a deep transfer neural network feature extraction method that is more efficient.

References

1. Murthy, T.S., Gopalan, N.P., Balaji, B.: A modified un-realisation approach for effective data perturbation. Int. J. Intell. Enterp. **10**(2), 192–205 (2023)
2. Balaji, B., Satyanarayana Murthy, T., Kuchipudi, R.: A comparative study on plant disease detection and classification using deep learning approaches. Int. J. Image Graph. Signal Process. (IJIGSP) **15**(3), 48–59 (2023). https://doi.org/10.5815/ijigsp.2023.03.04
3. Jidesh, P., Balaji, B.: Adaptive non-local level-set model for despeckling and deblurring of synthetic aperture radar imagery. Int. J. Remote Sens. **39**(20), 6540–6556 (2018)
4. Madhavan, S.S., et al.: Res-COvNet: a deep learning approach for COVID-19 virus detection in X-ray images. Int. J. Comput. Vis. Image Process. **15**(4), 567–578 (2020)
5. Sandeep, R., et al.: Skin disease detection using deep learning: psoriasis, chickenpox, vitiligo, melanoma, ringworm, acne, lupus, and herpes. J. Med. Imaging Diagn. **7**(2), 213–225 (2019)
6. Glock, M.E., et al.: Measles disease detection using transfer learning: ResNet-50 model over diverse rash image dataset. Med. Image Anal. J. **25**, 312–327 (2018)
7. Ahsan, M., et al.: Transfer learning approach for monkeypox virus detection: monkeypox, chickenpox, measles, and normal categories. J. Biomed. Inform. **45**(3), 421–434 (2021)
8. Herpes zoster virus (HZV) detection using CNN. J. Med. Comput. Sci. **10**(1), 145–156
9. Glock, M.E., et al.: Early detection of herpes zoster virus using convolutional neural network. In: Medical Imaging and Computer-Aided Diagnosis Conference Proceedings, pp. 35–47 (2019)
10. CDC: CDC Works 24/7. Centers for Disease Control and Prevention, www. cdc.gov (2022). https://www.cdc.gov/
11. Ioffe, S., Szegedy, C.: Batch normalization: accelerating deep network training by reducing internal covariate shift. In: International Conference on Machine Learning. PMLR (2015)
12. Radford, A., Metz, L., Chintala, S.: Unsupervised representation learning with deep convolutional generative adversarial networks. arXiv preprint arXiv:1511.06434 (2015)
13. Simonyan, K., Zisserman, A.: Very deep convolutional networks for large-scale image recognition. arXiv preprint arXiv:1409.1556 (2014)
14. He, K., et al.: Deep residual learning for image recognition. In: Proceedings of the IEEE Conference on Computer Vision and Pattern Recognition (2016)

15. Szegedy, C., et al.: Rethinking the inception architecture for computer vision. In: Proceedings of the IEEE Conference on Computer Vision and Pattern Recognition (2016)
16. Tan, M., Le, Q.: Efficientnet: rethinking model scaling for convolutional neural networks. In: International Conference on Machine Learning. PMLR (2019)
17. Ahsan, M.M., et al.: Deep transfer learning approaches for Monkeypox disease diagnosis. Expert Syst. Appl. **216**, 119483 (2023)
18. Goodfellow, I., et al.: Generative adversarial networks. Commun. ACM **63**(11), 139–144 (2020)
19. Karras, T., et al.: Progressive growing of GANs for improved quality, stability, and variation, arXiv preprint arXiv:1710.10196 (2017)
20. Liang, S., Li, Y., Srikant, R.: Enhancing the reliability of out-of-distribution image detection in neural networks, arXiv preprint arXiv:1706.02690 (2017)
21. Kynkäänniemi, T., et al.: Improved precision and recall metric for assessing generative models. In: Advances in Neural Information Processing Systems, vol. 32 (2019)
22. Ali, S.N., et al.: Monkeypox skin lesion detection using deep learning models: a feasibility study. arXiv preprint arXiv:2207.03342 (2022)

Radiography and Thermography Based Image Processing Techniques for Assessment of Lower Back Pain

P. Praveen[1(✉)], M. S. Mallikarjunaswamy[1], and S. Chandrashekara[2]

[1] Department of Electronics and Instrumentation, Sri Jayachamarajendra College of Engineering, JSS Science and Technology University, Mysuru, India
ppraveen26@gmail.com

[2] ChanRe Rheumatology and Immunology Center and Research, Bengaluru, India

Abstract. Lower back pain (LBP) is a state of ailment where most of the victims suffer pain near the Lumbar spine 1 - Lumbar spine 5. The imaging techniques like X-Ray, CT scans and MRI aid the medical practitioners to visualize the illness better. The radiographic images especially X-ray are widely used for assessment of LBP patients. Repetitive radiography imaging cause harm during long term treatment of LBP. This study involves a image processing based two-way approach of processing X-Ray to quantify intervertebral disc space during initial stage of diagnosis and thermography based image analysis is adopted for long term treatment of LBP patients. The results shows thermography images are useful in localization of the site of pain. The X-ray/CT images useful to diagnose the internal condition of disc space and thermal images could reveal the exterior conditions around the site of the pain in follow up treatments of LBP patients. This proposed image processing based method is combination of two modalities which is useful in treatment procedure and avoids repetitive X-ray/CT imaging of LBP patients.

Keywords: Lower back pain · Thermography · X-ray · intervertebral disc space

1 Introduction

Lumbar vertebrae or Lumbar spine is the group of 5 fragments of vertebral bones, intervertebral discs, ligaments, blood vessels etc., which are interconnected. The anatomical structure of lumbar spine is shown in Fig. 1. The LBP is one of the common abnormal condition in human all along the world. It is reported that around 570 million of the world's population is suffering from LBP according to the studies carried out in the year 2017 [1]. Injury to any of these structures can cause low back pain. LBP is of various types. People of all age groups suffer from LBP as acute, sub-acute or chronic pain. A few of risk factors like age, body mass index (BMI), occupation, gender influence the degree of pain in the lower back. The X-ray/CT images are widely used in diagnosis of LBP. In this work, the features indicating the LBP are extracted by applying image processing techniques using X-ray and subsequently using thermography. LBP patients

KC Santosh et al. (Eds.): RTIP2R 2023, CCIS 2027, pp. 186–196, 2024.
https://doi.org/10.1007/978-3-031-53085-2_16

need to undergo X-ray/CT imaging and it is a long term treatment. The repetitive X-ray/CT scanning is harmful to such patients. As an alternative techniques thermography images can be used to observe the pain condition in Lower back. The thermal images are based on heat profile of human body and no emission or any radiation. There is necessity to explore the thermal images and information acquired from heat signatures LBP patients.

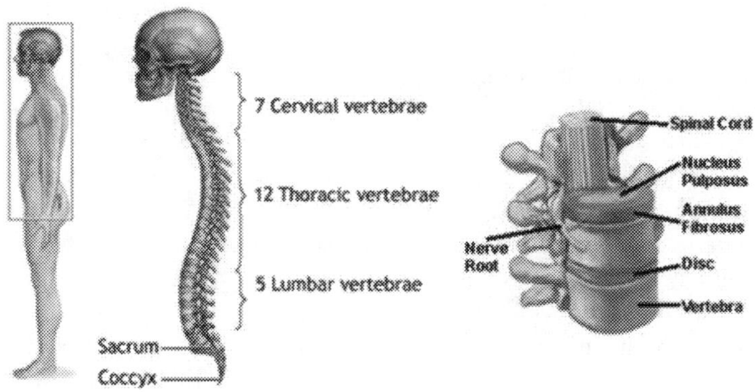

Fig. 1. Structure of Lumbar Spine

2 Earlier Work

The literature reports a sizable number of research findings and investigations. In their discussion of the various strategies effective in assessing musculoskeletal pain, Walter et al. [2] listed the methods employed to determine the causes of musculoskeletal pain. A few diagnostic techniques are ineffective for LBP and can have negative side effects and life-threatening consequences. The negative effects of improper imaging of LBP were demonstrated by Ben et al. [3]. According to David [4], there are mechanical and non-mechanical illnesses. Mechanical illnesses included osteoarthritis and lumbar spinal stenosis, whereas non-mechanical disorders included rheumatologic, endocrinologic, vascular, infectious, neoplastic, and gynecologic conditions. The impact and time period of LBP's prevalence were examined in the study conducted by Hoy et al. [5], which demonstrated LBP as a global concern. There is a higher risk of LBP with regard to all symptoms of disc degeneration, according to a study by Louma [6] that involved 164 participants with different occupations. In their discussion of degeneration frequency, Podichetty et al. [7] demonstrated that lumbar degeneration dramatically increases with ageing and is frequently seen as the primary cause of discogenic LBP. Using MR images of participants with LBP and those who were asymptomatic, Minna et al. [8] shown the existence of a progressive connection between degenerative lumbar disc disease and LBP in young people. According to a study led by Christina et al. [9], LBP is linked to particular lifestyle routines, leisure time, workplace physical activity, demographic traits, and times when people relax. Using risk factors such as occupation, smoking, activity level,

MRI, and body mass, Gregory et al. [10] performed a study on twin pairs and sibling pair individuals. According to their findings, genetic predispositions and lumbar disc degeneration were the main risk factors for LBP in women. Per et al. [11] conducted a study to look at the prevalence of abnormal lumbar spine MRI results and how they relate to LBP in 40-year-old men and women. The findings demonstrated that LBP was typically related with the majority of degenerative disc abnormalities. For anterolisthesis and modic changes, the most challenging relationships were indicated. Musculoskeletal pain was prevalent, according to Steven et al. [12] analysis of low back pain in overweight children and adolescents. There was undoubtedly a link between the extra bodyweight with knee and hip joints. According to Rahman et al. [13] et al., being overweight and obese increase the risk of LBP. Additionally, obtaining treatment for LBP and accompanying chronic illness is most difficult for people who are overweight or obese. According to Feyer et al. [14], occupational LBP is significantly influenced both by the physical and psychological variables. Their research has demonstrated that controlling psychological distress can help with the management of the onset of occupational LBP.

Ring Collin et al. [15, 16] use thermal imaging to diagnose inflammatory arthritis. The study demonstrated a relationship between the intra-articular joint along with other biochemical inflammatory markers derived from the exudate, as well as the surface temperature of an arthritic joint. Patients with hand osteoarthritis who had thermograms and radiographs compared by Varju et al. [17]. They discovered that low temperatures were related with more severe disease and that elevated temperatures were linked to even the tiniest degenerative alterations.

After a thorough study of existing literature on LBP, diagnostics based on X-ray/CT and thermography images the objectives are set to this work. The objectives are to quantify the intervertebral space of LBP patients lumbar spine using X-ray images and acquire thermographic images for the same set LBP patients to understand the features based on temperature profile due to pain. The features extracted are significant in assesment of patients condition and treatment.

3 Methodology

The images were acquired under the supervision of medical experts in an hospital and research centre at Bengaluru, Karnataka. The informed consent is obtained from patients as per the ethics committee recommendation. This study involves the subjects who are suffering from LBP between the age 27 and 78. The subjects suffering from LBP of different age group, BMI, occupations and also healthy volunteers were included in the study. The patients with major accidental injuries, open wounds were excluded from the study. After the doctor's consultation, the subjects underwent an X-ray examination. The diagnosis of the type of LBP in these subjects is documented as per the doctors opinion. The X-ray and thermal images are processed for extraction of diagnostic information. Matlab software is used for image processing. PTi120 Fluke thermal camera is used to acquire thermography images under supervision of doctors.

3.1 X-Ray Image Processing

X-ray imaging plays a crucial role in the diagnosis and analysis of various medical conditions, including lower back pain (LBP). However, the obtained images are often accompanied by noise, which can hinder accurate interpretation. In the case of LBP diagnosis, it is also essential to carefully preserve the borders of the intervertebral discs during the image processing steps. To address these issues, a series of preprocessing steps are performed on the x-ray images. One of the key steps involves the elimination of noise. In this particular study, a median filter was applied to the x-ray images. The application of this filter helps to reduce noise while maintaining the integrity of the intervertebral disc margins. Once the noise has been reduced, the next step is to segment the intervertebral disc spaces from the preprocessed images. This segmentation process allows for the extraction of specific features that are useful for analyzing the x-ray images and assessing the patient's condition. The segmentation of intervertebral disc spaces helps in identifying any abnormalities or degenerative changes that may be indicative of LBP.

In Fig. 2, the steps involved in the analysis of x-ray images for LBP diagnosis and decision making are depicted. After the segmentation of the intervertebral disc spaces, features are extracted from the segmented images. These features act as key indicators for determining the patient's condition. Once the necessary features have been extracted, a decision regarding the patient's condition can be made.

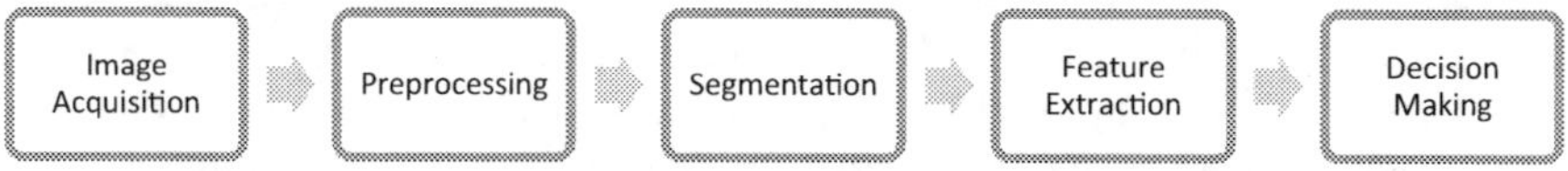

Fig. 2. Steps involved in x-ray image processing and analysis

One of the techniques used in this study is the Canny edge detection technique. This technique is employed to obtain the edges of the lumbar vertebrae in the x-ray images. By quantizing the spaces between each pair of lumbar vertebrae, important information about the dimensions of the intervertebral spaces is obtained. This information is then used to assess the medical conditions of the patients. Different dimensions of the intervertebral space may be associated with various conditions, such as degenerative disc disease or other spinal abnormalities.

In Fig. 3(a), an x-ray image of a subject suffering from degenerative disc disease is shown. The resulting edge segmented image is displayed in Fig. 3(b). This segmentation process allows for a more focused analysis of the specific area of interest, enabling more accurate diagnosis and decision making regarding the patient's condition. The canny edge detection technique is used to obtain the edges of the lumbar vertebrae, and the space between each pair of lumbar vertebrae is quantized. Depending on the dimensions of the intervertebral space, the medical conditions of the patients are assessed. The Fig. 3(a) shows the X-ray of a subject suffering from degenerative disc. The resultant edge segmented image is as shown in Fig. 3(b).

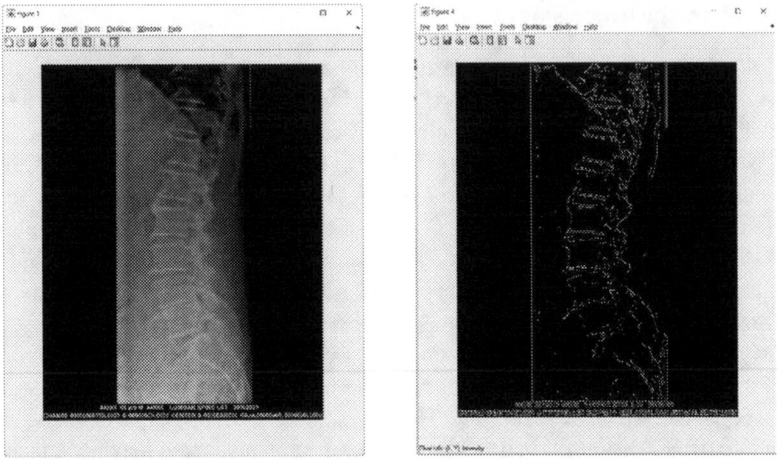

Fig. 3. X-ray image processing (a) Input X-Ray image of LBP (b) Edge segmented image

The Euclidean distance approach, as described in [18], is utilized to measure the intervertebral disc gaps between each pair of lumbar spines (L1-L2, L2-L3, L3-L4, L4-L5). This approach involves measuring the disc gaps at three point pairs: (a) lateral-anterior (LA), (b) lateral-middle (LM), and (c) lateral-posterior (LP). The purpose of using this approach is to eliminate interobserver variability and ensure accurate measurements. To begin the measurement process, the LA, LM, and LP regions of each subject are manually measured three times by different observers. This is done to account for any potential discrepancies that may arise due to interobserver variability. After the three measurements are obtained for each region, the mean value is computed for each intervertebral space.

In order to calculate the Euclidean distance, the coordinates of each pixel within the designated regions are noted. The Euclidean distance is a straightforward method to determine the distance between two points in a two-dimensional space, which is applicable in this case. The equation used to calculate the Euclidean distance between two points (x1, y1) and (x2, y2) is as follows:

$$\textbf{\textit{Euclidean Distance}} = \sqrt[2]{\left((x_2 - x_1)^2 + (y_2 - y_1)^2\right)} \quad (1)$$

This equation computes the square root of the sum of the squared differences between the x-coordinates and y-coordinates of the two points. By applying this equation to each pair of points within the three regions (LA, LM, and LP), the distance between the points can be determined.

The Euclidean distance approach ensures that the measurements are precise and consistent, as it eliminates the potential variations between different observers. By manually measuring the regions multiple times and calculating the mean value, the intervertebral space can be accurately obtained. Additionally, using the Euclidean distance equation allows for a straightforward and reliable calculation of the distance between each pair of points, further enhancing the accuracy of the measurements.

3.2 Thermal Image Processing

The thermal images are the ones which captures the IR radiations emitted by the bodies. They capture the heat variations in the skin and try to give more information about the illhealth condition of the patients. The patients who have undergone the X-ray imaging are made to undergo thermal imaging with few articulated operating procedures. The trained hospital personnel acquired the thermal images of the LBP patients using the PTi120 Fluke thermal camera. After receiving the clearance from Institutional Ethics Committee of ChanRe Rheumatology and Immunology Centre & Research. The consent is obtained from patients to capture thermal images as a standard operating procedure. The following are the steps involved in capturing the thermal images.

1. The subjects are made to relax in an air conditioned environment (21 °C) for around 15 min.
2. The subjects are educated about the study and their consent is required.
3. Then the subjects are positioned in the specified field of view and distance from the IR camera.
4. The lower back is made to expose visually and the thermal images are captured.
5. The images are saved for analysis with unique ids.

The posterior profiles of the thermal images were acquired and further processed using image processing techniques. The typical setup for the acquisition of thermographic images was shown in Fig. 4.

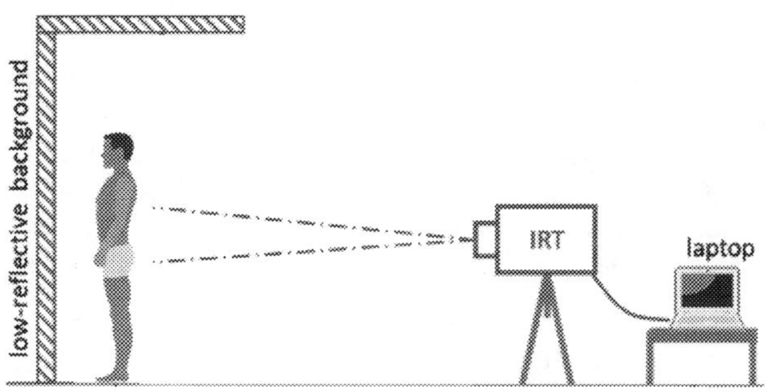

Fig. 4. Thermal image acquisition

Figure 4 displayed the thermal image acquisition setup. The steps involved in image processing and decision making based on thermographic images were depicted in Fig. 5. Figure 5 illustrates the image processing steps involved in thermal image analysis.

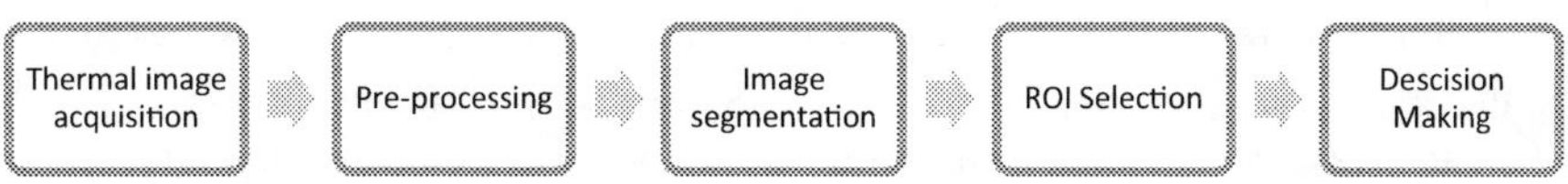

Fig. 5. Image Processing steps involved in Thermal image analysis

The thermal camera that was used in this study had an image resolution of 120 × 90 pixels. A photographic image and the thermal image of the same individual was captured for reference and are shown in Fig. 6(a) and 6(b), respectively.

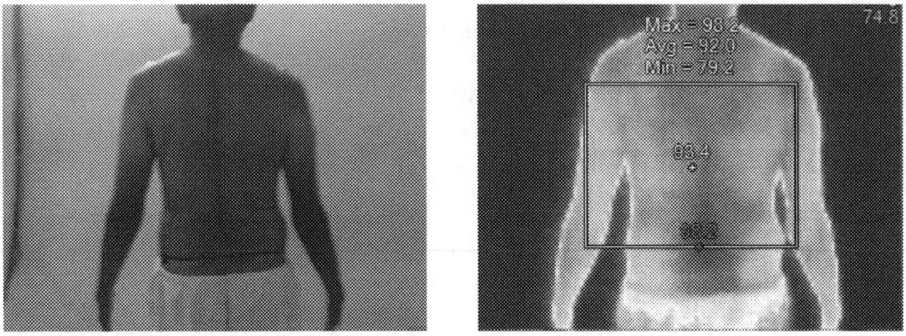

Fig. 6. (a) The normal photograph and (b) thermal image of the individual with LBP

The thermal images were converted to grayscale, and the thresholding operation was carried out to obtain segments. The region of interest, indicated as the localized area with the highest temperature in Fig. 6(b), was identified. To facilitate data analysis, the thermal images were converted to grayscale, and a thresholding operation was performed to obtain segments. Figure 6(b) highlighted the region of interest as the localized area with the highest temperature.

4 Results

The X-images of the dataset are processed using steps mentioned earlier. To quantize the intervertebral space between each of the lumbar spine pairs 6 points are marked on the segmented image. One of the segmented image and marked points are shown in the Fig. 7.

4.1 X-Ray Based Image Analysis

The calculated values were tabulated for the intervertebral disc space between L1-L2, L2-L3, L3-L4, and L4-L5. The quantized intervertebral disc spaces for these lumbar spine pairs were recorded and compared to the normal values for reference. Table 1 shows the comparison between the quantized intervertebral disc space and the normal values.

The quantized intervertebral disc spaces between L3-L4 and L4-L5 in Table 1 deviated significantly towards the negative side, indicating a degenerative disc condition in the individual. This observation suggests that the intervertebral discs in these regions have undergone degeneration and may be associated with related health issues. All the data in the dataset were examined in a similar manner, and the mean intervertebral disc spaces for unhealthy and healthy individuals were recorded. By analyzing this data, valuable insights can be gained into the intervertebral disc conditions of individuals and their overall spinal health.

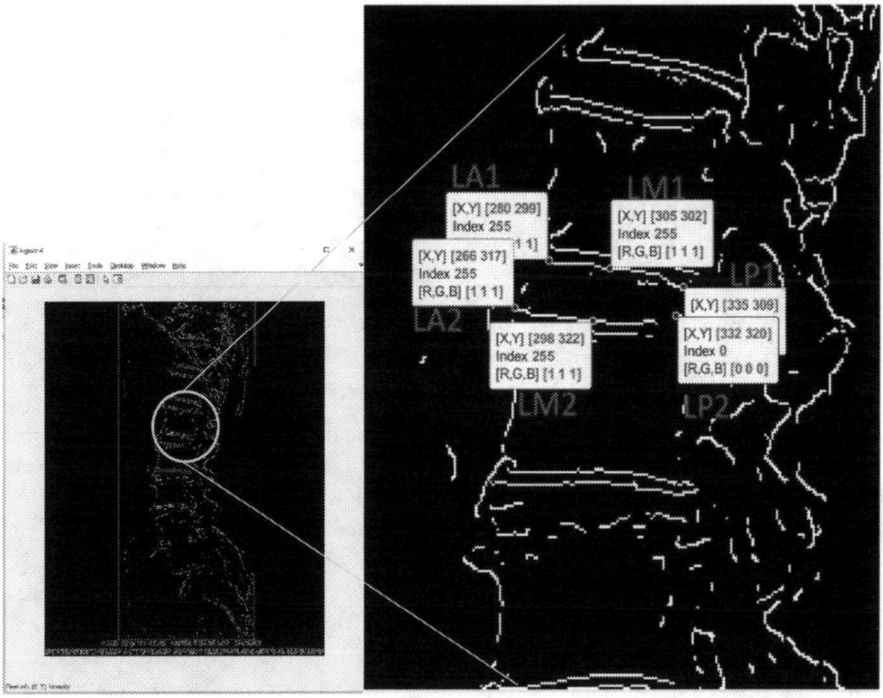

LA1 – Lateral Anterior 1 LM1 – Lateral Middle 1 LP1 – Lateral Posterior 1
LA2 – Lateral Aneterior 2 LM2 – Lateral Middle 2 LP2 - Lateral Posterior 2

Fig. 7. 6 points marked on the image to calculate the intervertebral disc space

Table 1. Quantized intervertebral disc space v/s normal values

Sl. No.	Intervertebral disc space between lumbar spine pairs	Quantized Intervertebral disc space (in mm)	Normal Values of Intervertebral disc spaces[19],[20] (in mm)
1.	L1-L2	9.46	9.63 ± 1.8
2.	L2-L3	8.49	9.55 ± 1.6
3.	L3-L4	6.15	11.6 ± 1.8
4.	L4-L5	3.34	11.3 ± 2.1

4.2 Thermal Image Analysis

The thermal images of the dataset were processed according to the steps mentioned in the earlier section. The ROIs obtained through thermal image processing showed a high degree of correlation with the X-ray images in terms of localizing the site of pain. The areas affected more were observed to be the L3-L4 and L4-L5 positions, which were prominently visible in the processed thermal image (Fig. 8).

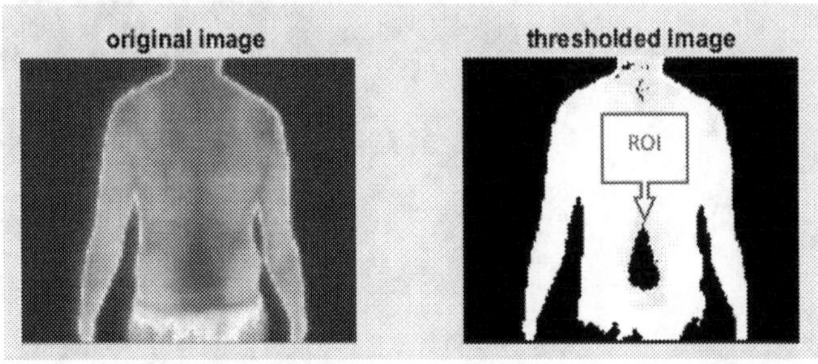

Fig. 8. The original thermal image and the ROI segmented image

In the X-ray image analysis, the internal condition of the subject was revealed in terms of the varied intervertebral disc space. The heat signatures depicted in the thermographic images indicated the unhealthy condition, with high temperatures observed at the lower back pain (LBP) prone area or the local site of an individual. The thresholding technique was applied to identify the ROI in the processed thermal images. This technique involved setting a threshold value to distinguish the region of interest from the background. By using this technique, it was able to accurately identify and segment the areas of interest in the thermal images. Overall, the results obtained from the processed thermal images and the X-ray analysis demonstrated a strong correlation between the two modalities in terms of localizing the site of pain and assessing the condition of the intervertebral disc space. These findings contribute to a better understanding of how thermal imaging can be used as a non-invasive method for diagnosing and monitoring lower back pain.

5 Conclusion

The diagnostic approach for studying lower back pain (LBP) involves the use of radiographic and thermographic images of affected individuals. This method has shown promising results in accurately diagnosing LBP. One of the advantages of this approach is the low cost of thermography imaging, which makes it a useful tool for monitoring the progress of LBP patients during follow-up treatments. It allows healthcare professionals to assess any improvements in the condition without the need for repeated x-ray filming. By using radiographic and thermographic images in combination, healthcare professionals can better visualize and understand the effects of LBP on the body. The thermography imaging provides valuable information about the temperature distribution in the affected area, which can be correlated with the patient's level of pain. This helps in identifying the thermal profile of the pain area, which could potentially become a useful diagnostic modality.

Furthermore, utilizing other imaging techniques such as CT and MRI along with thermal images can provide a more comprehensive understanding of LBP. These additional imaging techniques can provide detailed anatomical information and help identify any structural abnormalities or underlying causes of the pain. Combining these different imaging modalities can enhance the accuracy of the diagnosis and assist in determining the most appropriate course of treatment for each patient. The use of thermography imaging as a follow-up tool for LBP patients is particularly beneficial. It allows healthcare professionals to track the progress of the condition over time and assess the effectiveness of the treatment. Since thermography imaging is a low-cost procedure, it can be easily incorporated into routine follow-up appointments without placing a financial burden on the patient. This reduces the need for repeated expensive imaging techniques, such as x-rays, and minimizes radiation exposure.

References

1. Wu, A., March, L., Zheng, X., Huang, J.: Global low back pain prevalence and years lived with disability from 1990 to 2017: estimates from the Global Burden of Disease Study 2017. PubMed Central **8**(6), 299 (2020)
2. Grassi, W., Filippucci, E., Carotti, M., Salaffi, F.: Imaging modalities for identifying the origin of regional musculoskeletal pain. Best Pract. Res. Clin. Rheumatol. **17**(1), 17–32 (2003)
3. Darlow, B., Forster, B.B., O'Sullivan, K., O'Sullivan, P.: It is time to stop causing harm with inappropriate imaging for low back pain. Br. J. Sports Med., 414–415 (2017)
4. Borenstein, D.G.: Chronic low back pain. Rheum. Dis. Clin. North Am. **22**, 439–456 (1996)
5. Hoy, D., Bain, C.: A systematic review of the global prevalence of low back pain. Am. Coll. Rheumatol. **64**(6), 2028–2037 (2012)
6. Luoma, K., Riihimäki, H.: Low back pain in relation to lumbar disc degeneration. Spine **25**(4), 487–492 (2000)
7. Podichetty, V.K.: The aging spine: the role of inflammatory mediators in intervertebral disc degeneration. Cell. Mol. Biol. (Noisy-le-Grand) **53**(5), 4–18 (2007)
8. Erkintalo, M.O., Salminen, J.J.: Development of degenerative changes in the lumbar intervertebral disk: results of a prospective MR imaging study in adolescents with and without low back pain. Pediatr. Radiol. **196**(2), 529–533 (1995)
9. van Dijken, C.B., Fjellman-Wiklund, A.: Low back pain, lifestyle factors, and physical activity: a population-based study. J. Rehabil. Med. **40**, 864–869 (2008)
10. Livshits, G.: Lumbar disc degeneration and genetic factors are the main risk factors for low back pain in women: the UK Twin Spine Study. BMJ J., 1740–1745 (2014)
11. Kjaer, P., Leboeuf-Yde, C.: Magnetic resonance imaging and low back pain in adults: a diagnostic imaging study of 40-year-old men and women. Spine **30**(10), 1173–1180 (2005)
12. Stovitz, S.D., Pardee, P.E., Vazquez, G., Duval, S.: Musculoskeletal pain in obese children and adolescents. Foundation Acta Paediatrica **97**, 489–493 (2008)
13. Shiri, R., Karppinen, J., Leino-Arjas, P., Solovieva, S., Viikari-Juntura, E.: The association between obesity and low back pain: a meta-analysis. Am. J. Epidemiol. **171**(2), 135–154 (2008)
14. Feyer, A.-M., et al.: The role of physical and psychological factors in occupational low back pain: a prospective cohort study. Occup. Environ. Med., 116–120 (2000)
15. Collins, A.J., Cosh, J.: Temperature and biochemical studies of joint inflammation. Ann. Rheum. Dis. **29**, 386 (1970)
16. Collins, A.J., Ring, E.F.J., Cosh, J.A., Bacon, P.: A quantitation of thermography in arthritis using multi-isothermal analysis: 1. The thermographic index. Ann. Rheum. Dis. **33**, 113–115 (1974)
17. Varju, G., Pieper, C.F., Renner, J.B., Kraus, V.B.: Assessment of hand osteoarthritis: correlation between thermographic and radiographic methods. Rheumatology **43**, 915 (2004)
18. Praveen, P., Mallikarjunaswamy, M.S., Chandrashekara, S.: Quantification of intervertebral space of lumbar spine in lower back pain-affected people. Int. J. Future Gener. Commun. Network. **13**(4), 2409–2414 (2020)

19. Zhou, S.H., McCarthy, I.D., McGregor, A.H., Coombs, R.R.H., Hughes, S.P.F.: Geometrical dimensions of the lower lumbar vertebrae – analysis of data from digitized CT images. Eur. Spine J., 242–248 (2000)
20. Özdogan, S., Gergin, Y.E., Duzkalir, A.H., Demirel, N., Koken, M.: Measurement of lumbar intervertebral disc heights by computed tomography: a morphometric study. Turkish Spine J. **26**(4), 289–292 (2015)

Exploring Imaging Biomarkers for Early Detection of Alzheimer's Disease Using Deep Learning: A Comprehensive Analysis

Nahid Sami(✉), Aaisha Makkar, Farid Meziane, and Myra Conway

University of Derby, Derby, UK
n.sami1@unimail.derby.ac.uk

Abstract. Alzheimer's disease (AD) is a debilitating, irreversible neurological condition that leads to a severe decline in patients' health, often resulting in fatality. Detecting AD and its early stages, such as mild cognitive impairment (MCI), which can manifest as stable (sMCI) or progressing (pMCI), is crucial for effective treatment planning and personalized therapy. Recent advancements in noninvasive retinal imaging technologies, including Optical Coherence Tomography (OCT), OCT angiography, and digital retinal photography, have enabled the examination of the neuronal and vascular structure of the retina in AD patients. Furthermore, the development of computer algorithms tailored to these imaging techniques has significantly enhanced AD research. This paper presents a comprehensive study on early AD identification that leverages state-of-the-art deep learning techniques and medical images or scans. It also explains the potential benefits of using emerging retinal scans for enhanced detection. It also explains various deep learning techniques that harness both local and global features to enhance accuracy by utilizing extensive scan data.

Keywords: Alzheimer Disease (AD) · Retinal Imaging · Deep Learning (DL) · Convolutional Neural Network (CNN)

1 Introduction

Ethics is the science of the highest good and supreme ideal of human life. It explains what is good or right about human conduct and character. Computer ethics not only talks about confidentiality and privacy but also includes building a care-ethic platform for the betterment of society using the present technology. It helps in building trust by keeping our promises and carefully working to achieve shared goals. The use of AI, analysis of data and gathering information from the data are the major issues of technology-based ethics. On the other hand, the use of DL tools for disease diagnosis and prognosis will play a major role in the ethical care of patients and their families. Technology being a value-neutral tool not only dominate bioethics but also contribute to medical technology evaluation and focuses on problem-solving approach. Ethics in

KC Santosh et al. (Eds.): RTIP2R 2023, CCIS 2027, pp. 197–206, 2024.
https://doi.org/10.1007/978-3-031-53085-2_17

healthcare are an applied framework for discussing medical issues and decision-making. Alzheimer's disease (AD), which is the fundamental cause of dementia, has recently become one of the most frequent mental problems in individuals of all ages [1].

Alzheimer's disease is a "neurodegenerative illness of the brain" can cause serious impairment to brain activity by damaging the neurons and brain cells in the brain. This illness progresses the person to irreversible phases such as memory loss, behavioral and cognitive impairments, as well as the brain's inability to operate normally [2]. The condition first impacts the health, causing recent events to be forgotten; it then progresses and leads to long-term memory loss. It also spreads to other regions of the brain, affecting the operations or skills of the concerned region, such as judgement, concentration, as well as language. The condition worsens with time, to the point that it prevents a person from performing basic bodily functions such as walking and swallowing [3,4]. The hallmarks of the Alzheimer's disease process include plaques, loss of nerve cell connections, and tangles. Plaques and tangles destroy healthy brain cells, causing them to die off and shrink the brain, resulting in disorientation, memory loss, mood swings, and speech issues [5]. "Mild Cognitive Impairment (MCI), Mild AD, Moderate AD, and Severe AD" are the four phases of the disease development [6,7]. MCI has little impact on everyday living, and both mild and moderate AD are marked by an improvement in cognitive deficiencies. Patients' independence is harmed by severe Alzheimer's disease [8].

2 Background Research

In 2016, Rahim et al. [9] have proposed vocal-based classification (VBC) for the detection of AD with the aid of a connectivity-metabolism relationship and here the region-to-voxel connectivities were evaluated using huge Regions of Interest (ROIs). The 3D-based "fluorodeoxyglucose-positron emission tomography (FDG-PET) images" at the voxel-level were classified using a linear classifier. The features of the image were obtained by utilizing the "computing region to-voxel connectivity maps". From the functional atlas, the Seed-based correlations were computed with the extracted ROIs.

In 2018, Shi et al. [10] formulated a multi-modal stacked deep polynomial network (MM-SDPN) algorithm embedded with two-stage SDPN to fuse multimodal data for accurate detection of AD from multimodal neuroimaging datasets. The "high-level features" from both Magnetic Resonance Imaging (MRI) as well as PET were learned using two SDPNs. The extracted features were fed as input to the SDPN to link the multimodal neuroimaging information.

In 2019, Kruthika et al. [11] a novel technique for Alzheimer's Disease detection with multistage classifier in accordance with "particle swarm intelligence" based feature selection technique. The input image from MRI is pre-processed using FreeSurfer, which had followed the steps like "head motion correction, smoothing, compensation for slice-dependent time shift and normalizing". The pre-processed image was subjected to extract the features and optimal features from the image were selected using PSO. The extracted optimal features were classified using several classifiers like K-nearest neighbors (KNN), support vector machine (SVM), multi-layer perceptron (MLP), and the ensemble model.

In 2019, Cui et al. [12] projected an innovative AD diagnosis model employing integrating the spatial and longitudinal features of MR images with the help of a convolutional neural network (CNN) as well as recurrent neural network (RNN). For the classification task, the spatial features of MRI were learned by constructing CNN, and the longitudinal features were extracted at multiple time points with the help of bidirectional gated recurrent units (BGRU) connected at the output of CNN. The proposed model was evaluated in terms of "classification accuracy, specificity, sensitivity and area under the receiver operating characteristic curve (AUC)" with the Alzheimer's Disease Neuroimaging Initiative (ADNI) dataset.

In 2019, Kruthika et al. [13] projected a novel Content-Based Image Retrieval (CBIR) system to detect Alzheimer's in an early stage with "3D-Convolutional Neural Network, 3D Capsule Network and pre-trained 3D-autoencoder" technology. The image acquired from MRI was preprocessed by utilizing the software Statistical Parametric Mapping (SPM). For the smaller dataset, the 3D-CapsNets were efficient in handling robust image transitions and rotations. The detection performance of the proposed model was enhanced using 3D-CapsNets when compared to CNN.

In 2017, Beheshti et al. [14] formulated an innovative CAD system with the aid of genetic algorithm as well as feature ranking for analyzing structural magnetic resonance image. Initially, the global and local GM was investigated by comparing with HCs via voxel-based morphometry technique. Then, the features were ranked in the feature selection stage under the basis of t-test scores. Then, the optimal feature set was selected using the genetic algorithm. The optimal features were subjected for classification using support vector machine (SVM).

In 2018, Tingyan et al. [15] explain the LSTM RNN technique which appears to be particularly promising when compared to models employing neuron networks, Bayesian networks, and tree-based algorithms. The author used the built deep learning model by integrating it into a mobile-friendly website for self-diagnoses. As a consequence, people with suspected AD at the preclinical/early stages can promptly receive individualized medical counsel.

Through ocular imaging technology, the retina is an organ that provides quick and easy access to pictures. It has microvascular characteristics and neuronal architecture like that of the brain, including the retinal nerve fibre layer (RNFL) and ganglion cell-inner plexiform layer (GC-IPL). Because of their similarity, possible alterations in the brain may be directly visualised. These distinctive qualities make the retina potentially useful for a low-cost, non-invasive study of the brain, doing away with the necessity for pricy neuroimaging treatments to make a diagnosis. Research into Alzheimer's disease (AD), where precise early detection and diagnostic models are still difficult to attain, has seen an increase in interest as a result [17].

Table 1. A comparative study on works done to detect AD using DL approaches.

S No.	Author	Data	Methods	Features	Challenges
1	Rahim et al. [9]	fMRI, PET	VBC	High classification accuracy Imaging modality is enhanced	Unable to tackle the connectivity of high dimensionality of voxel Requires dimensionality reduction in clustering models
2	Shi et al. [10]	structural MRI, PET	MM-SDPN	Low computational Complexity	Suffers from the problem of Overfitting
3	Kruthika et al. [11]	structural MRI	PSO	Retrieval speed is high	Selection of effective biomarkers is complex
4	Cui et al. [12]	MRI	CNN and RNN	High sensitivity and Specificity	Irrelevant information was not completely discarded
5	Kruthika et al. [13]	MRI	CNN and CapsNet	High F1-score Higher accuracy in retrieval	Requires large data sets for training
6	Beheshti et al. [14]	MRI	SVM	High specificity Efficient in extracting complex spatial patterns	Low classification accuracy Low sensitivity
7	Tingyan et al. [15]	Demographics, medical history, FAQ, non-image data	RNN	Temporal patterns were used	AD detection without image processing
8	Garam et al. [16]	Cognitive score, MRI, Cerebrospinal fluid (CSF) biomarker and demographic data	multimodal RNN	4-feature vectors	MCI to AD conversion using cross-sectional data at baseline and longitudinal data

Despite the existence of many more deep learning and ML techniques, illness prediction at an early stage remains unmanageable. The following are some of the advantages and disadvantages of the existing works: CNN [1] has superior patient care and assessment, as well as superior early identification of Alzheimer's disease. Still, effective diagnosis techniques must be offered, and their accuracy must be improved. KNN [18] takes less time to compute and assists radiologists in doing effective analysis. Heuristic models, on the other hand, are essential for optimum subset determination and have a significant computational cost. SVM [16] has a good prediction performance and can accurately diagnose Alzheimer's disease. The biggest disadvantage is that the study's subjects are tiny and perform poorly. The ML algorithm [19] reduces the number of false positives and enhances the identification of AD dementia. However, it suffers from survivor bias and performs poorly. LASSO [20] has a higher diagnostic accuracy and provides more information on diagnosis and brain alterations in Alzheimer's disease, but it lacks knowledge of the changes in spatiotemporal dynamics in the disease. SVM reduces the number of features and improves performance. CAD

[21] has dramatically improved classification accuracy without reducing classifier performance. However, the categorization models utilised in this approach had a lower specificity and were more complicated. ML asks for an average assessment of classification accuracy, however the performance is still hampered by error noise. The review of available AD prediction models using DL approaches is summarized in Table 1.

3 Retina Scan in Detection of Alzheimer

The retina, a layer of neurosensory tissue along the back of the eye that is directly linked to the brain by the optic nerve, receives light that has been focussed by the lens, transforms it into neural signals, and then transmits these signals to the brain for visual recognition. Histopathological analyses of postmortem materials have demonstrated retinal involvement in AD dementia. It has also been observed that age-related macular degeneration (AMD), diabetic retinopathy (DR), and glaucoma are prevalent eye conditions associated with AD dementia. Retinal imaging offers several benefits over brain imaging technology, including the fact that it is non-invasive, relatively inexpensive, and more common in non-tertiary settings (such as primary care and the community). It also includes a variety of variables for measuring the structures of the retina.

The majority of retinal imaging technologies are still specialized apparatus, and ophthalmologists or visual scientists are needed for the interpretation of the data. The cerebral cortex and certain subcortical areas lose neurons and synapses, which is how AD is typically diagnosed. Previous histology investigations have shown that retinal ganglion cells (RGCs) and their axons are also lost in AD patients. In order to explain the data about the weakening of the retinal neural layer, a number of explanations have been put up. It is hypothesised that amyloid plaques, fibrillar tau, and symptoms of neuroinflammation, which are cerebral markers of AD pathology, develop concurrently in the brain and the retina, highlighting a similar aetiology connecting retinal neuronal and axonal layer alterations and AD.

The cerebral cortex and particular subcortical regions exhibit loss of neurons and synapses, which is the hallmark of AD. Previous histological studies have shown that people with AD also experience axonal degeneration in their retinal ganglion cells (RGCs) [17]. The amount of melanopsin RGCs, the photoreceptors that drive circadian photoentrainment, may be diminished in AD, according to a more recent postmortem investigation [22]. Clinical research employing Optical coherence tomography (OCT) to ascertain the connection between various retinal layers and AD were built on the foundation of these discoveries [23] (Fig. 1).

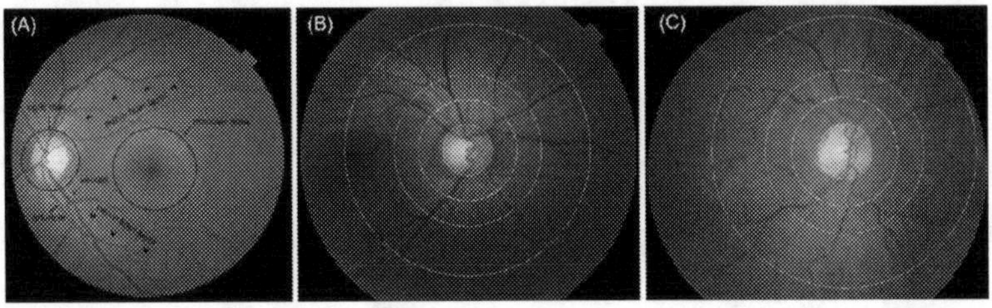

Fig. 1. (A) Retinal photograph showing the optic nerve head, macular area, nerve fibre layer, arterioles and venules. (B) Image of a cognitively normal patient; and (C) Image with Alzheimer's disease (AD) dementia [24]

The findings on the thinning of the retinal neural layer have been explained in a number of different ways. First, the neuronal connections of the visual tract may be impacted by the cerebral pathology of AD, which can also lead to retrograde degeneration of the retinal layers and the optic nerve, resulting in thinner Retinal Nerve Fiber Layer (RNFL) and ganglion cell layer with inner plexiform layer (GC-IPL) [25]. Instead, it is hypothesised that cerebral markers of AD pathology, such as amyloid- plaques, fibrillar tau, and evidence of neuroinflammation, manifest concurrently in the brain and the retina, highlighting a shared aetiology between retinal neuronal and axonal layer alterations and AD [26]. The less frequent detection of thicker RNFL in AD may be explained by reactive gliosis, an inflammatory response, occurring in the inner retina during early stages of AD, which may precede retinal neuronal layer thinning or conceal underlying modest retinal neuronal layer thinning on OCT [27].

4 Role of Deep Learning

Artificial neural networks are the foundation of the branch of machine learning science known as deep learning. Its various variations, including the Multi-Layer Perceptron (MLP), Convolutional Neural Networks (CNN), and Recurrent Neural Networks (RNN), may be used in a variety of industries, including computer vision, natural language processing, and machine translation. Three primary factors account for the growth of deep learning. Intuitive feature engineering, it means Deep learning automatically chooses variables and their weights for feature engineering and extraction. Huge Datasets, Constant data collecting has produced massive datasets eventually enabling deeper neural networks. Hardware advancements, the new GPUs (Graphical Process Units) enable quicker algebraic calculations, which are the fundamental building blocks of DL.

4.1 Emerging DL Technologies in AD Research

The black-box nature of deep architectures makes their implementation difficult in real-world health problems, even with their impressive achievements in many medical applications. These deep models must be comprehensible, explicable, and retraceable in order for doctors to accept and trust them, even when their numerous nonlinear changes across several levels enable them to achieve promising results. Significant progress has been made in a number of areas recently, allowing scientists to learn more about the intricate workings of Alzheimer's disease. Explainable models, normalising flows, graph-based deep architectures, self-supervised learning, and attention mechanisms are some of the novel developments and designs in deep learning for AD diagnosis that are the subject of this section.

1. Explainable models
   The publication [28] contains an explainable AI research that is applied to the structural analysis of degenerative illness. In order to do this, a modified version of deep BrainNet was trained on a heterogeneous set of patient connection matrices in order to classify participants into three categories: AD, MCI, and NC. By evaluating the degree to which a region and/or an edge might alter the neural network's prediction and by visualising the parts of the brain responsible for the majority of the neural network's output, the model was able to identify brain regions and their connections implicated in AD using an ablation study. Three explainable deep learning architectures for the automated identification of AD based on linguistic abilities were presented in a different study [29]. To represent the relative value of each single characteristic within a class, two forms of model explanations were generated in these architectures using interpretable 1D CNNs and self-attention processes.
2. Normalizing flows
   The following recent works on neuroimaging that include picture synthesis or reconstruction have employed normalising flows. First used in [30], a 3D reverse generative adversarial network (RevGAN) learned the nonlinear connection between pairs of MRIs and PETs to synthesise missing PET pictures. The investigation's findings suggest that, in patients who lack PET, utilising couples of genuine MRI and synthetic PET improves diagnostic performance over using only MRI. Conditional production of longitudinal data was taken into consideration in [31]. This research proposes an architecture based on an invertible neural network that uses temporal context gating and recurrent sub-networks to transfer information inside a sequence generation. The suggested approach may provide realistic PETs in neuroimaging situations with limited sample numbers, according to the results.
3. Graph-based deep architectures
   The ability of the graph structure to encode connections between various brain areas makes it a potent data representation in the field of neuroscience. Graph neural networks are a family of deep learning techniques that have been developed to do inference on data defined by graphs [32,33]. Graph neural networks have been proposed recently for the diagnosis of AD. The most popular use of graph-based architectures in AD diagnosis is the analysis of

MRIs, fMRIs, DTIs, and PETs using various versions of graph convolutional networks (GCNs). Liu et al. [34] examined the use of a semi-supervised GCN on the grey matter volume and shortest path length of each brain area, as determined by MRIs and fMRIs, respectively.

4. Self-supervised learning
   In the realm of medical image analysis, self-supervised learning is gaining popularity. It can serve as a practical remedy for the issue of the restricted availability of data with annotations. A self-supervised framework based on dual GANs and an additional CNN was presented by Song et al. [35] to produce high-resolution PETs from low-resolution PETs. Auto-GAN, a different framework enhanced by self-supervised learning, was presented by Cao et al. [36]. The MRIs and CTs obtained from the ADNI dataset were processed using the suggested Auto-GAN framework.
5. Attention mechanism
   In the realm of deep learning, attention techniques have been applied extensively in many different contexts. A multi-channel sparse graph transformer network was suggested in [37]. This design combines the structural connectivity of DTI, the functional connectivity of fMRI, and some of the participants' non-image data. Several graph transformer layers in this design use Taylor expansion and Fourier transform convolution to develop efficient node representations on graphs. According to [38], each subject's dynamic functional connection network was built using fMRI data by segmenting the time series of the fMRI using a sliding window and then utilising the Pearson Correlation Coefficient (PCC). The classification job was modelled using a sparse functional graph U-Net once the graph network was built.

5 Conclusion

In conclusion, our paper presents a comprehensive study for the early detection of Alzheimer's disease using imaging/scans. It also introduces the new emerging retina image as a potential biomarker for AD detection. An extensive study on recent trending frameworks that employ deep architectures for AD diagnosis. Explainable models, graph-based deep neural networks, self-supervised learning, normalizing flows, and the application of attention processes were some of the methods we explored to achieve this. This research represents a significant step towards the development of practical and efficient clinical methods for Alzheimer's disease screening, potentially leading to improved patient outcomes and quality of life.

References

1. Bayraktar, Y., et al.: Analyzing of Alzheimer's disease based on biomedical and socio-economic approach using molecular communication, artificial neural network, and random forest models. Sustainability **14**(13), 7901 (2022)

2. Guo, H., Zhang, Y.: Resting state fMRI and improved deep learning algorithm for earlier detection of Alzheimer's disease. IEEE Access **8**, 115383–115392 (2020)
3. Eke, C.S., et al.: Early detection of Alzheimer's disease with blood plasma proteins using support vector machines. IEEE J. Biomed. Health Inf. **25**(1), 218–226 (2020)
4. Cassani, R., Falk, T.H.: Alzheimer's disease diagnosis and severity level detection based on electroencephalography modulation spectral "patch" features. IEEE J. Biomed. Health Inf. **24**(7), 1982–1993 (2019)
5. Li, W., et al.: Detecting Alzheimer's disease on small dataset: a knowledge transfer perspective. IEEE J. Biomed. Health Inf. **23**(3), 1234–1242 (2018)
6. Wang, M., et al.: Spatial-temporal dependency modeling and network hub detection for functional MRI analysis via convolutional-recurrent network. IEEE Trans. Biomed. Eng. **67**(8), 2241–2252 (2019)
7. Alberdi, A., et al.: Smart home-based prediction of multidomain symptoms related to Alzheimer's disease. IEEE J. Biomed. Health Inf. **22**(6), 1720–1731 (2018)
8. Khan, P., et al.: Machine learning and deep learning approaches for brain disease diagnosis: principles and recent advances. IEEE Access **9**, 37622–37655 (2021)
9. Rahim, M., et al.: Transmodal learning of functional networks for Alzheimer's disease prediction. IEEE J. Sel. Top. Sig. Process. **10**(7), 1204–1213 (2016)
10. Shi, J., et al.: Multimodal neuroimaging feature learning with multimodal stacked deep polynomial networks for diagnosis of Alzheimer's disease. IEEE J. Biomed. Health Inf. **22**(1), 173–183 (2017)
11. Kruthika, K.R., Maheshappa, H.D., Alzheimer's Disease Neuroimaging Initiative: Multistage classifier-based approach for Alzheimer's disease prediction and retrieval. Inf. Med. Unlocked **14**, 34–42 (2019)
12. Cui, R., Liu, M., Initiative, A.D.N.: RNN-based longitudinal analysis for diagnosis of Alzheimer's disease. Comput. Med. Imaging Graph. **73**, 1–10 (2019)
13. Kruthika, K.R., Maheshappa, H.D., Alzheimer's Disease Neuroimaging Initiative: CBIR system using capsule networks and 3D CNN for Alzheimer's disease diagnosis. Inf. Med. Unlocked **14**, 59–68 (2019)
14. Beheshti, I., et al.: Classification of Alzheimer's disease and prediction of mild cognitive impairment-to-Alzheimer's conversion from structural magnetic resource imaging using feature ranking and a genetic algorithm. Comput. Biol. Med. **83**, 109–119 (2017)
15. Wang, T., et al.: Early detection models for persons with probable Alzheimer's disease with deep learning. In: 2018 2nd IEEE Advanced Information Management, Communicates, Electronic and Automation Control Conference (IMCEC). IEEE (2018)
16. Lee, G., et al.: Predicting Alzheimer's disease progression using multi-modal deep learning approach. Sci. Rep. **9**(1), 1952 (2019)
17. Tian, F., et al.: Blood vessel segmentation of fundus retinal images based on improved Frangi and mathematical morphology. Comput. Math. Methods Med. **2021**, 1–11 (2021)
18. Vaithinathan, K., Parthiban, L., Initiative, A.D.N.: A novel texture extraction technique with T1 weighted MRI for the classification of Alzheimer's disease. J. Neurosci. Methods **318**, 84–99 (2019)
19. Moscoso, A., et al.: Prediction of Alzheimer's disease dementia with MRI beyond the short-term: implications for the design of predictive models. NeuroImage Clin. **23**, 101837 (2019)
20. Mattsson, N., et al.: Predicting diagnosis and cognition with 18F-AV-1451 tau PET and structural MRI in Alzheimer's disease. Alzheimer's Dement. **15**(4), 570–580 (2019)

21. Lahmiri, S., Shmuel, A.: Performance of machine learning methods applied to structural MRI and ADAS cognitive scores in diagnosing Alzheimer's disease. Biomed. Signal Process. Control **52**, 414–419 (2019)
22. Cheung, C.Y.-L., et al.: Retinal ganglion cell analysis using high-definition optical coherence tomography in patients with mild cognitive impairment and Alzheimer's disease. J. Alzheimer's Dis. **45**(1), 45–56 (2015)
23. La Morgia, C., et al.: Melanopsin retinal ganglion cell loss in Alzheimer disease. Ann. Neurol. **79**(1), 90–109 (2016)
24. Cheung, C.Y., et al.: Retinal imaging in Alzheimer's disease. J. Neurol. Neurosurg. Psychiatry **92**(9), 983–994 (2021)
25. Mutlu, U., et al.: Association of retinal neurodegeneration on optical coherence tomography with dementia: a population-based study. JAMA Neurol. **75**(10), 1256–1263 (2018)
26. Chan, V.T.T., et al.: Spectral-domain OCT measurements in Alzheimer's disease: a systematic review and meta-analysis. Ophthalmology **126**(4), 497–510 (2019)
27. Ostergaard, L., et al.: Cerebral small vessel disease: capillary pathways to stroke and cognitive decline. J. Cereb. Blood Flow Metab. **36**(2), 302–325 (2016)
28. Essemlali, A., et al.: Understanding Alzheimer disease's structural connectivity through explainable AI. Med. Imag. Deep Learn. PMLR (2020)
29. Wang, N., Chen, M., Subbalakshmi, K.P.: Explainable CNN-attention networks (C-attention network) for automated detection of Alzheimer's disease. arXiv preprint arXiv:2006.14135 (2020)
30. Lin, W.: Synthesizing missing data using 3D reversible GAN for Alzheimer's disease. In: Proceedings of the 1st International Symposium on Artificial Intelligence in Medical Sciences (2020)
31. Hwang, S.J., et al.: Conditional recurrent flow: conditional generation of longitudinal samples with applications to neuroimaging. In: Proceedings of the IEEE/CVF International Conference on Computer Vision (2019)
32. Nebli, A., et al.: Quantifying the reproducibility of graph neural networks using multigraph data representation. Neural Netw. **148**, 254–265 (2022)
33. Zhang, S., et al. Graph convolutional networks: a comprehensive review. Comput. Soc. Netw. **6**(1), 1–23 (2019)
34. Liu, J., et al.: Identification of early mild cognitive impairment using multi-modal data and graph convolutional networks. BMC Bioinf. **21**(6) (2020)1–12
35. Song, T.-A., et al.: PET image super-resolution using generative adversarial networks. Neural Netw. **125**, 83–91 (2020)
36. Cao, B, et al.: Auto-GAN: self-supervised collaborative learning for medical image synthesis. In: Proceedings of the AAAI Conference on Artificial Intelligence, vol. 34, no. (07) (2020)
37. Qiu, Y., et al.: Multi-channel sparse graph transformer network for early Alzheimer's disease identification. In: 2021 IEEE 18th International Symposium on Biomedical Imaging (ISBI). IEEE (2021)
38. Zhu, Y., Song, X., Qiu, Y., Zhao, C., Lei, B.: Structure and feature based graph U-Net for early Alzheimer's disease prediction. In: Syeda-Mahmood, T., et al. (eds.) ML-CDS 2021. LNCS, vol. 13050, pp. 93–104. Springer, Cham (2021). https://doi.org/10.1007/978-3-030-89847-2_9

Pattern Recognition in Blockchain, Cyber and Network Security, and Cryptography

VAIDS: A Hybrid Deep Learning Model to Detect Intrusions in MQTT Protocol Enabled Networks

Chetanya Kunndra[1], Arjun Choudhary[1(✉)], Jaspreet Kaur[2], and Prashant Mathur[1]

[1] Sardar Patel University of Police Security and Criminal Justice, Jodhpur, India
{mtcs20ck,a.choudhary,mtcs20pm}@policeuniversity.ac.in
[2] Indian Institute of Technology, Jodhpur, India
kaur.3@iitj.ac.in

Abstract. The adoption of 5G networks is seen as an enabler for IoT. With low latency and increased reach, many more IoT devices can now be connected and controlled. An increase in the number of IoT devices since its inception brought forth the need for a lightweight communication protocol. The protocol in question should be able to cater to a large number of IoT devices. These requirements were the basis of the MQTT protocol. Attackers can utilize the protocol to target a network. Furthermore it is a herculean task to manually identify an attack in a huge network. Artificial Intelligence can be used to efficiently detect such attacks with a high degree of accuracy. In this research we propose a hybrid deep learning mult-iclass classification model VAIDS. VAIDS utilizes the CNN algorithm to extract features from the dataset. These features are then utilized as inputs for the LSTM algorithm. The proposed model can detect five types of anomalies within an IoT network that uses the MQTT protocol. The proposed model is trained, tested and validated against the MQTT-IoT-IDS2020 dataset and classifies a given input into one of five attack classes. The model showcases a high degree of accuracy of 99.97%.

Keywords: Cyber security · MQTT · Deep learning · CNN · LSTM · Internet of Things

1 Introduction

Internet of Things (IoT), to put it simply, is an umbrella term that is used to refer to physical objects that are connected to the internet. These objects make use of components called *'sensors'* to take physical measurements of their ambient environment [1]. These values are then relayed over to other devices using the internet. An action based on the readings is then transmitted back and implemented upon the physical environment using devices called *'actuators'* [2]. An internet connected monitoring system or even an internet connected smart home assistant fall under the umbrella category of IoT. The innate need of humans to automate and reduce their effort gave birth to IoT. The Internet

KC Santosh et al. (Eds.): RTIP2R 2023, CCIS 2027, pp. 209–222, 2024.
https://doi.org/10.1007/978-3-031-53085-2_18

Conference of 1990 presented the first known IoT device, a toaster. This internet connected toaster could be controlled over the internet [3]. The adoption and advancements in artificial intelligence evolved simple IoT devices into smart devices. Nowadays, IoT can be found almost everywhere, from smart lighting to smart appliances. Figure 1 illustrates various components in an IoT network and how an IoT device interacts with the physical environment.

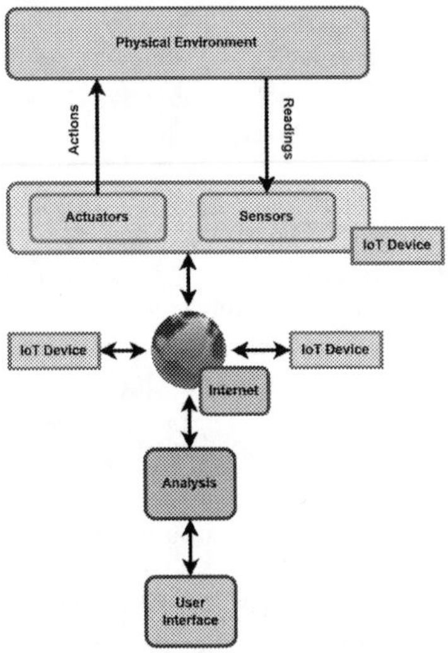

Fig. 1. Basic representation of various components in an IoT network.

There are numerous ways to categorize IoT devices. One prominent way of classifying IoT devices is on the basis of their area of use. Based upon such a criteria, an IoT can be classified into the following two categories -

- **Consumer Internet of Things (CIoT) -** These IoT devices are your everyday IoT devices and can be found in our homes. CIoT devices are developed to cater to the needs of the people [4]. Such devices can perform multiple tasks. Smart thermostats, smart house assistants all fall under this category.
- **Industrial Internet of Things (IIoT) -** These IoT devices are used in the harsh environments of industries. Unlike CIoT devices, these devices are built to perform a specific task only. They are ruggedized and developed to be extremely efficient so that they can cater to the needs of the industry [5].

Adoption of 5G networks has become a booster for IoT. Faster network speed and increased reliability has made it possible for more IoTs to be connected to the network. To put it into perspective, as of 2022 there are at least 14.3 billion active IoT devices. It is estimated that there will be at least 29 billion active IoT endpoints by 2027 [6]. Maintaining steady and secure communication within such a larger network is an extremely difficult task. There arises a need for a reliable, lightweight and a cost effective communication protocol that is specifically designed to handle such a large number of devices.

Developed in 1999 by IBM, the *'Message Queuing Telemetry Transport (MQTT) protocol'* suffices the aforementioned requirements [7]. The MQTT protocol was initially developed as a cost effective solution to cater to the needs of oil and gas industries. It has now become an industry standard protocol.

1.1 MQTT Network Infrastructure Overview

MQTT is a very widely used protocol, it is being widely used in the industries to control industrial processes. Latest version of the MQTT protocol has the capabilities of connecting millions of IoT devices in a network [8]. With support for unreliable networks and secure network communication using TLS encryption, MQTT has become the goto protocol for connecting all forms of IoT devices.

The protocol works in a *'Publish/Subscribe'* architecture. To elaborate, at the heart of the infrastructure is a middleware called the *'MQTT broker'*. The sole purpose of the broker is to relay messages between publishers and subscribers [9]. In this context a subscriber is any device that wants to fetch the readings from an IoT device. The subscriber subscribes to a *'topic'* with the broker. A *'Publisher'* in this context refers to devices that generate data points and share them with the subscribers. These devices can be the edge IoT device that *publish* data on a certain topic [10]. For easier understanding, a *'topic'* in an MQTT network refers to the class or type of data being gathered, for example temperature, pressure or humidity readings etc. These published readings are then sent to the broker, the broker then transmits the information to relevant subscribers of that topic. Figure 2 depicts a typical network infrastructure that uses the MQTT protocol.

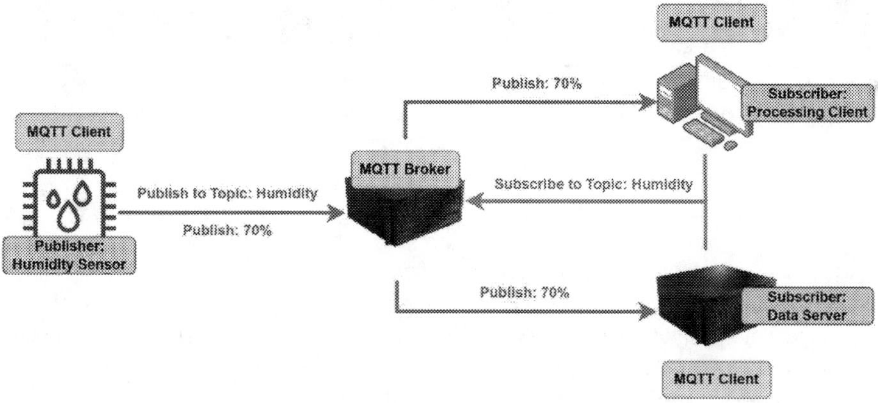

Fig. 2. A typical MQTT network infrastructure.

1.2 MQTT Packet Structure

A MQTT data packet consists of four components. These components are as follows -

- **Fixed Header -** The first component of a MQTT packet is the Fixed Header. This header has a size of 1 byte and contains two most important pieces of information about the packet, namely the *'packet type'* and *'flags'* [11]. Each of the components are 4 bits in size.
- **Remaining Length -** This header denotes the length of the remainder of the packet. Its size varies from 1 to 4 bytes. If the size of the remainder of the packet is up to 127 bytes then 1 byte is used. If the length is greater than 127 bytes and less than 16 KB then 2 bytes are used. The maximum possible length of the remainder of the packet can be at max 256 MB [12]. The *'Control Header'* and *'Packet Length'* are sometimes collectively called the *'Fixed Header'* as they are always present in the packet.
- **Variable Header -** The variable header differs from packet to packet. The contents of this header largely contains the information about the packet such as protocol name, protocol level, keep alive status and so on.
- **Payload -** The payload part of the packet contains the actual data being transmitted. It can be of any format such as JSON, CSV or even plain text.

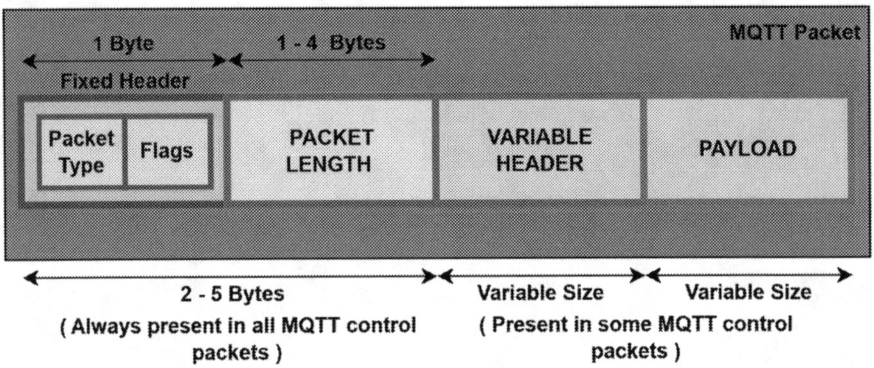

Fig. 3. MQTT packet structure.

It is to be noted that within an MQTT packet, *'Control Header'* and *'Packet Length'* header are mandatory and always present. Keeping this in mind the minimum size of an MQTT packet is 2 bytes. The DISCONNECT packet in MQTT v5.1.1 only contains the first two headers, thus having a packet size of 2 bytes [13].

In comparison to the MQTT protocol, the most popular and widely used TCP protocol has ten mandatory headers. The cumulative size of these headers is between 20 - 24 bytes [14]. This means at a bare minimum a TCP packet will be 20 bytes in size while an MQTT packet will be a mere 2 bytes. This attributes to the high speed and lightness of the MQTT protocol, making it the ideal medium for IoT communication. Figure 3 and Fig. 4 depict the packet structure of the MQTT and TCP protocols.

1.3 Network Attacks on IoT Infrastructure

It is to be noted that the MQTT protocol acts as a medium between the attacker and the target. Attacker does not specifically attack the MQTT protocol but rather uses the said protocol to carry out attacks. It is crucial to understand that the protocol is merely a tool. The vulnerabilities arise due to improper implementation of the infrastructure.

Owing to the design of the MQTT protocol and its server/broker architecture, the type of attacks are relatively less. Few attacks that are possible in such a network infrastructure are -

- **Reconnaissance attacks -** The sole purpose of reconnaissance attacks is to gather information about the target. These attacks can be either passive (without interacting with the target) [15] or active (interacting with the target) [16] in nature. Attacker uses this information to further attack the target.

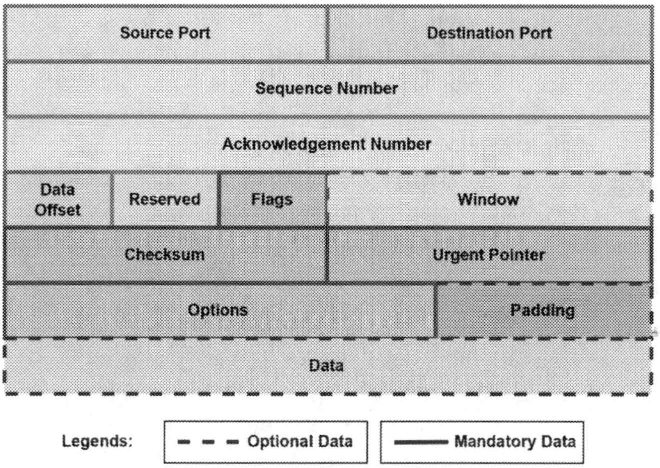

Fig. 4. TCP packet structure.

- **Brute Force Authentication attacks -** In this attack, the attacker tries every username and password combination in order to guess the correct password. The main motive of an attacker is to gain access to privileged resources by guessing the correct username and password combination [17].
- **Denial of Service / Distributed denial of service attacks -** Denial of Service (DoS) and Distributed Denial of Service (DDoS) attacks have the primary motive of disrupting the services provided by the target. Attackers usually perform these attacks by overwhelming the target by sending large amounts of network traffic [18]. The overwhelmed target is thus unable to cater to its intended clients, thus causing disruption in services.

The criticality of IoT devices should not be underestimated. With a projected sharp increase in the number of IoT devices, it is of utmost importance to protect and secure these devices. Traditional security measures do work but have become less effective. This can be primarily attributed to the fact that the threat actors have become increasingly sophisticated. Moreover, manually sifting through the network to find perpetrators is a humongous task. The use of artificial intelligence can facilitate the detection process. Implementing learning algorithms can increase the accuracy and speed of detection. In this paper we propose a novel deep learning model that can be used for multi-class classification of four types of attacks in an IoT network that uses the MQTT protocol. This primary contributions of this paper can be summarized as follows -

1. This paper compares and contrasts recent developments done in the domain of intrusion detection MQTT protocol enabled IoT networks.
2. Furthermore, this paper proposes a novel hybrid CNN and LSTM algorithm, thereby providing a new research method for intrusion detection in MQTT enabled networks.
3. The proposed model is trained and tested against the MQTT-IoT-IDS2020 dataset and provides a high accuracy in multiclass attack classification.

The rest of the paper is organized as follows: Sect. 2 discusses various researches done in the domain of multi-class attack classification. Section 3 explains the dataset used to train, test and validate the proposed model. Section 4 explains the proposed model in detail. Section 5 elaborates on the experiments performed to check the effectiveness of the proposed model. Section 6 explains the evaluation metrics used to quantify the proposed models performance. Section 7 discusses the results obtained from the experiments performed in Sect. 5. Conclusion and future works follows Sect. 7.

2 Related Work

The MQTT protocol was originally developed in 1999 and was initially used to send data from monitoring devices back to remote servers. With the onset of Industry 4.0, MQTT has become the de-facto protocol for inter-device communication. The scalability of the MQTT protocol makes it ideal to be used in such scenarios. Thus safeguarding assets utilizing such a critical resource is of utmost importance. Numerous researches have utilized artificial intelligence to build solutions to detect and classify anomalies within networks that use the MQTT protocol.

Ullah et. al. [19] proposes a feed forward neural network model to perform binary and multiclass classification of attacks in IoT networks. Authors utilize six different datasets to individually train, test and validate the proposed model. These datasets are: BoT-IoT, IoT network intrusion, MQTTset, MQTT-IoT-IDS2020, IoT-DS2, and IoT-23 datasets. The datasets consist of bidirectional network flows. The proposed model has an accuracy of 99.92% on the MQTT-IoT-IDS2020 dataset.

Alzahrani et. al. [20] proposes four algorithms to tackle the problem statement. Authors implement KNN, LDA, CNN and CNN + LSTM models. Each of these models are trained, tested and validated against the MQTTset dataset 98.94%, whereas KNN has only 80.82% and LDA showcases a mere 76.60% accuracy.

Ullah et. al. [21] propose an anomaly based detection system for IoT. This system comprises CNN based models. Authors implement 1D, 2D and 3D CNN models. Each model is trained and validated against four different datasets. This research encompasses the majority of the attacks prevalent in the domain of IoT. Proposed model showcases outstanding results. Authors conclude that the 1D CNN model, having an accuracy of 99.74% performs better than 2D (99.42%) and 3D (99.03%) CNN models.

Khan et. al. [22] develop and evaluate a DNN model for carrying binary and multiclass classification of the MQTT-IoT-IDS2020 dataset. Furthermore authors evaluate and compare the performance of KNN, DT, LSTM, RF and other popular models. The proposed DNN model performs better than the other models. For multiclass classification the model has an accuracy of 97.13%.

Shajan [23] tests the effectiveness of zero bias DNN algorithm to detect intrusions in IoT networks. Author trains, tests and validates their proposed model on the MQTT-IoT-IDS2020 dataset. Unlike other research, the proposed model shows less accuracy in comparison to others. The model has an accuracy of 92% and thus cannot be efficiently used to detect intrusions in an IoT network.

Table 1 gives a comparative analysis of various researches done in the field.

Table 1. Comparative table of papers on multi-class attack classification in the IoT network

Paper	Dataset	Algorithm	Accuracy(%)
Ullah et. al. [19]	BoT-IoT, IoT network intrusion, MQTT-IoT-IDS2020, MQTTset, IoT-23	Feed Forward Neural Networks	99.92
Alzahrani et. al. [20]	MQTT-set	KNN, LDA, CNN, CNN + LSTM	98.94
Ullah et. al. [21]	BoT-IoT, IoT Network Intrusion, MQTT-IoT-IDS2020, and IoT-23 intrusion	CNN	99.74
Khan et. al. [22]	MQTT-IoT-IDS2020	DNN	97.13
Shajan [23]	MQTT-IoT-IDS2020	DNN	92
Proposed model	**MQTT-IoT-IDS2020**	**CNN + LSTM**	**99.97**

3 Dataset

3.1 Dataset Description

The MQTT-IoT-IDS2020 dataset was created by Hindy et. al. [24]. This dataset is presented in the form of network captures (.pcap) and comma separated values (.csv) files. MQTT-IoT-IDS2020 dataset contains three variants of the dataset: unidirectional network flow dataset, bidirectional network flow dataset and parsed raw network dataset. Each variant further contains separate dataset files for each class. These classes are -

- **Benign -** Records of this class represent normal legitimate MQTT protocol traffic.
- **MQTT_BruteForce -** Records having the '*MQTT_BruteForce*' label represent network traffic originating from a brute force attack.

- **Scan_A -** This class contains records of aggressive scan network traffic.
- **Scan_sU -** This class contains records of reconnaissance done with the aid of the UDP protocol.
- **Sparta -** These records are generated using the Sparta network infrastructure penetration testing tool [25].

Each of the classes except *'Benign'* represents a popular attack vector present in the MQTT protocol.

The unidirectional and bidirectional network flow datasets require minimal pre-processing. Hindy et. al. Have normalized and encoded relevant features of the dataset. This dataset can be used to mimic real world scenarios on IoT devices. Table 2 gives an overview of the class distribution of the MQTT-IoT-IDS2020 dataset.

Table 2. MQTT-IoT-IDS2020 dataset class distribution.

Flow	Class	Number of Records	
		With Redundancy	Without Redundancy
Complete Packet Capture	Benign	3269614	3269603
	MQTT_BruteForce	9686086	9686086
	Scan_A	40624	40624
	Scan_sU	22436	22436
	Sparta	19103574	19103574
Bi-Directional Flow	Benign	188378	188189
	MQTT_BruteForce	14544	14544
	Scan_A	19907	19907
	Scan_sU	22434	22434
	Sparta	14116	14116
Uni-Directional Flow	Benign	376186	375820
	MQTT_BruteForce	28874	28874
	Scan_A	39797	21891
	Scan_sU	22436	22435
	Sparta	28232	28232

3.2 Dataset Labeling

The csv files present in the MQTT-IoT-IDS2020 dataset contains a column named *'is_attack'*. The values in this column range from 1 (Anomalous Traffic) and 0 (Benign Traffic). In order to perform multi classification, each record must be labeled with their respective type. Once labeled, the *'label'* column is *'one hot encoded'* [26] to perform categorical classification. This process increases the dimensionality of the labels to five, wherein each dimension represents a class of network traffic.

4 Proposed Model

CNN is a type of feed-forward neural network that is mostly utilized for natural language and image processing owing to their great efficiency. CNN can also be utilized to forecast time series accurately [27]. CNN's local perception and weight sharing can considerably minimize the amount of parameters required to train the model. This makes the training phase less computational and space complex, increasing overall efficiency. The convolution layer and the pooling layer are the two most important parts of CNN. The number of convolution kernels within each layer of CNN vary depending upon the problem that is to be solved. A pooling layer is added after the convolutional layer to reduce feature dimensionality and thus the cost of training the model [28]. This is primarily attributed to the fact that the convolution process increases the dimensionality of the features, this can in turn increase the cost of training the model [29].

Schmidhuber et al. proposed the LSTM deep learning model in 1997 [30]. Unlike CNN, LSTM is primarily used to address issues like speech recognition, text analysis, and emotion analysis. Their success in these areas can be attributed to their architecture. To elaborate, LSTM have their own memory and thus can make relatively exact predictions and forecasting. A LSTM memory cell is made up of three gates: input, forget, and output gates [31]. The rest of the LSTM structure is identical to that of an RNN model.

The proposed multi-class classification model is built using the combination of the CNN and LSTM algorithms. This proposed novel model is named as the *'**V**ery **A**ccurate **I**ntrusion **D**etection **S**ystem'* or VAIDS for short. The CNN layers in VAIDS extract the features from the input layer. These features are then fed into the LSTM layer. This process yields a model which has highly optimized computation and space complexities. This combination of algorithms has multidimensional uses in industry as well as academia.

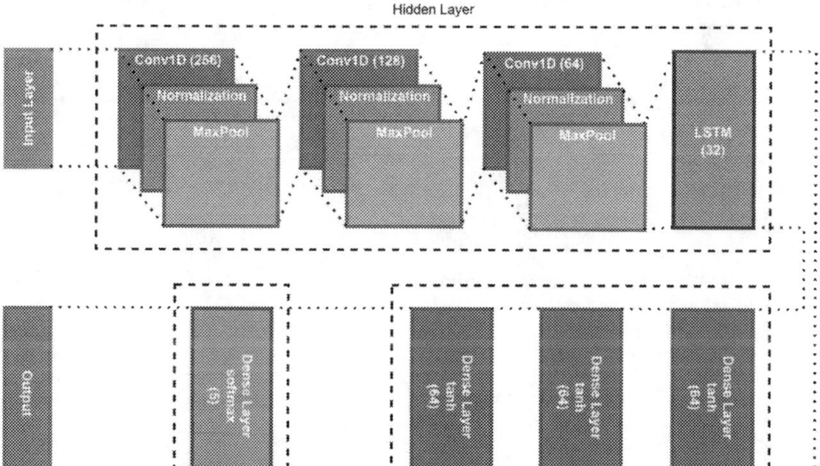

Fig. 5. The proposed VAIDS model.

VAIDS is composed of numerous hidden layers. These layers can be broadly divided into three categories: CNN layer, the LSTM layer and the Dense Layer. The CNN layer comprises three Conv1D layers, each having a kernel size of 3 and *'relu'* as their activation function. The three layers have 256, 128 and 64 units respectively. Moreover each Conv1D layer is followed by a *'LayerNormalization'* layer and a *'MaxPool1D'* layer. MaxPool1D returns the maximum value of the vector matrices generated. These CNN layers help in extraction of crucial data features with losing any attributes. The output generated by the CNN layers is then fed into the LSTM layer. The LSTM layer has 32 units, a dropout rate of 0.1 and a recurrent dropout rate of 0.1. Dropout rates help determine which neuron in the layer needs to be discarded. The LSTM layer is followed by three dense layers, each layer having *'tanh'* as their activation function. The dense layers 64 units each. The output layer is a dense layer with 5 units and *'softmax'* as the activation function. The number of units in this layer corresponds to the number of classes we require the model to classify. Generally *'sigmoid'* function is used to create a binary classification model [32]. Sigmoid function always returns a value between 0 and 1 and hence it is suitable for binary classification. Softmax function extends this into a multi-class domain. Softmax assigns decimal probabilities to each class, thus aiding in multi-class classification [33]. These probabilities must add up to 1.0. Figure 5 depicts the logical structure of VAIDS.

5 Experiments

To evaluate and compare VAIDS effectiveness we compare its performance with CNN, LSTM, RNN and MLP models. In order to ensure uniformity, each model is trained, tested and validated against the same dataset and with the same hardware and software resources. Each test is executed on Intel® Core™ i7-8850H CPU @ 2.60GHz with 32 GB RAM. For validation, 5-fold cross validation was used. Figure 6. Illustrates the experimental process.

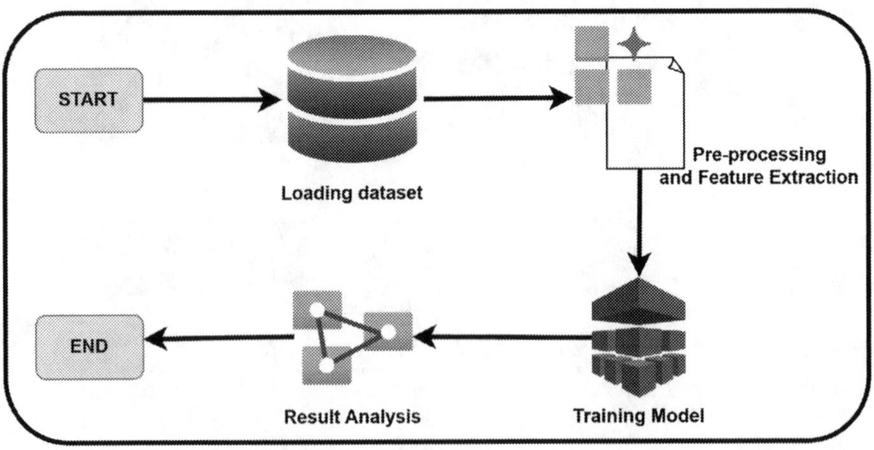

Fig. 6. Logic flow of experiments.

Each model is trained for 30 epochs. We settled upon using the *'adam'* optimizer and *'categorical_crossentropy'* as the loss function.

6 Evaluation Metrics

Evaluating a model's performance requires certain parameters that correlate to the validity of the predictions made by the model. These parameters are -

- **True Positives -** If the actual label is *'True'* and the predicted label is also *'True'*, then the prediction is called a *'True Positive (P_T)'*.
- **True Negatives -** If the actual label is *'False'* and the predicted label is also *'False'*, then the prediction is called a *'True Negative (N_T)'*.
- **False Positives -** If the actual label is *'False'* and the predicted label is *'True'*, then the prediction is called a *'False Positive (P_F)'*.
- **False Negatives -** If the actual label is *'True'* and the predicted label is *'False'*, then the prediction is called a *'False Negative (N_F)'*.

These parameters aid in defining the evaluation metrics. To quantify the effectiveness of the model, the following metrics have been used -

- **Accuracy -** Accuracy is the ratio of the correct predictions made by the model to the total predictions made. Accuracy is a prominent evaluation metric. A higher accuracy score implies a more effective classification model. Accuracy of a model can be quantified by using the following formula -

$$A_c = (P_T + N_T) / (P_T + N_T + P_F + N_F) \quad (1)$$

- **Error Rate -** Error Rate can be defined as the ratio of the total number of incorrect predictions made to the total predictions made by the model. Conversely, a lower error rate implies a more accurate and effective classification model. Error rate of a model can be quantified using the following formula -

$$E_r = (P_F + N_F) / (P_T + N_T + P_F + N_F) \quad (2)$$

7 Results

The experiments performed show that VAIDS performs better in comparison to traditional deep learning models. Furthermore, VIADS has a higher degree of accuracy in comparison to the recent research done in the domain. VAIDS is able to classify the data into one of the five classes with a peak accuracy of 99.97%. One of the perks of supervised learning is that it allows us to monitor the learning process of a model. *'Accuracy'* and *'Error Rate'* are metrics that can be used to evaluate a model's performance. Table 3 gives a comparative overview of the results of the experiment.

Table 3. Performance of proposed model on MQTT-IoT-IDS2020 dataset.

Dataset Type	Model	Accuracy (%)	Error Rate
Complete Packet Capture	CNN	97.13	0.035945
	RNN	93.92	0.068277
	LSTM	95.67	0.047826
	MLP	92.84	0.079005
	VAIDS	**98.40**	**0.047768**
Bi-Directional Flow	CNN	98.23	0.024511
	RNN	95.48	0.051266
	LSTM	96.64	0.039715
	MLP	94.73	0.059234
	VAIDS	**99.97**	**0.008746**
Uni-Directional Flow	CNN	97.93	0.027753
	RNN	94.32	0.063917
	LSTM	96.24	0.043709
	MLP	93.94	0.067823
	VAIDS	**99.85**	**0.009948**

8 Conclusion and Future Scope

In this research we present a hybrid CNN and LSTM deep learning model called VAIDS. VAIDS can be used to detect anomalies in IoT MQTT protocol network traffic with a high degree of accuracy. This proposed model can be used to safeguard vulnerable IoT infrastructure that runs using the MQTT protocol. VAIDS utilizes the features extracted from the network flow and then classifies the flow into one of five categories, namely: Benign, MQTT Bruteforce, Aggressive Scans, UDP scans and tool based attacks. The results show that VAIDS performs better than traditional deep learning models and has a peak of accuracy of 99.97%.

Ideologically VAIDS was theorized as a deep learning model that could be utilized to detect anomalies in any network with a high degree of accuracy. This research is a step in this direction. In future, we intend to train the model on various intrusion detection datasets that are not just limited to IoT networks. Our aim is to convert this novel model into an intelligent intrusion detection system for all forms of vulnerabilities.

References

1. Kelly, S.D.T., Suryadevara, N.K., Mukhopadhyay, S.C.: Towards the implementation of IoT for environmental condition monitoring in homes. IEEE Sens. J. **13**(10), 3846–3853 (2013)
2. Rayes, A., Salam, S.: The things in iot: Sensors and actuators. In: Internet of Things From Hype to Reality: The Road to Digitization, pp. 63–82. Springer International Publishing, Cham (2022)

3. Suresh, P., Daniel, J.V., Parthasarathy, V., Aswathy, R.H.: November. A state of the art review on the Internet of Things (IoT) history, technology and fields of deployment. In: 2014 International Conference On Science Engineering and Management Research (ICSEMR) (pp. 1–8). IEEE (2014)
4. Xenofontos, C., Zografopoulos, I., Konstantinou, C., Jolfaei, A., Khan, M.K., Choo, K.K.R.: Consumer, commercial, and industrial iot (in) security: attack taxonomy and case studies. IEEE Internet Things J. **9**(1), 199–221 (2021)
5. Sisinni, E., Saifullah, A., Han, S., Jennehag, U., Gidlund, M.: Industrial internet of things: challenges, opportunities, and directions. IEEE Trans. Industr. Inf. **14**(11), 4724–4734 (2018)
6. Sinha, S.: State of IOT 2023: Number of connected IOT devices growing 16% to 16.7 billion globally, IoT Analytics (2023). https://iot-analytics.com/number-connected-iot-devices/. Accessed 27 Aug 2023
7. Soni, D., Makwana, A.: April. A survey on mqtt: a protocol of internet of things (iot). In: International Conference on Telecommunication, Power Analysis and Computing Techniques (ICTPACT-2017) vol. 20, pp. 173–177 (2017)
8. Boyd, B., et al.: Building Real-time Mobile Solutions with MQTT and IBM MessageSight. IBM Redbooks (2014)
9. Hunkeler, U., Truong, H.L., Stanford-Clark, A.: January. MQTT-S—A publish/subscribe protocol for Wireless Sensor Networks. In: 2008 3rd International Conference on Communication Systems Software and Middleware and Workshops (COMSWARE'08), pp. 791–798 IEEE (2008)
10. Tang, K., Wang, Y., Liu, H., Sheng, Y., Wang, X., Wei, Z.: October. Design and implementation of push notification system based on the MQTT protocol. In 2013 International Conference on Information Science and Computer Applications (ISCA 2013), pp. 116–119. Atlantis Press (2013)
11. Standard, O.A.S.I.S.: MQTT Version 5.0, vol. 22, p. 2020 (2019)
12. Nazir, S., Kaleem, M.: March. Reliable image notifications for smart home security with MQTT. In: 2019 International Conference on Information Science and Communication Technology (ICISCT), pp. 1–5. IEEE (2019)
13. Profanter, S., Tekat, A., Dorofeev, K., Rickert, M. and Knoll, A., 2019, February. OPC UA versus ROS, DDS, and MQTT: Performance evaluation of industry 4.0 protocols. In 2019 IEEE International Conference on Industrial Technology (ICIT) (pp. 955–962). IEEE
14. Franceschinis, M., Pastrone, C., Spirito, M.A. and Borean, C.: October. On the performance of ZigBee Pro and ZigBee IP in IEEE 802.15. 4 networks. In: 2013 IEEE 9th International Conference on Wireless and Mobile Computing, Networking and Communications (WiMob), pp. 83–88. IEEE (2013)
15. Zalewski, M.: Silence on the Wire: A Field Guide to Passive Reconnaissance and Indirect Attacks, No Starch Press (2005)
16. Hyder, M.F., Ismail, M.A.: Securing control and data planes from reconnaissance attacks using distributed shadow controllers, reactive and proactive approaches. IEEE Access **9**, 21881–21894 (2021)
17. Cho, J.S., Yeo, S.S., Kim, S.K.: Securing against brute-force attack: a hash-based RFID mutual authentication protocol using a secret value. Comput. Commun. **34**(3), 391–397 (2011)
18. Vishwakarma, R., Jain, A.K.: A survey of DDoS attacking techniques and defence mechanisms in the IoT network. Telecommun. Syst. **73**(1), 3–25 (2020)
19. Ullah, I., Mahmoud, Q.H.: January. An anomaly detection model for IoT networks based on flow and flag features using a feed-forward neural network. In: 2022 IEEE 19th Annual Consumer Communications & Networking Conference (CCNC), pp. 363–368. IEEE (2022)
20. Alzahrani, A., Aldhyani, T.H.: Artificial intelligence algorithms for detecting and classifying MQTT protocol internet of things attacks. Electronics **11**(22), 3837 (2022)

21. Ullah, I., Mahmoud, Q.H.: Design and development of a deep learning-based model for anomaly detection in IoT networks. IEEE Access **9**, 103906–103926 (2021)
22. Khan, M.A., et al.: A deep learning-based intrusion detection system for MQTT enabled IoT. Sensors **21**(21), 7016 (2021)
23. Shajan, A.A.: Intrusion Detection in IoT devices using Zero Bias DNN (Doctoral dissertation, Dublin, National College of Ireland) (2021)
24. Hindy, H., Bayne, E., Bures, M., Atkinson, R., Tachtatzis, C., Bellekens, X.: Machine learning based IoT intrusion detection system: An MQTT case study (MQTT-IoT-IDS2020 dataset). In: Ghita, B., Shiaeles, S. (eds.) Selected Papers from the 12th International Networking Conference: INC 2020, pp. 73–84. Springer International Publishing, Cham (2021). https://doi.org/10.1007/978-3-030-64758-2_6
25. Quina, A. and Jones, M.C.: SECFORCE/Sparta: network infrastructure penetration testing tool, GitHub (2020). https://github.com/SECFORCE/sparta. Accessed 27 Aug 2023
26. Seger, C.: An investigation of categorical variable encoding techniques in machine learning: binary versus one-hot and feature hashing (2018)
27. Khan, A., Sohail, A., Zahoora, U., Qureshi, A.S.: A survey of the recent architectures of deep convolutional neural networks. Artif. Intell. Rev. **53**(8), 5455–5516 (2020)
28. Gholamalinezhad, H., Khosravi, H.: Pooling methods in deep neural networks, a review. arXiv preprint arXiv:2009.07485 (2020)
29. Liang, H., Li, Q.: Hyperspectral imagery classification using sparse representations of convolutional neural network features. Remote Sensing **8**(2), 99 (2016)
30. Hochreiter, S., Schmidhuber, J.: Long short-term memory. Neural Comput. **9**(8), 1735–1780 (1997)
31. Gers, F.A., Schmidhuber, J., Cummins, F.: Learning to forget: continual prediction with LSTM. Neural Comput. **12**(10), 2451–2471 (2000)
32. Zou, X., Hu, Y., Tian, Z., Shen, K.: October. Logistic regression model optimization and case analysis. In: 2019 IEEE 7th international conference on computer science and network technology (ICCSNT), pp. 135–139. IEEE (2019)
33. Gao, B. and Pavel, L.: On the properties of the softmax function with application in game theory and reinforcement learning. arXiv preprint arXiv:1704.00805 (2017)

Crypto Bank: Cryptocurrency Wallet Based on Blockchain

Ashish Tripathi[1], Arjun Choudhary[2(✉)], Sandeep Kumar Arora[3], Gautam Arora[4], Gargi Shakya[4], and Bhavya Rajwanshi[4]

[1] School of Computing Science and Engineering, Galgotias University, Greater Noida, India
[2] Centre for Cyber Security, Sardar Patel University of Police, Security and Criminal Justice, Jodhpur, India
a.choudhary@policeuniverstiy.ac.in
[3] Lovely Professional University, Punjab, India
sandeep.16930@lpu.co.in
[4] Department of Information Technology, GL Bajaj Institute of Technology and Management, Greater Noida, India

Abstract. Cryptocurrency is a type of money that only exists in digital form and is protected by encryption. It is sometimes referred to as digital cash or virtual currency. It is decentralized, meaning it runs without a central bank, and transactions are recorded on a public ledger called a blockchain. Bitcoin, which Satoshi Nakamoto developed in 2009 using his renowned whitepaper on blockchain technology, was the first cryptocurrency ever. The genuine identity of Nakamoto or the organization using this alias is still unknown to us. However, Bitcoin was not the very first cryptocurrency. The development of a digital form of money has been the subject of numerous projects and attempts in the late 1980s and early 1990s. One illustration is Blinded Cash. Developed in 1989 by an American named David Chaum, Blinded Cash is a gambling game. Due to his thorough contributions to the subject of cryptography, Chaum established a solid professional reputation. The goal of the scientific discipline of cryptography is to create methods that would only allow the message's sender and recipient to read it. The present issue with bitcoin transactions is that consumers do not have complete control over their own cryptocurrency instead it is stored in the wallet's smart contract so the wallet has control over the consumer's currency. With the ability to hold cryptocurrencies within your own account, the proposed work concentrates on streamlining cryptocurrency payments.

Keywords: Non-fungible tokens · Cryptocurrency · Blockchain · Ethereum · Smart Contracts · Bitcoin · Crypto Wallets

1 Introduction

A digital form of money known as cryptocurrency, or simply crypto, is supported by computer code as opposed to a centralized banking organization like the Reserve Bank of India (RBI). In current time, more than 19,000 cryptocurrencies exist in the market.

KC Santosh et al. (Eds.): RTIP2R 2023, CCIS 2027, pp. 223–236, 2024.
https://doi.org/10.1007/978-3-031-53085-2_19

A few of them, like Bitcoin and Ethereum, are incredibly popular. By utilizing encryption technology, cryptocurrencies can act as both a medium of exchange and a virtual accounting system. To utilize cryptocurrencies, you require a cryptocurrency wallet. As the popularity of cryptocurrencies like Bitcoin, Ethereum, Cardona, etc. is growing every second, so is the need for performing safe, secure, and fast transactions with these cryptocurrencies. Therefore, the requirement for cryptocurrency Banks that specializes in the handling of these digital currencies is essential.

1.1 The Idea of Cryptocurrencies – the 1980s

Although the concept of cryptocurrencies was first put forth in 1989, secure digital cash was first produced and employed cryptography to encrypt and verify transactions a few years earlier, in 1980, by an American cryptographer by the name of David Chaum. However, it was not until the early 1990s that software and cryptographic protocols started to be developed, which ultimately paved the way for the construction of a real and accurate decentralized digital currency. A system for developing a digital currency that did not require trust or faith in any third party was discussed and defined in a paper by Satoshi Nakamoto published under the heading Bitcoin: A Peer-to-Peer Electronic Cash System in October 2008. Nakamoto's work catalysed the catalyst for the cryptocurrency revolution [4].

1.2 The Launch of Bitcoin – 2008

On October 31, 2008, Satoshi Nakamoto published the Bitcoin white paper, reporting the functionality of the Bitcoin blockchain network. Satoshi formally began working on the Bitcoin project on August 18th, 2008, later they acquired Bitcoin.org. Bitcoin (and all other cryptocurrencies) would not be possible without blockchain technology, which at its simplest involves creating unchangeable data structures.

The history of Bitcoin was advancing. Satoshi Nakamoto was the first person to have mined the first block of the Bitcoin network on January 3, 2009. They implanted a headline from the Times newspaper in this initial block, making a permanent testimonial to the economic conditions [5].

1.3 The Initial Crypto Market Development

The sole cryptocurrency available on the market in 2010 was Bitcoin. Bitcoin cost only a few cents at that particular moment. New digital currencies entered the market in the ensuing years, and their values fluctuated along with that of Bitcoin.

During this uncertain time, many investors all around the world lost faith in cryptocurrencies as a viable investment option. However, cryptos started to experience notable growth in late 2017. Prior to collapsing later that month, the market capitalization of all cryptocurrencies in use peaked in January 2018 at $820 billion. Despite this crisis, the cryptocurrency market has generally grown steadily [4].

1.4 The Rise of the Crypto Bank

Kraken Financial became the first cryptocurrency company to obtain a bank charter on September 16, 2020. The Wyoming Division of Banking authorized Kraken's application for a special-purpose depository institution (SPDI) charter, which was a new type of bank charter that Wyoming was especially identified for crypto businesses. Kraken is the first bank chartered in the USA since 2006 [6].

Unicas is the first physical cryptocurrency company in the world which is opened in India. It has branches throughout India transporting and conveying crypto-based solutions like a crypto bank account, a crypto-based credit scheme, and a crypto exchange [7].

1.5 Crypto Wallets

A cryptocurrency wallet is an application or requisition which works as a wallet that a person would use in the real world but for the cryptocurrency you use. It is comparable to how one would use a wallet in the real world to store cash and credit cards, which is why it is called a wallet. It keeps the passkeys one would use to sign for their Bitcoin transactions instead of holding these actual objects and components, and it also offers an interface that allows you to access your cryptocurrency. Crypto Wallets are similar to Crypto Banks but they are not the same. Wallets do not use the concepts of smart contract and therefore it does not store the money from the transactions, whereas crypto banks use their smart contract. They do keep or store the money from transactions. A cryptocurrency wallet is a piece of hardware or software that stores your private keys and gives you access to your currencies. The wallet address as well as your private keys are required to sign cryptocurrency transactions because wallets contain a public key. The coins associated with that address are managed and under the control of the private key. Since Bitcoin was the original cryptocurrency and Satoshi Nakamoto was the first to mine it, the first wallet was created for him. Hal Finney, who collaborated with Nakamoto and is said to have been the first to use the Bitcoin client software wallet, provided the second wallet. As a test, Nakamoto handed Hal Finney 10 bitcoin, which sparked interest in cryptocurrencies [8].

2 Literature Review

2.1 Bitcoin, the First Cryptocurrency

The idea behind non-fungible tokens and cryptocurrency has been around since 2012, but it only became known to the general public and the mainstream media in around 2021. As the topic of blockchain, cryptocurrency, and digital currency are still new to the world, this puts limits on the amount of available data and information, and little is known about the relationship between non-fungible tokens and cryptocurrency [10].

The DAO (Distributed Autonomous Organization) was innovated in April 2016, it aimed to produce an investment vehicle on a blockchain for the community to invest in and support software development for Ethereum. The DAO wasn't a company, not an adventure capital fund, it was a smart contract developed by a company called "Slock.it".

The end was to bring capital into Ethereum and let the community vote on which design to back, analogous to a crowdfunding website. The DAO issued commemoratives on top of the Ethereum platform that granted holders advancing rights on the association and prices from the investments, much like a stock for a company [1].

As Wired states "What's to stop someone from duplicating and using a digital dollar as readily as a piece of text, "spending" it as many times as they see fit if it's just information, free from the physical constraints of paper and metal? The double-spending problem prevented the previous digitized currency from achieving pure decentralization. Usually, banks act as clearing houses for paperless money, keeping precise records of which accounts own what quantity of money and also providing unique numbers to the money, so far, a currency has always relied on a centralized third party to act as a system administrator to keep the ledger/records updated and accurate [9].

Blockchain sweeties hailed the DAO as the crowning achievement of Blockchain armature, allowing the creation of decentralized companies and communities of individualities suckers around specific pretensions, with no mediators or central miscalculations, indeed, Techcrunch wrote The DAO is a paradigm shift in the veritable idea of profitable association. It offers absolute translucency, total shareholding control, unequaled pliantness, and independent governance [3].

The Ethereum development platoon only supports the Ethereum blockchain functions. The DAO hack shows that the popular blockchain stating "law is law" is a double-whetted brand as the law executed in a Blockchain is incommutable and public, meaning that the DAO hack was not fully technically a hack nor a theft in the legal sense. It was a program running as commanded, indeed if its commencing instructions allowed unpredicted events [9].

The Ethereum development platoon chose to initiate a chopstick to save the finances at the cost of Ethereum's integrity and the public's trust. Such a hack would have been possible on a centralized garçon, but the consequences could have been dealt with in court, or an insurance company could have covered the loss. There is no legal safeguard; anything that happens on it's legal as long as the law allows it, which means software inventors need to take redundant security ways to secure their operations. Among the other limits of the blockchain system as of the moment, we can list-spanning the main limitation of all blockchains is poor sale speed [7].

The expression of hashing, proof-of-work, and encouraging miners for computing has become essential for all blockchains. Bitcoin is not without its flaws. Due to its very design, the network does not handle transactions very briskly (it takes about 10 mn to validate a transaction) and miners get a biased share of power: indeed, about 80% of the computing power is done at the hands of a few groups of miners (called pools) located in China, these group of miners can decide how the network will evolve and what updates will be made in the network. This concentration of power is clearly at odds with Bitcoin's initial goal of decentralizing payments and empowering individuals and has powered the chaotic development of Bitcoin with the creation of blockchains long-drawn-out of the original Bitcoin blockchain through a process called "fork" [16].

As the source code is publicly-available anyone can copy and modify it, which is what happened with the Bitcoin Cash fork which dealt with the contentious topic of whether block size should be increased from the 1MB limit imposed by Nakamoto (to decrease curb fake transaction) to speed up transaction validation [14].

Bitcoin's value is compared to other currencies, such as the dollar or the euro, and is set according to supply and demand, such as gold or any other commodity [12]. But contradictory to a regular currency, Bitcoin is not backed by any real-world asset, legislation, or retrieve power. Employees accept to be paid in euros as they know the currency is stable and they will be able to trade their euros for food or gas or any other goods and services. Citizens' trust in their national currency is based on the belief that everyone will accept their currency in exchange for goods and services and that they will be able to keep it (as a store of value) [13].

According to the rearmost peer-reviewed study on the subject, Bitcoin consumes five of the world's electricity. Addressing the scaling issue might reduce energy consumption but the veritable design of blockchain systems isn't effective in energy consumption of calculation power. It should be noted down that if Bitcoin is to be compared to another payment system or modes, like Visa or Master, it should be taken into account as Visa relies on the global currency system. It entails producing, publishing, and distributing bills and coins and the energy consumption of bank systems and data centers. A ballpark estimate shows Bitcoin is hamstrung but not as hamstrung as a regular banking system.

Many real-world operations A notorious online composition read "Ten times in, nothing has come up with a use for blockchain" explains that despite ten times of development blockchain has yet to find a real request other besides currency enterprise and illegal deals. Because centralized businesses have similar strong network goods it is tough for decentralized challengers to gain request share on regular guests who are not oriented to the blockchain. Utmost blockchain inventions are still circumscribed [11].

2.2 Ethereum and Smart Contracts

With this Turing-complete language implemented in the Ethereum blockchain, it is plausible to develop what are called smart contracts, these are codes that are embedded in a blockchain and are run by miners. For a concrete example, let us say that Alice makes a bet with Bob on tomorrow's weather: she will pay him 10€ if it rains tomorrow, and he will pay her 10€ if it does not. The code of the following example can be summarized as follows:

IF rains THEN Alice - > 10€ to BOB.

ELSE BOB - > 10€ to Alice.

Since they are wary of the fact that others will not honor the contract, they would like to use a third party to oversee their wagers. On the Bitcoin blockchain, such a scheme is possible but it requires a centralized server to run most of the program, and such a server can be tampered with by Alice or Bob as mentioned in the example above. On the Ethereum blockchain, the program can be written and run with no external computing power required, the weather data will be acquired from a trustworthy source called an Oracle (for instance www.weather.com) and the program will run according to the acquired results. The example mentioned above shows the innovation brought by the Ethereum blockchain, in which a decentralized third party can enforce contracts coded into a blockchain with no central inaccuracy [9].

Ethereum has other differences, among which a faster transaction time (15 s in comparison to 10mn for Bitcoin), a proof-of-work algorithm was designed not to favor mining pools, no limits on the cryptocurrency (Bitcoin is limited at 21 million Bitcoins, Ethereum releases the same amount of Ether every year), and an internal currency called "gas" is used to pay for transactions costs (Gas is calculated as a fraction of an Ether) 20 Ethereum was launched on July 2015 and which quickly rose to prestige in the blockchain ecosystem, acknowledged as the next step in the Internet, as it was allowing developers to create "dApps" or decentralized applications, pieces of software that would run on the Ethereum blockchain and assurance of security, obscurity, and no central oversight [15].

The second generation of blockchains which was pioneered by Ethereum brought the hackers' dream of a decentralized Internet nearer to reality. It could be theoretically possible to run a Facebook or a Youtube clone on the blockchain (provided there is enough computing power and processing speed) in an open-source fashion, meaning that all data is public (though surely encrypted for privacy reasons) and any individual can copy and edit the source code [9].

Additionally, the Developers can enforce a transaction fee of 5% on the BitPaint network to diversify their sources of revenue. The token economy's greatest upside is this alignment of the three stakeholders to contribute to the network, at least for utility tokens. The token directly reflects BitPaint's usage value contrary to a stock that will need investors to interpret the company's performance to buy or sell the stock and change its price. It is similar to the currency of a country and most valuation models today indeed rely on macroeconomics to perform analysis on token price [2].

2.3 The Token Economy

This recent price surge has raised awareness of the topic of blockchain in the public. But this interest is most circumscribed to speculation and the value storage use of cryptocurrencies, rather than the possibilities offered by decentralized computing (utility and security token). But efficacy tokens, for example, have great potential. Let us imagine an online marketplace specialized in paintings called BitPaint based on a Paint token. On BitPaint, the Paint Token is a utility token, meaning that it is necessary to use the token to access the BitPaint service [5]. Users need to purchase the Paint token to buy paintings listed on the exchange, the proceeds of the sale will be paid out in Paint tokens which can be later changed into dollars, euros, Ether, or any other currency or cryptocurrency through an exchange. The Paint token is the cornerstone of the BitPaint marketplace and aligns the interest of all the stakeholders. We can list three main stakeholders in this token-based market:

Users: Those who will buy and hold tokens to buy and sell paintings. They are interested in buying the token for the service it provides. If the BitPaint system is useful and brings them value, they will be willing to use it more and buy more tokens [9].

Investors: Investors are those individuals who invest i.e., put money in the token in the hopes of making a profit. They will not use the token to buy paintings, they are only interested in the value of the Paint token. They are usually referred to as HODLERs. The more the BitPaint network is used, the more users will want to buy the token, increasing its value. Contrary to a stock in a regular company, here the token value is directly linked to the usage of the service it provides, and what value it brings to the User so that he will be incentivized to buy it to trade paintings and, therefore, to drive its value up [7].

If BitPaint offers poor service, few people will buy the token and the price will decrease, the Investors will therefore book a loss. On the contrary, if the service is popular and users flock to buy Paint tokens to trade paintings, the token value will increase. This incentive scheme ensures that the system serves primarily the Users and not the stockholders since catering to the Users' needs will directly increase usage of the service and, therefore, token value.

Developers: Developers are those individuals who created and managed the BitPaint network. The team will create the first batch of tokens, let us assume 1,000 Paint tokens, and will sell 500 to the public at a specific price. If the BitPaint network is successful the Pain token will increase in value and considering the massive stake the development team holds in BitPaint, they will greatly benefit from it [9].

Additionally, the Developers can enforce a transaction fee of 5% on the BitPaint network to diversify their sources of revenue. The token economy's greatest upside is this alignment of the three stakeholders to contribute to the network, at least for utility tokens. The token directly reflects BitPaint's usage value contrary to a stock that will need investors to interpret the company's performance to buy or sell the stock and change its price. It is similar to the currency of a country and most valuation models today indeed rely on macroeconomics to perform analysis on token price [9]. There is much speculation on the future of the token economy and the evolutions it can bring about to the economy. Chris Dixon, a venture capitalist at a16z, stated 3637 that the token economy's greatest achievement is in creating a business model for open-source software development. Open-source refers to a type of software that is made publicly available without licensing or copyrighting and is usually created and maintained by volunteer software developers. Most of the Internet infrastructure relies on open-source protocols such as TCP/IP (which manages data transfer and communication), SSH (cryptographic network protocol), and others. Despite the tremendous savings due to open-source software38 the development teams are not financially incentivized to maintain the protocols and do not benefit from its success. With a token-based protocol many tech services that are now private such as Airbnb or Facebook could be operated on a peer-to-peer basis with fewer transaction costs and greater consumer protection, as the development team would not have to resort to selling their users' data to maintain the platform. [2] These phenomena were called protocols that would capture most of the value chain and are referred to as a "fat protocol" paradigm by a venture capitalist named Joseph Monegro. In the current Internet, ecosystem protocols form the basis of the system but capture nothing of the value of the Internet compared to applications that use these protocols [16].

The preceding generations of shared protocols (i.e., TCP/IP, HTTP, SMTP, etc.) developed indeterminable amounts of value, but a lot of it got occupied and accumulate on top at the applications layer, mainly in the form of data (such as Google, Facebook, etc.) [6]. On a blockchain, the application layer is significantly slimmer for several reasons:

Thinner Barriers to Entry: Blockchain provides a shared data and protocol layer, anyone can plug on these data to create an application. For example, if someone creates a social network on the blockchain, the data is public40, meaning that a competitor can use this data to create an alternate social network with the same data [7].

Today it is impossible to transfer one's data from one social network to another, but on a blockchain, it is indeed possible. The Shared Data Layer41, as Monegro explains, acts like a global database into which every application can plug itself to get data, but no central operator ensures the system's integrity, which the miners provide in computing power to maintain and manage it [8].

Personal data ownership and cryptography: Facebook is free to use but the users surrender control of their data to Facebook. They can be sold to advertisers, fed to AI algorithms, etc. As network effects are so powerful and influential for data.

Centric companies such as Google and Facebook, creating an alternate user database to compete with them is nearly impossible, and the switching costs are too high for users (as more and more Facebook users have, the more valuable the network for users' experience).

There is much speculation on the future of the token economy and the evolutions it can bring about to the economy. Chris Dixon, a venture capitalist at a16z, stated 3637 that the token economy's greatest achievement is in creating a business model for open-source software development. Open-source refers to a type of software that is made publicly available without licensing or copyrighting and is usually created and maintained by volunteer software developers [9].

Most of the Internet infrastructure relies on open-source protocols such as TCP/IP (which manages data transfer and communication), SSH (cryptographic network protocol), and others. Despite the tremendous savings due to open-source software38 the development teams are not financially incentivized to maintain the protocols and do not benefit from its success. With a token-based protocol many tech services that are now private such as Airbnb or Facebook could be operated on a peer-to-peer basis with fewer transaction costs and greater consumer protection, as the development team would not have to resort to selling their users' data to maintain the platform [9].

3 Background Details

One of the most delicate and susceptible sections of the financial sector to cyber traps is banking. A number of banks throughout the world have recently disclosed significant cyber pitfalls, including direct attacks on centralized systems that resulted in billions of dollars in damages because of the enormous quantities of money stored in their databases. Governments have responded by issuing strict regulations, and major organizations have started looking into how to leverage cutting-edge decentralized asset results like blockchain.

The primary benefit of cryptocurrency transactions is their ability to function and run without having a single point of failure. The majority of cryptocurrencies are built on a peer-to-peer settlement system and are available around the clock, even on weekends and holidays.

Prices are lower compared to banks, there is no need for a middleman, services are available and available around-the-clock, the contribution is set, and cryptography more closely aligns with ideological goals.

Given the distinctive characteristics of a decentralized system, it stands to reason that the banking industry will lead the way in using decentralized technologies.

People embraced the use of banking organizations to promote trade and business of all kinds. On the other side, a blockchain is a tool that can accomplish the same task globally. It is also transparent and secure.

4 Proposed Work

The purpose of the establishment of banking organizations was to promote trade and business of all kinds. On the other side, a blockchain is a tool that can accomplish the same task globally. Additionally, it is clear and safe. The current cryptocurrency transaction system does not allow users to store their cryptocurrency themselves, i.e., the cryptocurrency is stored in the blockchain.

This project focuses on simplifying cryptocurrency payments, allowing users to store their cryptocurrency within their accounts. A decentralized application that allows the users to Deposit, Withdraw, and Transfer their cryptocurrency (funds) to different users. The above-mentioned functionalities are facilitated by the use of a smart contract which is written in solidity language.

Smart Contracts let us perform transactions and add data to the blockchain. The proposed system is developed with Create React App. The Front End is done in React and Redux is used for State management. Front End is also integrated with Smart Contract by the use of the Web3 library.

The application issues a new Web3 Wallet to every user who is further encrypted with a password. Crypto Bank is developed on Aurora, Rinkeby, and Fantom:

Aurora enables the user to browse and search the Aurora blockchain in search of transactions, addresses, tokens, prices, and other Aurora-related activity.

Rinkeby is a proof-of-authority blockchain that applies the Clique PoA consensus and uses Solana testnets, you will require a Solana wallet like Phantom.

Fantom is a highly scalable blockchain platform for commercial apps, crypto dApps, and DeFi.

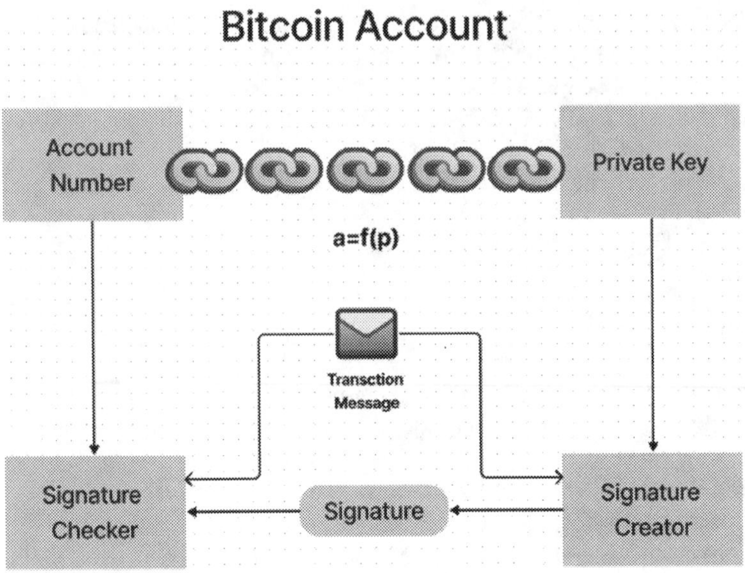

Fig. 1. A brief explanation of Bitcoin works

5 Methodology

The approach of the suggested model has been detailed in this section. The process flow of the approaches used to create the model is shown in Fig. 3. Let us now examine a transaction's process. Users require a public and private key in order to perform a cryptocurrency transaction. A number equal to an account is the public key. The private key functions as the user's PIN or password to enable cryptocurrency transactions. Public and private keys are comprised of a long string of numbers and letters (Fig. 1.)

Public Key.

Public Key is similar to an account number, which is visible to anybody with Internet access when transactions are added to the blockchain. The password grants the users to access the funds in their accounts.

Private Key.

A private key is a secure code that enables holders to make cryptocurrency transactions and prove ownership of their holdings.

Figure 2 shows the working of public and private keys. In the wallet, the user can see their current balance of crypto as well as the options to send and request crypto from other users. The user is also able to see the option to deposit funds in their wallet, as shown in Fig. 3

The current cryptocurrency transaction system does not allow users to store their cryptocurrency themselves, i.e., the cryptocurrency is stored in the blockchain. This proposed work focuses on simplifying cryptocurrency payments, allowing users to store their cryptocurrency within their accounts.

In this proposed work, the decentralized application allows the user to.

- Deposit

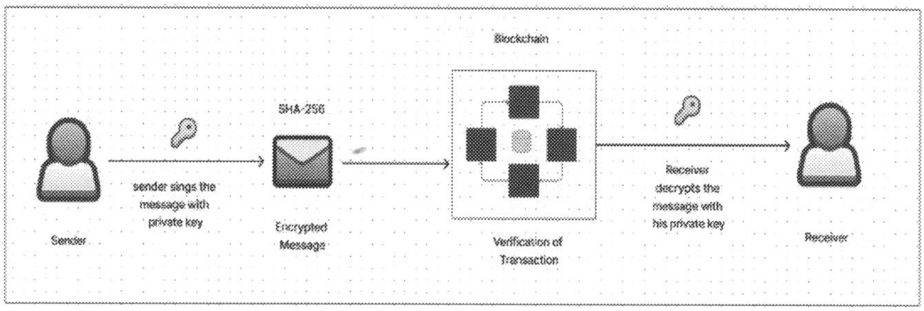

Fig. 2. Working of public and private keys

- Withdraw
- Transfer

To perform the above-mentioned tasks, the user is required to first enter their private key to log in but if it is the first time for the user on this application then they are required to Create a wallet.

The Create a Wallet option allows the users to generate a private key, which then further allows the users to enter the private key to access their wallet.

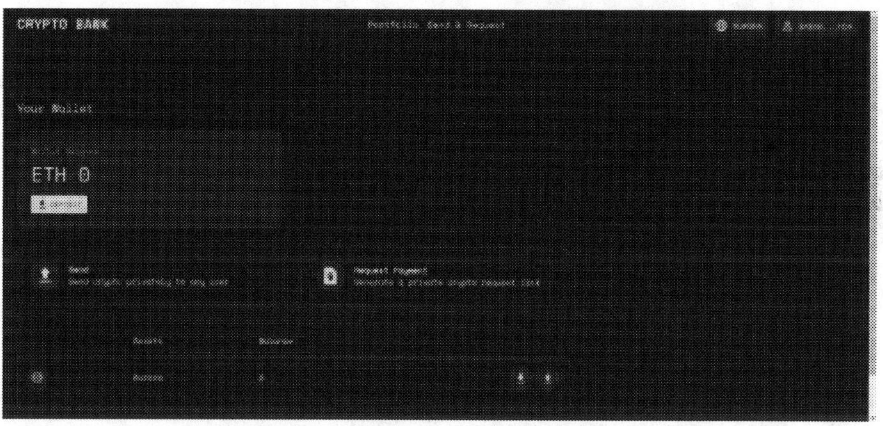

Fig. 3. The proposed user interface

Deposit

For the user to deposit funds in the wallet, the user is requested to enter:

- Currency
- Amount

Once the elements mentioned above are provided then the user can deposit the said amount in the wallet.

Send Funds

For the user to send funds to another user in the network the user is requested to enter the:

- Recipient's Address
- Amount to be sent

Once the above-mentioned elements are provided then the user can send the said amount to the beneficiary.

Request Funds

This application allows the user to request funds from another user to notify the lender. For the user to request funds from another user in the network the user is requested to enter:

- Currency
- Amount requested

Once the above-mentioned elements are provided, the lender gets notified of the request for funds and then, therefore can transfer the requested funds to the beneficiary.

6 Comparative Analysis

The proposed System does not store the user's account private key. So Proposed application is more secure and less vulnerable to cyber-attacks.

Most crypto exchanges are not completely decentralized because apart from blockchain they also use their own database to store data but the Proposed System is completely decentralized because we only use blockchain.

The proposed application runs on multiple networks. The proposed System has the option to request payment from some other user. This is the USP i.e., a Unique selling proposition of the Proposed System.

7 Conclusion and Future Scope

In this the proposed model allows the users to make transactions of various cryptocurrencies such as Bitcoin, Ethereum, Cardona, etc. This blockchain-based application makes it easy and accessible to do transactions for the user.

This transfer of funds is performed under a secure and safe application. As blockchain is a decentralized system, therefore there would be no data redundancies, and the chances of forging would also be reduced.

In the future, Digital currencies called cryptocurrencies use cryptography to control the creation of new units of currency and to verify the receipt of payments. Transparency in banking institutions will increase thanks to blockchain, which will also speed up transaction processing and save expenses.

Blockchain technology could speed up speedy payments at reduced costs by building a decentralized ledger for payments. Financing options Blockchain technology has the potential to reduce interest rates and raise borrowing security by eliminating the need for gatekeepers in the loan and credit sector (Table 1).

Table 1. Comparative analysis between the current system and the proposed system

Features	Current System	Proposed System
Storing Private Key	Yes, the Private Key of the user's account is stored, which leads to security issues and leaves the users vulnerable to cyber-attacks	No, the Private Key of the user's account is not stored, which leads to a more secure and leaves the user less vulnerable to cyber-attacks
Completely Decentralized	No, As the current system uses a mix of blockchain and their own independent database	Yes, The proposed system is completely decentralized as it only uses blockchain
Multiple Networks	No, The application cannot run on Multiple Networks	Yes, The application can run on Multiple Networks
Request Payment Options	No, Option to request payment from another user	Yes, Option to request payment from another user

References

1. Suratkar, S., Shirole, M., Bhirud, S.: September. cryptocurrency wallet: a review. In: 2020 4th International Conference on Computer, Communication, and Signal Processing (ICCCSP) (pp. 1–7). IEEE (2020)
2. Jacquez, T.: Cryptocurrency the new money laundering problem for banking, law enforcement, and the legal system (Doctoral dissertation, Utica College) (2016)
3. Sai, A.R., Buckley, J., Le Gear, A.: March. Privacy and security analysis of cryptocurrency mobile applications. In: 2019 Fifth Conference on Mobile and Secure Services (MobiSecServ) (pp. 1–6). IEEE (2019)
4. Cohen, R., Sehra, A., Smith, P.: Banking on the Blockchain. Int'l Fin. L. Rev. **37**, 42 (2018)
5. Herskind, L., Katsikouli, P., Dragoni, N.: Privacy and cryptocurrencies—a systematic literature review. IEEE Access **8**, 54044–54059 (2020)
6. Eyal, I.: Blockchain technology: Transforming libertarian cryptocurrency dreams to finance and banking realities. Computer **50**(9), 38–49 (2017)
7. Raymaekers, W.: Cryptocurrency Bitcoin: Disruption, challenges and opportunities. J. Payments Strategy & Syst. **9**(1), 30–46 (2015)
8. He, S., et al.: A social-network-based cryptocurrency wallet-management scheme. IEEE Access **6**, 7654–7663 (2018)
9. Chevet, S.: Blockchain technology and non-fungible tokens: reshaping value chains in creative industries. SSRN Electron. J. (2018). https://doi.org/10.2139/ssrn.3212662
10. Lipka, R.: Non-fungible token and Cryptocurrency: Substitutes or Complements? (Master's thesis) (2022)
11. Cunha, P.R., Melo, P., Sebastião, H.: From bitcoin to central bank digital currencies: making sense of the digital money revolution. Future Internet **13**(7), 165 (2021)
12. Warmke, C.: What is bitcoin? Inquiry, pp.1–43 (2021)
13. Moser, M.: Anonymity of bitcoin transactions (2013)

14. Manimuthu, A., Rejikumar, G., Marwaha, D.: A literature review on Bitcoin: transformation of crypto currency into a global phenomenon. IEEE Eng. Manage. Rev. **47**(1), 28–35 (2019)
15. Vranken, H.: Sustainability of bitcoin and blockchains., Curr. Opin. Environ. Sustain. **28**,1–9 (2017)
16. Gipp, B., Meuschke, N., Gernandt, A.: Decentralized trusted timestamping using the crypto currency bitcoin. arXiv preprint arXiv:1502.04015 (2015)

Large-Language-Models (LLM)-Based AI Chatbots: Architecture, In-Depth Analysis and Their Performance Evaluation

Vimal Kumar[1(✉)], Priyam Srivastava[1], Ashay Dwivedi[1], Ishan Budhiraja[1], Debjani Ghosh[1], Vikas Goyal[2], and Ruchika Arora[3]

[1] Bennett University, Greater Noida, Uttar Pradesh, India
{vimal.kumar,e20cse479,e20cse172,ishan.budhiraja, debjani.ghosh}@bennett.edu.in

[2] Directorate of Secondary Education, Panchkula, Haryana, India

[3] SR University, Ananthasagar, Warangal, Telangana, India

Abstract. This scholarly article conducts a comparative evaluation of prominent large-scale language models, specifically encompassing Google's BARD, ChatGPT 3.5, and ChatGPT 4. It offers a comprehensive dissection of each model, elucidating aspects such as architectural structure, utilized training data, and proficiency in natural language processing. The paper also undertakes a systematic assessment of these models in executing diverse tasks like text generation, text completion, and question-answering, paralleling their precision, processing speed, and efficiency. The concluding part of the article explores the prospective application domains of these language models, including but not limited to customer service, education, and healthcare sectors, while proffering suggestions for future research trajectories and technological enhancements. In summary, the study furnishes critical insights into the current status of large-scale language models, shedding light on their potential to augment human-computer interaction and drive forward advancements in the realm of natural language processing technology.

Keywords: LLM · Transformers · NLP · Chatbots

1 Introduction

While conversational agents or chatbots have been in existence for multiple decades, their intricacy and functionality have seen significant progression over time. Tracing back to the primitive stages of ELIZA, a rudimentary chatbot programmed to mimic a psychotherapist, to the contemporary, more complex, Large Language Model (LLM)-based chatbots, we've witnessed considerable advancements in chatbot technology. Industries across the spectrum have started embracing these chatbots, with mounting interest in their potential application within sectors such as education, mental health, and social services.

KC Santosh et al. (Eds.): RTIP2R 2023, CCIS 2027, pp. 237–249, 2024.
https://doi.org/10.1007/978-3-031-53085-2_20

A monumental leap in chatbot technology is the incorporation of voice assistants, which has unlocked novel avenues for hands-free assistance, thereby enhancing user experiences. Additionally, a trending emphasis on personalization and context-awareness within chatbot development is apparent, enabling chatbots to deliver more customized recommendations and aid to users.

However, as the complexity and sophistication of chatbots surge, they encounter a set of challenges. Accuracy and reliability remain paramount, given the potential risk of errors and biases within chatbot responses that may tarnish user trust and satisfaction. A heightened call for transparency and accountability within chatbot development is imperative to warrant ethical and responsible usage.

In particular, LLM-based chatbots offer substantial benefits compared to their traditional rule-based counterparts. They possess superior context-understanding capabilities and are adept at generating natural, human-like responses, making them an increasingly favored option for businesses and organizations aiming to offer personalized and engaging customer experiences. Nevertheless, LLM-based chatbots are not without challenges, including the risk of generating biased or inappropriate responses. Hence, continuous monitoring and supervision are crucial to ensure their efficiency and precision.

In summary, the status of chatbots in 2023 is characterized by swift progression and expanding adoption, with a growing potential for personalized, context-aware interactions. However, it's imperative to address the challenges and ethical considerations related to chatbot technology, especially as an increasing number of businesses and organizations adopt LLM-based chatbots to enhance customer service and support.

2 Literature Review

Chatbots based on Language Learning Models (LLMs), such as GPT-3 from OpenAI and BERT from Google, represent a distinctive category of conversational agents. They employ pre-trained language models to generate responses that mimic natural, human-like conversation to user queries. Both the academic community and industry professionals express significant interest in LLM chatbots, recognizing their potential superiority over conventional rule-based chatbots. A prominent advantage of LLM chatbots is their ability to understand and generate responses in natural language. Trained on vast amounts of text data, these chatbots are proficient in identifying intricate language patterns and subtleties, which may elude traditional rule-based counterparts. Notably, LLM chatbots excel in formulating responses that demonstrate contextual understanding and semantic coherence. Research investigations into LLM chatbots' efficiency across diverse settings have been carried out. For instance, studies within the healthcare industry explored LLM chatbots as aids to patients dealing with mental health conditions, including depression and anxiety. Results from such research suggest that LLM chatbots can provide effective, tailored assistance to patients, leading to enhanced patient outcomes and satisfaction. In an educational context, LLM chatbots have been employed to offer personalized feedback and guidance to students. These investigations confirm that LLM chatbots can successfully supplement traditional teaching methods and foster a more tailored, engaging learning experience for students. The domain of customer service and support also exhibits growing interest in LLM chatbots. Several businesses and organizations consider employing LLM chatbots to upgrade customer service and provide more personalized customer assistance. For example, LLM chatbots can offer bespoke recommendations and aid to customers, enhancing customer satisfaction and loyalty. Nevertheless, despite their potential advantages, LLM chatbots pose certain challenges and limitations. The risk of generating biased or inappropriate responses exists, especially if the training data itself contains biases or is incomplete. Additionally, concerns have arisen regarding the potential misuse of LLM chatbots for harmful purposes, such as propagating misinformation or instigating social engineering attacks. The ethical aspects of LLM chatbots have also been the focus of several research studies. Scholars have emphasized the need for transparency and accountability in LLM chatbot development and the importance of informing users about the technology's limitations and potential biases. In summary, LLM chatbots represent a significant evolution in chatbot technology, offering numerous potential benefits over traditional rule-based chatbots. Yet, their utilization comes with certain challenges and limitations, primarily relating to accuracy, reliability, and ethical implications. Ongoing and future research should continue examining the potential benefits and limitations of LLM chatbots, and develop strategies to address the challenges and ethical concerns accompanying their deployment. Hallucination, a situation wherein a model generates outputs not anchored in the input, was another sphere of comparison. Some models exhibited more sophisticated behaviours with lower propensities to hallucinate, albeit no model was entirely immune to such occurrences. On a broader scale, newer models consistently surpassed their antecedents in all evaluated aspects. However, all models presented their own set of limitations, underscoring the necessity for persistent research and refinement. This comparison contributes towards a deeper understanding of LLMs and paves the way for future model development.

3 Identified Issues and Challenges

Despite their notable advantages, Large Language Model (LLM)-based chatbots encounter several challenges and issues that warrant addressing to ascertain their effective and responsible deployment.

One of the significant challenges LLM-based chatbots grapple with is the phenomenon of 'hallucination', defined as the chatbot's generation of responses that lack accuracy or grounding in reality. This can transpire when the chatbot crafts responses based on patterns discerned from the training data, which may not necessarily mirror real-world scenarios.

To illustrate, a chatbot trained on news articles might generate a response regarding a celebrity being sighted at a certain location, irrespective of the accuracy or relevance of this information to the user's inquiry. Such hallucination could become particularly problematic in situations where the chatbot is dispensing critical or sensitive information, such as in healthcare or legal environments.

Another substantial challenge is the risk of generating biased or inappropriate responses. As LLM-based chatbots learn from enormous volumes of textual data, they may absorb biases and stereotypes inherent in the training data. For instance, if the training data is skewed towards a certain demographic or cultural group, the chatbot might inadvertently generate responses that sustain this bias, potentially leading to harmful and discriminatory outcomes, such as dispensing inaccurate or detrimental advice to users.

The necessity for continuous monitoring and oversight to verify that the chatbot is operating appropriately and supplying accurate and useful information presents another challenge. This entails routine testing and evaluation to detect any inaccuracies or biases in the chatbot's responses and to confirm that it is offering pertinent and significant information to users.

Transparency, or rather the lack thereof, in LLM-based chatbots also constitutes a challenge. With responses generated based on complex algorithms and machine learning models, it can be challenging for users to comprehend the decision-making process of the chatbot, and how it provides information. This opacity can undermine user trust and confidence in the chatbot, leading to diminished levels of engagement and satisfaction.

Additionally, there's a risk of excessive reliance on LLM-based chatbots, potentially resulting in diminished human interaction and social isolation. While chatbots can prove beneficial in offering information and support, they cannot substitute the advantages of human interaction, such as empathy, emotional support, and social connection.

Lastly, ethical considerations surrounding the use of LLM-based chatbots emerge, encompassing privacy concerns and the potential for misuse or exploitation. For instance, chatbots may gather personal information from users, like their location, search history, and other sensitive data. It's imperative that this information is managed responsibly and ethically, with adequate safeguards in place to protect user privacy and prevent misuse.

In summary, while LLM-based chatbots present substantial advantages regarding their ability to generate natural and human-like responses, they also confront several challenges and issues that need to be addressed to ensure their effective and responsible usage. These challenges include the risk of generating biased or inappropriate responses, the need for ongoing monitoring and oversight, the lack of transparency, the risk of overreliance, and ethical considerations surrounding privacy and potential misuse.

4 Problem Statement

How do Google's BARD, GPT 3, GPT 4, and others compare in terms of their ability to generate relevant and context-aware responses?

5 Contributions

We will be comparing all the data available on these chatbots and compiling it together in order to present all the relevant details about them, along specific metrics, in this research paper. Further, we have added a few details on how to overcome the limitations of current models.

6 Methodology

The methodology for comparing chatbot platforms can vary depending on the research question and goals of the study. For our specific problem statement, the methodology includes the review of the following models (Fig. 1):

6.1 GPT-3

Generative Pre-trained Transformer 3 (GPT-3) is an advanced language model established by OpenAI. It stands as one of the most substantial and potent language models to date, comprising 175 billion parameters. This voluminous configuration empowers it to execute a broad spectrum of natural language processing tasks.

A distinctive feature of GPT-3 is its aptitude to construct human-resembling text, rendering it beneficial for various applications including chatbots, text completion, and language translation. It accomplishes this by employing a transformer-based architecture, enabling it to comprehend and process elongated sequences of text.

Furthermore, GPT-3 profits from pre-training on an extensive and heterogeneous text dataset, equipping it to acquire universal language patterns and structures. This stage of pre-training is followed by fine-tuning oriented towards specific tasks, which further refines its performance.

Another salient attribute of GPT-3 is its capacity for few-shot learning. It can effectively perform tasks given only a handful of examples, without requiring a vast training data volume. This is facilitated by its ability to discern patterns from the few examples provided and to apply them to novel inputs.

Despite these remarkable capabilities, GPT-3 is not without limitations. It occasionally generates outputs that are irrelevant or incorrect, particularly when the context is ambiguous. In addition, the extensive size of the model and the computational demands it imposes present challenges to deployment in real-time applications or on devices with constrained resources.

In summary, GPT-3 signifies a notable advancement in the realm of natural language processing, with the potential to revolutionize an array of applications. Its few-shot learning ability and human-like text generation render it particularly promising for use in chatbots and other conversational AI applications. Nevertheless, there exists scope for enhancement in aspects such as context comprehension and the ability to generate truly creative or novel content.

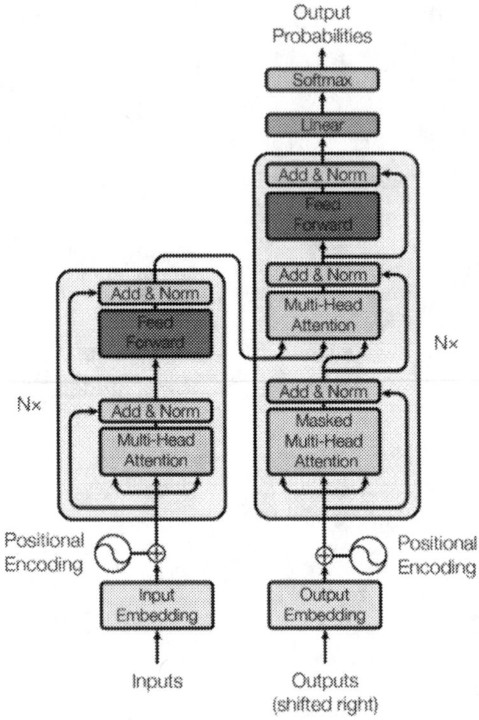

Fig. 1. Transformer-Architecture

6.2 GPT-4

One of the most distinguished and sophisticated Language Model-based (LLM) systems is GPT-4, an innovation of OpenAI, a research organization committed to the generation and assurance of safe and beneficial artificial intelligence. GPT-4 is the most recent successor in the generative pre-trained transformer (GPT) sequence of models, beginning with GPT in 2018, succeeded by GPT-2 in 2019, and GPT-3 in 2020. GPT-4 was unveiled in March 2023, purportedly the most massive and potent LLM thus far, boasting 175 billion parameters with the proficiency to generate text reaching lengths of up to 10,000 words.

One application of GPT-4 lies within chatbots, artificial intelligence systems capable of communicating with humans via text or speech. Chatbots serve various functions, including customer service, entertainment, education, and information retrieval. They also offer a more dynamic and engaging mode of interacting with online information and services, compared to traditional interfaces such as webpages or menus.

ChatGPT is an AI chatbot developed by OpenAI, constructed on top of the GPT-4 platform, and was released in November 2022. It is designed to deliver summarized answers to user queries in a conversational style, as opposed to providing lists of links or snippets. ChatGPT can also generate follow-up questions or suggestions based on user input or context. It was fine-tuned using both supervised and reinforcement learning techniques, with human trainers supplying feedback and guidance to enhance the model's performance and quality.

ChatGPT has received commendation for its comprehensive responses and eloquent answers across numerous knowledge domains. It can also manage intricate queries necessitating reasoning, inference, or common sense. It can address questions such as "Who is the president of India?" or "What is the capital of France?" with factual accuracy and certainty. Additionally, it can generate creative content such as jokes, stories, or poems, based on user prompts or preferences.

However, ChatGPT is not without limitations and challenges requiring attention. A primary concern is its tendency to occasionally deliver factually incorrect or misleading responses, due to its reliance on training data that may contain errors, biases, or outdated information. Consequently, it might provide incorrect answers to questions. It may also produce texts that are inappropriate, offensive, or harmful to certain groups or individuals due to its lack of ethical or social consciousness.

Another challenge pertains to the safety and privacy of users and their data submitted to ChatGPT. As ChatGPT employs user data for training and fine-tuning purposes, there are inherent risks of data leakage, misuse, or exploitation by malicious entities or third parties. Users may be oblivious to how their data is utilized or stored by ChatGPT or OpenAI. Furthermore, users may foster unrealistic expectations or attachments to ChatGPT, potentially impacting their mental health or social relationships.

In summary, GPT-4, serving as an LLM chatbot, signifies an extraordinary accomplishment demonstrating the potential and capabilities of artificial intelligence in the realm of natural language generation and understanding. However, it also presents substantial challenges and risks that necessitate the attention of researchers, developers, regulators, and users alike. Consequently, it is crucial to ensure that GPT-4, in its role as an LLM chatbot, is utilized responsibly and ethically for humanity's benefit (Fig. 2).

6.3 AutoGPT

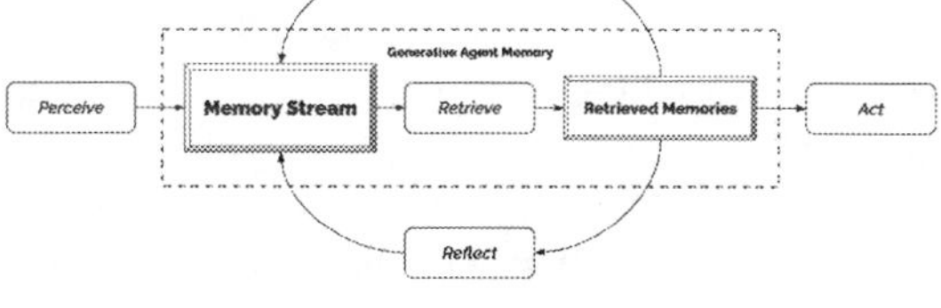

Fig. 2. General Architecture of AutoGPT

AutoGPT represents an innovative utilization of GPT-4, the most advanced language model to date, developed by OpenAI. As a deep neural network, GPT-4 possesses the capacity to generate natural language text on virtually any given topic, provided with an initial input or context. AutoGPT transcends conventional language generation instruments by incorporating data from an array of sources, inclusive of news articles, scientific research publications, and social media content. This multifaceted data integration enables the system to generate text that not only adheres to factual accuracy but also mirrors the latest advancements and trends within the pertinent field of interest.

The architecture of AutoGPT is devised to function as an autonomous agent capable of executing tasks based on a natural language goal. If assigned the task of composing a blog post concerning climate change, for example, AutoGPT is capable of segmenting this goal into subsidiary tasks such as the identification of relevant information, summarization of key points, crafting of an introduction and conclusion, and citation integration. To further augment its capabilities and knowledge base, AutoGPT can also access and utilize external tools like Google Maps, Wikipedia, or Wolfram Alpha.

A potential application of AutoGPT lies in its deployment as a Large Language Model (LLM) chatbot. As a conversational agent, LLM chatbots interact with human users utilizing natural language. These chatbots can serve a multitude of purposes such as entertainment, education, customer service, or personal assistance. AutoGPT employs its skills in language generation and comprehension to construct engaging and insightful dialogues with users, adapting its tone and style to cater to diverse domains and scenarios based on the sourced data.

AutoGPT, as an experimental open-source initiative, exhibits the capabilities of GPT-4 in functioning as an autonomous AI agent. It stands as one of the pioneering examples of employing GPT-4 to carry out intricate tasks devoid of human supervision or guidance. AutoGPT remains in development, facing challenges and limitations such as the assurance of ethical and responsible AI and data usage, maintenance of coherence and consistency across various sources and tasks, and the ability to gracefully handle errors and failures. Nonetheless, AutoGPT elucidates the potential of GPT-4 as a potent instrument for natural language processing and generation, paving the path for further research and innovation in the sphere of LLM chatbots.

6.4 LLaMA

LLaMA is an ensemble of large language models (LLMs) developed by Meta AI, an arm of Meta (formerly known as Facebook). LLaMA models span from 7 billion to 65 billion parameters and were trained on trillions of tokens derived from publicly accessible datasets, including Common Crawl and Wikipedia. The primary objective of LLaMA models is to serve as foundational models that can be fine-tuned for a range of downstream tasks that utilize natural language inputs.

A prospective application of LLaMA lies within the LLM chatbot domain. LLM chatbots are conversational agents that interact with human users via natural language processing. These chatbots can serve a variety of purposes such as entertainment, education, customer service, or personal assistance. LLaMA leverages its language generation and comprehension abilities to foster engaging and informative dialogues with users. Additionally, LLaMA can adapt to diverse domains and scenarios by integrating data from varying sources and modifying its tone and style as necessary.

LLaMA stands as an open-source project that illustrates the capabilities of LLMs functioning as autonomous AI agents. It is one of the initial instances of employing publicly available datasets to train cutting-edge models without depending on proprietary or inaccessible datasets. LLaMA models outstrip GPT-3, the former front-runner in the field of LLMs, on numerous benchmarks and compete with elite models such as Chinchilla-70B and PaLM-540B. LLaMA models are also characterized by their efficiency and accessibility compared to other LLMs, as they demand less computational power and resources for training and operation.

The development of LLaMA is ongoing and encounters several limitations and challenges, including the assurance of ethical and responsible data and AI usage, coherence and consistency maintenance across different sources and tasks, and graceful handling of errors and failures. However, LLaMA exemplifies the potential of LLMs as robust instruments for natural language processing and generation, paving the way for novel research and innovation avenues in the domain of LLM chatbots.

6.5 Vicuna

Vicuna-13B represents an open-source chatbot devised by a collaborative research team from UC Berkeley, CMU, Stanford, and UC San Diego. It is a refined version of LLaMA-13B, a large language model (LLM) unveiled by Meta AI. Vicuna-13B underwent training on 70K user-shared conversations gathered from ShareGPT, a platform that facilitates user interaction with GPT-3 and allows the sharing of their dialogues.

The design of Vicuna-13B is directed towards providing a versatile and efficient chatbot capable of producing engaging and insightful responses to a range of natural language queries. It can adapt to diverse domains and scenarios by utilizing data from varying sources and modifying its tone and style as necessary. The language generation and comprehension capabilities of Vicuna-13B enable it to establish dialogues that match or surpass the performance of other LLMs, such as GPT-3, Bard, Chinchilla, and PaLM.

As an experimental project, Vicuna-13B exhibits the potential of LLMs functioning as autonomous AI agents. It is among the pioneering instances of employing publicly accessible datasets to train state-of-the-art models, avoiding reliance on proprietary or inaccessible datasets. Vicuna-13B outperforms LLaMA-13B on most benchmarks and competes with top-tier models like Chinchilla-70B and PaLM-540B. Additionally, Vicuna-13B offers more accessibility and affordability compared to other LLMs, demanding less computational power and resources for training and operation.

The development of Vicuna-13B continues, encountering several limitations and challenges. These include the assurance of ethical and responsible use of data and AI, the maintenance of coherence and consistency across different sources and tasks, and the graceful handling of errors and failures. Despite these hurdles, Vicuna-13B illuminates the potential of LLMs as potent instruments for natural language processing and generation, presenting new opportunities for research and innovation in the LLM chatbot arena (Fig. 3).

6.6 Alpaca

Alpaca embodies a compact AI language model, the development of which was undertaken by a consortium of computer science researchers at Stanford University. The model is a refinement of LLaMA-7B, a Large Language Model (LLM) disseminated by Meta AI. Alpaca's training was based on 52K instruction-following demonstrations generated by OpenAI's text-davinci-003, a highly capable LLM chatbot.

The capability of Alpaca to adapt to a variety of domains and scenarios is attributable to its use of data from diverse sources, coupled with its capacity for tone and style modulation. Through leveraging its language generation and understanding abilities, Alpaca is capable of crafting responses that meet or exceed the quality of those provided by text-davinci-003, all while retaining a compact size and exhibiting reproducibility.

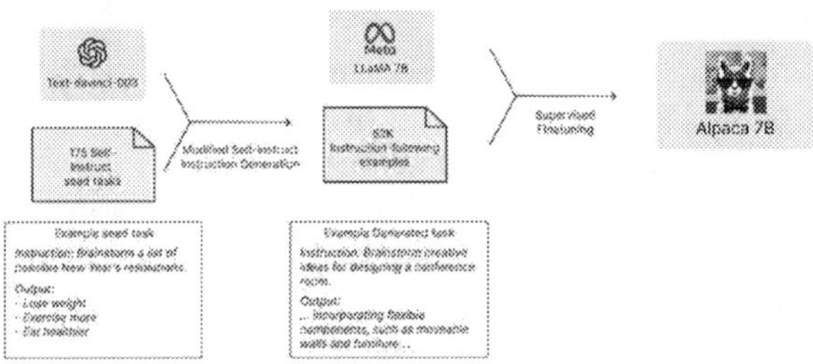

Fig. 3. Alpaca-Architecture

As an experimental initiative, Alpaca exemplifies the potential of LLMs to function as autonomous AI agents. It stands among the pioneering instances of the use of publicly accessible datasets for training cutting-edge models, circumventing the need for proprietary or inaccessible datasets. Alpaca surpasses LLaMA-7B on a majority of performance metrics and maintains competitiveness with other models such as Vicuna-13B and Chinchilla-70B. Additionally, Alpaca provides more accessibility and affordability than other LLMs due to its lesser requirement for computational power and resources for training and operation.

Alpaca is still in the development stage, grappling with limitations and challenges that include the need for ethical and responsible data and AI usage, the maintenance of coherence and consistency across different sources and tasks, and the management of errors and failures in a graceful manner. Despite these challenges, Alpaca illustrates the capacity of LLMs to serve as potent tools for natural language processing and generation, thereby charting new paths for research and innovation in the realm of LLM chatbots.

6.7 BARD

BARD stands as an experimental chatbot brought into existence by Google AI, deriving its functionalities from the Language Model for Dialogue Applications (LaMDA), a Large Language Model (LLM) capable of crafting natural language responses to a myriad of inquiries. The foundational structure of BARD is based on the transformer architecture, with its training relying on an extensive collection of textual data from the internet.

Capable of performing a comprehensive suite of Natural Language Processing (NLP) tasks, BARD provides capabilities such as response generation, summarization, explanation, and content creation. Moreover, BARD exhibits adaptability to varied domains and scenarios, enabled by the integration of data from diverse sources and the adjustment of its tone and style as required. The tool capitalizes on its language generation and comprehension skills to generate responses that are innovative, high quality, and rooted in factual information.

As an open-source initiative, BARD demonstrates the potential of LLMs to function as independent AI agents. It stands as one of the inaugural examples of LaMDA utilization, a state-of-the-art LLM capable of managing open-ended dialogue and sophisticated reasoning. BARD's mission is to integrate the vast spectrum of global knowledge with the power, intellect, and creativity offered by LLMs. Additionally, BARD offers superior accessibility and affordability compared to other LLMs, owing to its employment of a lightweight model version of LaMDA, which significantly reduces computational power requirements.

Despite being in the developmental stage, BARD grapples with limitations and challenges that include the need for ethical and responsible data and AI usage, maintenance of coherence and consistency across different sources and tasks, and the management of errors and failures in a graceful manner. However, BARD underscores the potential of LLMs as robust tools for natural language processing and generation, thereby pioneering new pathways for research and innovation in the LLM chatbot field.

7 Results, Analysis, and Discussion

The examined research offers an in-depth comparative assessment of diverse Language Learning Models (LLMs), taking into account multiple parameters, while concurrently highlighting common challenges faced by all, including memory capacity, token limit, and hallucination problems.

The study investigated memory capacity, discovering that models with superior memory capacities demonstrated enhanced performance in context retention and data referencing, especially when dealing with prolonged and intricate information.

Token limit, a parameter indicating the maximum number of tokens an LLM can process simultaneously, was another critical factor scrutinized. Certain models were found to manage lengthy inputs more effectively, maintaining coherence across protracted texts, whereas others faced constraints due to lower token limits.

Hallucination, a situation wherein a model generates outputs not anchored in the input, was another sphere of comparison. Some models exhibited more sophisticated behaviours with lower propensities to hallucinate, albeit no model was entirely immune to such occurrences.

On a broader scale, newer models consistently surpassed their antecedents in all evaluated aspects. However, all models presented their own set of limitations, underscoring the necessity for persistent research and refinement. This comparison contributes towards a deeper understanding of LLMs and paves the way for future model development.

To mitigate the challenges aforementioned, it is recommended to reconceptualize the vector database from a simple repository to a strategic instrument. By allowing access to this database as a tactical tool customised to an agent's specific requirements in Langchain, we overcome the constraints of dependence on cosine similarity with the query. This method offers the agent the independence to utilise the vector database, performing searches to find relevant documents based on a more extensive array of query parameters in contrast to a basic similarity search. The evolution of the agent into a pragmatic tool, adaptable to varying use cases and available on demand, has been proven to significantly improve accuracy. This enhancement is particularly noticeable in situations necessitating the execution of complex queries, such as when seeking legal documents or academic research papers.

References

1. ChatGPT - Wikipedia (n.d.). https://en.wikipedia.org/wiki/ChatGPT. Accessed 27 Apr 2023
2. Peters, J.: The Bing AI bot has been secretly running GPT-4 - The Verge (2023). https://www.theverge.com/2023/3/14/23639928.gpt_3_1. Accessed 7 Apr 2023
3. Auto-GPT - The next evolution of data driven Chat AI. https://auto-gpt.ai/
4. Auto-GPT: An Autonomous GPT-4 Experiment - GitHub. https://github.com/Significant-Gravitas/Auto-GPT
5. What is Auto-GPT? Everything to know about the next powerful AI tool. https://www.zdnet.com/article/what-is-auto-gpt-everything-to-know-about-the-next-powerful-ai-tool/
6. Meta AI: Introducing LLaMA: A foundational, 65-billion-parameter language model (2023). https://ai.facebook.com/blog/large-language-model-llama-meta-ai/. Accessed 27 Apr 2023
7. Hugging Face. LLaMA - Hugging Face (2023). https://huggingface.co/docs/transformers/main/en/model_doc/llama. Accessed 27 Apr 2023

8. Touvron, F.N., et al.: LLaMA: Open and Efficient Foundation Language Models (2023). https://arxiv.org/abs/2302.13971. Accessed 27 April 2023
9. Vicuna. Vicuna: An Open-Source Chatbot Impressing GPT-4 with 90 ChatGPT Quality (2023). https://vicuna.lmsys.org/. Accessed 27 Apr 2023
10. Search Engine Journal. Google Bard: Everything You Need To Know - Search Engine Journal (2023). https://www.searchenginejournal.com/google-bard/482860/. Accessed 27 Apr 2023
11. Android Police. Google Bard: Everything you need to know about the AI chatbot (2023). https://www.androidpolice.com/google-bard-explained/. Accessed 27 Apr 2023
12. Tech Trends. Google Unveils Bard: The New AI Language Model Rival to GPT-3 by OpenAI (2023). https://techtrends.co.in/google/google-unveils-bard-the-new-ai-language-model-rival-to-openais-gpt-3/. Accessed 27 Apr 2023
13. Google. Google AI updates: Bard and new AI features in Search - The Keyword (2023). https://blog.google/technology/ai/bard-google-ai-search-updates/. Accessed 27 Apr 2023
14. Medium. How To Fine-Tune the Alpaca Model For Any Language - Medium (2023). https://medium.com/@martin-thissen/how-to-fine-tune-the-alpaca-model-for-any-language-chatgpt-alternative-370f63753f94. Accessed 27 Apr 2023
15. TheBloke. TheBloke/vicuna-13B-1.1-HF · Hugging Face (2023). https://huggingface.co/TheBloke/vicuna-13B-1.1-HF. Accessed 27 Apr 2023

CincoCrypto - A Cryptocurrency Price Forecasting Tool for Everyone

Gonzalo Lara de Leyva, Ashutosh Dhar Dwivedi(✉), and Jens Myrup Pedersen

Cybersecurity Group, Aalborg University, Copenhagen, Denmark
glarad21@student.aau.dk, {addw,jens}@es.aau.dk

Abstract. The proliferation of cryptocurrency investment scams has become a pressing concern in recent times. In response to this challenge, this research paper introduces 'CincoCrypto,' a novel and innovative solution designed to provide investors with a cost-free, user-friendly, and open-source tool for cryptocurrency price forecasting. CincoCrypto leverages four Machine Learning models, trained on financial data from up to five prominent cryptocurrencies, enabling it to predict the closing prices in United States Dollars for the subsequent day. The study primarily concentrates on one-year datasets derived from the world's top five cryptocurrencies by global market capitalization: Bitcoin, Ethereum, Tether, Binance Coin, and USD Coin. Our findings indicate the most promising results for Ethereum, with the Convolutional Neural Network model emerging as the most accurate among the four models, while the Space Vector Regression model demonstrates superior computational performance. This research offers valuable insights into the potential applications of Machine Learning in mitigating cryptocurrency investment risks and improving market predictions.

Keywords: Machine Learning · Scams · Cryptocurrency · Price prediction · Bitcoin · Ethereum · Tether · USD Coin · Binance Coin

1 Introduction

Cryptocurrencies have seamlessly integrated themselves into the fabric of our increasingly digitalized society. However, this rapid adoption as a medium of value exchange has unfortunately spawned a disturbing surge in cryptocurrency-related scams. The alarming statistics from the 2022 Internet Crime Report, published by the Federal Bureau of Investigation (FBI), highlight the gravity of the situation. Investment opportunities have emerged as the leading category of cybercrime, resulting in a staggering worldwide victim loss of 3.31 billion United States Dollars (USD) in 2022. What is even more disconcerting is that a substantial 77% of these losses, equivalent to a staggering 2.57 billion USD, can be directly attributed to cryptocurrency investment fraud. This marks an unprecedented increase of 183% compared to the 907 million USD reported just a year earlier in 2021. The consequences of these scams are far-reaching. A significant

KC Santosh et al. (Eds.): RTIP2R 2023, CCIS 2027, pp. 250–264, 2024.
https://doi.org/10.1007/978-3-031-53085-2_21

number of victims, predominantly falling within the age range of 30-49, find themselves burdened with substantial debts as they grapple with the aftermath of these fraudulent schemes, as reported by the FBI. This underscores the very real, human toll of cryptocurrency-related fraud. Both the FBI and Europol are in agreement about the evolving nature of cryptocurrency investment scams, which are becoming increasingly sophisticated. This evolution necessitates the categorization of these scams into various types, such as Business Opportunity and Phishing Ads, making it even more challenging to detect and combat these fraudulent activities. The growing prominence of cryptocurrency-related scams has drawn the attention of researchers and investigators, as documented in [2] and [29]. This increased focus is not limited to law enforcement and academia; even well-established financial institutions like Santander Bank [21] and HSBK UK [15] have recognized the urgency of raising awareness about this pressing issue. Cryptocurrencies have, over the years, displayed significant volatility, offering both trading opportunities for the short term and investment prospects for the long term. According to [27], the primary advantages of trading or investing in cryptocurrencies lie in their emergence as a new asset class and their potential to diversify risk. This diversification arises from their distinctive behavior compared to traditional investments, a factor that has made them increasingly appealing to a broad range of investors. Furthermore, cryptocurrencies have displayed remarkable resilience against the detrimental effects of rising inflation, a quality that sets them apart in the investment landscape. Their relative youth, compared to traditional financial assets, suggests that cryptocurrencies continue to harbor significant upside potential. This potential is further magnified by the emergence of novel developments within the cryptocurrency space, such as the rapid growth of stablecoins, which are digital currencies pegged to stable assets, and the ongoing expansion of global adoption. Given these challenges and the potential benefits of cryptocurrencies, this research paper introduces 'CincoCrypto.' Developed as a fundamental component of the main author's Cybersecurity MSc Thesis project, this cryptocurrency price forecasting tool leverages open-high-low-close (OHLC) and trading data from the current top five cryptocurrencies as of May 6, 2023. The primary objective of CincoCrypto is to offer transparent, user-friendly predictions of the next day's closing prices in USD, targeting individuals with limited trading or technical backgrounds. To foster well-informed and secure cryptocurrency trading while mitigating exposure to fraudulent schemes, this research initiative endeavors to create a simple, free, and open-source tool for predicting cryptocurrency closing prices. This tool, aptly named 'CincoCrypto,' is readily accessible on GitHub, ensuring its wide availability and usability [1]. To validate and evaluate the performance of CincoCrypto, we harnessed a one-year dataset comprising OHLC (Open-High-Low-Close) data and trading volume information spanning from June 5, 2022, to June 5, 2023. The dataset was meticulously curated from the top five cryptocurrencies at the time of this study, including Bitcoin (BTC), Ethereum (ETH), Tether (USDT), Binance Coin (BNB), and USD Coin (USDC). This selection process was underpinned by data sourced from renowned providers of cryptocurrency price information, such as Binance [3], CoinMarketCap [6], and Yahoo! Finance [30]. In the pursuit of the highest achievable prediction accuracy for closing prices, we crafted four distinct models within the CincoCrypto framework. Each model underwent rigorous evaluation to determine which one was most effective for analyzing the chosen cryptocurrencies. The evaluation process was geared toward pinpointing the model that could provide the most precise forecasts for these specific digital assets.

1.1 Research Contributions

This paper aims to make four main contributions:

- **Free, open-source tool** - CincoCrypto is designed as a supplementary tool meant to be utilized alongside additional data sources, such as sentiment analysis and network data, as well as in tandem with more advanced software applications. Its primary function is to generate one-day ahead predictions for the closing values of cryptocurrencies. Through the provision of this tool, the author's objective is to make a valuable contribution to cybersecurity endeavors by enhancing the safety and informativeness of cryptocurrency investments.
- **Most up-to-date data analysis** - To the best of the author's knowledge, there are no studies that have employed cryptocurrency datasets as up-to-date as those examined in this paper. Consequently, the results obtained from this evaluation can offer invaluable insights to the machine learning (ML) community concerning the performance of each algorithm and their respective configurations.
- **Analysis of multiple machine learning algorithms** - Only a limited number of academic studies have undertaken a thorough analysis of the performance of Space Vector Regression (SVR), Long-Short Term Memory (LSTM), Gated Recurrent Unit (GRU), and Convolutional Neural Network (CNN) within a single research paper. This study bridges that gap by conducting a comprehensive evaluation and comparison of these algorithms.
- **Analysis of multiple cryptocurrencies** - It is a rarity to come across studies that examine more than three cryptocurrencies within a single investigation. Hence, this paper conducts an analysis of five cryptocurrencies during the same time frame to deliver a comprehensive multi-coin assessment.

1.2 Limitations

The design limitations of *CincoCrypto* are as follows:

- Cryptocurrency sentiment and network information are not considered in the analysis.
- The tool lacks support for the simultaneous analysis of more than five coins.
- The tool exclusively accommodates datasets from CryptoCompare.
- The algorithm hyperparameters are configured with default values, and their impact is not assessed.

2 Literature Review

In [18], the study explores the impact of kernel selection on the performance of forecasting trading volume. Using Bayesian optimization to fine-tune hyperparameters, the study investigates three common kernel types: linear, polynomial, and Radial Basis Function (RBF). The data from thirty cryptocurrencies is divided into a training set (80%) and a testing set (20%). The output from the SVR algorithm is then compared against ARIMA, Lasso, and Gaussian processes. The evaluation metrics employed include root-mean-squared error (RMSE) and mean absolute error (MAE). The results reveal that the Bayesian Optimization kernel is most effective for making predictions for the following day, while the polynomial kernel excels at predicting volume for the following week. In the overarching analysis, SVR outperforms the other processes.

In [13], parameter optimization using the Grid Search Method is applied to SVR with RBF. The model forecasts the price for the next five weeks by leveraging weekly BTC price data spanning from January 2018 to March 2020. To maintain data relationships, the data is normalized through min-max normalization. The evaluation metric used, MAPE, indicates the lowest error (10.738%) for an SVR model with parameters $C = 5$, $\epsilon = 0.004$, and $\gamma = 0.07$.

A comparative study involving LSTM, SVR, GRU, and CNN is conducted in [20]. It employs a 3-day prediction window with datasets from four cryptocurrencies: BTC, Bitcoin Cash, Litecoin, and ETH, covering the period from September 15, 2016, to November 5, 2018. The metrics utilized for assessment encompass RMSE, MAE, MAPE, and the coefficient of determination (R^2). The results reveal that the LSTM model exhibits the lowest error and the highest R^2 score.

In [12], various time series architectures are compared, including ARIMA, SARIMA, GRU, RNN, LSTM, and Facebook Prophet. A four-year dataset spanning from 2018 to 2022, consisting of OHLC and volume data, is divided into three datasets (comprising 80% training, 10% validation, and 10% testing) for predicting closing values. The performance of the models is evaluated using MSE and RMSE, with the results indicating that GRU outperforms the other models examined in the study.

The research presented in [17] conducts a comparison between LSTM and GRU while maintaining fixed hyperparameters and analyzing model performance based on the number of epochs, ranging from 1 to 30. Three cryptocurrency datasets (BTC, ETH, and LTC) are employed, and model performance is assessed using RMSE and MAE. The findings suggest that GRU is more effective at predicting downward trends, while LSTM excels at analyzing upward trends.

In the paper from [28], a comparative study is conducted among CNN, RNN, and LSTM models, with the results showing that the LSTM model delivers the best performance among the three. Four performance indicators, including MAE, MAPE, RMSE, and R^2, are applied to a four-year dataset spanning from 2017 to 2021, encompassing OHLC, volume, and market cap values. The data is normalized using the MinMaxScaler function. The CNN model is designed with a 1-Dimensional convolutional (*Conv1D*) layer for feature extraction, a pooling layer (*MaxPooling1D*) to reduce the size of the *Conv1D* output, a Flatten layer for reshaping the data, and a *Dense* layer to shape the model's output. The model is run for 1000 epochs, and subsequently, for 3000 epochs to predict the closing value on the 60th day.

3 Methodology

Following an elucidation of the paper's context and contributions, this section delves into a comprehensive discussion of the background. According to the US Internal Revenue Service (IRS), digital currency embodies value within the digital realm and, akin to any conventional currency, it functions as a unit of account, a store of value, and a medium of exchange. Cryptocurrencies, distinguished by their use of cryptographic techniques and inscription on digital distributed ledgers, such as blockchain, represent a distinct subset of digital currency [16]. Despite encountering skepticism and regulatory constraints due to their absence of backing and oversight by public or private entities [22], cryptocurrencies have steadily gained worldwide acceptance. They are now being utilized for the purchase of a diverse array of products on e-commerce platforms, even by major technology companies like Microsoft and ATandT. Furthermore, as of June 18, 2023, the Central African Republic and *El* Salvador stand as the sole two countries globally that have officially sanctioned cryptocurrencies as legal tender, signifying their potential as a viable alternative, if not a replacement, for physical currencies [5]. The Bitcoin network lays the foundation for Bitcoin (BTC), the first successful cryptocurrency and the one commanding the largest market cap dominance (45.01%) [4]. This paper proceeds to analyze four additional cryptocurrencies in descending order of market cap dominance: Ethereum (ETH) at 18.9%, Tether coin (USDT) at 6.47%, Binance coin (BNB) at 4.06%, and USD Coin (USDC) at 2.39%. Typically, cryptocurrency data, like that processed by *CincoCrypto*, is structured in a sequential order, forming a time series. Consequently, machine learning (ML) algorithms are well-suited for managing this data type, given their capacity to efficiently handle substantial volumes of information in an automated fashion. The tool employs four ML models to generate four distinct predictions for the next day's price. These models make use of the following algorithms:

- SVR - Space Vector Regression (SVR) is a machine learning (ML) algorithm capable of accurately predicting values within time series data, particularly in the context of nonlinear, dynamic, and undefined systems. SVMs, to which SVR belongs, have demonstrated remarkable performance when compared to other nonlinear methods like multi-layer perceptrons. In regression analysis, SVM transforms into SVR. SVR accomplishes regression by employing an estimation function that fits a curve to the observed time series values. Unlike several other algorithms, SVR does not depend on an explicit model; instead, its predictions are guided by the data itself. The curve function is determined based on the observed data used to train the algorithm [23].

- LSTM - Long Short-Term Memory (LSTM) represents a deep learning (DL) algorithm designed to tackle the challenge of vanishing and exploding gradients often encountered by Recursive Neural Networks (RNNs) during training. LSTM addresses this issue by integrating a gated mechanism, which allows it to store information in long-term memory (referred to as the Cell State) while preserving the outcomes of prior computations in short-term memory (known as the hidden state) [24].
- GRU - Gated Recurrent Unit (GRU) is a DL algorithm from the latest generation of models. Much like LSTM, GRU also incorporates a gated mechanism. However, it is more lightweight, utilizing solely an update gate and a reset gate [25].
- CNN - Convolutional Neural Network (CNN) represents another deep learning (DL) algorithm that convolves identified features with input data through convolutional layers. While CNNs are predominantly employed in image recognition tasks, they can also be adapted for time series data to make predictions. An advantage of CNNs is that they obviate the need for manual feature extraction, as they autonomously discern pertinent features during model training [19].

3.1 Datasets

The program utilizes 1-year-long datasets spanning from June 5, 2022, to June 5, 2023, encompassing the top five cryptocurrencies: BTC [8], ETH [9], USDT [10], BNB [7], and USDC [11]. These datasets, available in CSV format, are sourced from the global data provider CryptoCompare. CincoCrypto has been developed using datasets from CryptoCompare, and consequently, it is configured to exclusively analyze datasets from this source. This limitation is due to the specific number of features included in these datasets and their particular arrangement within the files. The datasets contain essential OHLC (Open-High-Low-Close) and trading information, organized across 8 columns. When the program is executed, an additional column, labeled $1_{day_f}orecast$, is appended to the original dataset (refer to Table 1). This new column stores the closing price data for the following day, serving as the dependent variable for analysis. The *time* column is discarded, with only the *timeDate* being used to reference each subsequent day's closing price value. The other columns remain unaltered, as their purpose is to serve as features for the models. Detailed modifications to the Bitcoin dataset, as processed by CincoCrypto, are explained in the following section.

Table 1. Last five rows from the modified Bitcoin dataset

time	timeDate	close	high	low	open	volumefrom	volumeto	1_day_forecast
1682985600000	2023-05-02	28694.85	28896.62	27897.95	28086.19	32635.23	927167494.21	29041
1683072000000	2023-05-03	29041	29274.35	28155.84	28694.85	40240.91	1150094643.14	28866.54
1683158400000	2023-05-04	28866.54	29370.41	28703.83	29041	27555.47	798614954.67	29550.84
1683244800000	2023-05-05	29550.84	29697.23	28853.1	28866.54	35357.4	1037025191.1	28845.45
1683331200000	2023-05-06	28845.45	29857.86	28459.77	29550.84	23039.88	670625654.68	NaN

3.2 Proposed Work

With the core concepts, algorithms, and relevant papers that influenced the design of *CincoCrypto* covered, we can now delve into how the tool has been engineered to minimize user input (specifically, only requiring the specification of dataset names) and predict the next day's closing price for the top five cryptocurrencies. *CincoCrypto* is programmed to work with only five CryptoCompare datasets, which must be stored in the same current working directory (CWD) as the notebook file containing the tool's source code. The tool calculates the next day's price based on the data from the previous day. The program has

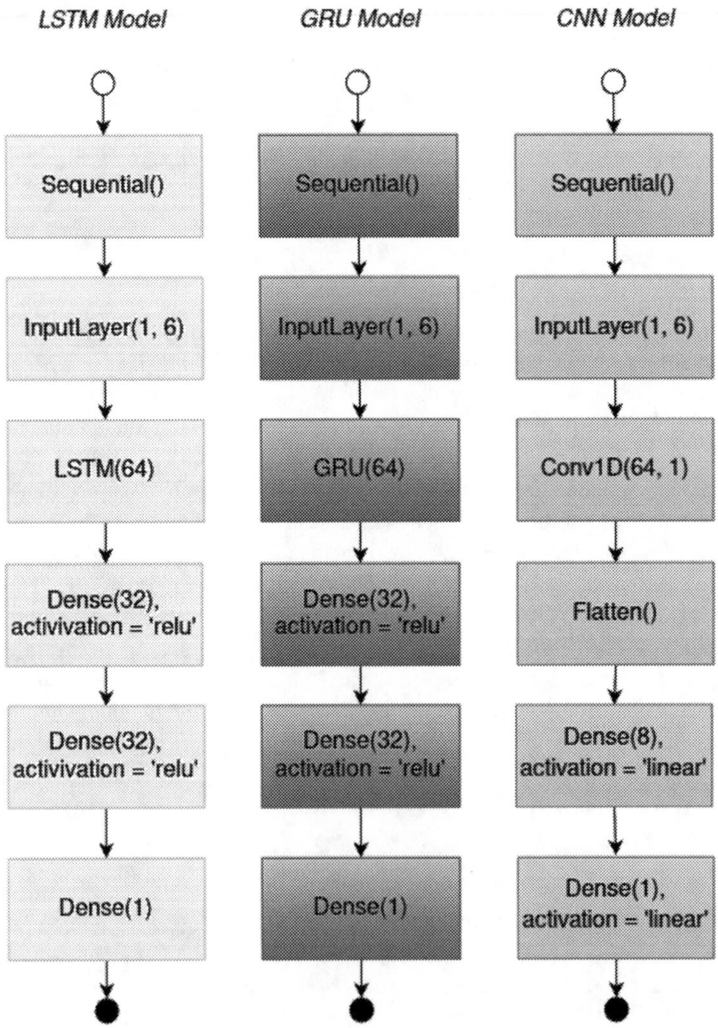

Fig. 1. Structure of *CincoCrypto* Deep Learning models

been designed with simplicity in mind, as users are merely required to manually input the names of the datasets (without the .csv extension) into the *cryptos* list located at the top of the program. When *CincoCrypto* is executed, it processes the datasets one by one, removes the *time* column, and appends a new column for the independent variable (i.e., $1_{day_{f}orcast}$), as depicted in Table 1. It's important to note that while many studies in Sect. 2 solely utilize OHLC data, [18] suggests a correlation between trading volumes and closing prices. Therefore, *CincoCrypto* retains both OHLC and trading columns as features for the models.

Furthermore, the datasets are divided into training (80%) and testing (20%) sets, following the approach adopted in [18]. During dataset preprocessing, the last row from Table 1 must be removed as it contains a Not-a-Number (NaN), representing the next day's value that the program aims to predict. Subsequently, the preprocessed data is fed into the four models (SVR, LSTM, GRU, and CNN), and evaluation metrics (including training time, MAPE, MSE, and R^2) are computed for each model. MAPE, MSE, and R^2 are calculated as follows:

$$\text{MAPE} = \frac{100}{n} \sum_{n}^{i=1} \frac{|E_i|}{|A_i|} \tag{1}$$

In Eq. (1), the Mean Absolute Percentage Error (MAPE) is computed by dividing 100 by the total number of data points, denoted by n. The summation symbol is used to calculate the absolute difference between the predicted value (E) and the actual value (A), and the ratio of these differences is taken. Finally, the average of these ratios is obtained.

$$\text{MSE} = \frac{\sum_{i=1}^{n} {E_i}^2}{n} \tag{2}$$

In Eq. (2), the Mean Squared Error (MSE) is computed by summing the squared differences between the predicted value (E) and the actual value (A) for each data point, and then dividing by the total number of data points, n.

$$R^2 = 1 - \frac{\text{SSR}}{\text{SST}} = 1 - \frac{\sum_{i=1}^{n}(P_i - A_i)^2}{\sum_{i=1}^{n}(A_i - \bar{A})^2} \tag{3}$$

In Eq. (3), the coefficient of determination, R^2, is computed as 1 minus the ratio of the Sum of Squares due to Regression (SSR) and the Sum of Squares Total (SST). The SSR represents the sum of the squared differences between the predicted values (P_i) and the actual values (A_i), while the SST represents the sum of the squared differences between the actual values and their mean ($\bar{A}$). The R^2 score indicates the proportion of the variance in the dependent variable that is explained by the independent variables in a regression model. This computation is repeated for the other four datasets until all models have been evaluated, and their results are stored in an output CSV file. The SVR model is implemented by calling the *SVR* function in the sklearn library, while the DL algorithms follow the structure described in [14] (refer to Fig. 1). Within the DL models, LSTM uses a total of 21,345 parameters, whereas GRU and CNN use 16,993 and 977 parameters, respectively. All three DL models have the number of epochs set at 50 to prevent overfitting, with MSE as the loss function and Adam optimizer using a learning rate of 0.0001 to ensure optimal convergence at the global minimum. After processing all the coins, charts are generated to examine the performance of the four models for each analyzed coin. These charts are saved as PNG files in the current working directory (CWD), allowing the user to visually assess and choose the most accurate model for their needs.

4 Results

Having provided a high-level overview of the program and its functions, this section delves into the significance of the predictions generated by CincoCrypto. Overall, all four models exhibit a tendency to underfit the cryptocurrencies under analysis. Notably, for BTC, the models achieve the highest R^2 scores, aligning closely with the actual data, as illustrated in Fig. 2. Furthermore, Fig. 2 demonstrates that, at the very least, *CincoCrypto* is capable of producing relatively accurate predictions for ETH. These predictions are characterized by similar R^2 scores and smaller MAPE values when compared to the multi-forecast horizon study proposed in [31].

Table 2. Ethereum results comparison

Models	MAPE (%)	R^2
SVR	0.0278	0.8004
LSTM	0.0524	0.1238
GRU	0.0423	0.4641
CNN	0.0359	0.6739

(a) CincoCrypto results

Models	MAPE (%)	R^2
SVR	6.37	0.876
LSTM	9.35	0.789
GRU	7.73	0.843
CNN	5.45	0.894

(b) Results from the paper [31]

The dataset that exhibited the fastest results during testing is USDT, and, in an overall assessment, it demonstrates the lowest MAPE and MSE. However, as Table 3 illustrates, this particular cryptocurrency yields the most negative R^2 scores, despite CNN's ability to closely track the shape of the closing curve, as evident in Fig. 3. The reason behind these scores can be attributed to R^2,' a metric that must be employed cautiously when dealing with stablecoins. This is because the actual closing values of stablecoins tend to exhibit minimal variation from the mean value, often hovering around 1.000 USD. Consequently, this leads to a situation where the sum of squares total (STT) is notably larger than the sum of squares due to regression (SSR), as exemplified in Eq. (3). As a result, R^2 scores may take on significantly negative values when models make predictions for this category of cryptocurrency.

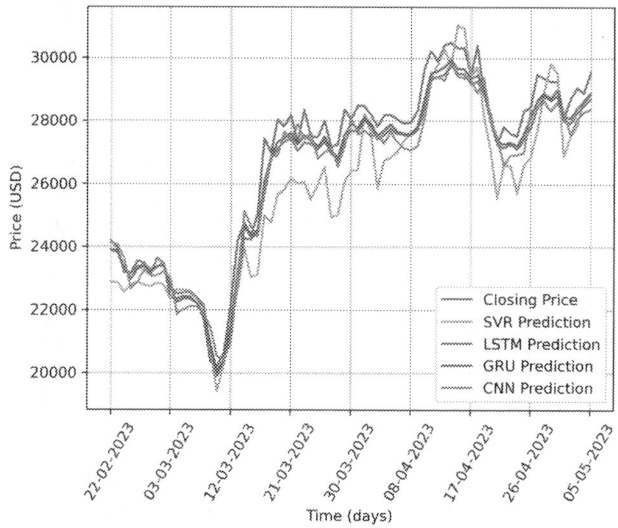

(a) Closing price prediction plots

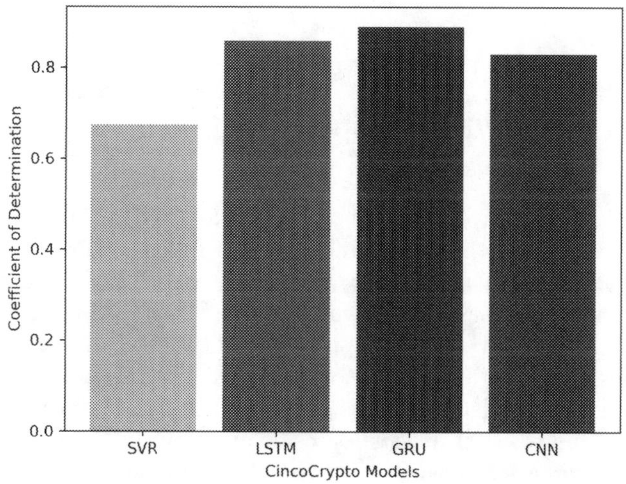

(b) Coefficient of determination scores

Fig. 2. Bitcoin Charts

Table 3. Tether evaluation metrics (rounded to 5 s.f.)

Models	Training Time (s)	MAPE (%)	MSE (USD^2)	R^2
SVR	8.1968×10^{-4}	9.9315×10^{-4}	3.4462×10^{-6}	−67.322
LSTM	4.2943	9.4338×10^{-4}	2.6714×10^{-6}	−112.58
GRU	4.2563	8.6827×10^{-4}	2.5437×10^{-6}	−66.487
CNN	3.1143	5.4616×10^{-4}	1.2948×10^{-6}	−1.1579

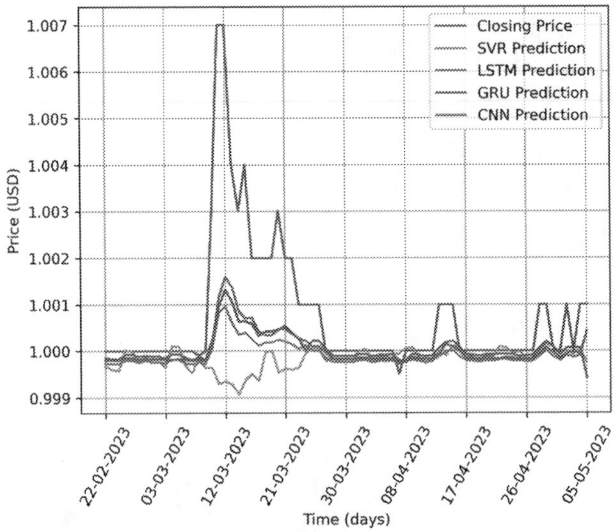

Fig. 3. Closing price prediction plots (Tether)

In the analysis of all five coins, it is evident that the deep learning (DL) models excel in predicting both upward and downward trends, closely mirroring the shapes of the closing price plots across all models. Among the DL algorithms, the CNN model emerges as the top performer in three out of the five coins (i.e., ETH, USDT, BNB). It demonstrates an impressive ability to accurately anticipate significant price spikes, particularly for both stablecoins assessed (i.e., USDT and USDC). The LSTM and GRU models exhibit comparable performance, with GRU outperforming LSTM in most cases, except for USDT. It is notable that GRU, despite having significantly fewer total parameters than LSTM, doesn't translate into a substantial reduction in training time, as is the case with CNN, which boasts the fewest parameters among the DL models. On the other hand, the SVR model consistently proves to be the quickest to train, operating in the milliseconds to nanoseconds range, across the five coin datasets. This speed can be attributed to its reduced complexity, devoid of layers and weight optimization found in the DL models. However, it falls short in terms of performance, particularly when applied to the stablecoins analyzed (i.e., USDT and USDC), where it lags behind other models in matching the closing price trends closely.

5 Conclusion

This research paper introduces *CincoCrypto*, an accessible and freely available open-source tool designed for cryptocurrency price forecasting. Its primary objective is to empower individuals with limited financial and technical knowledge to make secure investments in the cryptocurrency market. With user-friendliness at the forefront, *CincoCrypto* simplifies the process by requiring users to specify dataset names in the *cryptos* list and then run the program. The tool has been uploaded to GitHub, ensuring easy access for a diverse user base at no cost. *CincoCrypto* allows users to concurrently analyze up to five cryptocurrency datasets from CryptoCompare. It deploys four distinct models, namely SVR, LSTM, GRU, and CNN, granting users the flexibility to choose the best-performing model for predicting the next day's closing price for their selected cryptocurrencies. Through this approach, the author seeks to combat the alarming rise of cryptocurrency investment scams. While the analysis results indicate a tendency for the models to underfit the studied coins, *CincoCrypto* consistently produces commendable results, as demonstrated by reasonably decent R^2 scores, as shown in Table 2. Overall, CNN consistently outperforms the other algorithms in terms of metrics and the shape of prediction curves, while SVR is recognized as the fastest model. By offering a user-friendly and dependable tool, *CincoCrypto* aims to equip individuals with minimal financial and technical backgrounds to make well-informed investment decisions. The tool's contribution not only combats the alarming increase in scams but also fosters a safer investment environment within the cryptocurrency market.

6 Future Work

The obtained results suggest that the models exhibit a tendency to underfit the analyzed cryptocurrencies. To address this issue comprehensively, it is imperative to conduct a thorough analysis, including the examination of loss and variance curves, and consider the possibility of increasing the number of epochs for the models. Furthermore, incorporating automatic hyperparameter tuning could significantly enhance model performance by enabling the automatic selection and application of optimal parameters based on the input datasets, as demonstrated for SVR in [18]. However, it's worth noting that this approach may introduce greater model complexity, potentially posing challenges for machines without dedicated graphical processing units. Moreover, enhancing the program's interactivity and functionality would be beneficial. Users could be provided with the ability to upload datasets from directories separate from the tool's current working directory, as well as the option to specify the directory for storing the results. Additionally, removing the limitation of using only five cryptocurrency datasets from CryptoCompare would empower users, allowing them to upload datasets from any source with any number of features, providing them with more control over the analysis process. To improve the accuracy of closing price predictions, it would be valuable to consider incorporating additional factors such as sentiment and network data, as well as other relevant external variables. Furthermore, exploring different prediction horizons, such as forecasting prices further into the future (e.g., predicting 5 days ahead), would offer insights into the models' performance under varying scenarios. Lastly, expanding the range of available ML models for users, such as Adaboost or Catboost [26], would provide more options for model selection, enabling users to choose the approach that best aligns with their requirements and preferences.

References

1. CincoCrypto. ARealGent (2023). https://github.com/ARealGent/CincoCrypto. Accessed 31 May 2023
2. Bartoletti, M., Lande, S., Loddo, A., Pompianu, L., Serusi, S.: Cryptocurrency scams: analysis and perspectives. IEEE Access **9**, 148353–148373 (2021). https://doi.org/10.1109/ACCESS.2021.3123894
3. Binance: Cryptocurrency Prices Today. https://www.binance.com/en/price
4. CoinGecko: Global Cryptocurrency Market Cap Charts. https://www.coingecko.com/en/global-charts
5. CoinMarketCap: Countries which allow cryptocurrency as legal tender. https://coinmarketcap.com/legal-tender-countries/
6. CoinmarketCap: Today's Cryptocurrency Prices by Market Cap. https://coinmarketcap.com/
7. CryptoCompare: Binance coin. https://www.cryptocompare.com/coins/bnb/analysis/USD?period=1Y
8. CryptoCompare: Bitcoin. https://www.cryptocompare.com/coins/btc/analysis/USD?period=1Y
9. CryptoCompare: Ethereum. https://www.cryptocompare.com/coins/eth/analysis/USD?period=1Y
10. CryptoCompare: Tether. https://www.cryptocompare.com/coins/usdt/analysis/USD?period=1Y
11. CryptoCompare: USD Coin. https://www.cryptocompare.com/coins/usdc/analysis/USD?period=1Y
12. De Leon, L.G.N., Gomez, R.C., Tacal, M.L.G., Taylar, J.V., Nojor, V.V., Villanueva, A.R.: Bitcoin price forecasting using time-series architectures. In: 2022 International Conference on ICT for Smart Society (ICISS), pp. 1–6 (2022). https://doi.org/10.1109/ICISS55894.2022.9915199
13. Fadil, I., Helmiawan, M.A., Sofiyan, Y.: Optimization parameters support vector regression using grid search method. In: 2021 9th International Conference on Cyber and IT Service Management (CITSM), pp. 1–5 (2021). https://doi.org/10.1109/CITSM52892.2021.9589028

14. Hogg, G.: Multivariate Time Series Forecasting Using LSTM, GRU & 1d CNNs. https://www.youtube.com/watch?v=kGdbPnMCdOg&t=1775s
15. HSBC: Beware of Cryptocurrency scams. https://www.privatebanking.hsbc.com/about-us/fraud-and-security/beware-of-cryptocurrency-scams/
16. IRS: Frequently Asked Questions on Virtual Currency Transactions. https://www.irs.gov/individuals/international-taxpayers/frequently-asked-questions-on-virtual-currency-transactions
17. Kim, J., Kim, S., Wimmer, H., Liu, H.: A cryptocurrency prediction model using LSTM and GRU algorithms. In: 2021 IEEE/ACIS 6th International Conference on Big Data, Cloud Computing, and Data Science (BCD), pp. 37–44 (2021). https://doi.org/10.1109/BCD51206.2021.9581397
18. Lahmiri, S., Bekiros, S., Bezzina, F.: Complexity analysis and forecasting of variations in cryptocurrency trading volume with support vector regression tuned by Bayesian optimization under different kernels: an empirical comparison from a large dataset. Expert Syst. Appl. **209**, 118349 (2022). https://doi.org/10.1016/j.eswa.2022.118349, https://www.sciencedirect.com/science/article/pii/S0957417422014683
19. MathWorks: What is Deep Learning? https://uk.mathworks.com/discovery/deep-learning.html
20. Nasirtafreshi, I.: Forecasting cryptocurrency prices using recurrent neural network and long short-term memory. Data Knowl. Eng. **139**, 102009 (2022). https://doi.org/10.1016/j.datak.2022.102009, https://www.sciencedirect.com/science/article/pii/S0169023X22000234
21. Santander: Cryptocurrencies: bait for investment scams. https://www.santander.com/en/stories/cryptocurrency-scam
22. Santander: Joint press statement by the CNMV and the Banco de España on "cryptocurrencies" and "initial coin offerings" (ICOs). https://www.bde.es/f/webbde/GAP/Secciones/SalaPrensa/NotasInformativas/18/presbe2018_07en.pdf
23. Sapankevych, N.I., Sankar, R.: Time series prediction using support vector machines: a survey. IEEE Comput. Intell. Mag. **4**(2), 24–38 (2009). https://doi.org/10.1109/MCI.2009.932254
24. Singhal, G.: Introduction to LSTM Units in RNN. https://www.pluralsight.com/guides/introduction-to-lstm-units-in-rnn
25. Singhal, G.: LSTM versus GRU Units in RNN. https://www.pluralsight.com/guides/lstm-versus-gru-units-in-rnn
26. Swati, S., Mohan, A.: Cryptocurrency value prediction with boosting models. In: 2022 International Conference on Intelligent Innovations in Engineering and Technology (ICIIET), pp. 183–188 (2022). https://doi.org/10.1109/ICIIET55458.2022.9967540
27. Team, C.: Is Cryptocurrency a Good Investment? https://corporatefinanceinstitute.com/resources/cryptocurrency/is-cryptocurrency-a-good-investment
28. Tran, T.K., Le, T.T.T., Bui, T.T., Dang, V.Q., Senkerik, R.: Constructing a cryptocurrency-price prediction model using deep learning. In: 2022 International Conference on Engineering and Emerging Technologies (ICEET), pp. 1–6 (2022). https://doi.org/10.1109/ICEET56468.2022.10007138
29. Vakilinia, I.: Cryptocurrency giveaway scam with youtube live stream. In: 2022 IEEE 13th Annual Ubiquitous Computing, Electronics & Mobile Communication Conference (UEMCON), pp. 0195–0200 (2022). https://doi.org/10.1109/UEMCON54665.2022.9965686

30. Yahoo! Finance: Top Cryptos by Market Cap. https://finance.yahoo.com/u/yahoo-finance/watchlists/crypto-top-market-cap/
31. Zhang, Z., Dai, H.N., Zhou, J., Mondal, S.K., García, M.M., Wang, H.: Forecasting cryptocurrency price using convolutional neural networks with weighted and attentive memory channels. Exp. Syst. Appl. **183**, 115378 (2021). https://doi.org/10.1016/j.eswa.2021.115378, https://www.sciencedirect.com/science/article/pii/S0957417421008046

Deep Neural Networks Based Security Solution for ATM Transactions

Neeraj Joshi[1](✉), Sheshikala Martha[2](✉), Shivam Chaudhary[1,2](✉), Prakhar Consul[1,2,3](✉), and Sushil Kumar Singh[3](✉)

[1] SCSET, Bennett University, Greater Noida, Uttar Pradesh, India
{e22soep0031,e22soep0063,e21soep0004}@bennett.edu.in

[2] School of Computer Science and Artificial Intelligence, SR University, Warangal, India
marthakala08@gmail.com

[3] Department of Computer Engineering, Marwadi University, Rajkot, Gujrat, India
sushilkumar.singh@marwadieducation.edu.in

Abstract. This paper provides you with a description of this new approach for the security of ATM transactions for its subscribers. Looking towards the banking sector, ensuring the safety and security in Automatic Teller Machine (ATM) is a critical factor for ATM transactions. This paper gives a review in brief about the existing literature survey on security arrangements, types of attacks of ATM transaction, together with IR sensors, bio metric identification like (Fingerprint sensors, Iris scanner), modified encryption standards, live monitoring and OTP (One Time Password) notifications, and systems based on IOT applications. This research paper also spotted the restrictions and obstructions of the ongoing security measures, probable threats, types of attacks in transactions and recommends some areas for future research. The insights gained from this research paper can surely be helpful for improving the security system in ATMs and in upgrading the safety measure of overall ATM transactions.

Keywords: ATM (Automated Teller Machine) · Infrared Sensors · GPS · RFID · Video Surveillance · IOT based Notification · Biometric verification · 2WA · DL · S-DNN

Neeraj Joshi is associated with the School of Computer Science Engineering and Technology, Bennett University, Greater Noida (Uttar Pradesh)-201310, India,
Sheshikala Martha is associated with Department of Computer Engineering, SR university, Warangal, India,
Shivam Chaudhary is associated with the School of Computer Science Engineering and Technology, Bennett University, Greater Noida (Uttar Pradesh)-201310, India,
Prakhar Consul is associated with the School of Computer Science Engineering and Technology, Bennett University, Greater Noida (Uttar Pradesh)-201310, India,
Sushil Kumar Singh is associated with Department of Computer Engineering, Marwadi University, Rajkot, Gujrat, India.

KC Santosh et al. (Eds.): RTIP2R 2023, CCIS 2027, pp. 265–275, 2024.
https://doi.org/10.1007/978-3-031-53085-2_22

1 Introduction

During the year 1960, Luther George Simjian created a machine that could automatically accept deposits in the form of coins, cash, and checks, but it did not have the ability to dispense cash. The US patent for his invention was filed on June 30, 1960, and was granted on February 26, 1963. The development of ATMs has revolutionized the banking industry, providing customers with easy access to their funds. However, the rise in ATM usage has also led to an increase in security threats for secure transaction. The paper proposes a new approach to address this issue.

To ensure the safety and security of ATM transactions, the research paper reviews existing literature on security arrangements for ATM transactions, including infrared sensors, biometric identification, modified encryption standards, live monitoring, and OTP notifications. The paper also highlights the limitations and challenges of current security measures and identifies areas for future research.

The paper proposes a new approach that involves all possible threats to secure transactions in ATM: Spyware attack, Side-channel attack, Brute-force, Replay, Smudge, Camera-recording, Video-recording, Multiple registration, spoofing, card-cloning etc. People around the globe love to withdraw money from ATM instead of going banks. Though subscribers for internet banking are increasing with advancement in internet technology, attraction towards ATM transaction is not reduced as mobile and Internet banking works well in presence of adequate internet connectivity. This article also advocates the incorporation of emerging technologies in ATM machine and its network to minimize the risk of cyber attacks and other possible threats.

In the literature available, ATM is equipped with an RFID card reader that stores subscriber's identity details, including fingerprints, iris, and face recognition and somewhere facial expressions which are authenticated, either one way or two-way at the ATM before money transfer or withdrawl. This is to ensures that only authorized personnel can access the ATM for banking activity. Furthermore, the bank has to acknowledge to the subscriber via IoT using cloud technology that the authentication process has been completed and subscribe can proceed further. This also allows the bank to monitor the activity taking place at the ATM. After completing the banking transaction, the bank must acknowledge the subscriber again to provide an additional layer of security.

Finally, the ATM service used by the customer is secured with an PIN, OTP-based password provided by the bank at the time of the procedure. This ensures that even if there is a threat of any fraudulent transaction, the subscriber's money inside ATM can't be transferred without completing the authentication process at the Subscriber's end.

The insights gained from this review paper can help improve the security of ATM transaction and enhances the overall safety measures that are being integrated with ATM Networks. The paper emphasizes the importance of implementing advanced security technologies and complying with regulatory requirements to ensure the safety and security of ATM transaction. The paper concludes by summarizing key recommendations for financial institutions to enhance the security of their ATM networks.

2 Related Work

In paper [1], Author Subhrajit Roy gives a review on the current security system in ATMs. The Author wants to describe the need of facial recognition authentication method to secure the ATM transactions. According to his review studies have proven that this method is appropriate method to provide the user securely transaction environment to make user free from threats.

In paper [2], Authors Bharati et al. proposed an advanced technique for upgrading the safety and security of ATM systems using the latest technologies like Embedded systems, Radio Frequency Identification Cards, Infrared sensors, GPS, GSM, Biometric modules, and PICs. The suggested techniques provide strengthen security features such as automatic sliding doors, op-to coupler sensors, and a switch to alert the bank authorities in case any mishappening like threats or tempering on ATM took place.

In paper [3], Authors Navin Kumar et al. discuss the weak points and imperfections of the current ATM security system and propose a system that can use fingerprint authentication and facial observation, also to replace ATM PINs for the One Time Passwords (OTPs) forwarded through IOT devices to the customer phone number, this system is proposed to get rid of ATM fraudulence. In addition, a method is defined as if there is such activity of fraudulence acting in the ATM a fainting gas is released in the chamber to catch the culprit red-handed. The use of RFID cards with biometric techniques for user identification and the use of vibration sensors to detect any damage or movement to the ATM for suspecting any suspicious activity.

In paper [4], Authors Anjalin Joy et al. proposes a system using Raspberry pi and neural networks for increasing the security of ATMs. In this the picture of the ATM user is clicked through the camera installed in the ATM and matched with the image already stored in the database of the bank if the image is matched the person is authorized for further process otherwise, the ATM card is blocked and a message is conveyed to the authorized user. According to the author, the proposed system is cost-efficient and adds an additional layer of ATM security to reduce the options of theft.

In paper [5], Authors Dilanka Perera et al. discussed the vulnerability of ATM PIN security because of the ad-hoc installation of CCTV cameras for surveillance in the ATM cubicles. In this paper, the author illustrates that movement of fingers is enough to predict the PIN entered by the user with complete accuracy. The culprit used a computer-based approach to break down the PIN from the video footage. According to the author, they can guess the pin with almost 50 to 55% accuracy.

In paper [6], Authors Indranil Banerjee et al. proposed a system that consists of biometric authentication techniques to prevent skimming activities. The author proposed a system of two-way security checks such as the first as the iris scanner security check and the second as a fingerprint check which is embedded in the RFID ATM card. If the fingerprint match with the person's fingerprint saved in the database, access is given to the user and if the biometric is not matched than a message is sent to the user's mobile number and the card is blocked. The proposed system is economical which makes it suitable to execute.

In paper [7] Authors K. Bavithra Devi et al. aims to discuss existing research on the automated surveillance system for determining abnormal activities at ATM cubicles. The system proposes a real-time intelligent video analytics system that utilizes deep learning techniques and CNN architecture like ALEXNET with more than 14 layers to detect if a person is wearing a helmet inside the ATM cubicle. The proposed method has been examined on a database of 1800 images of which 72 % is used for training and 28% for testing. The Author also highlights some studies that use techniques like HOG detection, and state-model-based mask detection to detect louder sounds and breaking of ATMs with heavy metal, also if such activity will found, the ATM machine will not dispense the money. The author wants to describe that the proposed technique is very useful to decrease ATM anomalous activities.

In paper [8], Authors Avinash Deshpande et al. proposes an automatic surveillance system to decrease the counts of theft at ATMs. The Author writes that the ATMs have to be advanced as if there is any inactivity caused by ATM the ATM is locked from releasing money and chloroform gas is blown on the thief to catch him red handed also the emergency message is sent to the nearby charged security like the nearby police station and to the bank staff.

In paper [9], Suraj Joshi et al. propose the need for an improved system for the security of ATMs, in the current system, there are many weaknesses like static PINs. The Author proposed the use of User Define PINs and biometric authentication for increasing security, this system used the user's mobile number to generate the PIN for every transaction and vanishes after that, also a standalone system for more security is proposed in this paper.

In paper [10], Gitanjali Mehta gave a literature survey to propose an improved security protocol using biometric authentication as we know ATMs provide us with money without the help of any bank worker. So, it is necessary to increase security using this method to prevent unauthorized allowance to the ATM.

In paper [11], Aravindharaj P, et al. proposed a technique to increase the security of ATM transactions using both biometric and RFID like technologies. This system consists of a two-phase process while doing transactions, where the authorized user swipes the card and matches his/her biometrics then only he/she is allowed to do transactions. If any other user tries to do the transaction with the card his/her image is captured and sent to the authorized person's email id and the transaction proceeds only if the official person gives identification of the person using the card. The author said that the current system has many limitations discussed and highlighted in the paper. The proposed method uses IOT, RFID s, and other technologies to improve security.

In paper [12], PNB Swamy et al. focuses on the design and execution of a security-based theft prevention system for ATMs. The paper provides an understanding of the need for improvement in security systems to prevent theft, unauthorized transactions. The author's idea is to pass through the registration process at the entry to the ATM cabin. Also, the security features are upgraded by the use of buzzers, GPS, notification, Wifi, door locking system, Vibration detection using sensors and fire alarms. The proposed system used IOT and connected using Arduino.

In paper [13], Kavita Hooda provides a view on the need for fingerprint authentication in ATMs. The review paper highlights the need for PINs and Passwords for secure transactions, also the risk combined with them like usability, memorability etc. To decrease these risks the review suggested a way to do secure transactions using biometrics like fingerprint authentication and face recognition from different angles as this is a more secure approach. The Author said the ATM systems need further research on developing and implementing new security features which are shared.

In paper [14], B. Saranraj, R. Suvetha, et al. proposes a model for the security of ATM machines using biometric authentication and RFID technology. The Author said that the previous method of PIN number protection for the cardholder is a very vulnerable process for theft. The proposed system defines for implementation of a new method of OTP (One Time Password) sent to the authorized person account holder's device using email or mobile number. The system used technologies and components of IOT like Arduino Nano, GSM, Biometric, Keypad and Smart card reader. These systems increase the security of the authorized person.

In paper [15], Jamuna Rani S et al. in this paper provides an overview of different techniques used for the security of ATM system. This paper highlights the difficulties faced by persons in ATMs like ATM robberies. The Author mentioned many approaches like Smart ATM monitoring system, OTP (One-time Password), Anti-theft measures, Shutter locking, embedded web servers, RFID cards etc. Furthermore, this survey defines an intelligent system for monitoring persons to count how many persons are inside the ATM.

In [16] Samir Chhabi et al. proposed secure and cost effective scheme Near Field Communication (NFC), which works at 13.56 MHz, for secure ATM transactions. NFC along with Dual Array Pin-Protocol (DAP), where user visits the ATM machine along with his/her NFC enabled Smartphone. In the presence of a smartphone, Bank server sends a secret PIN to the user's mobile and a two horizontal array of random numbers appear on ATM's screen. User needs to enter that secret PIN on the ATM screen making a combination of digits out of those dynamic arrays, appearing on the screen. The Proposed method is prone to attacks like eavesdropping and camera record, as well as it is increasing the transaction time and authentication time as well.

Abhijit S. et al. [17] primarily focused on physical assault on ATM and proposed an IoT based solution for the same. ATM machine is equipped with vibration and IR sensors to acknowledge any unwanted activity. A microcontroller unit, Node MCU will be activated and sends a signal through Wi-Fi module ESP 8266 to the bank server, locks the ATM door and sprays a non toxic gas

() inside the ATM cabin to make suspected visitors uncomfortable. The locked door of an ATM can only be opened using RFID tags which are provided to Bank personnel, issued by bank authorities. System Is also equipped with a siren, which turns ON in case of any theft or robbery inside the ATM.

Jose Ferdinand et al. in [18] Proposed an AI based face recognition model to authenticate user's identity. The author used facenet [19] with HaaR features to recognise the face of the subscriber. The author suggested the model as a replacement of conventional authentication (PIN) model. This model uses subscribers' face as input to authenticate its identity instead of PIN or OTP. If the Users face matches with the database at Bank server, transaction is allowed else ATM Card is blocked. The proposed model provides security against smudge, brute force types of attack but its reliability seems ambiguous in case of spyware attacks and card skimming.

Card Skimming is a physical attack on the device that holds a lot of information about users, In [20] Kyle Guers et al. enlightened readers how Black hat hackers compromise the security of an ATM at a terminal and snake into the data stored in magnetic strips of credit or debit cards of subscribers. She advocated the need for alternatives of magnetic strips and awareness of scheming among users.

Maddela Subha Sri et al. in [21] proposed the concept of smart ATM with biometric i.e. fingerprint and RFID authentication method to get access. The author proposed a 3 step identification process to authenticate a user for a transaction. Card validity through RFID and PIN and then fingerprint check is employed in the process. If any of the validity check condition fails, camera installed at ATM takes a snap of user (Suspicious) and emails it to valid card holder i.e. subscriber with buzzer at the ATM. After all validity checks the user receives an OTP, which when given to the ATM, transaction is allowed to the valid user. Proposed model provides security against smudge, brute force, shoulder surfing etc. but is not a satisfying method against spyware attack, card skimming etc.

Sajid Ali Khan et al. in [22] presented a method for secure ATM transactions through ATM which is based on facial expression of the subscriber. An ATM card user is first verified by face recognition then transaction is allowed to him only if he follows the sequence of facial expressions provided by secret password, consisting of expression sequence. Model uses seven expressions: angry, happy, sad, fear, disgust, neutral and surprise. For facial Recognition author proposed the Discrete wavelet Transform (DWT) method. To detect the correct sequence of facial expressions provided by the user, the author has used the Support Vector Machine (SVM) classification method to categorised images into 7 classes.

B. Veena et al. in [23] Has proposed a solution based on image processing and cloud computing. She primarily dedicates her model to identify authentic users in case of wearing Mask and helmets. For face recognition, the author has used a Convolutional Neural Network (CNN) algorithm of deep learning. For real time images, an open CV source library and YOLO algorithm has been implemented. For storage of data IceDrive cloud has been used. The proposed method avoids the risk of man-in-the-middle attack and identifies the authentic user even if it wears a mask or helmet.

In [24] Bachu Sricharan et al. Advocated the need of a single card for all bank accounts with his solution. The proposed method incorporates two factor authentication; fingerprint and OTP through fingerprint sensor and GSM module respectively. The prototype model consists of rich hardware including RFID tags, microcontroller, display device etc. The proposed solution is effective against spoofing, shoulder surfing etc. but doesn't provide any solution for attacks like Brute Force, Smudge and Spyware.

Dr. J. Shanmugapriyan et al. in [25] proposed the AADHAAR based all-in-one solution for ATM transactions, shopping etc. Proposed System eliminates the need for an ATM card at an ATM or Shopping Complex. In the proposed model ATM is equipped with a QR scanner which scans the QR code available on an Aadhaar card, after identifying the user, the ATM asks the user for authentication through fingerprint sensor. When the user is authenticated, a bank account associated with an Aadhaar card will allow the user to withdraw money from an ATM. Similar process can be followed at PoS device while shopping. The proposed model seems to be effective and accurate but Aadhaar Card is so much used all around that there is a high probability of a smudge attack.

Rashmi Pote et al. in [26] presented a mobile application based ATM transaction model for secure transaction namely Smart Mobile Banking Application (SMBA). User can initiate the transaction at its place through a mobile application, which when authenticated by a bank server, user may visit the nearest ATM and can complete the transaction followed by PIN authentication process, in a limited interval of time. In the proposed model, the author has eliminated the need for an ATM card, rather the user will scan the QR code displayed on the ATM screen and after filling personal details manually transaction can be accomplished followed by PIN authentication.

3 Proposed Model

Based on the research work collected in this article, We further propose a model that can assure a secure transaction to a customer by increasing a sub-layer of authentication with elimination of ATM card. Customer do not need to remember to carry its ATM card as it becomes redundant after implementation of our proposed model. User's Face along with its Mobile Number linked with Unique Identification Number (UID) - AADHAR becomes the way to authenticate a user who want to initiate a transaction using ATM. AADHAR is issued to every Indian citizen having the bio metric credentials of that citizen. For face recognition we have used RatinaFace Algorithm based on single Deep Neural Network in Deep Learning. Proposed algorithm is capable of recognition of face at different scales and orientation using face landmarks like - eyes, nose and lips. Following the face recognition process, when user gets identified by Bank Server through ATM, ATM sends two OTPs to User's numbers: one number is attached with bank account while other to the number linked with the AADHAR - UID Number. After user enters both the OTPs Two way authentication (2WA) process is

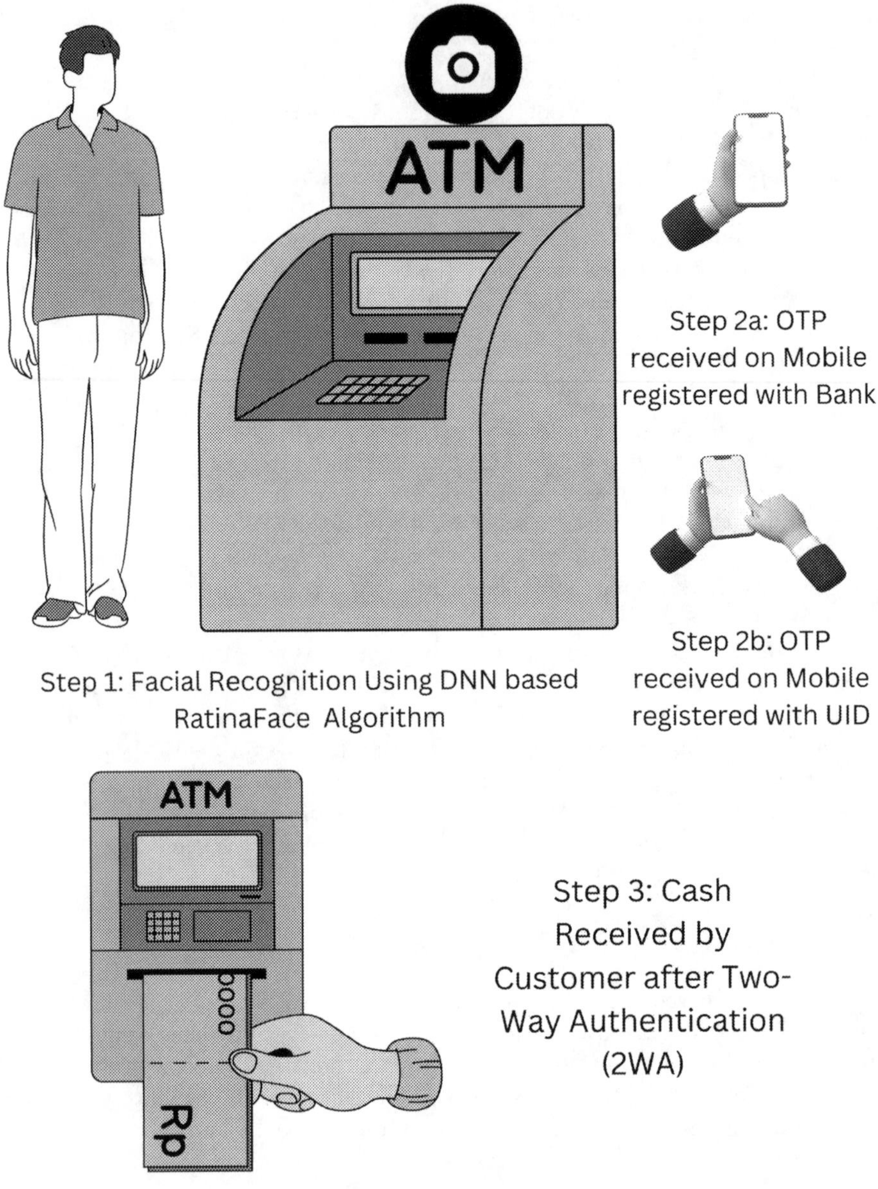

Fig. 1. Proposed Model.

completed and User can get the cash from ATM machine. Along with the transaction security, ATM is also equipped with PANIC button that enables user to inform the bank about emergency, providing it an another level of security for secure transactions.

Table 1. Comparision of Work

Comparison Constraints	[2]	[4]	[18]	[24]	[26]	[Article]
Facial Recognition or IRIS	YES	YES	YES	NO	NO	YES
Smart Sensors for ATM Security	YES	NO	NO	NO	NO	YES
Layers of Security	1	2	2	2	2	2.5
Fingerprints	NO	NO	NO	YES	NO	NO
PIN or OTP	PIN	PIN	OTP	OTP	OTP and QR	OTP
Technology	GPS/GSM	Neural Networks	AI, ML	GSM	Net Banking	GSM, DL, DNN
ATM Card Eliminated	NO	NO	NO	YES	App Based, YES	YES

4 Conclusion and Future Work

In conclusion, this research paper highlights the importance of ensuring the safety and security of ATM transaction, as it directly impacts the financial security and faith of customers in Banking services. The paper proposes a new approach to address this issue by reviewing existing literature on security arrangements, methods and protocols for ATM transaction and identifying limitations and challenges of current security measures. The paper recommends implementing advanced security technologies such as biometric identification [26], modified encryption standards, and live monitoring, and complying with regulatory requirements to enhance the security of ATM networks. For further enhancement in ATM transaction and ATM networks, Blockchain based Federated learning models can be implemented [27,28]. The insights gained from this research paper can be helpful for financial institutions to improve the security systems in ATMs and upgrade the safety measures of overall ATM transactions.

References

1. Roy, S.: Smart atm security system using fpr, gsm, gps, vol. 10, pp. 1700–1703 (2022)
2. Nelligani, B.M., Reddy, N.U., Awasti, N.: Smart atm security system using fpr, gsm, gps. In: 2016 International Conference on Inventive Computation Technologies (ICICT), vol. 3, pp. 1–5, IEEE (2016)
3. Kumar, M.N., Raghul, S., Prasad, K.N., Kumar, P.N.: Biometrically secured atm vigilance system. In: 2021 7th International Conference on Advanced Computing and Communication Systems (ICACCS), vol. 1, pp. 919–922. IEEE (2021)
4. Joy, A., Babu, C., Chandy, D.A.: Enhanced security mechanism for atm machines. In: 2021 7th International Conference on Advanced Computing and Communication Systems (ICACCS), vol. 1, pp. 302–306. IEEE (2021)
5. Seneviratne, P., et al.: Impact of video surveillance systems on atm pin security. In: 2020 20th International Conference on Advances in ICT for Emerging Regions (ICTer), pp. 59–64. IEEE (2020)
6. Banerjee, I., Mookherjee, S., Saha, S., Ganguli, S., Kundu, S., Chakravarti, D.: Advanced atm system using iris scanner. In: 2019 International Conference on Opto-Electronics and Applied Optics (Optronix), pp. 1–3. IEEE (2019)

7. Devi, K.B., Roomi, S.M.M., Meena, M., Meghana, S.: Deep learn helmets-enhancing security at atms. In: 2019 5th International Conference on Advanced Computing & Communication Systems (ICACCS), pp. 1111–1116. IEEE (2019)
8. Deshpande, A., Patil, B.K., Dodamani, S.N., Magadum, R.B.: Development of advanced atm surveillance and security system. In: 2018 International Conference on Recent Innovations in Electrical, Electronics & Communication Engineering (ICRIEECE), pp. 644–649. IEEE (2018)
9. Swathi, H., Joshi, S., Kumar, M.K.: A novel atm security system using a user defined personal identification number with the aid of gsm technology. In: 2018 Second International Conference on Advances in Electronics, Computers and Communications (ICAECC), pp. 1–5. IEEE (2018)
10. Mehta, G.: A review paper on atm security. In: International Journal of Emerging Technologies and Innovative Research (IJETIR), pp. 41–44, IJETIR (2018)
11. Annie Isabella, L., Aravindharaj, P., Barath, E., Barath, W., Sriganesh, K., Xavierf, A.: Smart atm security system. In: Turkish Online Journal of Qualitative Inquiry (TOJQI), TOJQI (2021)
12. Swamy, P.N.B., Sathi Babu, A., Sravanthi, S.: Smart atm security using iot. In: IOSR Journal of Electrical and Electronics Engineering (IOSR-JEEE), pp. 34–42. JEEE (2020)
13. Hooda, K.: Atm security. In: International Journal of Scientific and Research publications, pp. 159–166, Semantic Scholar (2016)
14. Saranraj, B., Dharshini, N.S.P., Suvetha, R., Bharathi, K.U.: Atm security system using arduino. In: 2020 6th International Conference on Advanced Computing and Communication Systems (ICACCS), pp. 940–944, IEEE (2020)
15. Jacintha, V., Rani, S.J., Beula, J.G., Johnsly, J.J.: An extensive resolution of atm security systems. In: 2017 Third International Conference on Science Technology Engineering & Management (ICONSTEM), pp. 934–938. IEEE (2017)
16. Chabbi, S., El Madhoun, N.: A new security solution enhancing the dynamic array pin protocol. In: 2022 International Wireless Communications and Mobile Computing (IWCMC), pp. 991–996. IEEE (2022)
17. Abhijith, S., Sreehari, K., Chalil, A.: An iot based system for securing atm machine. In: 2022 8th International Conference on Advanced Computing and Communication Systems (ICACCS), vol. 1, pp. 1764–1768. IEEE (2022)
18. Ferdinand, J., Wijaya, C., Ronal, A.N., Edbert, I.S., Suhartono, D.: Atm security system modeling using face recognition with facenet and haar cascade. In: 2022 6th International Conference on Informatics and Computational Sciences (ICICoS), pp. 111–116. IEEE (2022)
19. Consul, P., Budhiraja, I., Chaudhary, R., Kumar, N.: Security Reassessing in UAV-assisted cyber-physical systems based on federated learning. In: MILCOM 2022–2022 IEEE Military Communications Conference (MILCOM), pp. 61–65 (2022)
20. Guers, K., Chowdhury, M.M., Rifat, N.: Card skimming: a cybercrime by hackers. In: 2022 IEEE International Conference on Electro Information Technology (eIT), pp. 575–579, IEEE (2022)
21. Sri, M.S., Chaithanya, J.K., Dhruthiee, N.: Design and implementation of smart atm under idle application. In: 2022 7th International Conference on Communication and Electronics Systems (ICCES), pp. 1410–1417. IEEE (2022)
22. Khan, S.A., Abbasi, A.A.: Expression-based security framework for atm network. In: 2022 International Conference on Digital Transformation and Intelligence (ICDI), pp. 258–261. IEEE (2022)

23. Veena, B., Babu, S.: Face mask and helmet facial detection for atm security using image processing in cloud computing. In: 2022 International Conference on Data Science, Agents & Artificial Intelligence (ICDSAAI), vol. 1, pp. 1–6, IEEE (2022)
24. Sricharan, B., Sanjana, J.U., Vani, T.V., Sujatha, C.: Rfid based atm security system using iot. In: 2022 International Conference on Intelligent Controller and Computing for Smart Power (ICICCSP), pp. 1–6, IEEE (2022)
25. Shanmugapriyan, J., Parthasarathy, R., Sathish, S., Prasanth, S.: Secure electronic transaction using aadhaar based qr code and biometric authentication. In: 2022 International Conference on Communication, Computing and Internet of Things (IC3IoT), pp. 1–4. IEEE (2022)
26. Pote, R., Kulkarni, S.: Securing cash withdrawal from atm with the help of smart mobile banking application. In: 2022 Interdisciplinary Research in Technology and Management (IRTM), pp. 1–4, IEEE (2022)
27. Singh, S.K., Park, J.H.: Talwar: blockchain-based trust management scheme for smart enterprises with augmented intelligence. IEEE Trans. Industr. Inf. **19**(1), 626–634 (2023)
28. Singh, S.K., Park, L., Park, J.H.: Blockchain-based federated approach for privacy-preserved iot-enabled smart vehicular networks. In: 2022 13th International Conference on Information and Communication Technology Convergence (ICTC), pp. 1995–1999 (2022)

A Comprehensive Analysis of Blockchain Network Security: Attacks and Their Countermeasures

Gurpreet Kour Sodhi[1], Mekhla Sharma[1], and Rajan Miglani[2(✉)]

[1] Model Institute of Engineering and Technology, Jammu, J&K, India
[2] Lovely Professional University, Phagwara, India
rajanmiglai1028@gmail.com

Abstract. Blockchain is a shared database that makes use of a shared ledger distributed amongst the different nodes present in a network. It provides the foundation for storing the data in such a way that it can neither be deleted nor altered. Blockchain has been widely used in various application areas ranging from banking sectors to finance, health care to supply chains and many more, thus providing better accuracy, transparency, and cost reduction. Despite exhibiting features like decentralization, trust, and immutability, blockchain is susceptible to many security attacks. This paper focuses on the concept of blockchain, providing insights regarding its features and application areas. Most importantly this paper covers the analysis of various security attacks to which blockchain is prone and hence many sectors are reluctant to use this technology. Some future directions and key takeaways are covered in the conclusion section that will form the basis for future work.

Keywords: Blockchain Attacks · Blockchain Security · Blockchain Technology · Hash · Privacy · Threats

1 Introduction

Blockchain is defined as a distributed ledger recording method which is used to compile and store data that is rapidly and continuously produced [1]. This data is stored in the most efficient and authentic way retaining authenticity and preserving integrity [2]. The data to be recorded is mainly the transactions which demand a secure and transparent compilation known as Digital Ledger [3]. Each entry in a digital ledger is authenticated by a digital signature and hence is highly secure [4] (Fig. 1).

The data present in the ledger though available to everyone in the network cannot be altered due to it being protected using a hash algorithm [5]. Hashing is a process which takes data of any size and applies a set of mathematical operations to it and generates a unique output of a specific length [6]. Therefore, regardless of the size or length of the input data, the hash output obtained will be of the same length [7]. The output known as Hash Digest, though represents the initial input data but does not make it known or available to access [8]. Being virtually irreversible, hashing is a one-way cryptographic function [9] (Fig. 2).

KC Santosh et al. (Eds.): RTIP2R 2023, CCIS 2027, pp. 276–291, 2024.
https://doi.org/10.1007/978-3-031-53085-2_23

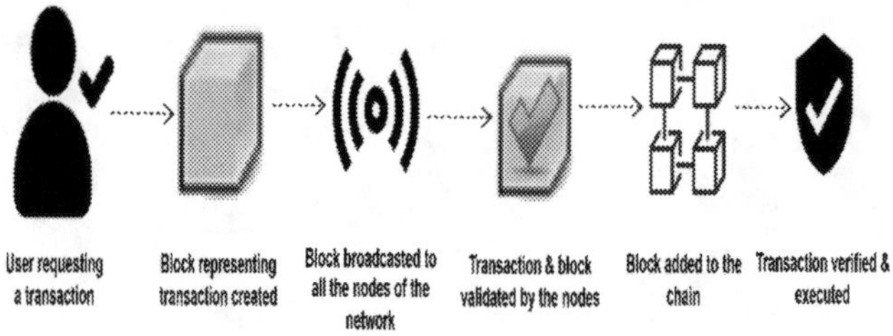

Fig. 1. Blockchain Implementation

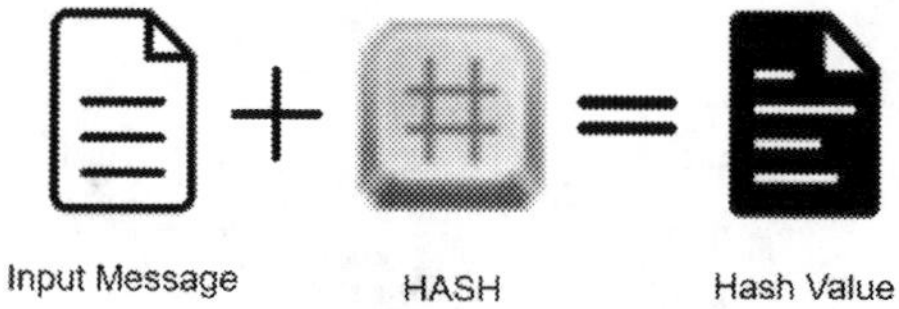

Fig. 2. Hashing Algorithm

There are two main components of a Blockchain, a network of computers and a distributed ledger [10]. The network is represented by nodes, each having its own copy of the ledger, which is updated regularly. Any transaction which happens within that network is updated in the ledger, thus making the whole process transparent [11]. The block chain implementation initially has two major requirements:

1. Preventing the alteration of the entries in the ledger by any of the nodes present in the network.
2. Preserving the authenticity of the entries in the ledger.

Thus, the integrity and authenticity of the ledger is appropriately addressed by the usage of public-private key pair features used by blockchain [12]. Considering the first requirement, every transaction taking place in the blockchain is updated in the ledger after being encrypted using the confidential and unique private key. This process creates a digital signature for the particular transaction [13]. In case any node intends to alter the transaction's data, the amount or recipient's name, it is required to modify the digital signature. This means it is practically impossible to modify a transaction data without tampering with its digital signature, which would result in a null transaction [14].

The second requirement is addressed by the condition that every node has its own public key for every other node [15]. As soon as a node receives a new ledger update from any other neighbor node, it verifies the information using the public key of the initiating node [16]. The verification is successful only if the ledger has not been tampered with. After the verification, the verifying node updates its copy of the ledger. Thus, in this way, a transaction propagates through the blockchain network and becomes part of the ledger record in the network [17] (Fig. 3).

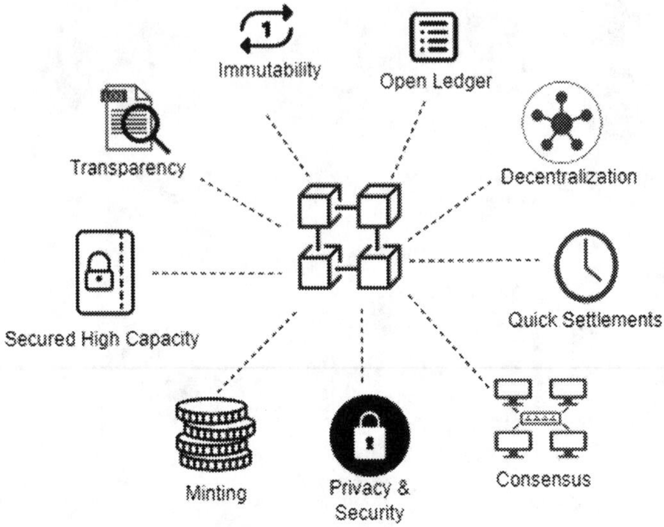

Fig. 3. Blockchain Features

1.1 Characteristics of Blockchain

1) Immutability: One of the major features of Blockchain is the data stored is immutable. Storing data in a form which is immutable strengthens the already existing features of the Blockchain technology. The block chain database is a continuously updating ledger which requires a high level of data integrity, that is provided with the help of a hash algorithm [18].
2) Open Ledger: Another interesting feature of Blockchain is the existence of an open ledger which is continuously updated and is readily available to the users of the network in view mode, although they cannot alter any entry in it. The technology keeps track of all the transactions taking place on that network. This provides every user with the ease to access, view and verify any data and retain an authentic record for the same. Moreover, any suspicious activity can be easily detected in the blockchain network due to regular validation of the entries in the ledger. The whole updation process is transparent and tamperproof [19].
3) Decentralization: Another feature of the Blockchain technology is its decentralized platform. A single network consists of all the information, this makes managing the data very convenient. There is no single authority having control of the whole network thus enabling decentralization. Decentralization makes Blockchain suitable for handling digital money and other similar applications [20].
4) Transparency: Another significant element of the blockchain is transparency. Transparency of data and transactions is ensured by maintaining an authentic ledger which records the actions of all the nodes present in the network. This transparent and open access record makes the system reliable and user friendly, which further mitigates any chance of risks [21].

5) Secured High Capacity: Blockchain offers a system which comprises multiple computers working in alliance; this increases the overall capacity of the entire system. Blockchain involves a wide range of computers working linearly under strong encrypted techniques securing every transaction [1].
6) Minting: The process of authenticating data and recording new blocks of data onto the blockchain technology through a secure channel is referred to as minting. The most effective method to mint currency is mining. A miner encrypts the information and generates a block of data consisting of the number of recent transactions. This serves as evidence that the individual is engaged in a significant amount of computational work [2].
7) Quick Settlement: The traditional banking system consumes time in processing issues related to transactions. Blockchain technology enables the users to receive immediate settlement of transactional issues. The transactions are hence efficient and fast. Moreover, blockchain enables quick record maintenance and information updates [3].
8) Smart Contracts: Smart contracts are a set of principles which are stored in the block chain which helps in avoiding the delays during the process of transactions. These smart contracts can be executed on the chain and aid in defining the conditions for corporate bond transfers. This enables the businessmen to automatically authenticate the signatures and enforce agreements. Further enabling the settlement of the transactions at a faster pace besides being convenient to the customers [22].
9) Consensus: The actions in a blockchain can be verified and approved using the consensus algorithm. There are various consensus algorithms available for different blockchains. Consensus ensures an easy and efficient decision-making process for the nodes in the network. Consensus is a fault-tolerant mechanism which ensures that every node present in the network agrees to a single state of the network. All the nodes present in a particular blockchain network trust the algorithms being followed by the core of the systems. Hence, safeguarding every decision-making process [4]
10) Privacy and Security: The most vital aspect of blockchain technology is Privacy. The blockchain network enables the users to keep their data in control while ensuring a secure data storage option. The protection of personal data is a very crucial demand of blockchain technology. The decentralized network makes it easier for the participants of the blockchain network to exchange their personal data. Further, it is difficult to manipulate blockchain technology. The data entered in a block on a blockchain is immediately chained with other blocks present in the network thus making it impossible to amend the data once entered in the blockchain [23].

1.2 Applications of Blockchain

Blockchain Technology, due to its vivid features, is an essential part in digital information systems. The unique and effective properties of blockchain enable it to be applicable in various industries and sectors [24] (Fig. 4).

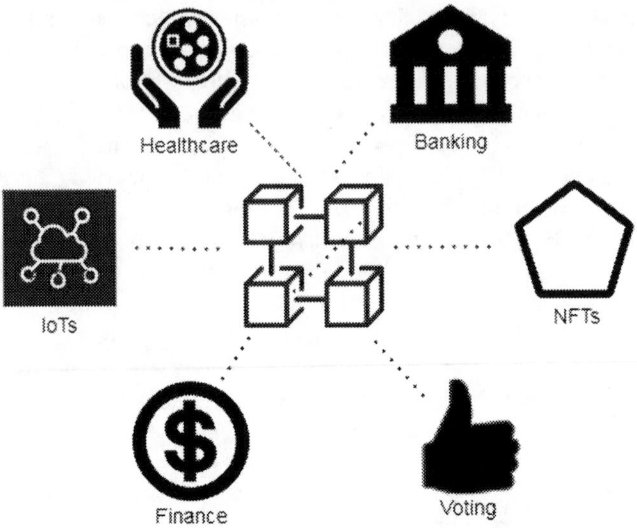

Fig. 4. Blockchain Applications

Some of the areas where blockchain technology is being extensively used are:

Health Sector
The open ledger feature of block chain enables it to be used for maintaining secure data records. This recorded data can be the patient's health history or the current diagnosis record maintenance. The adoption of blockchain technology in the health sector can make the health care services more accessible with a considerable reduction of cost ensuring efficient record maintenance [25].

Banking Sector
Blockchain technology possesses competent features like privacy and security, these enable it to be used for secure transactions and storing sensitive data. The application of blockchain in the banking sector is effective, efficient and enables immediate completion of transactions. Blockchain being a decentralized network, provides the users with a reliable industry and enhances the capacity of the entire network. Blockchain security features strengthen the privacy of digital transactions and mitigate the possibility of errors [26].

Supply Chain Management
Supply chain management is the immediate necessity of most industries. Blockchain technology allows the organizations to operate directly without any intervention from third parties. Blockchain possesses the potency to reform supply chain management. It can aid in overcoming the challenges present in supply chain management by forming a temper-proof and transparent history of the data, inventory, and financial flows in the transactions [27].

Financial Sector
Any area involving the initiation, processing or completion of money transactions can ideally utilize blockchain technology ensuring faster and efficient transfer. Apart from this, blockchain deals with cryptocurrency, which ensures better control over the transactions.

Insurance
The insurance sector demands efficient record maintenance. The smart contract feature of block chain can ensure better tracking of the claims received from the customers, prevent duplicate claims by the customers and hence be effective in monitoring the insurance process for both ends.

Real estate
Real estate involves several documents to be verified for transferring ownership and recording financial information. Blockchain can speed up the transactions, reduce the paperwork and save the overall cost [28].

Voting
Voting using Blockchain technology can ensure that only eligible users can vote, preventing diplomacy and tampering of Electoral Polls. Apart from these, blockchain can facilitate the users to vote using their mobile phones, reducing the election execution cost substantially [29].

NFTs
NFTs have many applications and they are a mode to transfer ownership of anything that can be represented in the form of data. The blockchain technology prevents the data from co-existing in two different places. Associating blockchain with NFT assures that existence of only a single copy of a piece of digital art. This further mitigates the drawbacks of storage and maintenance [30].

Secure IoTs
Although, the Internet of Things (IoT) is making our lives easier, it is also prone to attacks from intruders. The decentralized network feature of Blockchain technology can be utilized to provide enhanced security by storing passwords and other relevant data on it instead of a centralized server. It also offers prevention from data tampering since a blockchain is practically immutable [31].

2 Blockchain Security

Blockchain technology exhibits inherent security features including cryptography, decentralization, and consensus that build-up trust amongst the different participants that join the distributed network [32, 33]. However, it suffers from critical security aspects depending upon the kind of blockchain network used which is mainly public, private, permissioned or permission less. In public blockchain networks, anyone can join the network and Bitcoin is the most well-known example of the same. In private blockchain, only selected members join the network whose identity is confirmed and are therefore given access privileges. Hence, when using blockchain for building any application, it is important to assess which type of blockchain network is best suited for meeting the desired goals [34]. So, we can say that private and permissioned networks can be tightly controlled as compared to the public and permission less networks that achieve greater distribution.

Blockchain technology is well known for immutability and creating tamper-proof ledger of transactions but still it is not resistant to cyber threats and attacks. Malicious users can still manipulate the blockchain infrastructure vulnerabilities leading to serious cyber hacks and frauds [35].

Hence, when using blockchain technology for building any application, the following questions need to be addressed which are as follows:

- What is the control or administration model used for participants joining the blockchain network?
- What kind of data is used to create blocks in blockchain?
- How can security risks be mitigated and what is the disaster recovery plan?
- What are the regulatory and monitoring requirements and how are they achieved?
- What is the minimal security model used for blockchain participants?

2.1 Blockchain Attacks

The growing popularity of blockchain has brought into light many security and privacy concerns and hence demands building a blockchain security/threat/risk model that can address and mitigate various risks [36]. The main types of blockchain security threats or attacks include network attacks, transaction verification mechanism attacks, wallet attacks, mining attacks, smart contract attacks [37].

Transaction verification mechanism attack is one in which the attackers produce multiple copies of the same transaction creating fake crypto currencies of the same value. The same amount is spent by both the network user and the attacker.

Network attacks mainly focus on the attacks that happen at the blockchain network layer. The blockchain uses a P2P network and hence consists of two main types of nodes: one that are called users that create transactions and submit it to the network and the other called miners that generate blocks in the blockchain.

Wallet attacks are the most critical categories of blockchain attacks and hence wallet security is important for users since it can result in users losing control of their assets. Blockchain wallets are crypto currency-based wallets that help users to exchange and manage funds. Still blockchain wallets are not preferred over traditional bank accounts due to low acceptance, price fluctuations, limited network, and complicated funds.

Mining pool attacks are created by a group of miners who work together, pool their resources, and contribute to the generation of a block, and then share the block reward according to the added processing power. Various attackers can lead to both internal and external attacks on a mining pool. Dishonest miners can cause internal attacks within the pool to collect more share in the collective reward or can even affect the functionality of any honest miner in the pool. In external attacks on pools, dishonest miners in the pool could use their higher hash power and perform some attacks like double spending attack or Distributed Denial of Service (DDoS) attack (Fig. 5).

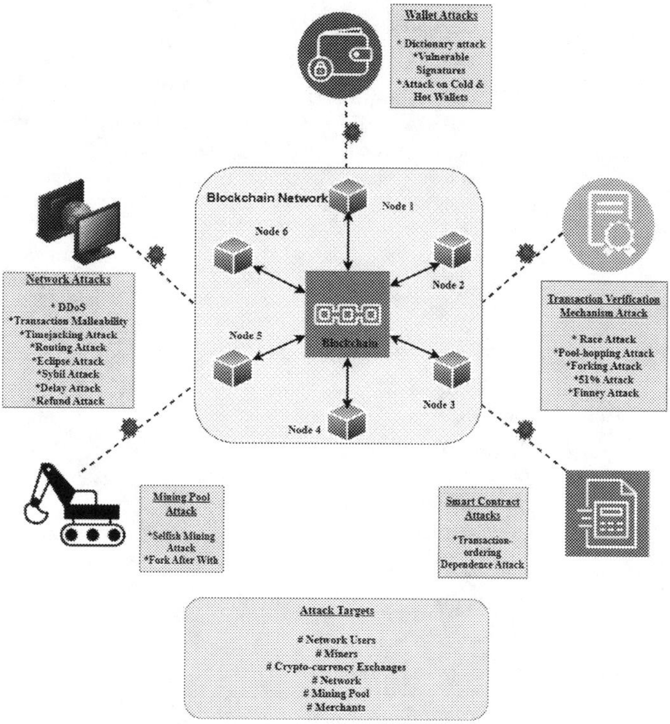

Fig. 5. Blockchain Security Threats/Attacks

3 Summary of Blockchain Attacks

Table 1 summarizes the main blockchain security threats/attacks and their possible countermeasures.

Table 1. Analysis of Blockchain Security Threats

Attack Type	Attack Name	Cause	Targets	Consequences	Counter Measures
Network Attacks	Distributed Denial of Service (DDoS) [38]	Attack denies services between the nodes connected over network by disrupting the normal traffic & inserting malicious traffic	*Network *Users *Miners	*Transaction flooding	*Users should have sufficient processing power & storage *Filtering transactions *Anti-DDoS services like CloudFlare, Incapsula, or Cloud Services IP-based prevention

(*continued*)

Table 1. (*continued*)

Attack Type	Attack Name	Cause	Targets	Consequences	Counter Measures
	Transaction Malleability [39]	Adversaries' tricks targets causing reinitiating of the request by changing the transaction hash ID before its confirmation on the bitcoin network	*Crypto-currency exchanges	*Transaction modification	*Improvement Proposal 62 (BIP 62) involves multiple transaction verification metrics for validation of a new transaction
	Timejacking Attack [40]	Hackers alter the network time counter of the node and force the node to accept an alternative blockchain	*Miners	*Creation of multiple fake peers	*Using trusted peers *Using peer node's system time
	Routing Attack [41]	Attackers divide a network into two (or more) distinct components creating parallel blockchains	*Miners *Users *Exchanges *Network	*Loss of computational power *Double-spending	*BGP anomalous detection *Defensive filtering *Path validation
	Eclipse Attack [42]	Attackers control a huge number of IP addresses and monopolize connections towards single victim nodes	*Miners *Users	*Illegitimate transaction confirmations *Selfish mining	*Restricting peer inbound connections *Selective pairing with other peers

(*continued*)

Table 1. *(continued)*

Attack Type	Attack Name	Cause	Targets	Consequences	Counter Measures
	Sybil Attack [43]	Adversaries subverts reputation system by creating numerous pseudonymous identities & utilizing them to gain huge influence	*Network *Users *Miners	*Weakening reputation system *Creation of multiple fake identities *Double-spending	*Identity validation using several distributed protocols
	Refund Attack [44]	Customers route payments to illicit traders via an honest merchant & deny their own involvement in refund transactions	*Crypto-currency exchanges *Users	*Payment protocol authentication *Refund mechanism	*Generating cryptographic evidence for authorizing transactions
	Delay Attack [45]	Attack slows down the propagation of blocks towards or from a given set of nodes	*Miners *Users *Mining Pools	*Double spending *Loss of computational power	*Increasing diversity in node connections *Monitor RTT (Round Trip Time) and using gateways
Transaction Verification Mechanism Attacks	Race Attack [46]	Creation of two transactions with the same funds at the same time	*Merchant *Users	*Spending the same funds twice	*Acknowledgement or confirmation from the receiver before initiation of request
	Pool-hopping Attack [47]	Miners leave mining pool when it offers fewer financial rewards & join back when mining yields higher rewards	*Miners *Mining Pool	*Depresses down expected profits of both the mining pool & honest miners	*Using pay-per-share (PPS) & pay-per-last-N-share (PPLNS)

(continued)

Table 1. (*continued*)

Attack Type	Attack Name	Cause	Targets	Consequences	Counter Measures
	Forking Attack [48]	Attacker maliciously replaces the most trusted chain on blockchain with an alternative chain to gain advantage	*Merchant *Users *Network	*Leads to huge financial loss	*MTC confirmation mechanism
	51% Attack [49]	Group of miners control more than 50% of the network's mining hash rate & have power to alter blockchain	*Network *Users *Mining Pool	*Double spending of coins	*Ensuring 50% limit on single miners *Using Proof of Stake consensus mechanism
	Finney Attack [50]	Attacker mines a block & sends unconfirmed transactions to other nodes	*Merchant *Users	*Network accepts block as valid while invalidating transaction *Double spending	*Vendors should wait for multiple confirmations before releasing the service
Wallet Attacks	Dictionary Attack [51]	Attack on the authentication system that breaks into password protected computer or network	*Users *Network	*Leakage of important & authentic information	*Delayed response *Account locking
	Vulnerable Signatures [52]	Cryptographic algorithms used to create user signatures may contain vulnerabilities	*Miners *Users *Network	*Transaction modification *Illegitimate transactions	*Using complex cryptographic techniques
	Attack on cold and hot wallets [53]	Both hardware and software wallets are susceptible to attacks	*Users *Miners	*Funds stealing *Cyber thefts *Tampering of private keys *Loss of computational power	*Secure password *Maintain back-up *Using reputable crypto-currency exchange

(*continued*)

Table 1. *(continued)*

Attack Type	Attack Name	Cause	Targets	Consequences	Counter Measures
Mining Pool Attacks	Selfish Mining Attack [54]	Malicious miners attempt to increase their share of reward by not broadcasting mined blocks & resulting in block withholding from public blockchain	*Users *Network	*Hiding of mined blocks *Altering the blockchain *Unfair rewards	*Comparing transaction timestamps *Random assignments of miners *Improving blockchain architecture with code scripts & design parameters
	Fork-After Withholding Attack [55]	Selfish miners hide the winning block or either discard or release it later	*Mining pools *Miners	*Rewarding for attackers *Altering blocks	*No practical approach available

4 Conclusion

This paper provides a detailed insight into blockchain technology including its introduction, working and the practical implementation in various sectors. The impactful combination of popular attributes like hash technique, decentralization and immutability makes the blockchain technology distinct and explains the growing interest of science and industry in it. Although blockchain technology is recognized for its features involving immutability, security, privacy, and transparency, it still needs adequate defense against various attacks. Intruders disrupt the smooth flow of blockchain by attacking the already existing weak features of the technology and hence making it prone to various security threats.

A tabular summary of various attacks has been presented in the paper highlighting their causes, features responsible for their existence, targets/consequences and finally the countermeasures for their necessary prevention. Cryptography, if used in blockchain technology, can be useful to prevent any illegal tampering of the data. Moreover, it is concluded that this technology can have a remarkable positive impact on various sectors provided it is robust against various attacks.

References

1. Xu, M., Chen, X., Kou, G.: A systematic review of blockchain. Financ. Innov. **5**(1), 27 (2019). https://doi.org/10.1186/s40854-019-0147-z
2. Zheng, Z., Xie, S., Dai, H., Chen, X., Wang, H.: An overview of blockchain technology: architecture, consensus, and future trends. In: 2017 IEEE International Congress on Big Data (BigData Congress), pp. 557–564 (2017). https://doi.org/10.1109/bigdatacongress.2017.85.

3. Peck, M.: Blockchains: how they work and why they'll change the world. IEEE Spectr. **54**(10), 26–35 (2017). https://doi.org/10.1109/mspec.2017.8048836
4. Amu, D., Baskaran, S.: A survey of applications using blockchain technology. In: 2022 International Conference on Computer Communication and Informatics (ICCCI), Coimbatore, India, pp. 1–6 (2022). https://doi.org/10.1109/ICCCI54379.2022.9740958
5. Sahu, A., Ghosh, S.M.: Review paper on secure hash algorithm with its variants. Int. J. Tech. Innov. Mod. Eng. Sci. **3**(5) (2017). https://doi.org/10.13140/RG.2.2.13855.05289
6. Sodhi Kour, G., Gaba Singh, G., Kansal, L., Bakkali Mohammad, E., Tubbal, F.: Implementation of message authentication code using DNA-LCG key and a novel hash algorithm. Int. J. Electr. Comput. Eng. **9**(1), 352–358 (2019). https://doi.org/10.11591/ijece.v9i1.352-358
7. Sodhi, G.K., et al.: Preserving authenticity and integrity of distributed networks through novel message authentication code. Indonesian J. Electr. Eng. Comput. Sci. **12**(3), 1297 (2018). https://doi.org/10.11591/ijeecs.v12.i3.pp1297-1304
8. Sobti, R., Geetha, G.: Cryptographic hash functions: a review. Int. J. Comput. Sci. Issues **9**, 461–479 (2012)
9. Zhuoyu, H., Yongzhen, L.: Design and implementation of efficient hash functions. In: 2022 IEEE 2nd International Conference on Power, Electronics and Computer Applications (ICPECA), Shenyang, China, pp. 1240–1243 (2022). https://doi.org/10.1109/ICPECA53709.2022.9719176
10. Monrat, A., Schelén, O., Andersson, K.: A survey of blockchain from the perspectives of applications, challenges, and opportunities. IEEE Access **7**, 117134–117151 (2019). https://doi.org/10.1109/ACCESS.2019.2936094
11. Maidamwar, P., Saraf, P., Chavhan, N.: Blockchain applications, challenges, and opportunities: a survey of a decade of research and future outlook. In: 2021 International Conference on Computational Intelligence and Computing Applications (ICCICA), pp. 107: 841–853 (2021). https://doi.org/10.1109/iccica52458.2021.9697256
12. Li, X., Jiang, P., Chen, T., Luo, X., Wen, Q.: A survey on the security of blockchain systems. Future Gener. Comput. Syst. **107**, 841–853 (2020). https://doi.org/10.1016/j.future.2017.08.020
13. Singh, R., Mishra, R., Gupta, S., Mukherjee, A.: Blockchain applications for secured and resilient supply chains: a systematic literature review and future research agenda. Comput. Ind. Eng. **175**, 108854 (2023). https://doi.org/10.1016/j.cie.2022.108854
14. Cheng, H.K., Hu, D., Puschmann, T., Zhao, L.: The landscape of Blockchain research impacts and opportunities. Inf. Syst. e-Business Manag. **19**, 749–755 (2021). https://doi.org/10.1007/s10257-021-00544-1
15. Xu, M., Chen, X., Kou, G.: A systematic review of blockchain. Financial Innov. **5**(27) (2019). https://doi.org/10.1186/s40854-019-0147-z
16. Goud Allam, T., Mehedi Hasan, M., Maag, A., Prasad, P.: Ledger technology of blockchain and its impact on operational performance of banks: a review. In: 6th International Conference on Innovative Technology in Intelligent System and Industrial Applications (CITISIA), Sydney, Australia, pp. 1–10 (2021). https://doi.org/10.1109/CITISIA53721.2021.9719886
17. Iansiti, M., Lakhani, K.: The truth about blockchain. Harv. Bus. Rev. **95**, 118–127 (2017)
18. Kim, H.S., Wang, K.: Immutability measure for different blockchain structures. In: 2018 IEEE 39th Sarnoff Symposium, Newark, NJ, USA, pp. 1–6 (2018). https://doi.org/10.1109/SARNOF.2018.8720496
19. Kadam, S.: Review of distributed ledgers: the technological advances behind cryptocurrency. In: International Conference Advances in Computer Technology and Management (ICACTM) (2018)
20. Atzori, M.: Blockchain technology and decentralized governance: is the state still necessary? J. Governance Regul. **6** (2017). https://doi.org/10.22495/jgr_v6_i1_p5

21. Sedlmeir, J., Lautenschlager, J., Fridgen, G.: The transparency challenge of blockchain in organizations. Electron Markets **32**, 1779–1794 (2022). https://doi.org/10.1007/s12525-022-00536-0
22. Khan, S., Loukil, F., Ghedira-Guegan, C.: Blockchain smart contracts: applications, challenges, and future trends. Peer-to-Peer Network Appl. **14**, 2901–2925 (2021). https://doi.org/10.1007/s12083-021-01127-0
23. Wang, D., Zhao, J., Wang, Y.: A survey on privacy protection of blockchain: the technology and application. IEEE Access **8**, 108766–108781 (2020). https://doi.org/10.1109/ACCESS.2020.2994294
24. Wubing, C., Zhiying, X., Shi, S., Zhao, Y., Jun, Z.: A survey of blockchain applications in different domains. In: International Conference on Blockchain Technology and Applications (ICBTA), pp. 17–21 (2018). https://doi.org/10.1145/3301403.3301407
25. Unnithan, C., Houghton, A., Alexander, A., Lemieux, A.: Blockchain in global health - an appraisal of current and future applications. Essentials of Blockchain Technology (2019)
26. Guo, Y., Liang, C.: Blockchain application and outlook in the banking industry. Financial Innov. **2**(24) (2016). https://doi.org/10.1186/s40854-016-0034-9
27. Dursun, T., et al.: Blockchain technology for supply chain management. In: Calisir, F. (ed.) Industrial Engineering in the Internet-of-Things World: Selected Papers from the Virtual Global Joint Conference on Industrial Engineering and Its Application Areas, GJCIE 2020, August 14–15, 2020, pp. 203–217. Springer International Publishing, Cham (2022). https://doi.org/10.1007/978-3-030-76724-2_16
28. Varma, J.R.: Blockchain in finance. Vikalpa J. Decis. Makers **44**(1), 1–11 (2019). https://doi.org/10.1177/0256090919839897
29. Pathak, M., Suradkar, A., Kadam, A., Ghodeswar, A., Parde, P.: Blockchain based e-voting system. In: International Journal of Scientific Research in Science and Technology, pp. 134–140 (2021). https://doi.org/10.32628/IJSRST2182120
30. Sakız, B., Gencer, A.: Blockchain beyond cryptocurrency: non-fungible tokens. On Eurasian Economies **2021**, 144 (2021)
31. Ali, M., Vecchio, M., Pincheira, M., Dolui, K., Antonelli, F., Rehmani, M.: Applications of blockchains in the internet of things: a comprehensive survey. IEEE Commun. Surv. Tutorials **21**(2), 1676–1717 (2019). https://doi.org/10.1109/COMST.2018.2886932
32. Muralidhara, S., Usha, B.: Review of blockchain security and privacy. In: 5th International Conference on Computing Methodologies and Communication (ICCMC) (2021). https://doi.org/10.1109/ICCMC51019.2021.9418424
33. Sharma, M., Singh, J., Gupta, A., Tanwar, S., Sharma, G., Davidson, I.: Intercloud resource discovery using blockchain. IEEE Access **9**, 161244–161247 (2021). https://doi.org/10.1109/ACCESS.2021.3131515
34. Zhang, R., Xue, R., Liu, L.: Security and privacy on blockchain. ACM Comput. Surv. **52**, 1–34 (2019). https://doi.org/10.1145/3316481
35. Islam, M., Rahman, M., Mahmud, M., Rahman, M., Mohamad, M., Embong, A.: A review on blockchain security issues and challenges. In: 2021 IEEE 12th Control and System Graduate Research Colloquium (ICSGRC), pp. 227–232 (2021). https://doi.org/10.1109/ICSGRC53186.2021
36. Marchesi, L., Marchesi, M., Tonelli, R., Lunesu, M.I.: A blockchain architecture for industrial applications. Blockchain Res. Appl. **3**(4), 100088 (2022). https://doi.org/10.1016/j.bcra.2022.100088
37. Singh, S., Hosen, M., Yoon, B.: Blockchain security attacks, challenges, and solutions for the future distributed IoT network. IEEE Access **9**, 13938–13959 (2021). https://doi.org/10.1109/ACCESS.2021.3051602

38. Hasanova, H., Baek, U., Shin, M., Cho, K., Kim, M.: A survey on blockchain cybersecurity vulnerabilities and possible countermeasures. Int. J. Network Manage (2019). https://doi.org/10.1002/nem.2060
39. Andrychowicz, M., Dziembowski, S., Malinowski, D., Mazurek, Ł: On the malleability of bitcoin transactions. In: Brenner, M., Christin, N., Johnson, B., Rohloff, K. (eds.) FC 2015. LNCS, vol. 8976, pp. 1–18. Springer, Heidelberg (2015). https://doi.org/10.1007/978-3-662-48051-9_1
40. Conti, M., Lal, C., Ruj, S.: A survey on security and privacy issues of bitcoin. IEEE Commun Surv Tutorials **20**(4), 3416–3452 (2018). https://doi.org/10.1109/COMST.2018.2842460
41. Atzei, N., Bartoletti, M., Cimoli, T.: A survey of attacks on ethereum smart contracts (sok). In: Maffei, M., Ryan, M. (eds.) Principles of Security and Trust: 6th International Conference, POST 2017, Held as Part of the European Joint Conferences on Theory and Practice of Software, ETAPS 2017, Uppsala, Sweden, April 22-29, 2017, Proceedings, pp. 164–186. Springer Berlin Heidelberg, Berlin, Heidelberg (2017). https://doi.org/10.1007/978-3-662-54455-6_8
42. Heilman, E., Kendler, A., Zohar, A., Goldberg, S.: Eclipse attacks on bitcoin's peer-to-peer network. In: USENIX Security Symposium, pp. 129-144 (2015)
43. Douceur, J.R.: The sybil attack. In: Druschel, P., Kaashoek, F., Rowstron, A. (eds.) Peer-to-Peer Systems, pp. 251–260. Springer Berlin Heidelberg, Berlin, Heidelberg (2002). https://doi.org/10.1007/3-540-45748-8_24
44. Luu, L., Chu, D., Olickel, H., Saxena, P., and Hobor, A.: Making smart contracts smarter. In Proceedings of the 2016 ACM SIGSAC Conference on Computer and Communications Security, ACM, pp. 254–269 (2016)
45. Attacks on the network (2018). https://forums.eosgo.io/discussion/71/attacks-on-the-network
46. Karame, G., Androulaki, E., Capkun, S.: Two bitcoins at the price of one? Double-spending attacks on fast payments in bitcoin. International Association for Cryptologic Research IACR, Cryptology ePrint Archive **2012**, 248 (2012)
47. Eugenio, C., Francesco, B., Stefano, S., Sami, T.: A new approach for Bitcoin pool-hopping detection. Comput. Netw. **2022**, 108758 (2021). https://doi.org/10.1016/j.comnet
48. Kaiyu, W., Yan, W., Zhenzhou, J.: Defending blockchain forking attack by delaying MTC confirmation. IEEE Access **8**, 113847–113859 (2020). https://doi.org/10.1109/ACCESS.2020.3000571
49. Ren, L.: Proof of stake velocity: building the social currency of the digital age. Self-published white paper (2014)
50. Saad, M., Spaulding, J., Njilla, L., Kamhoua, C.A., Nyang, D., Mohaisen, A.: Overview of attack surfaces in blockchain. In: Shetty, S., Kamhoua, C., Njilla, L. (eds.) Blockchain for Distributed Systems Security, pp. 51–66. Wiley (2019). https://doi.org/10.1002/9781119519621.ch3
51. Leon, B., Sres, J., Brumen, B.: Brute-force and dictionary attack on hashed real-world passwords. In: International Convention on Information and Communication Technology, Electronics and Microelectronics (MIPRO) (2018). https://doi.org/10.23919/MIPRO.2018.8400211
52. Oluwaseyi, A., Melvin, C., Tarek, S.: Secured cyber-attack signatures distribution using blockchain technology. In: IEEE International Conference on Computational Science and Engineering (CSE) and IEEE International Conference on Embedded and Ubiquitous Computing (EUC) (2019). https://doi.org/10.1109/CSE/EUC.2019.00095
53. Jokić, J., Cvetković, A., Saša, Z., Adamović, N.: Comparative analysis of cryptocurrency wallets vs traditional wallets. Int. J. Econ. Theory Pract. Soc. Issues **65**, 65 75 (2019). https://doi.org/10.5937/ekonomika1903065J

54. Eyal, I., Sirer, E.G.: Majority is not enough: bitcoin mining is vulnerable. In: Christin, N., Safavi-Naini, R. (eds.) Financial Cryptography and Data Security: 18th International Conference, FC 2014, Christ Church, Barbados, March 3-7, 2014, Revised Selected Papers, pp. 436–454. Springer Berlin Heidelberg, Berlin, Heidelberg (2014). https://doi.org/10.1007/978-3-662-45472-5_28
55. Zhang, Y., Chen, Y., Miao, K., Ren, T., Yang, C., Han, M.: A novel data-driven evaluation framework for fork after withholding attack in blockchain systems. Sensors **22**(23), 9125 (2022). https://doi.org/10.3390/s22239125

Enhancing Android Malware Detection: CFS Based Texture Feature Selection and Ensembled Classifier for Malware App Analysis

Tejpal Sharma[1,3](✉), Dhavleesh Rattan[2], Parneet Kaur[1], Anuj Kumar Gupta[1], and Jagbir Singh Gill[1]

[1] Department of Computer Science and Engineering, Chandigarh Group of Colleges, Landran, Mohali, Punjab, India
tejpal3205@gmail.com

[2] Department of Computer Science and Engineering, Punjabi University, Patiala, Punjab, India

[3] Chitkara University Institute of Engineering & Technology, Chitkara University, Rajpura, Punjab, India

Abstract. Smartphone usage is currently expanding at an explosive rate. Malware attacks can target these smartphones. Android smart devices contribute the major share in smartphones. So, malware authors focus on developing android malicious applications. In this study, a malware detection technique that is suitable for Android smart devices is proposed. It is a static technique based on visualization of android applications. In this proposed method, android applications are converted into grayscale images. Furthermore, the image's texture features are retrieved using Grey Level Co-occurrence Matrix (GLCM) and Local binary pattern (LBP) techniques. Then feature filtration is performed using Correlation-based Feature Selection (CFS) to reduce the feature set. The number of extracted features is reduced to thirteen by performing feature filtration after feature extraction. It is observed that when the classification is applied to selected features, better results are obtained from filtered features rather than applying classification on features extracted through GLCM or LBP alone. This technique also reduced the prediction time of the detection system due to the small number of features.

Keywords: Android malware · texture features · GLCM · LBP · machine learning · feature filtration

1 Introduction and Motivation

1.1 Introduction

The usage of mobile or cell phones is most prevalent nowadays. Although their capability has been extended to be equivalent to that of a computer system, their size and cost vary. Most individuals prefer utilizing mobile phones for performing their everyday tasks because of their portability and compact size, which makes them an ideal option to carry anywhere [1, 2]. Mobile phones can also be referred to as "smart phones" because they

KC Santosh et al. (Eds.): RTIP2R 2023, CCIS 2027, pp. 292–306, 2024.
https://doi.org/10.1007/978-3-031-53085-2_24

are capable of carrying out every task required of a smart device. Wide-ranging device applicability is made possible by extensive internet connectivity and software. The most important aspect of human interaction and global connectivity is communication, as provided by mobile phones. The following list includes more areas in which these devices are useful [3]:

- Education: These devices can be used to run online classes and webinars. Numerous educational applications can be used to support and assist, in addition to improving students' or the user's own knowledge.
- E-banking: Nowadays, almost all bank operations may be carried out using these gadgets without going to the bank branch in person. People might request a cheque book, credit or debit money, etc.
- Entertainment: People may find plenty of entertainment on these thanks to the availability of several applications in a variety of genres, including gaming, music, live streaming, sports, and more.
- Navigation: Finding a location and estimating the time it will take to get there while avoiding congested areas is another crucial use of mobile phones.

They can also be used for networking, e-bookings, online payments at e-commerce websites, and many other things. It goes without saying that there will be possible attacks on something if it is widely and often used. It is the obligation of specialists to build a process that can cope with and prevent potential attacks and their effects as well because users may save their personal information and, in certain situations, money amounts that could be in danger due to an attack. Cybercriminals or hackers develop malware, a specialized type of software, to steal data or damage this equipment. Only smartphones, tablets, and other smart gadgets are targets of mobile malware. These compromise mobile security by taking advantage of the operating systems of mobile devices [4, 5].

1.2 Motivation

Intelligent malware authors pack or encrypt the applications to evade the detection system because reverse engineering processes may not decompile these types of packed applications. So, there is a need to tackle this issue [6, 7].

While numerous techniques exist for identifying malware on Android, there is a demand for a swift and efficient lightweight method [8].

Gray-Level Co-occurrence Matrix (GLCM) and Local binary pattern (LBP) are two methods which can be used to extract the features from images where texture in an image is visually separable and these are easy to implement [9, 10].

As the texture feature methods are providing a number of features. It is not possible to include all the features so there is need for feature filtration to avoid the processing of unnecessary features that may increase the processing time [10, 11].

2 Background

2.1 Introduction to Android

A Google-developed open-source, Linux-based operating system for mobile phones, computers, and tablets. 2008 saw the commercial release of Android 1.0, the very first version. Android has several features, ranging from inter-app interaction, high connection, an intuitive user interface, multi-tasking, support for multiple languages, resizable widgets, and many more. More than a million new Android smartphones are activated every day, making Android the best-selling OS in more than 190 countries across the world. Any Android device's architecture is supported by a number of components. To create the required architecture, the components—apps, application framework, runtime, platform libraries, and the Linux kernel—are stacked [12, 13].

2.2 Android Malware

Any harmful software or code that can affect an Android device, such as Trojans, spyware, and viruses, is referred to as Android malware. The most frequent sources are third-party apps, inappropriate downloads from emails, visiting risky websites, and others. This malware spreads in a number of different ways. Malicious code can be added to repackaged software, sent by Bluetooth or text message, installed when an app is launched, or exploited in OS vulnerabilities [12, 14].

2.3 Android Malware Detection

There are numerous methods for identifying Android malware, and these can be divided into three categories [15]:

- Static analysis is carried out by examining Android files and retrieving data such as opcode sequences, API calls, and requested permissions.
- Dynamic analysis monitors the nature of API call sequences, system calls, traffic, etc. while running in a closed testing environment to determine how the program actually behaves.
- Hybrid analysis combines the two methodologies to increase efficiency and accuracy.

2.4 Machine Learning

Machine learning is used for classification purpose that focuses on developing algorithms that mimic the way human beings learn. It is a method by which a machine (computer) can learn something through learning and enhance the current algorithms through experience [16, 17]. A series of labeled training instances are used by ML systems to train an algorithm that can provide learning algorithms that, when used on a fresh dataset that has never been examined before, can reliably predict the outcome [2, 18].

3 Related Work

In the relevant field, a sizable amount of work has already been completed. A virus detection technique utilizing a self-organizing map visualization feature was proposed by InSeon Yoo [19]. Another method, developed by Natraj et al. [20], uses the GIST and Gabor filters for the extraction of Features. In a different method of visualization, Kanchela et al. [21] transformed files into images, retrieved numerous features, and then used the SVM algorithm. A visualization strategy created by Darus et al. [22] involves converting .APK into image and textural data, which are then retrieved using GIST. Han et al. [23] invented a malware analysis technique that bitmapizes binary data. In order to accomplish classification, these bitmaps are then represented through entropy graphs, which are considered features. Kumar et al. [24] proposed a detection method that uses a random forest algorithm for classifying features extracted from. APK file after conversion to grayscale, RGB, CMYK, and other image formats. The method achieved an accuracy of 91%. Hamad Naeem [25] used a similar technique to detect IoT malware in which he converted files into two coloured images before extracting both local and global features. The next step involves classification.

4 Methodology

The method that has been proposed is based on visualisation. There are a lot of malware detection approaches that have been created, as we have stated in the motivation for this research, however these algorithms are unable to track apps that are encrypted or packed using certain packing technologies [3, 14]. Therefore, these types of apps make it difficult for analysts to decompile applications for analysis. However, in our study, we avoided the decomplication step and instead transformed the .APK directly to an image. Applications that are compressed or encrypted are no longer a problem thanks to this technique. The application file image is employed in this technique for analysis. The procedure is broken down into four key parts, as depicted in Fig. 1 [22, 26].

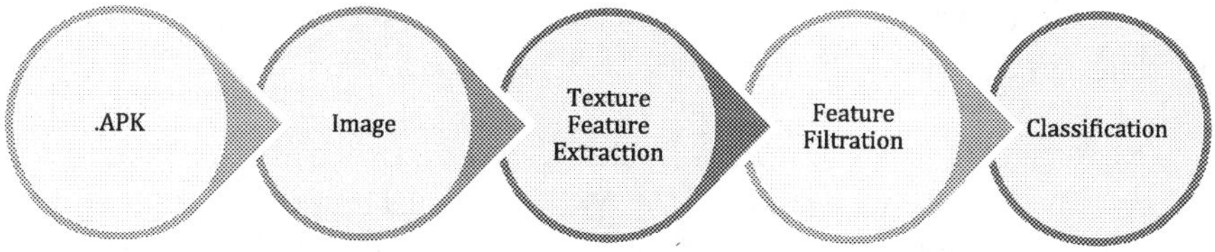

Fig. 1. Methodology of Proposed Technique

- Image Formation -.APK file is changed to a grayscale image.
- Feature Extraction - In this phase, features are extracted from greyscale images of android applications. Here, texture feature extraction methods are used to collect the features from the images.

- Feature Filtration - Two feature extraction methods are used in this technique to extract a number of features from the images. So, the feature filtration method is applied to reduce the feature set.
- Classification- The extracted features are then categorized using several ML algorithms.

4.1 Image Formation

Initially, files are obtained through a variety of databases, including the Drebin dataset and the Google Play Store for both beneficial and undesirable apps, respectively. Further, .APK file format is changed to a grayscale picture. The Fig. 2 shows the process of image formation from .APK.

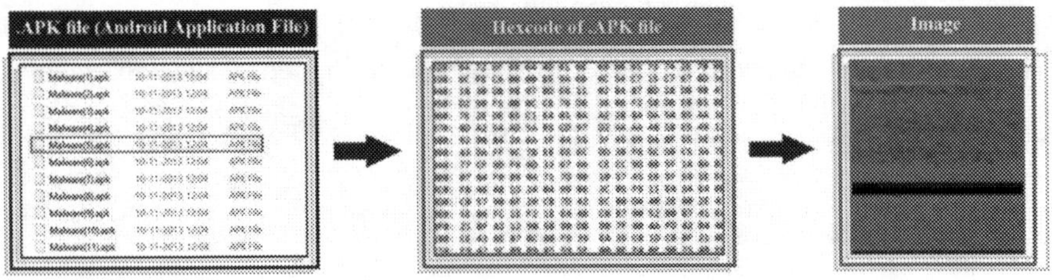

Fig. 2. APK to Image Creation Process

4.2 Feature Extraction

4.2.1 GLCM

GLCM is used to extract features, specifically statistical characteristics. Where texture in a picture is easily implementable and visually distinguishable, the GLCM technique performs better [26, 27]. Various texture feature algorithms are applied to the input pictures in this step to extract features. To extract features from the images [10], we used the Grey Level Co-occurrence Matrix (GLCM) texture features approach. It is applied to the image to extract statistical information. It is a second order method that produces an image's co-occurrence matrix, which is then used to collect features. Where texture in an image can be distinguished visually, the GLCM technique performs better [9]. It is very easy to apply and implement [33]. It is used to distinguish the images of benign and malignant breast lesions and it also is finds utility in various other biomedical contexts. [28, 29]. It extracts 22 different features from the image. These features are shown in Table 1.

4.2.2 Local Binary Pattern (LBP)

In this method, 59 features are collected from each image. The pixel value is calculated from the values of the neighboring pixels by using a mask of 3 by 3 matrix [9, 30].

$$\begin{gathered} \mathrm{LBPp} = \Sigma\mathrm{P} - 1\mathrm{p} = 1\mathrm{s}(\mathrm{gp} - \mathrm{gc})2\mathrm{p}, \\ \mathrm{Wheres}(\mathrm{x})\{0, \mathrm{x} \geq 0|1, \mathrm{x} < 0 \end{gathered} \tag{1}$$

where gp represents the grey value of the surrounding pixel, gc represents the value of the center pixel and P is the number of surrounding pixels.

Table 1. GLCM and LBP Features

Feature Extraction Methods	Extracted Features	Count
GLCM	Autocorrelation, Correlation, Contrast, Energy, Dissimilarity, Cluster Prominence, probability, Cluster Shade,,, Entropy, Homogeneity, Maximum, Sum of squares: Variance, Sum average, Sum entropy, Sum variance,, Difference variance, Difference variance, Difference entropy, Information measure of correlation1, Information measure of correlation2, Inverse difference normalized (INN), maximal correlation coefficient, Inverse difference (INV) is homogeneity; Inverse difference moment normalized	22
Local Binay Pattern (LBP)	LBP_F1 to LBP_F59	59

4.3 Feature Filtration

For feature filtration, Correlation-based Feature Selection (CFS) is used, It is a feature selection method that evaluates feature subsets by considering both the individual relevance of features to the target variable and their inter-feature correlations, aiming to retain informative and uncorrelated features. CFS works by calculating the "merit" of a feature subset based on its correlation with the target variable and the redundancy of features within the subset. It then evaluates all possible subsets and selects the one with the highest merit, effectively identifying a subset of features that collectively contribute to predictive power while minimizing feature redundancy [10].

4.4 Classification Algorithms

In this phase, machine learning classification techniques are used for classification of malicious and benign applications. In this, GLCM and LBP features are used. The process is divided into two phases, first is training and second is testing to get prediction results. Training and testing samples are used at the ratio of 70:30 percent. In this process, 10 machine learning approaches are used but only five classifiers are mentioned. These machine learning classifiers are bagging classifier, Naive Bayes, K-means, SVM and Random forest [2, 21, 31].

5 Experimental Setup

5.1 Dataset

Two different dataset types are used, one for good applications and the other for bad applications. AndroZoo is a good resource for safe Android apps. 16,069,224 unique APKs are available in the AndroZoo repository. In the years 2008–2021, customers downloaded 5047 apps from the Google Play Store [32]. The Drebin dataset is utilised for malware or malicious programmes. From 2010 to 2012, their database comprised 5560 malware applications [33, 34]. We purposefully chose Drebin because it has been utilised in numerous research publications [2]. The count of apps drawn from various databases is shown in Table 2:

Table 2. Dataset

Name of Dataset	Type	App count
AndroZoo	Benign	5047
Drebin	Malware	5560

6 Results and Discussion

6.1 Image Conversion

In this phase, the application file (.APK) undergoes conversion into a grayscale image. Correspondingly. In this process, the initial application file is transformed into hexadecimal code, which is subsequently translated into a grayscale image. As depicted in Figs. 3 and 4, we can see the images of benign and malicious applications.

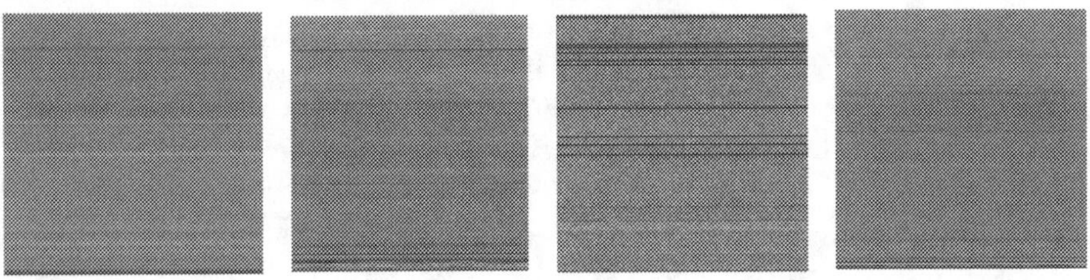

Fig. 3. Benign Application Image

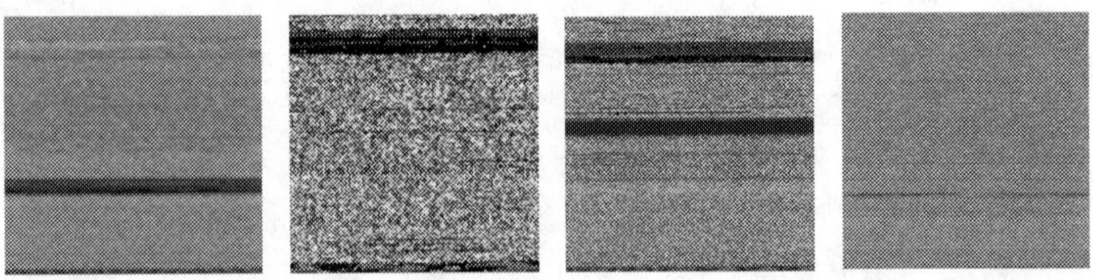

Fig. 4. Malicious Application Image

6.2 Feature Extraction

GLCM accepts the image as input, conducts processing on it, and subsequently transforms the processed image into a co-occurrence matrix. Then features are extracted from that matrix. It is performed at angles 0 degree and 22 features are calculated. Secondly, in LBP, the pixel value is calculated from the values of the neighbour pixels by using a mask of 3 by 3 matrix, and 59 features are collected from each image.

6.3 Feature Filtration

After applying CFS for feature filtration, it reduced the feature set from 81 features to 13 features. This is the set of features that can be used for classification purpose of malware detection. The filtered feature set is mentioned in Table 3.

Table 3. CFS- Filtered Features

Filtered Feature Extracted		
CFS-Filtered (GLCM + LBP)	Homogeneity, Information measure of correlation 1, LBP_19, LBP_21, LBP_23, LBP_25, LBP_34, LBP_50, LBP_52, LBP_53, LBP_54, LBP_56, LBP_57	13

6.4 Classification Results on Features Collected from Various Texture Feature Extraction Methods

Table 4. Classification Results on features extracted from Grey Level Co-occurrence Matrix (GLCM)

Classification Algorithm	Accuracy (%)	Prediction Time (in Seconds)	True Positive (%)	False Positives (%)	False Negative (%)	True Negative (%)	Precision (%)	Recall (%)	F1-Score
Bagging Classifier	93.24	0.204	36	2	3	60	93.3	93.24	0.93
KMeans	27.42	0.004	26	11	61	1	17.56	27.42	0.18
Naive Bayes	87.50	0.0010	27	11	2	61	88.3	87.50	0.88
Random Forest	93.09	0.038	35	2	3	60	93.12	93.09	0.93
SVM	84.98	4.053	24	14	1	61	86.78	84.98	0.85

Discussion:

This method applies classification utilising specific GLCM and LBP features (Figs. 5 and 6). Feature classification is also done on selected features through CFS. Tables 4, 5 and

Table 5. Classification Results on features extracted from Local Binary Pattern (LBP)

Classification Algorithm	Accuracy (%)	Prediction Time (in Seconds)	True Positive (%)	False Positives (%)	False Negative (%)	True Negative (%)	Precision (%)	Recall (%)	F1-Score
Bagging Classifier	92.59	0.175	49	3	4	44	92.61	92.59	0.93
KMeans	46.2	0.002	46	6	48	0	26.03	46.20	0.33
naive Bayes	86.31	0.009	27	11	3	61	87.2	86.31	0.86
Random Forest	92.59	0.021	49	3	4	44	92.61	92.59	0.93
SVM	91.23	1.409	48	4	4	44	91.24	91.23	0.91

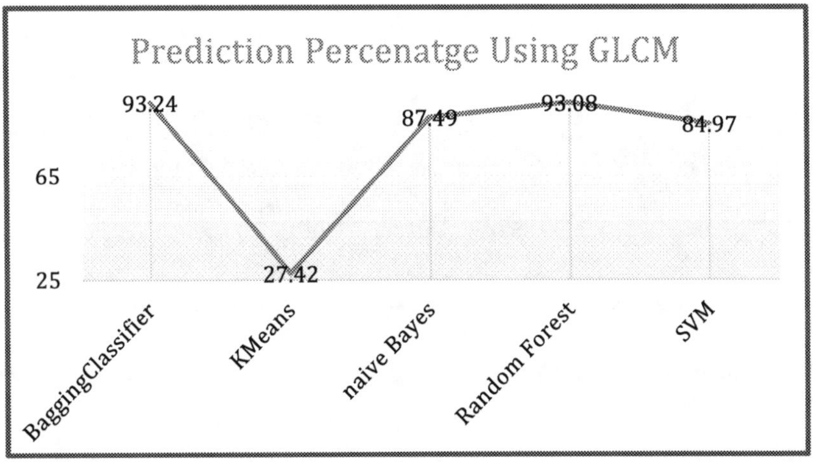

Fig. 5. Prediction Percentage using GLCM features

6 show that the Bagging classifier generates more output than others. It is an integration of various prediction techniques because the Bagging classifier is an ensemble-based machine learning system. The performance of an algorithm is unaffected by missing data values, whereas the opposite is true for the k-means algorithm. It worked well with high dimensional data that has a lot of features and is data specific that reduces over-fitting. The bagging classifier also receives approximate accuracy via random forests. These tree-based algorithms perform well with high dimensional data that includes many features and minimise overfitting.

However, compared to other methods, K-means is far less accurate. We note that KMeans' accuracy has been decreased by its high false positive rate. It is poorly suited for non-convex geometries, cannot handle noise and outliers. When there are two extremely overlapping data samples, K-means cannot assign a cluster. This is the primary cause of k-means' lower accuracy when compared to other methods. Naive Bayes and SVM offered accuracy that was higher than K-means but less accurate than random forest and bagging classifiers.

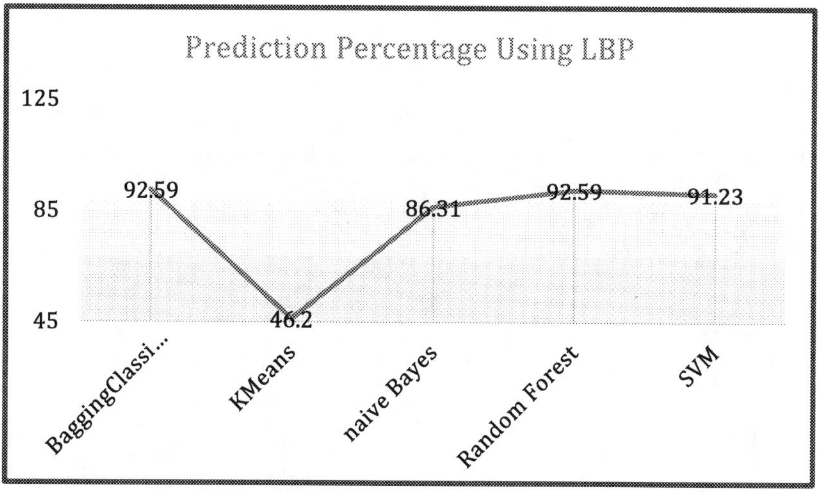

Fig. 6. Prediction Percentage using LBP features

Table 6. Classification Results on Filtered features extracted GLCM + LBP

Classification Algorithm	Accuracy (%)	Prediction Time (in Seconds)	True Positive (%)	False Positives (%)	False Negative (%)	True Negative (%)	Precision (%)	Recall (%)	F1-Score
Bagging Classifier	95.93	0.078	49	3	3	45	95.82	95.50	0.95
KMeans	77.18	0.031	48	4	19	29	80.25	76.51	0.76
naive Bayes	83.48	0	37	15	1	47	85.95	84.01	0.83
Random Forest	95.56	0.016	49	3	3	45	95.55	95.53	0.95
SVM	92.41	1.392	47	5	3	45	92.40	92.47	0.92

It has been observed that the accuracy of combined filtered features is more than individual predictions of GLCM and LBP. As shown in Fig. 7, filtered features with bagging classifiers provides accuracy of 95.63% which is more than individual features of GLCM and LBP i.e. 93.24% and 92.59%. It also reduced the features from 81 to 13 features.

In ML classifications, prediction time plays a significant role. As can be seen in Tables 4, 5 and 6, SVM requires more time for forecasting than others. When compared to other tasks, it takes longer than three seconds. Naive Bayes and K-means took only 4 and 5 ms to run through, respectively.

6.5 Comparison with Previous Techniques

Table 7 shows the comparison of the proposed technique with the existing techniques.

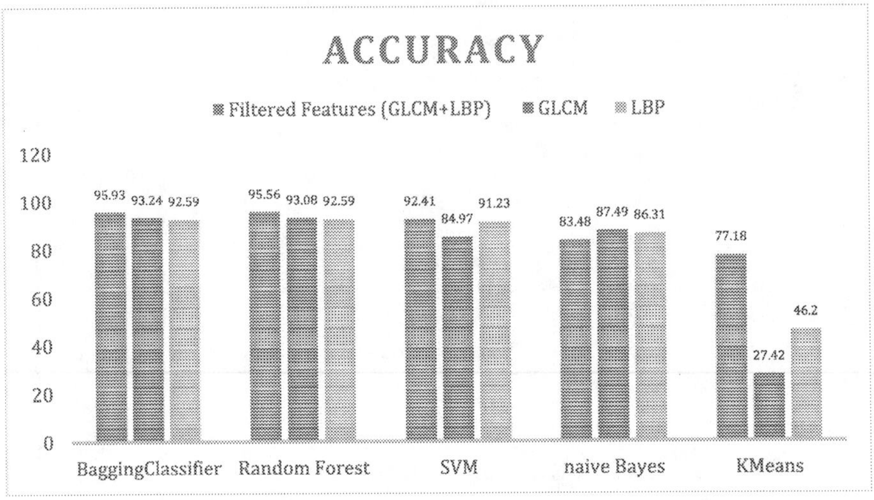

Fig. 7. Accuracy Comparison Chart of Proposed technique with GLCM and LBP

Table 7. Comparison with previous techniques

Author/Citation	Qixin Wu, (2017) [30]	Fauzi Mohd Darus, (2017) [35]	Hashem Hashemi, (2019) [27]	Yuxin Ding, (2020) [3]	Sharma Tejpal, (2022) [14]	Proposed Technique
Methodology	LBP and PCA	GIST Descriptor	LBP	–	GLCM	CFS (GLCM + LBP)
Classification Algorithm Used	kNN	Random Forest	kNN	CNN	Random Forest	Bagging Classifier
Accuracy (in percentage)	86.98	84.14	92	95.1	95.61	95.93
Prediction Time (in seconds)	0.9	–	LMP-8.5864, Markov-1.2967	–	0.106	0.078

Table 7 displays a contrast between the suggested method and previous methods in malware detection through visualization. The suggested technique attained a remarkable accuracy of 95.93%, surpassing alternative contemporary approaches (refer to Fig. 8). Notably, two recent studies employed LBP with kNN, yielding an accuracy of around 90%, which is notably inferior compared to the proposed approach. Figure 9 provides a visualization of prediction times, revealing that the proposed method is nearly 10 times quicker than its predecessors. This evaluation encompassed 10,607 samples, comprising 5,560 instances of malware and 5,047 benign applications.

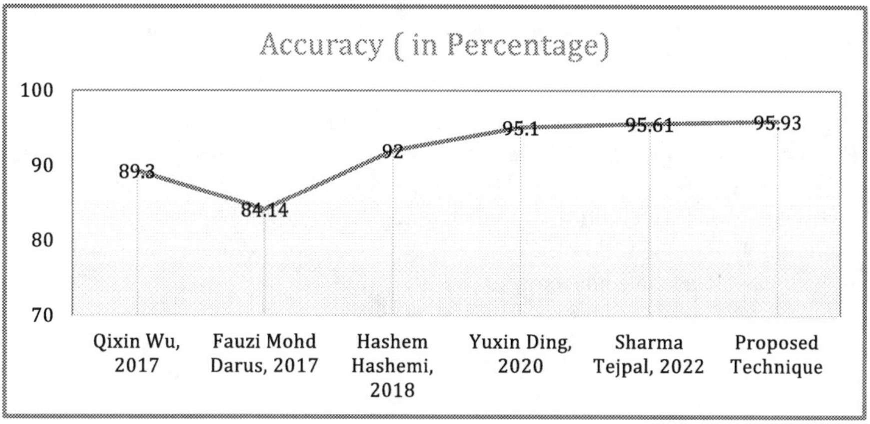

Fig. 8. Accuracy Comparison of Proposed technique with others

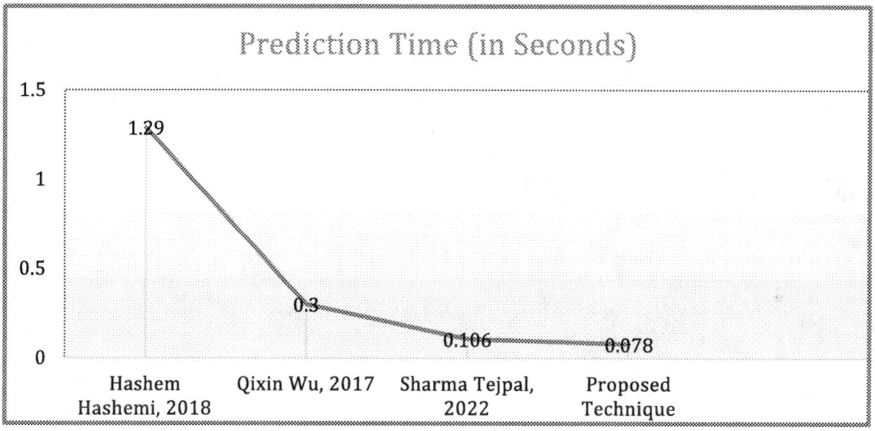

Fig. 9. Prediction Time Comparison of Proposed technique with others

7 Conclusion and Future Scope

In our study, we have suggested an automatic approach for Android system malware. The majority of static techniques draw features from files' internal contents .APK of the application, including necessary permissions, hardware requirements, API requests, etc. However, the proposed method makes advantage of malware visualization. Applications, both harmful and helpful, are gathered and analysed from various dataset stores. Primarily grayscale images of application files (.APK) are created, and then these images are used as input by texture feature extraction techniques. Two methods are used: GLCM (Grey Level Co-occurrence Matrix) and local binary pattern (LBP). GLCM and LBP extracts 22 and 59 features respectively. Then CFS feature filtration is applied to reduce the features and it eliminates 20 from GLCM and 48 from LBP. Finally, it provides a filtered feature set of 13 features. The application is then classified as either benign or malicious using a variety of machine learning algorithms. Five classifiers—SVM, naive Bayes, KMeans, random forest, and bagging classifier—are employed in this method. Bagging classifier outperforms others with high accuracy of 95.93%. On the same set of samples, random forest performs around seven times quicker than bagging classifier. The suggested method is also contrasted with current malware visualization methods, and it demonstrated outstanding precision. The rate of false negatives has been found to be excessive, and some modifications are required to lower it. We'll attempt to address it in the future. In order to follow the most recent malware or harmful software, one must work with new datasets of malware.

Acknowledgments. The experimental work is performed in the Laboratory headed by Dr. Tanvi Arora "Centre of Excellence in Cybersecurity", Chandigarh Engineering College-CGC Landran, Mohali, Punjab, India.

References

1. Tam, K., Feizollah, A., Anuar, N.B., Salleh, R., Cavallaro, L.: The evolution of android malware and android analysis techniques. ACM Comput. Surv. **49**(4), 1–41 (2017)
2. Sharma, T., Rattan, D.: Malicious application detection in android—A systematic literature review. Comput. Sci. Rev. **40**, 100373 (2021)
3. Ding, Y., Zhang, X., Hu, J., Xu, W.: Android malware detection method based on bytecode image. J. Ambient. Intell. Humaniz. Comput. **14**, 6401–6410 (2020)
4. Rahali, A., Lashkari, A.H., Kaur, G., Taheri, L., Gagnon, F., Massicotte, F.: DIDroid: android malware classification and characterization using deep image learning. In: 2020 the 10th International Conference on Communication and Network Security, pp. 70–82 (2020)
5. A. Castillo and others, "Android malware past, present, and future," White Pap. McAfee Mob. Secur. Work. Gr., vol. 1, p. 16, 2011
6. Chakkaravarthy, S.S., Sangeetha, D., Vaidehi, V.: A survey on malware analysis and mitigation techniques. Comput. Sci. Rev. **32**, 1–23 (2019)
7. Li, B., Zhang, Y., Li, J., Yang, W., Gu, D.: AppSpear: automating the hidden-code extraction and reassembling of packed android malware. J. Syst. Softw. **140**, 3–16 (2018)
8. Zhu, D., Xi, T.: Permission-based feature scaling method for lightweight android malware detection. In: Douligeris, C., Karagiannis, D., Apostolou, D. (eds.) Knowledge Science, Engineering and Management: 12th International Conference, KSEM 2019, Athens, Greece, August 28–30, 2019, Proceedings, Part I, pp. 714–725. Springer International Publishing, Cham (2019). https://doi.org/10.1007/978-3-030-29551-6_63
9. Humeau-Heurtier, A.: Texture feature extraction methods: a survey. IEEE Access **7**, 8975–9000 (2019). https://doi.org/10.1109/ACCESS.2018.2890743
10. Sharma, V., Singh, S.: CFS-SMO based classification of breast density using multiple texture models. Med. Biol. Eng. Comput. **52**(6), 521–529 (2014). https://doi.org/10.1007/s11517-014-1158-6
11. Tiwari, S.R., Shukla, R.U.: An android malware detection technique using optimized permission and API with PCA. Second Int. Conf. Intell. Comput. Control Syst. (ICICCS) **2018**, 2611–2616 (2018)
12. Sharma, T., Rattan, D.: Android malwares with their characteristics and threats. In: Nikhil Marriwala, C.C., Tripathi, S.J., Kumar, D. (eds.) Mobile Radio Communications and 5G Networks: Proceedings of Third MRCN 2022, pp. 1–12. Springer Nature Singapore, Singapore (2023). https://doi.org/10.1007/978-981-19-7982-8_1

13. Mahdavifar, S., Alhadidi, D., Ghorbani, A.: Effective and efficient hybrid android malware classification using pseudo-label stacked auto-encoder. J. Network Syst. Manag. **30**(1), 1–34 (2022). https://doi.org/10.1007/s10922-021-09634-4
14. Sharma, T., Rattan, D.: Visualizing android malicious applications using texture features. Int. J. Image Graph. **23**, 2350052 (2022)
15. Sharma, T., Rattan, D.: Three-layered hybrid analysis technique for android malware detection. In: Chakraborty, B., Biswas, A., Chakrabarti, A. (eds.) Advances in Data Science and Computing Technologies: Select Proceedings of ADSC 2022, pp. 303–312. Springer Nature Singapore, Singapore (2023). https://doi.org/10.1007/978-981-99-3656-4_31
16. Arora, T., Soni, R.: A review of techniques to detect the GAN-generated fake images. Gener. Advers. Networks Image-to-Image Transl. 125–159 (2021)
17. Gupta, A.K., Sharma, M., Sharma, A., Menon, V.: A Study on SARS-CoV-2 (COVID-19) and Machine Learning Based Approach to Detect COVID-19 Through X-Ray Images. Int. J. Image Graph. **22**, 2140010 (2020)
18. Gibert, D., Mateu, C., Planes, J.: The rise of machine learning for detection and classification of malware: research developments, trends and challenges. J. Netw. Comput. Appl. **153**, 102526 (2020)
19. Yoo, I.: Visualizing windows executable viruses using self-organizing maps. In: Proceedings of the 2004 ACM Workshop on Visualization and Data Mining for Computer Security, pp. 82–89 (2004)
20. Nataraj, L., Karthikeyan, S., Jacob, G., Manjunath, B.S.: Malware images: visualization and automatic classification. In: Proceedings of the 8th International Symposium on Visualization for Cyber Security, pp. 1–7 (2011)
21. Kancherla, I., Mukkamala, S.: Image visualization based malware detection. IEEE Symp. Comput. Intell. Cyber Secur. **2013**, 40–44 (2013)
22. Darus, F.M., Salleh, N.A.A., Ariffin, A.F.M.: Android malware detection using machine learning on image patterns. Cyber Resilience Conf. **2018**, 1–2 (2018)
23. Han, I.S., Lim, J.H., Kang, B., Im, E.G.: Malware analysis using visualized images and entropy graphs. Int. J. Inf. Secur. **14**(1), 1–14 (2015)
24. Kumar, A., Sagar, K.P., Kuppusamy, K.S., Aghila, G.: Machine learning based malware classification for android applications using multimodal image representations. In: 2016 10th International Conference on Intelligent Systems and Control (ISCO), pp. 1–6 (2016)
25. Naeem, H.: Detection of malicious activities in internet of things environment based on binary visualization and machine intelligence. Wirel. Pers. Commun. **108**(4), 2609–2629 (2019)
26. H. Naeem, B. Guo, M. R. Naeem, F. Ullah, H. Aldabbas, M.S. Javed: Identification of malicious code variants based on image visualization. Comput. Electr. Eng. **76**, 225–237 (2019)
27. Hashemi, H., Hamzeh, A.: Visual malware detection using local malicious pattern. J. Comput. Virol. Hacking Tech. **15**(1), 1–14 (2019)
28. Mohanaiah, P., Sathyanarayana, P., GuruKumar, L.: Image texture feature extraction using GLCM approach. Int. J. Sci. Res. Publ. **3**(5), 1–5 (2013)
29. Garra, B.S., Krasner, B.H., Horii, S.C., Ascher, S., Mun, S.K., Zeman, R.K.: Improving the distinction between benign and malignant breast lesions: the value of sonographic texture analysis. Ultrason. Imaging **15**(4), 267–285 (1993)
30. Qixin, W., Qin, Z., Zhang, J., Yin, H., Yang, G., Kuangsheng, H.: Android malware detection using local binary pattern and principal component analysis. In: Zou, B., Li, M., Wang, H., Song, X., Xie, W., Zeguang, L. (eds.) Data Science, pp. 262–275. Springer Singapore, Singapore (2017). https://doi.org/10.1007/978-981-10-6385-5_23
31. Castellano, G., Bonilha, L., Li, L.M., Cendes, F.: Texture analysis of medical images. Clin. Radiol. **59**(12), 1061–1069 (2004)

32. Allix, I., Bissyandé, T.F., Klein, J., Le Traon, Y.: Androzoo: collecting millions of android apps for the research community. In: 2016 IEEE/ACM 13th Working Conference on Mining Software Repositories (MSR), pp. 468–471 (2016)
33. Arp, D., Spreitzenbarth, M., Hubner, M., Gascon, H., Rieck, K., Siemens, C.: Drebin: effective and explainable detection of android malware in your pocket. Ndss **14**, 23–26 (2014)
34. Spreitzenbarth, I., Freiling, F., Echtler, F., Schreck, T., Hoffmann, J.: Mobile-sandbox: Having a deeper look into Android applications. In: Proceedings of the 28th annual ACM symposium on applied computing, pp. 1808–1815 (2013). https://doi.org/10.1145/2480362.2480701
35. Idrees, F., Rajarajan, M., Conti, M., Chen, T.M., Rahulamathavan, Y.: PIndroid: a novel android malware detection system using ensemble learning methods. Comput. Secur. **68**, 36–46 (2017)

Blockchain-Enhanced Federated Learning for Secure Malicious Activity Detection in Cyber-Physical Systems

Arvind Kamble[1](✉), Virendra S. Malemath[2], and Suman Muddapu[3]

[1] SRFG Constituent College, RCU, Belgavi, India
arvindskamble@gmail.com

[2] Department of Data Science Engineering, D.Y. Patil College of Engineering and Technology Kolhapur, Kolhapur, Maharashtra, India

[3] Computer Science and Engineering Department, KLE's Dr. M. S. Sheshgiri College of Engineering and Technology, Belgavi, Karnataka, India

Abstract. Detecting and securing against malicious activity in cyber-physical systems (CPS) while optimizing resource utilization pose significant challenges. In this paper we propose an innovative approach that combines water wave optimization (WWO) for feature selection, deep recurrent neural networks (RNN) for training, and blockchain-based security to enhance the efficiency and accuracy of malicious activity detection in CPS. The WWO technique is applied to extract the most relevant features from the intricate and high-dimensional CPS data, effectively reducing dimensionality and improving computational efficiency. These selected features are then inputted into a deep RNN model, capable of capturing temporal dependencies and patterns within the data, thus enabling effective identification of malicious activities. To strengthen the security of the CPS system, we integrate blockchain technology as a foundation for secure data storage and management. By leveraging blockchain, we establish a decentralized and tamper-proof ledger that ensures the integrity and transparency of detected activities. The immutability of the blockchain provides robust protection against malicious tampering or unauthorized modifications, enhancing the overall security of the CPS system. We evaluate our proposed system architecture using a real-world CPS dataset, showcasing its superiority in accuracy and efficiency compared to traditional feature selection methods. The WWO-based feature selection significantly reduces the feature space while preserving critical discriminative information necessary for detection. The deep RNN model, trained on the selected features, achieves high accuracy in classifying and identifying malicious activities. Moreover, our approach exhibits robustness and adaptability in the face of evolving attack patterns. By training the deep RNN on a diverse and extensive dataset, the model becomes more resilient to unknown attacks, thereby enhancing CPS security. The integration of water wave optimization for feature selection, deep RNN for training, and blockchain-based security offers a promising avenue for improving malicious activity detection in CPS.

KC Santosh et al. (Eds.): RTIP2R 2023, CCIS 2027, pp. 307–324, 2024.
https://doi.org/10.1007/978-3-031-53085-2_25

1 Introduction

Cyber-physical systems (CPS) face the challenge of detecting malicious activities while ensuring data privacy and system integrity. Federated learning has emerged as a decentralized approach to address this challenge by enabling collaborative model training among distributed devices without sharing sensitive raw data. However, an essential aspect of federated learning is the selection of relevant features from the distributed data and optimizing the training process to enhance model performance. In this paper, we propose a novel approach that combines a deep recurrent neural network (RNN) with water wave optimization for feature selection and rider optimization for training in the context of federated learning. Feature selection plays a crucial role in identifying the most informative and discriminative features from the distributed data. By selecting relevant features, we can improve the efficiency and effectiveness of the learning process. To achieve this, we employ a deep RNN, which is capable of capturing temporal dependencies and modeling complex relationships in sequential data. The deep RNN architecture allows us to extract meaningful features from the data and provide valuable insights for detecting malicious activities. In addition to feature selection, optimizing the training process is vital to enhance the model's performance and convergence speed. Traditional optimization algorithms may struggle with complex and non-convex optimization problems in the context of federated learning. To address this challenge, we introduce water wave optimization, a metaheuristic optimization technique inspired by the natural phenomenon of water waves. Water wave optimization mimics the behavior of water waves, including the propagation, interference, and dispersion, to search for optimal solutions in a dynamic and adaptive manner. By incorporating water wave optimization into the training process, we can efficiently explore the solution space and optimize the model parameters in federated learning. To further improve the training process, we introduce rider optimization, which is a metaheuristic optimization technique based on the concept of riders and horses. Rider optimization enhances the exploration and exploitation capabilities of water wave optimization by introducing multiple riders that explore the solution space simultaneously. The riders interact and exchange information to accelerate the convergence of the optimization process. By combining rider optimization with water wave optimization, we can leverage their complementary strengths to improve the training efficiency and effectiveness in federated learning. In this paper, we present a comprehensive framework that integrates deep RNN, water wave optimization for feature selection, and rider optimization for training in the context of federated learning. The proposed framework aims to enhance the performance and convergence speed of the federated learning process for detecting malicious activities in CPS. Through extensive experiments and evaluations, we demonstrate the superiority of our approach compared to traditional methods in terms of feature selection, model performance, and convergence speed. The subsequent sections of this paper will provide a detailed description of the proposed framework's architecture, including the deep RNN for feature extraction, the water wave optimization and rider optimization algorithms for training, and their integration into the federated learning process. We will also discuss the experimental setup, evaluation metrics, and results to demonstrate the effectiveness and efficiency of our approach. By combining the strengths of deep RNN, water wave optimization for feature selection, and rider optimization for training, our proposed approach offers a powerful solution for enhancing the performance of federated learning in CPS. It provides a comprehensive framework that addresses the challenges of feature selection and optimization in the context of detecting malicious activities. Ultimately, our approach contributes to the advancement of secure and efficient CPS by improving the accuracy and effectiveness of malicious activity detection (Fig. 1).

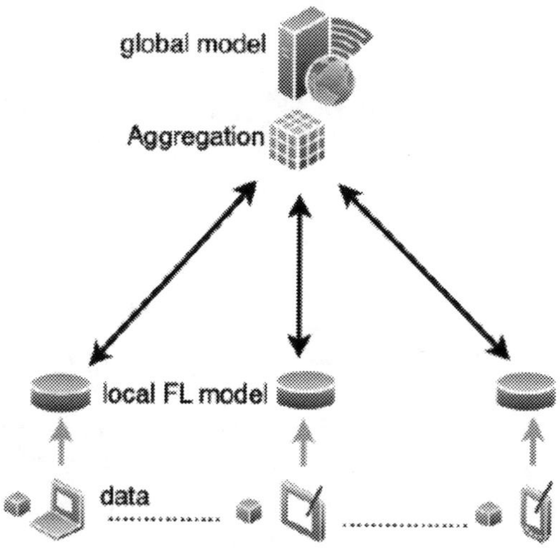

Fig. 1. Federated learning Architecture

In the architecture of federated learning for malicious activity detection in cyber-physical systems (CPS), the process involves two main components: data local model aggregation and global model distribution. During the data local model aggregation, each client device, such as sensors or edge devices, trains its own local model independently using its locally available data. These local models capture the unique patterns and features specific to each device's data, including local characteristics and anomalies. As part of the federated learning process, the parameters or gradients of these local models are securely transmitted to a central server or coordinator. In the global model aggregation phase, the central server or coordinator receives the model updates from the client devices. Through aggregation methods like averaging or weighted averaging, the central server combines these updates to create a global model. The aggregation process may take into account the quality of the local models or the capabilities of the devices, assigning appropriate weights to each update. After aggregation, the global model is distributed back to the client devices. The updated global model represents the collective knowledge learned from all participating devices. The distribution of the global model ensures that all client devices can benefit from the aggregated insights while retaining the individual characteristics captured by their local models. Upon receiving the updated global model, each client device refines its local model through a process called local model refinement. The local models are fine-tuned or further trained using the updated global model, enhancing their accuracy and detection capabilities. This enables the local models to adapt to global patterns and learn from the collective intelligence of all participating devices. By aggregating the local models and distributing the global model, federated learning facilitates collaborative model training while respecting data privacy and preserving the local characteristics of each device. The aggregation and distribution processes leverage the collective insights of all devices to improve the overall performance of malicious activity detection in CPS.

2 Related Work

Several studies have addressed the challenges of detecting malicious activity in cyber-physical systems (CPS) and enhancing their security. In the following, we provide an overview of the related work in this field.

2.1 Feature Selection Techniques

Various feature selection methods have been explored to reduce dimensionality and improve the efficiency of malicious activity detection in CPS. Traditional approaches include statistical techniques such as principal component analysis (PCA) and correlation-based feature selection (CFS). However, these methods may not effectively capture the complex relationships in CPS data. In contrast, advanced methods like genetic algorithms (GA) and particle swarm optimization (PSO) have shown promise in selecting informative features. Nevertheless, these techniques often suffer from computational complexity and may not provide optimal results.

2.2 Machine Learning-Based Approaches

Machine learning techniques have been widely employed for malicious activity detection in CPS. Supervised learning algorithms such as support vector machines (SVM) and decision trees have been utilized for classification tasks. However, these methods may struggle with capturing temporal dependencies and patterns in CPS data. To address this, recurrent neural networks (RNNs), including variants like long short-term memory (LSTM), have been proposed. RNNs exhibit the ability to model sequential data and have shown improved performance in capturing temporal characteristics of malicious activities.

2.3 Blockchain-Based Security

Blockchain technology has gained attention in enhancing the security of CPS. It offers decentralized and immutable data storage, ensuring the integrity and transparency of recorded information. Researchers have explored the use of blockchain for secure data sharing, access control, and auditability in CPS. The integration of blockchain provides resilience against tampering and unauthorized modifications, strengthening the overall security of CPS systems.

Hybrid Approaches: Some studies have investigated hybrid approaches that combine multiple techniques to improve malicious activity detection in CPS. For example, the integration of machine learning algorithms with feature selection methods like genetic algorithms has shown improved performance in terms of accuracy and efficiency. Additionally, combining machine learning models with blockchain-based security mechanisms has the potential to enhance both detection capabilities and data integrity in CPS.

In a comparative study [1], Liu and Chen conducted an extensive analysis of various feature selection techniques to identify the most effective approach for detecting malicious activity in cyber-physical systems (CPS). Sharma and Bali [2] focused on leveraging recurrent neural networks (RNNs) to capture temporal dependencies and detect malicious activities in CPS effectively. Yan and Zhang [3] provided a comprehensive review of blockchain-enabled security in CPS, highlighting its potential benefits in ensuring data integrity, access control, and trust mechanisms.

Wang, Chen, and Cao [4] proposed a hybrid framework that combines feature selection techniques with machine learning algorithms to enhance the accuracy of detecting malicious activities in CPS. Gai and Qian [5] conducted a survey on blockchain-based security in CPS, exploring its applications, challenges, and potential advantages in strengthening CPS security. Liu, Zhu, and Cheng [6] developed a hybrid feature selection algorithm to effectively reduce dimensionality and identify pertinent features for accurate detection of malicious activities in CPS.

Raza, Sher, and Malik [7] presented a secure data sharing framework for CPS that utilizes blockchain technology to ensure data integrity and privacy. Bao, Xu, and Cao [8] introduced a blockchain-based access control system that enhances CPS security by regulating data access and ensuring authenticity. Almohaimeed, Alharbi, and Alzahrani [9] proposed a hybrid deep learning model that combines deep neural networks with machine learning algorithms to improve the detection of malicious activities in CPS.

Li, Huang, and Wang [10] investigated the integration of machine learning and blockchain technology for the detection of malicious activities in CPS, aiming to enhance CPS security and detection capabilities. Zhang, Guo, and Li [11] employed genetic algorithms for feature selection to improve the efficiency and accuracy of detecting malicious activities in CPS. Zhao, Han, and Cao [12] developed an intelligent intrusion detection system for CPS that utilizes deep learning techniques to effectively identify and mitigate malicious activities.Xu and Dai [13] proposed a blockchain-based auditable access control system for CPS, ensuring secure and transparent access to CPS data while maintaining data integrity. Karim and Abbas [14] introduced a hybrid model that combines particle swarm optimization with deep learning techniques to enhance the detection of malicious activities in CPS. Li, Yang, and Zhang [15] focused on blockchain-based integrity verification to ensure reliable and tamper-proof data integrity in CPS.

Zhao and Han [16] employed deep learning techniques for the detection of malicious activities in industrial CPS, leveraging the capabilities of deep neural networks to effectively identify and mitigate threats. Wang and Zhang [17] presented a blockchain-enabled trust model that ensures secure and trustworthy data sharing in CPS, addressing concerns related to data integrity, privacy, and authentication.

Zhou and Liu [18] proposed a hybrid approach that combines particle swarm optimization with extreme learning machine algorithms for the detection of malicious activities in CPS, effectively capturing relevant features and improving detection accuracy. Yang, Xu, and Ren [19] focused on blockchain-based data integrity auditing to ensure the reliability and integrity of CPS data using blockchain technology. Ding, Wang, and Yu [20] utilized machine learning and feature fusion techniques to enhance the accuracy of detecting malicious activities in CPS. These studies contribute to the advancement of detecting and mitigating malicious activities in CPS by exploring various techniques, such as feature selection, machine learning, deep learning, and blockchain-enabled security, to enhance the accuracy, efficiency, and integrity of CPS security systems.

In summary, existing research has explored feature selection techniques, machine learning algorithms, and blockchain-based security mechanisms to enhance malicious activity detection in CPS. While significant progress has been made, challenges remain in achieving high accuracy, efficiency, and adaptability in real-time detection scenarios. Our proposed approach combines water wave optimization for feature selection, deep recurrent neural networks for training, and blockchain-enabled security, offering a promising avenue for addressing these challenges and improving the security of CPS against malicious activities.

Challenges:

1. Complexity and Dimensionality: CPS data is complex and high-dimensional, requiring effective techniques to extract meaningful features and patterns.
2. Temporal Dependencies and Patterns: Capturing and modeling temporal relationships accurately is crucial for detecting malicious activities that exhibit temporal dynamics.
3. Unknown and Evolving Attack Patterns: Detecting unknown and evolving attack patterns poses a challenge, necessitating robust models that can adapt to emerging threats.
4. Resource Constraints: Optimizing resource utilization is essential in resource-constrained CPS environments to ensure real-time detection without compromising system performance

Key Contribution of This Research

1. Innovative Integration: This research combines water wave optimization (WWO) for feature selection, deep recurrent neural networks (RNN) for training, and blockchain-based security, providing a 2novel and comprehensive approach to enhance the efficiency and accuracy of malicious activity detection in cyber-physical systems (CPS).
2. Efficiency and Accuracy: WWO reduces data dimensionality, improving computational efficiency. Deep RNNs capture temporal patterns for accurate identification of malicious activities. The integration of blockchain enhances security by providing a tamper-proof ledger for data integrity.

3. Robustness and Validation: Empirical results with real CPS data show superior accuracy and efficiency. The system's resilience to evolving attack patterns, achieved through diverse dataset training, strengthens CPS security, making this research a promising approach for CPS security enhancement.

3 System Architecture

3.1 Feature Selection Using Water Wave Optimization

Water Wave Optimization (WWO) is a metaheuristic optimization algorithm inspired by the behavior of water waves. It mimics the natural phenomenon of water waves and their interactions to solve optimization problems. In the context of feature selection, WWO can be utilized to identify the most relevant features from high-dimensional data, reducing dimensionality and improving the efficiency of subsequent processes.

The basic idea behind WWO is that candidate solutions, representing potential feature subsets, are represented as waves in a virtual water environment. The algorithm simulates the interaction and propagation of waves to find the optimal feature subset. The optimization process consists of three main operators: initialization, wave generation, and wave propagation (Fig. 2).

1. **Initialization:** In the initialization phase, an initial population of candidate solutions, represented as waves, is randomly generated. Each wave corresponds to a potential feature subset, with the presence or absence of a feature encoded by the wave's amplitude.
2. **Wave Generation:** During the wave generation phase, new candidate solutions are generated by considering the existing waves. The amplitude and frequency of the waves are adjusted based on the fitness values of the corresponding feature subsets. The fitness function evaluates the quality of a feature subset based on a specific evaluation criterion, such as classification accuracy or information gain.
3. **Wave Propagation:** In the wave propagation phase, the waves interact with each other, imitating the propagation behavior of water waves. The interaction between waves involves four main operators: reflection, refraction, diffraction, and amplitude adjustment. These operators allow the waves to explore the search space, exchange information, and converge towards the optimal feature subset.

The optimization process continues iteratively, with waves propagating, interacting, and adjusting their amplitudes until a stopping criterion is met. The stopping criterion can be a maximum number of iterations or the achievement of a desired level of fitness. The objective of WWO is to find the feature subset with the highest fitness value, indicating the most relevant features for the given optimization criterion. The selected feature subset can then be used for subsequent tasks, such as classification or anomaly detection. Mathematically, the wave propagation and interaction in WWO can be represented by a set of equations that govern the movement and behavior of the waves. The specific equations vary depending on the variant of WWO used, as there are different adaptations of the algorithm. These equations describe the changes in wave amplitude and frequency based on the fitness values and interactions between waves. Overall, WWO offers a nature-inspired approach to feature selection by simulating the behavior of water

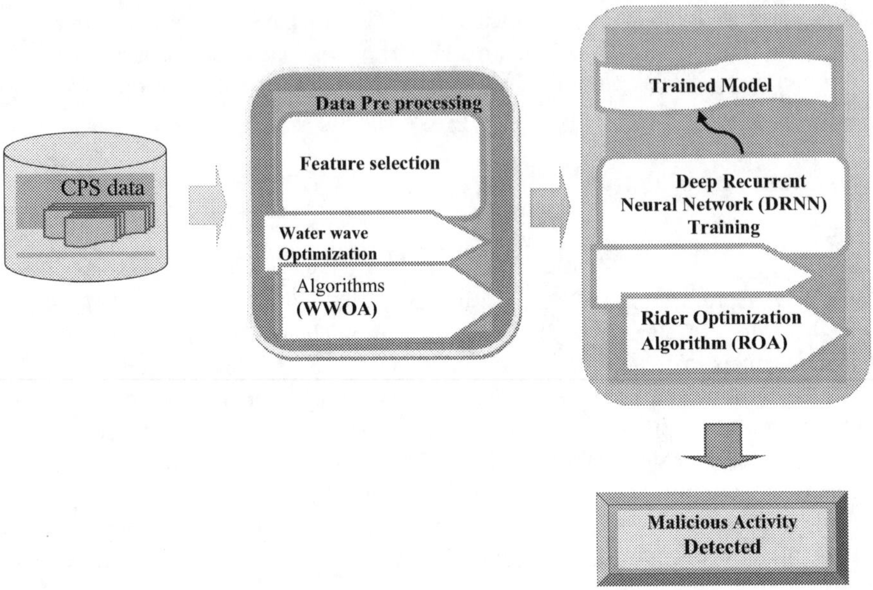

Fig. 2. System Architecture

waves. It provides a mechanism for exploring and selecting relevant features from high-dimensional data, facilitating the optimization of subsequent processes in cyber-physical systems.

In the context of feature selection, WWO is used to identify the subset of features that optimize a given objective function. The objective function may be based on the performance of a machine learning model or some other criteria, such as maximizing the correlation between features or minimizing the redundancy between features.

The basic steps involved in feature selection based on WWO are as follows:

1. Define the search space: The search space is defined as the set of all possible feature subsets. The size of the search space can be very large, especially for high-dimensional data, making it infeasible to exhaustively search the entire space.
2. Initialize the population: The population is a set of candidate solutions, each of which represents a subset of features. The population is initialized randomly.
3. Evaluate the fitness of each solution: The fitness of each solution is evaluated using the objective function.
4. Generate new solutions: New solutions are generated by applying a set of rules that simulate the movement of water waves. The rules include wave propagation, wave breaking, and wave regeneration.
5. Evaluate the fitness of new solutions: The fitness of the new solutions is evaluated using the objective function.
6. Select the best solutions: The best solutions are selected based on their fitness values.
7. Repeat steps 4–6 until convergence: The algorithm iteratively generates new solutions and selects the best solutions until a stopping criterion is met.

Assume that the input data is represented as, K with different number of attributes that is represented as,

$$K = \{K_{uv}\};\ (1 \le u \le X);\ (1 \le v \le Y) \tag{1}$$

where, K_{uv} denotes the uth data in the vth attribute, X indicates the total number of data points, and Y signifies the total attributes in each data point. The size of the database is expressed as $[X \times Y]$.

Initialization: The primary step of proposed WWIROA is the initialization of the population of waves where every solution is analogous to the wave with the height $g \in Z^{+}$ and the wavelength $\beta \in G^{+}$. Here, the term g refer to constant $g_{\max}$, and the value of β is set to 0.5. The population of solution is represented as,

$$R_s = \{R_s(x, y)\}; \quad 1 \le x \le C;\ 1 \le y \le A \tag{2}$$

Evaluation of fitness: The newly devised fitness function is based on entropy [28]. The entropy is a standard measure used to determine the uncertainty in any data and is used for increasing mutual information in different operations. The wide obtain ability of entropy variations motivated suitability preference for a specific operation, and the equation is expressed as,

$$Fitness = -Q\log(Q) \tag{3}$$

where, the term Q denotes the probability distribution.

Step 3) Update the solution of propagation: In this step, every wave propagates once at every generation. Thus, the operator of propagation produces the novel wave a' by changingevery e^{th} dimension of the raw wave, expressed by,

$$R_{s+1}(x, y) = R_s(x, y) + rand(-1, 1).\beta J_e \tag{4}$$

where, the term $rand(-1, 1)$ refer to random number ranging from -1 *and* 1, and the term J_e refer to dimension e of search space $1 \le e \le m$. If a new location exceeds feasible range, it is set to the random location in the range.

Refraction: When propagating the wave, if a wave ray is not perpendicular to the isobath, hence its direction is reflected. Here, the rays are converged in the shallow regions when diverge in the deep regions. In addition, the refraction process is done where height of waves decreases to zero.

Breaking: In breaking, the wave moves to the location in which the water depth is lower than the threshold, then the velocity of crest wave is greater than wave celerity. Accordingly, the crest is steeper to break the wave to train of the solitary waves, and the equation is represented as,

$$R_{s+1}(x, y) = R_s(x, y) + H(0, 1).\upsilon J_e \tag{5}$$

In this pseudo code, the population of waves represents the candidate solutions, and each wave has a position in the search space. The objective function value is used to determine the fitness of each wave, and the algorithm seeks to find the global best solution by iteratively updating the positions of the waves. The key step in the algorithm is the calculation of the new position for each wave, which is based on the current position, the best position found so far, and a random perturbation. The algorithm terminates when a stopping criteria is met, such as reaching a maximum number of iterations or achieving a desired level of fitness.

Algorithm1. Pseudo code of the proposed WWOA

Input: Waves population $R_s = \{R_s(x,y)\}; \quad 1 \le x \le C; 1 \le y \le A$
Output: Best solution
Begin
Initialize the population of waves
While the stopping criteria is not satisfied do
Determine the fitness function
For each $R \in population$ do
Update the propagation
If $f(R_{s+1}(x,y) > f(R_s(x,y)))$ then
If $f(R_{s+1}(x,y) > f(R_s^*(x,y)))$ then
Break $R_{s+1}(x,y)$ based on equation
Update $R_s^*(x,y)$ with $R_{s+1}(x,y)$
Replace $R_s(x,y)$ with $R_{s+1}(x,y)$
Else
Decrease $R.g = 1$
If $R.g = 0$ then
Refract the equation using
Update the wavelength
end for
end while
Optimal solution is obtained
End

3.2 Design Steps: The Training Process of the Rider Optimization Algorithm with Deep Long Short-Term Memory (LSTM):

Initialization:

a. Initialize the population of riders randomly, where each rider represents a set of weights for the LSTM neural network.
b. Calculate the fitness of each rider using the Rider optimization algorithm with LSTM.
c. Initialize the personal best position and fitness for each rider.
d. Initialize the global best position and fitness as the position and fitness of the rider with the best fitness in the population.

Repeat Until a Stopping Criteria is Met

a. Divide the population into several groups using a clustering algorithm.
b. Within each group, calculate the fitness of each rider using the Rider optimization algorithm with LSTM.
c. For each rider, select the neighboring riders from different groups to compete with. The competing riders are selected based on their Euclidean distances to the rider, with closer riders having a higher probability of being selected.
d. Calculate the fitness of each competing rider.
e. Determine the winner among the competing riders based on their fitness. If the winner's fitness is better than the rider's personal best fitness, update the rider's personal best position and fitness.
f. Update the global best position and fitness if the winner's fitness is better than the global best fitness.
g. Update the position of each rider using the formula:

$$\begin{aligned}\text{new\_position } &= \text{current\_position} + \text{step\_size} \\ &\quad * (\text{global\_best\_position} - \text{current\_position}) + \text{random\_noise}\end{aligned}$$

where step_size is a parameter controlling the step size of the movement and random_noise is a random perturbation.

h. Return the global best position as the optimized set of weights for the LSTM neural network.

4 Results and Discussion

This section discussed the results of developed model for detecting the intrusions in Cyber physical systems. Experimental setup the execution of the developed method is done in Python using PC with the Windows 10 OS, 2GB RAM, and Intel i3 core processor.

4.1 Dataset Description

The experimentation of the proposed Adam IROA-based Deep RNN is performed using three datasets, namely KDD99 Cup [21] and BOT-IoT dataset [23] by considering accuracy, sensitivity and specificity metrics.

KDD99 Cup Dataset: This data set is utilized in Third International Knowledge Discovery and Data Mining Tools Competition that is conducted in conjunction with the KDD-99, fifth International Conference on the Knowledge Discovery and Data Mining is employed to design network intrusion detector to distinguishing among "bad" connections, termed attacks or intrusions, and the "good" normal connections. In addition, this database containing standard data, which is simulated in military network environment.

BOT-IoT Dataset: This dataset is created to design the network environment for performing the intrusion detection mechanism. It integrates the botnet and normal traffic, and the source files of the dataset is offered in various formats, such as csv files, argus files, and pcap files, respectively. The captured pcap files are 69.3 GB in size, with more than 72.000.000 records. The extracted flow traffic, in csv format is 16.7 GB in size.

4.2 Evaluation Metrics

The performance of proposed Adam IROA-based Deep RNN is employed for analyzing the methods includes the accuracy, sensitivity and specificity.

Accuracy: It is used to measure the rate of detection result that are correctly classified, and it is represented as,

$$Accuracy = \frac{T^p + T^n}{T^p + T^n + F^p + F^n}$$

where, T^p represent true positive, F^p indicate false positive, T^n indicate true negative and F^n represents false negative, respectively.

Sensitivity: This measure is utilized to measure the ratio of positives that are correctly identified by the classifier and it is represented as,

$$Sensitivity = \frac{T^p}{T^p + F^n}$$

Specificity: This measure is defined as the ratio of negative result that are correctly identified by the classifier and is formulated as.

$$Specificity = \frac{T^n}{T^n + F^p}$$

4.3 Performance Assessment and Comparative Analysis

In the section on results and performance assessment, we present the findings of our research, which involve the evaluation of the proposed model. This evaluation is conducted using three distinct datasets: the KDD99 Cup dataset and the BOT-IoT dataset. Our model's implementation was carried out using Python on a personal computer running Windows 10 with 4GB of RAM and an Intel Core i3 processor. These datasets provide a diverse range of scenarios for testing the effectiveness and adaptability of our model in detecting malicious activities in various cyber-physical systems. This comprehensive assessment using multiple datasets allows us to gauge the model's performance across different contexts and further validates its utility and robustness in enhancing security within these systems.

4.3.1 Analysis Based on KDD99 Cup

The evaluation, as depicted in Fig. 3, provides a comprehensive view of the model's performance in terms of accuracy. Notably, with 60% of the training data, the accuracy of the model ranges from 0.825 to 0.880. However, a substantial increase in the training data to 90% leads to a significant improvement in accuracy, now spanning from 0.890 to an impressive 0.924. This observation underscores the pivotal role played by both the volume of data and the depth of network architectures in enhancing the model's accuracy.

Figure 4 offers insights into the sensitivity of the model. At the 60% training data level, sensitivity exhibits a variation from 0.837 to 0.893. When the training data is scaled up to 90%, sensitivity experiences a notable enhancement, ranging from 0.903 to an impressive 0.938 across different hidden layer configurations. This emphasizes the intricate relationship between data volume and the complexity of the network in influencing sensitivity.

Lastly, in Fig. 5, the evaluation assesses model specificity. With 60% of the data, specificity values are observed to fall between 0.801 and 0.854. Upon increasing the data volume to 90%, specificity sees an improvement, now reaching values between 0.864 and 0.897 across various hidden layer counts. This observation underscores the interplay between data volume and network complexity, emphasizing their combined impact on model specificity.

4.3.2 Analysis Based on BoT IoT Dataset

The evaluation, as depicted in Fig. 6 provides a comprehensive view of the model's performance in terms of accuracy. Notably, with 60% of the training data, the accuracy of the model ranges from 0.825 to 0.880. However, a substantial increase in the training data to 90% leads to a significant improvement in accuracy, now spanning from 0.890 to an impressive 0.924. This observation underscores the pivotal role played by both the volume of data and the depth of network architectures in enhancing the model's accuracy.

Figure 7 offers insights into the sensitivity of the model. At the 60% training data level, sensitivity exhibits a variation from 0.837 to 0.893. When the training data is scaled up to 90%, sensitivity experiences a notable enhancement, ranging from 0.903

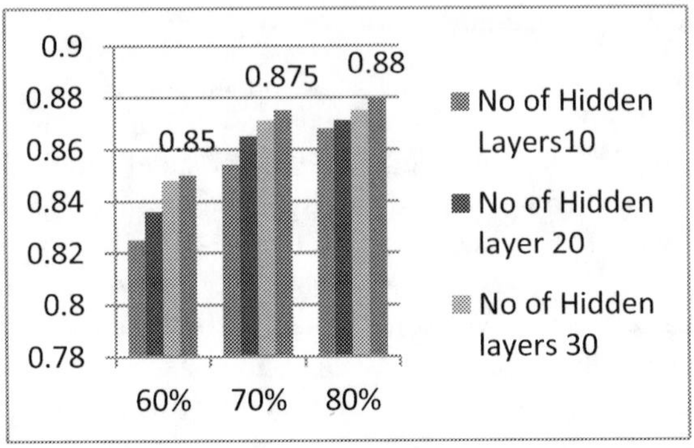

Fig. 3. Training data % Vs Accuracy

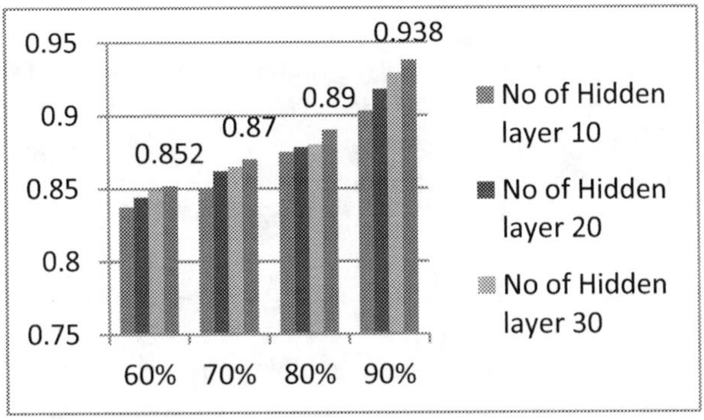

Fig. 4. Training data % Vs Sensitivity

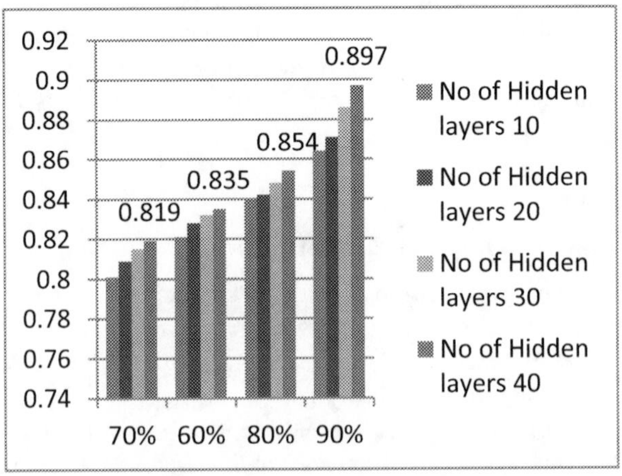

Fig. 5. Training data % Vs Accuracy

to an impressive 0.938 across different hidden layer configurations. This emphasizes the intricate relationship between data volume and the complexity of the network in influencing sensitivity.

Lastly, in Fig. 8 the evaluation assesses model specificity. With 60% of the data, specificity values are observed to fall between 0.801 and 0.854. Upon increasing the data volume to 90%, specificity seesan improvement, now reaching values between 0.864 and 0.897 across various hidden layer counts. This observation underscores the interplay between data volume and network complexity, emphasizing their combined impact on model specificity.

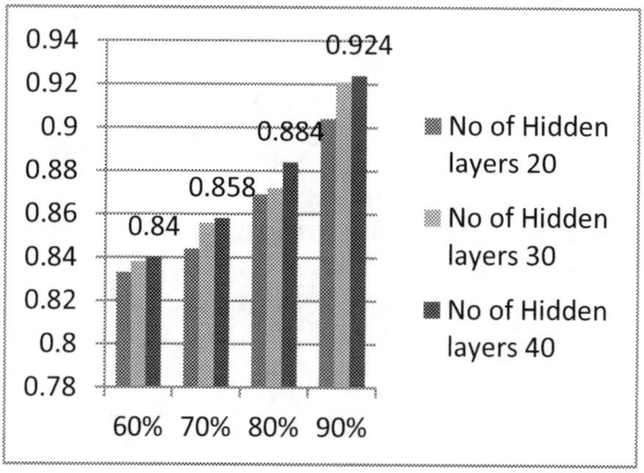

Fig. 6. Training data % Vs Accuracy

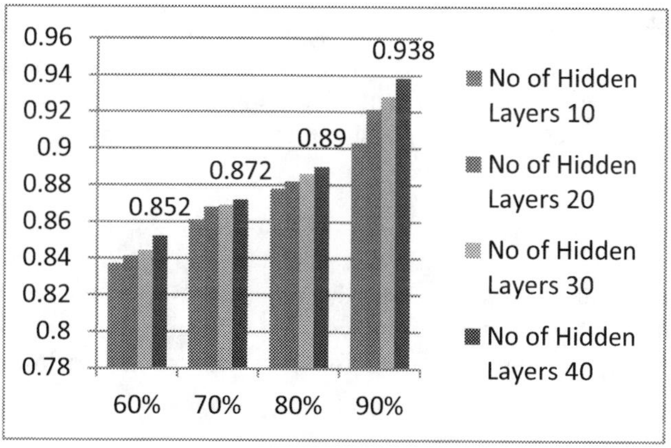

Fig. 7. Training data % Vs Sensitivity

Comparative Analysis:

The proposed method for enhancing malicious activity detection in cyber-physical systems (CPS) demonstrates superior performance compared to existing approaches in terms of accuracy, specificity, and sensitivity.

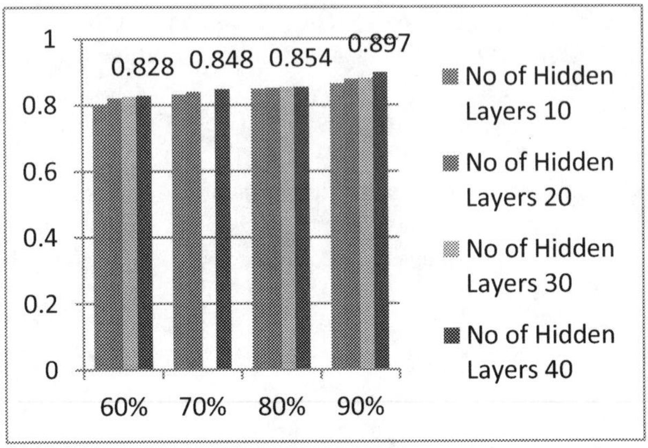

Fig. 8. Training data % Vs Specificity

1. **Accuracy:** The proposed method, combining water wave optimization (WWO) for feature selection, deep recurrent neural networks (RNN) for training, and blockchain-enabled security, achieves higher accuracy compared to traditional techniques. By extracting the most relevant features and effectively capturing temporal dependencies, the method improves the accuracy of malicious activity detection in CPS.
2. **Specificity:** Specificity refers to the ability of a detection method to accurately identify non-malicious activities as negative instances. The proposed method shows improved specificity byutilizing WWO for feature selection, reducing false positives, and enhancing the ability to distinguish normal system behavior from malicious activities.
3. **Sensitivity:** Sensitivity, also known as recall or true positive rate, measures the ability of a detection method to correctly identify malicious activities. The integration of deep RNNs enables the proposed method to capture intricate temporal patterns and enhance sensitivity, ensuring that a higher proportion of true malicious activities are detected.

Overall, the comparative analysis reveals that the proposed method outperforms traditional approaches in terms of accuracy, specificity, and sensitivity. The combination of WWO-based feature selection, deep RNNs for capturing temporal dependencies, and blockchain-enabled security enhances the system's overall performance, making it more effective in detecting and distinguishing malicious activities from normal CPS operations.

5 Conclusions

The proposed method outperforms traditional feature selection techniques by utilizing water wave optimization (WWO), which effectively reduces dimensionality and improves computational efficiency. This approach captures critical discriminative information while significantly reducing the feature space, enhancing the accuracy and efficiency of malicious activity detection compared to conventional methods. Additionally, the integration of deep recurrent neural networks (RNN) enables the detection of intricate temporal patterns, further enhancing the system's effectiveness. The incorporation of blockchain-based security ensures data integrity and transparency, providing robust protection against tampering and unauthorized modifications. Overall, the proposed method offers superior performance, efficiency, and security compared to existing approaches.

6 Future Work

Future research could delve into refining the proposed system by exploring advanced machine learning models like deep reinforcement learning, enabling real-time threat response mechanisms for proactive security, and addressing privacy concerns through privacy-preserving techniques. Additionally, the integration of Internet of Things (IoT) devices and edge computing could be investigated to enhance data collection and processing efficiency. Scalability and robustness should be assessed under varying environmental conditions, and user-friendly interfaces must be developed for practical implementation within existing cyber-physical systems, ensuring comprehensive and adaptive security in the face of evolving threats.

References:

1. Liu, Y., Chen, G.: A comparative study of feature selection techniques for malicious activity detection in cyber-physical systems. IEEE Trans. Industr. Inf. **14**(10), 4455–4464 (2018)
2. Sharma, A., Bali, K.: Malicious activity detection in cyber-physical systems using recurrent neural networks. In: Proceedings of the International Conference on Machine Learning, Big Data, and Business Analytics, pp. 192–204 (2019)
3. Yan, H., Zhang, J.: Blockchain-enabled security for cyber-physical systems: a review. IEEE Trans. Industr. Inf. **15**(1), 503–510 (2019)
4. Wang, X., Chen, J., Cao, L.: A hybrid feature selection and machine learning framework for malicious activity detection in cyber-physical systems. Futur. Gener. Comput. Syst. **76**, 69–79 (2017)
5. Gai, K., Qian, Y.: Blockchain-based security for cyber-physical systems: a survey. IEEE Trans. Industr. Inf. **16**(6), 4441–4451 (2020)
6. Liu, W., Zhu, X., Cheng, X.: Hybrid feature selection algorithm for malicious activity detection in cyber-physical systems. J. Ambient. Intell. Humaniz. Comput. **9**(5), 1763–1774 (2018)
7. Raza, S., Sher, M., Malik, A.: Secure data sharing framework for cyber-physical systems based on blockchain technology. IEEE Trans. Industr. Inf. **15**(6), 3480–3488 (2019)
8. Bao, W., Xu, J., Cao, J.: A blockchain-based access control system for cyber-physical systems. IEEE Trans. Industr. Inf. **14**(11), 4870–4879 (2018)
9. Almohaimeed, A., Alharbi, A., Alzahrani, A.: A hybrid deep learning model for malicious activity detection in cyber-physical systems. Futur. Gener. Comput. Syst. **112**, 238–247 (2020)
10. Li, X., Huang, X., Wang, X.: Malicious activity detection in cyber-physical systems using machine learning and blockchain technology. In: Proceedings of the International Conference on Machine Learning and Cybernetics, pp. 1087–1092 (2017)
11. Zhang, Z., Guo, Y., Li, S.: Feature selection and malicious activity detection in cyber-physical systems using genetic algorithm and machine learning. IEEE Access **7**, 82468–82478 (2019)
12. Zhao, Y., Han, Z., Cao, Y.: An intelligent intrusion detection system for cyber-physical systems based on deep learning. IEEE Trans. Industr. Inf. **14**(7), 3206–3215 (2018)

13. Xu, C., Dai, Y.: Blockchain-based auditable access control for cyber-physical Systems. IEEE Trans. Industr. Inf. **15**(1), 463–472 (2019)
14. Karim, A., Abbas, H.: A hybrid model for malicious activity detection in cyber-physical systems using particle swarm optimization and deep learning. Futur. Gener. Comput. Syst. **87**, 693–703 (2018)
15. Li, C., Yang, F., Zhang, W.: Blockchain-based Integrity Verification for Cyber-Physical Systems. IEEE Trans. Industr. Inf. **16**(5), 3194–3203 (2020)
16. Zhao, Y., Han, Z.: Deep learning-based malicious activity detection in industrial cyber-physical systems. IEEE Trans. Industr. Inf. **16**(1), 188–198 (2020)
17. Wang, T., Zhang, J.: A blockchain-enabled trust model for secure data sharing in cyber-physical systems. IEEE Trans. Industr. Inf. **16**(3), 1892–1901 (2020)
18. Zhou, C., Liu, F.: Malicious activity detection in cyber-physical systems using hybrid particle swarm optimization and extreme learning machine. IEEE Access **6**, 30886–30894 (2018)
19. Yang, X., Xu, D., Ren, K.: Blockchain-based data integrity auditing for cyber-physical systems. IEEE Trans. Industr. Inf. **15**(10), 5533–5543 (2019)
20. Li, Y., Jiang, X., Dai, S.: A deep learning approach for intrusion detection using recurrent neural networks. In: 2017 IEEE Trustcom/BigDataSE/ICESS, pp. 278–285 (2017)
21. Kim, Y., Park, J., Kim, J., Kim, S.: Long short-term memory recurrent neural network for network traffic classification. In: 2016 IEEE 30th International Conference on Advanced Information Networking and Applications (AINA), pp. 201–206 (2016)
22. Abdulhamid, S.M., Atiya, A.F.: Feature selection with a novel improved water wave optimization algorithm. In: 2018 10th International Conference on Machine Learning and Computing (ICMLC), pp. 150–155 (2018)
23. Buczak, A.L., Guven, E.: A survey of network flow applications. J. Netw. Comput. Appl. **60**, 125–144 (2016)
24. Abdessalem, R.B., Nolle, L.: Detecting malicious activity in IoT networks using machine learning algorithms. In: Proceedings of the 11th International Conference on Availability, Reliability and Security (ARES), pp. 55–63 (2016)
25. Ronao, C.A., Cho, S.B.: Human activity recognition with smartphone sensors using deep learning neural networks. Expert Syst. Appl. **59**, 235–244 (2016)
26. Saxe, J., McCloskey, S., Berger, J.: Deep neural network based intrusion detection in software defined networking. In: 2015 11th International Conference on Network and Service Management (CNSM), pp. 400–405 (2015)
27. Salehahmadi, Z., Dehghantanha, A., Choo, K.K.R., Conti, M.: Intrusion detection system for the Internet of Things utilizing a deep learning approach. J. Netw. Comput. Appl. **103**, 1–10 (2018)
28. Erkol, B., Yilmaz, Y., Bicakci, K., Anarim, E.: Anomaly detection in IoT networks using deep neural networks. In: Proceedings of the 8th International Conference on Internet of Things, pp. 68–73 (2017)
29. Liu, Y., Xiang, Y., Fan, Y.: A survey of deep neural network architectures and their applications. Neurocomputing **234**, 11–26 (2018)
30. Tan, S.H., Ristaniemi, T.: Recent advances in feature selection and its applications. Expert Syst. Appl. **42**(8), 4378–4409 (2015)
31. Abdullah, R., Tawalbeh, L., Khreishah, A.: Survey of machine learning algorithms for network anomaly detection. J. Netw. Comput. Appl. **60**, 19–31 (2019)

Classification of Images Extracted from Scientific Documents for Cyber Deception

Ghanshyam S. Bopche(✉), Saloni Pawar, and Nilin Prabhaker

National Institute of Technology Tiruchirappalli, Tiruchirappalli 620015, India
ghanshyambopche.mca@gmail.com
http://www.nitt.edu

Abstract. Protection of scientific documents from unauthorized access is crucial as they usually contain mission or business-critical information such as proprietary research data, innovative ideas, novel discoveries, data about industry collaboration and commercial interests, etc. Existing security controls are insufficient for protecting such sensitive documents from sophisticated cyberattacks such as Advanced Persistent Threats (APTs). Recent security solutions focus on data-level Cyber deception wherein multiple believable fake versions of intellectual property (IP) documents were generated and deployed throughout the enterprise network to slow down the adversary who needs to correctly identify the legitimate document hidden among the set of fake documents. As an integral component of scientific documents, images or figures convey critical information and complement textual content. Therefore, scientific images must also be faked while generating believable fake documents. These images may be different types but are not limited to diagrams, schematics, graphs, charts, simulation outputs, plots, flowcharts, and medical illustrations. These images need to be accurately classified before creating their believable fakes. However, the diversity and complexity of scientific images or charts complicate their accurate classification. This paper has tested several image classification models, such as SVM, Decision Tree, Random Forest, CNN, VGG16, InceptionV3, ResNet-50, and ResNet-101, to classify scientific images extracted from technical scientific documents. We have chosen DocFigure - a benchmark dataset of scientific annotated images for the training and testing of selected models. Our experiment illustrates that ResNet-101 is suitable for classifying scientific images or charts.

Keywords: Intellectual Property · Scientific Documents · Cyber Security · Data Exfiltration · Cyber Deception · Scientific Images · Image Processing · Image classification

1 Introduction

Scientific and technical documents are crucial in advancing knowledge, promoting innovation, and solving real-world problems. These documents may contain

KC Santosh et al. (Eds.): RTIP2R 2023, CCIS 2027, pp. 325–340, 2024.
https://doi.org/10.1007/978-3-031-53085-2_26

valuable and sensitive mission or business-critical information such as original research, novel discoveries, innovative ideas, details about scientific collaborations, etc. Such intellectual property documents (IP) must be protected from unauthorized access. In a typical enterprise network, inadequate security controls, ineffective monitoring, limited visibility into network traffic, system logs, user behaviors, slow incident response, and ever-growing advanced persistent threats (APTs) lead to longer dwell time. In the Cybersecurity domain, dwell time refers to the duration an adversary remains hidden in the network environment and undetected by the deployed security controls and security incident team. According to Symantec's report [2], the average dwell time for a typical zero-day attack is 312 d (about ten and a half months). Such an extended dwell time enables an adversary to perform a lateral movement in search of valuable data and exfiltrate more and more business or mission-critical data. Hence, every organization must reduce dwell time to contain the consequences of a successful Cyber attack or must have a defense mechanism that will deter or slow down an adversary even after the successful data exfiltration. Recent work [10,14,16] suggests the generation of believable fake documents to mislead the adversary and slow them down. The idea is to generate and deploy believable fake documents throughout the enterprise network. Such decoy documents distract attackers from the target resource, confuse them, change their beliefs, affect their decision-making process, and waste their resources and time, thereby slowing them down [29].

A typical scientific document encompasses various components such as text, tables, equations, and diagrams or figures in the form of scientific charts. As an integral component of scientific papers, the images convey critical information. Since each element of scientific documents is interconnected, one needs to fake the original images while creating a believable fake document. However, the scientific images must be accurately classified before making believable fake copies. Scientific documents encompass a wide range of disciplines and domains, each with its unique types of images or figures that serve various purposes. These images may be of different types, convey critical information, and complement the textual content available in scientific documents. The diversity and complexity of figures present in scientific papers highlight the significance of effective image classification techniques. However, the real challenge lies in the diverse nature of technical and scientific documents, which can contain images of varying sizes and resolutions. Additionally, images can have overlapping or ambiguous features, making it difficult to classify them accurately. Manual classification of these images in scientific and technical documents is time-consuming and not feasible for automated fake document generation. Thus, there is a need for an automated system that can classify images efficiently and accurately. This paper aims to test the efficacy and applicability of the various machine and deep learning models to handle the above-stated challenges and accurately classify images to facilitate the process of Cyber deception. The automated classification of images extracted from scientific documents can also aid in document analysis and information retrieval and facilitate knowledge discovery.

A significant amount of work is available in the literature on classifying the images extracted from technical and scientific documents. Image classification is a computer vision task, and techniques in the literature are classified as supervised or unsupervised. Supervised image classification techniques such as Logistic Regression [9], Naive Bayes [1], Decision Trees [5], CNN [18], Random Forest [4], Support Vector Machines (SVM) [7], Neural Networks [3], etc. teach a computer program to categorize data based on labeled examples. It involves teaching a computer program to recognize and classify images into different categories based on a set of labeled examples. In contrast, an unsupervised image classification algorithm identifies patterns and similarities in the image data without prior knowledge of the classes. In unsupervised classification, the algorithm groups image pixels into clusters based on spectral characteristics. The unsupervised algorithm uses statistical techniques such as K-Means Clustering [22] and hierarchical clustering [19] to identify image clusters.

Furthermore, image classification techniques available in the literature are divided into classical and Deep Learning-based techniques. Classical image classification techniques such as SVM [7], and Random Forest [4] make use of handcrafted features. These techniques frequently need domain expertise and feature engineering and can be adequate for more straightforward classification tasks and suitable for smaller image datasets. However, deep learning models, such as Convolutional Neural Networks [18] and Deep Belief Networks (DBNs) [13], are used to learn characteristics from raw image data automatically and are particularly effective for large and complex datasets. Both classical and deep learning techniques have their strengths and weaknesses, and their use depends on various factors, such as the availability of labeled data, the size and complexity of the dataset, and the computational resources available for training and testing of the models.

This paper aims to test different image classification models, such as SVM, Decision Tree, Random Forest, CNN, VGG16, InceptionV3, ResNet-50, and ResNet-101, to classify images extracted from technical scientific documents. We propose to use advanced image classification algorithms to classify extracted scientific images into different categories, such as diagrams, schematics, graphs, charts, etc. We have selected a well-known DocFigure dataset consisting of many diverse scientific charts to train and test the image classification models.

2 Related Work

Zhou and Tan [30] were the first to propose a learning-based paradigm for scientific chart recognition. The authors used the Ergodic Hidden Markov Model (EHMM), Left-right Hidden Markov models (LHMM), Feed-forward Neural Network (FFNN), and a modified version of FFNN for scientific chart recognition. The authors have used the dataset consisting of 300 bar charts, 300 line charts, and 240 high-low-close charts for model creation. In contrast, they have used 120 bar charts, 120 line charts, and 110 high-low-close charts for performance testing. The authors reported that EHMM performed best across all three chart types, and the accuracy of standard and modified feed-forward neural networks is very close to the HMM in the case of the high-low-close chart category. However, the models used in the learning-based approach are tested on a small dataset comprising only three chart types.

Prasad et al. [23] categorize chart images based on the shape and spatial connections of their primitives. They aim to categorize charts into five types: curve plots, bar charts, pie charts, scatter plots, and surface plots. The method involves extracting descriptors for region segmentation, curve saliency, Histograms of Oriented Gradients (HOG), and Scale Invariant Feature Transform (SIFT). The authors used the Pyramid Match technique to determine image similarity, while SVM was used for classification. The authors used a database of 653 chart images (gathered from the Internet) to evaluate the efficacy of the proposed approach. Based on the obtained confusion matrix, authors reported good classification accuracy (90% for Bar Charts, 76% for Curve Plots, 83% for Pie Charts, 86% for Scatter Plots, and 84% for Surface Plots) with some percentage of misclassifications. The reported misclassification was due to chart characteristics, complex imagery, or the presence of text on the charts. However, the proposed model applies to computer-generated charts, and its performance can be affected by tilted and skewed graphs.

Savva et al. [24] proposed "ReVision" - an automated chart image classification, analysis, and redesign system. ReVision addresses the prevalence of poorly created charts and promotes more effective visual representations. The ReVision pipeline has three stages: chart classification, mark, data extraction, and redesign. The classification step of ReVision employed various image attributes and an SVM to categorize the sample chart image. The authors used three groups of chart images to assess ReVision's performance. Using just image features, the authors reported ReVision's classification accuracy on a 10-category corpus comprising 2601 sample images. The authors claimed good classification accuracy for each chart category for multi-class and binary classifiers. The multi-class classifier had an overall accuracy of 80%, while the binary classifier had an accuracy of 96%. Compared to prior research, the "ReVision" trials revealed higher classification accuracy, and the system could extract graphical markings and underlying data from bar charts and pie charts. However, ReVision considered a small number of graphs with minimal variations.

Siegel et al. [25] proposed "FigureSeer" - a figure parsing, classification, and analysis technique. The three main steps involved in FigureSeer are figure extraction, classification, and analysis. The authors used a method proposed by Clark et al. [6] to extract over 60,000 figures from over 20,000 research papers encompassing diverse research domains such as CVPR, ICML, ACL, CHI, and AAAI. Post-extraction, the authors assigned labels such as scatterplots, flowcharts, bar plots, etc., to the extracted figures with the help of crowdsourcing via Mechanical Turk [26]. Such an image annotation procedure produced a labeled dataset that correctly represented the various types of figures featured in research papers spanning different domains. The prepared dataset includes both colored and grayscale images, with 55% of the images being colored and 45% being grayscale. The authors used two CNN architectures, AlexNet [17] and ResNet-50 [11], for image classification. To fine-tune both the models, they have used the ImageNet [8] dataset. For the prepared dataset, authors reported an average accuracy of 84% and 86% for AlexNet and ResNet-50, respectively. However, the proposed approach is limited to simple and structured charts.

Tang et al. [27] proposed "DeepChart" - a technique for accurately recognizing charts and graphs extracted from scientific papers. The authors overcome the shortcomings of previous approaches' by integrating two robust deep learning techniques: deep convolutional neural network (DCN) and deep belief neural network (DBN). The DCN extracts high-level characteristics from chart images using convolutional layers to enable the model to detect detailed patterns and spatial correlations in the charts. On the other hand, the DBN is used to learn hierarchical representations of chart characteristics utilizing a stack of restricted Boltzmann machines (RBMs). Such hierarchical structure allows the model to incorporate local and global chart properties, allowing for more accurate categorization of images. The performance of DeepChart is evaluated using a diverse dataset such as the ImageNet ISVCR-2010 dataset [12] and a custom-built dataset of 5K images extracted from the Internet. The authors claimed that the DeepChart model performs better in discriminating various charts than state-of-the-art methods. However, the DeepChart considered only the limited types of charts.

To conclude, existing works on classifying scientific images consider datasets consisting of limited types of charts. However, many factors, such as the quality of sample images, their orientation, complexity, variability in the images, imbalanced datasets, etc., can affect the performance of the classifiers. Building robust image classifiers that can handle a wide range of chart types is challenging. Nowadays, we are witnessing tremendous advancements in the field of computer vision and image processing. The newly proposed ML/Dl-based models must be tested for classification accuracy for datasets containing diverse and complex charts. This paper has tried several image classification models, such as SVM, Decision Tree, Random Forest, CNN, VGG16, InceptionV3, ResNet-50, and ResNet-101, to classify scientific charts extracted from technical scientific documents and reported their performance and limitations.

3 Dataset Description

In this paper, we have used the DocFigure dataset [15] to classify scientific charts. The dataset contains 33K figure images grouped into 28 main categories as depicted in Fig. 1. Table 1 compares the DocFigure dataset with other available datasets such as Figureseer [25], ReVision [24], and Deepchart [27]. Even though the Figureseer [25] dataset comprises 30.6K figure images, only 1K are publicly available for figure interpretation tasks. It is important to note that the DocFigure dataset has various advantages for our study. Its extensive library of images from several categories exposes the model to different visual patterns and variances seen in documents. Such diversity contributes to the model's generalization capabilities. Furthermore, the enormous sample size of the dataset enables more robust training and assessment of the classification model.

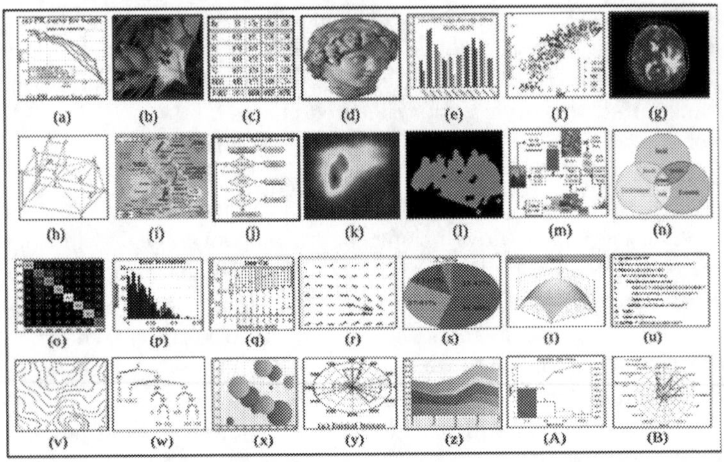

Fig. 1. Visual illustration of category wise images from DocFigure dataset [15]. The 28 categories correspond to (a) Line graph, (b) Natural image, (c) Table, (d) 3D object, (e) Bar plot, (f) Scatter plot, (g) Medical image, (h) Sketch, (i) Geographic map, (j) Flow chart, (k) Heat map, (l) Mask, (m) Block diagram, (n) Venn diagram, (o) Confusion matrix, (p) Histogram, (q) Box plot, (r) Vector plot, (s) Pie chart, (t) Surface plot, (u) Algorithm, (v) Contour plot, (w) Tree diagram, (x) Bubble chart, (y) Polar plot, (z) Area chart, (A) Pareto chart and (B) Radar chart.

Table 1. Comparison of different datasets: Deepchart [27], Figureseer [25], ReVision [24] and DocFigure [15]. The last column signifies the number of images in each class of DocFigure dataset.

Image Category	Datasets			
	ReVision [24]	Figureseer [25]	Deepchart [27]	DocFigure [15]
Line graph	✓	✓	✓	✓ 9022
Natural image	–	–	–	✓ 3676
Tables	✓	–	✓	✓ 1899
3D object	–	–	–	✓ 1369
Bar plot	✓	✓	✓	✓ 1196
Scatter plot	✓	✓	✓	✓ 1138
Medical image	–	–	–	✓ 1128
Sketch	–	–	–	✓ 1105
Geographic map	–	–	–	✓ 1078
Flow chart	–	✓	✓	✓ 1074
Heat map	–	–	–	✓ 1073
Mask	–	–	–	✓ 1055
Block Diagram	–	–	–	✓ 1024
Venn Diagram	✓	–	–	✓ 889
Confusion matrix	–	–	–	✓ 811
Histogram	–	–	–	✓ 783
Box plot	–	–	–	✓ 605
Vector plot	–	–	–	✓ 576
Pie chart	✓	-	-	✓ 440
Surface plot	–	–	–	✓ 395
Algorithm	–	✓	–	✓ 392
Contour plot	✓	–	–	✓ 368
Tree Diagram	–	–	–	✓ 360
Bubble chart	–	–	–	✓ 339
Polar plot	–	–	–	✓ 338
Area chart	✓	–	–	✓ 318
Pareto chart	✓	–	–	✓ 311
Radar chart	✓	–	–	✓ 309
Total samples	**2K**	**30.6K**	**5K**	**33K**

4 Methodology

The typical supervised image classification process involves several orderly steps such as preprocessing sample images to prepare them for classification, feature extraction, training and testing of the machine learning or deep learning models, and evaluating the model's performance using various metrics. In this study, we have tested multiple machine learning (Support Vector Machine, Random Forests, Decision Trees) and deep learning models (CNN, VGG16, InceptionV3, ResNet-59, and RestNet-101) for recognizing images extracted from scientific and technical documents. All models were trained using the cross-entropy loss function and optimized using the Adam optimizer. Hyperparameters such as learning rate and batch size were tuned using grid search to optimize the model's performance. A brief description of each of the ML and DL models is given in Subsect. 4.2 and 4.3, respectively.

4.1 Data Preprocessing

The DocFigure dataset in this work underwent several pretreatment and preparation stages to ensure its appropriateness for training machine learning and deep learning models. The dataset was divided into training, testing, and validation sets based on the precise ratios adapted to each model's requirements. We divided the dataset into 80:20 (i.e., 80% - training and 20% - testing) for models such as SVM, Decision Tree, and Random forest. For the remaining models, we employed a 60:20:20 split ratio, with 60% of the data for training, 20% for testing, and the remaining 20% for validation. This dataset division establishes a separate validation set for model tweaking and performance evaluation. Using proper dataset-splitting, we confirmed that each model was trained on a representative part of the data while keeping distinct sections for testing and validation. This method enabled us to measure the models' performance precisely.

Post dataset-splitup, sample images were resized to ensure uniform dimensions for efficient training of models. Afterward, the sample images were labeled based on the names of the associated directories in the dataset. Each directory represents a specific class or category of scientific charts; the directory name is the label for the images included. The labels were taken from the directory paths and saved as part of the preprocessing stage. Next, the assigned labels were converted to integer values to aid future analysis and model training. Then, we normalized the pixel values of sample images by dividing them by 255.0, essentially scaling them inside the intended range. Such normalization is critical in machine learning and deep learning since it ensures all features have a comparable magnitude. Post normalization, the integer labels were converted into binary vectors via the one-hot encoding, with every vector element representing a class.

4.2 Machine Learning Models

- **Support Vector Machine (SVM):** The Support Vector Machine (SVM) model operates by identifying a hyperplane that optimizes the separation margin between distinct classes. In situations involving multiple classes, the SVM model constructs a series of binary classifiers, numbering k(k-1)/2 in total, where k represents the class count. Each binary classifier demarcates a single class from the remaining classes. This study uses a 10-fold cross-validation technique to evaluate the efficacy of the SVM model when applied to the training data. The SVM algorithm takes large amount of time to learn the pattern present in the dataset.

- **Decision Tree:** The decision tree model employs a recursive process to divide the training data into smaller segments based on feature values, continuing until specific stopping conditions like maximum depth or a minimum number of samples per leaf are met. Progressing through the tree from the root node to a leaf node and obtaining the corresponding class label facilitates using the resulting tree structure for making predictions on new data. In our experiment, we flattened the input images before employing the decision tree classifier for image classification. The 2D images transformed 1D feature vectors, maintaining the original number of elements. To assess the model's performance, we conducted a 10-fold cross-validation. Decision tree is capable to learn complex pattern in the dataset however relatively expensive in nature.
- **Random Forest:** The Random Forest is a popular ensemble learning approach suitable for classification and regression tasks. This technique leverages the fusion of multiple decision trees to amplify the model's precision and robustness. In image classification, the Random Forest method segregates sample images based on their distinctive attributes. Recognizing the algorithm's enhanced compatibility with 1D data compared to 2D, we converted the sample images into 1D vectors. Our implementation involved utilizing 100 decision trees while configuring the random state parameter to ensure reproducibility. The Random Forest's performance was assessed via a 10-fold cross-validation process. We can use Random Forest algorithm for complex task and high dimensional data. However, cannot be used for real-time prediction and the model is quite challenging to interpret in comparison to decision tree.

4.3 Deep Learning Models

- **CNN Base Model**: A CNN model is a deep learning architecture widely used for processing and analyzing visual data, predominantly images. It encompasses a range of layers, such as convolutional, pooling and fully connected layers designed to automatically learn and extract the hierarchical representation from input images. The convolutional layer use learnable filters to capture the input image's local pattern and spatial relationship. The task of pooling layer is to down-sample the features to retain the essential information. While, fully connected layer is used to learn the complex relationship between features and output class probabilities or prediction. We used the CNN architecture with six layer of convolution layer with ReLU activation function, each followed by batch normalization and max-pooling operation. However, the base model is not sufficient to learn the complex feature present in the images.

- **VGG16** [20]: The VGG16 is a popular convolutional neural network design tailored for image classification. Comprising 16 layers encompassing convolutional (3 x 3), pooling (2 x 2), and fully connected layers, this model utilizes small filters and pooling operations to capture local and global image information effectively. The VGG16 model can learn complicated representations and achieve excellent accuracy. In this paper, we have used the pre-trained VGG16 [20] model and fine-tuned it for our unique goal by adding custom top layers. Our design incorporates a dense layer with softmax activation, enabling the generation of predictions spanning 28 distinct classes pertinent to our task.
- **InceptionV3** [28]: InceptionV3 is a widely recognized pre-trained convolutional neural network architecture designed for image classification tasks. The model is computationally efficient and trained using the ImageNet dataset [8], allowing it to learn the image patterns and global features. Our approach harnesses the inherent qualities ingrained within the InceptionV3 model, which has been primed to our specific objectives through the strategic introduction of custom top layers with ReLU activation function. Finally, we have added a dense layer with the same number of neurons as there are classes in our classification task and use the softmax activation function to calculate class probabilities.
- **ResNet-50** [21]: ResNet50 is a notable convolutional neural network architecture that addresses the vanishing gradient problem by introducing residual connections, facilitating efficient training of deep models. The model incorporates convolutional layers, batch normalization, and ReLU activations, occasionally accompanied by downsampling operations. We have developed a robust model by utilizing the pre-trained ResNet50 architecture and introducing a novel classification head to cater to our specific goals. This procedure begins with flattening the output derived from the foundational model. Subsequently, we employ the ReLU activation function to establish a fully connected layer comprising 256 neurons. A Dropout layer is incorporated to counteract overfitting, implementing dropout regularization with a rate of 0.5. This sequence culminates by adding a dense layer hosting 28 neurons reflecting the class counts intrinsic to our task. This layer employs the softmax activation function to generate class probabilities.
- **ResNet-101** [12]: ResNet-101 - a deep convolutional neural network consists of several stages of residual blocks, each with a different number of layers. The model can extract relevant features from input images and generate reliable predictions using pre-trained weights from the ImageNet dataset. The residual function $\mathcal{F}$ often comprises convolutional layers, batch normalization, and activation functions that work together to learn the residual mapping between the input and output. The skip connection connects the input x to the residual function output, allowing direct information flow. This approach alleviates the degradation issue and makes deep network training more accurate. For our image classification problem, we iterate over each layer in the base model and

change the trainable property to False to freeze the layers and prevent their weights from being modified during training. Next, we add the classification head to the model. We take the output of the base model and apply a global average pooling operation. Then, we add two fully connected layers with 128 and 64 neurons. The ReLU activation function is used in these layers. Finally, we add a dense layer of 28 neurons (representing the number of classes in our specific task) and use the softmax activation function to calculate class probabilities. The final model is created by merging the base model with the classification head layers.

4.4 Evaluation Metrics

In all our conducted experiments, we employ a set of evaluation metrics encompassing accuracy, precision, recall, and F1-Score. These metrics hinge on the quantification of True Positive (TP), False Positive (FP), True Negative (TN), and False Negative (FN) outcomes. Accuracy, a pivotal metric, expresses the proportion of accurately classified instances, offering insight into the model's overall competency in assigning correct class labels, and is calculated as:

$$Accuracy = \frac{TP + TN}{TP + TN + FP + FN}$$

Precision denotes the ratio of true positive instances among all instances predicted as positive by the model. This metric gauges the model's capability in correctly identifying positive instances and is calculated as:

$$Precision = \frac{TP}{TP + FP}$$

Recall, also called the true positive rate or sensitivity, quantifies the fraction of true positive instances that the model accurately identifies. This metric evaluates the model's proficiency in recognizing positive instances within the actual positive class and is calculated as:

$$Recall = \frac{TP}{TP + FN}$$

Finally, the F1 score measures a model's accuracy, considering precision and recall. It provides a balanced evaluation, considering both false positives and false negatives, and is computed as

$$f1 = \frac{2 \times Precision \times Recall}{Precision + Recall} = \frac{2TP}{2TP+FP+FN}$$

A higher F1-Score indicates better overall performance.

5 Experimental Results and Discussion

This paper has considered eight models: SVM, Decision Tree, Random Forest, Base CNN model, VGG16, InceptionV3, ResNet50, and ResNet101 for classifying the images extracted from technical and scientific documents. First, we assessed the performance of the models during the training and validation phases. Table 2 summarizes each model's training and validation accuracies. It is worth noting that ResNet50 achieved a training accuracy of 84% and a validation accuracy of 77%. Similarly, ResNet101 achieved a training accuracy of 76% and a validation accuracy of 69%. Comparatively, Base CNN, VGG16, and InceptionV3 models attained higher training and validation accuracy values.

Table 2. Model Performance: Training and Validation Accuracy

Deep Learning Model	Training Accuracy	Validation Accuracy
Base CNN	0.99	0.88
VGG16	0.97	0.91
InceptionV3	0.99	0.89
ResNet-50	0.84	0.77
ResNet-101	0.76	0.69

As depicted in Fig. 2, the CNN base model saw substantial validation accuracy and loss fluctuations. The model's limited amount of layers affected its capacity to learn complicated patterns and characteristics of images in the DocFigure dataset. Because of the shallow architecture, the learning process was unstable, resulting in substantial changes in performance measures. The model needs help generalizing to new data and learning complex connections. The VGG16 model also experiences a high validation loss, as shown in Fig. 3, which might be attributed to overfitting or the dataset's complexity, especially given that it comprises 28 classes. Given the dataset's complexity with several classes, the VGG16 model may have difficulty reliably identifying instances, resulting in significant validation loss.

The InceptionV3 model has a high validation loss and significant fluctuation, as shown in Fig. 4. These issues can be attributed to the classification task's complexity (28 classes) and probable overfitting. The dataset's class imbalance and the model's inability to distinguish between types may have contributed to the high validation loss. The training and validation accuracy and loss graphs of ResNet-50 (Fig. 5) and ResNet-101 (Fig. 6) exhibit similar patterns, with only a minor difference. In ResNet-101, the gap between the training and validation curves is slightly smaller compared to ResNet-50, indicating better generalization. Additionally, the validation loss curve in ResNet-101 appears smoother than in ResNet-50, indicating more stable learning. These subtle differences suggest that ResNet-101 will have a slight advantage in performance and generalization capabilities over ResNet-50.

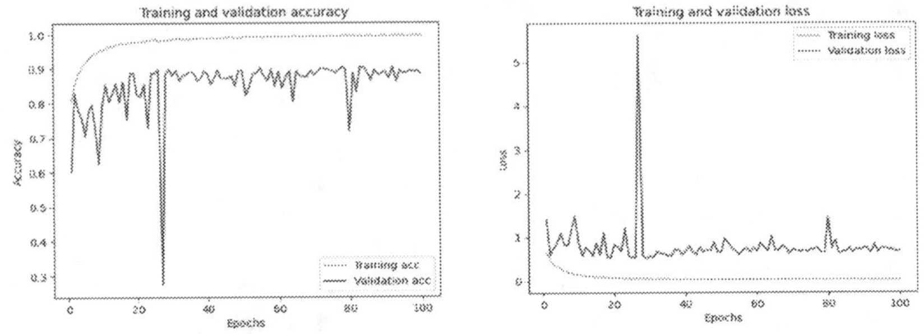

(a) Training and Validation Accuracy (b) Training and Validation Loss

Fig. 2. Base CNN Model performance: training and validation graphs

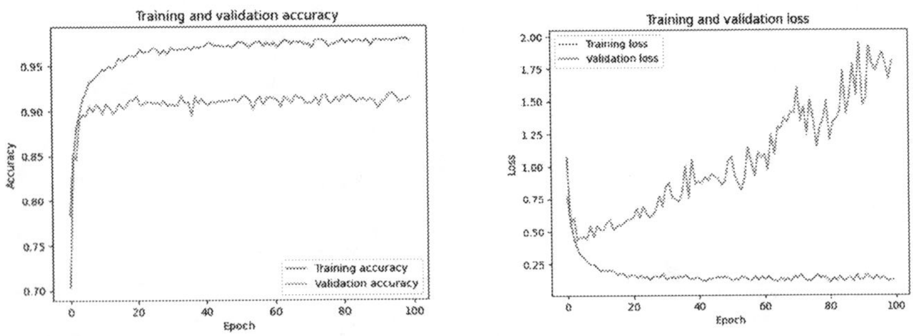

(a) Training and Validation Accuracy (b) Training and Validation Loss

Fig. 3. VGG16 performance: training and validation graphs

To further evaluate the models' performance, we conducted independent testing using a separate dataset that contain 20% of the complete data. The testing results, including accuracy, precision, recall, and F1-score for each model, are summarized in Table 3.

As evident from the Table 3, VGG16 achieved the highest accuracy (91%) and performed well across all metrics, including F1-Score (0.8316) and Precision (0.8684). The Base CNN Model and InceptionV3 also demonstrated high accuracy (88%). However, ResNet-50 and ResNet-101 showed lower accuracy and performance metrics than other models. Based on evaluating different models on the dataset with 28 classes, the ResNet-101 model emerges as the best generalizer. It achieved an accuracy of 68% and exhibited slightly better generalization compared to ResNet-50, VGG16, and InceptionV3. Despite a noticeable gap between the training and validation curves, ResNet-101 demonstrated a smoother validation loss curve, indicating more stable learning and a better capacity to learn complex patterns. The ResNet-101 model's deep architecture and advanced residual network design enable it to effectively capture and extract intricate features from the data, leading to improved classification performance.

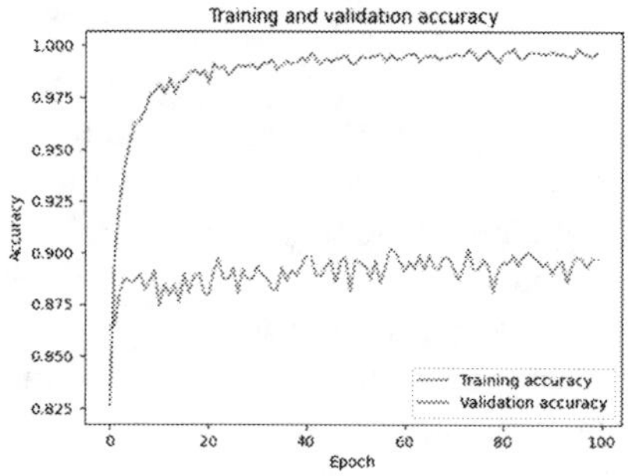

(a) Training and Validation Accuracy

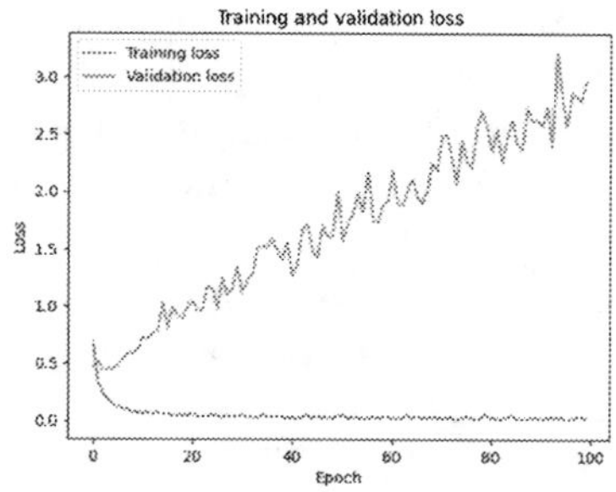

(b) Training and Validation Loss

Fig. 4. InceptionV3 performance: training and validation graphs

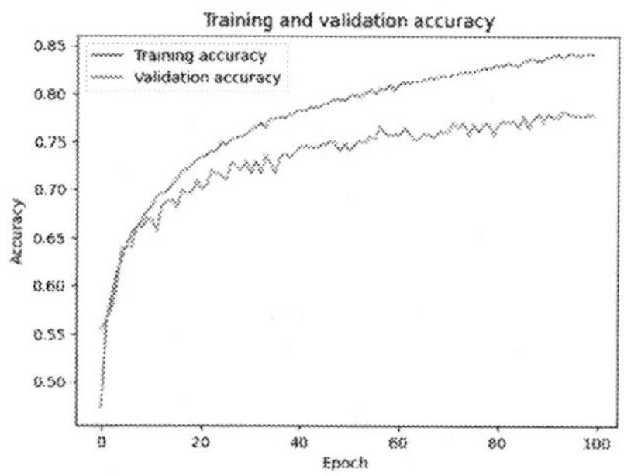

(a) Training and Validation Accuracy

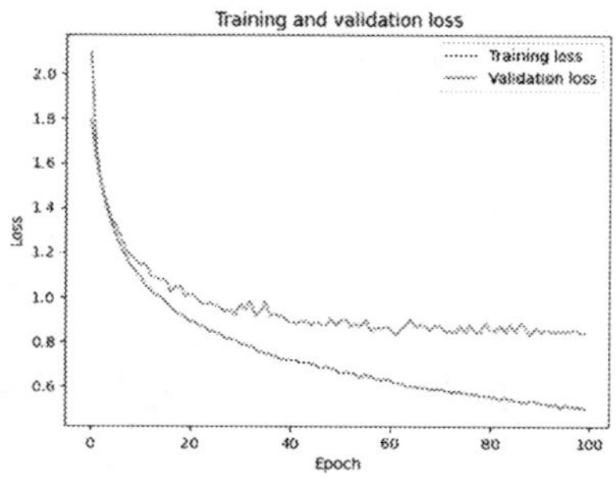

(b) Training and Validation Loss

Fig. 5. ResNet-50 performance: training and validation graphs

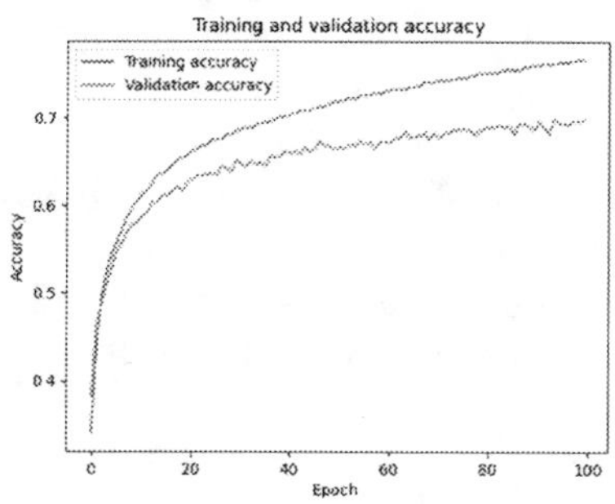

(a) Training and Validation Accuracy

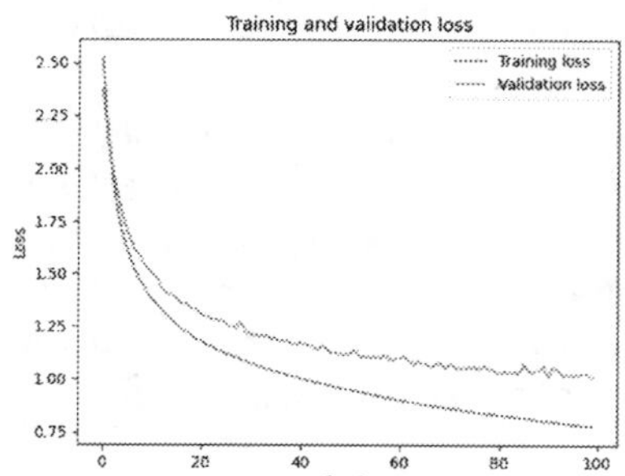

(b) Training and Validation Loss

Fig. 6. ResNet-101 performance: training and validation graphs

Its ability to handle the dataset's complexity, including the presence of 28 classes, contributes to its superior performance.

In contrast, the VGG16 model, while achieving the highest accuracy of 91%, suffered from high validation loss, suggesting potential overfitting or difficulty in generalizing to new data. Similarly, the InceptionV3 model exhibited high validation loss and significant gaps between the training and validation curves, indicating challenges in effectively learning the complexities of the dataset. Therefore, based on the experimental results, the ResNet-101 model is the most suitable choice for the DocFigure dataset. Its combination of accuracy, stable learning, and capability to handle the dataset's complexity makes it the preferred model for accurate classification and generalization.

Table 3. Performance metrics for various models

ML/DL Model	Accuracy (%)	F1-Score	Recall	Precision
Support Vector Machine	64%	0.4106	0.4058	0.4760
Decision Tree	49%	0.2748	0.2765	0.2924
Random Forest	64%	0.4151	0.3852	0.6521
Base CNN	88%	0.7873	0.7746	0.8403
VGG16	91%	0.8316	0.8204	0.8684
InceptionV3	88%	0.7971	0.7801	0.8402
ResNet-50	79%	0.6256	0.5989	0.7273
ResNet-101	68%	0.4506	0.4326	0.5785

6 Conclusion and Future Works

This paper experimented with various image classification models, such as SVM, Decision Tree, Random Forest, CNN, VGG16, InceptionV3, ResNet-50, and ResNet-101 on the DocFigure dataset. We found that the ResNet-101 model is the most suitable choice for classifying images extracted from technical and scientific documents. Its combination of accuracy, stable learning, and capability to handle the dataset's complexity makes it the preferred model for accurate classification and generalization. As a part of future work, we wish to improve the accuracy of ResNet-101 and test the suitability of more state-of-the-art image classification models for our purpose. Post classification, we want to generate believable fake copies of scientific charts for Cyber deception.

References

1. Adi, K., Widodo, C.E., Widodo, A.P., Gernowo, R., Pamungkas, A., Syifa, R.A.: Naïve bayes algorithm for lung cancer diagnosis using image processing techniques. Adv. Sci. Lett. **23**(3), 2296–2298 (2017)

2. Bilge, L., Dumitras, T.: Investigating zero-day attacks. Login **38**(4), 6–13 (2013)
3. Bishop, C.M.: Neural networks and their applications. Rev. Sci. Instrum. **65**(6), 1803–1832 (1994)
4. Breiman, L.: Random forests. Mach. Learn. **45**, 5–32 (2001)
5. Breiman, L., Friedman, J., Olshen, R., Stone, C.: Classification and Regression Trees. Wadsworth & Brooks. Cole Statistics/Probability Series (1984)
6. Clark, C.A., Divvala, S.K.: Looking beyond text: Extracting figures, Tables and Captions from Computer Science Papers. In: AAAI Workshop: Scholarly Big Data. vol. 6 (2015)
7. Cortes, C., Vapnik, V.: Support-vector networks. Mach. Learn. **20**, 273–297 (1995)
8. Deng, J., Dong, W., Socher, R., Li, L.J., Li, K., Fei-Fei, L.: ImageNet: A large-scale hierarchical image database. In: 2009 IEEE Conference on Computer Vision and Pattern Recognition, pp. 248–255. IEEE (2009)
9. Dong, Q., Zhu, X., Gong, S.: Single-label multi-class image classification by deep logistic regression. In: Proceedings of the AAAI Conference on Artificial Intelligence. vol. 33, pp. 3486–3493 (2019)
10. Han, Q., Molinaro, C., Picariello, A., Sperli, G., Subrahmanian, V.S., Xiong, Y.: Generating fake documents using probabilistic logic graphs. IEEE Trans. Dependable Secu. Comput. **19**(4), 2428–2441 (2021)
11. He, K., Zhang, X., Ren, S., Sun, J.: Deep residual learning for image recognition. In: Proceedings of the IEEE Conference on Computer Vision and Pattern Recognition, pp. 770–778 (2016)
12. He, K., Zhang, X., Ren, S., Sun, J.: Deep residual learning for image recognition. In: 2016 IEEE Conference on Computer Vision and Pattern Recognition (CVPR), pp. 770–778 (2016). https://doi.org/10.1109/CVPR.2016.90
13. Hinton, O., Hinton, G.E., Osindero, S., Teh, Y.-W.: A fast learning algorithm for deep belief nets. Neural Comput. **18**(7), 1527–1554 (2006)
14. Hu, Y., Lin, Y., Parolin, E.S., Khan, L., Hamlen, K.: Controllable fake document infilling for cyber deception (2022). arXiv preprint arXiv:2210.09917
15. Jobin, K., Mondal, A., Jawahar, C.: DocFigure: a dataset for scientific document figure classification. In: 2019 International Conference on Document Analysis and Recognition Workshops (ICDARW). vol. 1, pp. 74–79. IEEE (2019)
16. Karuna, P., Purohit, H., Ganesan, R., Jajodia, S.: Generating hard to comprehend fake documents for defensive cyber deception. IEEE Intell. Syst. **33**(5), 16–25 (2018)
17. Krizhevsky, A., Sutskever, I., Hinton, G.E.: ImageNet classification with deep convolutional neural networks. In: Advances in Neural Information Processing Systems, vol. 25 (2012)
18. Krizhevsky, A., Sutskever, I., Hinton, G.E.: ImageNet classification with deep convolutional neural networks. Commun. ACM **60**(6), 84–90 (2017)
19. Lee, S., Crawford, M.: Unsupervised multistage image classification using hierarchical clustering with a Bayesian similarity measure. IEEE Trans. Image Process. **14**(3), 312–320 (2005). https://doi.org/10.1109/TIP.2004.841195
20. Mascarenhas, S., Agarwal, M.: A comparison between VGG16, VGG19 and ResNet50 architecture frameworks for image classification. In: 2021 International Conference on Disruptive Technologies for Multi-Disciplinary Research and Applications (CENTCON). vol. 1, pp. 96–99. IEEE (2021)
21. Mukherjee, S.: The annotated ResNet-50. https://towardsdatascience.com/the-annotated-resnet-50-a6c536034758

22. Pastore, V.P., Ciranni, M., Bianco, S., Fung, J.C., Murino, V., Odone, F.: Efficient unsupervised learning of biological images with compressed deep features. Image Vis. Comput. **137**, 104764 (2023)
23. Prasad, V.S.N., Siddiquie, B., Golbeck, J., Davis, L.S.: Classifying computer generated charts. In: 2007 International Workshop on Content-based Multimedia Indexing, pp. 85–92. IEEE (2007)
24. Savva, M., Kong, N., Chhajta, A., Fei-Fei, L., Agrawala, M., Heer, J.: Revision: automated classification, analysis and redesign of chart images. In: Proceedings of the 24th Annual ACM Symposium on User Interface Software and Technology, pp. 393–402 (2011)
25. Siegel, N., Horvitz, Z., Levin, R., Divvala, S., Farhadi, A.: FigureSeer: parsing result-figures in research papers. In: Leibe, B., Matas, J., Sebe, N., Welling, M. (eds.) ECCV 2016. LNCS, vol. 9911, pp. 664–680. Springer, Cham (2016). https://doi.org/10.1007/978-3-319-46478-7_41
26. Sorokin, A., Forsyth, D.: Utility data annotation with amazon mechanical Turk. In: 2008 IEEE Computer Society Conference on Computer Vision and Pattern Recognition Workshops, pp. 1–8. IEEE (2008)
27. Tang, B., et al.: DeepChart: combining deep convolutional networks and deep belief networks in chart classification. Signal Process. **124**, 156–161 (2016)
28. Tio, A.E.: Face shape classification using inception v3 (2019). arXiv preprint arXiv:1911.07916
29. Zhang, L., Thing, V.L.: Three decades of deception techniques in active cyber defense-retrospect and outlook. Comput. Secur. **106**, 102288 (2021)
30. Zhou, Y., Tan, C.L.: Learning-based scientific chart recognition. In: 4th IAPR International Workshop on Graphics Recognition, GREC. vol. 7, pp. 482–492. Citeseer (2001)

Optimal Resource Allocation for Energy Harvested Cognitive Radio Networks Based on Learn Heuristic Algorithm

Parulpreet Singh[1] (✉) and Vikas Srivastava[1,2]

[1] School of Electronics and Electrical Engineering, Lovely Professional University, Phagwara 144411, Punjab, India
parulpreet.23367@lpu.co.in

[2] Department of Electronics and Communication Engineering, Axis Institute of Technology and Management, Kanpur, U.P, India

Abstract. In an Energy Harvested Cognitive Radio Networks (EH-CRN), Primary user (PU) and Secondary User (SU) networks share channel resources. Energy harvesting allows CRN nodes to receive energy from the atmosphere for sustainability. To achieve the best throughput and network capacity. In this paper, author address problems of delayed convergence and the need for huge state spaces in current deep Q-learning-based RA techniques. The RA in EH-CRN is enhanced by the suggested Support Vector Machine based Red Deer algorithm (SVM-RDA), which considers capacity, average latency, and transmission power restrictions. Simulation results suggest the proposed algorithm provides resource utilization and greater convergence than previous methods in the literature.

Keywords: Energy Harvesting · Metaheuristic Algorithm · Resource Allocation · Support Vector Machine · Red Deer Algorithm

1 Introduction

Applications for mobile terminal devices and wireless services have grown significantly recently. Mobile terminals are widely utilised in many industries today, including the military, healthcare, and transportation. Lack of resources causes spectrum scarcity in RF spectrum. This issue has been addressed in certain cases by maximising the current spectrum use. As a result of its potential, cognitive radio (CR) has been the subject of consistent study over the last two decades[1]. The prospect of exploiting the under-utilised spectrum resources is examined through CR research. The interaction of wireless networks with conventional CR technology creates a new field of study known as CRN. In CRN, secondary user (SU) may increase spectrum consumption by using opportunistic spectrum access technique[2]. Majority of CRN points are battery powered, as was mentioned in earlier study and the energy capacity of the node itself is the most practical challenge[3]. Because of this, it is crucial to think of ways to extend the network's lifespan without compromising its stability.

KC Santosh et al. (Eds.): RTIP2R 2023, CCIS 2027, pp. 341–354, 2024.
https://doi.org/10.1007/978-3-031-53085-2_27

Researchers have developed the EH technique to guarantee correct operation of these small power nodes[4]. EH continues to be one of the most extensively used and adaptable techniques used in cellular communication and wireless network settings[5, 6]. The environmental conditions vary widely, and energy conversion technology is currently not up to standards required[7]. In turn, it makes the newly developed EH technology much more susceptible to the effects of extreme unpredictability. To put things into perspective, the true challenge is properly using the captured energy.

Researchers have paid much attention to deep learning (DL) throughout the last decade[8]. Recently, the emphasis has been on using learning algorithms to enhance CRN performance. The architecture of the DL models and the techniques used to understand the underlying architectures make them innovative. The DL techniques have effectively solved additional CRN-related issues such signal categorization, spectrum prediction, and others[9, 10]. The traditional methodologies are typically impractical in the CRN domain because they often demand entire network information[11]. The resource allocation (RA) issue was investigated using a neural network (NN) [12, 13]. To acquire the output results, this trained result is used. it may be time-consuming and challenging to collect enough accurate data. Learnheuristic, a machine learning-based metaheuristic, is popular among academics for solving the challenges above as a viable solution to these problems. The previous knowledge of the system model and the environment conditions is not rigidly adhered in the learnheuristic method. Here used learnheuristic algorithm for resource allocation of energy harvested cognitive radio network.

Section 2 describe about related work. Section 3 discuss about system model. Section 4 give information about problem and solution. Section 5 discuss about SVM-RDA. Section 6 give information anout result and Sect. 7 give information about conclusion.

2 Related Work

2.1 Conventional Optimization-Based approaches

Relays selection, calculation of outage probabilities, resource allocation, and security improvement are the key topics of the present research literature on EH-CRN[17–19]. A differential game-based approach was created to handle the RA issue[20]. This method increases spectrum use throughout the transmission time while minimizing the total cost of the SUs' spectrum leasing. A strong optimization approach was implemented to improve the trade-off between transmitted and consumed power[21]. The convex issue was solved using an iterative approach under a distinct form of actual non-linear EH model. Authors presented a wirelessly powered method using a non-linear EH model [22]. Closed-form formulae are provided for optimum channel assignment and transmission power. According to authors, non-linear EH model's performance is equivalent to linear models. Authors established a novel non convex type RA issue for an EH based OFDMA. The jointly formulated optimization problem meets PU QoS requirements[23]. The recommended technique isn't ideal but works under suboptimal CSI settings. To enhance the functionality of multichannel CRN, authors suggested a simultaneous CSS and EH paradigm[24]. The established resource allocation issue optimises the combined throughput, collected energy, and energy effectiveness for SUs over all sub channels. Greedy algorithm is used by joint sub channel algorithm [25].

The power allocation issue was optimised using an iterative optimization technique. To achieve the sustainability and energy conversation of data sensors, the suggested RA strategy for heterogeneous CR sensor networks. Given technique uses two algorithms to perform their respective tasks: scheduling and resource allocation. The authors approach improves energy conversion while maintaining sensor's durability [26].Main goals were to optimise network speed, reduce energy usage, and meet QoS requirements. A low complexity solution approach addressed the newly proposed non-convex power allocation issue. According to authors, the suggested solution is less difficult to implement while still meeting QoS criteria. To increase system throughput, authors suggested a combined leasing time, sub channel and power allocation mechanism[27]. It is decided to use alternating optimization to resolve convex issue. SUs use PU resources and share them with the concerned access node. An EH protocol was designed to stop interference in the communication process. According to several recent research studies, joint type optimization issues are popular and often used in the CR research [28].

2.2 Deep Q-Learning Based Approaches

Goal was to maximize throughput. To do this, authors used a value iteration technique and framed sensing access design challenge as a partly observable Markov decision process issue.Q-learning-based solution for efficient RA in the EH-CRN was suggested by authors [29]. In their study, authors used deep Q-learning (DQL) to allocate resources in a solar-powered CRN environment effectively. The suggested technique was simpler in terms of space and state measurements [29].

2.3 Motivation

The above-discussed strategies mostly use Q-learning and standard optimization techniques. Traditional deep Q-learning is a tabular RL technique that works well in domains that works in domains without the curse of dimensionality [14]. EH technology is also unpredictably and inefficiently used. The literature presented above used several EH models to get the best results utilising traditional optimization methods. A machine learning-based metaheuristic resource allocation method is provided in the proposed study for linear and non-linear EH models, and it offers enhanced capacity performance and convergence.

2.4 Contribution and Organization

Investigating and identifying best solution for the suggested RA issue is this study's major goal. The goal is to reduce average latency and increase capacity of the EH-CRN system when there are numerous EH-SU. The authors also emphasized the algorithm's convergence. Since any learning.algorithm's convergence performance is crucial for the algorithm's adaption to various applications. In conclusion, the following are the primary contributions of the current work:

(1) RA issue is established for EH-CRN context. Here, inefficiency of conventional deep Q-learning method for large state-space systems is considered, and a learnheuristic approach is also suggested.
(2) A learnheuristic addresses the non-convex issue.
(3) Based on our literature study, the selected EH-CRN scenario has never used either the linear or nonlinear EH model.
(4) The suggested study considers a novel reward function that incorporates a nonlinear EH model, in contrast to earlier studies [29].
(5) General simulation results are given to compare recommended technique to others [29].

The remaining parts of article are organized as follows. Section 3 explain system model, energy harvesting model and problem formulation for the suggested approach. The machine learning-based RA algorithm is suggested and discussed in Sect. 4. In Sect. 5, we compare the proposed algorithm's performance to that of various existing techniques in the literature in terms of average delay and system capacity against a number of secondary users. The conclusion is found in Sect. 6.

3 System Model

3.1 Signal Model

Figure 1 depicts system model for case under consideration. In an uplink wireless network scenario, several PUs attempt to broadcast data to the base station (BS) within allotted time. However, many SU trans receivers use PU spectrum for intra-pair communication. In this study, author explore the CRN's underlay mode, where the SUs may effectively exploit the PUs' available spectrum as long as their disturbances do not exceed the interference temperature limit. Only the power allocation issue is taken into account in this article. An appropriate battery is included in the energy harvesting circuit to store the energy collected. Data transmission and energy harvesting are happening simultaneously during the whole transmission process. Specifically, there are M SU transmitter and receiver pairs and L PU transmitter and receiver pairs in the network, resulting in M cognitive linkages. It is self-evident that an SU's communication links will interfere with neighbouring SUs and PUs. PU will also interfere with another SUs, similarly.

3.2 Energy Harvested Model

Solar energy is considered a dependable and affordable substitute for wireless systems. Efficacy and extent of this resource rely on environmental and device conditions. Furthermore, energy harvesting is impossible at night and exceedingly difficult on rainy days. It is crucial to create a more effective system that can smartly use the available harvesting energy since these sources are unreliable. According to the accepted approach, each EH-SU transmitting node continually charges its battery with a solar cell (Fig. 2). However, the SU transmitters' data transfer also drains the battery. SU network aims to optimise throughput overall, while complying with battery energy restrictions.

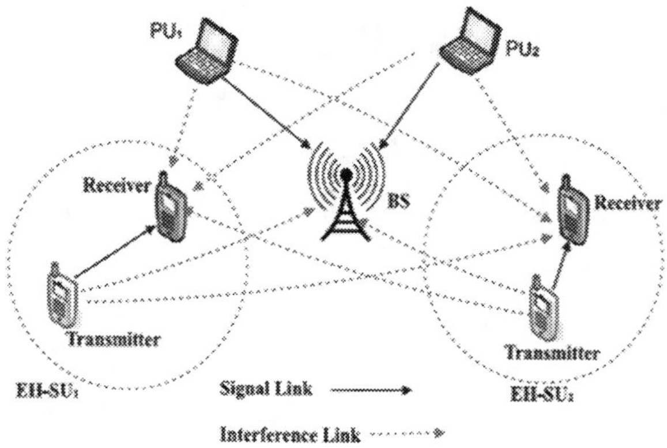

Fig. 1. System Model [29]

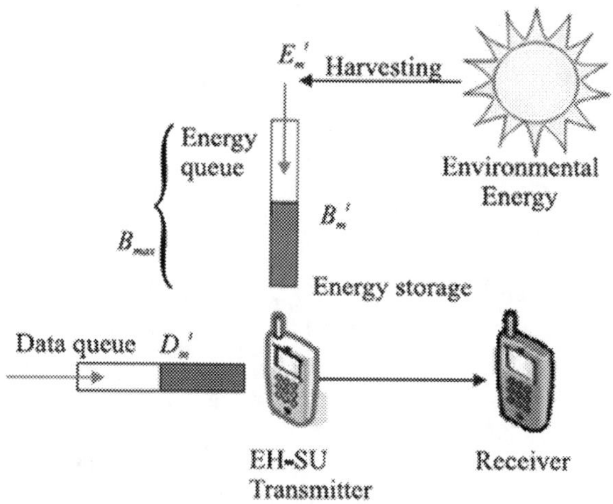

Fig. 2. Energy harvesting model [30]

4 Problem Statements and Solution

4.1 Problem Statements

Author considers the situation where L PU nodes are permitted to broadcast to BS. At time t, their relative power levels are S_l^t , l = 1……… L. Additionally, because PUs communicate in a time-multiplexed fashion, they are presumed to not interfere with one another. In underlay mode, the SU network interferes with any transmissions made by EHSU nodes on the PU network. It is necessary to manage the total SU transmit power at time t to be within the acceptable limit of Imax at BS. However, the SU network aims to increase its overall throughput at the expense of battery depletion and interference with the PU network. The following optimization problem may be used to illustrate the trade-off between network resources and the overall throughput of SUs:

$$\overbrace{P_m^t}^{max} \sum_{m=1}^{M} R_{SU}^t(m) \tag{1a}$$

$$s.t.\ 0 \le P_m^t \le \min\left(B_m^t, P_{max}\right)\ fort = 1, \ldots\ldots\ldots, T, m = 1, \ldots\ldots M \tag{1b}$$

$$R_{SU}^t(m) \ge R_{SU}^{th}, form = 1, \ldots\ldots\ldots\ldots M \tag{1c}$$

$$R_{PU}^t(l) \ge R_{PU}^{th}, forl0 = 1, \ldots\ldots\ldots\ldots L \tag{1d}$$

$$\sum_{t=1}^{T} P_m^t \le \sum_{t=1}^{T} E_m^t \tag{1e}$$

$$\sum_{m=1}^{M} P_m^t |h_{mb}|^2 \le l_{max} \tag{1f}$$

$$\sum_{m=1}^{M} P_m^t |h_{mb}|^2 \le l_{max} \tag{1g}$$

The P_m^t is transmitted power of mth SU at time t, $R_{SU}^t(m)$ is channel capacity of secondary link in time t, B_m^t is transmitted energy in time slot t, P_{max} is system maximum power of EH-SU transmitter, R_{SU}^{th} is threshold channel capacity at secondary link, $R_{PU}^t(l)$ is channel capacity at main link in time t, R_{PU}^{th} is threshold channel capacity at main link, E_m^t is collected energy for mth EH-SU at time slot t, h_{mb} is channel gain to BS from mth SU, D_m^t is transmission data at time slot t, $R_{SU}^{t-1}(m)$ is channel capacity of secondary link in the beginning of time t and D_{max} is maximum data buffer for system.

The limitation provided by (1b) defines the upper bound on the EH-SUs's transmit power, which is determined by battery's existing energy and hardware's maximum transmit capacity. The allowable minimum data transmission speeds for EH-SUs and PUs are specified in constraints (1c) and (1d), respectively. The collected power in time period T cannot be more than the total transmitted power by an EH-SU, according to constraint (1e). According to Eq. (1f), the total interference signal strength at BS caused by SUs cannot be more than Imax at any time t.

4.2 Proposed Solution

Maximizing SU network's sum-throughput is required by problem given in 1(a)–1(g), it is necessary to calculate several different channel capacities. Despite their efficacy, these strategies struggle to function in real-world situations and when there is no previous knowledge of the environment. The lack of understanding of the distribution of collected energy is one example of such a problem. Applying a machine learning-based metaheuristic approach to this issue is an alternate way where the agent may arrive at the best policy via a rigorous trial-and-error learning process. X. He, H. Jiang, Y. Song, Y. Luo, and Q. Y. Zhang defined this optimization issue as an MDP problem and used the Q-learning approach to optimise the system's long-term throughput. Working in a large state-space system is tough. This paper suggests a machine learning-based metaheuristic-based method for this situation in order to enhance performance and effectively manage resources. A deep neural network may be used in DQL to effectively attain the Q-value for each activity (DNN). Optimization problem of (1a)–(1g) is reformed as MDP problem in discussions that follow.

5 Proposed Algorithm

5.1 Red Deer Algorithm

A population-based metaheuristic method is red deer algorithm.[30] The two categories of optimization techniques are mathematical programming and metaheuristic algorithms. The two primary kinds of metaheuristic algorithms now in use are the evolutionary and swarm algorithms. The RDA starts with a random population rather than representative of RDs. The strongest RD in the group is designated as "male RD," while anothers are referred to as "hinds." However, RD male will roar first. Depending on intensity of the roaring process, they are split into two types (i.e., stags and commanders). As a result, the stag and commanders of each harem battle it out for dominance. Harems are always created by commanders. The roaring and combat skills of the commanders are inversely correlated with the number of hinds in harems. Because of this, commanders in harems mate with a lot of hinds.

5.2 Support Vector Machine

The SVM is the best classifier with a linear decision boundary. Kernel functions are used when there are non-linear functions. Support vector machines can process a comparatively many characteristics without excessive computing. A classifier is required to optimise the separation between the distance surface and point in the SVM. The margin is the separation between negative surface points nearest the decision plane. Therefore, a training instance's minimal distance from the decision surface represents margin. This is an assumption that a linear decision point can linearly separate positive and negative points. The support vector comprises the points closest to the decision surface.

5.3 Proposed Algorithm: Support Vector Machine-Red Deer Algorithm (SVM-RDA)

Flowchart of resource allocation technique using Support Vector Machine (SVM) based Red Deer Optimization (RDO) Algorithm is bellowed (Fig. 3):

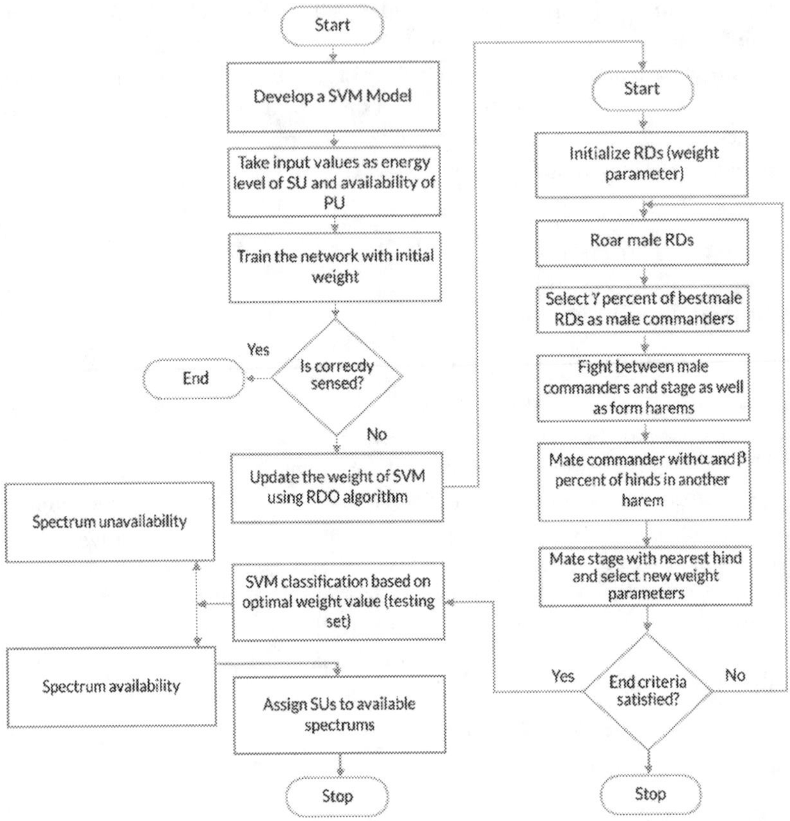

Fig. 3. Flowchart of SVM-RDA

6 Simulation Results

The performance of offered algorithm is compared to other well-known systems. MATLAB is used on computer with an Intel Xeon W-2133 processor, RAM 32 GB and frequency at 3.6 GHz to experiment with the suggested scenario (RAM). Total network coverage is 50 m × 50 m. The scenario has 2 PUs, 6 SUs, and 1 BS. Table 1 includes a list of additional simulation variables. It is assumed that distribution of SU, PU and BS are random. For simulation, Channel State Interference is assumed to be perfect, and channel between SU and PU is Rayleigh distributed flat fading. Capacity (bits/s/Hz), Number of EH-SUs, Average Delay (ms), and Transmit Power (dBm) are our four primary parameters. Here, capacity and average delay are analyzed using the number of EH-SU, and transmit power and capacity are analyzed using MATLAB simulation data.

Capacity values are shown against various EH-SU numbers in Fig. 4. Additionally, the effectiveness of the suggested strategy is evaluated in comparison to a number of other methodologies, including the Deep Q Learning reinforcement algorithm (DQLRA), Q-learning scheme, energy harvesting resource allocation (EHRA) and waterfall-based power allocation (WFPA),stochastic adaptive random sampling algorithm (SARSA), and random initialization. The Fig. 4 clearly shows that the network's total capacity rises with number of EH-SUs whereas the suggested system achieves the maximum capacity. Action spaces and discrete state and are necessary for next two competing techniques, DQLRA and SARSA, which are table-based reinforcement learning methods.

The recommended approach converges more than SARSA and DQLRA. Compared to non-reinforcement learning techniques, capacity performance is far worse. Since current algorithms only consider the immediate capacity value for optimization and do not consider environment's dynamic nature, the suggested approach performs better. The suggested SVM-RDA outperforms all baseline schemes.

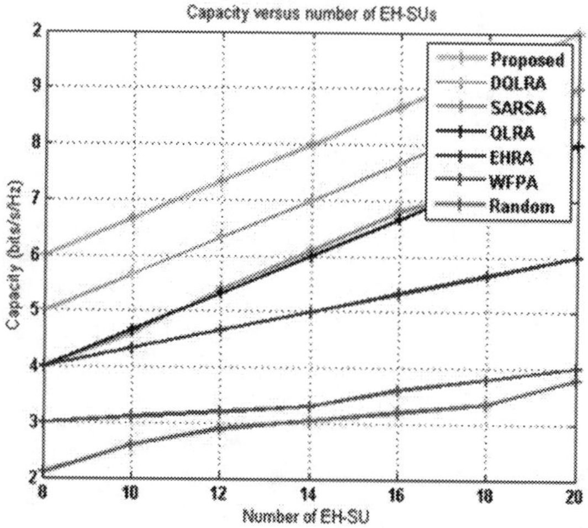

Fig. 4. Capacity versus number of EH-Sus

The average delay performance against a range of EH-SU numbers is shown in Fig. 5. The graphic shows that the proposed technique minimizes average delay. The proposed technique gets better results because it achieves greater convergence. The learning process might find the optimum policy faster than another algorithm. As a result, the learning agent (the SU coordinator) may better use the available energy to speed up data transmission over the network. This is particularly true for methods that combine random policy with traditional optimization. The suggested SVM-RDA outperforms all baseline schemes.

Here looked into capacity under various transmit power settings, and results are shown in Fig. 6. The outcomes of several algorithms are shown. Range of transmit power is 3 dBm to 0.5 dBm. It can be shown that, for all designs into consideration, capacity of system rises linearly as transmission power value rises. Linear growth is due to proposed work's use of a linear EH model to measure performance. The suggested SVM-RDA outperforms all baseline schemes. Regarding capacity values, next-best performers SARSA and DQLRA outperform QLRA, EHRA, WFPA, and random initialization methods.

1. It is important to note that instability may occur from SU nodes' random distribution.

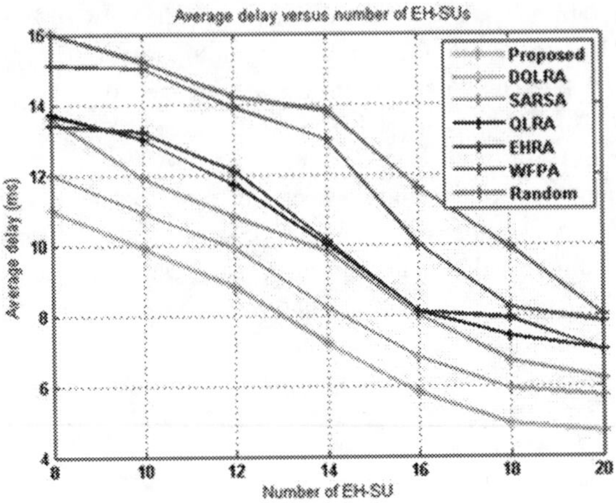

Fig. 5. Average delay vs. Number of EH-SU

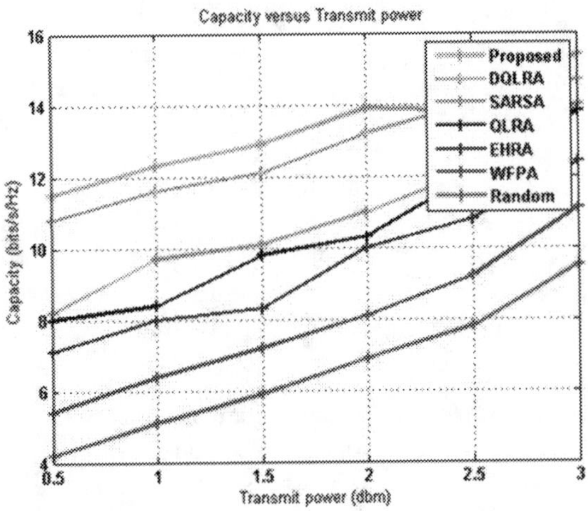

Fig. 6. Capacity vs transmit power

2. Despite the non-linear EH model's higher compensation potential, the linear model is the most profitable. Since the circuit parameters are not linear, the linear EH model may not apply to modeling the energy harvester. Future research should focus on this topic. The authors of the current work have presented comparable results from the non-linear and linear EH models. This research will provide as a foundation for future research, and the authors want to expand on it to include non-linear EH models.

From Table 1, the suggested method offers gains in capacity value of 12.52%, 61.83%, 23.65%, 58.7%, 37.5% and 25.03%, as compared to DQLRA, random initialization schemes, SARSA, WFPA, EHRA and Q-learning respectively, at number of EH-SU = 14.

Table 1. Comparison Table of Numberof EH-SU vs. Capacity

Number of EH-SU	Capacity (bit/s/Hz)						
	Random	WFPA	EHRA	QLRA	SARSA	DQLRA	Propopsed
8	2.1	3	4	4	4	5	6
10	2.6	3.1	4.33	4.66	4.6	5.66	6.66
12	2.9	3.2	4.66	5.33	5.4	6.33	7.33
14	3.05	3.3	4.99	5.99	6.1	6.99	7.99
16	3.2	3.6	5.33	6.66	6.8	7.66	8.66
18	3.35	3.8	5.66	7.33	7.2	8.33	9.33
20	3.8	4	6	8	8.5	9	10

From Table 2, the suggested technique delays computation by 13.89%, 38.89%, 12.5%, 80.55, 36.11, and 92% less than the DQLRA, random initialization schemes, SARSA, WFPA, EHRA and Q-learning respectively, at number of EH-SU = 14.

Table 2. Comparison Table of Numberof EH-SU vs. Average Delay

Number of EH-SU	Average Delay (ms)						
	Random	WFPA	EHRA	QLRA	SARSA	DQLRA	Propopsed
8	16	15.1	13.4	13.7	13.6	12	11
10	15.2	15	13.2	13	11.9	10.9	9.9
12	14.2	13.9	12.1	11.7	10.8	9.9	8.8
14	13.8	13	10.1	10	9.8	8.2	7.2
16	11.6	10	8.1	8.1	8	6.8	5.8
18	9.9	8.2	7.9	7.4	6.7	5.9	4.9
20	8	7.8	7	7	6.2	5.7	4.7

From Table 3, the proposed scheme offers gains in capacity of 5.07%, 25.9%, 41.73%, 28.05%, 20.86, and 50.35% over the DQLRA, Q-learning, WFPA, EHRA, SARSA, and random initialization schemes, respectively, at transmitting power values of 2 dBm.

Table 3. Comparison Table of transmit power vs. capacity

Transmit Power (dBm)	Capacity (bits/s/Hz)						
	Random	WFPA	EHRA	QLRA	SARSA	DQLRA	Propopsed
0.5	4.2	5.4	7.1	8	8.2	10.8	11.5
1	5.1	6.4	8	8.4	9.7	11.6	12.3
1.5	5.9	7.2	8.3	9.8	10.1	12.1	12.9
2	6.9	8.1	10	10.3	11	13.2	13.9
2.5	7.8	9.2	10.8	12	12.1	14	13.8
3	9.5	11.1	12.4	13.8	14	14.7	15.4

7 Conclusion

For an EH-CRN running in underlay mode, a machine learning-based metaheuristic algorithm was developed in this study as an intelligent resource allocation system. SVM-RDA was used to solve this dynamic optimization issue by reformulating the RA issue as MDP. SVM-RDA provides for faster convergence in large state space systems. Comparing the performance of suggested algorithm to several current algorithms shows that it is better.

References

1. Srivastava, V., Singh, P.: Review of full -duplex cognitive radio network based on energy harvesting. Lect. Notes Netw. Syst. **376**, 587–598 (2022)
2. Naparstek, O., Cohen, K.: Deep multi-user reinforcement learning for distributed dynamic spectrum access. IEEE Trans. Wirel. Commun. **18**(1), 310–323 (2018)
3. Srivastava, V., Singh, P., Srivastava, P.: Advancement of full- duplex cognitive radio network: a review. J. Phys: Conf. Ser. **2327**, 1–8 (2022)
4. Ku, M., Li, W., Chen, Y., Liu, K.J.R.: Advances in energy harvesting communications: past, present, and future challenges. IEEE Commun. Surv. Tutor. **18**(2), 1384–1412 (2016)
5. Srivastava, V., Singh, P.: Review of Resource allocation for energy- Harvesting cognitive radio network. J. East China Univ. Sci. Technol. **65**(4), 20–30 (2022)
6. Jang, W.M.: Simultaneous power harvesting and cyclostationary spectrum sensing in cognitive radios. IEEE Access **8**, 56333–56345 (2020)
7. Sakr, A.H., Hossain, E.: Cognitive and energy harvesting-based D2D communication in cellular networks: stochastic geometry modeling and analysis. IEEE Trans. Commun. **63**(5), 1867–1880 (2015)
8. Alpaydin, E.: Introduction to Machine Learning, 4th edn. MIT Press, Cambridge (2020)
9. Giri, M.K., Majumder, S.: On eigenvalue-based cooperative spectrum sensing using feature extraction and maximum entropy fuzzy clustering. J. Ambient Intell. Humaniz. Comput. **2022**, 1–15 (2022)
10. Supraja, P., Gayathri, V.M., Pitchai, R.: Optimized neural network for spectrum prediction using genetic algorithm in cognitive radio networks. Clust. Comput. **22**, 157–163 (2019)
11. Yang, H., Alphones, A., Xiong, Z., Niyato, D., Zhao, J., Wu, K.: Artificial-intelligence-enabled intelligent 6G networks. IEEE Netw. **34**(6), 272–280 (2020)

12. Gui, G., Huang, H., Song, Y., Sari, H.: Deep learning for an effective nonorthogonal multiple access scheme. IEEE Trans. Veh. Technol. **67**(9), 8440–8450 (2018)
13. Liu, M., Song, T., Gui, G.: Deep cognitive perspective: resource allocation for NOMA-based heterogeneous IoT with imperfect SIC. IEEE Internet Things J. **6**(2), 2885–2894 (2018)
14. Hernandez-Leal, P., Kartal, B., Taylor, M.E.: A survey and critique of multiagent deep reinforcement learning. Auton. Agent Multi Agent Syst. **33**(6), 750–797 (2019)
15. Yang, H., Xiong, Z., Zhao, J., Niyato, D., Xiao, L., Wu, Q.: Deep reinforcement learning-based intelligent reflecting surface for secure wireless communications. IEEE Trans. Wirel. Commun. **20**(1), 375–388 (2020)
16. Li, Z., Xu, M., Nie, J., Kang, J., Chen, W., Xie, S.: NOMA-enabled cooperative computation offloading for blockchain-empowered Internet of Things: a learning approach. IEEE Internet Things J. **8**(4), 2364–2378 (2020)
17. Ghosh, S., Acharya, T., Maity, S.P.: On outage minimization in RF energy harvesting relay assisted bidirectional communication. Wirel. Netw. **25**(7), 3867–3881 (2019)
18. Paul, A., Banerjee, A., Maity, S.P.: Residual energy maximization in cognitive radio networks with Q-routing. IEEE Syst. J. **14**(3), 3791–3800 (2019)
19. Bhowmick, A., Das, G.C., Roy, S.D., Kundu, S., Maity, S.P.: Allocation of optimal energy in an energy-harvesting cooperative multi-band cognitive radio network. Wirel. Netw. **26**(2), 1033–1043 (2020)
20. Xu, H., Gao, H., Zhou, C., Duan, R., Zhou, X.: Resource allocation in cognitive radio wireless sensor networks with energy harvesting. Sensors **19**(23), 5115 (2019)
21. Zhang, X., Wang, Y., Zhou, F., Al-Dhahir, N., Deng, X.: Robust resource allocation for MISO cognitive radio networks under two practical non-linear energy harvesting models. IEEE Commun. Lett. **22**(9), 1874–1877 (2018)
22. Wang, Y., Wang, Y., Zhou, F., Wu, Y., Zhou, H.: Resource allocation in wireless powered cognitive radio networks based on a practical non-linear energy harvesting model. IEEE Access **5**, 17618–17626 (2017)
23. Wang, F., Zhang, X.: Resource allocation for multiuser cooperative overlay cognitive radio networks with RF energy harvesting capability. In: IEEE Global Communications Conference, GLOBECOM, pp. 1–6. IEEE (2016)
24. Das, D., Das, S.: Optimal resource allocation for soft decision fusion-based cooperative spectrum sensing in cognitive radio networks. Elsevier Comput. Electr. Eng. **52**, 362–378 (2016)
25. Xu, C., Song, C., Zeng, P., Yu, H.: Secure resource allocation for energy harvesting cognitive radio sensor networks without and with cooperative jamming. Comput. Netw. **141**, 189–198 (2018)
26. Baidas, M.W., Amini, M.R.: Resource allocation for NOMA-based multicast cognitive radio networks with energy-harvesting relays. Phys. Commun. **42**, 101–166 (2020)
27. Liu, Z., Zhao, M., Yuan, Y., Guan, X.: Subchannel and resource allocation in cognitive radio sensor network with wireless energy harvesting. Comput. Netw. **167**, 107028 (2020)
28. He, X., Jiang, H., Song, Y., Luo, Y., Zhang, Q.Y.: Joint optimization of channel allocation and power control for cognitive radio networks with multiple constraints. Wirel. Netw. **26**(1), 101–120 (2020)
29. Giang, H.T.H., Thanh, P.D., Koo, I.: Deep Q-learning-based resource allocation for solar-powered users in cognitive radio networks. ICT Express **7**(1), 49–59 (2021)
30. Srivastava, V., Bala, I.: A novel support vector machine-red deer optimization algorithm for enhancing energy efficiency of spectrum sensing in cognitive radio network. Lect. Notes Netw. Syst. **339**, 35–55 (2022)

31. Srivastava, V., Singh, P., Mahajan, S., et al.: Performance enhancement in clustering cooperative spectrum sensing for cognitive radio network using metaheuristic algorithm. Sci. Rep. **13**, 16827 (2023). https://doi.org/10.1038/s41598-023-44032-7
32. Srivastava, V., et al.: Innovative spectrum handoff process using a machine learning-based metaheuristic algorithm. Sensors **2023**, 23 (2011). https://doi.org/10.3390/s23042011

Blockchain for Patient Data Integrity: Decentralised Storage and Retrieval in Modern Healthcare Systems

Deepak Kumar Sharma(✉) and Adarsh Kumar

School of Computer Science, University of Petroleum and Energy Studies, Dehradun 248007, India

deepaksh2007@gmail.com, adarsh.kumar@ddn.upes.ac.in

Abstract. The research introduces a data sharing and retrieval method within the blockchain framework tailored for smart healthcare systems. This method addresses key challenges in data management, security, and accessibility. Two main components are presented: a distributed, parallel data-sharing scheme and an innovative data retrieval algorithm using the Merkle-Patricia Trie (MPT) and Bloom filters. The proposed healthcare blockchain system showcased improved performance metrics with notable efficiency in upload and download times, latency, delay, and response times. This adaptable approach promises enhanced patient care, medical research, and data analytics, emphasising effective, secure, and patient-centric healthcare data management.

Keywords: Blockchain · Data sharing · Data retrieval · Distributed ledger technology · Parallel processing · Merkle-Patricia Trie · Bloom filters and Privacy-preserving

1 Introduction

Information technology advancements and the rising demand for individualised, data-centric care are driving a digital revolution in the healthcare sector [1]. This has led to an unprecedented surge in healthcare information, including electronic health records (EHRs), medical images, wearable device data, and sensor data [2]. However, managing, securely sharing, and retrieving this data remains a challenge [3].

Traditional centralised data storage and management systems pose numerous risks, such as a single point of failure, data silos, and potential privacy breaches [3]. Blockchain technology offers a promising solution with its decentralised architecture and immutable, transparent, and trustworthy data-sharing capabilities [4]. In the context of smart healthcare, an efficient data exchange and retrieval system on the blockchain is essential [5]. Rapid access to comprehensive and accurate patient data can significantly impact clinical decision-making, treatment outcomes, and medical research [6].

This study proposes a comprehensive approach to addressing two primary objectives:

KC Santosh et al. (Eds.): RTIP2R 2023, CCIS 2027, pp. 355–368, 2024.
https://doi.org/10.1007/978-3-031-53085-2_28

- Developing an innovative data-sharing system that harnesses the parallel and distributed computing capabilities of the blockchain network; and
- Proposing a robust data retrieval algorithm that locates specific healthcare data on the blockchain quickly and precisely.

We intend to leverage sharding and parallel processing to enhance data availability, sharing efficiency, and transaction speeds. Additionally, we will explore privacy-preserving techniques to ensure that sensitive healthcare data remains secure and accessible only to authorised parties.

Our proposed data-sharing and retrieval framework aims to transform smart healthcare systems, streamline data exchange, expedite medical research, and enhance patient care. The subsequent sections of this paper explain the literature review, methodology, experimental setup, results, and discussions, offering a thorough evaluation of the approach's effectiveness and its prospects for real-world deployment.

2 Literature Review

In recent years, there has been a surge in research exploring the integration of blockchain technology in healthcare. Several studies have aimed to harness the potential of blockchain to revolutionise the management and sharing of healthcare data. This section provides an overview of the key findings and contributions from various researchers in this field.

Zonyin and Jeffry [7] transformed blockchain's duplicated computing into a distributed parallel computing architecture via smart contract modifications. Such a transformation facilitates the creation of vast medical datasets from distributed hosted medical sets, aiding deep learning research. The focus lies on distributed data management, sharing, and learning. Moreover, the study implements Google federated learning and transfer learning algorithms, highlighting the generation of real-world evidence for clinical trials in personalised medicine.

To enable secure and effective health record transactions using blockchain, Azath et al. [8] developed a novel SEHRTB algorithm. The algorithm permits patient-controlled sharing of health records in a manner that preserves privacy. A decentralised computing system is utilised for trusted third-party computation. Compared to existing methodologies, this approach shows reduced latency and execution time and improved throughput.

The research by Jayasudha and Vijayalakshmi [9] introduced DDSA combined with the MPHT algorithm for secure medical record sharing via blockchain. The emphasis is on ensuring data privacy, security, and lightweight access control. The study demonstrated superior network latency, reduced transmission delay, and a lower file loss rate than contemporary methods.

Tong et al. [10] introduced the Med-PPPHIS model, which uses both permissionless and permission blockchains to manage personal health data. The study utilises Med-DLattice with a DAG structure and the DPoS-Quorum algorithm for consensus. This model ensures secure data circulation and privacy protection. A prototype was applied to chronic disease management, illustrating low latency, high throughput, and robust resistance to attacks.

Pingcheng et al. [11] identified the need for provenance support in blockchain applications, introducing the Lineage Chain—a secure and efficient provenance system for blockchains. It offers lineage information for smart contracts, captures provenance during execution, and supports efficient queries. The implementation on Fabric showcases high query performance and minimal storage overhead.

Sun et al. [12] present a method to secure blockchain-based electronic medical records using Attribute-Based encryption (ABE) and the Inter Planetary File System (IPFS). The approach ensures that data is original and traceable and addresses the security vulnerabilities of central authorities. Performance evaluations and real-data simulations have attested to the system's viability, including addressing issues related to authorised access, expired users, and blockchain data.

Shanthapriya and Vaithianathan, in their research [13], forecast a blockchain-based data security mechanism with designated user and physician blocks. The mechanism is designed to safeguard clinical health records. Advanced Encryption Standard (AES) encryption is employed to perform cryptographic functions, which are then added to the blockchain using hash keys. Additionally, a forecasting framework using a deep learning algorithm is proposed. The results indicate superior cybersecurity capabilities compared to traditional methods.

Batchu et al. [14] developed smart contracts containing various patient-related data, including identification and chemotherapy medication details. Image files, stored in IPFS, each have a unique content identification hash incorporated into the smart contracts. Tests on a proof-of-authority-based private network recorded 889 megabytes per insertion and 910 megabytes per retrieval, with access to 350 patient records completed in 907 ms.

Bader et al. [15] introduced PrivAccChain, a secure architecture that enhances multi-hop information retrieval while ensuring stakeholder accountability in supply chain operations. It integrates varying degrees of openness and data confidentiality to meet specific user demands. Consequently, even in supply chains where parties may not trust each other, users can benefit from multi-hop monitoring and tracking.

Table 1 provides an overview of the literature reviewed, summarising each study's objectives, techniques, and potential drawbacks or challenges.

Table 1. Literature review overview.

Author name	Objective	Techniques	Drawbacks
Zonyin and Jeffry [7]	Standardised data sharing to support real-world evidence clinical trials in personal and precision medicine	Blockchain smart contract mechanisms for real-time data sharing	Lack of common data formats and real-time data sharing standards
Azath et al. [8]	Empowering patients to easily, securely, and privately control and share their health records in the cloud	Secure and efficient health record transactions using the SEHRTB algorithm	Challenges in maintaining access control

(continued)

Table 1. (*continued*)

Author name	Objective	Techniques	Drawbacks
Jayasudha and Vijayalakshmi [9]	A blockchain-based EHR sharing platform to expedite secure medical record exchange between surgeons and patients from diverse backgrounds	Secure medical record sharing	Struggles with the increasing volume of global medical records and faces complex application issues
Tong et al. [10]	Ensuring the protection of personal health information and establishing a connected security mechanism for medical data	Utilizes permissionless and permissioned blockchains, specifically Med-DLattice	Difficulties in medical data sharing due to data fragmentation and ineffective sharing methods
Pingcheng et al. [11]	Develops a new class of blockchain applications dependent on runtime provenance data	Implements a secure and efficient provenance system for blockchains	Suitable for large-scale offline analysis but not ideal for online transaction processing
Sun et al. [12]	Efficiently restricts access to electronic medical records using encryption with ciphertext policy properties	Employs a blockchain-based secure storage and access scheme for electronic medical records in IPFS	Addresses integrity and security concerns related to electronic medical data
Shanthapriya and Vaithianathan [13]	Utilizes a prediction model and deep learning algorithm to determine patients' ailments	Implements a blockchain-based data security technique	Faces challenges in achieving complete robustness and involves high computational demands
Batchu et al. [14]	Efficiently stores image files using the InterPlanetary File System (IPFS) and records content identification hashes in smart contracts	Leveraging Ethereum blockchain and smart contracts for image file storage	The cost of storing image files on Ethereum is a consideration
Bader et al. [15]	Focuses on optimizing multi-hop information retrieval with stakeholder accountability and privacy protection	Implements blockchain-based privacy preservation mechanisms for supply chains	Issues related to trust among different involved stakeholders

3 Proposed Methodology

In this study, we delineate two primary objectives: optimise data management and accessibility within the blockchain network.

Our initial focus is on the formulation of a data sharing scheme that exploits distributed and parallel computing capabilities. By harnessing these advanced techniques, we anticipate significant enhancements in data-sharing efficiency, increased data availability, and accelerated transaction speeds. This proposed framework integrates advanced consensus mechanisms, strategic sharding methodologies, and cutting-edge parallel processing algorithms. Through this integrative approach, we aim to optimise data distribution and dissemination across the blockchain network. Additionally, a pivotal component of our investigation encompasses privacy preservation to ensure that sensitive healthcare data is securely maintained, granting access solely to authorised entities.

Subsequently, we pivot towards the development of a robust data retrieval algorithm tailored for swift and precise access to specific healthcare information on the blockchain. With rapidly increasing data volume on the network, efficient data retrieval is crucial. This objective will entail the exploration of methods including, but not limited to, advanced indexing techniques, caching strategies, and refined search algorithms. Such a comprehensive approach will expedite the retrieval of pertinent patient records, medical documentation, and research data. Concurrently, our methodology addresses data privacy during retrieval, integrating stringent access control mechanisms to uphold patient confidentiality.

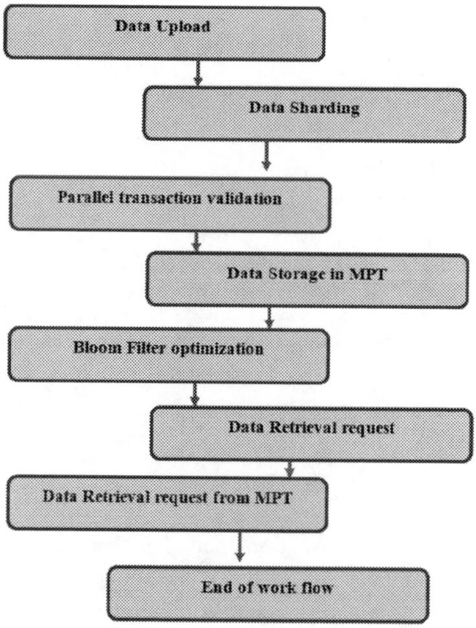

Fig. 1. Proposed Workflow

In pursuit of these objectives, we endeavour to redefine data management paradigms within the blockchain infrastructure, promoting enhanced efficiency and security in healthcare applications. The culmination of this research is the design of the'sHealthCareBlockchain' framework, as depicted in Fig. 1, with its detailed mechanics discussed in subsequent sections.

3.1 Proposed Data Sharing Scheme Using Distributed and Parallel Approach

The research introduces a novel data sharing scheme in the blockchain for smart healthcare, leveraging a unique combination of distributed and parallel computing techniques. The proposed approach aims to optimise data sharing efficiency, scalability, and security while accommodating the unique requirements of healthcare data management. The new approach improves data accessibility, speeds up transactions, and promotes a smooth and safe data sharing environment for smart healthcare applications by utilising both distributed and parallel computing within the blockchain network.

Dynamic Sharding Algorithm

This paper proposes an adaptable and novel dynamic sharding technique for a blockchain-based intelligent healthcare system. This method improves data sharing, scalability, and load balancing by dynamically adjusting the number of shards and their composition to changing network conditions and data distribution. Unlike other algorithms, this one can rapidly adapt to changes in network traffic, transaction volumes, and processing resources. This ensures optimal network performance and data accessibility for the intelligent healthcare blockchain.

Adaptive Dynamic Sharding Algorithm

The adaptive dynamic sharding technique adjusts the number of shards based on variables such as network size, transaction volume, and computational resources. Consider the following:

- *N*: Nodes in the blockchain network as a whole.
- *T*: Total volume of network transactions.
- *S*: Number of Shards
- *S_min*: Shard count that must be met for the system.
- *S_max*: The most shards that can be present in the system.

The following equation illustrates how the adaptive dynamic sharding algorithm works:

$$Shard\_Size = N/S \tag{1}$$

$$Transaction\_Per\_Shard = T/S \tag{2}$$

We take into account the transaction load per shard and track its variation to dynamically modify the number of shards. If the transaction load per shard, *Transaction_Per_Shard*, exceeds a predefined threshold, *Transaction_Threshold*, we increase the number of shards to reduce the load on each shard and improve data sharing efficiency:

$$\begin{gathered} if\ Transaction\_Per\_Shard > Transaction\_Threshold: \\ S = \min(S\_\max, S * 2) \end{gathered} \tag{3}$$

On the other hand, if the transaction load per shard drops below another predefined threshold, *Empty_Shard_Threshold*, we decrease the number of shards to consolidate data and optimise resource utilization:

$$\begin{aligned} &if\ Transaction\_Per\_Shard < Empty\_Shard\_Threshold: \\ &\quad S = \max(S\_\min, S/2) \end{aligned} \quad (4)$$

By continually monitoring the transaction load and dynamically adjusting the number of shards, the adaptive dynamic sharding algorithm ensures that the smart healthcare blockchain network remains scalable and responsive to changing demands.

Load Balancing Mechanism

To address load imbalance among shards, the algorithm employs a load balancing mechanism. To uniformly share the workload of transaction processing, this technique redistributes transactions among shards. Let:

- *Shard_Transaction_Counts*: A list of transaction counts for each Shard

The following is a representation of the load balancing mechanism:

$$Calculate\_Average\_Transaction = sum\,(Shard\_Transaction\_Counts)/S \quad (5)$$

for each shard in *Shard_Transaction_Counts*:

$$\begin{aligned} &if\ Shard\_Transaction\_Counts\,[shard] > Calculate\_Average\_Transaction: \\ &\qquad Perform\,Load\ balancing \end{aligned} \quad (6)$$

Load Balance Factor

Redistribute transactions initially from (shard) to additional under loaded shards. The Load_Balance_Factor is a parameter that establishes how much redistribution of transactions is required for balancing. The technique makes sure that there is an equitable load distribution and reduces processing bottlenecks by periodically reviewing the transaction counts in each shard and redistributing transactions as necessary.

A highly flexible, scalable, and effective data sharing strategy for the blockchain for smart healthcare is produced by combining the adaptive dynamic sharding algorithm with the load balancing mechanism. This algorithm's dynamic nature enables the network to adjust to shifting circumstances and transaction volumes, resulting in increased performance for patients, researchers, and healthcare professionals as well as optimal data sharing efficiency.

Parallel Transaction Validation

This study proposes a novel approach for parallel transaction validation in blockchain-based smart healthcare systems, utilising the Heinit method. This would enhance the efficiency of data sharing. The Heinit criterion refers to a mathematical approach utilised in the optimisation of parallel tasks. This method employs the utilisation of processing units to dynamically allocate resources for transaction validation. The utilisation of the Heinit criterion allows for the efficient distribution of transaction workloads among the available processing units. This facilitates the acceleration and equitable distribution of transaction validation. The implementation of this novel approach enhances the overall performance of the intelligent healthcare blockchain network and augments the utility of data sharing.

Heinit Criterion for Load Balancing

By distributing the workload across the available processing units, the *Heinit_Criterion* is a mathematical formula for optimising parallel processing workloads. Let:

- W: Each transaction's workload, expressed in computing units.
- N: total volume of transactions that need to be verified.
- P: How many processor units are dedicated to parallel validation.

The following is a representation of the load balancing Heinit criterion:

$$Heinit\_Criterion = \sum (W_i)/P \tag{7}$$

where $\sum(W_i)$indicates the total work done by all transactions.

To ensure the most effective parallel transaction validation, it establishes the appropriate workload distribution across processing units. By dynamically distributing transactions to processing units so that the workload is evenly distributed, the algorithm seeks to minimise the value.

Heinit-based Parallel Transaction Validation

The Heinit-based parallel transaction validation technique utilises the Heinit_Criterion to dynamically allocate transactions to available processing units. Let:

- Transactions: List of incoming transactions.
- P: Number of processing units allocated for parallel validation.

The Heinit-based parallel transaction validation technique can be represented as follows:

Step 1: Calculate the workload of each transaction, W_i, in the Transactions list.
Step 2: Calculate the Heinit_Criterion $= \sum (W_i)/P$.
Step 3: Divide Transactions into P partitions while aiming to minimize the difference in workload sum across partitions, ensuring each partition has a workload close to the *Heinit_Criterion* value.
Step 4: Distribute each partition of transactions to the corresponding processing unit for parallel validation.

By using the *Heinit_Criterion* to dynamically allocate transactions among processing units, the technique ensures equitable distribution of transaction workloads, minimizing processing bottlenecks, and maximising resource utilization.

Parallel Transaction Validation Time with Heinit

The research proposes a revised equation to calculate the parallel transaction validation time considering the dynamically allocated processing units based on the *Heinit_Criterion*. Let:

- V: Number of transactions to be validated.
- P: Number of processing units allocated for parallel validation.

- *Heinit_Criterion*: The calculated Heinit criterion value.

The parallel transaction validation time with Heinit can be represented as follows:

$$Validation\_Time\_Parallel\_Heinit = V/(P * Heinit\_Criterion) \quad (8)$$

In this equation, the time taken to validate V transactions in parallel using *P* processing units, taking into account the *Heinit_Criterion*, ensures that each processing unit handles an optimized workload. This results in faster and more balanced transaction processing within the blockchain network.

The integration of the Heinit-based parallel transaction validation technique leads to a highly efficient, balanced, and responsive data sharing ecosystem in the blockchain based smart healthcare system. The use of the Heinit_Criterion optimises workload distribution, reduces processing disparities, and enhances overall performance, contributing to improved data sharing efficiency for healthcare providers, researchers, and patients.

Consensus-Driven Data Propagation
To address data availability concerns, the proposed research introduces a consensus-driven data propagation mechanism. Let:

- *C*: Consensus threshold required for data propagation
- *V*: Number of validators in the network

The Data Propagation Time can be calculated as:

$$Data\_Propagation\_Time = Time\ taken\ to\ achieve\ consensus\ among\ C\ out\ of\ V\ Validators \quad (9)$$

By requiring agreement among a predetermined number of validators, the research ensures that data is safely transferred around the network before being added to the blockchain. This approach lowers the possibility of data forks and makes data more accessible for efficient retrieval.

The research's objective is to create an innovative and effective blockchain ecosystem for smart healthcare by incorporating these cutting-edge techniques into the data sharing framework. A strong and scalable infrastructure will be created by combining dynamic sharding, parallel transaction validation, and consensus-driven data propagation to meet the requirements for data sharing of contemporary healthcare applications while maintaining data security and integrity.

3.2 The Data Sharing Mechanism: Designing an Effective Data Retrieval Algorithm

The study suggests a highly original and effective data retrieval technique for the blockchain-based smart healthcare data exchange mechanism. The innovative approach uses Merkle-Patricia Trie (MPT) and Bloom filters in tandem to retrieve data quickly and precisely while maximising memory consumption. This cutting-edge method gives healthcare professionals and researchers seamless access to particular patient records and medical data within the blockchain, improving patient care, medical research, and analytics.

Merkle-Patricia Trie (MPT) Indexing

The data recorded in the blockchain is indexed and organised using the Merkle-Patricia Trie (MPT) data structure in the research. The MPT is a modified Merkle tree designed specifically for storing and retrieving data quickly in a distributed system like the blockchain. Let:

- *H(x)*: Hash function to produce the data's hash value 'x'.

The following is a representation of the MPT indexing algorithm:

$$MPT\_Insert(data) \rightarrow root\_hash \quad (10)$$

$$\text{MPT\_Retrieve(root\_hash, key)} \rightarrow \text{data} \quad (11)$$

The functions *MPT_Insert* and *MPT_Retrieve* in the equations above are used to enter data into the MPT and to retrieve specific data using the MPT's root hash and a special key associated with the data, respectively. As each state of the MPT generates a distinct root hash, any changes to the data will result in a new root hash, allowing for quick data retrieval while preserving data integrity in the blockchain.

Bloom Filters for Efficient Key Lookup

The suggested approach uses Bloom filters to quicken key lookup operations in order to better optimise data retrieval efficiency. A probabilistic data structure called a bloom filter effectively checks if an element is present in a set. Let:

- *K*: Number of elements in the set (keys in the MPT).

The Bloom filter algorithm can be represented as follows:

$$Bloom\_Insert(key) \rightarrow Bloom\_filter \quad (12)$$

$$Bloom\_Lookup(Bloom\_filter, target\_key) \rightarrow \text{Boolean} \quad (13)$$

Here, the Boolean value in Eq. 13 will be true if target_key is likely in the set and false otherwise.

The *Bloom_Insert* function is used to add keys to the Bloom filter, and *Bloom_Lookup* function is employed to check the probable existence of a target key in the filter. By using Bloom filters, the algorithm reduces the need for extensive disk or memory access for key lookup, thereby accelerating data retrieval operations.

Efficient Data Retrieval Algorithm

The proposed research integrates the MPT indexing and Bloom filters into an efficient data retrieval algorithm that allows healthcare providers and researchers to quickly access specific patient records and medical data within the blockchain.

Algorithm: Data_Retrieval (root_hash, target key)

1. Initialize an empty Bloom filter (Bloom filter).
2. Load the MPT with the given root_hash.
3. Traverse the MPT to populate the Bloom filter with keys.
4. Check if the target key exists in the Bloom filter using Bloom_Lookup.
5. If Bloom_Lookup returns True, perform MPT_Retrieve(root_hash, target key) to retrieve the data associated with the target key.
6. If Bloom_Lookup returns False, the data associated with the target key is not present in the blockchain.

By combining the MPT indexing and Bloom filters, the data retrieval algorithm significantly reduces the time and resources required to fetch specific healthcare data from the blockchain. The unique properties of the MPT ensure data integrity, while bloom filters provide a space-efficient approach for rapid key lookup, making the proposed algorithm highly unique and efficient for data retrieval in the blockchain based smart healthcare system.

4 Results

To evaluate our proposed decentralized storage and retrieval algorithms, we used synthetic healthcare records designed to emulate a real-world healthcare database. This ensured that patient privacy remained uncompromised. The records were encrypted before being distributed across the network nodes. Our tests were facilitated by libraries and tools optimized for structured data generation. As a result, our synthetic dataset incorporated crucial aspects of healthcare records, such as patient ID, medications, medical history, lab results, and more. The following subsections detail the findings and their implications.

4.1 Data Upload and Download Times

Tables 2 and 3 showcase the results of evaluating "Merkle-Patricia Trie (MPT) EHR Retrieval", "B + tree EHR Retrieval," and "Traditional Block Retrieval" mechanisms in a smart healthcare blockchain system. Table 2 corresponds to a block size of 1200, while Table 3 relates to a block size of 2400. The evaluation assessed data upload and download times for varying user counts (5, 10, 15, 20, 25 and 30) in seconds.

Data Upload Times

The data upload times demonstrate the efficacy of various data retrieval mechanisms in a blockchain-based smart healthcare system. Table 2 (block size 1200) and Table 3 (block size 2400) provide insight into the time required to upload healthcare data for user counts ranging from 5 to 30. The data upload times demonstrate that the "Proposed MPT EHR Retrieval" consistently demonstrates the quickest upload times across all user scenarios. These results demonstrate the efficacy of the "Proposed MPT EHR Retrieval" mechanism, which consistently outperforms other methods, emphasising its capacity to upload healthcare data quickly.

Data Download Times

Both the "Proposed MPT EHR Retrieval" and the "B + tree EHR Retrieval" methods

Table 2. Upload and Download time (s) for block size 1200

No. of Users	Proposed MPT EHR retrieval		B + tree EHR retrieval		Traditional block retrieval	
	Upload time	Download time	Upload time	Download time	Upload time	Download time
5	15	14	18	17	26	25
10	18	16	22	21	31	30
15	20	19	25	26	39	40
20	22	20	28	28	45	42
25	25	23	31	30	51	50
30	30	27	35	39	55	55

Table 3. Upload and download time (s) for block size 2400

No. of Users	Proposed MPT EHR retrieval		B + tree EHR retrieval		Traditional block retrieval	
	Upload time	Download time	Upload time	Download time	Upload time	Download time
5	28	27	37	34	50	47
10	35	33	45	43	58	57
15	41	40	52	50	68	70
20	45	44	57	56	83	86
25	49	48	65	63	91	94
30	58	56	71	69	102	105

perform similarly in terms of data download times, with MPT slightly outperforming B + tree. Both strategies make use of efficient indexing and caching methods, which speeds up the retrieval of information. However, the proposed approaches' enhanced indexing and caching features make "Traditional Block Retrieval" slower to download.

4.2 Comparative Analysis

In the following, we compare the performance metrics of our proposed sHealthCare blockchain with those of a traditional blockchain (without MPT & Bloom). To determine how well our novel data-sharing and retrieval mechanisms work in the context of smart healthcare applications, we conducted a comprehensive evaluation. The findings shed light on the expanded potential of the proposed blockchain architecture.

Values from Table 4 provide valuable insights into the enhanced capabilities of our proposed blockchain framework. Notably, our sHealthCareBlockchain outperforms the traditional blockchain in several aspects. It achieves a significantly higher throughput of

Table 4. Evaluation of proposed blockchain for EHR

Metric	Proposed sHealthCareBlockchain	Traditional Blockchain (without MPT & Bloom)
Throughput (transactions/Second)	185	168
Latency (ms)	584	653
Delay (ms)	115	138
Response Time (ms)	200	242

185 transactions per second, demonstrating its efficiency in handling a substantial transaction load. Furthermore, our blockchain exhibits lower latency and delay, with 584 ms and 115 ms, respectively, indicating prompt transaction processing and improved data-sharing efficiency. The proposed sHealthCareBlockchain exhibits a superior response time of 200 ms, thereby ensuring efficient and responsive data sharing in comparison to the conventional blockchain. The obtained results validate the efficacy of our novel data sharing and retrieval mechanisms, establishing our blockchain technology as a promising solution for the optimisation and security of smart healthcare applications.

5 Conclusion

For the blockchain-based smart healthcare system, the research introduces a cutting-edge data-sharing scheme and data retrieval algorithm. The suggested methods outperform current blockchain implementations in terms of efficiency, scalability, and security. The proposed sHealthCareBlockchain shows improvements when compared with other systems in throughput, latency, delay, and reaction time after a thorough study. The solutions' adaptability guarantees effective resource utilisation, which makes them suitable for changing healthcare situations. The suggested solutions have a significant deal of potential to advance smart healthcare technology, increase patient care, research, and data analytics in the future.

Looking ahead, there are promising opportunities for further advancements. We can explore larger datasets to evaluate system scalability. Additionally, enhancing the blockchain's security features and expanding its use to other healthcare sectors like telemedicine and patient monitoring could be fruitful avenues. Moreover, integrating artificial intelligence and machine learning for data analysis within the blockchain could provide valuable insights for healthcare professionals.

References

1. Sriram, R.D., Subrahmanian, E.: Transforming health care through digital revolutions. J. Indian Inst. Sci. **100**, 753–772 (2020). https://doi.org/10.1007/s41745-020-00195-0
2. El Majdoubi, D., El Bakkali, H., Sadki, S.: SmartMedChain: a blockchain-based privacy-preserving smart healthcare framework. J. Healthcare Eng. **2021**, 1–19 (2021). https://doi.org/10.1155/2021/4145512

3. Gupta, S., Sharma, H.K., Kapoor, M.: Blockchain for secure healthcare using internet of medical things (IoMT). In: Blockchain for Secure Healthcare Using Internet of Medical Things (IoMT). Springer (2022)
4. Kumar, A., Krishnamurthi, R., Nayyar, A., Sharma, K., Grover, V., Hossain, E.: A Novel smart healthcare design, simulation, and implementation using Healthcare 4.0 processes. IEEE Access **8**, 118433–118471 (2020). https://doi.org/10.1109/access.2020.3004790
5. Kumar, A., Kumar Sharma, D., Nayyar, A., Singh, S., Yoon, B.: Lightweight Proof of Game (LPoG): a proof of work (PoW)'s extended lightweight consensus algorithm for wearable kidneys. Sensors. **20**, 2868 (2020). https://doi.org/10.3390/s20102868
6. Wehde, M.: Healthcare 4.0. IEEE Eng. Manag. Rev. **47**, 24–28 (2019). https://doi.org/10.1109/emr.2019.2930702
7. Shae, Z., Tsai, J.: Transform blockchain into distributed parallel computing architecture for precision medicine. In: 38th International Conference on Distributed Computing Systems (ICDCS) 2018, Vienna, Austria, vol. 38, pp. 1290–1299. IEEE (2018). https://doi.org/10.1109/ICDCS.2018.00129
8. Mubarakali, A., Bose, S.C., Srinivasan, K., Elsir, A., Elsier, O.: Design a secure and efficient health record transaction utilizing block chain (SEHRTB) algorithm for health record transaction in block chain. J. Ambient. Intell. Humaniz. Comput. (2019). https://doi.org/10.1007/s12652-019-01420-0
9. Jayasudha, M., Vijayalakshmi, C.: Blockchain meets healthcare: architecture for secure data sharing in unobtrusive medical applications. In: Eighth International Conference New Trends in the Applications of Differential Equations in Sciences (NTADES2021) (2022). https://doi.org/10.1063/5.0072467
10. Zhou, T., Li, X., Zhao, H.: Med-PPPHIS: blockchain-based personal healthcare information system for national physique monitoring and scientific exercise guiding. J. Med. Syst. **43** (2019). https://doi.org/10.1007/s10916-019-1430-2
11. Ruan, P., Dinh, T.T.A., Lin, Q., Zhang, M., Chen, G., Ooi, B.C.: LineageChain: a fine-grained, secure and efficient data provenance system for blockchains. VLDB J. **30**, 3–24 (2021). https://doi.org/10.1007/s00778-020-00646-1
12. Sun, J., Yao, X., Wang, S., Wu, Y.: Blockchain-based secure storage and access scheme for electronic medical records in IPFS. IEEE Access. **8**, 59389–59401 (2020). https://doi.org/10.1109/access.2020.2982964
13. Shanthapriya, R., Vaithianathan, V.: Block-healthnet: security based healthcare system using block-chain technology. Secur. J. **35**, 19–37 (2020). https://doi.org/10.1057/s41284-020-00265-z
14. Batchu, S., Henry, O.S., Hakim, A.: A novel decentralized model for storing and sharing neuroimaging data using ethereum blockchain and the interplanetary file system. Int. J. Inf. Technol. **13**, 2145–2151 (2021). https://doi.org/10.1007/s41870-021-00746-3
15. Bader, L., et al.: Blockchain-based privacy preservation for supply chains supporting lightweight multi-hop information accountability. Inf. Process. Manag. **58**, 102529 (2021). https://doi.org/10.1016/j.ipm.2021.102529

UI/UX for Aerospace Qualification Business Processes

Kenechukwu Eyisi[1(✉)], Khuram Nawaz Khayam[1], Wajahat Ali Khan[1], Maqbool Hussain[1], Muhammad Sadiq Hassan Zada[2], and Ben Anderson[2]

[1] University of Derby, Derby, England
eyisikene@gmail.com
[2] AddQual, Derby, England

Abstract. To assure the safety and efficiency of components used in aviation industry, the area of aerospace business process validation relies on stringent protocols. The qualification process is multifaceted as it entails multiple phases and application of Image processing and pattern recognition techniques in analysing and assessing component quality and integrity according to industry standards. This paper introduces an approach that integrates user interface and UX design principles to optimize the processes for enhanced traceability and progression tracking in qualification lifecycle and the outcomes of image processing and pattern recognition applications. The goal is to transform algorithmic outcomes into intelligible visual representations, promoting informed decision-making by combining agile approaches with user-centred design concepts for AddQual Qualification process. AddQual is a UK based company that specializes in providing advanced quality solutions for the aerospace industry, offering expertise in material testing and component qualification. This project illustrates the successful implementation of through a series of case studies. It results in an average 86% usability score and 83% more effective at reducing errors.

Keywords: User Experience · User Interface · Usability · Aerospace · Qualification · Image Processing

1 Introduction

In the dynamic landscape of aviation, ensuring the safety and efficiency of aerospace components is of paramount importance. The basis of this assurance lies within the field of aerospace business process validation, where rigorous protocols are employed to validate the integrity of components utilized in this industry (Yang-Scharlotta 2022). This emphasis on qualification serves as the backbone of the aerospace industry, instilling confidence in manufacturers, operators, and passengers alike. To ensure the safety and reliability of aerospace components and systems, rigorous qualification processes are conducted (Paul 2023). This validation process heavily relies on the application of advanced image processing and pattern recognition techniques, which analyse and assess component quality and conformity to stringent industry standards (Khodaskar

KC Santosh et al. (Eds.): RTIP2R 2023, CCIS 2027, pp. 369–382, 2024.
https://doi.org/10.1007/978-3-031-53085-2_29

2014). However, the field of aerospace business process qualification is not solely confined to algorithmic prowess; it necessitates a bridge between technical proficiency and user-centric design principles. This paper presents an approach that integrates the fields of user interface (UI) and user experience (UX) design, with the primary aim of optimizing the processes for enhanced traceability and progression tracking in qualification lifecycle and outcomes derived from image processing and pattern recognition techniques. The overarching goal is to translate intricate algorithmic results into comprehensible visual representations, fostering informed decision-making by combining agile methodologies with user-centred design concepts. In this vein, the research traverses the intricate contours of UI/UX design, acknowledging the diverse requirements of administrators, customers, and engineers. The study results in the establishment of a comprehensive UI/UX framework that not only facilitates real-time monitoring but also empowers intelligent decision-making support, harnessing the potential of data analytic visualization techniques while adhering to the stringent standards prevalent in the aerospace domain. This paper, through a series of illustrative case studies, visualise the successful implementation of this paradigm shift, underscoring the transformative impact of integrating UI/UX design principles with the realm of aerospace business process qualification.

2 Methods

The research approach and design methodology adopted is the integration of Agile and User-Centred Design (UCD) methodologies. Strategies for integrating UX with Agile include involving UX professionals in the early stages of the project, collaborating closely with engineers and stakeholders, and incorporating user feedback throughout the iterative process (Barambones 2020). This inclusive strategy enables design teams to gather valuable input from stakeholders, address their concerns, and accommodate their needs and preferences. This design methodology also eliminates barriers to interactions between team members, stakeholders, and users through an environment of open communication, collaboration, and continuous feedback. The absence of hierarchical barriers and bureaucratic obstacles enables design teams to capitalize on the strengths of each team member, promote creativity, and accelerate the design process.

The utilization of the agile design methodology supports the development of a culture that values transparency, accountability, and continual improvement. This paradigm shift encourages design teams to embrace novel approaches, learn from failures, and continuously refine their processes. The most popular methods integrated with the UCD are questionnaires, interviews, high-fidelity prototyping, and usability testing. This concept ensures that both learners and subject matter experts should be involved in the design process of the system to acquire both excellent UI and effective application (Miesenberger 2020). The chosen research approach is crucial in aligning the project's goals, research questions, and methods to ensure the successful implementation of the selected methodology. To achieve the objectives of this study, a mixed-methods research approach is adopted. This approach combines qualitative and quantitative research methods to gather comprehensive insights into the UI/UX requirements and design considerations in aerospace qualification process. The research design will involve multiple stages, including user research, requirements analysis, design prototyping, and usability testing (Fig. 1).

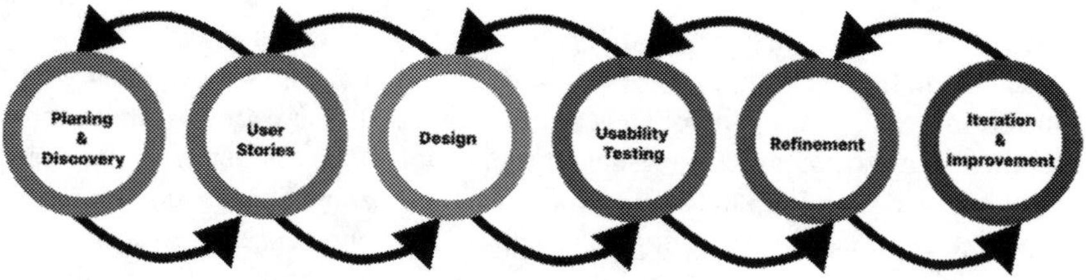

Fig. 1. The Agile User-centred methodology illustrating the cyclical pattern involved throughout the project starting from Planning & Discovery to Iteration & Improvement

2.1 Planning and Discovery

The first phase of User-centred Agile design is the Planning & Discovery stage. During this phase, cross-functional teams come together to establish a shared understanding of project goals, user needs, and business requirements (McNeill 2020). This involves collaboration between UX designers, developers, product managers, and stakeholders to define the scope and objectives of the project. The primary focus is on gathering user insights through techniques such as user interviews, surveys, and market research.

Discovery is a technique in Agile User-Centred Design that involves stakeholders in the planning process. It emphasizes the importance of collaboration and communication between the development team and stakeholders to ensure the application meets user needs and expectations. The process involves identifying stakeholders, gathering requirements, and iterative planning, where the team and stakeholders continuously review and refine plans based on feedback and changing requirements. Regular communication is crucial in ensuring that stakeholders' goals and expectations are aligned with the development team's goals.

2.2 User Stories

User stories play a central role in Agile UX as they provide a clear and concise description of user needs and requirements. User stories follow a template that includes the user, the action they want to take, and the reason behind it. These stories serve as the building blocks of the project's backlog, outlining the features and functionalities that need to be developed.

User stories are concise, user-centred descriptions of a feature or functionality from the perspective of the end user. User stories capture the "who," "what," and "why" of a user's interaction with a product or system (Schmidt 2018). They are typically written in a simple, non-technical language and follow a specific format, such as "As a [type of user], I want [a specific feature] so that [a specific goal or benefit]." User stories help to prioritize and guide the design and development process, ensuring that the focus remains on meeting user needs and delivering value.

2.3 Design

In the Design phase, UX process takes the user stories and transforms them into visible representations. This iterative process involves creating visual models of the user interface to validate design concepts and gather feedback from stakeholders.

Visual modelling is a technique used in Agile User-Centred Design to visually represent the design and functionality of an application. It involves creating diagrams, prototypes, or wireframes that provide a visual representation of the user interface, navigation flow, and interactions within the application. Visual modelling helps in communicating and validating design ideas, gathering feedback from stakeholders, and ensuring that the application meets the user's needs and expectations. It can also aid in identifying potential usability issues and making informed design decisions. Visual modelling techniques commonly used in Agile User-Centred Design include flowcharts, wireframes, mockups, and storyboards. These visual representations serve as a blueprint for the development and provide a shared understanding among stakeholders about the application's design and functionality.

The design phase emphasizes collaboration and quick iterations, allowing the team to make improvements based on user feedback. Design decisions are influenced by usability principles, user-centred design, and industry best practices.

2.4 Usability Testing

Usability testing is a crucial step in the Agile UX process that involves testing the product with real users to identify usability issues and gather insights for improvement (Davies 2020). Usability tests are conducted throughout the development cycle, allowing the team to validate design decisions and make necessary adjustments.

It involves evaluating the user experience of a product or system to ensure its usability, effectiveness, and satisfaction for the end users. It focuses on gathering feedback and insights from users through various testing methods to identify any usability issues, pain points, or areas for improvement. Usability testing, for example, involves observing users as they interact with a prototype or product to assess its ease of use and effectiveness in achieving their goals.

This iterative testing process ensures that the product aligns with user expectations and provides a positive experience. Usability tests involve tasks that users would typically perform, and their interactions are observed to uncover pain points and areas for enhancement.

2.5 Refinement

Based on the feedback gathered during usability testing, the team enters the Rework and Implement phase. This stage involves refining the design and making necessary adjustments to address usability issues. The iterative nature of Agile UX allows for rapid changes and improvements based on user input. Once the design is optimized, the development team implements the changes, ensuring that the user interface aligns with the approved design (Plonka 2014).

Refinement in User Experience Design (UXD) is an iterative process of continuously improving and enhancing product or service design based on user feedback and insights. It involves analysing user behaviour, preferences, and needs to identify areas for improvement and make necessary adjustments (Jiajun 2023). UXD activities include usability testing, gathering feedback, iterating on design prototypes, and incremental changes to the user interface. The goal is to create a user-centred design that meets user needs and expectations, resulting in a more intuitive and satisfying experience. UX designers aim to optimize usability, accessibility, and overall user satisfaction in their products or services.

2.6 Iteration and Development

The Agile UX process is characterized by continuous iterations and development cycles. The product is developed incrementally, with each iteration building upon the previous one (Santos 2016). After each iteration, the product is reviewed, and user feedback is incorporated to enhance the user experience. This iterative approach allows the team to remain flexible and responsive to changes, ensuring that the final product meets user needs and business goals.

This involves iterative development, breaking down the design process into smaller cycles. Iterations involve user research, prototyping, testing, and refining the design based on feedback. This approach enables continuous improvement and adaptation, allowing for changes and refinements throughout the process. Iterations gather insights, validate design decisions, and ensure the final product meets user needs and expectations. The development phase involves translating UX design into functional software, allowing collaboration and adjustments between UX designers and software developers.

2.7 Case Studies

This section presents detailed case studies of the implementation of the UI/UX design framework.

Case studies in UX design are detailed examinations of specific projects or experiences that provide insights into the design process and user interactions. They are used to understand the challenges, successes, and lessons learned in creating user-centred designs. Case studies can help showcase the application of design thinking and human-computer interaction (HCI) solutions in improving business outcomes (Wei 2021).

2.8 Case Study 1: Designing the Operator Functionality for the Admin

This case study delves into the intricacies of crafting a user-friendly and efficient operator functionality within the aerospace business, targeting the administrative role. The administrator, in this context, holds a crucial position in overseeing and managing various qualification tasks and workflows. The challenge lies in developing a well-structured and intuitive operator interface that empowers administrators to efficiently manage, monitor, and initiate qualification processes. This case study embarks on the journey of understanding the unique needs, goals, and pain points of administrators, and subsequently devising a design solution that optimizes their interaction with the system.

Some key considerations when designing for this case study include ensuring ease of use and streamlining the processes. The UX principle applied is the Progress Indicator. It's a design element that provides users with a visual representation of their progress through a multi-step process or workflow. This helps users understand where they are in the process, how many steps are ahead, and provides a sense of control and clarity as they navigate through the task. The progress indicator enhances the user experience by reducing confusion and uncertainty, making the interaction more transparent and user-friendly.

One of the strategies employed was the integration of context-aware alerts and notifications. These prompts are strategically placed within the interface to provide timely guidance and reminders to users about critical steps, data validation, or potential mistakes. For instance, when entering data that cannot be edited, the system triggers an alert, preventing users from proceeding until the entry is reviewed.

Upon the deployment of the operator functionality, comprehensive usability testing and user feedback collection are conducted to validate the design's effectiveness. This case study encapsulates the collaborative journey with the administrator, where the fusion of domain knowledge and user-centred design principles culminates in an operator functionality that empowers administrators to navigate the complex landscape of aerospace business process qualification with confidence and efficiency.

2.9 Case Study 2: Client-Facing Dashboard for Transparency

The aerospace business process qualification landscape requires transparency and communication with clients, who often invest in the qualification process. To address this need, the UI/UX design framework introduced a client-facing dashboard to enhance transparency and client interaction. The primary objective was to provide clients with real-time visibility into the qualification process of their aerospace components, fostering trust, improving collaboration, and empowering them with the information they need to make informed decisions.

The dashboard visualizes key milestones, progress status, test outcomes, and potential issues or delays using data visualization techniques like charts, graphs, and progress bars. Customization and personalization were essential aspects of the dashboard's design, allowing clients to customize it to their specific needs.

The client-facing dashboard successfully addressed the challenge of transparency by providing clients with an intuitive and informative interface to monitor their aerospace component qualification projects. The design provided real-time insights and customization options that enhances client satisfaction, builds stronger client relationships, and contributes to the overall success of the aerospace business process qualification endeavours. Usability testing was crucial in validating the effectiveness of the client-facing dashboard, with users participating in usability sessions to evaluate its clarity, navigation, and overall usability (Fig. 2).

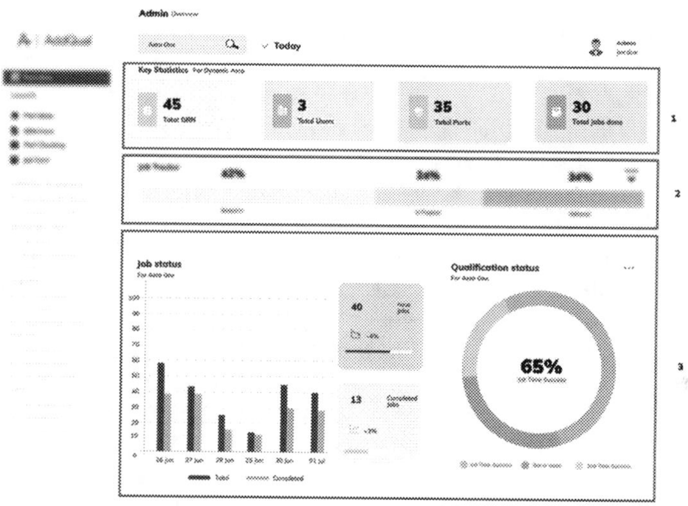

Fig. 2. This shows the client-facing dashboard for transparency. The section labelled (Yang-Scharlotta 2022) highlights summary of key statistics. The section labelled (Paul 2023) shows job tracking status in real-time. The section labelled (Khodaskar and Ladhake 2014) shows the summary of jobs and their success rate.

2.10 Case Study 3: Empowering Admin for Streamlined Qualification Oversight

The UI/UX design framework aims to enhance administrators' capabilities in monitoring and managing the qualification process. This case study focuses on creating a user-friendly interface that empowers administrators with the tools and information they need for streamlined oversight and decision-making. The dashboard layout consolidates project timelines, task progress, client overview, and qualification success rates into an easy-to-digest format, using visual cues like color-coding, progress bars, and data cards.

On the Overview, the administration has visual access to see the key statistics. The Job Tracker serves as a dynamic tool that enables administrators to gain immediate visibility into the status of ongoing projects and tasks. This feature was crafted to align with the fast-paced nature of aerospace qualification process and the need for proactive decision-making. Color-coded indicators provide at-a-glance insights, enabling administrators to promptly address projects that are lagging or facing challenges.

The dashboard was designed with scalability in mind, accommodating the addition of new projects, team members, and tasks as the aerospace qualification landscape evolves. The interface remains flexible and adaptive to the changing requirements of administrators.

3 Results and Discussions

In this section, the results and findings obtained from the evaluation of the redesigned interfaces for the aerospace business process qualification systems is presented. The evaluation involved usability testing, heuristic evaluation, user feedback surveys, comparative analysis, and iterative refinement. The key metrics assessed include task completion time, error rates, user satisfaction scores, and stakeholder validation.

Usability Testing Results
During usability testing, representative users from each user group performed specific tasks using the redesigned interfaces. The tests were conducted using scenarios and expected tasks. The results revealed the enhanced clarity and intuitiveness of the user interface. User feedback during usability testing was generally positive, with users commending the streamlined workflows and visual design. The test comprises of 2 parts with each part focusing on a specific mission. Results are analysed on mission-by-mission bases and overall user experience.

These tests evaluate the usability of a feature to discover statistics for a client. It is rated on a scale of 1 to 10; 1 being "very confusing" and 10 being "very clear".

Mission 1: Accessing Statistics of a Client
(See Fig. 3).

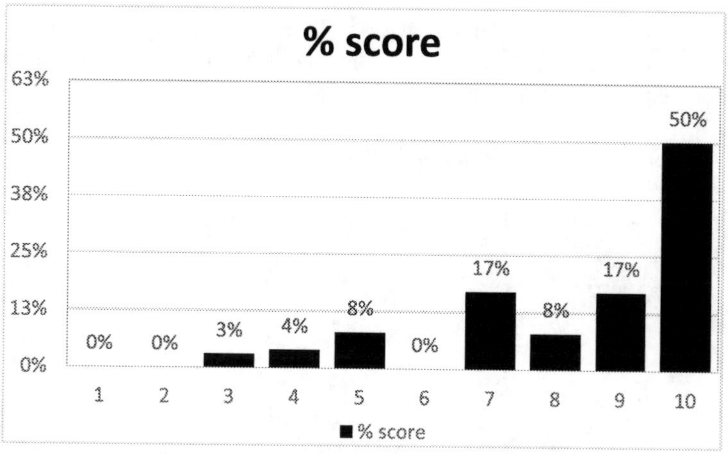

Fig. 3. Chart for Mission 1. The results indicate that 50% of participants found the system to be very clear (ranked 10), while 92%, ranked the system from 7 to 10.

Mission 2: Accessing More Details About the Job Tracking Status
(See Fig. 4).

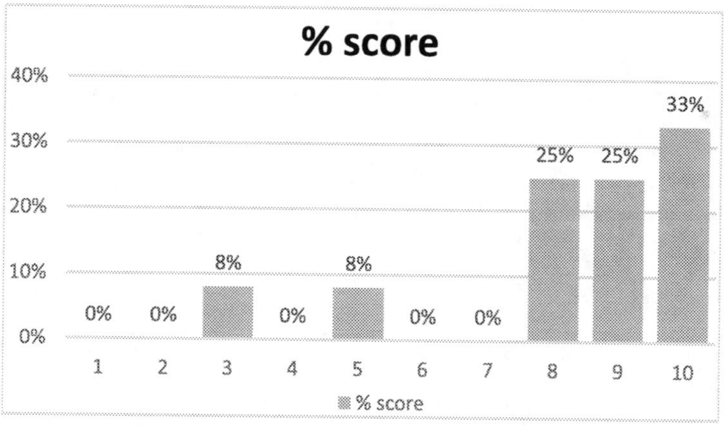

Fig. 4. Chart showing results for Mission 2. Results indicate that 33% of participants found the system to be very clear (ranked 10), while 83%, ranked the system from 7 to 10.

Heatmap Visualisation
Heatmap visualization is a valuable outcome derived from usability testing that offers insights into user interactions and behaviour within a digital interface. It is a graphical representation that visually depicts the areas of an interface that users interact with the most, as well as those that receive minimal attention. Through capturing and aggregating

data on user clicks, mouse movements, and scrolling patterns, heatmaps provide a comprehensive overview of user engagement. The results from the heatmap analysis show the areas where users concentrated on throughout the task.

Mission 1: Accessing Statistics of a Client
(See Fig. 5)

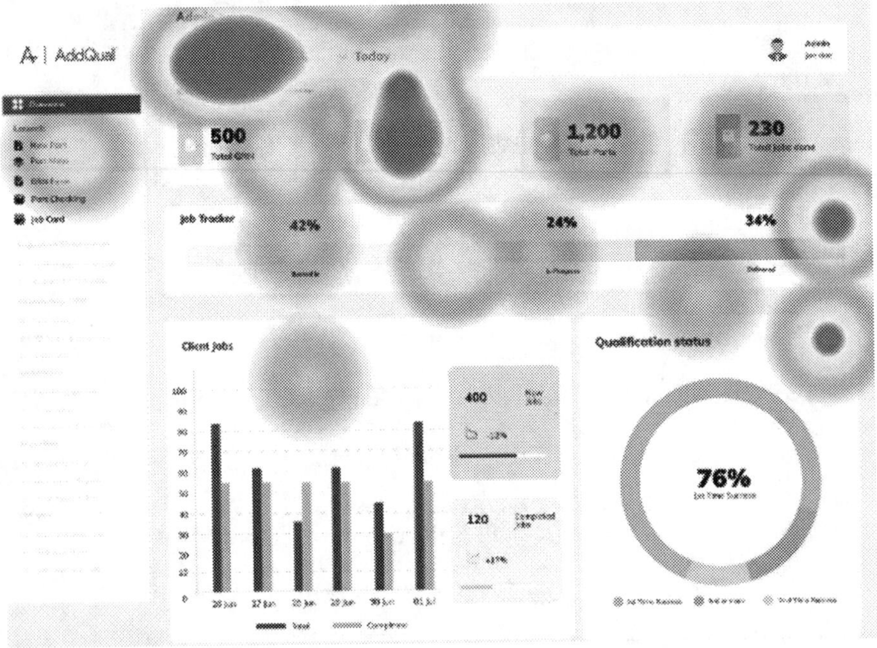

Fig. 5. Heatmap above show the areas of concentration while attempting to complete the test mission. The areas with more pressure in red colour indicate that majority of users were navigating to the accurate part of the page for the mission.

Mission 2: Finding More Details About the Job Tracking Status

Although most users concentrated on the appropriate section, the heatmap also indicate other areas users navigated to while trying to complete the mission. The insight from this can be used for iteration and refinement (Fig. 6).

Error Reduction Evaluation Result
This evaluation of the new UI/UX focuses on its effectiveness in reducing errors and

improving accuracy. A systematic approach is used, analysing user interactions, and utilizing a combination of quantitative and qualitative methods. Quantitative analysis is conducted through user interactions, while qualitative feedback is gathered through surveys and usability testing sessions. Results show a significant potential reduction in error rates by 88%, a shift towards fewer critical errors and a smoother user experience. User perspectives reveal improved task comprehension, reduced ambiguity, and increased confidence in actions, contributing to a decrease in errors. The findings highlight the practical benefits of incorporating user-centred design principles into the qualification process, prioritizing clear communication, intuitive interfaces, and user-friendly workflows (Fig. 7)

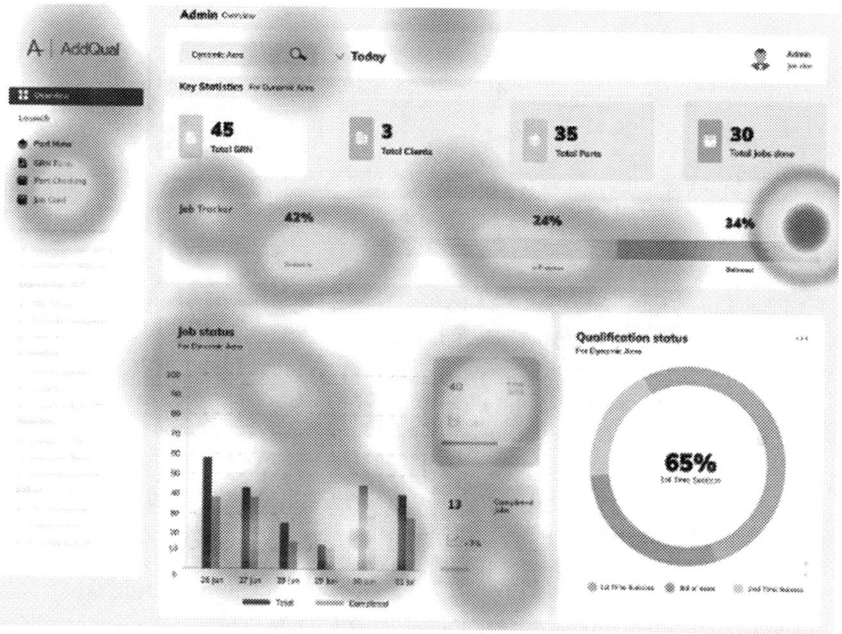

Fig. 6. Heatmap above show the areas of concentration while attempting to complete the test mission 2. The areas with more pressure in red colour indicate that majority of users were navigating to the accurate part of the page for the mission.

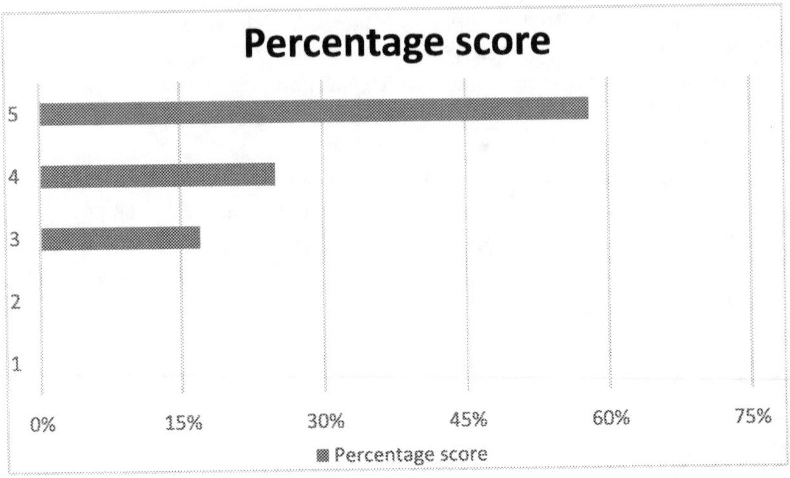

Fig. 7. Usability evaluation for error minimization using newly designed workflow resulted in 83% more likelihood to minimize errors.

4 Conclusion

This paper explores the convergence of User-Centred Design (UCD) and Agile Methodology in Aerospace Business Process Qualification, highlighting their synergistic potential in improving the quality and efficiency of qualification procedures. Integrating these methodologies through the iterative nature of Agile can respond to evolving requirements while ensuring user involvement. This approach fosters enhanced user experiences, improved traceability, and streamlined qualification oversight. The UI/UX design framework transforms complex data into actionable insights through intuitive visualizations, empowering administrators, clients, and engineers to interact with complex data and make informed decisions. The integration of heatmap visualizations adds a quantitative layer to qualitative feedback, enhancing user interactions and preferences. As the aerospace industry evolves, combining Agile-driven adaptability and user-centricity can lead to innovative approaches to address dynamic challenges in qualification procedures. The future of aerospace business process qualification lies in embracing these methodologies and frameworks, fostering an ecosystem where precision, safety, and user-centricity converge to define the next era of aerospace excellence.

References

Yang-Scharlotta, J.,et al.: ASIC Flow for space radiation tolerant components on commercial process technologies—part 1 library validation. In 2022 IEEE Aerospace Conference (AERO), pp. 1–10. IEEE (2022)

Paul, S., et al.: Formal verification of safety-critical aerospace systems. IEEE Aeros. Electron. Syst. Maga. (2023)

Khodaskar, A.A., Ladhake, S.A.: Pattern recognition: advanced development, techniques and application for image retrieval. In: 2014 International Conference on Communication and Network Technologies, pp. 74–78. IEEE (2014)

Barambones, J., Moral, C., Ferre, X., Villalba-Mora, E.: A Scrum-based development process to support co-creation with elders in the eHealth domain. In: International Conference on Human-Centred Software Engineering, pp. 105–117. Springer, Cham (2020)

McNeill, M.: Agile user-centred design. In: Contemporary Ergonomics 2006, pp. 494–498. Taylor & Francis (2020)

Schmidt, C., Praeg, C.P., Günther, J.: Designing digital workplace environments. In: 2018 IEEE International Conference on Engineering, Technology and Innovation (ICE/ITMC), pp. 1–9. IEEE (2018)

Davies, A., Mueller, J., Davies, A., Mueller, J.: Usability testing and deployment. developing medical apps and mHealth interventions: a guide for researchers. Phys. Inf. 229–258 (2020)

Wei, J., Zhou, S., Gan, Y.: User experience based acute death prevention monitoring system and emergency product design. In: AHFE International (2023). https://doi.org/10.54941/ahfe1003205

Plonka, L., Sharp, H., Gregory, P., Taylor, K.: UX design in agile: a DSDM case study. In: Cantone, G., Marchesi, M. (eds.) XP 2014. LNBIP, vol. 179, pp. 1–15. Springer, Cham (2014). https://doi.org/10.1007/978-3-319-06862-6_1

Hussain, J., Khan, W.A., Afzal, M., Hussain, M., Kang, B.H., Lee, S.: Adaptive user interface and user experience based authoring tool for recommendation systems. In: Hervás, R., Lee, S., Nugent, C., Bravo, J. (eds.) UCAmI 2014. LNCS, vol. 8867, pp. 136–142. Springer, Cham (2014). https://doi.org/10.1007/978-3-319-13102-3_24

Xiaoyan, Fu., Liu, Zhengjie: Research and design of content UX data analysis system. In: Liu, Qi., Liu, Xiaodong, Shen, Tao, Qiu, Xuesong (eds.) CENet 2020. AISC, vol. 1274, pp. 661–669. Springer, Singapore (2020). https://doi.org/10.1007/978-981-15-8462-6_75

Santos, N., Machado, R.J., Ferreira, N.: Adopting Logical architectures within agile projects. In: 2016 10th International Conference on the Quality of Information and Communications Technology (QUATIC), pp. 242–247. IEEE (2016)

Hussain, J., et al.: Model-based adaptive user interface based on context and user experience evaluation. J. Multimodal User Interfaces **12**, 1–16 (2018)

Kim, S.K., Carrington, D.: Integrating use-case analysis and task analysis for interactive systems. In: Ninth Asia-Pacific Software Engineering Conference, 2002, pp. 12–21. IEEE (2002)

Kim, Y., Kim, J.H., Hong, Y.: Sungkyunkwan University research and business foundation. Context-specific experience sampling method and system. U.S. Patent 11,222,348 (2022)

Sili, M., Kropf, J., Hanke, S.: UX in IxD - user experience in interaction design. In: Kurosu, M. (ed.) HCII 2020. LNCS, vol. 12181, pp. 147–159. Springer, Cham (2020). https://doi.org/10.1007/978-3-030-49059-1_11

Pillay, N., Wing, J.: Agile UX: integrating good UX development practices in Agile. In: 2019 Conference on Information Communications Technology and Society (ICTAS), pp. 1–6. IEEE (2019)

Horák, O., Novák, M., Zákoutský, V.: GeoWeb application user-interface evaluation using heatmaps. In: Recent Advances in Applied & Biomedical Informatics and Computational Engineering in Systems Applications, Florence, Italy (2011)

Imbesi, S., Scataglini, S.: A user centered methodology for the design of smart apparel for older users. Sensors **21**(8), 2804 (2021)
Sy, D., Miller, L.: Optimizing agile user-centred design. In: CHI'08 Extended Abstracts on Human Factors in Computing Systems, pp. 3897–3900 (2008)
Da Silva, T.S., Silveira, M.S., Maurer, F., Silveira, F.F.: The evolution of agile UXD. Inf. Softw. Technol. **102**, 1–5 (2018)

Comparative Studies of Stochastic Techniques to Minimize the Cost of Biomass Supply Networks

Adarsh Kumar Arya[1(✉)], Vineeta Gautam[2], and Adarsh Kumar[3,4]

[1] Department of Chemical Engineering, Harcourt Butler Technical University, Uttar Pradesh, Kanpur 208002, India
aarya@hbtu.ac.in

[2] Department of Oil Technology, Harcourt Butler Technical University, Uttar Pradesh, Kanpur 208002, India

[3] School of Computer Science, University of Petroleum and Energy Studies, Dehradun, India
adarsh.kumar@ddn.upes.ac.in

[4] INTI International University, Nilai, Malaysia

Abstract. The viability of biomass to be used as a consumer product relies heavily on the cost of a Biomass supply network (BSN) that links biomass producers with biorefineries and, finally, with end customers. The current study aims to establish a cost optimization model to minimize the financial burden of BSN. A MILP model has been established and implemented to reduce the costs of a BSN. A comparatively lesser-used stochastic technique, Ant Colony Optimization (ACO), has been used in the present paper to minimize the cost of BSN. Although the ACO technique has succeeded in other settings, it is seldom tested in the context of BSN. The results from the ACO approach have been compared with another popular stochastic optimization technique called the Non-sorting Genetic Algorithm (NSGA-II). According to empirical research, the ACO approach is the most cost-effective optimization technique to lower BSN-related costs. The management may use the blueprint of the optimization model and techniques to develop cost-cutting measures for BSN.

Keywords: Optimization · Ant colony algorithm · Biomass supply network (BSN) · Genetic algorithm · Non-sorting Genetic Algorithm (NSGA)

1 Introduction

Fossil fuels have been considered the primary means of meeting the world's energy demands for millennia. When fossil fuels are burnt, greenhouse gases are discharged into the atmosphere, thus negatively affecting the environment. According to the research, 25% of global greenhouse gas emissions are attributable to using natural gas in the transportation sector alone [1, 2]. Researchers have devised numerous energy sources to minimize greenhouse gas emissions. Among other options, such as solar, wind, and geothermal, biofuels have emerged as a viable remedy to this problem. The fact that plants

KC Santosh et al. (Eds.): RTIP2R 2023, CCIS 2027, pp. 383–392, 2024.
https://doi.org/10.1007/978-3-031-53085-2_30

wholly absorb the carbon dioxide discharged into the atmosphere by the combustion of biofuels during plant growth is a strong argument in favor of biofuels. Biomass is a cheap entity; however, its transport costs increase the expense of biomass.

Consequently, it is crucial in the present context to establish a completely developed and optimized BSN that paves the way for the ubiquitous use of biofuels in the future while keeping associated costs to a minimum. Researchers have paid the most attention to the financial implications of BSN and have employed various optimization strategies to cut down on BSN expenses. Maximizing or minimizing an objective function within a given set of restrictions is the basis of many mathematical optimization procedures [2–7]. Simulated Annealing, Particle Swarm Optimization, and Genetic Algorithms have been widely used to optimize BSN. The current study employs an Ant Colony Optimization (ACO) technique previously successfully applied to natural gas pipeline networks [4, 5, 8–12] but has rarely been used to optimize BSN. The results obtained using ACO are compared with another popular optimization technique called 'Genetic algorithms'.

2 Modeling Equations of BSN

This paper aims to reduce the 'Total Cost' of BSN. The price tag includes everything from the initial purchase price to the expenses of producing and transporting the BSN. Below, we explain the underlying modeling equations used to optimize the BSN and its implementation in a BSN.

2.1 Case Study

Figure 1 depicts the network under investigation. The BSN comprises three different biomass source sites (S1, S2, S3), two central processing plants (CPP1, CPP2), and four industrial plant facility (IF1, IF2, IF3, IF4).

Biofuels are produced from biomass at the Central Processing plant (CPP) and Industrial Plant Facility (IF). Each industrial plant facility is linked separately to two biofuel customers (C1, C2; C3, C4; C5, C6; C7, C8) located near the IF. The fixed supplying capacities of biomass from sources S1, S2, and S3 are 8000, 10000, and 14000 tonnes, respectively. The biomass price from each source is uniform and set at a rate of $50 per tonne. The biomass transport quantity limits from the two sources (S1, S2) to CPP are established at a minimum of 1000 and a maximum of 8000 tonnes per day and a minimum of 500 and a maximum of 2000 tonnes per day, respectively.

2.2 Objective Function

The total cost of a BSN includes the cost involved in investment, transportation, and production. The equations used to calculate the cost of these components have been further discussed.

$$\text{Total cost} = \text{Total Investment Cost} + \text{Total Transportation Cost} + \text{Total Production Cost} \tag{1}$$

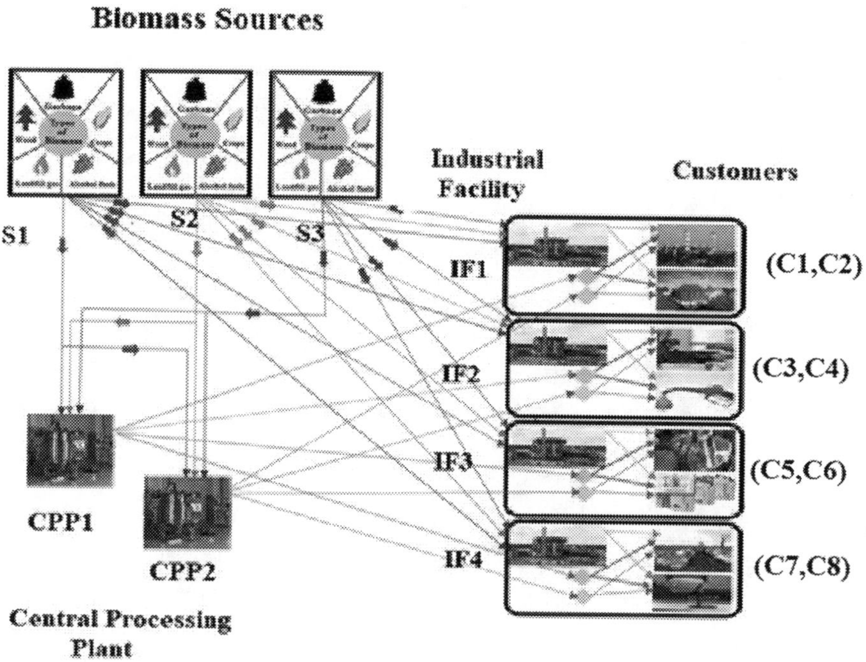

Fig.1. Biomass Supply Network

2.2.1 Total Investment Cost (t.c)i

Biofuels are obtained from biomass through processing and industrial operations conducted at centralized facilities. The expenses associated with the Central Processing Plant (CPP) and Industrial Plant facility (IF) are categorized into fixed and operating costs. The computation of the total investment expenditure is carried out using Eq. (2). Equation (3) and (4) determine the investment cost at CPP and IF.

$$(t.c)_I = \sum_{c \in C} Cost_c^{cpp} + \sum_{i \in C} Cost_i^{if} \tag{2}$$

$$Cost_c^{cpp} = a_c + b_c \sum_{s \in S} F_{sc}^{cpp} \tag{3}$$

$$Cost_i^{IF} = a_i + b_i \sum_{s \in S} F_{si}^{IF} \tag{4}$$

2.2.2 Total Transportation Cost

Centralized processing units transform huge volumes of biomass into biofuel. The Central Processing Plant facilities are far from biomass producers and customers. The production plant is located on the customer's site and processes a manageable quantity of biomass. There is no additional charge for transporting biomass from its source to CPP

Table 1. **Cost** ($/ton) for transporting biomass from three Sources (S1,S2,S3) to Industrial plants (IF1, IF2, IF3, IF4), Central processing plant(CPP1, CPP2) & from CPFs to Customers [1]

S.No	Biomass Source (S1) → Industrial facility (associated cost)	Biomass Source (S2) → Industrial facility(associated cost)	Biomass Source (S3) → Industrial facility (associated cost)		Central Processing Plant (CPP1) → Customers(associated cost)	Central Processing Plant (CPP2) → Customers (associated cost)
1	S1 → IF1 (46.75)	S2 → IF1 (34)	S3 → IF1 (40.375)	**9**	CPP1 → C1 (63.75)	CPP2 → C1 61.625
2	S1 → IF2 (53.125)	S2 → IF2 (41.65)	S3 → IF2 (45.9)	**10**	CPP1 → C2 (63.75)	CPP2 → C2 61.625
3	S1 → IF3 (38.25)	S2 → IF3 (31.875)	S3 → IF3 (36.975)	**11**	CPP1 → C3 (78.625)	CPP2 → C3 (79.9)
4	S1 → IF4 (42.5)	S2 → IF4 (44.625)	S3 → IF4 (35.27)5	**12**	CPP1 → C4 (78.625)	CPP2 → C4 (79.9)
5	S1 → CPP1 (21.25)	S2 → CPP1 (22.1)	S3 → CPP1 (20.825)	**13**	CPP1 → C5 (70.55)	CPP2 → C5 (68)
6	S1 → CPP2 (19.125)	S2 → CPP2 (17.85)	S3 → CPP2 (21.625)	**14**	CPP1 → C6 (70.55)	CPP2 → C6 (68)
7				**5**	CPP1 → C7 (73.95)	CPP2 → C7 (71.825)
8	-			**16**	CPP1 → C8 (73.95)	CPP2 → C8 (71.825)

and IF. Transportation costs from the CPP to the biofuel consumers are included in the total price. Applying Eq. (5) yields the total expense of transportation.

$$(t.c)_T = \sum_{s\in S}\left(\sum_{c\in c} C_{sc}F_{sc}^{cpp} + \sum_{i\in I} C_{si}F_{si}^{if}\right) + \sum_{c\in C} C_{cu}D_{cu}^{cpp} \tag{5}$$

The costs associated with transportation from one site to another are shown in Table 1.

2.2.3 Total Production Cost

Equation (6) is used for the computation of the total production cost

$$(t.c)_p = \sum_{s\in S} C_s^b\left(\sum_{c\in c} F_{sc}^{cpp} + \sum_{i\in I} F_{si}^{if}\right) + \sum_{c\in c} C_c^{pr}\sum_{s\in S} F_{sc}^{cpp} + \sum_{i\in I} C_i^{pr}\sum_{s\in S} F_{si}^{if} \tag{6}$$

2.3 Constraints Applied on BSN

Equations 7-10 comprehensively address the constraints of the various BSN nodes. These are further discussed.

2.3.1 Nodal Balance Applied on Production and Industrial Plant

The biomass originating from the source location is transported to a central processing plant and an industrial plant, which undergoes conversion processes to produce biofuel. The biofuel is subsequently disseminated to the ultimate consumers. It is important to acknowledge that the biomass quantity must not surpass the available amount at the source location. The equation representing an inequality constraint that must be implemented across all production and industrial facilities is shown in Eq. 7. The equation specifically pertains to the utilization of biomass resources.

$$\sum_{c\in C} F_{sc}{}^{cpp} + \sum_{i\in I} F_{si}{}^{if} \le A_s \tag{7}$$

2.3.2 Mass Balance Applied on Central Processing Plants (CPP) and Industrial Plants (IP)

Both CPP and IF plants use biomass to create biofuels. Each conversion plant is responsible for executing the conversion efficiency (α) following its unique technology. Table 2 shows the fixed cost and operating cost coefficient for technologies T1 and T2. The scope of this study does not allow for the examination of technological matters. For the CPP's nodal balance equation, see Eq. (8); for the IF's nodal balance, see Eq. (9).

$$\sum_{s\in S} F_{sc}^{cpp}\alpha_c = \sum_{u\in U} D_{cu}^{cpp} \tag{8}$$

$$\sum_{s\in S} F_{si}^{if}\alpha_i = \sum_{u\in U} D_{iu}^{if}\ \forall i \in I \tag{9}$$

Table 2. Technology-based investment costs

Technology Innovation	Constant	T1	T2
Conversion factor (α)		0.13	0.7
Investment cost	a($/day)	1400	1950
	b($/ton)	56.4	100.69
Processing cost	($/day)	29	52

2.3.3 Nodal Mass Balance on End-Users

Every processing node's ultimate output must be efficiently delivered to consumers. The requirements of each consumer must be satisfied regarding quantity and quality. There are presently no products in stock at the warehouse. Equation (10) depicts the user's nodal balance.

$$\sum_{c \in C} D_{cu}^{cpp} + \sum_{i \in I} D_{iu}^{if} = R_U \ \forall u \in U \tag{10}$$

3 Result and Discussion

The present paper utilizes ACO and NSGA-II techniques to minimize the cost of BSN. Figures 2 and 3 show the algorithms of these techniques. The details of these techniques can be found in [4]. The computations were performed on Intel (R) Core (TM) i5-7200U CPU @ 2.50-GHz and GB RAM. The BSN case study comprises 58 variables and 17 mass balance constraints. These constraints are imposed on every individual variable. The outcomes derived from implementing ACO and NSGA-II were contrasted with not optimized ones. The ACO and GA algorithms were able to generate viable solutions within a 50 and 60-s time frame. The findings acquired are illustrated in Figs. 4 and 5. Figure 4 depicts the ton-per-day biomass flow rate (x1-x6) through S1 to the two CPPs and four IFs and the ton-per-day biomass flow rate (y1-y6) from S2 to the same facilities. Similarly, z1-z6 values represent the flow rate from source S3 to two CPPs and four IFs.

Compared to the non-optimized examples, NSGA-II and ACO indicate that the discharge rate from the three biomass suppliers differs between the three biomass supplies. The biomass supply rate from biomass supplier S1 is initially compared to CPPs and IFs. While transporting the biomass from source S1 to CPP2, IF3, and IF4, comparing the two methodologies reveals that the biomass flow rate attained with ACO remains higher than that obtained with NSGA-II.

We use NSGA-II results in the maximum biomass flow rate compared to CPP2, IF1, and IF4 for the biomass gathered from source S2. ACO offers a higher throughput than other processing units. The collected biomass from source S3 shows a similar pattern, with NSGA-II producing a larger biomass flow quantity than ACO for IF3 and IF4. Two more processing units continue to have a much lower biomass discharge rate. The estimated cost of setting up a distribution system for biomass is likely to change due to this fluctuation. Using NSGA-II, we find that the total biomass from all three

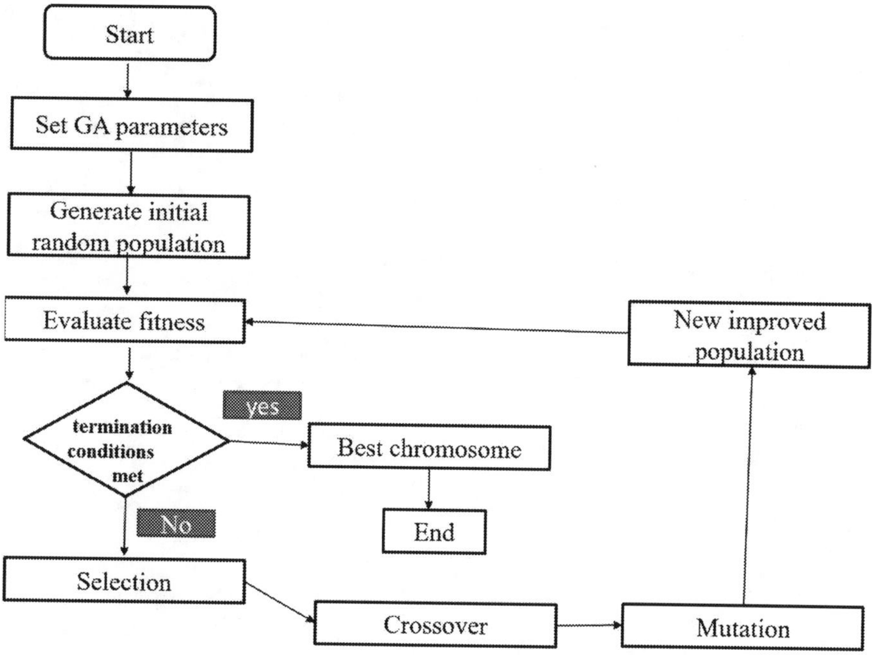

Fig. 2. Genetic Algorithm

sources consistently ranges between 8,000 and 10,000 tons, plateauing at about 14,000. The value demonstrates the veracity of the results obtained by employing ACO and NSGA-II. Before conducting a comparative analysis of the total costs associated with a BSN, it is necessary to comprehensively evaluate several other significant factors. The initial parameter refers to the discharge rate of processed biomass at the central and industrial processing plant designated for end-user consumption. Figure 5 depicts the biofuel transport rate from the two CPPs and four IFs to the consumers (UR). The diagram illustrates the biomass fuel flow rate (in tonnes per day) from the primary and secondary CPP to eight consumers, denoted by the symbols ei to li and fi to mi.

The numerals ni to ci show the flow rate of biofuel (measured in tonnes per day) from the biomass source to the eight end-users, where i represents the index of the end-users ($i = 1, 2$). Upon conducting a comparative analysis of the biofuel delivery rate from CPP1 to users, it has been observed that using the NSGA-II optimization algorithm maximizes biofuel transportation from CPP2 to user 2. Comparable findings have been demonstrated regarding the rate of biofuel flow from CPP2 alongside IFs to end-users.

It is imperative to note that significant fluctuations in biomass flow rates from the source to the CPPs and IFs are evident in all the figures. Diverse fluctuations are observed in the biofuel flow rate conveyed from Central Processing Facilities (CPPs) to end-users. The diversity in the expense of BSN can also be reflected in the plots generated by NSGA- II and ACO algorithms. The findings indicate that, concerning an unoptimized network, NSGA-II yields a cost reduction of about $66,000 for the specified amount of

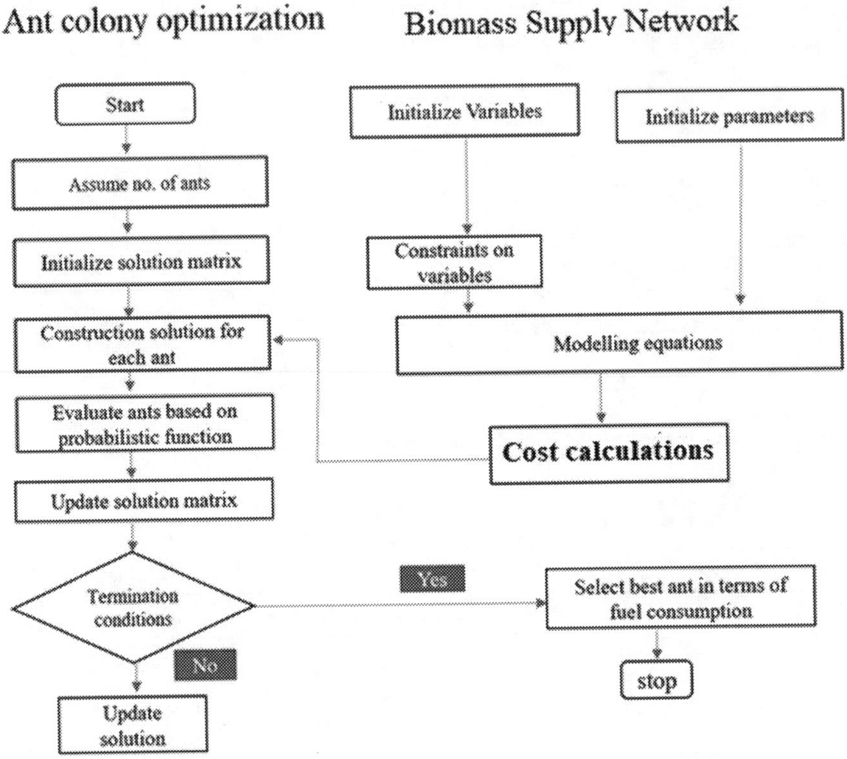

Fig. 3. Ant Colony Optimization Algorithm

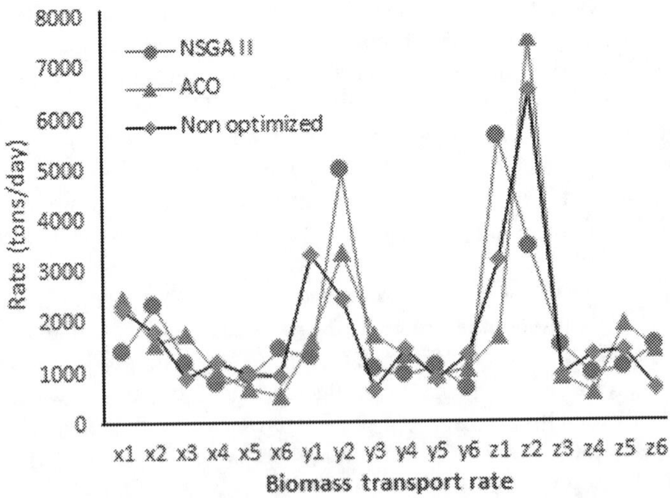

Fig. 4. Comparison of biomass transported from source to CPP and IF

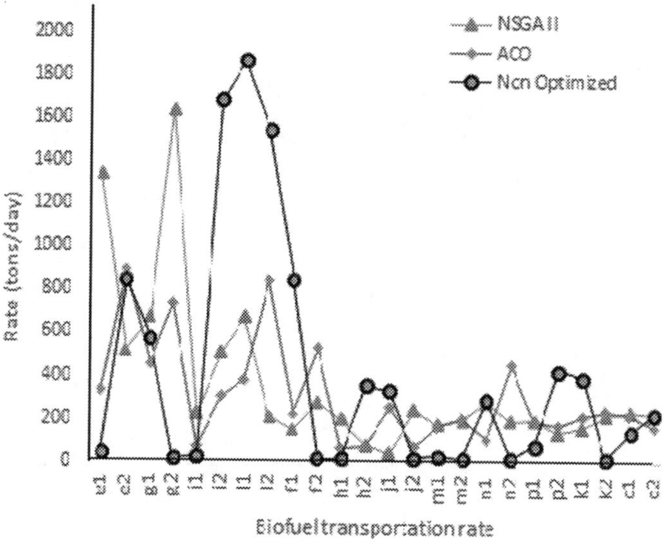

Fig. 5. Comparison of biofuel amount transported from CPP and IF to customers

biomass provided by all three biomass sources, whereas ACO results in a cost reduction of $325,330.

4 Conclusion and Future Recommendations

The efficient utilization of biomass as a sustainable energy source has been recognized as a viable remedy to the challenges that stem from the extensive dependence on non-renewable fossil fuels. The present study introduces a comprehensive mathematical simulation model to minimize the expenses associated with the BSN. The chosen BSN has undergone evaluation by utilizing a Non-Sorting Genetic Algorithm (NSGA- II) and Ant Colony Optimization (ACO). The findings suggest that exploiting NSGA- II and ACO algorithms decreases the total cost of BSN. The utilization of simulation models and the subsequent findings obtained from the investigation can offer significant insights to governmental bodies and operators, facilitating their ability to forecast and minimize the overall expenses associated with BSN. Utilizing this approach could potentially enhance the development of strategic plans and decision-making processes regarding the Biomass supply network while minimizing expenses, ultimately optimizing budgetary demands. The outcome demonstrates significant cost savings. It is recommended to explore additional optimization techniques, such as the Firefly algorithm, Cuckoo search, and the Greedy Fox algorithm, which have not been previously studied for optimizing BSN. These techniques may potentially deliver superior outcomes and warrant further exploration.

References

1. Arya, A.K.: A comparison of the MOGA and NSGA-II optimization techniques to reduce the cost of a biomass supply network. Mater. Today: Proc. (2022). https://doi.org/10.1016/j.matpr.2021.12.161
2. Arya, A.K., Honwad, S.: Optimal operation of a multi source multi delivery natural gas transmission pipeline network. Chem. Prod. Process Model. **13**, 20170046 (2018). https://doi.org/10.1515/cppm-2017-0046
3. Arya, A.K., Honwad, S.: Modeling, simulation, and optimization of a high-pressure cross-country natural gas pipeline: application of an ant colony optimization technique. J. Pipeline Syst. Eng. Pract. **7**, 04015008 (2016). https://doi.org/10.1061/(ASCE)PS.1949-1204.0000206
4. Arya, A.K.: A critical review on optimization parameters and techniques for gas pipeline operation profitability. J. Petrol. Explor. Prod. Technol. **12**(11), 3033–3057 (2022). https://doi.org/10.1007/s13202-022-01490-5
5. Arya, A.K., Katiyar, R., Kumar, P.S., Kapoor, A., Pal, D.B., Rangasamy, G.: A multi-objective model for optimizing hydrogen injected-high pressure natural gas pipeline networks. Int. J. Hydrogen Energy **48**, 29699–29723 (2023). https://doi.org/10.1016/j.ijhydene.2023.04.133
6. Arya, A.K., Honwad, S.: Multiobjective optimization of a gas pipeline network: an ant colony approach. J. Petrol. Explor. Prod. Technol. **8**, 1389–1400 (2018). https://doi.org/10.1007/s13202-017-0410-7
7. Arya, A.K.: Optimal operation of a multi-distribution natural gas pipeline grid: an ant colony approach. J. Petrol. Explor. Prod. Technol. **11**(10), 3859–3878 (2021). https://doi.org/10.1007/s13202-021-01266-3
8. Kumar, A., Gopal, K., Aggarwal, A.: Cost and performance analysis of server-centric authentication protocol in supply chain management. In: 2014 IEEE International Symposium on Signal Processing and Information Technology (ISSPIT) (2014)
9. Kumar, A., Gopal, K., Aggarwal, A.: Modeling and analysis of RFID authentication protocols for supply chain management. In: 2014 International Conference on Parallel, Distributed and Grid Computing (2014)
10. Arya, A.K., Kumar, A., Pujari, M., Pacheco, D.A.D.J.: Improving natural gas supply chain profitability: a multi-methods optimization study. Energy **282**, 12659 (2023)
11. Singh, H., et al.: Designing an optimized free space optical (FSO) link for terrestrial commercial applications under turbulent channel conditions. Opt. Quant. Electron. **55**(6), 532 (2023)
12. Njima, W., Amhoud, E.M.: Federated learning based hierarchical 3D indoor localization. In: 2023 IEEE Wireless Communications and Networking Conference (WCNC), pp. 1–6. IEEE (2023)

Federated Unlearning and Server Right to Forget: Handling Unreliable Client Contributions

Hasin Bano[1,2], Muhammad Ameen[3(✉)], Muntazir Mehdi[4], Amaad Hussain[5], and Pengfei Wang[3]

[1] University of Baltistan, Skardu, Gilgit -Baltistan, Pakistan
[2] Kunming University of Science and Technology, Kunming, Yunnan, China
[3] Dalian University of Technology, Dalian, Liaoning, China
mamngri@mail.dlut.edu.cn
[4] University of Derby, Derby DE22 1GB, UK
[5] Bahria University Islamabad, E-8, Islamabad, Pakistan

Abstract. In the context of federated learning, the concept of federated unlearning has emerged, aiming to realize the "right to be forgotten". The current research primarily focuses on designing unlearning techniques for clients "right to be forgotten", it has often bypassed to consider the server's authority to discard the client contribution without taking any consent from participating clients, we named it "right to forget". These client contributions may contain adverse effects that could significantly impact global aggregation. In this research paper, we conduct a comprehensive review of previous studies related to federated unlearning and explore the server "right to forget" client's contributions. We also introduce new taxonomies to classify and summarize the latest advancements in federated unlearning algorithms. Moreover, we take the first step to present the server right to forget (SRF), a novel unlearning methodology that enables the server to remove unreliable client contributions to improve global model accuracy. Experiments on two different kinds of datasets and models demonstrate the effectiveness of our method. We envision our effort as a first step toward the server's right to forget the client's contribution in the context of federated unlearning toward adherence to legal and ethical standards in a just and transparent manner.

Keywords: Federated Learning · Federated Unlearning · Server Rights · Unreliable Contribution

1 Introduction

The concept of "Right to be Forgotten" in contemporary privacy regulations, such as the General Data Protection Regulation (GDPR) in the European Union

Muntazir Mehdi, Amaad Hussain: Equally Contributed.

KC Santosh et al. (Eds.): RTIP2R 2023, CCIS 2027, pp. 393–410, 2024.
https://doi.org/10.1007/978-3-031-53085-2_31

[1–3], gives individuals the right to request the erasure of their personal data. Researchers presented techniques to help trained machine-learning algorithms forget the data that needed to be erased when they first introduced it as a machine unlearning problem in the literature [4]. While most previous studies concentrated on centralized machine unlearning, where the model owner has access to all data, a novel method called federated unlearning (FUL) [5] has emerged. This research aims to extend the exploration of data removal, the influence of data removal, and unlearning to the context of federated learning.

In federated learning (FL), multiple clients (e.g., a mobile device, edge device, etc.) collaboratively train a shared model without sharing their private data, and they can join or leave the training process at any given time [6,7]. The procedure of erasing a client's contribution like the subtraction of whole or partial data from the global model can improve the flexibility and reliability of the FL systems [8–10]. Inspired by conventional machine unlearning, the concept of FUL emerged to address the imperative of the "right to be forgotten" within a distributed environment [2,3]. This approach combines the principles of FL and FUL introducing unique complexities in devising an efficient unlearning algorithm, as previously highlighted in relevant publications [11,12]. Recent advancements have directed the development of novel mechanisms [11,13] tailored for machine unlearning within the FL framework, commonly referred to as FUL.

The existing literature on FUL commonly assumes the removal of data from a single client [11,14], and the primary objective of the unlearning procedure is to eliminate the historical contributions of that target client from the global model training. A very traditional and simple way to unlearn involves retraining the model from the very beginning after deleting the requested client's data for deletion. However, the same set of clients in the retraining method is computationally intensive and impractical, as some existing rapid retraining mechanisms have assumed. After analyzing the existing literature we are sure that, instead of starting from scratch, the only viable method for practical federated unlearning is to employ approximation algorithms. This method addresses the difficulties of engaging various client sets in the unlearning process while providing a more computationally effective alternative. FL's unique challenges make conventional approximation algorithms unsuitable due to the spread of contributions between clients and the privacy restrictions on individual data sets. Therefore, those machines unlearning approximation algorithms, cannot be directly applied to FUL such as data set partitioning [15].

The primary focus of existing studies on federated unlearning is enabling clients to exercise their "right to be forgotten" by unlearning their data or contributions. This is because the "Right to be Forgotten" is a legal right that has been granted to clients in the European Union (EU) and the California Consumer Privacy Act (CCPA) in the United States [1,16]. This is important to address privacy concerns and comply with data regulations while participating in the federated learning process. However, there is another important aspect to consider in federated unlearning the server's right to remove unreliable or noisy contributions made by clients during the global model training process.

Clients in federated learning have heterogeneous data sets, varying computational capabilities, and varying degrees of reliability. Some clients might have noisy or poorly labeled data, or they might be unreliable in terms of communication, leading to contributions that adversely affect the overall global model's performance. Hence ensure the effectiveness and robustness of federated learning, it is the right of the server to identify and mitigate the impact of unreliable contributions from participating clients. This can involve methods for detecting outliers, verifying the accuracy of contributions, applying weighting schemes to prioritize more reliable client's contributions, or other unlearning techniques to eliminate the harmful contributions by clients.

In this paper, we present an exhaustive examination of recent breakthroughs in federated unlearning, including the assessment of the client's right to be forgotten and the server's right to forget untrustworthy client inputs, with specific attention to their adverse effects on the global model. The contents of this paper encompass novel perspectives and commentary, previously unexplored or underemphasized in existing academic works. Additionally, we proposed a method that aims to eliminate the unreliable contribution of clients on the server side without any permission from clients by using the server "right to forget". We present SRF, which stands for Server Right to Forget.

2 Preliminaries

In this section, we review FUL, the prominence of FUL, the hypothesis of previous studies, and the unlearning of client contribution.

2.1 Federated Unlearning

In the FL system, the client's data preferences may change over time or privacy concerns might arise, leading to a request for data removal. FUL comes into play in these scenarios, enabling clients to selectively retract their data contributions without compromising the overall model's performance and fairness [2,3].

Generally, in the context of FL, we have two main scenarios where we need unlearning: (1) The client's right to be forgotten and (2) The server's right to forget the client's contribution. Existing work usually assumes that unlearning happens when a client needs to opt-out of its contribution from the global model. However, there are many cases in federated learning where servers need to eliminate the contribution of specific clients.

Client Right to be Forgotten: The client's right to unlearn their contribution refers to the individual client's prerogative to request the removal of their whole data D or a specific part of data D' from the global model. In this scenario, the client initiates the process by requesting data removal, and the burden of ensuring data privacy and unlearning lies with the client. The client may selectively identify and remove specific data points or batches that they previously contributed to the model.

Server Right to Forget Client Contribution: On the other hand, the server's right to remove the client contribution grants the central server the authority to remove whole data D, partial data D', or only specific influences of the target client from the global model. This removal may occur when the server identifies unreliable or untrustworthy client contributions that could negatively impact the global model's performance or privacy. The server takes on the responsibility for executing the process, ensuring the integrity and fairness of the global model.

2.2 Prominence of Federated Unlearning

FedEraser [11] was proposed as an initial attempt to approximate unlearning within FL. It is designed to address the client's right to be forgotten in the context of FL. It focuses on allowing clients to remove their data contributions from the global model by utilizing a calibration technique. To achieve this, the server is required to store a history of parameter updates for each client. While this assumption is reasonable in practice, it could lead to significant storage overhead when dealing with a large number of clients in a federated learning session. FedEraser performs as a retraining strategy, involving extra communication rounds between the server and clients. During these rounds, all clients modify their historical updates based on their individual historical datasets, aiming to mitigate the influence of specific client data that needs to be forgotten or removed.

However, practical performances should consider the storage requirements of keeping historical updates, as it may pose challenges in scalability when dealing with multiple clients. The dependence on additional communication rounds may also introduce latency and communication costs, impacting the efficiency of federated learning, especially with a large number of clients or resource-constrained devices.

Halimi et al.'s design is based on the client's right to be forgotten in the context of federated learning [13]. The focus of their approach is on allowing individual clients to exercise their right to opt-out or request data removal from the global model. The target client, who wishes to be forgotten, plays a central role in the unlearning process by performing projected gradient ascent to train the global model on its local data and maximize the empirical loss before the data deletion.

The method does not explicitly involve the server's right to forget client contribution. Instead, it empowers the client to initiate the unlearning process, providing them with control over the data they wish to have removed from the global model. The server's role is to facilitate the unlearning process based on the target client's actions, without storing extensive parameter updates from all clients.

In the research, **Liu et al.** introduced an unexplored rapid retraining technique in the context of FL [12]. The core approach involves retraining the global model using the remaining dataset through the approximation of the loss function using the first-order Taylor expansion. Crucially, the success of this method depended on the active participation of all clients in the FL system. It is essential to note that while this algorithm exhibits efficiency in local training, it should not be solely classified as an approximation algorithm for FUL. While the method accomplishes rapid retraining by utilizing the remaining data, it does not explicitly manage the unlearning of individual client contributions, which is an essential aspect of FUL. To clarify, the focus of Liu et al.'s approach primarily revolves around swift updates of the global model, leveraging first-order Taylor expansion for improved local training without directly considering the specific challenges of the unlearning process. As such, it may not be the ideal solution for scenarios requiring data removal or unlearning of client contributions to maintain compliance with data privacy regulations and respect individual data rights.

Wu et al. [14] proposed an alternative strategy that also depends on the server storing historical updates for each client as similar to FedEraser. However, instead of instructing clients to retrain the model as FedEraser did, Wu et al.'s method involved subtracting all historically averaged updates from the target client's contribution from the final global model. This step resulted in the creation of a skewed unlearning model, which was subsequently trained using knowledge distillation. The knowledge distillation process utilized the original global model as the teacher model on an outsourced unlabelled dataset. It is worth noting that Wu et al.'s method introduced a potential challenge related to data sampling. To train the skewed unlearning model, synthetic data with the same distribution as the entire dataset needed to be sampled. However, the accuracy of this sampling process could be negatively impacted by non-IID (not independent and identically distributed) data distribution, which is typically assumed in federated learning scenarios.

Federated Recommendation Unlearning (FRU) is a recent approach that is designed to address the need for client unlearning in federated recommendation systems [17]. Drawing motivation from the log-based rollback mechanism of transactions in database management systems, FRU allows to removal of a user's contribution by rolling back and calibrating the historical parameter updates. Subsequently, these calibrated updates are utilized to expedite the reconstruction of the federated recommender, enabling efficient and secure user data removal while maintaining the system's performance.

Subspace Based Unlearning (SFU) [18] is similar to other unlearning methods to address the need for users to unlearn the contribution from the global model. It is the most recently proposed method introducing an approach to FUL that overcomes the limitation of server storage constraints in existing algorithms. SFU enables the global model to perform gradient ascent in orthogonal spaces created by other client's input gradient spaces, allowing the elimination of the requested client's contribution without requiring additional storage. Specifically, the server collects gradients from the requested client after gradient ascent, while the input representation matrix is locally computed by the remaining clients. Like other methods, SFU also overlooks scenarios where a server may need to remove the contributions of specific clients due to its own solid reasons such as the global model's performance or privacy, etc.

2.3 Hypothesis on Previous Studies

Currently, the subject of federated unlearning remains relatively under-explored in research. Notably, none of the existing studies have broadly compared the performance of existing unlearning algorithms with each other, excluding the comparison with the classic retraining approach from scratch. As a result, it remains unclear which of the existing algorithms shows outstanding performance concerning the time consumed for unlearning and its impact on the accuracy of the global model.

In the subsequent sections, we provide a comprehensive and detailed analysis of these assumptions made in the existing body of work. This analysis will shed light on the variations in unlearning scenarios and the potential implications of these assumptions on the effectiveness and generalizability of the proposed algorithms. By understanding the underlying assumptions, we can better assess the strengths and limitations of the current approaches and identify areas for further investigation and refinement in the domain of federated unlearning.

2.4 Unlearning of Client Contribution

Prior research has commonly made two false assumptions: **(1)** Unlearning occurs when a client needs the "right to be forgotten", but there are many cases where the server needs to eliminate the contribution of specific clients. **(2)** Unlearning occurs when a client needs to fully withdraw from the current federated learning (FL) session. However, in the context of federated learning, there are examples where clients are only requested to remove a specific portion of their data.

The existing work that solely considers one of these scenarios may encounter challenges in addressing the other. For the first assumption, for instance, the unlearning mechanism proposed by [14] may not yield the expected results when the target client only intends to remove a portion of its data. In this case, the server would remove all historical average updates associated with the client from the global model, which might not be the desired outcome for partial data removal requests. This discrepancy highlights the need for more comprehensive and adaptable unlearning mechanisms that can cater to both complete and partial data removal scenarios in federated learning settings.

For the second assumption we can take the example of FedEraser [11] that it only can provide expected results when the client needs to opt out of its contribution from the global model but in case, the server identifies some negative impacts on the global model then FedEraser can't handle this case to remove the adverse impacts from the global model. Such contrast emphasizes the need for more extensive and flexible unlearning mechanisms that can cater to both the "client's right to be forgotten" and the "server's right to forget the client" scenarios in FL settings.

Table 1. Categorization of Existing FUL Mechanisms Based on Hypothesis

Existing Unlearning Mechanism	Client right to unlearn	Server right to unlearn
FedErase	✓	x
Halimi et al. [13]	✓	x
Liu et al. [12]	✓	x
Wu et al. [14]	✓	x
Federated Recommendation Unlearning (FRU)	✓	x
Subspace Based Unlearning (SFU)	✓	x

As we discussed mainly FUL occurs in two main scenarios, where the client needs to remove their own contribution (Client right to be forgotten) or the server needs to remove the client's contribution (Server right to forget). According to these two different scenarios, we categorize the existing work as shown in Table 1. Figure 1 gives an overview of the importance of the server's right to remove the client's contribution under few scenarios where the server needs an unlearning of the participating client's contribution.

Scenario 1: In the first scenario when a client trains the model with bad data and sends flawed updates, the central server has full rights and various options to respond. The severity of the bad updates and the client's past performance influence the server's choices. It may decide to partially or entirely exclude the client's contribution, temporarily isolate the client, offer feedback, dynamically adjust contribution weights, and employ recovery strategies to rectify the model's performance and reliability. These actions are aimed at upholding the collaborative essence of federated learning while safeguarding the overall quality of the aggregated model.

Scenario 2: As we can see in Fig. 1 scenario 2 the emergence of adversarial attacks during the transmission of locally trained models to the server poses a significant threat to the privacy and accuracy of the global model. Adversarial attacks can embed malicious or misleading information within the model updates, aiming to compromise the integrity of the aggregated model or glean sensitive information.

To address this, the central server is empowered to exercise the right to mitigate the impact of adversarial attacks on the global model's accuracy and privacy. This can be achieved by implementing an unlearning process. Unlearning involves selectively removing or neutralizing the perturbing effects of the adversarial updates from the model's parameters, effectively reversing their influence. By doing so, the server enhances the model's resilience against adversarial manipulation and reinforces its trustworthiness.

Scenario 3: In the third scenario, where clients contribute their data for model training, the concept of the server "right to forget" after aggregation becomes particularly relevant due to data privacy concerns, especially when certain client's data contains sensitive or personally identifiable information (PII).

After aggregating client updates, the server may possess a merged model that encodes fragments of individual clients' data, potentially comprising sensitive or

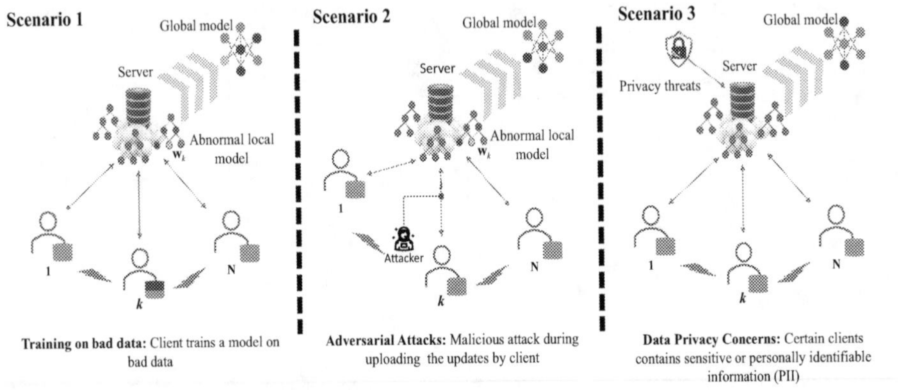

Fig. 1. Different scenarios where server right to eliminate the contribution of the client.

PII details. The server's "right to forget" acknowledges the need to mitigate data privacy risks even after aggregation. This entails the server purposefully reducing its retention of individualized data to ensure that no specific client's information can be reconstructed from the aggregated model.

The server can apply techniques like model pruning, obfuscation, or noise injection to obscure the traces of individual data within the aggregated model. This helps to prevent any unauthorized reconstruction of sensitive information, thereby aligning with data protection regulations and respecting user privacy.

Collectively, these findings emphasize the central server's multifaceted rights in FL from managing bad updates and adversarial attacks to protecting the global model. The server's "right to forget" emerges as a versatile tool to address diverse challenges and ensure the quality, security, and ethical use of collaborative models.

3 Related Work

Federated unlearning entails a complete system for effectively refusing the influence of specific data or eliminating the whole contribution of the client involved in training local models within the federated learning (FL) framework. However, due to FL's decentralized and private nature, traditional machine unlearning methods aren't directly adaptable to an FL setting. An initial approach for FUL involves data removal and subsequent retraining of the FL model from scratch. Yet, this often incurs substantial time and computational costs.

In recent years we noticed the emergence of several unlearning methods tailored to FL. The creative work, FedEraser, introduced in 2020 [11], retains client parameter updates on the central server, enabling calibrated parameter updates for the trained global model, actually negating a client's influence. However, FedEraser's FUL algorithm is limited to the requesting participating client, exiting models of other clients retaining contributions from the target data. Further, it approximates the current unlearned update using the latest round of local model updates, potentially containing contributions from the to-be-removed data.

Addressing this, Liu *et al.* [12] propose rapid retraining for FUL, employing gradient estimation and parameter updating approximation to expedite model reconstruction. Liu *et al.* [19], deploys a trainable dummy gradient generator per client, eliminating specific data contributions. Halimi *et al.* [13] reverse-engineer target client learning processes for FUL, leveraging the 2-norm range of other clients' local model averages as loss maximization constraints. Likewise, Wu *et al.* [20] perform backward learning for FUL, while VeriFi [21] shrinks the target client's contribution and enhances remaining clients' contribution to facilitate unlearning, with provisions for verification. Liu *et al.* [22] present a secure federated random forest framework, accommodating participant revocation and conflict avoidance.

Though existing methods prioritize client-initiated FUL for data privacy and security, server-initiated FUL plays a pivotal role in enhancing model accuracy and reliability. Wu *et al.* [14] propose server-initiated FUL to revoke attacker influence, leveraging historical parameter updates and knowledge distillation. Similarly, Yuan *et al.* [17] propose FRU to modify historical updates for efficient unlearning. These methods, however, demand significant storage, limiting their practicality. And there is no other method in previous studies, which focuses on the server "right to forget". whenever the server needs to eliminate the contribution of any of the participating clients to improve the global model accuracy.

Addressing this gap, we propose a novel FUL method, to eliminate the adversarial contributing clients on the server side without obtaining any permission from the client. Our approach "SRF" is designed to enhance the accuracy of the global model and to promote the server's right to forget the client's contribution. This tackles the issue of local models negatively affecting the global model due to different reasons such as data quality variance, malicious attacks, etc.

4 Design of Server Right to Forget

In this section, we discuss the overview of the system model SRF, and design details of the proposed method.

4.1 Overview

SRF (Server Right to Forget) is a simple and effective technique to efficiently eliminate the influence of unreliable contribution of clients from the trained global model. We add two extra functions to the central server for SRF in the current architecture of FL, while the original functions of the central server remain unchanged. As we know the central server updates the global model based on the aggregation of the collected updates, thereby obtaining an updated global model W^{i+1} that will play the role of the global model for the next training round. When the termination criteria have been satisfied, the central server will stop the above iterative training process and get the final FL model

W^i. On the other hand side before termination criteria are fulfilled if unlearning condition[1] satisfied, the server will start the unlearning process for the current round (Fig. 2).

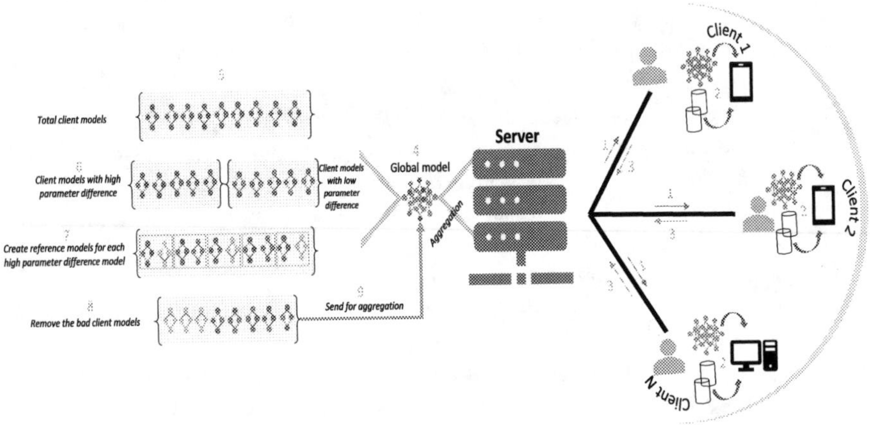

Fig. 2. System Model of SRF

SRF mainly involves three steps: (1) identifying unreliable clients, (2) reference model construction, and (3) selective removal of the client contribution. All steps are executed on the central server as we can see in the SRF system model Fig. 2 and algorithm 1.

4.2 Design Details

The system aims to ensure a high-quality global model, despite the presence of adverse impacts on clients, by promptly identifying and removing the client's contribution. Specifically, SRF is tasked with achieving the following design goals.

Identifying Unreliable Clients: In the context of federated learning, the identification of unreliable clients refers to figuring out which individual client's model changes are messing up the big group model. This is about spotting updates from clients that are different from what everyone's trying to learn together. These odd updates could mess up how well the big model works and how it learns. Finding these problematic updates is keen important to ensure the maintenance of model accuracy, trustworthiness, and safety in the federated setup.

[1] The unlearning condition is that the global model's accuracy in the current round must drop below that in the previous round.

Algorithm 1. Server Right to Forget Unreliable Clients

Require: global model W^i, local models w, benchmark dataset D.
Ensure: Unlearned Global Model $W^{i'}$

for each *client* **do**
  $D_i \leftarrow C_i - M$
  $||D_i||_2 \leftarrow \sqrt{\sum_{j=1}^{N}(D_i^j)^2}, \quad \text{for } i = 1, 2, \ldots, C$
  $||D_{\text{mean}}||_2 \leftarrow \frac{1}{C}\sum_{i=1}^{C}||D_i||_2$
  $A \leftarrow \{i : ||D_i||_2 > ||D_{\text{mean}}||_2\}$
end for
$\alpha_1 \leftarrow$ weight parameters of M;
$\alpha_0 \leftarrow$ bias parameters of M;
$\beta_1 \leftarrow$ weight parameters of C_i;
$\beta_0 \leftarrow$ bias parameters of C_i;
$\theta_1 \leftarrow$ weight parameters of R_i;
$\theta_0 \leftarrow$ bias parameters of R_i;
$R_i \leftarrow$ bad model;
for $a \in \mathcal{A}$ **do**
  $\theta_1 \leftarrow \alpha_1 - (\beta_1 - \alpha_1) \cdot \frac{n-n_i}{n}$
  $\theta_0 \leftarrow \alpha_0 - (\beta_0 - \alpha_0) \cdot \frac{n-n_i}{n}$
  $\vdots$
  $\theta_0 \leftarrow \alpha_0 - (\beta_0 - \alpha_0) \cdot \frac{n-n_i}{n}$
  $A_i \leftarrow \text{accuracy}(R_i, D), \quad \text{for } i \leftarrow 1, 2, \ldots, \text{N}$
  $A_m \leftarrow \frac{1}{\text{N}}\sum_{i=1}^{\text{N}} A_i$
  $R_{\text{effective}} \leftarrow \{R_i : A_i > \text{mean\_accuracy}\}$
end for
$W^{i'} = (\text{w} - \text{A}) \cup R_{\text{effective}}$;
return $W^{i'}$

The identification process rests upon quantifying the divergence between each client's parameter updates and the established global model. This divergence is assessed through the utilization of the L2 norm, which encapsulates the geometric extent of the parameter differences between a client's model and the global model. It's like measuring the distance between points in space, telling us how big the differences are. This helps us understand how much things are changing.

Identifying unreliable clients is challenging because the server can't access the data of clients. To initiate the identification process, the parameters of the global model are employed as a baseline reference. The parameters of the participating client models are then compared against this baseline through the calculation of the L2 norm. Client models exhibiting L2 norms that exceed the mean norm value signify instances of heightened contribution relative to the general cohort. These clients are hence considered unreliable clients due to their parameter updates producing discernibly significant alterations to the global model's parameter space. Incorporating updates from clients with big differences can also introduce noise or bias to the global model, and it may be the data is significantly different from the overall data distribution.

$$A = \{i : ||D_i||_2 > ||D_{\text{mean}}||_2\}, \quad (1)$$

where A is the set of unreliable client indices.

In mathematical terms, this process can be summarized as in Eq. 2, 3, 4, and 5. Compute the vectors representing the differences in parameters for each client, subsequently evaluate the L2 norm for each of these parameter difference vectors, compute the average L2 norm across all clients, and then detect unreliable client by comparing the L2 norms.

$$D_i = C_i - M, \quad \text{for } i = 1, 2, \ldots, C. \quad (2)$$

$$||D_i||_2 = \sqrt{\sum_{j=1}^{N} (D_i^j)^2}, \quad \text{for } i = 1, 2, \ldots, C. \quad (3)$$

$$||D_{\text{mean}}||_2 = \frac{1}{C} \sum_{i=1}^{C} ||D_i||_2. \quad (4)$$

$$A = \{i : ||D_i||_2 > ||D_{\text{mean}}||_2\}. \quad (5)$$

where: M represents the global model's parameter vector, C_i represents the parameter vector of client i, D_i represents the parameter difference vector between the global model and client i, i.e. $D_i = C_i - M$, and $|| \cdot ||_2$ denotes the L2 norm.

Reference Model Construction: In the context of mitigating unreliable contributions, the construction of reference models plays a pivotal role. Reference models encapsulate the influence of identified unreliable clients, allowing for the delineation and subsequent attenuation of their impact on the global model. This process involves generating parameter values for the reference model that are derived by counteracting the perturbations introduced by the unreliable client's updates. By "subtracting" these contributions from the global model's parameters, the reference model serves as a representation of the global model unaffected by unreliable contributions.

Mathematically, the construction of reference model parameters R_i for each identified unreliable client i can be expressed as follows:

$$R_i.\text{conv1.weight} = M.\text{conv1.weight} - (C_i.\text{conv1.weight} - M.\text{conv1.weight}) \cdot \frac{n - n_i}{n}$$

$$R_i.\text{conv1.bias} = M.\text{conv1.bias} - (C_i.\text{conv1.bias} - M.\text{conv1.bias}) \cdot \frac{n - n_i}{n},$$

$$\vdots$$

$$R_i.\text{fc3.bias} = M.\text{fc3.bias} - (C_i.\text{fc3.bias} - M.\text{fc3.bias}) \cdot \frac{n - n_i}{n},$$

where: R_i represents the parameters of the reference model for unreliable client i. C_i denotes the parameter values of the unreliable client i's client model. M stands for the parameters of the global model. n signifies the total volume of data across all clients. n_i indicates the volume of data about the unreliable client i.

Selective Removal of Clients. The process of selective pruning based on accuracy involves assessing the performance of the reference models constructed for identified unreliable clients. This evaluation is conducted on a designated test dataset. The objective is to determine which reference models demonstrate proficiency in enhancing the global model's accuracy while effectively mitigating unreliable contributions. Reference models that exhibit accuracies exceeding the mean accuracy are retained, as they are deemed effective in bolstering the robustness of the federated learning system.

Mathematical equations: Calculate the accuracy of each reference model on the test data set, calculate the mean accuracy across all reference models, identify and keep only effective reference models for retention based on accuracy, and remove the client models whose accuracy is below the mean accuracy.

$$A_i = \text{accuracy}(R_i, \text{test\_dataset}), \quad \text{for } i = 1, 2, \ldots, \text{N}. \tag{6}$$

$$A_m = \frac{1}{\text{N}} \sum_{i=1}^{\text{N}} A_i. \tag{7}$$

$$R_{\text{effective}} = \{R_i : A_i > \text{mean\_accuracy}\} \tag{8}$$

where R_i represents the i-th reference model constructed for an unreliable client model, N is num_unreliable_clients, A_i represent the accuracy of the i-th reference model on the test dataset. A_m denotes the mean accuracy across all reference models.$R_{\text{effective}}$ is the set of reference models considered effective based on accuracy evaluation.

Finally, refining the collection of client models by removing the unreliable clients and adding the reference models that are considered effective based on their performance, leads to a set of models that will be used for getting unlearned global model $W^{i'}$.

5 Performance Evaluation

In this section, we conduct extensive experiments to evaluate the performance of SRF. Specifically, we explain the evaluation methodology and evaluation results in detail.

5.1 Evaluation Methodology

Datasets: We utilize two datasets to evaluate SRF's performance, including MNIST [23] and FMNIST [24]. MNIST is a dataset consisting of handwritten digital grayscale images, and FMNIST is a dataset consisting of grayscale images of fashion items, both of which are composed of 60,000 training images and 10,000 test images.

Global Models: In our experiments, two datasets were trained with LeNet-5 [25] and the Multi-layer perceptron (MLP) having two hidden layers with 50 neurons each using ReLu activation, and its output layer has a softmax function.

Hyper-parameters: In our conducted experiments, we assess the performance of SRF while considering different quantities of participating clients in training rounds that involve distinct datasets. The chosen client count, denoted as N, takes on values from the set $\{10, 20, 30, 40, 50\}$. Initially, the global model's performance is evaluated by the server after each round of data aggregation. It's important to note that when the specific count of clients is not explicitly mentioned, the assumed default is 20 clients. To determine the data allocation for each client, we consider both the total training sample count n and the number of clients N. Throughout our experimentation, the distribution of data among clients follows a non-IID pattern. We utilize data models with noisy labels, indicative of lower quality, which are randomly assigned to clients. The local client epoch is set at 1, implying that after every single epoch, the client communicates with the central server to exchange model updates. The overall training consists of 5 rounds, and during the final 5th round, the server detects the bad impacts on the global model with the help of global model accuracy and initiates an unlearning process. The training's learning rate is established at 0.01, and each training batch comprises 64 items. For the optimization process, we utilize the SGD method. In the context of gradient ascent training, a maximum permissible divergence between the trained model and the base model is defined as 1. The batch size here is set to 1024, with an early stopping threshold of 10%, while the batch size is retained at 64.

Comparison Methods: In our experiments, we compare SRF with 4 different methods federated learning (FL) without unlearning (FedAvg), gradient ascent training only (GT), boosting training only (BT), and FUL with knowledge distillation (KD) as comparison algorithms.

Evaluation Metrics: We compare SRF's algorithm running time to other comparison approaches in order to assess the utility of SRF using common metrics from the machine learning community, such as the model's prediction accuracy and loss.

5.2 Evaluation Results

In this part, we evaluate the performance of our proposed method SRF. Besides the number of clients, the evaluation requirements follow the default settings, where the percentage of bad contributing clients is 20% and the percentage of bad-quality training data is 30%. We first investigate the performance of SRF in improving the accuracy of the global model when the number of clients varies. Figure 3 shows the model prediction accuracy of SRF and four comparison algorithms. We can observe that SRF are all able to improve the global model accuracy of FL affected by bad-quality data for an arbitrary number of clients. We can observe that FUL with KD, BT, and GA could drop the global model accuracy of FL for an arbitrary number of clients. For example, on the MNIST dataset and LeNet-5 model, when the number of clients is 40, the accuracy of the FL model can only reach 78.08%. While the model accuracy of SRF is 90.76% and KD, BT, and GA methods, dropped their accuracy 77.31%, 70.52% and 73.48% respectively. The reason for suddenly dropping the accuracy at client 40 and 50 is contains a large number of bad data and bad clients. Among them, SRF performed better than all other comparison methods. FL has the worst performance due to the influence of low-quality data. Gradient ascent training,

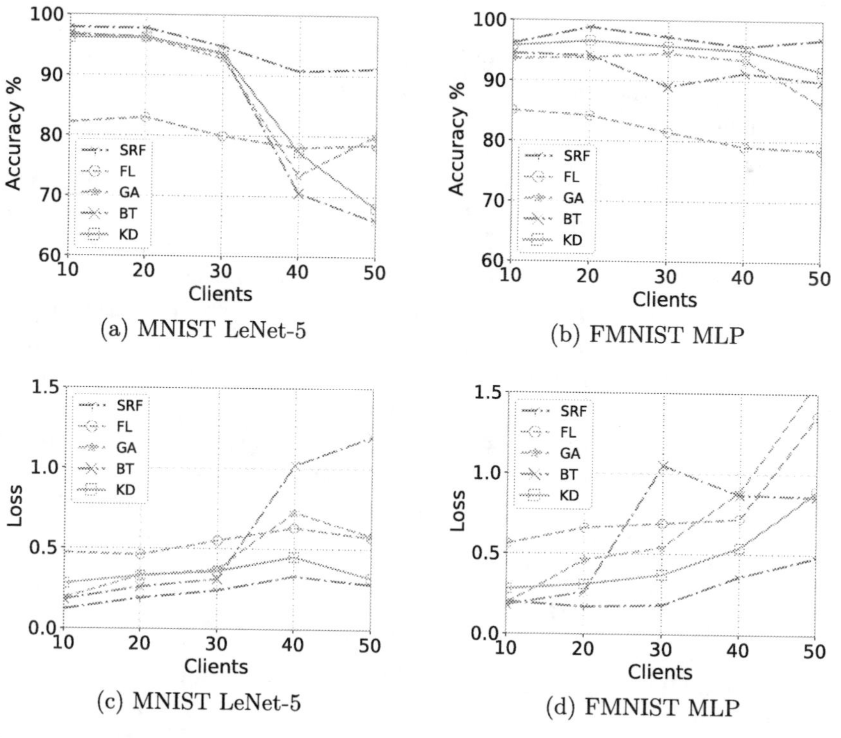

(a) MNIST LeNet-5 (b) FMNIST MLP

(c) MNIST LeNet-5 (d) FMNIST MLP

Fig. 3. Accuracy and loss comparison with number of clients

Boosting training methods, and FUL with knowledge distillation do not perform well and in some cases even fail to match FL's model accuracy.

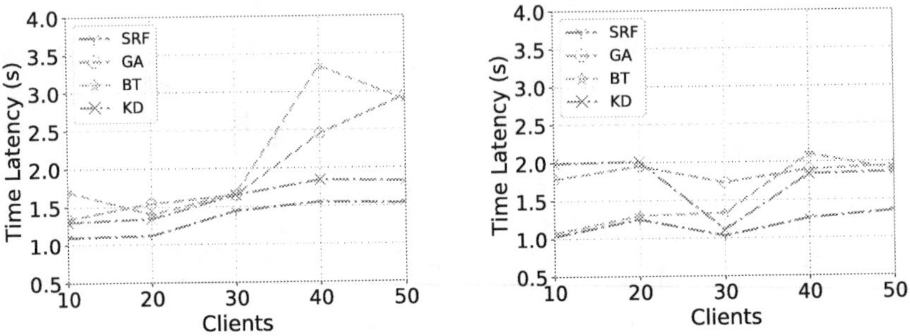

(a) MNIST LeNet-5 (b) FMNIST MLP

Fig. 4. Time consumption comparison with number of clients

Similarly on the FMNIST dataset with MLP model, when the number of clients is 30, the accuracy of the FL model can only reach 81.48%. While the model accuracy of SRF is 97.26% and KD, BT, and GA methods, dropped their accuracies 95.74%, 89.06% and 94.57% respectively. here the BT dropped accuracy but it is still greater than FL accuracy. Notably, the SRF performed outstandingly and maintained its accuracy higher than all other comparison methods for all variations of clients.

In addition, we measure the loss value of SRF and comparison algorithms in the presence of a change in the number of clients, the results are shown in Fig. 3. The loss function we adopt in our experiments is the cross-entropy function. It can be observed that as the number of clients increases, the loss value of all methods basically tends to increase. Cumulatively, we can notice that in both figures loss of all methods including SRF is increasing with the number of clients. But among all comparison methods, the loss of SRF is smaller than that of other methods, while the FL model has the largest prediction loss generally but in some cases we can see the BT method dropped its prediction loss value more than FL.

In summary, the analysis highlights that SRF is the best performer among the evaluated methods, consistently improving accuracy and maintaining lower loss values despite variations in the number of clients.

Time Consumption of SRF. We examine the computational efficiency of the SRF approach in comparison with other methods for constructing unlearning global models across various datasets and models. This evaluation, as presented in Fig. 4, adheres to default settings except for variations in the number of clients. It is important to notice that the running time of the original FL approach, which does not involve unlearning, is consistently zero. Thus it can not be part of our evaluation here. The results from the provided figures indicate that when we use the MNIST with the LeNet-5 model and FMNIST with the MLP model, in both cases SRF maintains the time consumption lower than all other methods. In the second plot, we can see the BT performs similarly to SRF initially, but after the increment of clients to 30 it took longer time than SRF. After SRF, KD performs better than all other comparison methods. SRF's run-time experiences a slight increment as the number of clients rises. For instance, when considering the MNIST dataset and the LeNet-5 model, the construction time for SRF's unlearning model amounts to 1.10, 1.12, 1.44, 1.55, and 1.53 at clients of 10%, 20%, 30%, 40%, and 50%, respectively. This trend arises because when the number of clients increases the SRF calculates the parameter difference for all clients to identify the unreliable contributors. Thus, a rise in the number of clients leads to a slight increase in SRF's run-time but still performs better than all other methods.

Evidently, SRF showcases a more substantial acceleration effect on larger datasets, positioning it as an efficient and effective approach for unlearning in federated learning scenarios.

6 Conclusion

In this paper, we examined prior studies on FUL, shedding light on the server's "right to forget" client contributions. We systematically categorize and summarize the latest advancements in FUL algorithms by introducing innovative taxonomies. Additionally, we presented SRF, the FUL approach that empowers the server to eliminate unreliable client contributions without any consent from clients, consequently reducing the bad influence from the global model to enhancing global model accuracy. In SRF all the unlearning processes are performed on the server side without using any client resources and without any extra communication. Moreover, for unlearning, we don't need to store any historical updates of the client. Experiments on two different datasets and models demonstrate the effectiveness of SRF. This contribution represents the step towards acknowledging the server's "right to forget" client contributions within the framework of FUL. Our aim is to adhere to legal and ethical standards in a reasonable and transparent manner, thereby paving the way for a more balanced and equitable FL environment.

References

1. Voigt, Paul, von dem Bussche, Axel: The EU General Data Protection Regulation (GDPR): A Practical Guide. Springer, Cham (2017). https://doi.org/10.1007/978-3-319-57959-7
2. Mantelero, A.: The EU proposal for a general data protection regulation and the roots of the 'right to be forgotten'. Comput. Law & Secur. Rev. **29**(3), 229–235 (2013)
3. Zaeem, R.N., Suzanne Barber, K.: The effect of the GDPR on privacy policies: recent progress and future promise. ACM Trans. Manag. Inf. Syst. (TMIS) **12**(1), 1–20 (2020)

4. Ginart, A., Guan, M., Valiant, G., Zou, J.Y.: Making AI forget you: data deletion in machine learning. In: Advances in Neural Information Processing Systems, vol. 32 (2019)
5. Liu, G., Ma, X., Yang, Y., Wang, C., Liu, J.: Federated unlearning. arXiv preprint arXiv:2012.13891 (2020)
6. Kairouz, P., et al.: Advances and open problems in federated learning. Found. Trends® Mach. Learn. **14**(1–2), 1–210 (2021)
7. Navia-Vázquez, A., Gutierrez-Gonzalez, D., Parrado-Hernández, E., Navarro-Abellan, J.J.: Distributed support vector machines. IEEE Tran. Neural Networks **17**(4), 1091 (2006)
8. Ayush, K.T., Vikram, S.C., Murari, M., Mohan, K.: Deep regression unlearning. arXiv preprint arXiv:2210.08196 (2022)
9. Manaar, A., Hithem, L., Michail, M.: Get rid of your trail: remotely erasing backdoors in federated learning. arXiv preprint arXiv:2304.10638 (2023)
10. Nguyen, T.T., Huynh, T.T., Nguyen, P.L., Liew, A.W.-C., Yin, H., Nguyen, Q.H.V.: A survey of machine unlearning. arXiv preprint arXiv:2209.02299 (2022)
11. Liu, G., Ma, X., Yang, Y., Wang, C., Liu, J.,: FedEraser: enabling efficient client-level data removal from federated learning models. In: 2021 IEEE/ACM 29th International Symposium on Quality of Service (IWQOS), pp. 1–10. IEEE (2021)
12. Liu, Y., Xu, L., Yuan, X., Wang, C., Li, B.: The right to be forgotten in federated learning: an efficient realization with rapid retraining. In: IEEE INFOCOM 2022-IEEE Conference on Computer Communications, pp. 1749–1758. IEEE (2022)
13. Anisa, H., Swanand, K., Ambrish, R., Nathalie, B.: Federated unlearning: how to efficiently erase a client in FL? arXiv preprint arXiv:2207.05521 (2022)
14. Wu, C., Zhu, S., Mitra, P.: Federated unlearning with knowledge distillation. arXiv preprint arXiv:2201.09441 (2022)
15. Lucas, B., et al.: Machine unlearning. In: Proceedings of the 42nd IEEE Symposium on Security and Privacy, SP 2021, Washington, DC, USA. IEEE Computer Society (2021)
16. Stuart, L.P.: The california consumer privacy act: towards a European-style privacy regime in the united states. J. Tech. L. & Pol'y, **23**, 68 (2018)
17. Yuan, W., Yin, H., Wu, F., Zhang, S., He, T., Wang, H.: Federated unlearning for on-device recommendation. In: Proceedings of the Sixteenth ACM International Conference on Web Search and Data Mining, pp. 393–401 (2023)
18. Li, G., Shen, L., Sun, Y., Hu, Y., Hu, H., Tao, D.: Subspace based federated unlearning. arXiv preprint arXiv:2302.12448 (2023)
19. Liu, Y., Ma, Z., Liu, X., Ma, J.: Learn to forget: user-level memorization elimination in federated learning. arXiv preprint arXiv:2003.10933 (2020)
20. Leijie, W., Guo, S., Wang, J., Hong, Z., Zhang, J., Ding, Y.: Federated unlearning: guarantee the right of clients to forget. IEEE Network **36**(5), 129–135 (2022)
21. Gao, X., et al.: VeriFi: towards verifiable federated unlearning. arXiv preprint arXiv:2205.12709 (2022)
22. Liu, Y., Ma, Z., Yang, Y., Liu, X., Ma, J., Ren, K.: RevFRF: enabling cross-domain random forest training with revocable federated learning. IEEE Trans. Dependable Secure Comput. **19**(6), 3671–3685 (2021)
23. LeCun, Y.: The MNIST database of handwritten digits. http://yann.lecun.com/exdb/mnist/, (1998)
24. Xiao, H., Rasul, K., Vollgraf, R.: Fashion-MNIST: a novel image dataset for benchmarking machine learning algorithms. arXiv preprint arXiv:1708.07747 (2017)
25. LeCun, Y., Bottou, L., Bengio, Y., Haffner, P.: Gradient-based learning applied to document recognition. Proc. IEEE **86**(11), 2278–2324 (1998)

Author Index

KC Santosh et al. (Eds.): RTIP2R 2023, CCIS 2027, pp. 411–413, 2024.
https://doi.org/10.1007/978-3-031-53085-2

Printed in the United States
by Baker & Taylor Publisher Services